The Yorkshire County Cricket Club Limited

W0007672

Editor:
GRAHAM HARDCASTLE

Production Editor:
JAMES M. GREENFIELD

Records and Statistics
Yorkshire First Eleven:
JOHN T POTTER
Yorkshire Second Eleven:
HOWARD CLAYTON

Official Photographers:
SIMON WILKINSON, ALEX WHITEHEAD
and ALLAN MCKENZIE. *SWpix.com*

Published by
THE YORKSHIRE COUNTY CRICKET CLUB LTD
EMERALD HEADINGLEY CRICKET GROUND
LEEDS LS6 3BU
Tel: 0344 504 3099   Fax: 0113 278 4099
Internet: http://www.yorkshireccc.com
e-mail: cricket@yorkshireccc.com

Solicitors: *Auditors:*
DLA PIPER UK LLP   Garbutt and Elliott Audit Ltd
Medical Officer: Dr NIGEL MAYERS, MBChB, MRCGP
Burley Park Medical Centre, 273 Burley Road, Leeds LS4 2EL

The opinions expressed by contributors are not necessarily those of the Board.

TELEPHONE AND FAX NUMBERS

EMERALD HEADINGLEY CRICKET GROUND

Tel: 0344 504 3099
Fax: 0113 278 4099

NORTH MARINE ROAD, SCARBOROUGH **Tel: 01723 365625**
Fax: 01723 364287

SHIPTON ROAD, YORK **Tel: 01904 623602**

ST GEORGE'S ROAD, HARROGATE **Tel: 01423-525000**

© The Yorkshire County Cricket Club Ltd 2021

Produced by:

Great Northern Books
PO Box 1380, Bradford, BD5 5FB
www.greatnorthernbooks.co.uk

ISBN: 978-1-914227-07-3

CONTENTS

Colour Plates — Facing Pages 32 and 256

Officers for 2020

PATRONESS

THE DUCHESS OF KENT

PATRONS

DAVID LASCELLES, EARL OF HAREWOOD   LORD HAWKE
The EARL OF MEXBOROUGH

HONORARY LIFE MEMBERS

Mr J G BINKS
Mr H D BIRD, OBE,
Hon. D (Univ) LLD
Sir GEOFFREY BOYCOTT
Mr D BYAS
Mr D GOUGH
Dr K HOWARD, OBE

Mr R A HUTTON
Mr R ILLINGWORTH, CBE
Mr D S LEHMANN
Mr D E V PADGETT
Mr R K PLATT
Mr S R TENDULKAR
Mr M P VAUGHAN, OBE

PRESIDENT

Mr G A COPE

VICE-PRESIDENTS

Mrs J BAIRSTOW
Mr B BOUTTELL
Mr I M CHAPPELL
Mr M COWAN
Mr S FIELDEN
Mr D S HALL, CBE, TD
Mr R A HILLIAM
Mr S J MANN
Mr K H MOSS MBE

Mr J W T MUSTOE
Mr D M RYDER
Mr R A SMITH, TD, DL
Mr W B STOTT
Mr K TAYLOR
Mr A L VANN
Mr D WARNER
Mr J D WELCH

Changes announced after February 22 will be recorded in the 2022 edition of the Yorkshire County Cricket Club Yearbook

---

Stars align for Superchargers

The Northern Superchargers women's squad as of February 2021, with five further squad places to fill: Lauren Winfield-Hill (captain), Hollie Armitage, Nicola Carey (overseas), Alice Davidson-Richards, Helen Fenby, Alyssa Healy (overseas), Bess Heath, Beth Langston, Katie Levick, Linsey Smith.

Officials of the Yorkshire County Cricket Club

President

T R Barker	1863	R A Smith	
M J Ellison	1864-97	TD, LLB, DL	1999-2004
Lord Hawke	1898-1938	David Jones CBE	2004-6
Rt Hon Sir F S Jackson		Robert Appleyard	2006-8
	1939-1947	Brian Close CBE	2008-10
T L Taylor	1948-1960	Raymond Illingworth CBE	
Sir W A Worsley Bart			2010-12
	1961-1973	Geoffrey Boycott OBE	
Sir K Parkinson	1974-1981		2012-13
N W D Yardley	1981-1983	Harold 'Dickie' Bird OBE	
The Viscount Mountgarret			2014-15
	1984-1989	John H Hampshire	
Sir Leonard Hutton	1989-1990		2016-17
Sir Lawrence Byford		Richard A Hutton	2017-18
QPM, LLD, DL	1991-1999	Geoff A Cope	2018-2020

Chairman

A H Connell, DL	1971-1979	GA Cope	2002
M G Crawford	1980-1984	R A Smith TD, LLB, DL	
H R Kirk	1984-1985		2002-5
B Walsh, QC	1986-1991	C J Graves	2005-15
Sir Lawrence Byford		S J Denison	2015-18
CBE, QPM, LLD, DL		R A Smith TD, LLB, DL	
	1991-1998		2018-20
K H Moss MBE	1998-2002	C N R Hutton	2020-

Secretary

Geo Padley	1863	J H Nash	1931-1971
J B Wostinholm	1864-1902	J Lister	1972-1991
F C (Sir Fredk.) Toone		D M Ryder	1991-2002
	1903-1930		

Company Secretary

B Bouttell	2002-5	P Hudson	2014-
C Hartwell	2011-14		

Officials of the Yorkshire County Cricket Club

Captain

R Iddison	1863-1872	J V Wilson	1960-1962
J Rowbotham	1873	D B Close	1963-1970
L Greenwood	1874	G Boycott	1971-1978
J Rowbotham	1875	J H Hampshire	1979-1980
E Lockwood	1876-1877	C M Old	1981-1982
T Emmett	1878-1882	R Illingworth	1982-1983
Hon M B (Lord) Hawke		D L Bairstow	1984-1986
	1883-1910	P Carrick	1987-1989
E J R H Radcliffe	1911	M D Moxon	1990-1995
Sir A W White	1912-1918	D Byas	1996-2001
D C F Burton	1919-1921	D S Lehmann	2002
Geoff Wilson	1922-1924	A McGrath	2003
A W Lupton	1925-1927	C White	2004-6
W A Worsley	1928-1929	D Gough	2007-8
A T Barber	1930	A McGrath	2009
F E Greenwood	1931-1932	A W Gale	2010-16
A B Sellers	1933-1947	G S Ballance	2017-18
N W D Yardley	1948-1955	S A Patterson	2018-
W H H Sutcliffe	1956-1957	D J Willey	2020-
J R Burnet	1958-1959		*(T20 only)*

Treasurer

M J Ellison	1863-1893	M G Crawford	1963-1979
M Ellison, jun.	1894-1898	J D Welch	1980-1984
Chas Stokes	1899-1912	P W Townend	1984-2002
R T Heselton	1913-1931		
A Wyndham Heselton			
	1932-1962		

Chief Executive

C D Hassell	1991-2002	Colin J Graves	2012-13
Colin J Graves	2002-5	Mark Arthur	2013-
Stewart Regan	2006-10		

YORKSHIRE PRIDE TRIUMPHS THROUGH YEAR OF TRAGEDY

By Graham Hardcastle

There are many words which could be used to describe the last 12 months or so. Many of them, however, can't be used within the pages of this publication. But the very first word I thought of when thinking about Yorkshire Cricket was pride.

Pride in the players for getting out there and playing amidst difficult circumstances surrounding Coronavirus, the men enhancing their first-class credentials in the process and building confidence ahead of this summer's County Championship campaign.

Pride in the club's staff for dealing with a horrid situation and in those who worked tirelessly to ensure everything behind the scenes was correct and ready to ensure cricket could be played in August and September.

And, last but by certainly no means least, pride in the club's members, 85 percent of whom donated their 2020 membership fees to the club and dealt with the frustrations of not seeing live cricket so admirably. We can't wait to see you back around the county grounds this summer.

There were stages around last April and May where I wondered whether a 2021 yearbook would be published, but thankfully here we are with some great content, including some reflections on memorable matches gone by. A huge thanks goes to all the contributors and, as ever, to James Greenfield for his tireless work in putting the latest edition together.

I particularly enjoyed delving into the story of Yorkshire's YTS and Academy programmes, the former which started in the late eighties. It is without doubt one of the county's greatest success stories given the players provided to England over the last 30 years. And it will continue on the same lines for years and years to come, no doubt.

It had been suggested to me to really get stuck into an article on the impacts of Coronavirus within the club. But, while we have a couple of pieces on the matter, including from member Roger Statham, it has been decided to leave anything in depth alone for now, given the pandemic is not yet over and things are ever changing.

Results were mixed in 2020. Topping the Bob Willis Trophy North Group, only just missing out on a Lord's final, was definitely encouraging, while the Vitality Blast provided yet more frustration in the form of a group stage exit. In terms of the women, the Northern Diamonds were brilliant in reaching the Rachael Heyhoe Flint Trophy final at Edgbaston.

It was a great pleasure to watch a host of youngsters progress their games and build a platform ahead of more normal campaigns to come.

There is plenty to look forward to in 2021, both domestically and internationally. An Indian Test Match at Emerald Headingley and the venue's first ever T20 International between England and Pakistan are just two. Away from home turf, later in the year Eoin Morgan and Joe Root tackle a T20 World Cup in India and an away *Ashes* series.

Five professional women's contracts within the Northern Diamonds set-up will undoubtedly strengthen that area of the game, while arguably the *Hundred* is more important for the development of the women's game than the men's.

With the addition of Dom Bess and the development of the up-and-comers, it would be no surprise to see Steve Patterson lift this year's revamped County Championship title and with it the Bob Willis Trophy if things go perfectly. A long overdue third Finals Day appearance would be most welcome for T20 captain David Willey.

The biggest goal for 2021 must be to get back to normality and for the return of spectators to grounds. Fingers crossed, that happens.

Enjoy reading this edition of the *Yearbook*. It has been a pleasure to put together. And enjoy the summer. It promises so much.

Test call for Seconds stalwart

Yorkshire Second-team scorer John Virr earned a Test call-up last summer.

Virr has been scoring for the Seconds for five years — 2020 would have been his sixth had there been cricket at that level — but he was redeployed across the Pennines to score for two Test matches at Emirates Old Trafford between England and the West Indies and England and Pakistan.

Alongside Lancashire's Second-team scorer Garry Morgan, himself a Yorkshireman, Virr also oversaw a West Indies intra-squad warm-up game in late June.

COUNTY FIXTURES — 2021

LV= INSURANCE COUNTY CHAMPIONSHIP
(All four-day matches)

Date			Opponents	Venue
THU	**8-11**	**APRIL**	**GLAMORGAN**	HEADINGLEY
Thu	15-18	April	Kent	Canterbury
Thu	22-25	April	Sussex	Hove
THU	**29-2**	**APRIL/MAY**	**NORTHAMPTONSHIRE**	HEADINGLEY
THU	**6-9**	**MAY**	**KENT**	HEADINGLEY
Thu	13-16	May	Glamorgan	Sophia Gardens
Thu	27-30	May	Lancashire	Old Trafford
THU	**3-6**	**JUNE**	**SUSSEX**	HEADINGLEY
Sun	4-7	July	Northamptonshire	Wantage Road
SUN	**11-14**	**JULY**	**LANCASHIRE**	SCARBOROUGH
Mon	30-2	August/September	Divisional Stage	TBC
Sun	5-8	September	Divisional Stage	TBC
Sun	12-15	September	Divisional Stage	TBC
Tues	21-24	September	Divisional Stage	TBC
Mon	*27-1*	*September/October*	*Bob Willis Trophy Final*	*Lord's*

VITALITY BLAST (Twenty20)

THU	**10**	**JUNE**	**BIRMINGHAM**	HEADINGLEY
Fri	11	June	Durham	Riverside
TUE	**15**	**JUNE**	**LEICESTERSHIRE**	HEADINGLEY
Wed	16	June	Worcestershire	New Road
FRI	**18**	**JUNE**	**DURHAM**	HEADINGLEY
SUN	**20**	**JUNE**	**DERBYSHIRE**	HEADINGLEY
WED	**23**	**JUNE**	**WORCESTERSHIRE**	HEADINGLEY
Fri	25	June	LEICESTERSHIRE	Grace Road
SAT	**26**	**JUNE**	**NORTHAMPTONSHIRE**	HEADINGLEY
Wed	30	June	Birmingham	Edgbaston
FRI	**2**	**JULY**	**LANCASHIRE**	HEADINGLEY
Fri	9	July	Nottinghamshire	Trent Bridge
Sat	17	July	Lancashire	Old Trafford
Sun	18	July	Derbyshire	Chesterfield
Tue	24-27	August	Quarter-Finals	TBC
Sat	*18*	*September*	*Finals Day*	*Edgbaston*

ROYAL LONDON ONE-DAY CUP (50-overs)

THU	**22**	**JULY**	**SURREY**	SCARBOROUGH
Sun	25	July	Leicestershire	Grace Road
WED	**28**	**JULY**	**NORTHAMPTONSHIRE**	SCARBOROUGH
Sun	1	August	Somerset	Taunton
TUE	**3**	**AUGUST**	**WARWICKSHIRE**	YORK
FRI	**6**	**AUGUST**	**NOTTINGHAMSHIRE**	YORK
Sun	8	August	Derbyshire	Chesterfield
Thu	12	August	Glamorgan	Sophia Gardens
Sat	14	August	Quarter-Final	TBC
Tue	17	August	Semi-Final	TBC
Thu	*19*	*August*	*Final*	*Trent Bridge*

OTHER MATCHES

Tue	20	July	Northumberland ....TBC

(National Counties 50-over Friendly)

INTERNATIONAL MATCHES PLAYED AT HEADINGLEY

SUN	**18**	**JULY**	**SECOND T20I** ....ENGLAND V. PAKISTAN
WED	**25-29**	**AUGUST**	**THIRD TEST** ....ENGLAND V. INDIA

SECOND ELEVEN CHAMPIONSHIP
(All four-day matches)

Mon	19-22	April	Gloucestershire ....Bristol
Mon	26-30	April	Surrey ....Guildford
Mon	3-6	May	Essex ....Billericay
MON	**10-13**	**MAY**	**LANCASHIRE** ....SCARBOROUGH
MON	**17-20**	**MAY**	**NOTTINGHAMSHIRE** ....YORK
MON	**24-27**	**MAY**	**DURHAM** ....HOME, TBC
MON	**28-1**	**JUNE/JULY**	**WARWICKSHIRE** ....WEETWOOD
Mon	5-8	July	Leicestershire ....Kibworth
MON	**16-19**	**AUGUST**	**DERBYSHIRE** ....WEETWOOD
Tue	31-3	August/September	Lancashire ....Chester BH
Mon	6-9	September	Glamorgan ....Away, TBC
MON	**13-16**	**SEPTEMBER**	**WORCESTERSHIRE,** ....SCARBOROUGH

SECOND ELEVEN TWENTY20

Tue	1	June	Nottinghamshire ....Away, TBC
			(Two games)
THUR	**3**	**JUNE**	**DURHAM** ....WEETWOOD
			(Two games)
Mon	7	June	Derbyshire ....Away, TBC
Tue	8	June	Leicestershire ....Away, TBC
Thu	10	June,	Lancashire ....Liverpool
MON	**14**	**JUNE**	**DERBYSHIRE** ....HOME, TBC
TUE	**15**	**JUNE**	**LEICESTERSHIRE** ....HOME, TBC
THU	**17**	**JUNE**	**LANCASHIRE** ....WEETWOOD
Thu	24		Finals Day ....TBC

Further friendlies and possible One-Day Trophy fixtures are still to be confirmed.

YORKSHIRE IN VITALITY WOMEN'S T20 (Group One North)

Sun	25	April	10.30am: Cumbria ....Cumbria, TBC
			1.30pm: Scotland A
MON	**3**	**MAY**	**10.30AM: NORTH EAST WARRIORS** ....HARROGATE CC
			4.30PM: CUMBRIA
SUN	**9**	**MAY**	**10.30AM: LANCASHIRE** ....HARROGATE CC
			4.30PM: NORTH EAST WARRIORS
Sun	16	May	1.30pm: Cumbria ....Lancashire TBC
			4.30pm: Lancashire

All fixtures are part of daily triple headers at the above venues. Away venues had not been confirmed at the time of print. Please check www.yorkshireccc.com for further details, plus information on any friendly fixtures arranged.

Finch supercharges back...

Australia limited-overs captain Aaron Finch, left, returns to Emerald Headingley this summer to lead the Northern Superchargers into the inaugural Hundred campaign.

Batsman Finch played across two years as Yorkshire's overseas in 2014 an 2015, scoring 415 runs in eight County Championship matches and contributing to back-to-back titles.

"I can't claim much (credit) in that regard, but it was great to see how hard everyone was working at the club," he said. "So to get the success on the back of that was outstanding.

"There were some seriously talented players there, and it would have been a shame had Yorkshire not won a couple of titles in that period. For it to come together the way it did, with us dominating the competition, it was unbelievable.

"I had a couple of great years there, and I loved every bit of it. It's a pretty special place up North, and I can't wait to get back."

THE HUNDRED, PRESENTED BY CAZOO

All Northern Superchargers fixtures are double headers with the men's and women's teams at the same venue. Women will play in the afternoon and men in the evening.

SAT	**24**	**JULY**	**WELSH FIRE**	.................HEADINGLEY
Mon	26	July	Trent Rockets	.....................Trent Bridge
Wed	28	July	Manchester Originals	...................Old Trafford
SAT	**31**	**JULY**	**OVAL INVINCIBLES**	.............HEADINGLEY
Tue	3	August	London Spirit,	......................Lord's
Sat	7	August	Southern Brave	......................Ageas Bowl
THU	**12**	**AUGUST**	**MANCHESTER ORIGINALS**	... HEADINGLEY
TUE	**17**	**AUGUST**	**BIRMINGHAM PHOENIX**	......HEADINGLEY
Fri	20	August	Eliminator 2nd place v 3rd place	...........The Oval
Sat	21	August	Final 1st place v winner of Eliminator	........Lord's

WOMEN'S REGIONAL T20, NORTHERN DIAMONDS

SAT	**26**	**JUNE**	**NORTH WEST THUNDER**	.......HEADINGLEY
Fri	2	July	Sunrisers	...................Chelmsford
Sat	10	July	Western Storm	...........................Taunton
WED	**25**	**AUGUST**	**SUNRISERS**	...............................TBC
SAT	**28**	**AUGUST**	**WESTERN STORM**	................RIVERSIDE
Mon	30	August	North West Thunder	........................TBC
Sun	5	September	Finals Day	...............................TBC

RACHAEL HEYHOE FLINT TROPHY,
NORTHERN DIAMONDS

SAT	**29**	**MAY**	**CENTRAL SPARKS** ....**HEADINGLEY**	
Mon	31	May	Lightning ....TBC	
Sat	5	June	Sunrisers ....TBC	
SAT	**12**	**JUNE**	**SOUTH EAST STARS** ....**HEADINGLEY**	
FRI	**10**	**SEPTEMBER**	**WESTERN STORM** ....**RIVERSIDE**	
SUN	**12**	**SEPTEMBER**	**NORTH WEST THUNDER** ....**RIVERSIDE**	
Sat	18	September	Southern Vipers ....TBC	
Wed	22	September	2nd v 3rd playoff ....TBC	
Sat	25	September	Final ....TBC	

YORKSHIRE ACADEMY IN THE YPL NORTH LEAGUE

SAT	**24**	**APRIL**	**SCARBOROUGH** ....**WEETWOOD**
Sat	1	May	Woodhouse Grange ....Woodhouse Grange
Sat	8	May	Castleford ....Castleford
Sat	15	May	Dunnington ....Dunnington
SAT	**22**	**MAY**	**DRIFFIELD** ....**WEETWOOD**
Sat	29	May	Acomb ....Acomb
MON	**31**	**MAY**	**YORK** ....**WEETWOOD**
SAT	**5**	**JUNE**	**SHERIFF HUTTON BRIDGE** ......**WEETWOOD**
Sat	12	June	Harrogate ....Harrogate
SAT	**19**	**JUNE**	**CLIFTON ALLIANCE** ....**WEETWOOD**
Sat	26	June	York ....Clifton Park
Sat	3	July	Scarborough ....Scarborough
SAT	**10**	**JULY**	**WOODHOUSE GRANGE** ....**WEETWOOD**
Sat	17	July	Stamford Bridge ....Stamford Bridge
SAT	**24**	**JULY**	**CASTLEFORD** ....**WEETWOOD**
SAT	**31**	**JULY**	**DUNNINGTON** ....**WEETWOOD**
Sat	7	August	Driffield Town ....Driffield
SAT	**14**	**AUGUST**	**ACOMB** ....**WEETWOOD**
Sat	21	August	Sheriff Hutton Bridge ....Sheriff Hutton Bridge
SAT	**28**	**AUGUST**	**HARROGATE** ....**WEETWOOD**
MON	**30**	**AUGUST**	**STAMFORD BRIDGE** ....**WEETWOOD**
Sat	4	September	Clifton Alliance ....Clifton Alliance

YORKSHIRE ACADEMY FRIENDLIES

WED	**21-22**	**APRIL**	**DURHAM** ....**MIDDLESBROUGH**
Sun	9	May	Nottinghamshire ....Away, TBC
SUN	**23**	**MAY**	**NOTTINGHAMSHIRE** ....**HOME, TBC**
Tue	1-3	June	Durham ....Away, TBC
Sun	27	June	Warwickshire ....Away, TBC
SUN	**4**	**JULY**	**WARWICKSHIRE** ....**HOME, TBC**

YORKSHIRE PREMIER LEAGUE CUP

Sat	18	September	Final ....TBC

*** All dates and venues, across all teams, are subject to change
as a result of the Coronavirus pandemic. ***

THE COMPETITIONS EXPLAINED

LV= INSURANCE COUNTY CHAMPIONSHIP

The 18 counties have been split into three conferences of six. The top two in each conference after 10 games advances into a four-game top group to fight for the County Championship title — the winner taking that honour.

The top two sides after the extra four games — but not against the team they advanced with — in August and September then play off for the Bob Willis Trophy in an end-of-season Lord's final.

The middle two teams and bottom two teams in each of the initial conferences also make up separate "leagues" and play for placings in the final four games.

This has been billed as a trial. The current plan is to revert to Divisions One and Two in 2022.

VITALITY BLAST

After a shortened version last summer, this year's Blast reverts to type. The counties are split into two regional groups of nine, with 14 games. Yorkshire will play the majority of their opponents at home and away, but not all.

The top four teams in the table advance to the quarter-finals ahead of the traditional Finals Day in late September at Edgbaston. The top two teams — four in total across the North and South — all win the right to host their quarter-final. Unfortunately, a clash of dates with the Emerald Headingley Test Match in August means Yorkshire would have to forfeit home advantage should they qualify first or second.

ROYAL LONDON ONE-DAY CUP

This competition was last summer's "fall guy" as Coronavirus bit. It returns this year in almost the same format as in 2019.

This time the counties have been split into two non-regionalised groups of nine. Each will play eight matches — four at home, four away.

The top three in each table advance to the knockout stages. The top team qualifies direct to the semi-final, while the second and third teams play each other in an effective quarter-final. The winners advance to the semi-final, with the final played at Trent Bridge.

THE HUNDRED, PRESENTED BY CAZOO

The ECB's brand-new competition and brand-new format. Essentially, each game will be 100 balls per side, both for the men and the women, with a number of new playing conditions within that.

Each of the eight teams plays eight group fixtures, including their nearest rivals twice. Northern Superchargers play the Manchester Originals twice.

Every fixture date will see the men and women play double headers at the same venue, with the competitions identical in their format.

The top team after the group stage advances directly into the final on August 21. The previous day the second and third-placed teams play off in an Eliminator for the right to advance to the final.

RACHAEL HEYHOE FLINT TROPHY

The 50-over competition played between the eight women's Regional Centres of Excellence returns this summer in an expanded format.

This was played last summer in a short and sharp regional burst as a means of getting women's cricket played amidst Coronavirus. This summer each team plays everybody else once in the group stage — non-regionalised. The Diamonds have four games at home and three away.

The "finals series" is exactly the same as the Hundred. The top team after the group stage advance directly to the September 25 final. On September 22 the second and third-placed teams play off for the right to fight for the trophy.

WOMEN'S REGIONAL T20

This is a newly introduced competition for the Diamonds and their seven counterparts, and it will be played either side of the Hundred to give players the best chance to prepare for that particular competition.

In the Regional T20 the eight teams are split into two non-regionalised groups of four with six group games — three at home and three away. The champions will be decided at Finals Day on September 5.

The best placed group winner advances directly to the final. Beforehand, the other group winner plays the best second-placed team as a means to qualify for the final.

Century Captain: Joe Root walks off the field late on the third day of England's Second Test against Sri Lanka in Galle on January 24, 2021, after a sublime innings of 186. Root had scored 228 — the fourth double-century of his Test career — in the first Test of a 2-0 series victory. He celebrated his 100th Test cap — 47 of them as captain — in the first of the series that followed against India. *(Photo: Danny Reuben)*

TOP-OF-THE-TREE MAESTRO STAYS CLOSE TO HIS ROOTS

By Graham Hardcastle

There have been many significant influences during Joe Root's stellar career with Yorkshire and England, one which reached the 100 Test caps milestone in India at the start of February. Childhood friend Josh Varley is certainly one of them.

Root and Varley, the first-team captain at the pair's home club Sheffield Collegiate and a respected young coach, go way back. "I've known Joe ever since he started playing cricket really," Varley said on the eve of Root's magical 100th Test appearance in the first of a four-match series at Chennai.

"We went to the same school, and our parents are really good friends. Dore Primary School was our first school, then we went on to King Ecgberts. It was then probably Year 10 and Year 9 that Joe and Billy (Joe's younger brother) went to Worksop College. I'm two school years below Joe (aged 30) and one below Bill.

"It would have been aged seven or eight that I remember first coming across Joe."

Varley was name-checked in the media last summer by Joe as someone he leans on coaching-wise a lot when time allows. It is no surprise, given how close the pair are. "Their family home is close to mine, and we were about a 10-minute walk away from the club, Abbeydale, as youngsters," Josh continued. "We've obviously now both moved out, and we're actually a bit closer to the club.

"In school holidays, instead of being 9-3 in school, it was 9-3 down at the nets. It was hard graft, probably harder than school actually. Mind you, for Joe he probably saw a 9-3 session in the nets as down time. He will have done longer sessions in his time, no doubt.

"His attitude towards practice has always been first class. He's never been afraid of asking for help or advice, and he was never scared of coming up against older players as a young lad. All myself and Bill wanted to do was smash it out of the nets and throw it as hard as we could. For Joe, there was a lot more thinking from a young age."

It was in late 2012 that Joe made his Test debut in Ahmedabad. Varley recalls his feelings of pride and how those were mirrored by many at

Joe the bowler: Root takes a wicket with his off-spin in Yorkshire's last Vitality Blast match of 2020 against Derbyshire at Emerald Headingley.
(Photo: Paul Butterfield)

Sheffield Collegiate: "Matt, his dad, rang me late on to tell me it was happening, and the club was full at around 3am to watch him. It was a fantastic occasion."

Circumstances mean that did not happen in February, but Varley was up at the crack of dawn and tuned in at home.

"I love my cricket," he said. "I love watching Yorkshire and England, and it's a massive bonus that I get to watch my pal at the same time."

Captain Root started 2021 in fine style with scores of 228 and 186 in the 2-0 series win in Sri Lanka on the back of some extensive work with Varley over the last 12 months or so. He then became the first player in history to score a double-century — 218 — in their 100th Test appearance at Chennai. "We worked together two or even three times a week just before he went to New Zealand last winter," Varley said. "It's great for my coaching to be able to work with someone like him.

"I absolutely love it, and listening to him talk about the game is brilliant. He has done wonders for me as a coach. But I can be wanging it down at him as hard as I can with a brand-new ball, and he makes it look like I'm bowling 55mph spin at him. His class just shows through."

Varley recently left his post as junior head coach at Sheffield Collegiate, and now runs a business in liquidation: "I'm working with a couple of other guys heavily involved with the cricket club, so I can easily get time off," he said. "If Joe ever needs me, it's not a problem."

So what are his best memories of a young Mr Root? "I played a lot with Joe from the juniors, and I could name you a lot of standout innings that he played," he said.

"But the one that I always go back to was in 2012 when Collegiate's firsts were struggling, and we didn't win many games at all.

"It was probably the last league game I played with Joe. He had only just played for Yorkshire a couple of days beforehand, and England Lions not too long before that.

"But he came back with his dad, and they both played. He got 90-odd, and we won away at Doncaster.

"And that day summed him up as a person. He was desperate to help us out as a young team. I knew it beforehand, but a lot of our other lads didn't really know him.

"They soon realised what a great bloke he was and how approachable he

Dear old pals...Root with coach Josh Varley before they get down to serious business.
(Photo: Josh Varley Archive)

was. It is not unusual at all to see him walking around the boundary at Collegiate when he has a Saturday off, and he's so approachable — signing autographs, talking to people. He never leaves a bad impression on anybody."

Root sailed beyond 8,000 Test runs in Sri Lanka in January, and is very much in range of Sir Alastair Cook's national record of 12,472.

"I really don't see why he shouldn't break all manner of records, and break them by quite a bit because he's such a fit and strong lad," Varley said. "He should have another six years in his prime at least.

"If I could have handpicked a place for him to start this year Sri Lanka would have been very high up on my list. I think he's in the top two or three in the world in terms of playing against spin."

JOE CAN GO ON TO 200 TEST CAPS, SAYS SIR GEOFFREY

Sir Geoffrey Boycott, the only other Yorkshireman to reach the 100 Test Match milestone, believes Joe Root has every chance of doubling up his number of Test caps. Boycott has praised Root's career achievements to date, but insists the 30-year-old has so much more to give English cricket.

In February Root became the 15th England player to play 100 Tests or more. Sir Geoffrey is one of the previous 14, having played 108 Tests between 1964 and 1982, as are fellow knights Ian Botham, Andrew Strauss and Alastair Cook — who leads the way with 161 appearances, with current seamers Jimmy Anderson and Stuart Broad either side of the 150-mark.

With a fair wind Boycott fully expects Sheffield-born Root to sail beyond them all and break another significant record in the process. "To get 100 is special," Sir Geoffrey said. "Any century in cricket is special. But Joe can go and get 200 caps, no doubt.

"As long as he can maintain his enthusiasm and enjoyment of the game, there's no reason why he can't reach 200 Tests and score more runs than anybody ever has, even Sachin Tendulkar's 15,000.

"The more you play, the more the travel and the hotels can wear you down. If that doesn't affect him, he maintains the enthusiasm and he doesn't get a serious injury, there's no reason why not."

If you look down the list of 15 England players who have made it to 100, including Root, seven have played their entire careers in the 21st Century: Cook, Anderson, Broad, Ian Bell, Kevin Pietersen and Strauss.

Three more — Alec Stewart, Mike Atherton and Graham Thorpe — also finished their careers in the 21st Century.

"Please don't get me wrong, and I'm not trying to belittle what is a fantastic achievement," Boycott said, "but it is not quite as big a milestone as it was in days gone by. Joe's only 30, he's been playing nine years and has got 100 Tests to his name. He can play another seven or eight years, and Test matches are coming thick and fast. There are 17 for England this year.

"The first icon in cricket was W G Grace in the 1890s and early 1900s. He only played 22 in his whole career, and he played into his early fifties. You can't compare any of us on figures because it's completely unfair, especially on someone like W G, who only played his 22

Tests and played on uncovered pitches. To judge Joe's quality he should be put up against the best batsmen of today, who are Virat Kohli, Steve Smith and Kane Williamson. He is good enough to be up there in that bracket every year. He has the talent and the youthful exuberance to do it."

Root is younger than each of Kohli, Smith and Williamson, and has played more Tests than them. Whereas Root has topped 8,000 career runs, none of the others have done so yet.

Boycott also thinks Root can get better during the second half of his career: "I actually think it might have done Joe some good to have a bit of time off at the start of this Covid-19 virus to study and think about his batting a bit more.

"He hasn't been bad at all in recent years. He's still been scoring runs, but he hasn't been influencing matches as much as he could have. The real key is how you influence matches and earn wins or draws for your side. The last few years, up until his two superb innings in Sri Lanka, you would have to say that Ben Stokes has overtaken Joe in that regard, even though I believe Joe is a better player than Ben is, more technically correct."

Sir Geoffrey has long been aware of Root's talents, but it was actually another Boycott who tipped him for international honours: "I first saw Joe with Rachael (Geoffrey's wife) when I was living in Jersey and he was about 14," he explained.

"The Yorkshire Academy kids were brought over by Steve Oldham. He brought an Under-16s team across with Joe in it at 14 because he was thought of as being that good.

"I went to one of their matches, and he wasn't actually playing because his equipment had been lost. So he was 12th man, with Steve talking to him and teaching him about the game — 'Why do you think the captain's moved the field, why has he got a man there, where would you put him?'

"Steve did a brilliant job coaching the youngsters, and brought on a lot. The following day we saw him bat when his kit had arrived, and it was Rachael who actually said, 'He'll play for England, that lad'. I said, 'Right, let's see'. She was dead right.

"We had them at our house over there each year they came for around three years. They used our swimming pool at the house, and then we had a barbecue with them. I kept tabs on him from then on.

"I was then on the board at Yorkshire. He was a terrific player, and it was a case of when and not if he would make it. Nobody at the club had any doubts."

48 HOURS IN MUMBAI AND THE BEGINNING OF A COVID YEAR

By Graham Hardcastle

English cricket was put through the mill in 2020 by Coronavirus, both at international and domestic level. In many respects it was a miracle that England's entire international summer, plus a two-month domestic campaign, was played from July onwards.

How did it all start? For Yorkshire the first sign of problems came with the senior squad's early March preseason tour to Mumbai.

What was to be a near fortnight-long tour turned into, for most of the party, a manic 48 hours in which one training session was completed before a mad dash home amidst the threat of UK borders closing. Then followed lockdown, player and staff furlough, and a shortened summer.

Yorkshire made the decision to travel to Mumbai on March 11, following medical and ECB advice. Six bowlers had travelled a week early alongside coach Rich Pyrah and physiotherapist Kunwar Bansil to get a head start before the full complement of 19 and a handful of backroom staff would assemble for training and matches in a cricket-crazy city.

Unfortunately, things escalated so quickly that continuing with the tour scheduled to end on March 24 was simply impossible.

"There were a lot of discussions before we travelled," explained Andrew Gale, whose job as first-team coach quickly turned into head of travel logistics. "Should we go? Shouldn't we? But we did our due diligence and spoke to the ECB.

"We sat the players down, repeated the messages we'd got to put them at ease. We didn't want to put them at risk. That was our first priority. And we were told it was fine. I remember our doctor saying, 'You've got more chance of catching malaria than you have Coronavirus'. At that time it just didn't feel real, but when we got there things just turned rapidly. It became very chaotic."

The *White Rose* party, led by Gale, landed in Mumbai at approximately 6am on Thursday, March 12, before a full training session the following day. "We had a fantastic session," Gale continued. "It was a glimpse of what we were going to get for the tour — we had numerous net bowlers, the facilities were fantastic.

"But Martyn (Moxon, Director of Cricket) was getting in touch,

What might have been: Matthew Fisher working out at Parsee Gymkhana, Mumbai, ahead of the order to get out.

telling me that things were escalating back home. Then, the final call came from him, saying, 'Look, they'll potentially shut the (UK) borders. We can't afford for the squad to be stuck outside that. It was then for me, Kunwar and Sachin, who was running our tour as a host, to come up with a plan to get the squad home."

A backroom staff afternoon run around the streets of Mumbai gave them a brief glimpse of India's passion for the game: "Anyone with any cricket clothing gets swamped. I'm not sure they knew who we were, but they still asked for selfies and autographs!" Gale laughed. "It's a fantastic country, it really is."

Then, at an early-evening team meal, the players were informed of the new plan. "We said, 'We're going home ASAP. Have your tea, pack your bags and get ready to go. We're looking at a number of flights tonight. We might leave at 11pm — just be ready'.

"We ended up leaving at 1.30-2am for a couple of 5am flights to Manchester and Birmingham because we couldn't get everyone on one flight," Gale explained. "It was one of the most stressful things I've had to deal with in my life."

Even at that stage there was little clue as to what would follow: "Coming back on the flight, I was thinking that a worst-case scenario would see us miss maybe four or five weeks of the season," Gale said. "Then it just got to the stage where I stopped thinking about it, because every time I looked forward there was a stumbling block.

"Everything was changing so fast."

On the following Friday, March 20, the England and Wales Cricket Board announced a delay of all professional cricket until May 28, a delay later extended until England began their summer programme against the West Indies on July 8. County cricket started on July 24, with Yorkshire hosting Lancashire in a two-day friendly ahead of competitive action on August 1.

Yorkshire placed the majority of their operational staff on furlough on March 26, the players and coaching staff following on April 6. Of the cricket department only cricket-operations manager Cecilia Allen and Moxon were not furloughed.

Following the end of the two-month summer, however, with the Government's extension of business support, every member of the club's staff was the subject of some form of furlough until the end of April 2021, including flexi-furlough, where only a certain number of hours would be worked and the Government would pay 80 per cent of a worker's wage up to £2,500 per month.

While the furlough scheme ran from March 2020 to April 2021 staff also took a three-month salary reduction over the summer of up to 20 per cent. A small number of redundancies were unavoidable across the business, which was facing losses of up to £2m before various initiatives such as credit options for 2021 or membership donations.

An incredible 85 per cent of qualified members donate their fees.

"It was great we had a season because, at stages, it looked so far away," said Gale. "The work that's gone on behind the scenes at the club — people from the outside won't have seen it — has been phenomenal.

"Martyn Moxon, for example, has worked himself into the ground. Sam Hinchliffe (Operations Director), Kunwar Bansil and Mark Arthur (Chief Executive) have been absolutely brilliant."

For new chairman Roger Hutton and vice-chairman Neil Hartley it proved to be a baptism of fire. "It wasn't quite what we were expecting, I must say! It's been a testing year," Hutton said, "but at least I've learnt more than I would have done otherwise. For me, whilst it's been extraordinarily challenging in many ways it's also been very rewarding.

"Rather than coming to some games and watching players perform on the pitch, I've got to understand in much more depth what goes on behind the scenes. I've seen a lot of skill. It's a really impressive organisation that is going places.

"You can talk a lot about frustration and disappointment throughout the last 12 months, but actually, in hard times you end up understanding a lot about character, loyalty, commitment and team spirit. And you've seen that right across the club in spades.

"In terms of the way the players have dealt with the difficult mental position they've been in, and their willingness to continue to commit and wellbeing on the line has been remarkable. They and the club should be very proud.

"This was the year when the light shone equally brightly on the club's staff and executive staff.

"The hard work, ingenuity and commitment has been equally astonishing in challenging times such as accepting furlough or working on reduced pay.

"Hosting matches for other clubs and solutions — some of the work Sam and Martyn have done — processes to get games on — has been adopted across the game.

"There is disappointment in that when I came in the club was on an incredible high after the *Ashes* Test in 2019 and the squad assembled on the field was one which had a great chance of silverware.

"We nearly achieved that in the

NEIL HARTLEY: Became Vice-Chair to Roger Hutton.

Bob Willis Trophy, but a few things went against us — weather and England call-ups. But my level of optimism ahead of this year, a fuller summer, is every bit as high.

"In terms of the club's financial future I'm extremely confident. Having seen how the executive staff have dealt with the issues thrown at them, how members and sponsors have continued to support us, makes you realise the future is bright."

Ajmal lead bowling coach

Former Yorkshire and England seamer Ajmal Shahzad has been appointed as Derbyshire's lead bowling coach for 2021 and beyond, replacing former *White Rose* pacer Steven Kirby.

SO NEAR, WITH JORDAN RIVER OF EMERGING TALENT

By Andrew Bosi

Players and supporters experienced conflicting emotions, and the prospect of no county cricket for the first time since the Second World War gave way to hope and some trepidation as a shortened summer began on August 1. Without a call to the armed services to occupy their time or league cricket at which to hone skills, how prepared could furloughed players be? Most relied on close relatives for throwdowns or back gardens for exercise regimes.

England were running two bio-secure squads in parallel, impacting on availability. Gary Ballance was absent through illness, while Tim Bresnan had announced a pre-season departure to Warwickshire, citing the need to clear space for the next generation. His obvious successor, Matthew Waite, was then injured on the eve of the first game at Durham.

Thus it was Jordan Thompson, an unknown quantity outside the *Broad Acres*, who was propelled into the side. He had looked the part among a lacklustre team performance at Guildford in 2019, and now he was to prove the find of the season, winning matches with either bat or ball, highlighted by 98 in the win at Nottingham and five wickets in the home victory against Leicestershire.

As was the case for Bresnan, a change of scene refreshed the skills of Dawid Malan, whose weight of runs went a long way to filling the gap created by the loss of Ballance — 332 in three four-day matches, including a maiden career double-hundred in the rain-soaked draw versus Derbyshire at Emerald Headingley.

The format of the Bob Willis Trophy, with one of the three group winners missing out on the late September Lord's final, suggested that batting bonus points would be key. While a low-scoring opening round match against Durham at Emirates Riverside ensured Yorkshire had time to win in the face of indifferent weather, the lack of bonus points effectively left the side in fifth place across the country. The depth of Yorkshire's pace attack — superb Ben Coad and Matthew Fisher shared 10 wickets — and a pleasing unbeaten 66 from Harry Brook saw Yorkshire home chasing 171.

Then Coad and Fisher fell prey to injury ahead of the following

COMING OF AGE: Jordan Thompson lofts Leicestershire's Arron Lilley for four during his first-innings 62 at Emerald Headingley. He took 5-31 in the visitors' second innings.

week's trip to Trent Bridge. Thompson came of age with his swashbuckling 98 and then three wickets in a comfortable final-day defence of 188 as Jonny Bairstow made a winning return to county action. Seamer Dom Leech, who removed Haseeb Hameed in both innings, debuted — one of three with George Hill and Jack Shutt making their first-class bows across five games.

The first home wicket was conducive to batting points. Yorkshire took them all against North Group leaders Derbyshire, thanks largely to Malan, but the attack was not strong enough to enforce the follow-on or even take maximum bowling points in the face of 400-6 declared. Rain forced a draw in a game which Steven Patterson and company would have hoped to let them leapfrog the leaders. Still, with two games remaining, they were very much in contention for Lord's.

Malan was called up and Bairstow recalled to England duty for the following *Roses* match, though Adam Lyth responded with a century. But more inclement weather limited the points from a second drawn match. The only consolation was that Essex had endured even more disruption from the weather in the South Group. With the top two in the Central Group — Somerset and Worcestershire — meeting in the last round that group seemed certain to provide one of the finalists. Yorkshire's task was thus to beat Leicestershire at Headingley...and overhaul Derbyshire and Essex.

Another impressive bowling performance secured a routine win, but only maximum batting points would have kept Yorkshire in the hunt. After some brilliance from Coad with the ball, Jonny Tattersall and Brook kept hope alive for a while — both made significant progress in this truncated season. Derbyshire's final-round defeat by Lancashire ensured Yorkshire had the consolation of easily topping the Northern Group, while they claimed more batting bonus points than either of the finalists. Ultimately, it just was not to be.

Given a fair crack of the whip with availability, Patterson's team will be confident of making it to Division One from their 2021 conference in the new four-day structure. Patterson continued to exercise great control with the ball in 2020, a trait shared by the excellent Coad. The acquisition of Dom Bess from Somerset will provide wickets and runs and ensure Shutt continues his development alongside a Test incumbent.

The most important addition for Yorkshire in 2021 will be spectators in grounds as they hopefully cheer the team on to four-day silverware.

For the future — not the present...

Yorkshire's County Age Group programme played a combined total of 31 matches across six teams after recreational cricket was given the go-ahead from late July.

Under-10s, 11s, 12s, 13s, 14s and 15s all played meaningful cricket, allowing players to progress and coaches to select squads for upcoming assignments such as winter training and this summer's programme.

"All matches were played with the emphasis being on learning, rather than win or lose," explained Yorkshire's CAG performance manager Jim Love.

Intra-squad games (12 in total) were played from Under 10s-12s, while local rivals Durham, Lancashire and Nottinghamshire were opponents for Under 13s-15s, whose groups played a combined total of 19 matches, allowing future Pathways squads to be selected — Gold 2 (Under 15s), Gold 3 (Under 14s) and Gold 4 (Under-13s).

No Under-18s cricket was played, but the Gold 1 for that age-group squad has been selected in conjunction with YCCC staff.

GENIUS WITHIN: Yorkshire Coach Andrew Gale believes Ben Coad, above, has "real genius" within him as a new-ball seamer, best shown during the Bob Willis Trophy win over Leicestershire at Headingley with his fabulous match figures of 8-41.

VIKINGS MOURN TOO MANY MATCHES THAT GOT AWAY

By Graham Hardcastle

Weird and not so wonderful is the best way to sum up Yorkshire's campaign in 2020. On the face of it five defeats and only three wins from 10 games was in keeping with previous disappointment in this format, though there were certainly mitigating circumstances — chiefly in the form of four players missing for the final four games in line with Coronavirus guidelines.

Captain David Willey and wife Carolynne tested positive for the disease, and Matthew Fisher, Tom Kohler-Cadmore and Josh Poysden had all been in close contact with them away from cricket, meaning they also had to self-isolate for 14 days.

Yorkshire lost the three games immediately after they were ruled out, ensuring a dramatic fall from quarter-final contention. The end result? The county have still qualified for only two finals days in 18 attempts, having finished second bottom in the North Group.

A campaign in which Ben Birkhead, George Hill, Matthew Revis, James Wharton and Sam Wisniewski all debuted returned other obvious positives — two wins over Derbyshire which bookended things, the emergence of Will Fraine as a powerful finisher and Test captain Joe Root reminding England of his all-round *T20* credentials ahead of this year's World Cup in India.

The Blast started with a rain-soaked No Result against Nottinghamshire at Emerald Headingley on Thursday, August 27. It was the second successive year this fixture, on the opening night, had been washed out without a ball bowled. The televised match was abandoned at 7.05pm, half an hour before the scheduled start.

Next up was Derbyshire at Emerald Headingley three days later to start a Bank Holiday double header, and given the Vikings' recent record against the Falcons in *T20* cricket the hosts would have been forgiven for heading into this fixture with some trepidation. But there was not one bit of it as they racked up 220-5 after stand-in captain Kohler-Cadmore — Willey was away with England — elected to bat first.

Adam Lyth and Root shared 84 for the second wicket to underpin a dominant innings, with Lyth hitting 61 off 32 balls and Root 64 off 40. Those two shared five leg-side sixes, and laid the platform for Fraine to crash five sixes in only 16 balls, his 44 giving the hosts their eighth score of 220 or more in *T20* history.

The visitors crumbled to 38-5 inside nine overs, and could only limp to 121-9, signalling a 99-run victory for Yorkshire to end a run of six successive Blast defeats against Derby.

Fisher returned an impressive 3-21 from four overs, while Root struck twice in the fifth over to remove key left-handers Billy

Over the top: Test captain Joe Root shares a stand of 84, including five sixes with Adam Lyth against Derbyshire at Emerald Headingley.

Godleman and Leus du Plooy (20-4). Poysden also claimed two wickets in an encouraging return after suffering a fractured skull in July 2019.

Twenty four hours later Andrew Gale and co travelled down the M1 to Trent Bridge for a Bank Holiday Monday clash with Nottinghamshire. A couple of weeks earlier the *White Rose* had claimed a superb Bob Willis Trophy win, defending a target of 188 on the final day. In first-class cricket Nottinghamshire had not won since June 2018, but in *T20* they are a very different proposition. Blast champions in 2017, they had also reached Finals Day in 2016 and 2019, and went on to win this competition as well.

Ultimately, this proved to be a six-wicket defeat as the Outlaws chased down 191 to win with four balls to spare, but Yorkshire were mightily frustrated at letting this one slip through their grasp. At 168-3 early in the 18th over they were very much on track to top the 200 mark for the second day running. Silky Root and belligerent Lyth hit 65 off 43 balls and 53 off 29, but Root was one of seven wickets to fall for only 22 runs in the last 16 balls. Luke Fletcher finished with 5-43.

Yorkshire quickly reasserted their authority thanks to wickets for Lyth, who took the new ball with his off-spinners, and Fisher as they reduced the score to 16-2 in the second over. Alex Hales drilled Lyth to mid-off before Joe Clarke was caught at cover. Again the contest swung as Ben Duckett hit a superbly inventive 86 off 53 balls, sharing a stand of 85 for the third wicket with opener Chris Nash (51) and gaining further support via 21s from captain Dan Christian and unbeaten Tom Moores. The hosts needed 30 off the last three overs and 19 off the last two, only for 14 to come off Fisher in the last but one.

Vikings suffered their second No Result in four games on Wednesday, September 2, as their clash with Leicestershire at Emerald Headingley was washed out. Afternoon rain left puddles on the outfield, and the fixture was abandoned at 6.40pm, 10 minutes after the scheduled start.

A hard-working unbeaten 85 from Kohler-Cadmore proved the feature of a dominant Yorkshire batting performance in a 29-run win over Durham at Emirates Riverside on Friday, September 4.

Opener Kohler-Cadmore smashed five sixes, all clearing long-off or long-on, as the Vikings amassed a daunting 198-3, also including a blistering 36 not out off 15 balls from Fraine. Kohler-Cadmore's highest score of the summer in all formats came off only 57 balls, and was supplemented by scores in the 20s for Lyth, Root and Harry Brook.

Durham threatened Yorkshire's pursuit of a second win in five North Group games, reaching 77-0 in the eighth over, but impressive spinners Poysden (3-32 from four overs) and Root (2-29 from four) dragged things back to leave Durham 152-6 in the 17th. They were bowled out for 169, with new captain Willey, back from England ODI duty, claiming three late wickets. Yorkshire's dominance with the bat was highlighted by the fact Willey, a notoriously destructive striker, did not make it to the crease. Durham opener Graham Clark, who reached a 26-ball fifty and 68 off 39, got them ahead of the Duckworth Lewis Stern requirement as rain started to fall, but they crumbled after the excellent start as spin prospered.

Third-placed Vikings moved to six points at the halfway stage in the group games, two behind joint leaders Nottinghamshire and Lancashire in the pursuit of a quarter-final berth, but things were about to take a turn for the worse after a week-long break for four-day cricket.

On Friday, September 11, Yorkshire travelled to the Fischer County Ground, Grace Road, to take on Leicestershire. And they lost a game they should have won. Irish overseas Gareth Delany starred with ball and then bat in a Foxes heist which saw them chase down a target of 189 to consign the visitors to a three-wicket defeat off the last ball. Delany's part-time leg-spin accounted for two wickets before he opened the batting with 60 off 40 balls.

Having been invited to bat, Yorkshire's innings was a strange one. They flew out of the blocks courtesy of Lyth's 71 off 46 balls — his third fifty in four Blast innings — helping them to reach 98-1 in the 10th over, but they slipped to 124-5 in the 15th as spin squeezed through the middle. Fraine was run out without facing a ball, while Willey, Lyth and Brook also fell before the innings was revived to 188-6 by Jordan

HUNDRED HERO: Yorkshire's Joe Root celebrates his brilliant century in the first Test against India in Chennai on February 5. Root became only the third Englishman and the ninth batsman to score a century in their 100th appearance...and he went on to turn it into a stunning double-century the following day — 218 — becoming the first player ever to achieve the feat in this milestone appearance. *(Photo: BCCI).*

CENTURY IN CAPS: Opening batsman Dom Sibley congratulates captain Root, who has just reached 100 in his third successive Test after raising his bat twice in Sri Lanka. Root receives his 100th Test cap, below, from England vice-captain Ben Stokes, who will represent the Emerald Headingley-based Northern Superchargers in this summer's inaugural Hundred competition. *(Photos: BCCI and Danny Reuben).*

JOINING THE MEMBERS: Test captain and batting star Joe Root and former Yorkshire and England paceman Darren Gough, who have both been honoured by the Queen with the award of the MBE.

TESTIMONIAL FOR ADAM LYTH: 2021 will be special for Yorkshire's experienced left-handed opener — a *Roses* game at his home ground of Scarborough and a Testimonial year deferred from 2020 because of the complications surrounding the Coronavirus pandemic.

ACTION MAN: Jordan Thompson, brilliant with bat, ball and in the field last season. The all-action all-rounder will hope 2020 was the launchpad for a memorable career.

WORLD NO.1: Dawid Malan, who was signed by Yorkshire in late 2019. The left-hander made an immediate impression with his double hundred against Derbyshire in the Bob Willis Trophy, and was named by the ICC as the best T20 batsman on the planet, courtesy of his exploits for England.

CRACKING ON: Harry Brook, 22, hits out on his way to a half century against Leicestershire in the Bob Willis Trophy. Harry ended 2020 with his maiden T20 fifty, a match-winning effort against Derbyshire at Emerald Headingley as his batting developed significantly with 447 runs across both formats.

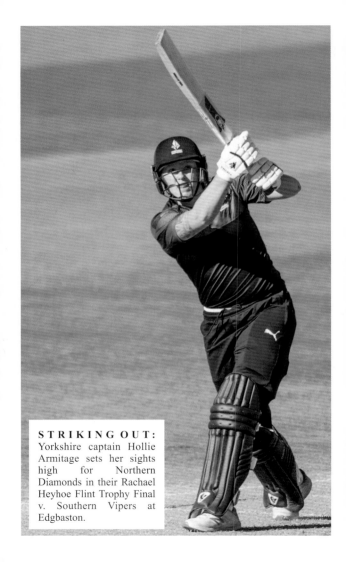

STRIKING OUT: Yorkshire captain Hollie Armitage sets her sights high for Northern Diamonds in their Rachael Heyhoe Flint Trophy Final v. Southern Vipers at Edgbaston.

Happy landing: Harry Brook catches Durham's Graham Clark off Adam Lyth's bowling at Emerald Headingley.

Happy return: Josh Poysden, who was back with leg-spin after suffering a sickening injury in 2019.

Thompson's blistering 44 off 19 balls. The Vikings should have posted 200 plus, yet they were still ahead of the game at halfway.

That theory was strengthened with Leicester 61-2 in the eighth over and a long way behind the rate. But that was when Delany and South African captain Colin Ackermann turned things around with an 88-run stand in seven overs, including 28 off Thompson in the 14th over.

Delany fell, leaving Ackermann to steer the chase with 58 off 34. Lyth was left defending nine off the last over and three off the last ball, which seamer Ben Mike clubbed for six down the ground. A disconsolate Lyth admitted afterwards: "That's one game we should really have won."

On-field drama was followed by drama off it as the Vikings' knockout chances went up in smoke. Willey, Fisher, Kohler-Cadmore and Poysden met up the day after the Leicester defeat and, with Willey testing positive for Coronavirus, the other three were ruled out of the rest of the group stage.

Yorkshire were hoping to find out the results of Willey's test on Monday, September 14, the day of the home *Roses* clash at Emerald Headingley. Had it come back negative all four would have been able to play. They were sitting outside the ground until 5.30pm, an hour before the start time, waiting for a text from the NHS. Confirmation was not actually provided until the Wednesday.

It meant coach Gale's preparations were heavily disrupted: he had to pick two teams to face Lancashire — one if the four could play and one if they could not. He ended up fielding the latter, including batsman Wharton, 19, for his first-team debut. Dawid Malan also made his *T20* debut for the Vikings, having been released from England's ODI bubble to play, but even his inclusion was not enough to prevent defeat.

Yorkshire, with stand-in captain Lyth electing to bat, made an excellent start of 62-1 after six overs, but Lyth's 36 was the top-score of an innings which subsided badly to 145-9. Malan was next best with 27.

Matthew Parkinson and Luke Wood claimed three wickets apiece for a Lancashire side whose Christmases had all come at once. Not only were they facing an under-strength side, they were able to absorb three dropped catches before recovering their chase from a wobble at 77-4 in the ninth over. Captain Dane Vilas (44) and Rob Jones (38) shared an unbroken 71 for the fifth wicket, meaning Yorkshire lost by six wickets with 2.1 overs remaining.

Yorkshire were four points behind the Lightning in second place in the North with three games remaining. Even with the cushion of knowing they could finish third in the group and still advance as one of the two best third-placed teams they were still up against it. Heading into their next fixture, against Durham at Emerald Headingley on Wednesday, September 16, they realistically had to win their remaining three games to have any chance of qualification. It was not to be.

Durham comfortably defended a target of 148 as the hosts lost by 43 runs. Yorkshire's third successive defeat came in a fixture which saw both sides struggle with the bat. Durham were 40-0 after four overs, only to be bowled out for 147. Duanne Olivier impressed with 2-16 from four overs in his first Blast outing of the summer after Lyth elected to bowl.

Yorkshire then slipped to 73-6 in the 11th over of their chase and lost

Setting the pace: Matthew Fisher, on the attack against Brooke Guest, of Derbyshire, had eight wickets from four matches before a Covid19 alert took him out of the contest.

with 20 balls remaining, new-ball seamer Matty Potts claiming 3-14 from three overs. Opener Clark's brisk 28 got Durham off to a flyer, only for Olivier to drag things back alongside Lyth and Thompson, who both claimed two wickets, and excellent off-spinner Jack Shutt with one. Wickets tumbled in the Vikings reply as they lost Lyth, Malan — for a golden duck — and Brook inside the first four overs as the score fell to 22-3. Not surprisingly, with experience lacking, they failed to recover.

The following evening, Thursday, September 17, Yorkshire were back across the Pennines against Lancashire at Emirates Old Trafford, a clash the visitors went into knowing they were all but out of quarter-final contention, if not mathematically.

The frustration of having to go into it under strength — Root returned after the end of England's international summer, however — remained. But, make no bones about it, this was a fixture the *White Rose* should have won. Root returned an excellent all-round display in front of the Sky TV cameras, raising hopes that the first Blast win against Lancashire since August 2017 could be achieved.

Root took 2-25 from four overs as Lancashire fell from 132-1 in their 15th over to finish on 167-6, opener Liam Livingstone top-scoring with 69 and Steven Croft hit 58. Left-arm wrist spinner Wisniewski, an 18-year-old debutant who bowled two encouraging overs for 15, was one of five Vikings spinners used.

All-rounder Root then hit a classy 64 off 39 balls as the Vikings reached 115-1 in the 13th over, sharing 91 with Lyth (45). The pair were two of three run-outs, Fraine the other, all coming back for a second as the score crumbled to 156-6 after 19 overs. Jonny Tattersall and debutant Revis failed to hit 12 off Saqib Mahmood in the last over, Vikings finishing on 160-6 and losing by seven runs to put the final nail in the coffin of their qualification hopes. In a team meeting afterwards, Root and Lyth both accepted blame for not seeing their side over the line, having been well set at the crease.

Yorkshire returned to Emerald Headingley on Sunday, September 20, to face Derbyshire in the final group game and their last of 2020 in either format. The visitors were actually the hosts, given their Incora County Ground was being used as a biosecure venue for England's women.

Even though quarter-final places were not on the line there was plenty to play for. Had the Vikings lost they could have finished bottom of the North Group. They were also aiming to secure the double over a Falcons side who had done exactly that over Yorkshire in each of the previous three seasons. A difficult week was ended in style with a thrilling six-wicket win off the last ball as Yorkshire recovered from 80-4 in the 12th over to overhaul a target of 168.

Root and Brook both hit fabulous half-centuries in an unbroken stand of 91 for the fifth wicket, uniting for 8.2 overs. Root finished with 60 off 50 balls as the equation became nine off the last over, while Brook, who needed to get one off the last ball against seamer Dustin Melton, hit the winning runs to reach 50 off 29.

While Root's fifty was his fourth in five Blast innings, Brook was the one who provided the impetus from No.6 and took the lead role late on to post his first career fifty in 25 games and give Yorkshire their third win in 10 group games. Derbyshire posted 167-6, led by opener Tom Wood's meaty career-best 67 off 48 balls, and Ben Coad's 3-40 from four overs was also a career best. The Falcons would have been frustrated with their total after a platform of 100-0 after 12 overs through Wood and Godleman (49).

Coad, who recovered from conceding 25 in his first two overs, led the way during the second half of the innings with his first three-for in 12 *T20* appearances, removing Wood caught at deep mid-wicket pulling, Wayne Madsen caught at mid-off and Matt Critchley caught at cover.

ROSES BLAST: Will Fraine showed his power during the Vitality Blast campaign with 163 runs from eight innings at a strike-rate of 187.35, his 44 off 16 balls in the home win over Derbyshire including five sixes. Above: Will crashes a six against Lancashire Lightning at Emerald Headingley.

NORTHERN DIAMONDS

Captain: Lauren Winfield-Hill

Director of Cricket: James Carr   Coach: Danielle Hazell

RACHAEL HEYHOE FLINT TROPHY 2020 (50 overs)

2020 CHAMPIONS: Southern Vipers, who beat the Diamonds by 38 runs
with 7.4 overs remaining in the final at Edgbaston on September 27

NORTH GROUP TABLE

*4 points awarded for a win, plus 1 bonus point for any team that
achieves victory with a run rate 1.25 times that of the opposition*

		P	W	L	T	NR	NRR	PTS
1	Northern Diamonds	6	5	1	0	0	1	23
2	Central Sparks	6	3	3	0	0	-0.285	13
3	Thunder	6	2	4	0	0	-0.515	9
4	Lightning	6	2	4	0	0	-0.113	8

Southern Vipers topped the South Group, winning all six of their games,
three of them with a bonus point.

NORTHERN DIAMONDS 2020 RHF TROPHY SQUAD

Player	Date of Birth	Birthplace	Type
L Winfield-Hill (Captain)	August 16, 1990	York	RHB, WK
H J Armitage	June 14, 1997	Huddersfield	RHB, LB
K H Brunt	July 2, 1985	Barnsley	RHB, RAF
A Campbell	June 6, 1991	Newcastle upon Tyne	LHB
L Dobson	June 10, 2001	Scarborough	RHB
H L Fenby	November 23, 1998	Stockton	LB
P C Graham	October 23, 1991	Steeton	RAMF
J L Gunn	May 9, 1986	Nottingham	RHB, RAMF
B A M Heath	August 20, 2001	Chesterfield	RHB, WK
R H M Hopkins	July 19, 1992	Nottingham	RHB
S L Kalis	August 30, 1999	Delft, Holland	RHB
B A Langston	September 6, 1992	Harold Wood	RAF
K A Levick	July 17, 1991	Sheffield	LB
A L MacDonald	October 3, 1991	Kingston-upon-Thames	LHB, RAM
N R Sciver	August 20, 1992	Tokyo, Japan	RHB, RAMF
L C N Smith	March 10, 1995	Hillingdon	SLA
R Slater	November 20, 2001	Glens Fallls	LAM
E F Telford	April 5, 1999	Penrith	RAM
L Tipton	March 19, 2002	Sunderland	RHB

End of an era runs hard into the next

SPARKLING DIAMONDS SHORT OF FINAL CUTTING EDGE

By Graham Hardcastle

The Northern Diamonds enjoyed an excellent start to their competitive life as one of the eight new women's Regional Centres of Excellence, reaching the final of the 50-over Rachael Heyhoe Flint Trophy, only to be beaten by Southern Vipers in the late September final.

Effectively replacing the Yorkshire Diamonds, who played in four years of the *T20* Kia Super League, this side's existence will see it represent Yorkshire, Durham and Northumberland — something they did with vigour in 2020. The Heyhoe Flint Trophy was drawn up at late notice by the ECB once domestic cricket was given the go-ahead after the first Coronavirus lockdown — eight teams split into two regional groups, each team playing six games and the top of each group advancing to the final.

Diamonds raced out of the blocks, winning their first four matches. In the end they lost only one in the group phase — by six wickets against Central Sparks at Emerald Headingley on September 13 — and advanced with comfort.

The squad included many who had performed well while wearing the *White Rose* in the KSL: Hollie Armitage, Helen Fenby, Bess Heath, Beth Langston and Katie Levick. Then they were able to make use of England players Katherine Brunt, Nat Sciver, Linsey Smith and Lauren Winfield-Hill at either end of the competition.

They got off to an excellent start with Bank Holiday wins over the Sparks at Edgbaston on Saturday, August 29, and another Midlands side, Lightning, at Durham's Emirates Riverside on the Monday.

All England players were available before heading into a training camp ahead of a late summer *T20* series against the West Indies at Derby, and all four shone across the two aforementioned fixtures, highlighted by five wickets against the Sparks for seamer Brunt and a century against the Lightning for her wife, Sciver.

Winfield-Hill made a winning start as captain, her 72 off 71 balls helping to secure a nine-wicket win chasing 145 against the Sparks after Brunt's superb 5-20 from nine overs, four of them bowled. The win over

the Lightning was more hard-fought. Sciver, a star of the world game, showed all her class to fashion a recovery from 84-6 in the 22nd over after Winfield-Hill had elected to bat. She took the lead in an 84-run partnership for the seventh wicket with Alex MacDonald (28) as her 104 off 113 balls ensured a score of 226-9.

There was more peril on the horizon for the Diamonds as captain Kathryn Bryce, who had taken the new ball and claimed 5-29 from 10 overs, posted 71 not out from No.3 in the order. England opener Tammy Beaumont hit 51 and the other Bryce, Sarah, 57. Lightning were 117-1 and 152-2 but subsided badly to 217-7.

Sciver struck twice in the 37th over as the score became 152-4, while Smith and experienced Jenny Gunn were miserly and bagged two wickets apiece.

The return clash with Lightning followed on Saturday, September 5, at Leicestershire's Fischer County Ground, Grace Road, and again the Diamonds had to dig deep to secure a victory — by two wickets with seven balls remaining as they chased a target of 227.

Now without their England players, Langston, Gunn, Armitage and MacDonald each claimed two wickets as the hosts were bowled out for 226, a target which proved competitive across the board.

The Diamonds slipped to 7-2 in the seventh over and 119-7 in the 30th, with off-spinner Lucy Higham claiming three wickets. Thankfully, the visitors had the experience of for-

JENNY GUNN: Call to talk World Cup star out of retirement was inspired.

**Better late: Netherlands international Sterre Kalis shrugs off
three successive ducks as she drives on to 87 for Northern
Diamonds against Central Sparks at Emerald Headingley.**

mer England one-day World Cup winners Gunn and Langston to count
on. They shared a controlled and sensible stand of 81 in 15 overs for the
eighth wicket, Langston hitting 37. When she departed at 200-8 in the
45th Gunn kept her cool to finish on 50 not out off 72 balls with four
fours, seamer Phoebe Graham chipping in with 15 unbeaten.

Aged 34, Gunn had to be coaxed out of retirement ahead of the campaign by Head Coach Danielle Hazell, a call which proved to be inspired
as this contribution was supplemented by more to follow.

Next up was the *Roses* battle. We say '*Roses'* in inverted commas
given the other influences — the North West Thunder were represented
not only by Lancashire, but Cheshire and Cumbria, too. Still, the rivalry
remains even in a new competition. The two sides met at Liverpool's

Aigburth ground on Thursday, September 10, and it was a pretty comfortable 73-run win for the Diamonds, who made it four wins from four to put them on the brink of the final.

There was early trouble at 57-4 in the 17th over, including the loss of Netherlands international batsman Sterre Kalis for a third successive duck as she was bowled by an unplayable grubber from seamer Alice Dyson.

She left the field with arms outstretched as if to say: "What am I supposed to do with that?"

Hard in: Northern Diamonds' Beth Langston gathers cleanly from Linsey Smith to run out Southern Vipers's Tara Norris in the Rachael Heyhoe Flint Trophy Final at Edgbaston.

She need have had no fear as her luck was soon to change.

The Diamonds' recovery was led by left-hander MacDonald, aged 28, whose superb 110-ball 92 from No.5 included 10 fours and two sixes, and was filled with a fair share of sweep shots. Yorkshire all-rounder MacDonald, helped by 29s from Gunn and Graham and 23 from Heath, posted her highest domestic score in six years to underpin a commanding 248-8.

Against a youthful-looking Thunder side, coached by Barnsley-born former England coach Paul Shaw, it was a target which looked pretty safe. So it proved as the hosts lost regular wickets to limp to 175-8. New-ball seamer Langston and leg-spinner Armitage struck twice and MacDonald once, while Levick's leg-spin accounted for a magnificent 3-22 from 10 overs.

One more win would seal top spot in the North for a Diamonds side who had claimed two four-point wins and two with an additional bonus point — Sparks at Edgbaston and Thunder at Liverpool. But they would be made to wait as the second-placed Sparks kept the race alive with a six-wicket win at Emerald Headingley on Sunday, September 13.

The Diamonds were bowled out for 217, which included a stylish 87

How's that? The umpire's finger goes up as Northern Diamonds wicket-keeper Bess Heath catches Southern Vipers's Ella McCaughan off the bowling of Linsey Smith in the Rachael Heyhoe Flint Trophy Final at Edgbaston.

from No.3 Kalis, a 21-year-old with 17 *T20* international caps under her belt. Langston then struck with the second ball of the Sparks chase, only for captain and opener Eve Jones (77) and second-wicket partner Marie Kelly (49) to steer the ship towards harbour with a stand of 123. Two quick wickets, including Jones, left the score at 172-4 in the 40th over, but the Sparks, for whom new-ball seamer Liz Russell had earlier claimed four wickets, got over the line with 3.2 overs remaining.

It meant that going into the final round of games, the Diamonds were five points clear of the Sparks with a better net run rate. The Sparks had to beat Lightning with a bonus point and hope the Diamonds suffered a heavy home defeat at Emerald Headingley against the Thunder on Saturday, September 19. Neither happened, setting up a final against Southern Vipers eight days later.

Langston starred with 3-18 from 8.5 overs against the Thunder, while Graham, Levick and Gunn chipped in with two as the visitors slipped to 8-2 and lost their last seven wickets for 52 to be bowled out for 143 inside 43 overs. Only two players reached 20 for the Thunder.

In reply Kalis continued her impressive upturn in form with an

DANIELLE HAZELL   **LAUREN WINFIELD-HILL**   **HOLLIE ARMITAGE**

unbeaten 55 and was backed up by 36 from skipper Armitage and 26 not out from Gunn, securing a third bonus-point win with 20.2 overs remaining and six wickets in hand. So, to Edgbaston they went.

Levick spoke about how this new team had run with the progression shown by the Yorkshire Diamonds in the final year, 2019, of the Kia Super League competition. In that, they missed out on Finals Day by two points despite having won one more game than the Vipers, who qualified courtesy of claiming two bonus points.

All that was put to one side as the excitement grew for the Sunday, September 27, showdown in Birmingham. On the eve of the game, Winfield-Hill was released from the England *T20* squad to play — and she captained the side. It just was not to be as the Vipers won by 38 runs defending a target of 232.

The Diamonds certainly had their chances to win.

First of all, they dragged back an excellent Vipers start from 100-0 in the 24th over after Georgia Adams and Ella McCaughan (35) had threatened to make a mockery of Winfield-Hill's decision to bowl first. Spin dragged things back brilliantly. Levick claimed 3-49 from eight overs, including the big wicket of Adams for 80 — she moved to 500 competition runs in the process. Armitage claimed two, getting No.3 Maia Bouchier (28) caught at mid-on with a drag-down short ball. That, leaving the score at 150-2 in the 32nd over, proved a huge wicket as the innings stuttered to 231 all out.

In reply, the Diamonds were ideally placed at 74-1 in the 15th over, only to subside themselves to off-spinner Charlotte Taylor, whose 6-34 from 10 overs proved to be the competition's best haul. Kalis tried in vain to steer the ship out of trouble with 55, but a loss of six wickets for 36 through the middle of the innings was irreparable damage. They finished a hugely positive campaign bowled out for 193 inside 43 overs.

FROM BABY BOYCOTTS
TO COUNTY PROS

Some sporting nicknames can be amusing, some brutal and others difficult to live up to. Childhood buddies Will Fraine and Hollie Armitage are certainly doing a pretty decent job of living up to theirs.

The Yorkshire pair grew up at Huddersfield club Meltham, opened the batting together and won a decent amount of silverware in the process.

"I'm not so sure Hollie will want me to tell you this," *White Rose* batsman Fraine said. "But they used to call us Geoffrey and Geraldine Boycott. That's what we went by."

Fraine needn't have worried, with Armitage laughing: "Ah yes, ginger Geraldine. We were both in the Yorkshire pathway system. It's a long time ago, but they were good days."

The newly turned Northern Diamonds professional continued: "That nickname's actually a good memory for me, because maybe a girl mixing in a lads' team could have been quite awkward then. It's a bit more common now. But they just treated me as one of the lads. I loved it.

"They got stuck into me the same as anybody else."

Fraine, 24, continued: "Those nicknames came from the fact we used to block it loads. I was 10 or 11 when I first played there, and Hollie's a year younger. We played together at under-11s and 13s, and I captained. We won all the local competitions.

"From other sides there was a bit of, 'Ooh, there's a girl playing against us'. But they quickly realised she was an absolute gun. We also played a bit of second-team cricket together before I moved to Honley at 16 and then went down to Bromsgrove. That was when we lost touch a bit. But she's done really well, and progressed her career fantastically.

"I see her mum and dad down at Meltham still and Hollie sometimes when we're at training. We reminisce about the days when she was the slowest person ever between the wickets. She's not rapid now, but much quicker."

There has actually been very little crossover between the Yorkshire men's and women's senior squads, including the Northern Diamonds, who have only very recently come into existence.

"It's a shame we can't overlap more," Armitage said. "It would be great if we could do that and share experiences with the lads and just get to know each other. Obviously, myself and Frainey are mates, but I don't know many of the other lads. I hope it happens more with us being in

Opening pair: Hollie Armitage and Will Fraine, who started together at Meltham and are now professional cricketers.

and around Headingley for longer now that a few of us are professionals."

Fraine is proud of his own development from his days in the Huddersfield League to playing for his home county. But he is also proud of Armitage's progression: "It's great the way the women's game is going," he said. "It's getting so much more coverage, and Hollie's doing really well. That she's professional now is fully deserved."

Will played in Worcestershire's system as a teenager, and has a wealth of experience in league cricket having played in the Birmingham League. He believes it is a vital breeding ground for any young player determined to catch the eye.

"I started playing in the Meltham second team when I was 12," he said. "You get roughed up a bit, but you're playing against men. My dad (Mike) was massive on me playing at that level because sometimes, when you're playing against schoolboys, you can bully the opposition.

"But you find a lot out about a young lad coming up against some serious senior cricketers — league pros or paid players. Some can be internationals. It teaches you to grow up a bit as well.

"It really helped me to get picked up by a county.

"When I was down in Worcester I played a bit for the Academy. But I'd started playing in the Birmingham League, and I got two hundreds in three games (for Halesowen in 2014) and got thrown into training with the Worcester Academy. And they were all talking about it because no one else had really done that.

"If a young lad scores buckets on a Saturday it shows me that they're a real player. If you do something spectacular you will get noticed."

FIVE SIGN PROFESSIONAL FORMS

The following five players have turned professional with the Northern Diamonds:

Hollie Armitage: The Yorkshire women's captain and all-rounder has turned professional in a bid to kick on a career filled with promise. A top-order bat from Huddersfield and a rapidly improving leg-spinner, Armitage, 28, has made 25 appearances with the England Academy.

She has spent the last two winters playing grade cricket and coaching in Tasmania.

Phoebe Graham: Fast bowler, 29, who has played county cricket for Yorkshire, Nottinghamshire, Devon and Berkshire. She impressed with ball and bat for the Diamonds in last season's RHF Trophy, particularly with her economy rate of 3.87 across five appearances.

Steeton-born Graham has given up a job in marketing at Sky to turn pro. She is the daughter of the late local cricket legend Peter, who took 1,192 Bradford League wickets (1997-2001).

Jenny Gunn: A seam bowling all-rounder among the first 18 women to be offered a central contract by England in 2014. Her 15-year England career (2004-2019) brought three World Cup titles and five *Ashes* triumphs, while 136 ODI wickets puts her in England's all-time top five wicket-takers.

Gunn had retired before Diamonds coach Dani Hazell offered her a short-term deal last summer, and she did enough to return to full-time professional status.

Beth Langston: Essex-born opening bowler who is also proficient at the death, Langston has played six one-day and T20 internationals for England (2013-2016). Aged 28, she has played her cricket in the Yorkshire system since 2016, having debuted in county cricket for Essex as a 16-year-old.

In last summer's RHF Trophy she was the Diamonds' leading wicket-taker with 12, the joint third best in the competition.

Linsey Smith: A 25-year-old left-arm spinner with nine T20 caps for England in 2018 and 2019. A centrally contracted England player in 2019, she is hoping to get back to that level through standout performances with the Diamonds this summer.

Middlesex-born, Smith has played county cricket for Sussex and Berkshire, and played T20 cricket for the Yorkshire Diamonds in 2019. She claimed four RHF Trophy wickets for the Northern Diamonds last summer.

BOUNCING BACK WITH
VICTORIES HAT-TRICK

Yorkshire Women's first team played a series of T20 and 50-over friendlies through August and into September, enjoying an excellent start with three straight wins before a mixture of defeats, rain and a tie to end their campaign. Aside from 10 official fixtures there were some competitive training matches played to give players further opportunities to push for Northern Diamonds selection.

Sunday August 2, 2020, Harrogate CC

T20: Yorkshire (138-4) beat North East Warriors (98-8) by 40 runs.
T20: Yorkshire (113-5) beat North East Warriors (112-4) by five wickets.

Sunday August 9, 2020, Harrogate CC

T20: Yorkshire (142-4) beat North East Warriors (70-8) by 72 runs.
T20: Yorkshire (103-8) lost to North East Warriors (112-6) by nine runs.

Thursday August 27, 2020, Newton-le-Willows CC

50-overs: Yorkshire (39-2 in the 10th over) v. Lancashire (117 all out). Match abandoned.

Tuesday September 1, 2020, Eppleton CC

50-overs: Yorkshire (129 all out) lost to North East Warriors (131 all out) by two runs.

Sunday September 6, 2020, Harrogate CC

T20: Yorkshire (110-6) lost to Scotland (114-6) by four wickets.
T20: Yorkshire (87-2 after 16 overs) v. Scotland. Match abandoned.

Sunday September 13, 2020, Collingham & District CC

T20: Yorkshire (94-7) beat Nottinghamshire (56-9) by 38 runs.
T20: Yorkshire (99-4) tied with Nottinghamshire (99-6).

Alex MacDonald provided the standout performance with 4-16 in the rained off clash with Lancashire, while Hannah Buck hit 48 in one of the two meetings with Scotland.

Yorkshire also fielded teams at Under-17s, 15s and 13s level during the summer. The standout individual performances came from the Under-13s, Kate Cooper and Sarah Wood scoring half-centuries in a late September victory over Lancashire. Emily Roberts and Lucy Randle-Bissell both claimed five-wicket hauls in wins over Durham and Nottinghamshire.

Team work...at a distance: Yorkshire women observe the Coronavirus restrictions as they line up for their match against Lancashire at Newton-le-Willows CC on August 27.
(Photo: John Heald)

QUARTET OF DOUBLE-HEADERS

The Yorkshire women will play a series of T20 double-headers through late April and into May.

The Vitality T20 competition sees Yorkshire play in Group One North alongside Cumbria, Lancashire, North East Warriors and Scotland A.

The *White Rose*, coached by former Essex leg-spinner Tom Craddock, have two home dates, both at Harrogate CC, while venues for away trips were still to be confirmed at the time of print.

They begin their campaign with an away date in Cumbria on Sunday April 25, playing Cumbria (10.30am) and Scotland A (1.30pm).

Then it is the first of two successive home dates on Monday May 3 at Harrogate, facing North East Warriors at 10.30am and then Cumbria at 4.30pm. The following Sunday, May 9, they are at Harrogate again to host Lancashire at 10.30am and North East Warriors at 4.30pm.

The final round of fixtures goes across the Pennines on Sunday May 16, for clashes with Cumbria at 1.30pm and hosts Lancashire at 4.30pm.

While it is expected there will be no knockout cricket following the group stages, some further friendly fixtures are likely to be arranged leading into the Northern Diamonds schedule and also the women's Hundred.

OFF-SPIN STAR FOR *WHITE ROSE* AS CURTAIN FALLS ON LEGEND

By Graham Hardcastle

When, in the summer of 2019, Dom Bess was on loan at Yorkshire he regularly fielded the question: "'Would you be open to a permanent move to Emerald Headingley?"

With more than a year left on his contract at home county Somerset, he understandably kept his cards close to his chest.

But a couple of things were obvious.

One: He needed to be playing regular first-team cricket to accelerate his development, and it just wasn't happening at Taunton, given the presence of Jack

DOM BESS: Joining a *White Rose* "massively on the up".

Leach. Two: Yorkshire were keen to acquire his services. The hierarchy knew they were lacking an experienced four-day spinner, hence the recruitment of overseas duo Keshav Maharaj and Ravi Ashwin for 2020.

Coronavirus put the kibosh on those particular deals, giving fledgling off-spinner Jack Shutt more opportunities in the Bob Willis Trophy. But, when Bess became available, it was no surprise to see Yorkshire pounce on a 23-year-old offie with 10 Test appearances and 19 wickets to his name at the time.

Last year proved a hugely significant one for Bess. It started with him claiming the senior spinner's role in England's Test team, thanks to eight wickets in two appearances in South Africa, and ended with him signing a four-year deal with Yorkshire. "Hopefully the opportunities I can get at Yorkshire will develop my learning to kick on and play international

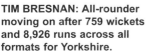

TIM BRESNAN: All-rounder moving on after 759 wickets and 8,926 runs across all formats for Yorkshire.

cricket for a long time," he said. "That is the ultimate goal, but I also want to be part of a Yorkshire side that are again winning Championships. I want us to be pushing for one-day and *T20* success as well. Last year, I certainly got the hint that the club want to push for the *T20* and 50-over competition.

"This club is massively on the up. I wouldn't be signing with a club if they didn't have big ambitions."

The big arrival of a rising star followed the big departure of club legend Tim Bresnan, who brought the curtain down on a 19-year career with the *White Rose* in mid-June, shortly before joining Warwickshire.

The 35-year-old former England all-rounder, a Championship-title winner in 2014 and 2015, was out of contract at the end of 2019 and opted to leave early to take up an opportunity at Edgbaston. "It has given me immense pride to represent the county for the best part of two decades," Tim said. "My Yorkshire cap is one of my proudest possessions. I didn't take this decision lightly, but now is the best time to move on. There is still plenty of fire in my belly, and I look forward to what the future brings. Hopefully, with me moving aside, the younger players will get their opportunity to kickstart their careers as well."

Debuting for Yorkshire in 2003, the *Ashes* and World *T20* winner went on to take 759 wickets and score 8,926 runs across all formats for the county, earning plaudits from teammates, coaches and supporters.

Seamer Matthew Fisher told a great tale about 'Brezzy': "When I was younger and coming into the dressing room he was in the England side and came back to Yorkshire. He had a boot sponsorship, and would give me boots most seasons. When he rang me up to tell me what was going on with him leaving, we talked a bit about the boot thing, and I'll always remember it. If I can get to the same point in my career I'd love to continue that kind of thing with another young player."

Three young players with limited or no first-team experience also departed for pastures new. Left-arm spinner James Logan's contract was not renewed. The 23-year-old is the Academy's record wicket-taker with 193 between 2014 and 2017. Seamers Ed Barnes and Jared Warner also departed, Barnes for Leicestershire and Warner for Gloucestershire.

TIMOTHY (TIM) THOMAS BRESNAN
FIRST-CLASS CRICKET FOR YORKSHIRE 2003 TO 2019

Right-hand batsman		Right-arm fast-medium bowler		
Born: Pontefract		February 28, 1985		
Debut for Yorkshire	v. Northamptonshire at Northampton	May 14, 2003		
Last played:	v. Kent at Leeds	September 16, 2019		
	Yorkshire Cap: July 19, 2006			

BATTING AND FIELDING

Season	M	I	NO	Runs	HS	Avge	100s	50s	Ct
2003	4	4	0	81	52	20.25	0	1	1
2004	10	15	3	143	35	11.91	0	0	3
2005	15	20	3	339	74	19.94	0	3	4
2006	10	14	1	249	91	19.15	0	1	4
2007	15	20	6	553	116	39.50	2	2	6
2008	14	20	5	506	84*	33.73	0	2	9
2009	10	14	2	372	97	31.00	0	1	5
2010	6	9	1	203	70	25.37	0	2	2
2011	3	5	1	175	87	43.75	0	1	1
2012	4	4	0	73	38	18.25	0	0	2
2013	4	5	1	66	38	16.50	0	0	1
2014	10	10	0	338	95	33.80	0	4	5
2015	18	25	5	907	169*	45.35	2	4	15
2016	12	21	4	731	142*	43.00	1	5	12
2017	12	16	0	330	61	20.62	0	1	9
2018	12	22	3	385	80	20.26	0	2	9
2019	4	8	0	143	58	17.87	0	1	1
	163	232	35	5594	169*	28.39	5	30	89

BOWLING

Seasons	Overs	Mdns	Runs	Wkts	Avge	Best	5wI
2003	79.1	16	259	7	37.00	3- 88	0
2004	160.3	31	557	17	32.76	3- 32	0
2005	459	87	1571	47	33.42	5- 42	1
2006	258.3	47	828	27	30.66	5- 58	1
2007	332	71	1090	34	32.05	4- 10	0
2008	421	77	1278	45	28.40	5- 94	1
2009	352.4	91	909	24	37.87	4-116	0
2010	188.2	42	538	17	31.64	5- 52	1
2011	97	27	252	13	19.38	4- 50	0
2012	130.2	31	397	14	28.35	5- 81	1
2013	130.2	31	393	16	24.56	4- 41	0
2014	331	76	947	30	31.56	4-112	0
2015	457.5	123	1482	48	30.87	5- 85	1
2016	318.1	76	997	35	28.48	5- 36	1
2017	262	56	934	30	31.13	4- 53	0
2018	279.5	48	969	35	27.68	5- 28	1
2019	82	17	262	6	43.66	2- 47	0
	4339.4	947	13663	445	30.70	5- 28	8

Centuries (5)

2007	116	v. Surrey	at The Oval
2007	101 *	v. Warwickshire	at Scarborough
2015	100 *	v. Somerset	at Taunton
2015	169 *	v. Durham	at Chester-le-treet
2016	142 *	v. Middlesex	at Lord's

5 wickets in an innings (8)

2005	5-42	v. Worcestershire	at Worcester
2006	5-58	v. Durham	at Chester-le Street
2008	5-94	v. Durham	at Leeds
2010	5-52	v. Kent	at Canterbury
2012	5-81	v. Gloucestershire	at Bristol
2015	5-85	v. Warwickshire	at Leeds
2016	5-36	v. Nottinghamshire	at Scarborough
2018	5-28	v. Hampshire	at Leeds

TEST MATCHES FOR ENGLAND
BATTING AND FIELDING

Seasons	M	I	NO	Runs	HS	Avge	100s	50s	Ct
2009-13/14	23	26	4	575	91	26.13	0	3	8

BOWLING

Seasons	Matches	Overs	Mdns	Runs	Wkts	Avge	Best	5wI	10wM
2009-13/14	23	779	185	2357	72	32.73	5-48	1	0

ALL FIRST CLASS MATCHES
BATTING AND FIELDING

Seasons	M	I	NO	Runs	HS	Avge	100s	50s	Ct
2003-20	202	278	43	6813	169*	28.99	7	34	107

Seasons	Matches	Overs	Mdns	Runs	Wkts	Avge	Best	5wI	10wM
2003-20	202	5590.4	1246	17367	562	30.90	5-28	9	0

LIST A CRICKET FOR YORKSHIRE 2001 TO 2019

Debut for Yorkshire   v. Kent at Leeds   June 10, 2001
Last played: v. Durham at Leeds   June 14, 2019

BATTING AND FIELDING

Season	M	I	NO	Runs	HS	Avge	100s	50s	Ct
2001	4	3	2	12	7	12.00	0	0	2
2002	21	12	6	76	22	12.66	0	0	2
2003	13	9	1	218	61	27.25	0	1	8
2004	22	15	4	227	49	20.63	0	0	3
2005	19	16	2	88	17	6.28	0	0	10
2006	7	3	1	97	47	48.50	0	0	2
2007	15	10	3	150	33	21.42	0	0	2
2008	16	9	2	134	55	19.14	0	1	3
2009	6	6	1	31	8*	6.20	0	0	2
2010	7	6	3	90	58	30.00	0	1	1
2011	1	1	0	9	9	9.00	0	0	0
2012	1	1	0	27	27	27.00	0	0	0
2013	1	1	0	0	0	0.00	0	0	0
2014	9	5	1	77	32	19.25	0	0	6
2015	9	7	0	132	43	18.85	0	0	2
2016	9	8	2	361	95*	60.16	0	3	2
2017	8	7	1	138	65	23.00	0	1	4
2018	7	7	2	140	41	28.00	0	0	2
2019	6	4	0	117	89	29.25	0	1	1
	181	130	31	2124	95*	21.45	0	8	52

BOWLING

Seasons	Overs	Mdns	Runs	Wkts	Avge	Best	4wI
2001	23	3	86	4	21.50	2-27	0
2002	122.5	7	549	14	39.21	2-27	0
2003	93.5	5	447	18	24.83	3-29	0
2004	150	14	753	19	39.63	3-31	0
2005	143.5	6	757	12	63.08	4-25	1
2006	53	3	297	9	33.00	3-46	0
2007	99.5	5	565	15	37.66	3-22	0
2008	111.1	14	485	24	20.20	4-31	1
2009	46	5	239	10	23.90	4-35	1
2010	55	2	309	12	25.75	3-40	0
2011	7	0	34	2	17.00	2-34	0
2012	5	0	46	1	46.00	1-46	0
2013	7	0	45	1	45.00	1-45	0
2014	75.2	6	371	15	24.73	4-28	1
2015	50.5	2	265	8	33.12	2-41	0
2016	62	6	335	10	33.50	2-22	0
2017	63	3	356	9	39.55	3-22	0
2018	57	3	338	7	48.28	2-39	0
2019	44	0	259	6	43.16	2-27	0
	1269.4	84	6536	196	33.34	4-25	4

4 wickets in an innings (4)

2005	4-25	v. Somerset	at Leeds
2008	4-31	v. Gloucestershire	at Bristol
2009	4-35	v. Sussex	at Leeds
2014	4-28	v. Worcestershire	at Leeds

ONE-DAY INTERNATIONALS FOR ENGLAND
BATTING AND FIELDING

Seasons	M	I	NO	Runs	HS	Avge	100s	50s	Ct
2006-15	85	64	20	871	80	19.79	0	1	20

BOWLING

Seasons	Overs	Mdns	Runs	Wkts	Avge	Best	4wI
2006-15	703.3	35	3813	109	34.98	5-48	4

ALL LIST A MATCHES
BATTING AND FIELDING

Seasons	M	I	NO	Runs	HS	Avge	100s	50s	Ct
2001-19	279	203	54	3221	95*	21.61	0	10	73

BOWLING

Seasons	Overs	Mdns	Runs	Wkts	Avge	Best	4wI
2001-19	2056.2	123	10794	315	34.26	5-48	8

T20 CRICKET FOR YORKSHIRE 2003 TO 2019

Debut for Yorkshire:	v. Derbyshire at Leeds		June 14, 2003
Last played:	v, Warwickshire at Birmingham		August 30, 2019

BATTING AND FIELDING

Season	M	I	NO	Runs	HS	Avge	100s	50s	Ct
2003	5	2	1	18	13*	18.00	0	0	2
2004	5	4	0	89	42	22.25	0	0	3
2005	8	8	5	102	25	34.00	0	0	2
2006	3	1	0	8	8	8.00	0	0	0
2007	8	5	1	50	25*	12.50	0	0	3
2008	9	8	3	58	15	11.60	0	0	4
2009	6	4	1	38	19*	12.66	0	0	1
2010	1	0	0	0	—	—	0	0	0
2011	3	1	1	25	25*	—	0	0	0
2012	2	2	0	24	18	12.00	0	0	0
2014	10	9	5	175	45*	43.75	0	0	5
2015	11	8	3	155	51	31.00	0	1	5
2016	15	13	4	180	29*	20.00	0	0	8
2017	12	10	5	105	24	21.00	0	0	3
2018	11	9	3	106	28*	17.66	0	0	5
2018/19	1	1	1	17	17*	—	0	0	0
2019	8	6	2	58	18	14.50	0	0	0
	118	91	35	1208	51	21.57	0	1	41

BOWLING

Seasons	Overs	Mdns	Runs	Wkts	Avge	Best	4wI
2003	18	0	116	7	16.57	3- 31	0
2004	18.2	0	143	3	47.66	1- 21	0
2005	26	0	210	10	21.00	3- 22	0
2006	7	0	45	6	7.50	3- 21	0
2007	18	0	146	5	29.20	2- 9	0
2008	34	0	244	8	30.50	2- 12	0
2009	23	0	157	7	22.42	3- 26	0
2010	4	0	21	1	21.00	1- 21	0
2011	11	0	106	2	53.00	1- 32	0
2012	7	0	40	2	20.00	2- 22	0
2014	36	0	262	9	29.11	2- 22	0
2015	26	0	263	5	52.60	1- 5	0
2016	44	2	353	21	16.80	3- 15	0
2017	39.3	2	338	17	19.88	6- 19	1
2018	29.5	0	312	5	62.40	3- 38	0
2018/19	3.4	0	41	2	20.50	2- 41	0
2019	15	0	121	8	15.12	2- 15	0
	360.2	4	2918	118	24.72	6- 19	1

4 wickets in an innings (1)

2017   6-19 v. Lancashire   at Leeds

T20 MATCHES FOR ENGLAND
BATTING AND FIELDING

Seasons	M	I	NO	Runs	HS	Avge	100s	50s	Ct
2006-13/14	34	22	9	216	47*	16.61	0	0	10

BOWLING

Seasons	Overs	Mdns	Runs	Wkts	Avge	Best	4wI
2006-13/14	110.3	1	887	24	36.95	3-10	0

ALL T20 MATCHES
BATTING AND FIELDING

Seasons	M	I	NO	Runs	HS	Avge	100s	50s	Ct
2003-20	182	132	52	1639	51	20.48	0	1	61

BOWLING

Seasons	Overs	Mdns	Runs	Wkts	Avge	Best	4wI
2003-20	571.1	5	4654	180	25.85	6-19	1

Hollie Armitage catches record

Yorkshire's Hollie Armitage equalled a Clarence CC record — male or female — on February 7 when she took five outfield catches in a Tasmanian women's grade 50-over fixture against North Hobart.

JARED DAVID WARNER
FIRST-CLASS MATCHES FOR YORKSHIRE
BATTING AND FIELDING

Seasons	M	I	NO	Runs	HS	Avge	100s	50s	Ct
2020	1	1	0	4	4	4.00	0	0	0

BOWLING

Seasons	Matches	Overs	Mdns	Runs	Wkts	Avge	Best	5wI	10wM
2020	1	9	0	23	1	23.00	1-23	0	0

LIST A MATCHES FOR YORKSHIRE
BATTING AND FIELDING

Seasons	M	I	NO	Runs	HS	Avge	100s	50s	Ct
2019	1	0	0	0	—	—	0	0	0

BOWLING

Seasons	Matches	Overs	Mdns	Runs	Wkts	Avge	Best	4wI
2019	1	5	0	32	0	—	0-32	0

JAMES EDWIN LOGAN
FIRST-CLASS MATCHES FOR YORKSHIRE
BATTING AND FIELDING

Seasons	M	I	NO	Runs	HS	Avge	100s	50s	Ct
2018-19	2	3	1	33	20*	16.50	0	0	1

BOWLING

Seasons	Matches	Overs	Mdns	Runs	Wkts	Avge	Best	5wI	10wM
2018-19	2	33	9	85	4	21.25	4-22	0	0

Winter sun shines on Yorkshire stars

Jonny Bairstow, Katherine Brunt, Tom Kohler-Cadmore, Dawid Malan, Adam Lyth, Duanne Olivier, Nat Sciver and Sam Wisniewski all spent time overseas this winter playing in the various domestic T20 leagues:

Jonny Bairstow —Sunrisers Hyderabad, Indian Premier League

Katherine Brunt — Melbourne Stars, Women's Big Bash

Tom Kohler-Cadmore — Pune Devils, Abu Dhabi T10 League and Peshawar Zalmi Pakistan Super League.

Dawid Malan — Hobart Hurricanes, Big Bash

Adam Lyth — Multan Sultans, Pakistan Super League and Delhi Bulls, Abu Dhabi T10 League

Duanne Olivier — Jaffna Stallions, Lanka Premier League.

Nat Sciver — Melbourne Stars, Women's Big Bash

Sam Wisniewski — Pune Devils, Abu Dhabi T10 League

Fashionista: Not content with taking wickets and scoring runs for Yorkshire, Blast captain David Willey, above, has turned his hand to fashion-designing.

The England all-rounder has helped to design the county's new T20 kit, produced by new partners, Nike, and Yorkshire have signed a contract with the world-leading sportswear brand to produce the county's playing, training and leisure wear for the next four years at least. Nike, who have in the past produced Team India's kit, have replaced Puma, who first partnered the *White Rose* in 2014.

"I've travelled the world playing T20 cricket for England and various teams and franchises," the all-rounder said. "I've seen what works well, and the club were keen to have my input into the new T20 kit, so it marries up with how we want to play — that attacking and fearless brand of cricket."

Yorkshire's non-stop gift to the cricket world

PLAYER PRODUCTION LINE THAT HAS NO END

Special Feature By Graham Hardcastle

The Yorkshire production line is a wonderful thing. The phrase 'Strong Yorkshire, strong England' has rung true for more than 150 years — right back to the county being founded in 1863. As Director of Cricket Martyn Moxon puts it, the county have nurtured their own and provided England with an abundance of talent "forever"

The Dazzler: Founder manager of Yorkshire Cricket School Ralph Middlebrook puts a burgeoning Darren Gough through his paces.

From early 1987 onwards the drive to produce top-class talent stepped up a notch with the opening of the Indoor School on the opposite side of St Michael's Lane to Emerald Headingley.

It was on February 1, 1987, that a £465,000 project was completed, the brainchild of then cricket chairman Tony Vann. It led to a successful Youth Training Scheme, the precursor to the Yorkshire Academy that continues to thrive to this day and is the envy of many a professional club worldwide, not just in England.

Leeds City Council cricket development officer Ralph Middlebrook, a Bradford League stalwart with an eye for talent, would relocate to be based at Headingley and guide the Government-funded YTS in conjunction with the *White Rose* county. The YTS would be a two-year rolling programme, employing eight players at any one time. The first were Jeremy Batty, Stephen Bethel, Richard Carlton and Paul Grayson, a future international and Yorkshire's current batting coach. It would eventually run until 1999, and of the 52 players enrolled five went on to play international cricket for England — Grayson, Darren Gough, Ryan Sidebottom, Chris Silverwood and Alex Wharf — while 19 others played first-class cricket.

"The other 28 made their mark in cricket in other ways and in other businesses," said Middlebrook proudly. "I'm just as pleased with David Nebard, who still does a shed load of work at Morley Cricket Club, as I am with Ryan Sidebottom. They are opposite each other on my list.

"Paul Machel still plays at Yeadon, and does the ground. Steven Bourne runs the second team at Hanging Heaton; Andrew Smith lives in New Zealand; Chris Leaf worked for Kippax making bats, and Adam Holroyd makes fire engines. Richard Robinson also does the ground at Weetwood. James Pipe is a physio at Nottinghamshire, and Richard Kettleborough is arguably the finest umpire in the world. Alex Wharf is also on the international umpiring panel.

"I'm immensely proud of them all."

So how were young players identified? "We advertised in the *Yorkshire Post*, but generally we knew the lads," explained Middlebrook, who is still heavily involved at Pudsey Congs CC.

"David Ryder and myself interviewed them with the parents, and explained living away from home, that type of thing. Between myself and David we organised the scheme. David was a guiding hand, and the money and Government papers went through him. The progress reports were done by me, but the county club had the authority to attract the scheme via the Government funding.

"We didn't have any girls, but they did come in on work experience.

"There was a public perception that Yorkshire was racist and elitist. We debunked that by having a variety of coaches from all walks of life — all ages, all colours and creeds, and both sexes. Two of our players, Antonio Richardson and Imam-ul-Haq, were West Indian and Pakistani.

"The lads got £27.50 the first year and their travel expenses paid. They also got a grant for accommodation. The second year they got £35 along with the same benefits. They also got a free tracksuit. But the opportunity to have YCCC on your CV whatever you were going to go into wasn't a bad thing at all."

Obviously, not all players would make it, but many lessons and skills learnt would be transferrable into other lines of work. Even if they did make it into the pro game lessons learned would still prove valuable later in life. Take international umpires Kettleborough and Wharf as examples. Ralph's son, James, a Championship winner with Yorkshire

Academy Class of 1991. Back row, left to right, Stuart Milburn, Richard Robinson, David Bates, Richard Kettleborough and Mark Broadhirst. Centre row: John Pearson (assistant coach), Stephen Bethel, Michael Brook, Stephen Bartle, Michael Foster, David Jarvis and David Batty (assistant coach). Front row: David Pennant, Glenn Roberts, Mike Bore (coach), Colin Chapman and Bradley Parker. *(Photo: Ron Deaton Archive.)*

is on the same path. Middlebrook said: "The lads helped with grounds-manship; there was office work, life-saving, a BTEC, coaching, fitness and cricket skills. They worked shifts to look after the Cricket School and took their coaching badges while with us.

"The BTEC (in Sport and Leisure) at Airedale and Wharfedale College went on throughout the year like a normal course. A typical week would be a day in the office with David Ryder, an afternoon of cricket nets with Arnie Sidebottom, Steve Oldham or myself. Chris Shaw also worked at the Cricket School for some time, so did Jim Love. They were duty officers."

In 1991, prior to England's Test series against the West Indies, a number of England players, Graham Gooch included, came to Yorkshire to use the indoor school for training, so impressed were the national hierarchy by its quality. Antonio Richardson ended up bowling to them — usually from 17 or 18 yards rather than the full 22 — to get them ready for the battery of West Indian quicks. He knocked Gooch's helmet off.

The light-bulb moment

It was a bit of a light-bulb moment for cricket chairman at the time Tony Vann which led to the acquisition and opening of Emerald Headingley's Indoor School in 1987.

Vann had been elected cricket chairman after Yorkshire's 1985 Annual General Meeting, defeating Brian Close by nine votes to eight. Shortly afterwards he headed down to watch the squad have a preseason net outdoors and, upon leaving, he noticed a "To Let" sign on the AIE Cables warehouse opposite the ground. The agents were BP Towler and Sons, with the company's senior partner, Peter Towler, being third-team captain at Vann's club, Alwoodley, who played in the Airedale and Wharfedale League.

A number of hurdles were cleared, and "To Let" became "Sold". An indoor-training facility was to built to replace the two-lane net in the winter shed at the Kirkstall Lane End approximately where the Carnegie Pavilion is today. Vann laughed: "They weren't very high, and Bob Appleyard used to complain that as a spin bowler you couldn't give the ball enough air because of the roof."

Make no mistake: in keeping with the acrimonious climate within the club at the time there were clashes and disagreements. But this is not the time to revisit such issues and reopen old wounds. It is one for celebrating the magnificent system which has produced many of England's greatest cricketers and give a nod to all who have played their part, from Vann at the start, to Bob Appleyard to current Academy lead coaches Ian Dews and Richard Damms and all those in between. Sir Geoffrey Boycott was integral to the formation and success of the Indoor School, particularly raising finances. But it is impossible to namecheck them all.

"When I saw the *To Let* sign I thought 'Wow'," Vann recalled. "The space was big enough for two six-a-side games to be played and eight nets in total. It was even bigger than the Indoor School at Lord's, which myself and Ralph Middlebrook went down to look at to get an idea of what we needed to do.

"A key thing was Leeds City Council had Ralph as cricket-development officer. They were one of very few councils with that kind of foresight, but they were using a small gym in one of their local schools. They straightaway saw the potential of Ralph coming to us and being the Indoor School manager. They continued to pay his salary.

"He was the one who found all of these young players with potential around Yorkshire. He did so through playing league cricket and all of his other contacts within the game. The credit for making it work on a day-to-day basis should go to him. Because the council wanted a home for Ralph they put up £120-130,000. Another £100,000 came from West

Cradle rebirth: Former Cricket Chairman and indoor-school pioneer Tony Vann greets Sir Geoffrey Boycott for the opening of the refurbished Yorkshire Cricket School in 2002.

Yorkshire Metropolitan County Council, who had to spend their money before being wound up. The Sports Council also gave us £50,000. We then raised around £200,000 ourselves.

"We would sell off eight lanes for sponsorship at £12,500 each for a five-year period. I had a Shell garage in those days, and I was telling the regional manager the story. So I got Shell, and Bryan Stott got British Gas. We also had other companies involved.

"That was £100,000 raised, with the other £100,000 raised via dinners and buy-a-brick, all those sorts of things. Within £5,000 we balanced the books. It cost the club almost nothing, and even made a profit every year but one out of the first 10. Even the loss year was only nominal. Ten years later £1m was spent upgrading it and putting in offices which weren't there in the first place. It was the first property the club owned, against which they are now able to borrow.

"At the start Leeds City Council contributed 60 percent of all over-heads on top of Ralph's salary. They couldn't have been fairer. A man called Mike Palmer-Jones was the one who had the vision on their part. It was a hell of a battle to get it through because there was opposition from within the cricket committee. I spent around 300 hours of my own time trying to get it going. I had no experience of that kind of thing, other than a love of cricket and an ability to pull things together."

The disagreements came as there were also moves to start up a Yorkshire Academy at Bradford Park Avenue led by Appleyard at around the same time. That actually opened at an initial cost of £30,000 on May 15, 1989, both schemes running concurrently for 10 years until the YTS was dissolved.

Three of the first YTS four — Jeremy Batty, Stephen Bethel and Paul Grayson — were among the first 11 taken onto the Academy. All aged 17-19, they were handed two-year summer contracts, with Steven Bartle, Richard Benson, Colin Chapman, Matthew Doidge, James Goldthorp, Darren Gough, Stuart Milburn and Bradley Parker the other eight. Only Gough had already debuted in Yorkshire's first team.

Despite the opposite views both the YTS and the Academy were and continue to be huge successes. Vann agrees.

"It's wonderful, phenomenal, and both have definitely played their part," he said. "It's what you work for — to produce your own. While I was in favour in the mid-eighties and early nineties of bringing in an overseas player, because all other counties had one and we didn't, there's nothing better than seeing 11 Yorkshiremen walk onto the field.

"The history is there, as are the bricks and mortar, and it's one of the thrills of my lifetime to know I've played my part in what has been achieved."

The only thing that was ours

Sir Geoffrey describes the opening of the Indoor School as a "huge" moment in Yorkshire's history, both on and off the field. The *White Rose's* icon player at the time, the England opener played a significant part in the purchase and development of the building.

The number of players who have honed their game in the St Michael's Lane centre and gone on to play for Yorkshire and England is quite remarkable...but Boycott insists it was the financial side of things which proved just as important.

"Yorkshire have always been known for producing their own players," he said. "That's why we have won more Championship titles than anybody else, and have provided more players for England than anybody else. But what you have to remember is that at that time Yorkshire owned nothing, not even the ground. We didn't own a stick anywhere else. We were always tenants. We lived year to year mainly on member subscriptions, and that building was the only thing that was ours.

"We had to practice in the old Tea Hut. In the summer it sold tea, coffee and sandwiches to the spectators. In the winter that was converted into two lanes of nets. It was a poor facility, but better than now't! So to open the Indoor School proper was very important for the senior players and the youngsters. For a number of reasons, that was a huge thing for the future of the club."

Times of their lives

"I had some of the best times of my life in that year or so at Headingley," says Richard Carlton, the first to take up a place on the Yorkshire Youth Training Scheme.

A wicketkeeper-batsman, Carlton arrived at headquarters aged 16 and left as a much more rounded 17-year-old despite being told he would not make it as a professional cricketer.

MARTYN MOXON: *White Rose* **great.**

He went straight into a job at the John Smeaton Leisure Centre in Leeds, and maintained a love affair with the game which brought him memorable experiences at home and abroad. Now in his early 50s and a self-employed builder, Carlton still plays at Pool in the Airedale and Wharfedale Senior League.

"I fancied a good go at the pro game, but I just wasn't quite there," he reflected. "Ralph, who was brilliant — I haven't a bad word to say about him — told me straight up, and I had to find another avenue. But I've still had a good career out of the game.

"I went to South Africa on three separate occasions, and played at the Wanderers Club in Johannesburg and did some coaching in a primary school over there. Being involved with Yorkshire certainly stood me in good stead. Even when I didn't make it into first-class cricket Ralph helped me to find a job in the Leisure Services.

"He marched me down to the council's offices, where a guy called Geoff Cooke, who went on to be England Rugby Union manager, was in charge and gave me a job. I worked in that for 15 years before going into the building game. Ralph led a fantastic scheme at Yorkshire. We were involved with the first team quite a bit. I loved it.

"I was actually there on my own for a couple of months at the very start. It was just me and Ralph before the other three lads began."

What about the transition from hoping to be a pro cricketer to working 9-5? "I found it quite easy," Carlton said. "The other stuff we did aside from the cricket gave you a real grounding. What we had to do was very similar to what you'd have to do working in the Leisure Services — cleaning the floor, maintenance, etc. The BTEC in Sport and Leisure Studies turned out to be perfect for me."

Launchpad for the stars

Martyn Moxon was one of many players who came through for Yorkshire and England without being involved with either scheme.

The county's current Director of Cricket played 10 Tests and eight one-day internationals, scoring 28,439 runs for Yorkshire across all formats between 1980 and 1997. He is, without doubt, a *White Rose* great, adding in his long-standing coaching and administration roles, including significant County Championship title involvement in 2014 and 2015.

"I came through age-group and league cricket, and was recognised that way for my performances," he reflected. "I then got my chance in the Second XI. I guess it was a move to more professionalism with the start of Academy and YTS schemes. They have both been great initiatives, giving young lads like Darren Gough a broader education.

"There's a lot of work done by coaches and staff with players from their formative years — 15 and 16 upwards. Without the help players get at that age it's hard to reach the heights many have — Gough, Silverwood, Root, Bairstow, Rashid and others. It's vitally important we are as professional as we can be in that development stage of a player's career. It takes time to develop players in any sport, but it's something Yorkshire believe in and has been a philosophy for forever."

Moxon agrees that seeing one of your own flourish is up there among the best feelings for any coach or supporter: "Absolutely," he said. "It's why people like Tony Vann and Ralph Middlebrook, massive cricket lovers, put in the time and effort to help to set up something which allows players to develop. It's also why players, or anyone for that matter, go into coaching.

"There's such a pleasure in seeing someone you've worked with achieve success, be it in league cricket or in international cricket. It's exactly the same. If they get a hundred or five wickets, and you've played a part towards that, that's the reason you do it."

England's big two

England's coach and captain, Chris Silverwood and Joe Root, were nurtured on both of Yorkshire's development schemes. Silverwood was an early YTS entry, and Root came through the Academy.

What's that phrase again? *Strong Yorkshire, strong England*.

Pontefract-born Silverwood, 46, enjoyed an impressive career with Yorkshire, Middlesex, Essex and England as a seamer before going into coaching with Essex.

With two years at the helm at Chelmsford he secured the County Championship Division Two title in 2016 and the

From little acorns...Joe Root tosses the coin to start the epic Third Specsavers Test Match at Emerald Headingley in 2019 as Australia captain Tim Paine and match referee Javagal Srinath await the outcome.

Division One crown in 2017. He immediately was appointed to the England coaching set-up, first as bowling coach and then as head coach.

Root, 30, from Sheffield, is one of the world's best batsman. He first wore the *White Rose* badge aged 11 and progressed through the age-groups and into the Academy, where he spent three years between 2007 and 2009. This summer he is likely to make his 300th international appearance across all formats.

Recalling Silverwood's YTS days, Ralph Middlebrook — the pair remain close friends — said: "One of my duties as Leeds City Council's cricket development officer was to try and resurrect Leeds Schools cricket, starting with Under-11s. We ran the Joe Lumb team, and I helped with the Lord's Taverners team as well.

"We went to the North East and Chris played. He took six for about 20 and bowled very quick. He was big, solid and dependable. I said, 'I'd like you to apply to come on the YTS scheme at Headingley. You just need to write a letter explaining your qualities and why you believe we should interview you'. A bit later on I got the letter: 'Dear Ralph. Will you please give me a job? Yours sincerely, Chris Silverwood.'

"From little acorns, big things grow!"

Root loved his time on the Academy, a big part of which was playing senior cricket in the Yorkshire Premier League: "In terms of playing in the Yorkshire League it was quite hard graft," he said.

"As a kid from Sheffield, playing home games at Weetwood in Leeds, it's like almost every game being an away game. It actually makes you really appreciate the opportunity to bat, because you've sometimes spent five hours in a car to Scarborough, Driffield and Hull. You don't want to mess it up!"

Amidst the pride of wearing the *White Rose* as a junior Root learnt valuable lessons as an Academy starlet, ones which will serve any current player in that age-group extremely well: "It's just like your schooling in a sense, almost an education in cricket. You're constantly learning about the different things when you play in that team. You're learning about the pressures of playing for a different badge.

"I'd been playing for Sheffield Collegiate beforehand, but there are a lot of guys in other teams who are either very jealous of you or just have too strong a desire to prove a point against the Academy. There are a number of things which are almost against you.

"You also have that inter-team rivalry which you don't have in other teams in the sense that everyone is trying to get themselves into the second team or even win a contract. You lose a bit of that team camaraderie. That's a shame, but it's part of your learning. You have to realise that to get the best out of yourself you still have to put the team first. I look at the guys who were most successful at county level or went on to play for England, and they would play the situation and not play for themselves.

"There were a number of players who fell away because they were so desperate to look after themselves. And it didn't work out for them."

> *"The message to the lads is: 'Let's get stuck in, and see if*
> *we can achieve your dream. If we can't, let's make sure*
> *that when you leave this place you always look back with*
> *fondness and say, 'I still love cricket. I still love Yorkshire,*
> *but I'm set up well for my next chapter'.*
> *"That, to us, is job done."*

Yorkshire Academy head coach Richard Damms knows just what it takes to keep the well oiled production line moving. He is perfectly placed in that regard.

As a teenager from Barnsley, he was invited onto the YTS scheme, joining the second cohort immediately after Jeremy Batty, Stephen

Didn't they do well? Yorkshire Cricket School's rising stars of 1992. Back row, left to right: Iam-ul-Haq, who played for England Schools Cricket Association Under-15s; Chris Silverwood, of Yorkshire and England and now England Head Coach; Alex Wharf, who played for Yorkshire, Nottinghamshire and Glamorgan before becoming an international umpire; Lee Baxter, who played for Yorkshire Cricket Association Under-19s and volunteered to face England paceman Devon Malcolm, and Ian Fisher, who played for Yorkshire, Gloucestershire and Worcestershire and is now the *White Rose* Strength and Conditioning Coach. Front row: Darren Wyrill, who left Yorkshire to join the Lord's groundstaff; Stephen Cockshott, a long-serving player at Farsley in the Bradord League; Ralph Middlebrook, founder manager of Yorkshire Cricket School; Craig Knight, later assistant groundsman for Manchester City AFC, and Chris Schofield, who advanced his career in coaching circles. *(Photo: Ralph Middlebrook Archive.)*

Bethel, Richard Carlton and Paul Grayson. Unfortunately, he was one of those who did not make it as a player, but it was a programme which set him up for a coaching career within the game. There are similarities between then and now, and obvious differences, one which you may not expect.

"The biggest difference from the YTS to now is that the YTS was full-time, five days a week. Now, we are part-time with the Academy," Damms explained. "The lads come in three days a week during the winter. They have a one-to-one and two group sessions every week. I think that's enough, because there's an added pressure on education nowadays. Education comes first."

RICHARD DAMMS
Academy Coach

Below Yorkshire's senior squad the pyramid for player development is: Age-group cricket, Emerging Players Programme, Academy and then Rookie — the only level which is full time. They are effectively the bridge between the Academy and professionals. Damms and company start their significant work with players at EPP level.

The subject of extracurricular activities away from fitness and skills with bat and ball is both a difference and a similarity to the YTS and today's programme: "There were lots of things we did back then, including coaching and things like groundsmanship to give you something to fall back on in case playing didn't work," Damms continued.

"Ralph (Middlebrook) always made sure we did our coaching badges. A bit like your driving licence — once you've got it, you've got it. Unfortunately, I wasn't good enough to make it as a player, but I fell in love with coaching. From that point on I've never not done any cricket coaching, culminating in the job I'm in now. It's something I've taken into this role. Comparing then and now, what we do now is more about becoming a professional cricketer with the emphasis on skills and fitness. The all-round other stuff is what myself, Ian Dews and the other coaches put into that as an addition.

"It's not necessarily what's in the programme, because that's run by the club and the ECB rather than Leeds City Council as it was back then. They are just things we urge. That's a direct result of my personal pathway. It's almost me saying to young lads, 'I went on this journey into playing. I wasn't good enough, but look at how I've stayed in the game'.

"We often tell lads that if they want to go to Australia or South Africa for a winter you're a more attractive proposition to clubs if you have your coaching badges as well because you can get stuck in with their juniors. If nothing else, going through your coaching badges furthers you as a leader, speaking in front of people, and that can only be good for you as a cricketer. Thankfully, the lads love that kind of thing. "Another thing we have is lifestyle sessions with Matthew Wood, our former opening batsman and now the Professional Cricketers' Association representative for us, Lancashire and Durham. He comes in on a Wednesday night during the winter.

"Those sessions deal with a multitude of things. Dealing with the media, finance, contracts. Things they probably get educated on at home or school. But we find they are more inclined to listen in a cricket environment. They are incredibly useful. And Woody is an outstanding practitioner. With his background as a player he just gets it."

One of the major positives to come out of the shortened 2020 summer was the progression at senior level of many young players, including first-team debuts for George Hill, Dom Leech, James Wharton and Sam Wisniewski. With Coronavirus having a major impact on the finances of county clubs it would seem that there will be more focus on homegrown players. Does that put an extra pressure on coaches like Damms?

"No, I just don't see it like that," he said. "I just see it as exciting. Take Matthew Weston as an example. He's a little left-handed opening batsman who has just come into the EPP. How good can he be? Who knows. Let's hope he can be as good as Adam Lyth. That's the excitement of it.

"I really hope the loan system doesn't move to a similar level you see in football, because in cricket we are always trying to find the next Ben Coad or the next Gary Ballance. Once we pass one up to the seniors we search for another."

Yorkshire have always been the envy of other counties when it comes to producing our own. But how successfully are things being done elsewhere? "There are plenty of other counties doing great stuff," Damms said, "but we do like to pride ourselves on always being one step ahead.

"We try to do lots of things to challenge and support our players. We are not just trying to produce cricketers for Yorkshire, we are trying to produce cricketers. If the path is blocked here they move on. We've seen that for decades. Jared Warner and Ed Barnes are the latest examples who have been snapped up by Gloucester and Leicester. If they don't make it as players anywhere, we still want to leave them well set up."

ROLL OF HONOUR

The following 20 players who have passed through Yorkshire's YTS and Academy programmes have progressed to international cricket for England.

Jonathan Bairstow

Gary Ballance

Gareth Batty

Tim Bresnan

Richard Dawson

Darren Gough

Paul Grayson

Gavin Hamilton

Matthew Hoggard

ROLL OF HONOUR

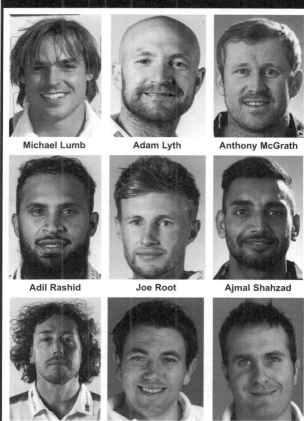

Michael Lumb

Adam Lyth

Anthony McGrath

Adil Rashid

Joe Root

Ajmal Shahzad

Ryan Sidebottom

Chris Silverwood

Michael Vaughan

ROLL OF HONOUR

**WHO
COULD
BE
NEXT?**

Alex Wharf   Craig White

Rookie who made it to the Palace

Yorkshire and England legend Darren Gough was awarded an MBE for his services to cricket in the Queen's Birthday Honour's list last October. The talismanic seamer and former Yorkshire captain claimed 1,486 wickets, added to 6,904 runs, during a 20-season career between 1989 and 2008, playing his part in County Championship (2001) and C&G Trophy (2002) title successes.

Gough played 219 times for England, including 58 Tests, and claimed 464 wickets. Only Gough with 234 and Jimmy Anderson with 269 have taken more than 200 one-day international wickets for England. Adil Rashid could be next to that milestone. He is now within 50 of that mark.

THE SECRET YORKSHIRE'S CUP HERO NEVER KNEW

By Graham Hardcastle

Jim's Midas Touch. That was the headline on the Bradford *Telegraph and Argus* match report after Yorkshire's Benson and Hedges Cup final triumph over Northamptonshire at Lord's in 1987. It remains a hugely popular memory for many Yorkshire supporters and players, not least for star of the show Jim Love. Not that Love sees it like that.

He may have hit a match-clinching 75 not out as the *White Rose*, chasing 245 in 55 overs, finished on 244-6 to win a thriller on fewer wickets lost following Northamptonshire's 244-7...but he insists there were other worthy recipients of the Gold Award which he claimed.

Had he been adjudicating on the award instead of England Test captain at the time Mike Gatting, the prize for man-of-the-match would likely have gone elsewhere. "It probably would, yeah," reflects the man who is now elite cricket age-group co-ordinator for the county.

"I thought the openers were outstanding, and the bowlers did a great job," Jim said. "I happened to be there at the end. That's what I think tipped it in my favour. Mike Gatting was the adjudicator, and he was a batsman. Who knows? If it was a bowler it may have gone that way. Everybody played a part on the day. That was the great thing."

The openers, Martyn Moxon and Ashley Metcalfe, laid the platform in the chase with a partnership of 97, hitting 45 and 47. Paul Jarvis earlier claimed 4-47 with the new ball, while Arnie Sidebottom returned 11 wicketless overs at a cost of only 40 and captain and left-arm spinner Phil Carrick went for only 30 runs in his 11 overs. Peter Hartley struck twice and Stuart Fletcher once.

Sidebottom was also there at the end, while Carrick earned high praise for sacrificing himself in a run-out mixup with Love. In another newspaper report, written by David Warner, Love praised his skipper, saying the incident highlighted the strong team spirit which contributed to the county's second piece of limited-overs silverware of the Eighties following the 1983 John Player League success.

Fast forward to the current day and last year, when the coronavirus pandemic reared its ugly head and forced the cancellation of the early stages of the county season: Yorkshire fans were asked to suggest classic

Victory with the totals level: Jim Love survives the last ball of the 1987 Benson and Hedges Cup final at Lord's, and Yorkshire win by virtue of losing one wicket fewer than Northamptonshire. The *White Rose* men in the middle did not realise that even if Love had not survived the trophy would still have gone to them. *(Photo: Mick Pope Archive.)*

matches for a club website feature, and the most popular response was this nail-biting win, which was Yorkshire's seventh out of seven in that competition.

"It was an interesting campaign. It just all seemed to go our way," Love said. "I remember the quarter-final at Headingley when Hampshire came. In those days the pitches were a bit sporting at Headingley, shall we say, and Hampshire came with not a bad side.

"But we pretty much knew we'd beaten them when we saw them looking at the pitch. They weren't just looking at it, they were on their hands and knees looking for ridges and things. We thought, 'They're reading far more into this than there is'. Then we beat Surrey reasonably well in the semi-final. And it was on to the big game!"

By that stage in his career, Love, then 32, had played three one-day internationals for England — he would not play any more — against Australia in the summer of 1981. He debuted at Lord's, and played in fixtures at Edgbaston and Headingley, posting scores of 15, 43 and three. So, how did they compare as occasions to a domestic Lord's final?

"I don't think there are similarities," he said. "It's completely different walking out there with your buddies who you've known for years to going to play internationals for England. For me, the B&H was a bigger occasion. I'm not trying to disrespect the one-day internationals because I'm hugely proud of them and enjoyed them. But it meant a bit more going out there with your mates from home."

Upon winning the toss on a lovely mid-July day Yorkshire opted to field first against a Northamptonshire side captained by Geoff Cook and including the likes of Wayne Larkins, Allan Lamb, David Capel and West Indies fast bowler Winston Davis.

All-rounder Capel, who had made his Test debut a week earlier against Pakistan at Headingley, top-scored for the Wantage Road side with an excellent 97. Like Love he batted at No. 5 and led a recovery from 48-3 and later 92-4.

"We definitely thought we could win it at halfway, no doubt," Love said. "We were quite pleased we'd only gone for 244, because it was a great wicket and a fast outfield. We knew if we got off to a good start we'd have every chance. That's what happened."

Love came to the crease at 103-3. Following a solid opening stand, Yorkshire had lost three wickets for six runs, and needed to rebuild: "It wasn't the best innings I've ever played, there's no doubt about that. I think it was first or second ball I got off the mark, and I still remember clearly how I did it. It was Nick Cook bowling, the left-arm spinner.

"I worked him through mid-wicket for one, and knew straightaway that if I didn't do anything stupid we'd win. It was just one of those surreal moments. Other times you have to work like hell for it. I'm not saying I didn't have to work for it, but I just knew."

At the start of the final over Yorkshire needed five runs to win outright with Love on strike against overseas quick Davis and Sidebottom for company.

"That was when we first knew the situation with the tie and fewer wickets lost," Love explained. "Dickie Bird, who was umpiring, told us. Apparently they made an announcement on the tannoy, but we couldn't hear it. So he had to tell us. Arnie and I knew exactly what we'd have to do at the very least."

Funnily enough, they didn't know the full story. Had Yorkshire lost a wicket and finished on 244-7 they would have still won, given that the second separator to fewer wickets lost was a runs count back to 30 overs. Whichever side had scored more after 30 overs of their innings would win, and that was in the Love and co's favour.

"No, we didn't know that," confirmed Love.

That meant that with one ball to go and the scores level Love thought he had to preserve his wicket to seal the silverware, which he duly did to spark celebrations which went on into the night.

Selfless captain: Phil Carrick raises the Benson and Hedges Cup at Lord's in 1987 after sacrificing himself in a run-out mixup with Jim Love. *(Ron Deaton Archive.)*

After the match Sidebottom found out that his father, Jack, had been rushed from the ground to hospital at around lunchtime with angina, meaning that while Love and the players were toasting their success in the dressing room Sidebottom was on his way to hospital, having been

Gold Award: Jim Love laden with honours after his undefeated innings of 75 that piloted Yorkshire home. Others in contention must have included bowler Paul Jarvis.
(Photos: Mick Pope and Ron Deaton Archives.)

given the news by his sister. Jack returned home to Barnsley a day or two later. Back at Lord's, a congratulatory call came in from the Duke of York, Prince Andrew. It was meant for captain Carrick, but was taken by cricket chairman Brian Close because the skipper was otherwise engaged with media duties.

Scheduling meant that Yorkshire's squad had to continue their celebrations on the team coach that evening because they were hosting Middlesex in a Sunday League clash at Scarborough next day.

"We won that game as well," added Love. "How, I've no idea. We celebrated just as hard, even though we had that game to play.

"We came up on a coach and stopped at Selby Fort Services overnight, and then drove to Scarborough the following morning. By that time the driver had done a fantastic job in covering all the seats up with bin liners. There was a fair celebration.

"Mike Gatting was on the bus with us as well, having a decent time. Maybe that's why we won the next day."

Love scored 14 in that clash, later admitting to David Warner that he was blown away by a standing ovation from the North Marine Road crowd as he strode to the crease: "I didn't know what was going on," he said. "I thought Geoff Boycott must be following me to the middle or something."

Benson & Hedges Cup — Semi-Final
Yorkshire v. Surrey

Played at Headingley, Leeds, on June 10, 11 and 12, 1987
Yorkshire won by 76 runs

Toss won by Surrey

Close of play: First Day, Surrey 41-3 (G S Clinton 11*, C K Bullen 2 *); Second Day, no play

YORKSHIRE

M D Moxon, c Richards b Bicknell	97
A A Metcalfe, c Thomas b Jesty	27
R J Blakey, c and b Bullen	2
K Sharp, c Lynch b Bullen	10
§ D L Bairstow, lbw b Clarke	45
J D Love, not out	40
* P Carrick, c Smith b Bicknell	0
A Sidebottom, lbw b Bicknell	0
P J Hartley, not out	7
P W Jarvis	
S D Fletcher	Did not bat
Extras b 2, lb 5, w 1, nb 2	10
Total (7 wkts, 55 overs)	238

FoW: 1-53, 2-68, 3-108, 4-186, 5-190, 6-190, 7-190

	O	M	R	W
Clarke	11	2	38	1
Thomas	8	1	70	0
Bicknell	11	2	29	3
Greig	3	0	21	0
Jesty	11	2	35	1
Bullen	11	1	38	2

SURREY

G S Clinton, b Sidebottom	69
D M Smith, c Fletcher b Sidebottom	5
A J Stewart, lbw b Sidebottom	0
M A Lynch, run out	6
C K Bullen, b Jarvis	33
T E Jesty, c Bairstow b Jarvis	5
§ C J Richards, b Hartley	8
* I A Greig, c Jarvis b Fletcher	6
D J Thomas, b Fletcher	3
S T Clarke, lbw b Fletcher	1
M P Bicknell, not out	1
Extras b 3, lb 8, w 12, nb 2	25
Total (48.2 overs)	162

FoW: 1-19, 2-19, 3-36, 4-114, 5-126, 6-137, 7-147, 8-152, 9-154, 10-162

	O	M	R	W
Sidebottom	8.2	1	29	3
Jarvis	7	1	21	2
Hartley	11	1	28	1
Fletcher	10	0	33	3
Carrick	11	2	33	0
Love	1	0	7	0

Gold Award: M D Moxon

Umpires: J Birkenshaw and D J Constant   Scorers: E I Lester and T Billson

Benson & Hedges Cup — Final
Northamptonshire v. Yorkshire

Played at Lord's Cricket Ground on July 11, 1987

Yorkshire won by losing fewer wickets with the scores level

Toss won by Yorkshire

NORTHAMPTONSHIRE

* G Cook, c Blakey b Jarvis	1
W Larkin, c Carrick b Hartley	15
R J Bailey, c Moxon b Fletcher	26
A J Lamb, c Bairstow b Jarvis	28
D J Capel, b Hartley	97
R G Williams, c Bairstow b Jarvis	44
D J Wild, b Jarvis	6
W W Davis, not out	10
§ D Ripley, not out	6
N G B Cook	
A Walker Did not bat	
Extras b 2, lb 3, w 2, nb 4	11
Total (7 wkts, 55 overs)	244

FoW: 1-3 (G Cook), 2-31 (Larkins), 3-48 (Bailey), 4-92 (Lamb), 5-212 (Williams) 6-226 (Wild), 7-232 (Capel)

	O	M	R	W
Jarvis	11	2	43	4
Sidebottom	11	1	40	0
Fletcher	11	1	60	1
Hartley	11	0	66	2
Carrick	11	2	30	0

YORKSHIRE

M D Moxon, b N G B Cook	45
A A Metcalfe, c Davis b Williams	47
R J Blakey, c Davis b Williams	1
K Sharp, b Williams	24
J D Love, not out	75
§ D L Bairstow, run out (G Cook/Ripley)	24
* P Carrick, run out (Bailey/G Cook)	10
A Sidebottom, not out	2
P J Hartley	
P W Jarvis	
S D Fletcher Did not bat	
Extras b 1, lb 4, w 4, nb 7	16
Total (6 wkts, 55 overs)	244

FoW: 1-97 (Moxon), 2-101 (Metcalfe), 3-103 (Blakey), 4-160 (Sharp), 5-223 (Bairstow), 6-235 (Carrick)

	O	M	R	W
Davis	11	1	37	0
Walker	11	0	62	0
Capel	11	0	66	0
N G B Cook	11	1	42	1
Williams	11	0	32	3

Gold Award: J D Love

Umpires: H D Bird and K E Palmer   Scorers: E I Lester and B H Clarke

Andrew Bosi is the chairman of the Yorkshire Southern Supporters' Group. He has been following the county home and away since 1966, and is also a regular watcher of the county's second-team games. Andrew usually provides the Yearbook with Championship match reports throughout the summer. So, instead of kicking his heels with a lack of cricket to report in 2020 we asked him to select six of his most memorable matches — one per decade — win, lose, draw or tie.

SIX GREAT MATCHES

1968

Worcestershire v. Yorkshire

A love affair started in the Malverns

Worcestershire won by 1 run

This writer's first Yorkshire games were in Worcestershire, two counties who performed strongly through the mid-sixties, particularly Brian Close's side. As Yorkshire claimed Championship titles in 1966, 1967 and 1968 the two sides won a game apiece at New Road and drew the other. The last of these was a thrilling Worcester win.

In 1966 the *White Rose* had built a good lead and came to New Road seeking a draw against the eventual second-placed finishers, which Close achieved with attritional cricket. The following year Yorkshire won by an innings, Ken Taylor making 160 not out.

So to 1968. Test calls depleted both sides, and the wicket was spin-friendly, highlighted by Fred Trueman bowling only 8.5 overs in the match. Geoff Cope and Don Wilson shared five wickets as Worcestershire limped to 101 all out. Yorkshire's first innings was well advanced by the close on day one, though an experienced seam attack ensured they slipped to 126 all out.

Yorkshire took the lead with seven wickets down, but this was the first season in which bonus points replaced those for first-innings lead. With no bonus points and due to bat last, a 25-run lead was not sufficient. This was also the first season in which qualification for overseas players had been relaxed.

Yorkshire continued with a homegrown side, but Worcestershire employed a young New Zealander with a liking for crease occupation. Glenn Turner did so for most of the second day for a princely 31. His

82

Spin duo: Left-hander Don Wilson and off-breaker Geoff Cope.

37-run stand with Jim Yardley, who made the highest score in the match of 43, proved crucial.

Eventually Trueman (3.5-2-3-2) came on to wrap up the innings for 163, but Wilson's match figures, 6-77 in 56 overs, were equally notable.

Yorkshire needed 139 with almost all of the third day remaining. In the final hour last pair Trueman and Tony Nicholson came together with 16 runs still needed. They managed only 14.

1976

Lancashire v. Yorkshire
Highlight of a drought summer

Yorkshire won by 109 runs

Yorkshire had not beaten the old enemy since their last Championship-winning year in 1968, and they were in danger of exceeding the winless run which surrounded the Second World War — they went without a *Roses* win from 1939 to 1954.

Geoff Cope made a half-century in the previous game as nightwatch-man, a win against Glamorgan at Middlesbrough, and came in first wicket down at Old Trafford. The ploy did not work, and Geoffrey Boycott (34) and Jim Love spent the opening morning rebuilding from

18-2, sharing 53. Love (38) had another stand of 50 with John Hampshire, who dominated the afternoon with some powerful drives on the way to 83.

He found a reliable partner in Phil Carrick, adding 86 for the seventh wicket — crucial in a low-scoring game. Yorkshire used all but eight of their allotted 100 overs to reach 260.

Lancashire began confidently in reply, but scored no more quickly, reaching 112-2 before "Rocker" Robinson claimed four of the top order and Graham Stevenson mopped up the tail, also with a four-for.

Yorkshire led by 93, and Boycott made sure the third innings did not implode to

Power play: John Hampshire on the way to a top-score 83.
(Photo: Mick Pope Archive.)

let Lancashire back into the game, scoring 103 not out. Cope had more success this time with 21, sharing the only half-century stand of an innings which was declared closed at 174-6 as soon as Boycott had reached three figures.

Lancashire never looked like making a fist of scoring 268 in the fourth innings. This time Stevenson made the early inroads before Cope secured 6-37, figures to be replicated by Carrick in the home *Roses* match the following year, also a victory, at Bradford.

A few minutes into the last hour in 1976 Yorkshire were comfortable winners by 109 runs. It was the highlight of a disappointing season. Yorkshire slipped from second to mid-table in the Championship, and achieved little in one-day cricket.

Pitch of two halves: Abbeydale Park, Sheffield, in the 1980s.

1983

Yorkshire v. Derbyshire
Defeat on a different pitch

Derbyshire won by 22 runs

In the early years at Abbeydale Park, Sheffield,, the groundsman was commended for pitches with good pace and carry, though fixture allocation did Yorkshire few favours: they encountered some fearsome quicks. Middlesex's Wayne Daniel, for example. Yorkshire narrowly escaped another great West Indian this time in Michael Holding — a treat in store three years later — but this was a pitch of two halves.

England off-spinner Raymond Illingworth took only one wicket in the match, while Phil Carrick (12-89) and Derbyshire Dallas Moir (9-159) enjoyed some of the best figures of their careers. Down the hill pace prospered. Derbyshire's Ole Mortensen never surpassed his first-innings and match figures of 6-27 and 11-89 in another 11 seasons.

Derbyshire won an invaluable toss and batted. Yorkshire reached 63-0 in reply to 225, but it was a pitch where you needed luck at the start of your innings to prosper. Only openers Geoffrey Boycott and Richard Lumb had any, and Yorkshire ended up 118 all out.

Only three bowlers were used in the second innings, Carrick bowling unchanged from the fifth over for seven wickets. Johnny Morris made a half-century, but the thorn in Yorkshire's side was Bob Taylor (33), undefeated for the second time in the match to set a 256 target.

Boycott abandoned his normal policy of watchful defence against the new ball on the way to 112 not out, and was perilously close to being caught at third-man in the opening over. Soon it became a matter of who could stay with him, and David Bairstow answered the call, sharing a

Brilliance in a left hand: Phil Carrick and Darren Lehmann

fifth-wicket stand of 92 to advance from 52-4. This left 105 runs needed, and the next significant stand was with Arnie Sidebottom — 35 for the seventh wicket. Crucially, he was dismissed as the weather closed in for a premature end to day two at 192-7, and the hosts could not recover, losing by 22 runs in a miserable season as they claimed the table's wooden spoon.

1998

Yorkshire v. Essex
Close shave at the seaside

Yorkshire won by 1 wicket

After allegedly costing Essex the 1989 title with bad batting at Southend, Yorkshire had a remarkably good Championship record against them in the following years, winning five encounters between 1991 and 1997. In 1998, that superiority was enhanced.

Heading to North Marine Road, Scarborough, in late August, Essex were languishing at the foot of the table while Yorkshire were riding high.

Until lunch on day three the game followed script: Yorkshire won the toss and exposed the visitors to a green wicket, with Gavin Hamilton claiming six wickets as they were despatched for 200.

Darren Lehmann then found gaps in a field set to block his favourite shots, though he was unluckily dismissed on 99 by Danny Law — failing to locate a ball that may have slipped from the bowler's hand and deflecting it via body onto the stumps.

Yorkshire led by 114, and with two more wickets for Matthew Hoggard, who had claimed two in the first innings, Essex (97-3) were still trailing at the close on day two. Hoggard's eventual five-wicket haul — a career first — left the hosts needing just 148.

Yorkshire were to make a dreadful hash of it, and as tea on day three approached they had slumped to 81-8 when newly capped Hamilton and fledgling

Purple patch: Gavin Hamilton

seamer Paul Hutchison united. Essex were over-reliant on Mark Ilott and Ronnie Irani following a back injury to new-ball exponent Neil Williams, and by grafting it out Hutchison enforced their rest.

When Hutchison was out for 30 with just six needed, having shared 61 with Hamilton, the reception he received surpassed any that year.

Hamilton was in the middle of a purple patch. Following immediately on from his famous Cardiff performance, when he hit two seventies and claimed 10 wickets in victory, his unbeaten 41 carried Yorkshire home again. The calm way another up-and-comer, Hoggard, smote the winning four confirmed Yorkshire's future had never looked brighter, with an emerging side finishing third.

2008

Somerset v. Yorkshire
Four days on the edge of a seat

Yorkshire won by 40 runs

The rock: Jacques Rudolph, whose 155 was the foundation for one of Yorkshire's most gripping victories.

When your sanity is questioned as the fifth pullover makes no impact and the game you watch drifts towards a dull draw, remember this fixture.

You might wait 20 years to see anything as gripping. It is a reminder that cricket at its best has no equal as a spectator sport.

This Yorkshire XI only played together twice, the other occasion being the Houdini escape from relegation at Hove later in the season when a draw against Sussex was enough to send Kent down.

Anthony McGrath won the toss at Taunton, and was batting serenely until he slapped a long-hop to third-man. Despite that Yorkshire passed 300 with only three wickets down, but what looked like a long tail failed to reach 400. Opener Jacques Rudolph top-scored with 155.

Somerset underperformed in reply. Marcus Trescothick emulated McGrath — two of Steve Patterson's only three bad balls took wickets, this one thanks to a brilliant Adil Rashid catch in the covers. The follow-on was saved when the last pair came together, Charl Willoughby's disdain for the MCC coaching book adding 38 for the last wicket.

Yorkshire's 114-lead looked less impregnable when both openers left without scoring. Good swing bowling from Alfonso Thomas reduced them to 104-6 in mid-afternoon on day three, but Rashid (30) and Richard Pyrah took Yorkshire almost to tea. Pyrah completed 50 with excellent support from David Wainwright and Patterson, and Somerset needed 323 in a possible 101 overs. Twelve were scored overnight.

Monday morning saw last-day queues. Somerset slipped to 54-4, though no further wicket fell before lunch and only one in the afternoon as their victory chance was revived. Patterson's economy was as influential as his two wickets, and when the asking rate reached six McGrath turned to Rashid. His two wickets, including centurion Zander de Bruyn, put Yorkshire back on top. They completed victory with 23 balls left.

2013

Middlesex v Yorkshire

Lees picks perfect venue for maiden century

Yorkshire won by 10 wickets

Yorkshire arrived at Lord's, for the first time since 1998, amidst great optimism, winning three of their first seven matches and losing only once.

The team coach had delivered them not to the Home of Cricket, but to Parliament for a 150th anniversary celebration hosted by North Yorkshire MP Nigel Adams on the eve of the game.

Adil Rashid had just completed three successive centuries, and his captain, Andrew Gale, was about to emulate him. Not even intermittent drizzle, causing five first-day interruptions, could disrupt Yorkshire, who elected to bat.

The delays put pressure on Alex Lees to complete a maiden century before close on day one, but in a

ALEX LEES: Calm assurance

show of calm assurance, the 20-year-old reached the landmark in the day's last-but-one over. Gale followed him to three figures next day, and the only minor setback was failing to secure a fourth batting point after lunch. They were bowled out for 390.

More bad weather limited Yorkshire to an early wicket to Steve Patterson, opening the bowling with Ryan Sidebottom. But these two and Liam Plunkett polished off Middlesex for 175 on the third day, aided by two splendid slip catches for Joe Sayers in what was to be his last-but-one match before retirement.

Middlesex were asked to bat again, and this time Rashid was the main destroyer with the aid of a smart stumping of Joe Denly by Andrew Hodd. The hosts ended the third day 78 behind with only six wickets left, and were all out for 219 before lunch, Rashid claiming 5-78, the

Three centuries on the bounce: Skipper Andrew Gale and leg-spinning all-rounder Adil Rashid in 2013, when both achieved this feat. Gale top-scored at Lord's with 103, and Rashid was the chief destroyer with 5-78 in Middlesex's second innings.

contest's best figures. The interval was delayed under a recent regulation change to enable the match to finish quicker, and the visitors' target was only five.

Yorkshire's 10-wicket victory was their first since 1987 against Middlesex. It was also the first in a sequence of four games at Lord's memorable for different reasons, including a couple of title-clinchers and deciders.

John Potter presents the scorecards for Andrew Bosi's Six Most Memorable Matches on the following pages.

County Championship
Worcestershire v. Yorkshire

Played at the County Ground, New Road, Worcester, on August 21, 22 and 23, 1968
Worcestershire won by 1 run on the Third Day

Toss won by Yorkshire   Worcestershire 15 points, Yorkshire 5 points

Close of play: First Day, Yorkshire 80-6 (Binks 12 *, Cope 0 *); Second Day, Worcestershire 161-7 (Yardley 43 *, Brain 3 *)

First Innings	WORCESTERSHIRE	Second Innings	
R G A Headley, b Cope	23	lbw b Hutton	8
G M Turner, run out	13	c and b Wilson	31
J A Ormrod, b Wilson	12	c sub b Wilson	28
C D Fearnley, lbw b Nicholson	11	lbw b Close	13
A R P Barker, lbw b Cope	3	b Cope	11
T J Yardley, b Cope	14	lbw b Trueman	43
* § R Booth, b Wilson	5	b Wilson	6
N Gifford, not out	9	b Wilson	3
B M Brain, lbw b Nicholson	4	b Nicholson	3
L J Coldwell, run out	0	(11) not out	1
R G M Carter, b Nicholson	0	(10) b Trueman	0
Extras b 4, lb 2, nb 1	7	Extras b 8, lb 7, nb 1	16
Total	101	Total	163

Bonus points — Yorkshire 5

FoW:	1st:	1-37	2-37	3-53	4-62	5-67	6-72	7-87	8-96	9-99	10-101
	2nd:	1-14	2-69	3-70	4-89	5-126	6-147	7-151	8-161	9-161	10-163

	O	M	R	W		O	M	R	W
Trueman	5	1	11	0	Trueman	3.5	2	3	2
Nicholson	17.2	5	36	3	Nicholson	10	3	22	1
Cope	13	5	26	3	Cope	19	8	31	1
Wilson	21	10	20	2	Wilson	35	15	57	4
Close	4	3	1	0	Close	15	8	23	1
					Hutton	10	3	11	1

First Innings	YORKSHIRE	Second Innings	
P J Sharpe, c Ormrod b Carter	5	run out	1
K Taylor, lbw b Coldwell	2	c Booth b Carter	6
D E V Padgett, b Brain	4	b Carter	0
J H Hampshire, b Coldwell	6	b Gifford	31
* D B Close, lbw b Brain	27	lbw b Carter	8
§ J G Binks, b Brain	22	c Ormrod b Brain	34
R A Hutton, c Booth b Brain	16	b Coldwell	19
G A Cope, b Carter	13	c Turner b Gifford	1
F S Trueman, b Carter	4	(10) lbw b Carter	12
D Wilson, b Brain	7	(9) c Barker b Coldwell	10
A G Nicholson, not out	4	not out	2
Extras b 12, lb 3, nb 1	16	Extras b 4, lb 4, w 1, nb 4	13
Total	126	Total	137

Bonus points — Worcestershire 5

FoW:	1st:	1-7	2-9	3-18	4-22	5-67	6-74	7-99	8-109	9-110	10-126
	2nd:	1-7	2-7	3-24	4-32	5-61	6-79	7-94	8-111	9-123	10-137

	O	M	R	W		O	M	R	W
Coldwell	20	4	32	2	Coldwell	18	8	28	2
Carter	19	5	30	3	Carter	19.4	4	36	4
Brain	24.2	10	37	5	Brain	17	4	26	1
Gifford	8	4	11	0	Gifford	19	9	34	2

Umpires: R S M Lay and G H Pope

County Championship
Lancashire v. Yorkshire

Played at Old Trafford, Manchester, on August 28, 29 and 31, 1976

**(The first innings of each match was limited to 100 overs.
The total overs for both teams in their first innings was limited to 200 overs)**

Yorkshire won by 109 runs on the Third Day

Toss won by Yorkshire — Yorkshire 17 points, Lancashire 5 points

Close of play: First Day, Lancashire 12-0 (Engineer 6 *, Kennedy 2 *); Second Day, Yorkshire 96-3 (Boycott 66 *, Hampshire 0 *)

	First Innings	YORKSHIRE	Second Innings	
* G Boycott,	c Engineer b Lee	34	not out	103
R G Lumb,	c Simmons b Lee	0	c Kennedy b Lever	0
G A Cope,	lbw b Lever	3	run out	21
J D Love,	c Abrahams b Simmons	38	hit wicket b Hughes	10
J H Hampshire,	b Lee	83	c Hayes b Ratcliffe	10
P J Squires,	c Hayes b Simmons	0	lbw b Hughes	6
§ D L Bairstow,	c and b Simmons	8	st Engineer b Hughes	13
P Carrick,	b Lee	57		
G B Stevenson,	b Lee	5		
A L Robinson,	not out	13		
S Silvester,	lbw b Simmons	3		
	Extras b 2, lb 2, nb 12	16	Extras b 1, lb 2, w 1, nb 7	11
	Total	260	Total (6 wkts dec)	174

Bonus points — Yorkshire 3, Lancashire 4

FoW: 1st: 1- 6 2-18 3-71 4-121 5-126 6-148 7-234 8-242 9-245 10-260
      2nd: 1-17 2-71 3-96 4-118 5-138 6-174

	O	M	R	W		O	M	R	W
Lever	18	3	59	1	Lever	15	4	27	1
Lee	34	8	75	5	Lee	15	6	44	0
Ratcliffe	5	0	14	0	Ratcliffe	22	3	61	1
Hughes	15	3	36	0	Hughes	7.5	4	15	3
Simmons	20	4	60	4	Simmons	9	3	16	0

	First Innings	LANCASHIRE	Second Innings	
§ F M Engineer,	lbw b Robinson	22	lbw b Silvester	11
A Kennedy,	c Love b Robinson	15	b Stevenson	7
H Pilling,	c Stevenson b Carrick	35	lbw b Stevenson	17
F C Hayes,	b Robinson	31	b Stevenson	25
J Abrahams,	c Robinson b Cope	13	c Stevenson b Cope	9
* D Lloyd,	c Love b Robinson	20	c Bairstow b Cope	15
D P Hughes,	not out	14	c Love b Cope	24
J Simmons,	b Stevenson	0	b Cope	8
R M Ratcliffe,	lbw b Stevenson	0	c Hampshire b Cope	2
P G Lee,	c Bairstow b Stevenson	8	not out	0
P Lever,	b Stevenson	0	c Carrick b Cope	28
	Extras b 4, lb 4, nb	9	Extras b 4, lb 6, nb 2	12
	Total	167	Total	158

Bonus points — Lancashire 1, Yorkshire 4

FoW: 1st: 1-30 2-55 3-112 4-122 5-142 6-154 7-155 8-155 9-163 10-167
      2nd: 1-17 2-29 3- 42 4- 68 5-91 6- 96 7-119 8-127 9-128 10-168

	O	M	R	W		O	M	R	W
Robinson	25	6	61	4	Robinson	6	1	15	0
Silvester	12	7	19	0	Silvester	5	0	14	1
Stevenson	10.1	3	25	4	Stevenson	13	3	30	3
Cope	18	9	38	1	Cope	18.2	10	37	6
Carrick	9	4	15	1	Carrick	27	13	50	0

Umpires: K E Palmer and A E G Rhodes

Schweppes County Championship
Yorkshire v. Derbyshire

Played at Abbeydale Park, Sheffield, on June 22, 23 and 24, 1983
Derbyshire won by 22 runs on the Third Day

Toss won by Derbyshire   Derbyshire 22 points, Yorkshire 4 points

Close of play: First Day, Yorkshire 76-6 (Dennis 0 *); Second Day, Yorkshire 194-7 (Boycott 92 *, Stevenson 1 *)

	First Innings	DERBYSHIRE		Second Innings	
I S Anderson, c Lumb b Sidebottom		14	(2) c Stevenson b Carrick		4
J E Morris, c Bairstow b Stevenson		0	(1) c Love b Carrick		58
A Hill, b Stevenson		12	c Love b Stevenson		4
* K J Barnett, b Carrick		95	st Bairstow b Carrick		2
R J Finney, c Boycott b Carrick		23	(7) lbw b Carrick		14
G Miller, c Athey b Illingworth		4	c Boycott b Carrick		2
W P Fowler, c Bairstow b Stevenson		16	(5) b Stevenson		8
C J Tunnicliffe, st Bairstow b Carrick		18	b Dennis		21
§ R W Taylor, not out		13	not out		33
D G Moir, c Athey b Carrick		0	c Boycott b Carrick		0
O H Mortensen, c and b Carrick		2	c and b Carrick		0
Extras b 3, lb 13, w 6, nb 6		28	Extras lb 2		2
Total		225	Total		148

Bonus points — Derbyshire 2, Yorkshire 4

FoW: 1st: 1- 1   2-28   3-50   4-141   5-146   6-180   7-180   8-220   9-220   10-225
     2nd: 1-23   2-28   3-47   4-76   5- 79   6-90   7- 94   8-145   9-146   10-148

	O	M	R	W		O	M	R	W
Dennis	10	3	24	0	Dennis	8	1	37	1
Stevenson	15	5	44	3	Stevenson	13	1	65	2
Sidebottom	16	3	32	1	Carrick	18	7	44	7
Carrick	23.4	8	45	5					
Illingworth	14	2	52	1					

	First Innings	YORKSHIRE		Second Innings	
G Boycott, c Anderson b Moir		33	not out		112
R G Lumb, lbw b Mortensen		28	c Miller b Moir		0
C W J Athey, c Taylor b Moir		0	st Taylor b Moir		12
S N Hartley, c Moir b Mortensen		2	lbw b Mortensen		4
J D Love, c Taylor b Moir		0	c Hill b Mortensen		8
S J Dennis, c Taylor b Mortensen		0	(11) c Fowler b Mortensen		17
§ D L Bairstow, c Taylor b Moir		4	(6) b Moir		44
G B Stevenson, c Taylor b Mortensen		3	(9) c Fowler b Mortensen		3
P Carrick, b Mortensen		15	(7) b Mortensen		1
A Sidebottom, c Taylor b Mortensen		7	(8) b Moir		19
* R Illingworth, not out		12	(10) b Moir		0
Extras b 2, lb 4, nb 5		11	Extras lb 5, w 5, nb 3		13
Total		118	Total		233

Bonus points — Derbyshire 4

FoW: 1st: 1-63   2-63   3-72   4-72   5- 72   6- 76   7- 78   8- 79   9- 91   10-118
     2nd: 1- 9   2-21   3-34   4-52   5-142   6-157   7-192   8-197   9-198   10-233

	O	M	R	W		O	M	R	W
Mortensen	16.4	5	27	6	Mortensen	24.1	3	62	5
Tunnicliffe	10	2	23	0	Tunnicliffe	11	2	37	0
Moir	17	6	45	4	Moir	34	7	114	5
Fowler	3	0	12	0	Miller	1	0	7	0

Umpires: R Julian and M J Kitchen

Britannic Assurance County Championship
Yorkshire v. Essex

Played at North Marine Road, Scarborough, on August 26, 27 and 28, 1998
Yorkshire won by 1 wicket on the Third Day

Toss won by Yorkshire

Yorkshire 23 points, Essex 5 points

Close of play: First Day, Yorkshire 40-1 (Vaughan 20 *); Second Day, Essex 97-3 (Hodgson 40 *, Irani 25 *)

First Innings	ESSEX	Second Innings	
* P J Prichard, c Wood b Hoggard	20	c Blakey b Hoggard	24
D D J Robinson, c Byas b Hamilton	42	b Hutchison	0
T P Hodgson, lbw b Middlebrook	13	lbw b Hamilton	54
S G Law, c Blakey b McGrath	47	c Blakey b Hoggard	2
R C Irani, c Blakey b Hoggard	22	c Middlebrook b Hoggard	43
A P Grayson, b Hamilton	11	lbw b Silverwood	57
D R Law, b Hamilton	6	lbw b Silverwood	29
§ B J Hyam, c Byas b Hamilton	14	b Hoggard	22
M C Ilott, lbw b Hamilton	3	b Silverwood	3
N F Williams, not out	7	c Lehmann b Hoggard	0
P M Such, c Blakey b Hamilton	0	not out	1
Extras b 1, lb 4, w 6, nb 4	15	Extras lb 14, nb 12	26
Total	200	Total	261

Bonus points — Essex 1, Yorkshire 4

FoW: 1-37 (Prichard), 2-75 (Hodgson), 3-82 (Robinson), 4-130 (Irani), 5-162 (Grayson),
1st 6-170 (S G Law), 7-176 (D R Law), 8-191 (Ilott), 9-196 (Hyam), 10-200 (Such)
FoW: 1-0 (Robinson), 2-45 (Prichard), 3-47 (S G Law), 4-125 (Irani), 5-151 (Hoggard),
2nd 6-195 (D R Law), 7-240 (Hyam), 8-254 (Grayson), 9-255 (Williams), 10-261 (Ilott)

	O	M	R	W		O	M	R	W
Silverwood	14	4	37	0	Silverwood	23	5	70	3
Hutchison	15	3	51	0	Hutchison	10	2	36	1
Hoggard	15	7	32	2	Hoggard	20	5	57	5
Hamilton	18.4	4	50	6	Hamilton	10	2	33	1
Middlebrook	3	1	10	1	McGrath	4	0	13	0
McGrath	8	3	13	1	Middlebrook	7	0	29	0
Lehmann	1	0	2	0	Lehmann	3	0	9	0

First Innings	YORKSHIRE	Second Innings	
* D Byas, c Hyam b Irani	12	c Hyam b Ilott	0
M P Vaughan, c Robinson b Irani	71	c S G Law b Irani	8
M J Wood, c S G Law b Irani	1	b Ilott	1
D S Lehmann, b D R Law	99	c Hyam b Irani	25
A McGrath, c Hyam b Ilott	0	lbw b Ilott	7
§ R J Blakey, c Hyam b Irani	51	lbw b Ilott	6
G M Hamilton, c Hyam b D R Law	13	not out	41
J D Middlebrook, c Hyam b Ilott	20	lbw b Irani	5
C E W Silverwood, c Hyam b Ilott	0	lbw b Irani	5
P M Hutchison, not out	6	lbw b D R Law	30
M J Hoggard, b Irani	5	not out	6
Extras b 8, lb 9, w 2, nb 17	36	Extras b 10, lb 2, nb 4	16
Total	314	Total (9 wkts)	150

Bonus points — Yorkshire 3, Essex 4

FoW: 1-40 (Byas), 2-42 (Wood), 3-200 (Lehmann), 4-203 (McGrath), 5-219 (Vaughan), 6-253
1st (Hamilton), 7-289 (Middlebrook), 8-297 (Silverwood), 9-308 (Silverwood), 10-314 (Hoggard)
FoW: 1-0 (Byas), 2-10 (Wood), 3-24 (Vaughan), 4-31 (McGrath), 5-51 (Lehmann),
2nd 6-51 (Blakey), 7-68 (Middlebrook), 8-81 (Silverwood), 9-142 (Hutchison)

	O	M	R	W		O	M	R	W
Ilott	20	4	64	3	Ilott	18	3	54	5
* Williams	8.5	1	26	0	Irani	18	4	55	3
D R Law	14	1	75	2	Grayson	4	1	14	0
Irani	21.2	9	47	5	D R Law	3.4	0	15	1
* Such	17.1	4	58	0					
Grayson	7	1	27	0					

* *First Innings:* Williams was unable to finish his ninth over. It was completed by Such

Umpires: D J Constant and V A Holder

Scorers: J T Potter and C F Driver

LV County Championship — Division 1
Somerset v. Yorkshire

Played at the County Ground, Taunton, on June 6, 7, 8 and 9, 2008
Yorkshire won by 40 runs at 6.04pm on the Fourth Day

Toss won by Yorkshire   Yorkshire 21 points, Somerset 5 points
Close of play: First Day, Yorkshire 339-6 (Bresnan 5 *, Patterson 1 *); Second Day, Somerset 220-9 (Kieswetter 53 *); Third Day, Somerset 12-0 (Trescothick 11 *, Edwards 1 *)

First Innings	YORKSHIRE		Second Innings	
J A Rudolph, c Kieswetter b Blackwell	155		c Langer b Willoughby	0
A Lyth, c Edwards b Willoughby	4		c Kieswetter b Caddick	0
* A McGrath, c Thomas b Phillips	26		b Thomas	21
A W Gale, b Blackwell	61		lbw b Thomas	58
§ G L Brophy, lbw b Blackwell	70		b Thomas	9
T T Bresnan, lbw b Willoughby	5		c Kieswetter b Blackwell	9
A U Rashid, lbw b de Bruyn	5		c Kieswetter b Willoughby	30
S A Patterson, c Edwards b Phillips	17		(10) not out	13
R M Pyrah, lbw b Willoughby	0		(8) b Thomas	51
D J Wainwright, b Willoughby	5		(9) b Blackwell	5
M J Hoggard, not out	10		b Thomas	2
Extras b 5, lb 4, w 1, nb 4"	14		Extras b 2, lb 4, nb 4	10
Total	372		Total	208

Bonus points — Yorkshire 4, Somerset 3

FoW: 1-14 (Lyth), 2-59 (McGrath), 3-185 (Gale), 4-315 (Brophy), 5-330 (Rudolph),
1st 6-335 (Rashid), 7-341 (Bresnan), 8-341 (Pyrah), 9-351 (Wainwright), 10-372 (Patterson)
FoW: 1-0 (Rudolph), 2-0 (Lyth), 3-78 (McGrath), 4-81 (Gale), 5-92 (Bresnan),
2nd 6-104 (Brophy), 7-146 (Rashid), 8-172 (Wainwright), 9-202 (Pyrah), 10-208 (Hoggard)

	O	M	R	W		O	M	R	W
Caddick	22	5	76	0	Willoughby	15	5	29	2
Willoughby	19	3	65	4	Caddick	11	1	34	1
Phillips	14.4	2	58	2	Blackwell	29	5	55	2
Thomas	16	4	57	0	Phillips	4	0	22	0
Blackwell	29	7	68	3	Thomas	18.3	4	46	5
de Bruyn	11	1	39	1	de Bruyn	5	1	16	0

First Innings	SOMERSET		Second Innings	
M E Trescothick, c Rashid b Patterson	51		c Wainwright b Bresnan	12
N J Edwards, lbw b Bresnan	13		c Wainwright b Bresnan	18
* J L Langer, c Brophy b Bresnan	4		c Rudolph b Patterson	10
J C Hildreth, lbw b Pyrah	42		lbw b Hoggard	2
Z de Bruyn, c Brophy b Patterson	12		b Rashid	103
I D Blackwell, b Rashid	1		c Brophy b Hoggard	64
§ C Kieswetter, not out	67		lbw b Patterson	41
B J Phillips, c Brophy b Bresnan	2		b Hoggard	7
A C Thomas, c Lyth b Patterson	28		b Rashid	5
A R Caddick, c Rudolph b Rashid	0		b Bresnan	0
C M Willoughby, c Rudolph b Hoggard	18		not out	0
Extras b 5, lb 9, w 2, nb 4	20		Extras b 8, lb 8, w 2, nb 2	20
Total	258		Total	282

Bonus points — Somerset 2, Yorkshire 3

FoW: 1-20 (Edwards), 2-24 (Langer), 3-98 (Hildreth), 4-130 (Trescothick), 5-130 (de Bruyn),
1st 6-132 (Blackwell), 7-143 (Phillips), 8-201 (Thomas), 9-220 (Caddick), 10-258 (Willoughby)
FoW: 1-25 (Trescothick), 2-33 (Edwards), 3-36 (Hildreth), 4-54 (Langer), 5-142 (Blackwell),
2nd 6-242 (Kieswetter), 7-255 (Phillips), 8-277 (Thomas), 9-282 (de Bruyn), 10-282 (Caddick)

	O	M	R	W		O	M	R	W
Hoggard	17.4	4	69	1	Hoggard	20	2	48	3
Bresnan	23	5	91	3	Bresnan	19.1	5	25	3
Pyrah	9	3	14	1	Rashid	22	3	60	2
Patterson	12	6	19	3	Patterson	16	1	56	2
Rashid	16	2	46	2	Wainwright	10	1	36	0
Wainwright	4	2	5	0	Pyrah	10	0	41	0

Umpires: B Dudleston and T E Jesty   Scorers: J T Potter and G A Stickley

LV County Championship — Division 1
Middlesex v. Yorkshire

Played at Lord's Cricket Ground on June 11, 12, 13 and 14, 2013
Yorkshire won by 10 wickets at 1.01pm on the Fourth Day

Toss won by Yorkshire

Close of play: First Day, Yorkshire 205-2 (Lees 100 *, Gale 61 *); Second Day, Middlesex 16-1 (Rogers 6 *, Denly 0 *); Third Day, Middlesex (2) 137-4 (Dexter 25 *, Simpson 20 *)

First Innings	YORKSHIRE		Second Innings	
A Lyth, c Dexter b Murtagh	11		not out	4
A Z Lees, c Simpson b Harris	100		not out	0
P A Jaques, c Simpson b Berg	20			
* A W Gale, lbw b Rayner	103			
J J Sayers, lbw b Murtagh	1			
A U Rashid, lbw b Harris	72			
§ A J Hodd, c and b Murtagh	13			
R M Pyrah, c Robson b Harris	1			
L E Plunkett, lbw b Rayner	26			
R J Sidebottom, st Simpson b Rayner	9			
S A Patterson, not out	2			
Extras b 2, lb 19, w 1, nb 10	32		Extras lb3	3
Total	390		Total (0 wkts)	7

Bonus points — Yorkshire 3, Middlesex 2   Score at 110 : 345-7

FoW: 1-32 (Lyth), 2-70 (Jaques), 3-215 (Lees), 4-220 (Sayers), 5-329 (Gale),
1st 6-343 (Rashid), 7-345 (Pyrah), 8-361 (Hodd), 9-387 (Sidebottom), 10-390 (Plunkett)

	O	M	R	W		O	M	R	W
Murtagh	32.3	3	93	3	Rayner	2	2	0	0
Collymore	19	6	51	0	Denly	1.4	1	4	0
Berg	28	5	103	1					
* Harris	14.3	3	48	3					
Dexter	9	2	23	0					
* Rayner	22.1	4	44	3					
Denly	3	0	7	0					

* *First Innings:* Harris was unable to finish his fifth over. It was completed by Rayner

First Innings	MIDDLESEX		Second Innings	
* C J L Rogers, c Hodd b Plunkett	27		c Hodd b Sidebottom	0
S D Robson, c Lyth b Patterson	5		b Rashid	46
J L Denly, c Sayers b Sidebottom	14		st Hodd b Rashid	31
A B London, c Sayers b Plunkett	28		lbw b Rashid	3
N J Dexter, lbw b Patterson	11		b Sidebottom	36
§ J A Simpson, b Plunkett	9		c Pyrah b Patterson	21
G K Berg, lbw b Patterson	54		c Pyrah b Rashid	38
O P Rayner, lbw b Plunkett	1		lbw b Plunkett	0
J A R Harris, lbw b Sidebottom	5		lbw b Patterson	14
T J Murtagh, not out	18		not out	5
C D Collymore, c Hodd b Patterson	5		c and b Rashid	3
Extras b 1, lb 11, nb 2	14		Extras b 9, lb 13	22
Total	175		Total	219

Bonus points — Yorkshire 3

FoW: 1-12 (Robson), 2-19 (Denly), 3-46 (Rogers), 4-59 (Dexter), 5-84 (Simpson),
1st 6-105 (London), 7-113 (Rayner), 8-141 (Harris), 9-169 (Berg), 10-175 (Collymore)
FoW: 1-0 (Rogers), 2-69 (Denly), 3-90 (Robson), 4-93 (London), 5-143 (Simpson),
2nd 6-155 (Dexter), 7-167 (Rayner), 8-209 (Harris), 9-209 (Berg), 10-219 (Collymore)

	O	M	R	W		O	M	R	W
Sidebottom	15	4	48	2	Sidebottom	11	5	17	2
Patterson	17.2	5	39	4	Patterson	16	6	40	2
Plunkett	15	1	50	4	Plunkett	13	2	46	1
Pyrah	8	1	26	0	Rashid	24.4	3	78	5
					Pyrah	6	1	15	0
					Lyth	1	0	1	0

Umpires: T E Jesty and D J Millns   Scorers: J T Potter and D K Shelly

96

PLUCKY THIRD AS ALL-ROUND GIANT TAKES HIS REST

By Anthony Bradbury

In 1920 Yorkshire had finished fourth in the County Championship. They had hopes of doing rather better in 1921, but clawed themselves only up to third position after a poor start. They might have climbed higher but for poor August weather against both Middlesex and Surrey which deprived them of almost certain victories. Middlesex and Surrey did then finish first and second in the Championship.

Yet Yorkshire did win 16 of their 26 Championship games and nine of their victories were by an innings. Against Northamptonshire they secured their largest ever margin of victory – by an innings and 397 runs – still a record. In this match at Harrogate they scored 548 runs for four wickets on the first day, and though Northamptonshire wilted they still bowled 122 overs. There is a lesson for today's players and administrators. The next day the visitors were bowled out twice by Emmott Robinson and Abe Waddington for 58 and 93. No other bowlers were used. Though in world cricket there have been more comprehensive victories this remains a startling result.

Batting honours were shared around several players, but it was neither Holmes nor Sutcliffe who topped the averages. In Championship cricket Edgar Oldroyd, aged 22, led the way at an average of 44.50 with four centuries. One, according to *Wisden*, was scored in strange circumstances. At Bramall Lane the hosts needed 263 runs to beat Hampshire. With Oldroyd batting they had reached 264-4, and the game was won. But Oldroyd was on 99 not out. The players should have left the field, but Tennyson went back to his mark. He bowled again and Oldroyd struck the ball for four. The scorers and umpires, and naturally Oldroyd, were content, and Oldroyd has for ever after been allowed to retain his century – and he made three more that season.

Perhaps the surprise batting package was Wilfred Rhodes. In 1920 his average for Yorkshire had been 27.30. In 1921 it jumped to 42.87. At the age of 43 he also achieved his highest score — 267 not out against Leicestershire at Headingley, made in less than five hours. He then took match figures of 7-66 as Leicestershire were crushed.

Other centurions in the season were Percy Holmes, Robinson, Roy

Kilner, George Macaulay, Norman Kilner, Cecil Tyson and the captain, Mr D C F Burton.

Tyson warrants a special mention. David Denton had retired in 1920, and there was a vacancy at the important No. 3 position. For the first game of the season at Southampton the 32-year-old league profession-al was chosen. He did bat one wicket down — and returned that compliment by scoring 100 not out and 80 not out.

He was the first Yorkshire player to score a hundred in his first game — yet he played only twice more for Yorkshire. His first-class career began and ended in May 1921.

Yorkshire historian Tony Woodhouse wrote: "Tyson claimed that working down the pit during the week was more remunerative than six-days-a-week county cricket."

CECIL TYSON: Mystery of debu-tant centurion who played only three times for Yorkshire.
(Photo: Ron Deaton Archive)

No mention of his two remarkable innings was made in an authorised *History of Yorkshire County Cricket 1903-1923* by the well known A W Pullin, "Old Ebor". Tyson had prob-ably upset authority, and Yorkshire may have had good hopes of a much younger batsman who was played occasionally. His name was Maurice Leyland, and in subsequent years he became a mainstay of Yorkshire and England batting.

One batsman of whom there very high hopes that year and who how-ever failed to score a century was Herbert Sutcliffe. He was far down the national batting averages at 30.12, but a *Wisden* writer was wise enough to write "he may yet find a place in representative elevens". Sutcliffe became an England player in 1924 and was to score 16 Test centuries and average 60.73 in Tests . He did score a 97 and a 95 in 1921.

With the bowling Yorkshire had true reason to remain proud of

Last bow: One of the greatest all-rounders the game has known, George Hirst, extreme left, takes the field at the Scarborough Festival for Yorkshire's match v. MCC.

(Photo: Mick Pope Archive)

Rhodes, who in all Yorkshire games took 128 wickets at 13.04 apiece, Macaulay with 101 wickets at 17.33 and Waddington 105 at 18.92. Then to give considerable help came the Yorkshire-born amateur and school-master Rockley Wilson, who from late July took 51 wickets at 11.13 with his teasing right-arm slow bowling. His presence in the side brought added skills and knowledge.

It was in 1921 that the mighty all rounder George Herbert Hirst made his last Championship appearances. He took two wickets in 42 overs and made 200 runs. His time as a competitive player was over and, aged 50 he was given a heart-warming farewell at the Scarborough Festival before continuing a career as a coach at Eton College.

Wicket-keepers with Yorkshire usually have worthy and sustained careers. Arthur Dolphin was the Yorkshire incumbent, having first appeared for the county in 1905, but in June 1921 he broke a wrist and was unable to play again that season. His able replacement was Reg Allen, not now a well remembered player. Yet Allen in the last championship game of the year, at Hove, gave an outstanding performance with six wickets, including four stumpings, in the Sussex second innings. Three stumpings were taken off the bowling of the great Rhodes. Both Allen and Rhodes would have been well pleased.

The rather terse Annual Report about 1921 in the 1922 Yearbook expressed satisfaction at team consistency, and (as always) expressed

Century teaser: How many names can you pick out from this photo of the match between Yorkshire and York and District XVI played at York on May 4 and 5, 1921? The scorecard for this game appears on Page 69 of the 1922 Report under Extra Matches. Archivist Ron Deaton has the names of the players — but sadly not the umpires or the three distinguished-looking gentlemen wearing suits. Back row, left to right: A Waddington, J J Munford, W Wilkinson, A Naylor, C W Shaw, Col. G L Crossman and H Haigh. Standing: N Kilner, J Pidcock, H H Dryland, G G Ellison, H K Longman, Capt. Humfrey and K G Chilman. Seated: R Kilner, R E F Tendal, W Rhodes, Sir A W. White, D C F Burton, S M Toyne, A Dolphin and E W Wrigley. On the ground: C T Tyson, P Holmes, H Sutcliffe, E Robinson and G G Macaulay.

Cecil Tyson, who scored a century on his Yorkshire debut in 1921, scored two and 36 in this match. In the York and District first innings he bowled 1.1 overs to take two wickets for one run, and in the second innings he bowled two overs, taking two wickets for five runs. Sir Archibald White, Yorkshire Skipper from 1912 to 1918, played for York and District, and the fact that he is seated alongside his successor, D C F Burton, suggests that he was leading the York and District team.

good hopes of younger players. The financial profit for the year was a record at £3,225, and membership of 5,000 was pleasing. At a "nominal subscription of One Guinea (plus 1s 6d tax) – about £55 today – there was an expressed hope for even more support. Aspirations did come to pass, and 1922 would bring more success to the club.

YORKSHIRE'S FIRST CLASS HIGHLIGHTS OF 1921

Wins by an innings (9)

Yorkshire (548-4 dec) defeated Northamptonshire (58 and 93) by an innings and 397 runs at Harrogate ***

Yorkshire (560-6 dec) defeated Leicestershire (154 and 164) by an innings and 242 runs at Leeds *

Derbyshire (37 and 103) lost to Yorkshire (377) by an innings and 237 runs at Chesterfield

Yorkshire (383-6 dec) defeated Northamptonshire (81and 108) by an innings and 194 runs at Northampton **

Yorkshire (373) defeated Warwickshire (97 and 136) by an innings and 140 runs at Sheffield *

Derbyshire (105 and 23) lost to Yorkshire (240) by an innings and 112 runs at Hull

Yorkshire (292-7 dec) defeated Essex (66 and 146) by an innings and 80 runs at Bradford

Yorkshire (306) defeated Gloucestershire (136 and 119) by an innings and 51 runs at Bradford **

Nottinghamshire (174 and 216) lost to Yorkshire (438-9 dec) by an innings and 48 runs at Nottingham ***

*, **, *** *Consecutive matches*

Wins by 200 or more runs (2)

Yorkshire (89 and 420) defeated Warwickshire (72 and 129) by 308 runs at Birmingham *

Yorkshire (213 and 316-6 dec) defeated Gloucestershire (165 and 106) by 258 runs at Spa Ground, Gloucester *

* *Consecutive matches*

Totals of 400 and over (6)

560-6 dec v, Leicestershire at Leeds
548-4 dec v. Northamptonshire at Harrogate *
489   v. Lancashire at Leeds *
452-8 dec v. Leicestershire at Aylestone Road, Leicester *
438-9 dec v. Nottinghamshire at Nottingham *
420   v. Warwickshire at Birmingham

* *Consecutive matches*

Opponents dismissed for under 100 (9)

23 v. Derbyshire at Hull
37 v. Derbyshire at Chesterfield
58 v. Northamptonshire at Harrogate
          — 1st innings
66 v. Essex at Bradford *
72 v. Warwickshire at Birmingham

81 v. Northamptonshire at Northampton
82 v. Middlesex at Sheffield *
93 v. Northamptonshire at Harrogate
          — 2nd innings
97 v. Warwickshire at Sheffield

* *Consecutive matches*

Century Partnerships (22)

For the 1st wicket (5)

129	H Sutcliffe and E Robinson	v. Hampshire at Sheffield
118	P Holmes and H Sutcliffe	v. Warwickshire at Sheffield
107	P Holmes and H Sutcliffe	v. Essex at Bradford
103	P Holmes and H Sutcliffe	v. Sussex at Dewsbury *

* This was the 10,000th First Class match played in all cricket

100	P Holmes and H Sutcliffe	v. Nottinghamshire at Nottingham

For the 2nd wicket (4)

160	P Holmes and E Oldroyd	v. Northamptonshire at Harrogate
143	H Sutcliffe and E Oldroyd	v. Gloucestershire at Spa Ground, Gloucester 2nd innings
135	H Sutcliffe and E Oldroyd	v. Hampshire at Sheffield
129	P Holmes and E Oldroyd	v. Gloucestershire at Spa Ground, Gloucester 1st innings

For the 3rd wicket (1)

105 *	C T Tyson and W Rhodes	v. Hampshire at Southampton

For the 4th wicket (3)

299	P Holmes and R Kilner	v. Northamptonshire at Harrogate
144	R Kilner and W Rhodes	v. Leicestershire at Leeds
102	P Holmes and E Robinson	v. Derbyshire at Chesterfield

For the 5th wicket (4)

276	W Rhodes and R Kilner	v. Northamptonshire at Northampton
105	E Robinson and W Rhodes	v. Sussex at Dewsbury
146	E Oldroyd and W Rhodes	v. Surrey at The Oval *
116	E Robinson and W Rhodes	v. Essex at Leyton *

* Consecutive matches

For the 6th wicket (2)

229	W Rhodes and N Kilner	v. Leicestershire at Leeds
178	E Robinson and D C F Burton	v. Derbyshire at Hull

For the 7th wicket (2)

215	E Robinson and D C F Burton	v. Leicestershire at Aylestone Road, Leicester
133 *	W Rhodes and M Leyland	v. Leicestershire at Leeds

For the 8th wicket (1)

113	G G Macaulay and A Waddington	v. Nottinghamshire at Nottingham

Centuries (18)

P Holmes (3)

277 *	v. Northamptonshire at Harrogate
150	v. Derbyshire at Chesterfield
132	v. Lancashire at Leeds

E Oldroyd (3)

144	v. Surrey at The Oval
127 *	v. Gloucestershire at Bradford
125	v. Warwickshire at Birmingham

Centuries *(Continued)*

W Rhodes (3)

267 * v. Leicestershire at Leeds
104 * v. Northamptonshire at Northampton
102 * v. Essex at Leyton

E Robinson (3)

135 * v. Leicestershire at Aylestone Road, Leicester
115   v. Sussex at Dewsbury
100   v. Derbyshire at Hull

R Kilner (2)

166   v. Northamptonshire at Northampton
150   v. Northamptonshire at Harrogate

D C F Burton (1)

110   v. Leicestershire at Aylestone Road, Leicester

N Kilner (1)

112   v. Leicestershire at Leeds

G G Macaulay (1)

125 * v. Nottinghamshire at Nottingham

C T Tyson (1)

100 * v. Hampshire at Southampton (on First Class debut)

5 wickets in an innings (31)

W Rhodes (8)

7- 80   v. Lancashire at Manchester
6- 38   v. Surrey at The Oval
6- 40   v. Warwickshire at Birmingham
6- 46   v. Leicestershire at Aylestone Road, Leicester
5- 27   v. Sussex at Hove
5- 74   v. Nottinghamshire at Huddersfield
5- 87   v. Australians at Bradford
5-108   v. Middlesex at Lord's

G G Macaulay (7)

6- 3   v. Derbyshire at Hull
6- 10   v. Warwickshire at Birmingham
6- 32   v. Derbyshire at Chesterfield
5- 33   v. Gloucestershire at Bradford *
5- 35   v. Northamptonshire at Northampton *
5- 57   v. Surrey at Leeds 1st innings *
5- 85   v. Surrey at Leeds 2nd innings
          * *Consecutive matches*

A Waddington (7)

6- 21   v. Northamptonshire at Harrogate
6- 41   v. Gloucestershire at Spa Ground, Gloucester
5- 34   v. Essex at Bradford
5- 40   v. Cambridge University at Cambridge
5- 41   v. Sussex at Dewsbury
5- 64   v. Kent at Tunbridge Wells
5- 77   v. Nottinghamshire at Nottingham

E Robinson (3)

6- 43   v. Northamptonshire at Harrogate
5- 16   v. Derbyshire at Chesterfield
5- 35   v. Warwickshire at Sheffield

5 wickets in an innings *(Continued)*

E R Wilson (3)

    7- 32 v. Middlesex at Sheffield

    7- 67 v. Sussex at Hove

    5- 54 v. Nottinghamshire at Huddersfield

R Kilner (2)

    5- 29 v. Nottinghamshire at Nottingham

    5- 34 v. Warwickshire at Sheffield

G W Bayes (1)

    5- 83 v. Hampshire at Sheffield

10 wickets in a match (4)

G G Macaulay (2)

    10- 65   (6-10 and 4-55) v. Warwickshire at Birmingham

    10- 142 (5-57 and 5-85) v. Surrey at Leeds

E Robinson (1)

    10- 70   (4-27 and 6-43) v. Northamptonshire at Harrogate

E R Wilson (1)

    11- 109 (7-67 and 4-42) v. Sussex at Hove

3 catches in an innings (6)

W R Allen (2)

    5   v. Northamptonshire at Northampton

    3   v. Australians at Sheffield

A Dolphin (2)

    4   v. Warwickshire at Birmingham

    3   v. Kent at Bradford

P Holmes (2)

    4   v. Nottinghamshire at Huddersfield

    3   v. Kent at Tunbridge Wells

3 dismissals in an innings (4)

W R Allen (3)

    6 (2ct, 4st) v. Sussex at Hove

    4 (3ct, 1st) v. Australians at Sheffield

    3 (1ct, 2st) v. Surrey at The Oval

A Dolphin (1)

    4 (3ct, 1st) v. Kent at Maidstone

5 catches in a match (2)

P Holmes (1)

    6 (4 + 2) v. Nottinghamshire at Huddersfield

W R Allen (1)

    5 (5 + 0) v. Northamptonshire at Northampton

Debuts (4)

In **First Class** cricket (4): C T Tyson, H D Badger, J T Bell and W R Allen

Caps awarded (2): G G Macaulay and E Oldroyd

100 YEARS AGO

YORKSHIRE AVERAGES 1921

ALL FIRST-CLASS MATCHES

Played 30   Won 17   Lost 5   Drawn 8

County Championship: Played 26   Won 16   Lost 3   Drawn 7

BATTING AND FIELDING *(Qualification 10 completed innings)*

Player	M.	I.	N.O.	Runs	H.S.	100s	50s	Avge	ct/st
W Rhodes	27	38	7	1329	267*	3	5	42.87	22
E Oldroyd	28	40	4	1469	144	3	8	40.80	21
P Holmes	27	39	2	1458	277*	3	5	39.40	29
H Sutcliffe	29	43	2	1235	97	0	8	30.12	17
E Robinson	30	40	3	1104	135*	3	5	29.83	16
R Kilner	30	41	0	1137	166	2	5	27.73	24
N Kilner	12	14	2	326	112	1	2	27.16	7
G G Macaulay	27	32	10	497	125*	1	1	22.59	32
D C F Burton	30	40	6	767	110	1	3	22.55	14
G H Hirst	7	10	0	212	64	0	2	21.20	4
W R Allen	20	22	7	279	41*	0	0	18.60	32/19
A Waddington	26	27	7	231	44	0	0	11.55	20
A Dolphin	10	14	1	113	38	0	0	8.69	18/7
Also played									
C T Tyson	3	5	2	232	100*	1	1	77.33	1
M Leyland	5	7	1	115	52*	0	1	19.16	1
E R Wilson	10	8	1	87	33*	0	0	12.42	7
G Wilson	3	4	0	40	31	0	0	10.00	2
G W Bayes	3	5	2	20	11	0	0	6.66	1
H D Badger	1	2	1	0	0*	0	0	0.00	1
J T Bell	2	3	0	0	0	0	0	0.00	

BOWLING

(Qualification 10 wickets)

Player	Overs	Mdns	Runs	Wkts	Avge	Best	5wI	10wM
E R Wilson	370	170	571	51	11.19	7-32	3	1
W Rhodes	857.2	288	1672	128	13.06	7-80	8	0
G G Macaulay	651.2	140	1751	101	17.33	6- 3	7	2
R Kilner	589.1	204	1147	61	18.80	5-29	2	0
A Waddington	679.3	124	1989	105	18.94	6-21	7	0
E Robinson	403.2	106	1157	55	21.03	6-43	3	1
G W Bayes	86	10	317	11	28.81	5-83	1	0
Also bowled								
H D Badger	27	2	111	6	18.50	3- 38	0	0
G H Hurst	42	11	70	2	35.00	1- 8	0	0
M Leyland	96	2	43	1	43.00	1- 10	0	0
E Oldroyd	29	3	96	2	48.00	1- 13	0	0
P Holmes	2	0	6	0	—	0- 6	0	0
H Sutcliffe	3	0	9	0	—	0- 9	0	0

CAPTAIN BOYCOTT SUPREME
AS STORM CLOUDS GATHER

By Anthony Bradbury

Sadly, this article may be one of several in the next decade that have to discuss a very turbulent period in the history of Yorkshire County Cricket Club. The tone can be set from the opening statement to the Annual Report of the Yorkshire Committee for 1971 — "It is with regret that your Committee has to report that the season of 1971 was, without doubt, the worst in the history of the club, both from a playing and financial point of view".

There were three competitions in 1971 — the County Championship, the knockout Gillette Cup and the 40-overs-per-side John Player League on Sundays. In the Championship Yorkshire were 13th, equalling their previous lowest position; they were knocked out of the Gillette Cup in their only match, and were 15th in the John Player League, two points ahead of the bottom side. In a Championship of 26 games they won only four times, and at one stage went 17 games without a victory, the worst sequence the county had ever known.

It did not help that within that sequence was a match against Somerset, for whom Brian Close was now playing and perhaps inevitable that he should score a century. The club had started the year with an acrimonious Annual General Meeting following the dismissal from the playing staff of Close, a highly successful and popular captain. The Annual Report for 1970 was then voted down and an *Action Group* of members seeking Committee change had been formed.

Low morale and uncertainty within the playing staff must have been present when the opening first-class game against Kent started on May 1. The new captain, Geoffrey Boycott, was absent, having broken his arm, and during the match Sharpe, Old and Cope all suffered nasty injuries. The end result was an innings defeat. There was a revival victory in the next match against Warwickshire, when Boycott scored 61 and 110. That was the start of a whole season of remarkable scoring by Boycott, who also had Test cricket to play. For Yorkshire he scored in 17 Championship games 2,197 runs with 11 centuries, a highest score of 233 and an astonishing average of 109.85. He became the first Englishman to average more than 100 per innings throughout a season.

Problems, though, arose in several directions at once. Other batsmen,

Stairway to paradise? Captain Geoffrey Boycott, extreme left, was to scale unprecedented heights as an English batsman, but for Yorkshire 1971 was a bitter disappointment. From the left and in ascending order: vice-captain Don Wilson, Philip Sharpe, David Bairstow, Phil Carrick, Peter Borrill, John Hampshire, John Woodford, Chris Old, Barrie Leadbeater, Mike Bore, Neil Smith, Richard Lumb, Andy Dalton, Tony Nicholson and Geoff Cope.

(Photo: Ron Deaton Archive)

some normally very proficient, failed to score as well as expected. Sharpe, Hampshire and Padgett in a total of 97 Championship innings managed only four centuries, and no batsman other than Boycott averaged above 35. Young players Woodford and Dalton were given good opportunities and scored a century apiece, but barely any other success.

With the bowling, only Nicholson played more than 20 games. Yet his average and that of Bore, Old and Cope was still above 25. Only Richard Hutton with 57 wickets and Don Wilson had averages below 20. Richard's all-round qualities did shine through, and he was selected for five Tests that summer, leaving him with good reason to feel pleased, as did match figures of 11-62 in a drawn Old Trafford *Roses* match.

But there was, too, a more general area of discontent. That partly arose from a failure to secure more batting points, an important aspect in gaining a good Championship position, and in pressing on firmly when the team had gained an advantage.

An example comes from the away match against Essex. Yorkshire declared at 421-5 in the 138th over, but obtained only two batting bonus points, then available for each 25 runs above 150 in the first 85 overs.

The first-wicket partnership had been 240 with, it should be said, Boycott well outscoring Sharpe, who was then run out for 92.

Nine times in 1971 Yorkshire had a first-innings score above 300, but they won only one of those matches...and it was not against Essex. These problems became associated with the captaincy.

Was Boycott too concerned with his own scores, and too often leaving others to force the pace? Were those thoughts true?

Young gun: Arnold Long appeals as 1971 centurion John Woodford turns to leg against Surrey.
(Photo: Mick Pope Archive)

Years later the highly experienced and fair Yorkshire cricket correspondent David Warner was to write: "Some felt that he put self before team...but others saw him as being gloriously successful at a time when those around him could not match his own standards. It is true that many spectators came to matches more in the expectation that Boycott would score a century than that Yorkshire would go on to win the match."

Inevitably, the pros and cons of this debate would rage on for years.

Off-the-field unhappiness was brewing with a proposal to build a football stand over a central part of the Bramall Lane ground at Sheffield, and ever increasing costs leading to a deficit of £12,000 for 1971. Brian Sellers did resign as the Cricket Chairman, and the

108

Practice makes perfect: Geoffrey Boycott, who reigned supreme as the Yorkshire and England batsman of 1971.
(Photo: Mick Pope Archive)

Committee was much reduced in size. The long serving Secretary John Nash, 41 years in post, retired with suitable plaudits.

Arthur Mitchell, the main coach, also departed, and his place was taken by Doug Padgett who would also captain the Second XI. The Seconds under the captaincy of Bob Platt had just won the Minor Counties Championship, so there were hopes for better success in 1972, though that success was to prove marginal.

It is noteworthy that the Committee 50 years ago did report "It is obvious that one day-matches have a great appeal with many of the public, and provided the team can prove successful in them, the many advantages are obvious".

Changes still slowly evolved.

Faithful servant: Yorkshire Secretary John Nash, who retired after 41 years in the post.

Who would have guessed that the young wicket-keeper David Bairstow and slow left-arm bowler Phil Carrick, chosen for one match, would in the years ahead each captain the club?

YORKSHIRE'S FIRST CLASS HIGHLIGHTS OF 1971

Wins by an innings (3)

Oxford University (168 and 102) lost to Yorkshire (447-5 dec) by an innings
and 177 runs at Oxford

Yorkshire (375-5 dec) defeated Nottinghamshire (142 and 102) by an innings
and 131 runs at Leeds

Northamptonshire (61 and 106) lost to Yorkshire (266-2 dec) by an innings
and 99 runs at Harrogate

Totals of 400 and over (3)

447-5 dec v. Oxford University at Oxford

422-9 dec v. Pakistanis at Bradford

421-4 dec v. Essex at Colchester

Opponents dismissed for under 100 (3)

61 v. Northamptonshire at Harrogate	87 v. Essex at Hull
75 v. Lancashire at Manchester	

Century Partnerships (18)

For the 1st wicket (5)

240	G Boycott and P J Sharpe	v. Essex at Colchester
196	A J Dalton and R A Hutton	v. Oxford University at Oxford
161	G Boycott and J D Woodford	v. Warwickshire at Middlesbrough
160	G Boycott and J D Woodford	v. Derbyshire at Chesterfield
134	G Boycott and R G Lumb	v. Warwickshire at Birmingham

For the 2nd wicket (5)

301	P J Sharpe and D E V Padgett	v. Glamorgan at Swansea
175	G Boycott and D E V Padgett	v. Derbyshire at Scarborough
150	G Boycott and P J Sharpe	v. Northamptonshire at Harrogate
129	G Boycott and D E V Padgett	v. Essex at Colchester
100	G Boycott and D E V Padgett	. Warwickshire at Middlesbrough

For the 3rd wicket (5)

186	G Boycott and J H Hampshire	v. Lancashire at Sheffield
182	G Boycott and J H Hampshire	v. Leicestershire at Bradford
169 *	G Boycott and J H Hampshire	v. Middlesex at Leeds
150	D E V Padgett and J H Hampshire	v. Oxford University at Oxford
139	G Boycott and J H Hampshire	v. Nottinghamshire at Leeds

For 5th wicket (1)

159	J H Hampshire and C Johnson	v. Sussex at Hove

For 6th wicket (1)

172	A J Dalton and D L Bairstow	v. Worcestershire at Dudley

For 9th wicket (1)

179	R A Hutton and G A Cope	v. Pakistanis at Bradford

Centuries (21)

G Boycott (11))

233	v. Essex at Colchester
182 *	v. Middlesex at Lord's — *Carried his bat* **
169	v. Nottinghamshire at Leeds
169	v. Lancashire at Sheffield
151	v. Leicestershire at Bradford
138 *	v. Warwickshire at Birmingham — *Carried his bat* ***
133	v. Derbyshire at Scarborough **
124 *	v Northamptonshire at Harrogate ***
112 *	v. Middlesex at Leeds
111	v. Hampshire at Bournemouth
110	v. Warwickshire at Middlesbrough
	, * *Consecutive matches*

J H Hampshire (3)

183 *	v. Sussex at Hove
116 *	v. Oxford University at Oxford
105 *	v. Gloucestershire at Sheffield

A J Dalton (2)

| 119 * | v. Worcestershire at Dudley |
| 111 | v. Oxford University at Oxford |

R A Hutton (2)

| 189 | v. Pakistanis at Bradford |
| 101 | v. Oxford University at Oxford |

D E V Padgett (1)

| 133 | v. Glamorgan at Swansea |

P J Sharpe (1)

| 172 * | v. Glamorgan at Swansea |

J D Woodford (1)

| 101 | v. Warwickshire at Middlesbrough |

5 wickets in an innings (14

R A Hutton (4)

6- 38	v. Lancashire at Manchester 1st innings
5- 24	v. Lancashire at Manchester 2nd innings
5- 54	v. Sussex at Hove
5- 58	v. Lancashire at Sheffield

A G Nicholson (3)

5- 48	v. Warwickshire at Birmingham
5- 54	v. Leicestershire at Bradford
5- 75	v. Warwickshire at Middlesbrough

D Wilson (3)

6- 35	v. Essex at Hull
6- 77	v. Worcestershire at Sheffield
5- 44	v. Glamorgan at Swansea

M K Bore (1)

| 6- 63 | v. Gloucestershire at Sheffield |

G A Cope (1)

| 5- 95 | v. Worcestershire at Sheffield |

J H Hampshire (1)

| 5- 37 | v. Nottinghamshire at Leeds |

C M Old (1)

| 5- 70 | v. Kent at Canterbury |

10 wickets in a match (1)

R A Hutton (1)

11-62 (6-38 and 5-24)   v. Lancashire at Manchester

3 catches in an innings (10)

D L Bairstow (10)

6	v. Lancashire at Manchester 1st innings
5	v. Derbyshire at Scarborough
5	v. Kent at Canterbury
4	v. Oxford University at Oxford
4	v. Surrey at Sheffield
3	v. Sussex at Hove
3	v. Lancashire at Manchester 2nd innings
3	v. Worcestershire at Sheffield
3	v. Warwickshire at Birmingham 1st innings
3	v. Warwickshire at Birmingham 2nd innings

3 dismissals in an innings (1)

D L Bairstow (1))

4 (2ct, 3st)   v. Essex at Hull

5 catches in a match (6)

D L Bairstow (6)

9 (6 + 3)	v. Lancashire at Manchester
6 (3 + 3)	v Warwickshire at Birmingham
5 (5 + 0)	v. Kent at Canterbury
5 (5 + 0)	v. Derbyshire at Scarborough
5 (4 + 1)	v. Oxford University at Oxford
5 (4 + 1)	v. Surrey at Sheffield

Debut (3

In First Class cricket: P D Borrill, A L Robinson and H P Cooper

Cap awarded (None)

Players charge with fire and rockets...

The Northern Superchargers men's 16-player squad for 2021: Aaron Finch, Harry Brook, Brydon Carse, Matthew Fisher, Tom Kohler-Cadmore, Chris Lynn, Adam Lyth, Callum Parkinson, Matty Potts, Adil Rashid, John Simpson, Ben Stokes, Olly Stone, Mujeeb Ur Rahman and David Willey — with one wildcard selection to add prior to the competition starting.

Other Yorkshire men's players involved in this summer's *Hundred* will include Jonny Bairstow (Welsh Fire), Joe Root and Dawid Malan (both Trent Rockets). This number could rise with wildcard selections much closer to the competition.

YORKSHIRE'S LIST A
HIGHLIGHTS OF 1971

Win by 100 or more runs (1)

Yorkshire (230-7) defeated Warwickshire (124) by 106 runs at Middlesbrough

Totals of 250 and over (None)

Opponents dismissed for under 100 (None)

Match aggregates of 450 and over (None)

Century Partnerships (3)

For 1st wicket (2)

143   G Boycott and J H Hampshire v. Leicestershire at Hull

121   G Boycott and J H Hampshire v. Hampshire at Bournemouth

For 2nd wicket (1)

116   G Boycott and D E V Padgett v. Warwickshire at Middlesbrough

Centuries (1)

J H Hampshire (1)

119   v. Leicestershire at Hull

4 wickets in an innings (4)

C M Old (2)

5-33   v. Sussex at Hove

4-38   v. Derbyshire at Harrogate

A L Robinson (1)

4-38   v. Surrey at The Oval

J D Woodford (1)

4-23   v. Warwickshire at Middlesbrough

3 catches in an innings (None)

3 dismissals in an innings (None)

List A Debuts (3): A L Robinson, H P Cooper and P J Squires

50 YEARS AGO

YORKSHIRE AVERAGES 1971

ALL FIRST-CLASS MATCHES

Played 27   Won 5   Lost 8   Drawn 14

County Championship: Played 24   Won 4   Lost 8   Drawn 12

BATTING AND FIELDING *(Qualification 10 completed innings)*

Player	M.	I.	N.O.	Runs	H.S.	100s	50s	Avge	ct/st
G Boycott	18	25	4	2221	233	11	6	105.76	5
J H Hampshire	27	40	5	1259	183*	3	4	35.97	13
P J Sharpe	17	27	3	823	172*	1	4	34.29	18
R A Hutton	21	28	4	697	189	2	0	29.04	21
D E V Padgett	23	35	1	866	133	1	5	25.47	19
A J Dalton	10	15	1	339	119*	2	0	24.21	3
B Leadbeater	21	32	5	645	69	0	2	23.88	12
J D Woodford	13	21	1	434	101	1	1	21.70	4
D L Bairstow	26	36	5	465	67*	0	2	15.00	64/6
C M Old	20	25	5	282	28	0	0	14.10	11
A G Nicholson	23	21	7	192	33	0	0	13.71	7
G A Cope	18	20	6	121	30*	0	0	8.64	5
D Wilson	19	21	4	143	37	0	0	8.41	20
M K Bore	17	19	4	60	16	0	0	4.00	7
Also played									
R G Lumb	4	6	1	163	65	0	2	32.60	2
C Johnson	6	8	0	165	53	0	1	20.62	8
H P Cooper	6	2	0	6	5	0	0	3.00	6
D Schofield	1	2	2	6	4*	0	0	—	0
P D Borrill	2	0	0	0	0	0	0	—	0
P Carrick	1	0	0	0	—	0	0	—	0
A L Robinson	3	0	0	0	—	0	0	—	1
N Smith	1	0	0	0	0	0	0	—	1

BOWLING *(Qualification 10 wickets)*

Player	Overs	Mdns	Runs	Wkts	Avge	Best	5wI	10wM
R A Hutton	508.3	140	1112	63	17.65	6 - 38	4	1
D Wilson	527.2	210	1095	60	18.25	6 - 35	3	0
A G Nicholson	678.5	195	1476	56	26.35	5 - 48	3	0
M K Bore	538.3	192	1184	44	26.90	6 - 63	1	0
C M Old	463	108	1226	45	27.24	5 - 70	1	0
Also bowled								
B Leadbeater	5	1	5	1	5.00	1 - 1	0	0
P D Borrill	36	14	61	5	12.20	2 - 6	0	0
J H Hampshire	33.5	8	123	8	15.37	5 - 37	1	0
J D Woodford	36.3	15	82	4	20.50	2 - 20	0	0
A L Robinson	73	24	153	6	25.50	2 - 22	0	0
H P Cooper	79	22	206	7	29.42	2 - 36	0	0
C Johnson	36.2	10	97	3	32.33	2 - 22	0	0
P Carrick	13	2	20	0	—	0 - 20	0	0
D E V Pagett	0.3	0	4	0	—	0 - 4	0	0
D Scofield	4	1	7	0	—	0 - 7	0	0

50 YEARS AGO

YORKSHIRE AVERAGES 1971

LIST A

Played 15   Won 5   Lost 10   Abandoned 2

BATTING AND FIELDING *(Qualification 4 completed innings)*

Player	M.	I.	N.O.	Runs	H.S.	100s	50s	Avge	ct/st
G Boycott	10	10	0	489	93	0	5	48.90	4
J H Hampshire	15	15	0	400	119	1	1	26.66	7
D E V Padgett	13	13	1	315	48	0	0	26.25	2
J D Woodford	13	13	1	270	41*	0	0	22.50	5
A J Dalton	8	8	0	153	55	0	1	19.12	5
R A Hutton	12	10	4	97	37	0	0	16.16	0
D L Bairstow	15	14	6	124	31	0	0	15.50	14/0
C Johnson	6	6	1	74	32	0	0	14.80	0
D Wilson	9	8	1	68	27*	0	0	9.71	2
PJ Sharpe	10	9	0	77	22	0	0	8.55	5

Also batted

Player	M.	I.	N.O.	Runs	H.S.	100s	50s	Avge	ct/st
B Leadbeater	7	7	4	153	32	0	0	51.00	1
C M Old	9	6	3	48	14*	0	0	16.00	3
P J Squires	1	1	0	14	14	0	0	14.00	0
M K Bore	10	3	2	10	10*	0	0	10.00	1
A G Nicholson	15	5	2	23	13*	0	0	7.66	0
A L Robinson	2	2	0	14	14	0	0	7.00	0
H P Cooper	8	4	1	18	10*	0	0	6.00	3
D Schofield	1	1	0	0	0	0	0	0.00	0
R G Lumb	1	1	1	0	0*	0	0	—	0

BOWLING *(Qualification 4 wickets)*

Player	Overs	Mdns	Runs	Wkts	Avge	Best	4wI	RPO
A L Robinson	16	0	81	6	13.50	4-38	1	5.06
C M Old	62	5	260	15	17.33	5-33	2	4.19
J D Woodford	65.3	5	280	15	18.66	4-23	1	4.27
R A Hutton	96	8	370	15	24.66	3-28	0	3.85
A G Nicholson	115.2	17	393	14	28.07	3-31	0	3.40
D Wilson	54	5	194	6	32.33	2-21	0	3.59
H P Cooper	60	9	243	7	34.71	2-17	0	4.05
M K Bore	76.4	11	356	8	44.50	3-35	0	4.64

Also bowled

Player	Overs	Mdns	Runs	Wkts	Avge	Best	4wI	RPO
C Johnson	2	0	5	1	5.00	1- 5	0	2.50
D Scofield	5	0	23	1	23.00	1-23	0	4.60

YORKSHIRE PASSAGES TO INDIA UNEARTHED EASTERN PROMISE

By Jeremy Lonsdale

We have become used to top English cricketers playing all around the world. A century ago opportunities were more limited, but not so for Yorkshire's professionals, several of whom had the chance to winter in India in the 1920s.

The annual coaching engagement came about through Lord Hawke's connections with the Maharaja of Patiala, one of the self-governing princely states within British-governed India. This was situated in the Punjab about 1,000 miles north of Bombay, now Mumbai. The Maharaja had captained the 1911 Indian side to England, was a well known figure in newspaper 'society' columns and had been developing local cricket for many years. He had beautifully laid-out cricket facilities in the grounds of his palace, and he wanted English professionals to go out and coach his side and his sons.

The political situation in India in the 1920s was increasingly unsettled as it was announced in July 1921 that George Hirst — in his final season with Yorkshire and almost 50 — and Wilfred Rhodes, now 44, had accepted engagements in Patiala. They left home in October, travelling through France to Marseilles, and then sailing for Bombay before taking a two-day journey by train to Patiala.

In November they appeared for the Europeans against the Hindus — where Rhodes scored 156 and took 7-26 and Hirst 6-33 — and against the Parsees — where Rhodes made 183 and took 12-59 in the match, and Hirst 62. During the second game, against a background of riots, the Prince of Wales, later Edward VIII, visited the packed ground in Bombay as part of a royal tour organised to try to popularise British rule. He met the players, and Hirst offered his bat to the Prince, who faced a couple of balls from a local bowler.

Much of the stay involved undemanding coaching of the Maharaja's team, although Rhodes also occupied himself taking photographs, some of which were later published in the *Leeds Mercury*. On his return in March 1922 Hirst spoke about his experiences, including the exhausting travel, while Rhodes said he had never played on a better wicket. They came back fit and well, although they had to look after themselves, buy-

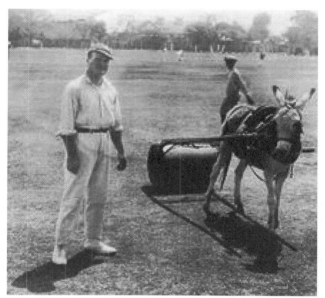

A word with the groundstaff: Roy Kilner, whose happy winters in India ended in his tragic death in 1928.
(Photo: Yorkshire Cricket Foundation)

ing food in a local bazaar. After the Championship-winning season of 1922 Rhodes returned to India the following autumn, this time with Roy Kilner, who was particularly successful in November, making 128 and 49 not out in one game. He enjoyed the trip, which he said mixed hard work and plenty of rest, and the pair accepted a further invitation for 1923-24. At the request of local players both professionals were prevented from participating in any important matches this time, but they still played local cricket.

Rhodes was impressed by the progress of the game in India, and commented enthusiastically about the sightseeing, the durbars and motoring trips in the hills. Kilner wrote that he had been surprised to see a lion — one of the Maharaja's pets — wandering round the ground at one match. He must have incurred the wrath of Rhodes by waking him in the middle of the night just to tell him it was raining, so unusual was the sight.

Rhodes returned the following winter, but with Kilner selected for the

MCC tour of Australia he was accompanied by Emmott Robinson. Rhodes had a good winter with the bat, but Robinson was troubled by injury. Both enjoyed the climate and the palace gardens, although not the snakes.

Rhodes remarked how strange it was to play with the Himalayas in the distance. Very interested in everything he saw, Rhodes observed there was still much to do to overcome caste prejudice.

Rhodes decided not to go in the winter of 1925-26, and although Kilner was lined up he eventually went to the West Indies with the MCC. Robinson was accompanied by Maurice Leyland and Abe Waddington.

Most, they held an hour's practice with the local team, but only played in matches on 13 days in the four months away. Otherwise, they were free except for coaching the Maharaja's sons two or three times a week. Leyland thought Patiala pleasant but very quiet, and they spent much of their time in their quarters in the cricket pavilion. They relaxed by playing tennis, bowls and billiards, and Waddington did some duck-shooting. They made visits to the bazaars and read old English newspapers to distract themselves.

Sartorial elegance: Legend Wilfred Rhodes off the field

Leyland, Rhodes and Arthur Dolphin travelled out in October 1926. The first ever MCC side to visit India, led by Arthur Gilligan, sailed at the same time, thoroughly underprepared for the arduous tour with only 13 players. Following injuries to MCC players, Dolphin and Leyland were called up for several, and so saw more of India than their predecessors. All three also appeared for the Maharaja's side against the MCC. On their return Dolphin said they had had a "wonderful time", although Leyland admitted he had enjoyed himself too much and would need to lose weight before the county season started.

The following winter's visit was characterised by controversy and tragedy. Interviewed on arrival in India in November 1927 about the appointment of Herbert Sutcliffe as Yorkshire captain, Kilner, Dolphin and Leyland expressed misgivings about the move from an amateur captain, although soon afterwards Sutcliffe turned down the offer anyway.

White Rose ambassadors: Roy Kilner, Arthur Dolphin in a sling, Wilfred Rhodes and Percy Holmes escape the English winter to enjoy a real Indian summer.

(Photo: Yorkshire Cricket Foundation)

Kilner then hit 283 not out for the Rajendra Gymkhana Club – including six sixes and 40 fours – in the All-India tournament in Delhi. In late March 1928 the Yorkshire trio began their journey home. Kilner became ill. He arrived in England muffled in sweaters and blankets, and was diagnosed as suffering from a form of enteric fever. He returned to Wombwell in an ambulance and entered hospital. Initial reports were optimistic, but he tragically died on April 5, 1928, aged 37.

Because of Kilner's terrible death no Yorkshire player went to India over the winter of 1928-29, but the following year Arthur Mitchell and Frank Dennis were invited, the first time such inexperienced players had been involved. Dennis wrote detailed letters home, recalling the deck games, dancing and fancy-dress competitions. Mitchell's wife also went out, and as well as cricket the players received numerous invitations to parties and big-game hunting trips. Both made big scores in local games, and Mitchell was very positive when he got home, commenting that with better coaching systems in place in the cities Indian cricket would develop quickly.

Throughout the 1920s several Yorkshire players spent their winters in India, despite long summers of Championship cricket. Although the journey was arduous the visits were a chance to earn extra money, make the most of their skills, and experience what was usually an undemanding adventure in exotic surroundings.

Jeremy Lonsdale is the author of *A Game Divided: Triumphs and Troubles in Yorkshire Cricket in the 1920s*, published by ACS Publications, 2020.

ROSES BY THE SEA WILL LIGHTEN OUR DARKNESS

By Roger Statham

When the first-class fixture list was published for 2020 it revealed the prospect of Yorkshire v. Lancashire at Scarborough, the first *Roses* fixture at the seaside for 29 years. We could look forward to four days in the mid-June sunshine at this historic cricket venue, which has hosted the old rivals only twice before in its history.

What better way to banish the trials of winter than to be lost in the reverie of all those cricket-festival days and the prospect of Fisher or Coad running in from the Trafalgar Road End to undo the Lancashire batsmen?

Practically every cricket great has played at Scarborough, when its festivals, like those at Cheltenham and so many other parts of the country, were played with a holiday joy that enhanced the strokeplay of so many batsmen. It was here that Joe Root, future England captain, stroked his first hundred and demonstrated that he could play with ease off the back foot.

But Scarborough's next chapter was to be delayed. The plague of Coronavirus arrived to frustrate the cricket season more successfully than had the battlefields of world wars.

It was as if the death of Bob Willis was an omen for the season, but it was then, of course, entirely fitting that his Trophy should provide a lifeline for the cricket deprived. After despair county members nationwide now had some positive focus for cricket imaginations and, for those so inclined, they could even sharpen the pencils for their scorebooks.

Disappointingly, the games had to be played to empty seats and benches, and those who were used to filling dates in their diaries as soon as the fixtures arrived had to be both diligent and inventive to find fulfilling cricket hours.

Assistance came through the announcement of international cricket bubbles, bio-secure Test Matches, ODIs and T20s. Most of all, it came through the bravery of all players from the West Indies, Pakistan, Australia and Ireland, coming to a country with such high Covid case rates. Home players, too, sacrificed personal and family lives in order to play. Credit has to go to them, the cricket boards of these countries and to the ECB for making these happen, and then the counties who enabled Bob's domestic cricket to take place.

Cricket-lovers had the BBC and Sky to thank most of all, as archives were opened early in the season and it was possible to listen to the rich voices of TMS past and relive genius with bat and ball. In the end we got through it all in what became an unexpectedly elongated season. But, without wanting to appear ungrateful, we could not really experience county cricket as we have grown to love it.

For us in Yorkshire no trips passed the gates of Harewood House through Meanwood and into Headingley. No parking in front of the houses of patient local residents before tripping to the ground with bags packed full of expectation and cushions to sit on.

Not since 1975 have I missed going to Headingley and, after 36 years of Yorkshire membership, the sense of loss of a cricket season has been more profound than I might ever have anticipated. But it never was anticipated was it?

This Covid virus belongs to the celluloid world of the horror movie, not to Lord's, The Oval, Emerald Headingley and the many other grounds that host the county game. There could be no away games at Old Trafford, Trent Bridge, Edgbaston, Chelmsford, Derby, Sophia Gardens or to Worcester for the cake. Not even that trip to Scarborough for a home game and driving back through the inspirational sunlit Ryedale, having been tempted again by fish and chips.

Such things are part of cricket memories, the best ones conjured by the nostalgia of actually sitting in a ground and remembering as the mind is jogged by a pull, a drive through the covers or beautiful bowling. A first *Roses* match in 1953...

Did I really see Hutton, Trueman, Wardle, Washbrook and Statham at Old Trafford? Later there was stubborn Boycott, the brutal batting of Lehmann, the talented strokeplay of a young Root and the Bairstows, father and son.

Now a whole host of yeoman fast bowlers, the always unlucky Sidebottom A with anguished howl, his talented left-arm son Ryan, who bowled some of the best opening spells I have ever seen. The ever willing Hoggard and the ebullient Gough gelling his hair for the camera after a spell at Middlesbrough that heralded his arrival on the scene.

Had we been able to sit at Headingley last summer there would have been talk of the 2019 *Ashes* Test most surely, as Ben Stokes's heroics were recalled. Remembering sharing four historic days with family and friends as Stokes and Jack Leach contrived to compile a batting partnership of unequal but immense proportions. Yes, we were there, the Statham clan — none of us is likely to forget it.

But we also missed the nods to regulars and the good-natured

At home with the greats: Roger Statham beneath John A. Blakey's portrait of legends Raymond Illingworth, Brian Close (standing), Fred Trueman and Sir Geoffrey Boycott.

exchanges with members from other counties. The visits to the East Stand Long Room for refreshment, a bite to eat and to stare at the Honours Board with the names of those who sparkled, extolling the exploits of those involved in more than a century of Test Cricket. Willis 8-43 and Botham 145 in 1981 now sit alongside Stokes 135 not out, Hazelwood 5-30 and Archer 6-45 in 2019.

The postscript to the season arrived with a further reminder of how Covid had impacted the county scene when YCCC wrote to ask for 2020 subscriptions to be donated by members. The thought of asking the Yorkshire contingent to pay for something they had not had raised a wry smile. However, the plea was very real, as repaying all members would add a further £500,000 to the county's deficit. Other counties have had to follow this course as the whole of cricket entered a survival struggle.

I have been so lucky, being able to spend so many years watching county cricket, enthralled by generations of players. A donation to keep it going is a but a small price. But our time will come again.

The *Roses* fixture at Scarborough has been rescheduled in 2021, this time in mid-July when the sun will shine again and Coad, Fisher, Patterson and Bess will triumph over Jennings, Davies, Livingstone and Vilas. What an occasion it promises to be, and it will be enjoyed all the more following the frustrations of the year gone by.

BEYOND THE SEA: Crowds bask in the North Marine Road sunshine as Yorkshire take on Nottinghamshire in 2019.

CRICKET ON HOLIDAY FOR 10 YEARS

The cricketing love affair between Yorkshire and Scarborough will be continuing for another 10 years after a new staging agreement was agreed, starting this summer.

North Marine Road will continue to host 10 days of Yorkshire cricket per summer, subject to unforeseen changes in the county schedule. As things stand, the 10 days are made up of two County Championship fixtures and two 50-over matches.

Yorkshire chief executive Mark Arthur said: "Scarborough is the jewel in our crown as far as I'm concerned, and the two things that people always look out for are the Scarborough fixtures and the Lancashire T20 at Emerald Headingley."

Scarborough CC chief executive Rob Richtering added: "Ten years is obviously a long time, and we're very grateful Yorkshire would make that commitment."

Yorkshire played their first county match at North Marine Road in 1874, a three-day draw with Middlesex. The venue has also hosted two men's one-day internationals — England v. West Indies in 1976 and England v. New Zealand in 1978.

It has also hosted five England women's Test Matches between 1951 and 2004 as well as three women's One-Day Internationals between 1998 and 2014.

STABLE THAT TURNED COLTS INTO THOROUGHBREDS

By Howard Clayton

RECORD CAPTAIN: R W Frank, whose contribution to Yorkshire County Cricket Club extended way beyond being a highly regarded Colts skipper. He made 17 appearances for the first team, served on the committee and was a vice-president.

(Photo: Ron Deaton Archive)

From 1862 to 1892 the Yorkshire second team were known as the Colts. The Second XI tag was first used on June 7, 1892, in a two-day match against Lancashire at Old Trafford, which the hosts won by one wicket. England batsman David Denton played, as did his older brother Joe.

Yorkshire first played in the Minor Counties Championship in 1900, and remained in the competition until 1910. They left at this point, but resumed in 1921. The Second XI Championship began in 1959.

For three seasons — 1959, 1960 and 1961 — Yorkshire ran a team in each competition before pulling out of the Second XI Championship at the end of 1961. They left the Minor Counties Championship in 1974, and concentrated solely on the Second XI competition from 1975.

All statistics include competitive and friendly fixtures played.

SECOND XI HONOURS

Minor Counties Championship: 1947, 1957, 1958, 1968 and 1971.

Second XI Championship: 1977, 1984, 1987 (shared with Kent), 1991 and 2003.

One-day Trophy: 1988 (beat Kent by 7 wickets), 1994 (beat Leicestershire by 4 wickets), 2009 (beat Lancashire by 2 wickets) and 2017 (beat Middlesex by 99 runs under *DLS method*).

T20: NA — Yorkshire were semi-finalists beaten by Hampshire at

Next in: Knocking on the first-team door in 1908, the Yorkshire Second XI who played Staffordshire at Rotherham on July 6 and 7. Back row, left to right: Umpire (unknown), B B Wilson, M W Booth, W Brown, A Turner and A Drake. Middle row: H Rudston, R W Frank (captain) and H Harrison. Front row: A Dolphin, C H Grimshaw and W H Micklethwait.

Staffordshire won by 102 runs, thanks to 11 wickets in the match for S F Barnes, who was England's leading Test match wicket-taker until he was eclipsed by A V Bedser in 1953.

This fixture saw the debut of locally born all-rounder Alonzo Drake, who had a fine record up to the outbreak of the Great War but died in 1919. Second Lieutenant Major Booth was killed in 1916 on the first day of the Somme offensive.

(Photo: Mick Pope Archive)

Arundel in 2017.

SECOND XI RECORDS

Number of players to have represented Yorkshire Seconds across all formats: 1,457. The first named player to represent Yorkshire was W Ainley in 1862, the 1,000th Barry Stead in 1959 and the latest Harris (Harry) Sullivan in 2019.

Home grounds used by Yorkshire Seconds up to 2019 across all formats: Yorkshire have played on 74 different grounds within the three ridings.

Most used home venue across all formats: Headingley 71 matches;

Major Raleigh C Chichester-Constable, Ernest F Holdsworth, who succeded Frank as captain, and Paul Booth, the Seconds' record wicket-taker. *(Photos: Ron Deaton and Mick Pope)*

COLIN CHAPMAN   **BRADLEY PARKER**   **CHRIS PICKLES**

GEOFF COPE   **KARL CARVER**   **HARRY SULLIVAN**

York CC, Clifton Park 57 matches; Harrogate CC, St George`s Road 48.
Record appearances: Championship — Colin Chapman 137 matches (1989 to 1998). One-day Trophy – Simon Guy 70 (1996 to 2009). T20

Minor Counties Champions 1947. Back row, left to right: H Halliday, E S Barraclough, K Smales, J H Wardle, R Aspinall, E I Lester, J T Lodge and H Sykes (scorer). Front row: J V Wilson, D V Brennan, J R S Raper (captain), C Walker and G A Smithson. *(Photo: Ron Deaton Archive).*

– Karl Carver 53 (2012 to 2019).

Most appearances as captain: Robert Wilson Frank (1900-1914) 167, and Brigadier Raleigh Charles Joseph Chichester-Constable (1925-1938) 147.

Record run-scorer: Championship – Bradley Parker 7,450, average 40.48 in 122 matches. One-day Trophy – Bradley Parker 1,885, average 34.90 in 64 matches. T20 – Jack Leaning 1,198, average 34.22 in 45 matches.

Record wicket-taker: Championship – Paul Booth 248, average 29.33 in 109 matches. One-day Trophy – Chris Pickles 53, average 21.54 in 39 matches. T20 – Karl Carver 43, average 16.25 in 53.

Highest individual Championship score: 273*. Richard Blakey v. Northamptonshire at Northampton on July 9-11, 1986.

Best Championship bowling performance: 9-27. Geoff Cope v. Northamptonshire at Northampton on May 14-15, 1979.

Highest individual one-day score: 166. Bradley Parker v. Northamptonshire at Wagon Lane, Bingley, on June 3, 1991.

Best one-day bowling performance: 6-21. Paul Booth v. Nottinghamshire at Thoresby Park, Nottinghamshire, on June 3, 1986.

Highest individual T20 score: 116*. Alex Lees v. Northamptonshire at Pudsey Congs on July 10, 2017.

Best T20 bowling performance: 5-20. Karl Carver v. Worcestershire at Barnt Green, Worcestershire, on June 25, 2015.

Highest team total: 585-8 dec v. Lancashire (Championship) at Scarborough on June 13-15, 2017.

Highest partnership: 358 for the fourth-wicket, Jonny Bairstow and Joe Root v. Leicestershire (Championship) at Lime Kilns Ground, Oakham, on June 2-4, 2009. Yorkshire required 402 to win and slipped to 44-3 before Bairstow (202*) and Root (163*) united to secure a seven-wicket victory.

First Yorkshire Second XI or Colts match: Yorkshire Colts v. All England XI, Lascelles Hall, Huddersfield, on September 11-13, 1862.

Yorkshire (69 and 99) lost to All England XI (92 and 79-6) by four wickets. Yorkshire fielded 22 players to the 11 of All England due to the strength of the visiting side. Yorkshire lost 21 wickets in each innings to All England's 10.

Did you know? On August 8, 1906, the Seconds took on Staffordshire in the Minor Counties Championship at the County Ground, Stoke-on-Trent. The game, scheduled for two days, was completed in four hours on the first day. Yorkshire were bowled out for 35 and 47, Sidney Francis Barnes taking match figures of 11-46 and his artner, Robert John Mee, 9-35. Staffordshire managed only 57 in their first innings (John Emmanuel Elms 6-25 and Charles Oyston 4-32) but needed only 4.5 overs to score 26-0 to win by 10 wickets.

There were no bowling changes throughout the match.

Howard Clayton, Yorkshire's second-team scorer between 2012 and 2017, has done extensive research on the county at this level. His findings are online at crickethistory.website.

Howard's favourite: The memory which stands out was my first game as official second-team scorer at Marton CC on April 11-13, 2012.

The game was against Durham Seconds in that very wet summer, with no play possible on the first two days. But it was particularly pleasant for me because it was with Marton CC in the North Yorkshire and South Durham CL (Division B) in April 1965 that I scored my first competitive match.

It started a path which led to five years with Marton, 11 years with Leeds/Bradford MCCU, six years with Yorkshire Seconds and 28 years with England Under-19s, including tours to Pakistan, Sri Lanka, New Zealand, South Africa (three tours) and four trips to Australia.

I also served six years as a Press Box scorer with ECB at internationals involving England around the country and, when with Yorkshire, six Test matches as opposition scorer for Sri Lanka, New Zealand, South Africa and the West Indies.

There was no competitive Second XI cricket played in 2020 due to the Coronavirus pandemic.

THE LIGHT AND THE DARK SIDE TO A YORKSHIRE LEGEND

By Graham Hardcastle

Just A Few Lines...the unseen letters and memorabilia of Brian Close   **By David Warner**   *(Great Northern Books £20*

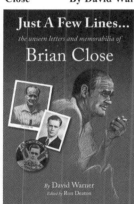

Given the rapidly changing face of communication, it is difficult to imagine Jonny Bairstow or Joe Root hand-writing personal letters back home from England tours to Australia, South Africa or India, as interesting as they would be.

Twitter and Instagram posts are all the rage nowadays, as are WhatsApp, Skype and Zoom calls. That just wasn't possible in Brian Close's day.

It is exactly why the excellent book, written by former Yorkshire cricket correspondent David Warner is so unique.

Warner and book editor Ron Deaton have collated letters to home written by legendary Close during the early stages of his illustrious near 30-year playing career.

Between 1949 and 1956 Close, the former Yorkshire and England captain who died aged 84 in 2015, wrote regularly to his best friend, John Anderson, detailing life on and off the field in entertaining and honest accounts. The letters (and autograph books filled on his behalf) to Anderson, who has also since died, were handed to Warner by Brian's widow, Vivien — the pair are friends and near neighbours in Baildon.

Close's first Test tour to Australia and New Zealand in 1950-51 is a central part of the book. Of the journey *Down Under* by boat and his exercise regime, Close writes: "I've managed to pull my (running) time for the mile well below five minutes. The mile is seven times around the deck house."

He was known to write immediately before going out to bat, and he detailed nights out or victories on championship golf courses such as Royal Melbourne.

With the great importance placed upon mental health in sport nowadays, it is fascinating to read a chapter entitled *Feeling the Strain*. On that same *Ashes* tour, which was disrupted by a groin injury, Close's mood became worryingly dark to contrast with the book's many lighter missives.

An all-round sportsman of some repute — he played football for Arsenal, Bradford and Leeds — Close's letter writing ceased in 1956 and gave way to telephone calls. To use a well known and apt phrase, Close's career ensured there was plenty to write home about.

A multiple Championship winner with the *White Rose* county, he played 22 Tests for England and three one-day internationals. His record of 34,994 first-class runs and 1,171 wickets is truly amazing, as is the feat of collating this fine book.

The Honorary Tyke   Inside Sachin Tendulkar's Summer at YCCC
Thomas Blow   *(Vertical Editions £11.99)*

Darren Lehmann may have been Yorkshire's greatest overseas player, but few could argue that Sachin Tendulkar is the greatest name to have worn the *White Rose*.

But while Lehmann, a left-handed wizard with the willow, amassed 14,599 runs across all formats between 1997 and 2006, India's adored *Little Master* was only at Headingley for one season in 1992 — or just less than a full summer to be precise.

He scored 1,671 runs in Championship and one-day cricket, including two centuries.

Tendulkar's stay in god's own country made history as he was the first overseas player to represent the county. He did so aged 19, and it says much about his talents that he was already a household name.

The story of that landmark year is told in this book written by Sheffield native Thomas Blow, whose day job sees him work for *The Cricketer* magazine. Blow's book is a short and sharp, but excellent, read. It is only 207 pages long, including a facts-and-figures section at the back. Rather than speak to the man himself, Blow draws information from various sources such as Tendulkar's autobiography and then speaks first hand to a number of Yorkshire teammates and opponents.

It is kind of apt that Tendulkar's first sporting hero was tennis legend John McEnroe because, when looking at Tendulkar's career record, it is fair to exclaim: "You cannot be serious!"

A player who scored a century on first-class debut for Mumbai aged 15 was famously only an injury replacement signing for Yorkshire after Australian fast bowler Craig McDermott pulled out of his original deal. Tendulkar went on to score August centuries against Lancashire and Durham shortly before returning home early for international duties.

Around chronicling Tendulkar's stay with the county, Blow writes of why Yorkshire had not previously employed an overseas player and about the wider topic of great foreign stars to grace the county game. The very first chapter is entitled *50 Years of Overseas Players*.

Blow starts the book with forewords from Jason Gillespie and Lehmann. Darren says: "Until Sachin Tendulkar played for them in 1992 they didn't have an overseas player — you had to be Yorkshire born and bred to play for the club. So to captain them just a decade later — and to be the club's first overseas captain — was a huge honour (for me).

"Sachin was one of the greatest players ever to play the game. When you saw him play you just thought, 'Wow, what a superstar he is. He can do anything, on and off the field'.

"I made my Test debut for Australia against India in 1998, when he scored 177 in Bangalore. To play against him was a great privilege. A really quiet, beautiful man who loves the game and played it really well; his technical ability was second to none."

Graham Hardcastle

The Men Who Raised The Bar   **Chris Waters**
(Wisden/Bloomsbury, £12.99)

Yorkshire Post cricket correspondent Chris Waters is on for a hat-trick of awards with his third book.

After earning notoriety with *Fred Trueman: The Authorised Biography* and *10 for 10: Hedley Verity and the Story of Cricket's Greatest Bowling Feat*, Waters has written his first book without a link to the White Rose county.

This is a book which would form the basis of a fabulous pub quiz question: can you name the 11 who, in the first instance, set the record for the highest individual batting score in Test cricket and then broke the records?

London-born Australian Charles Bannerman's 165 against England in 1877 set the bar before names such as Don Bradman, Wally Hammond, Len Hutton, Garry Sobers and Brian Lara (twice) raised it.

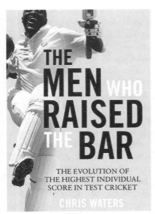

THE
MEN WHO
RAISED
THE BAR

THE EVOLUTION OF
THE HIGHEST INDIVIDUAL
SCORE IN TEST CRICKET

CHRIS WATERS

Like *10 for 10*, this is a Wisden/Bloomsbury published book and comes in exactly the same format. An almost pocket-sized publication, you could easily get through its 255 pages while sitting at Headingley or Scarborough watching a Championship game this summer.

A hall of fame dominated solely by Australians, Englishmen and West Indians, Waters dedicates a chapter to each player, telling their story and providing a scorecard for the feats in question.

While the majority of us will be familiar with the more recent exploits of Sobers, current record holder Lara (400 against England at Antigua in 1994) it is fascinating to learn more about the early pacesetters, especially Bannerman in the game's very first Test.

Having offered a simple catching chance in single figures, he was also struck a painful blow on the fingers. His innings was later curtailed as a result. So, the record books read *C Bannerman, retired hurt 165*.

Pardon the pun but, fingers crossed, this book can deliver Waters yet another gong to sit on his mantelpiece. This book is definitely worth a place on yours, Yorkshire Cricket fan or otherwise.

Graham Hardcastle

Gale's challenge to 2021 squad

Yorkshire Coach Andrew Gale summed up his side's performances in 2020: "Coming into the season, I challenged the players to compete in both competitions. We haven't done that in the Blast, but we were excellent in the Bob Willis.

"We've also had the chance to look at a number of players who wouldn't have had an opportunity in a normal season. They stood up and showed glimpses they can do it. Our challenge now is to improve them and fast-track them on the back of what they've learnt."

BRIAN BOLUS

By David Warner

Whitkirk-born Brian Bolus, right, who began an illustrious first-class career with Yorkshire before going on to play for Nottinghamshire, Derbyshire and England, died on May 6, 2020, aged 86.

Bolus had been an active member of the Yorkshire CCC Players' Association since its formation over a decade ago.

An aggressive batsman, he made his Yorkshire debut against MCC at Lord's in 1954. He went on to play in 107 matches for his native county, scoring 4,712 runs with seven centuries and a top score of 146 not out against Hampshire at Portsmouth in 1960.

He helped them to win the Championship three times, and he twice completed 1,000 runs in a season, his most prolific summer being in 1961 with 1,970 runs. A year later he was not retained. He joined Nottinghamshire in 1963, making the first of his seven England Test appearances in the same season.

Bolus was at Trent Bridge from 1963 to 1972, playing in 269 matches and completing 1,000 runs in each season. He captained Nottinghamshire in 1972 before moving on to Derbyshire, where he was captain from 1973 until his retirement at the end of the 1975 season.

He became the third player to represent three first-class counties and the first to captain different counties in consecutive seasons. While at Derby he hit the headlines at Chesterfield by sending off teammate and England fast bowler Alan Ward, who had declined to resume bowling.

In 1994 he joined Raymond Illingworth's England selection committee.

A popular cricketer with a cheery nature, Bolus was liked and respected throughout his, but it was during his time with Nottinghamshire that he will be best remembered. Nottinghamshire chairman Richard Tennant said: "Brian was a great cricketer, a wonderful ambassador for the club and a Nottinghamshire man through and through, despite his Yorkshire roots.

"We had seen little of Brian at Trent Bridge in recent times, but he will be sorely missed by everyone at the club where he was also a committee member and past president."

Former Yorkshire batsman Andrew Dalton, who played with and against Bolus, said: "I knew him very well as, of course, many of us did in those far off days in the 70s and 80s. One of my memories goes back to Trent Bridge, where he was opening the batting against us.

"Tony Nicholson was bowling well, and after Brian had padded Nick up, and the ball had gone over my head at cover — for runs, he then took a quick single and I ran him out at the bowler's end much to Nick's delight and Brian's chagrin. Of course, there wasn't really a run in it, and Brian just misjudged the call.

"Anyhow, we often went back to these type of anecdotes as we met up thereafter, and there are many more of that sort in our memory banks."

JOHN BRIAN BOLUS
FIRST CLASS CRICKET FOR YORKSHIRE 2004 TO 2015

Right-hand Batsman. Left-arm medium-pace bowler
Born: Whitkirk, Leeds January 31, 1934
Died: Nottingham May 6, 2020
Debut for Yorkshire; v. MCC at Lord's April 28, 1956
Last played: v. Northamptonshire at Sheffield July 14, 1962
Yorkshire Cap: September 29, 1960

YORKSHIRE BATTING AND FIELDING

Season	M	I	NO	Runs	HS	Avge	100s	50s	Ct
1956-62	107	179	18	4712	146*	29.26	7	22	45

YORKSHIRE BOWLING

Seasons	Matches	Overs	Mdns	Runs	Wkts	Avge	Best	5wI	10wM
1956-62	107	156.1	46	407	13	31.30	4-40	0	0

TEST MATCHES FOR ENGLAND
BATTING AND FIELDING

Seasons	M	I	NO	Runs	HS	Avge	100s	50s	Ct
1963-63/4	7	12	0	496	88	41.33	0	4	2

BOWLING

Seasons	Matches	Overs	Mdns	Runs	Wkts	Avge	Best	5wI	10wM
1963-63/4	7	6	0	16	0	—	0-16	0	0

MOLLIE STAINES

Mollie Staines, left, the only woman to gain a seat on the general committee of Yorkshire CCC, died aged 89 on October 22.

In winning a ballot for the vacant seat in the Dewsbury district in 1977, Miss Staines ended 114 years of all-male membership of the club's committee.

Having secured a comfortable win against two male candidates, she said: "I am just about beginning to realise that it is quite an achievement to have made Yorkshire cricket history. I am up in the air about it all, but I'll soon come down to earth and start doing whatever I can to help Yorkshire Cricket."

Savile Town-born Mollie was as good as her word, giving stalwart service on the committee until 1984, when she lost her seat to Philip Akroyd. She lived nearly all her life in the family home until moving to Dewsbury's Fieldhead Court Care Home approximately 16 months before her death.

Her love of Yorkshire CCC began when she went with a friend to Bradford Park , where Yorkshire were playing Gloucestershire in August 1947. The following winter her father bought her junior membership of Yorkshire for 10s. 6d. He always said it was the best money he had ever spent on her.

In those , Yorkshire's Annual General Meeting was held mid-week in January, and Mollie wrote regularly to the newspapers pointing out that few members were able to attend because of work and that Saturday would be more suitable.

In 1967 she collected 100 signatures on a petition to change the day and time of the AGM, and presented it to Yorkshire Secretary John Nash. Two years later, on Saturday, January 27, at noon, the AGM took place in the Grand Hotel at Sheffield, attended by about 250 members. Mollie always considered it her biggest achievement.

At the 2008 AGM at Headingley Mollie found herself one of the first three recipients of the President's Medal, awarded for outstanding service to Yorkshire. The other two that year were Geoff Holmes and Vivien Stone, who ran the ground's secondhand bookstall.

Perhaps most important of all to Mollie was the affection in which she was held down the years by scores of young Yorkshire players who went on to become household names. "Auntie Mollie", as she was known, followed their progress from their earliest days in the second team.

Yorkshire Coach and former first-team captain Andrew Gale said: "She was very supportive of us all, particularly when we were young players at the Academy and in the seconds, and she travelled far and wide to watch us play. She would walk round the boundary edge and have a good chat to us.

"Once, when she was unwell, I took some flowers and a card from the Academy lads to her home, and she was really made up. She always sent us Christmas cards, and would write letters when we had done well. She is a sad loss to us all. Yorkshire have lost one of their best supporters."

Yorkshire President Geoff Cope, who also grew up knowing Mollie, said: "It is always sad when you lose one of your keenest members, and Mollie gave an awful lot to the club, its players and to local cricket. From the lads' point of view she was always there at their benefit matches, helping to carry the buckets or assisting in other ways."

Mollie had attended Bingley Teacher Training College, and went on to become a junior school teacher in Batley and Dewsbury.

She was speaker secretary for the now defunct Heavy Woollen Cricket Society, and regularly attended meetings of the Northern and Wombwell societies.

Her funeral was conducted by the Right Reverend Chris Edmondson, the club's chaplain. Mourners who were unable to attend because of the Coronavirus restrictions were able to watch the service via webcast.

David Warner

DAVID PICKLES

David Pickles, right, one of the fastest bowlers in the country when he made his Yorkshire debut in 1957, died in his home town of Halifax on June 22, 2020, aged 84.

David, who claimed never to have received any coaching before joining the *White Rose*, made good enough progress in the second XI in his maiden season to be drafted into the first team by mid-July.

His searing pace ensured he formed a fearsome new ball partnership with Fred Trueman. In that season's last-but-one Championship match, he blasted through Somerset at Taunton with 7-61 in the first innings and 5-72 in the second to claim career-best match figures of 12-133. He opened the bowling on that occasion with left-arm fast bowler, Mike Cowan, who recalls: "David was certainly very quick and, to be honest, when he first came into the side I thought my place must be in jeopardy through having to make way for a better man. He and Fred were certainly a formidable pair."

David rounded off that summer with six wickets in a win over the MCC at Scarborough, clean bowling Bill Edrich, Doug Insole and Ted Dexter. He finished second to Trueman in Yorkshire's first-class averages with 37 wickets at 17.56 apiece.

The following summer he captured 42 wickets at 20.28, including 5-42 in the *Roses* clash at Old Trafford. But he went into rapid decline with an action which suggested he could not sustain his pace at first-class level over a long period of time. He managed only 17 wickets in the next two campaigns before leaving at the end of 1960. He played 41 matches for Yorkshire, taking 96 wickets at 21.47.

He represented Sowerby Bridge's first team aged 12, and was professional at Bradford League clubs Bowling Old Lane (1958 and 1959) and Baildon (1961). He also played for Halifax in 1965.

David left a widow, Jill, two sons and a daughter, and several grandchildren and great grandchildren.

David Warner

PETER SUTCLIFFE

Peter Sutcliffe, left, a Halifax-born off-spinner with the rather unique distinction of representing both Yorkshire's and Lancashire's second teams in the 1950s and 1960s, died aged 88 in early January.

Sutcliffe represented the *White Rose* seconds — he never played for the firsts — from 1951 to 1954, taking 67 wickets. They were summers in which Yorkshire's reserves would have given at least half the first-class counties a good match.

After national service in Cyprus he went to Loughborough and trained as a PE teacher, with work taking him to Watford and allowing him to play Minor Counties cricket for Hertfordshire before later appearances for Cumberland and Cheshire.

Sutcliffe moved into further education, training young teachers in Birmingham and Southport. For much of this period, he had been closely involved with the English Schools Cricket Association, and in 1971 was appointed the first director of coaching at the National Cricket Association, upon a recommendation from good friend Jack Ikin, the former Lancashire and England all-rounder.

His club sides included Southport and Birkdale in Lancashire and Staffordshire club Bignall End, the latter alongside Ikin.

Rather than appointing an ex-county player keen to stay in the game, the NCA had given their most important coaching post to a professional educator prepared to innovate with the aim of broadening cricket's appeal.

Sutcliffe set up the proficiency award scheme and insisted on equal opportunities being given to girls in primary school cricket. He wrote coaching books and devised courses for the various awards that aspiring coaches might earn. He cleared a path which his successors at the England and Wales Cricket Board have smoothed and modified. It is his most significant legacy to the game he loved.

In 1966, Sutcliffe played two games for Lancashire's second team, the last against Yorkshire at Old Trafford, taking 6-43 against a team containing three future Test cricketers.

Peter's off-spinning son, Simon, played against Yorkshire for Oxford University in 1980 and also represented Warwickshire in 1981 and 1982.

Your starter for 11. Who can name this Yorkshire team walking out at Weetwood, Leeds, on April 23, 1952, for a non-first-class match against Leeds University? Left to right: Johnny Wardle, Leonard Hutton, Norman Yardley, Eric Fisk, Frank Lowson, Freddie Trueman, Bob Appleyard, Harry Halliday, Eddie Leadbeater and Ted Lester. But can you spot the player almost hidden between Hutton and Yardley? He is Eric Sutton, whose death was reported in the 2020 _Yorkshire County Cricket Club Yearbook_ and who was deputising as wicketkeeper for Don Brennan.

(Photo: Ron Deaton Archive)

The Players

Steven Andrew PATTERSON
Right-hand batsman, right-arm medium-fast bowler
Born: Beverley, October 3, 1983
First-Class Cricket:
Debut: v. Bangladesh A at Leeds, 2005
Highest score: 63* v. Warwickshire at Leeds, 2016
Best bowling: 6-40 v. Essex at Chelmsford, 2018
One-Day:
Highest score: 25* v. Worcestershire at Leeds, 2006
Best bowling: 6-32 v. Derbyshire at Leeds, 2010
T20:
Highest score: 3* v. Derbyshire at Leeds, 2010
Best bowling: 4-30 v. Lancashire at Leeds, 2010

Autograph

Joe Edward ROOT
Right-hand batsman, right-arm off-spin bowler
Born: Sheffield, December 30, 1990
First-Class cricket:
Debut: v. Loughborough MCCU at Leeds, 2010
Highest score: 254 for England v. Pakistan
at Manchester, 2016
Highest for Yorkshire: 236 v. Derbyshire
at Leeds, 2013
Best bowling: is 4-5 v. Lancashire
at Manchester, 2018
One-Day:
Highest Score: 133* for England v. Bangladesh
at The Oval, 2017
Highest for Yorkshire: 83 v. Warwickshire
at Birmingham, 2017
Best bowling: 3-52 for England v. Ireland
at Lord's, 2017
Best bowling for Yorkshire: 2-14 v. Kent at Leeds, 2012
T20:
Highest score: 92* v. Lancashire at Manchester, 2016
Best bowling for England: 2-9 v West Indies at Kolkata, 2016-17
For Yorkshire: 2-7 v. Derbyshire at Leeds, 2020

Autograph

Autograph-hunters are advised not to use permanent markers on these pages

David Jonathan WILLEY

Left-hand batsman, left-arm fast-medium bowler
Born: Northampton, February 28, 1990

First-Class cricket:
Debut: for Northamptonshire v. Leicestershire
at Leicester, 2009
Debut for Yorkshire: v. Nottinghamshire
at Nottingham, 2016
Highest score: 104* for Northamptonshire
v. Gloucestershire at Northampton, 2015
Highest for Yorkshire: 46 v. Warwickshire at York,
2019
Best bowling: 5-29 for Northamptonshire
v. Gloucestershire at Northampton, 2011
For Yorkshire: 3-55 v. Surrey at Leeds, 2016

One-Day:
Highest score: 167 for Northamptonshire v. Warwickshire at Birmingham, 2013
Highest for Yorkshire: 131 v. Lancashire at Manchester, 2018
Best bowling: 5-62 for England Lions v. New Zealand A at Bristol, 2014
For Yorkshire: 4-47 v. Derbyshire at Derby, 2018

T20:
Highest score: 118 for Yorkshire v. Worcestershire at Leeds, 2017
Best bowling: 4-7 for England v. West Indies at Basseterre, 2019
For Yorkshire: 4-18 v. Northamptonshire at Leeds, 2019

Autograph

Adam LYTH

Left-hand batsman, right-arm medium bowler
Born: Whitby, September 25, 1987
First-Class cricket:
Debut: v. Loughborough UCCE at Leeds, 2007
Highest score: 251 v. Lancashire
at Manchester, 2014
Best bowling: 2-9 v. Middlesex at Scarborough,
2016

One-Day:
Highest score: 144 v. Lancashire at Manchester,
2018
Best bowling: 1-6 v Middlesex at Leeds, 2013

T20:
Highest score: 161 v. Northamptonshire
at Leeds, 2017
Best bowling: 5-31 v. Nottinghamshire
at Nottingham, 2019

Autograph

Gary Simon BALLANCE

Left-hand batsman, leg-break bowler
Born: Harare, Zimbabwe, November 22, 1989

First-Class Cricket:
Debut: v Kent at Canterbury, 2008
Highest score: 210 for Mid-West Rhinos v. Southern Rocks at Masvingo, Zimbabwe, 2011-12
For Yorkshire: 203* v. Hampshire at West End, Southampton, 2017

One-Day:
Highest score: 156 v. Leicestershire at Leeds, 2019

T20:
Highest score: 79 v. Birmingham at Birmingham, 2018

Autograph

Jonathan Marc BAIRSTOW

Right-hand batsman, wicket-keeper
Born: Bradford, September 26, 1989

First-Class Cricket:
Debut: v Somerset at Leeds, 2009
Highest score: 246 v. Hampshire at Leeds, 2016

One-Day:
Highest score: 174 v, Durham at Leeds, 2017

T20:
Highest score: 114 for Sunrisers Hyderabad v. Royal Challengers Bangalore at Hyderabad, 2019
For Yorkshire: 102* v. Durham at Chester-le-Street, 2014

Autograph

Adil Usman RASHID

Right-hand batsman, leg-break bowler
Born: Bradford, February 17, 1988

First-Class cricket:
Debut: v. Warwickshire at Scarborough, 2006
Highest score: 180 v Somerset at Leeds, 2013
Best bowling: 7-107 v. Hampshire
at Southampton, 2008

One-Day:
Highest score: 71 v. Gloucestershire at Leeds, 2014
Best bowling: 5-27 for England v.Ireland
at Bristol, 2017
Best bowling for Yorkshire: 5-33 v. Hampshire
at Southampton 2014

t20:
Highest score: 36* v Uva Next
at Johannesburg, 2012/13
Best bowling: 4-19 v. Durham at Leeds, 2017

Autograph

Tom KOHLER-CADMORE

Right-hand batsman, right-arm off-break bowler
Born: Chatham, August 19, 1994

First-Class Cricket:
Debut: For Worcestershire v. Hampshire
at West End, Southampton, 2014
Debut for Yorkshire: v. Somerset
at Scarborough, 2017
Highest score: 176 v. Leeds/Bradford MCCU
at Weetwood, Leeds, 2019

One-Day:
Highest score: 164 v. Durham at Chester-le-Street,
2018

T20:
Highest score: 127 for Worcestershire v. Durham
at Worcester, 2016
For Yorkshire: 96* v. Leicestershire at Leicester,
2019

Autograph

Benjamin Oliver COAD
Right-hand batsman, right-arm fast-medium bowler
Born: Harrogate, January 10, 1994
First-Class Cricket:
Debut: v. Durham at Chester-le-Street, 2016
Highest score: 48 v. Surrey at Scarborough, 2019
Best bowling: 6-25 v. Lancashire at Leeds, 2017
One-Day:
Highest score: 9 v. Hampshire at West End, 2018
Best bowling: 4-63 v. Derbyshire at Leeds, 2017
t20:
Highest score: 7 v. Lancashire at Leeds, 2020
Best bowling: 3-40 v. Derbyshire at Leeds 2020

Autograph

Harry Charrington BROOK
Right-hand batsman, medium-pace bowler
Born: Keighley, February 22, 1999
First-Class Cricket:
Debut: v. Pakistan A at Leeds, 2016
Highest score: 124 v. Essex at Chelmsford, 2018
Best bowling: 1-54 v. Somerset
at Scarborough, 2017
One-Day:
Highest score: 103 v. Leicestershire at Leeds, 2019
Best bowling: 0-19 v. Worcestershire at
Worcestershire, 2019
T20:
Highest score: 50* v. Derbyshire at Leeds, 2020
Best bowling: 1-13 v. Derbyshire at Leeds, 2020

Autograph

Dawid Johannes MALAN

Left-hand batsman, leg-break bowler
Born: Roehampton September 3, 1987

First-Class cricket:
Debut: for Boland v Border at Paarl, 2006
Debut for Yorkshire: v. Durham
at Chester-le-Street, 2020
Highest score: 219 v. Derbyshire at Leeds, 2020
Best bowling: 5-61 for Middlesex v. Lancashire
at Liverpool, 2012
Best bowling for Yorkshire: 2-24 v. Nottinghamshire
at Nottingham, 2020

One-Day:
Highest score: 185* for England Lions v. Sri Lanka
at Northampton, 2016
Best bowling: 4-25 for Prime Doleshwar Sporting Club
v. Partex Sporting Club at Savar, Bangladesh, 2014

T20:
Highest score: 117 for Middlesex v. Surrey at The Oval, 2019
Highest score for Yorkshire: 27 v. Lancashire at Leeds, 2020
Best bowling: 2-10 for Middlesex v. Essex at Lord's 2009
*Best bowling f*or Yorkshire: 0-16 v. Lancashire at Manchester, 2020

Autograph

Jordan Aaron THOMPSON

Left-hand batsman, right-arm medium-pace bowler
Born: Leeds, October 9, 1996

First-Class Cricket:
Debut: v. Surrey at Guildford, 2019
Highest score: 98 v. Nottinghamshire
at Nottingham, 2020
Best bowling: 5-31 v. Leicestershire at Leeds, 2020

One-Day:
Has not batted
Best bowling: 0-43 v. Durham at Leeds, 2019

T20:
Highest score: 50 v. Derbyshire at Chesterfield,
2019
Best bowling: 3-23 v. Derbyshire at Leeds, 2018

Autograph

Dominic Mark BESS

Right-hand batsman, right-arm off-break bowler
Born: Exeter, July 22, 1997

First-Class cricket:
Debut: for Somerset v. Pakistanis at Taunton, 2016
Debut for Yorkshire: v. Kent at Canterbury, 2019
Highest score: 107 for MCC v. Essex at Bridgetown,
Barbados, 2018
Highest score for Yorkshire: 91* v. Essex
at Leeds, 2019
Best bowling: 7-117 for Somerset v. Hampshire
at Taunton, 2017
Best bowling for Yorkshire: 3-45 v. Essex
at Leeds, 2019

One-Day:
Highest score: 24* for North v. South at Cave Hill,
Barbados, 2018
Best bowling: 3-35 for England Lions v. Pakistan A at Abu Dhabi, 2018
Awaiting Yorkshire debut

T20:
Highest score: 5* v. Worcestershire at Leeds, 2019
Best bowling: 2-30 v. Derbyshire at Chesterfield, 2019

Autograph

Matthew David FISHER
Right-hand batsman, right-arm fast-medium bowler
Born: York, November 9, 1997
First-Class Cricket:
Debut: v. Nottinghamshire at Nottingham, 2015
Highest score: 47* v. Kent at Leeds, 2019
Best bowling: 5-54 v. Warwickshire at Leeds, 2017
One-Day:
Highest score: 36* v. Worcestershire
at Worcester, 2017
Best bowling: 3-32 v. Leicestershire at Leeds, 2015
T20:
Highest score: 17* v. Birmingham at Birmingham,
2018
Best bowling: 5-22 v. Derbyshire at Leeds, 2015

Duanne OLIVIER
Right-hand batsman, right-arm fast bowler
Born: Groblersdal, South Africa, May 12, 1992
First-Class cricket:
Debut: for Free State v. North West
at Potchefstroom, 2011
Debut for Yorkshire: v. Leeds/Bradford MCCU
at Weetwood, Leeds, 2019
Highest score: 72 for Free State v. Namibia
at Bloemfontein, 2014
Highest score for Yorkshire: 24 v. Kent at Leeds,
2019
Best bowling: 6-37 for South Africa v. Pakistan
at Centurion, 2018
Best bowling for Yorkshire: 5-96 v.
Nottinghamshire at Nottingham, 2019

One-Day:
Highest score: 25* for Knights v. Lions at Kimberley, 2018
Highest score for Yorkshire: 8* v. Nottinghamshire at Nottingham, 2019
Best bowling: 4-34 for Knights v Lions at Kimberley, 2018
Best bowling for Yorkshire: 1-44 v. Lancashire at Leeds, 2019

T20:
Highest score: 15* for Jozi Stars v. Nelson Mandela Bay Giants at Johannesburg, 2018
Highest score for Yorkshire: 8 v. Durham at Leeds, 2020
Best bowling: 4-28 for Free State v. South West Districts at Oudtshoom, 2013
Best bowling for Yorkshire: 2-17 v. Durham at Leeds, 2020

Autograph

Jonathon Andrew TATTERSALL
Right-hand batsman, leg-break bowler
Born: Harrogate, December 15, 1994
First-Class Cricket:
Debut: v. Hampshire at West End, Southampton,
2018
Highest score: 135* v. Leeds/Bradford MCCU
at Weetwood, Leeds, 2019

One-Day:
Highest score: 89 v. Hampshire at West End,
Southampton, 2018

T20:
Highest score: 53* v. Durham at Leeds, 2018

Autograph

Joshua Edward POYSDEN

Left-hand batsman, leg-break bowler
Born: Shoreham-by-Sea, August 8, 1991

First-Class Cricket:
Debut: for Cambridge MCCU v Essex at
Cambridge, 2011
Debut for Yorkshire: v. Lancashire at Manchester,
2018
Highest score: 47 for Cambridge MCCU v. Surrey
at Cambridge, 2011
Highest score for Yorkshire: 20 v. Lancashire
at Manchester, 2018
Best bowling: 5-29 for Warwickshire v. Glamorgan
at Birmingham, 2018
Best bowling for Yorkshire: 3-128 v. Worcestershire
at Scarborough, 2018

One-Day:
Highest score: 10* for Unicorns v. Gloucestershire at Wormsley, 2013
Highest score for Yorkshire: 1 v. Lancashire at Leeds, 2019, and 1 v. Nottinghamshire
at Nottingham, 2019
Best bowling: 3-33 for Unicorns v. Middlesex at Lord's 2013
Best bowling for Yorkshire: 2-31 v. Leicestershire at Leeds, 2019

T20:
Highest score: 9* for Warwickshire v. Northamptonshire at Northampton, 2016
Highest score for Yorkshire: 0* v. Nottinghamshire at Nottingham, 2020
Best bowling: 4-51 for Warwickshire v. Derbyshire at Birmingham, 2015
Best bowling for Yorkshire: 3-32 v. Durham at Leeds, 2020

Autograph

William Alan Richard FRAINE

Right-hand batsman, right-arm medium pace bowler
Born: Huddersfield, June 13, 1996

First-Class Cricket:
Debut: For Durham MCCU v. Gloucestershire at
Bristol, 2017
Debut for Yorkshire: v. Essex at Leeds, 2019
Highest score: 106 v. Surrey at Scarborough, 2019

One-Day:
Highest score: 13 for Nottinghamshire v.
Lancashire at Manchester, 2018
Awaiting Yorkshire debut

T20:
Highest score: 44* v. Derbyshire at Leeds, 2020

Autograph

Matthew James WAITE

Right-hand batsman, right-arm fast medium bowler
Born: Leeds, December 24, 1995

First-Class Cricket:
Debut: v. Somerset at Taunton, 2017
Highest score: 42 v. Nottinghamshire at
Nottingham, 2018
Best bowling: 5-16 v. Leeds/Bradford MCCU
at Weetwood, Leeds, 2019

One-Day:
Highest score: 71 v. Warwickshire
at Birmingham, 2017
Best bowling: 4-65 v. Worcestershire
at Worcester, 2017

T20:
Highest score: 19* v. Glamorgan at Cardiff, 2016
Best bowling: 1-6 v. Glamorgan at Cardiff, 2016

Autograph

George Christopher HILL

Right-hand batsman, right-arm fast-medium bowler
Born: Keighley, January 24, 2001

First-Class Cricket:
Debut: v. Derbyshire at Leeds, 2020
Highest score: 29 v. Lancashire at Leeds, 2020
Best bowling: 1-27 v. Lancashire at Leeds, 2020

One-Day:
Awaits debut

T20:
Highest score: 14 v. Durham at Leeds, 2020
Best bowling: 1-9 v. Durham at Leeds, 2020

Autograph

Matthew William PILLANS
Right-hand batsman, right-arm fast bowler
Born: Westville, South Africa, July 4, 1991
First-Class Cricket:
Debut: for Northerns v North West at Pretoria, 2012
Debut for Yorkshire: v. Nottinghamshire
at Nottingham, 2018
Highest score: 56 for Leicestershire v.
Northamptonshire at Northampton, 2017
*Highest score fo*r *Yorkshire:* 8 v. Nottinghamshire
at Nottingham, 2018
Best bowling: 6-67 for Dolphins v. Knights
at Durban, 2015
Best bowling for Yorkshire: 2-34 v. Leeds/Bradford
MCCU at Weetwood, Leeds, 2019
One-Day:
Highest score: 31 v. Worcestershire
at Worcester, 2019
Best bowling: 5-29 v. Leicestershire at Leeds, 2019
T20:
Highest score: 34* for Leicestershire v. Warwickshire at Leicester, 2017
Highest score for Yorkshire: 8 v. Lancashire at Leeds, 2019
Best bowling: 3-15 for KwaZulu-Natal Inland v. Northerns at Bloemfontein, 2015
Best bowling for Yorkshire: 1-22 v. Durham at Chester-le-Street, 2020

Autograph

Jack William SHUTT
Right-hand batsman, right-arm off-break bowler
Born: Barnsley, June 24, 1997
First-Class Cricket:
Awaiting debut
One-Day:
Awaiting debut
T20:
Highest score: 0* v. Lancashire at Leeds, 2019
                0* v. Lancashire at Leeds, 2020
                0* v. Durham at Leeds, 2020
Best bowling: 5-11 v. Durham
at Chester-le-Street, 2019

Autograph

Thomas William LOTEN
Right-hand batsman, right-arm medium-fast bowler
Born: Huddersfield, June 13, 1996
First-Class Cricket:
Debut: v. Warwickshire at Birmingham, 2019
Highest score: 58 v. Warwickshire at Birmingham, 2019
One-Day:
Awaiting debut
T20:
Awaiting debut

Autograph

Autograph

Matthew Liam REVIS
Right-hand batsman, right-arm medium-fast bowler
Right-hand batsman, right-arm medium-pace bowler
Born: Steeton, November 15, 2001
First-Class Cricket:
Debut: v. Kent at Leeds, 2019
Highest score: 9 v. Kent at Leeds, 2019
One-Day:
Awaiting debut
T20:
Highest score: 0* v. Lancashire at Manchester, 2020

Autograph

Dominic James LEECH
Left-hand batsman, slow left-arm orthodox bowler
Right-hand batsman, right-arm medium-pace bowler
Born: Middlesbrough, January 10, 2001
First-Class Cricket:
Debut: v. Nottinghamshire at Nottingham, 2020
Highest score: 1 v. Nottinghamshire at Nottingham, 2020
Best bowling: 2-72 v. Derbyshire at Leeds, 2020
One-Day:
Awaits debut
T20:
Awaits debut

Teammates run for Dan

During the early stages of the UK's first Coronavirus lockdown last April many players and coaches connected with Yorkshire Cricket got involved in the *RunForDan* tribute in memory of the late Dan Woods, a prominent league cricketer with York CC, who lost his battle with cancer a month earlier.

Hundreds of teammates, opponents, cricket-lovers and those who knew the 32-year-old spinner from his job as a teacher joined to run, walk or cycle five kilometres to raise money for the Magnolia Centre at York, who provide support for cancer patients including Woods, diagnosed with an oesophageal tumour in the winter of 2018-19.

Former York teammates Jonny Tattersall, Ben Coad, Finlay Bean and Jack Leaning joined in to provide a strong Yorkshire CCC presence, as did Director of Cricket Martyn Moxon alongside his son Jonny.

All who took part did so in cricket whites on what would have been the first day of the Yorkshire Premier League North campaign on April 18.

YORKSHIRE'S FIRST-CLASS HIGHLIGHTS OF 2020

Win by 10 wickets (1)

   Leicestershire (124 and 161) lost to Yorkshire (252 and 37-0) at Leeds

Totals of 400 (1)

   400-6 dec   v. Derbyshire at Leeds

Century Partnerships (3)

For 2nd wicket (1)

   131   A Lyth and J M Bairstow   v. Nottinghamshire at Nottingham

For 5th wicket (1)

   200   D J Malan and J A Tattersall   v. Derbyshire at Leeds

For 6th wicket (1)

   116   J A Tattersall and J A Thompson   v. Leicestershire at Leeds

Centuries (2)

   A Lyth (1)

   103   v. Lancashire at Leeds

   D J Malan (1)

   219   v. Derbyshire at Leeds

5 wickets in an innings (2)

   B O Coad (1)

      5- 18   v. Leicestershire at Leeds

   J A Thompson

      5- 31   v. Leicestershire at Leeds

10 wickets in a match (None)

3 catches in an innings (2)

   A Lyth (1)

      3   v. Nottinghamshire at Nottingham

   J A Tattersall (1)

      3   v. Leicestershire at Leeds

5 catches in a match (None)

3 dismissals in an innings (None)

Debuts (5

In First Class cricket (3): J W Shutt, D J Leech and G C H Hill
In First Class cricket for Yorkshire (2): D J Malan and J D Warner

FIRST CLASS FACTFILE
BOB WILLIS TROPHY 2020

Compiled by John T Potter

Versus DURHAM at Chester-le-Street

1. J W Shutt made his First Class debut.
2. D J Malan made his First Class debut for Yorkshire.
3. D G Bedingham made his First Class debut in England.
4. J A Thomson's 3-16 in Durham's first innings was a career best.
5. A Z Lees's 106 in Durham's second innings made him the 11th player to score a century for and against Yorkshire. M J Lumb was the last to do this for Nottinghamshire in 2013.
6. C Rushworth took his 500th First Class wicket when he dismissed T Kohler-Cadmore in Yorkshire's second innings.

Versus NOTTINGHAMSHIRE at Nottingham

1. D J Leech made his First Class debut.
2. J A Thompson (98) scored his maiden First Class fifty in Yorkshire's first innings. His 3-6 in Nottinghamshire's second innings was also a career best.
3. T J Moores's 106 in Nottinghamshire's first innings was a career best.
4. D Olivier took his 450th First Class wicket when he dismissed B M Duckett in Nottinghamshire's second innings.

Versus DERBYSHIRE at Leeds

1. G C H Hill made his First Class debut.
2. D J Malan (219) scored his maiden First Class double-century.
3. Yorkshire's fifth-wicket partnership of 200 between D J Malan and J A Tattersall was their highest against Derbyshire, and was only eight short of passing Yorkshire's best for this wicket at Headingley, Leeds — 207 by G S Ballance and A U Rashid against Somerset in 2013.
4. The weather played a large part in this match with 626 minutes lost in the game due to rain and bad light.

BOB WILLIS TROPHY FACTFILE *(Continued)*

Versus LANCASHIRE at Leeds

1. G D Burrows made First Class debut.
2. J D Warner made his First Class debut for Yorkshire.
3. Yorkshire last played Lancashire in a Non-Championship First Class fixture in April 1997, a match in which G J Batty and M J Wood made their First Class debuts.
4. Once again the weather played a large part, with 884 minutes lost and no play on the final day.

Versus LEICESTERSHIRE at Leeds

1. B O Coad took his 150th First Class wicket when he dismissed S T Evans in Leicestershire's first innings.
2. J A Thompson's 5-31 in Leicestershire's second innings was his maiden five-wicket haul in an innings in First Class cricket.
3. No play was possible on day two due to rain.

Face shield for bowlers

Fast bowler Ben Coad and his brother Dan, through their Dac Sports clothing business, are close to completion in manufacturing a bowling face mask for T20 cricket.

The Coad brothers, with the help of Yorkshire physio Kunwar Bansil, have been working on designs to protect seamers and spinners when batsmen smash the ball straight back at them.

Nottinghamshire seamer Luke Fletcher was hit on the head in his follow-through during a Vitality Blast game in July 2017, and did not play again for nearly a year.

You may see Coad wearing his new mask in this summer's T20 competition. "It's almost a case of us waiting for a fatality to happen," he said. "And I want something to be in place before that happens."

Bob Willis Trophy 2020

Captain: S A Patterson

* Captain

§ Wicket-Keeper

Figures in brackets ( ) indicate position in Second Innings batting order,
where different from First Innings

DETAILS OF PLAYERS WHO APPEARED FOR YORKSHIRE IN 2020

Player	Date of Birth	Birthplace	First-Class debut for Yorkshire	Date Capped
S A Patterson	October 3, 1983	Beverley	August 3, 2005	May 16, 2012
A Lyth	September 25, 1987	Whitby	May 16, 2007	Aug 22, 2010
J M Bairstow	September 26, 1989	Bradford	June 11, 2009	Aug 17, 2011
B O Coad	January 10, 1994	Harrogate	June 20, 2016	Sept 18, 2018
T Kohler-Cadmore	April 19, 1994	Chatham	July 3, 2017	Feb 28, 2019
D Olivier	May 9, 1992	Groblersdal, South Africa	March 31, 2019	Mar 31, 2019
D J Malan	September 3, 1987	Roehampton	August 1, 2020	Aug 1, 2020
M D Fisher	November 9, 1997	York	April 19, 2015	
H C Brook	February 22, 1999	Keighley	June 26, 2016	
J A Tattersall	December 15, 1994	Harrogate	June 20, 2018	
W A R Fraine	June 13, 1996	Huddersfield	June 3, 2019	
J A Thompson	October 9, 1996	Leeds	June 10, 2019	
T W Loten	January 8, 1999	York	September 23, 2019	
J W Shutt	June 24, 1997	Barnsley	August 1, 2020	
D J Leech	January 10, 2001	Middlesbrough	August 8, 2020	
G C H Hill	January 24, 2001	Keighley	August 15, 2020	
J D Warner	November 14, 1996	Wakefield	August 22, 2020	

Bob Willis Trophy — North Group
Durham v. Yorkshire

Played at Emirates Riverside, Chester-le-Street, on August 1, 2, 3 and 4, 2020
Yorkshire won by 6 wickets

Toss won by Durham

Yorkshire 19 points, Durham 3 points

Close of play: First Day, Yorkshire 84-4 (Malan 24*, Brook 2*); Second Day, Durham 106-2 (Lees 58*, Bedingham 18*); Third Day, Yorkshire 103-3 (Malan 50*, Brook 23*)

First Innings	DURHAM		Second Innings	
A Z Lees, lbw b Fisher		8	b Fisher	106
S R Dickson, c Tattersall b Coad		11	c Tattersall b Patterson	14
C T Steel, c Tattersall b Thompson		9	run out (Coad/Tattersall)	11
D G Bedingham, c Fisher b Thompson		8	lbw b Patterson	77
G J Harte, not out		33	not out	29
J T A Burnham, b Coad		7	b Fisher	2
* § E J H Eckersley, lbw b Patterson		6	lbw b Fisher	0
P Coughlin, lbw b Thompson		3	lbw b Fisher	0
B A Raine, lbw b Fisher		7	b Thompson	0
M J Potts, c Fisher b Coad		10	c Kohler-Cadmore b Thompson	0
C Rushworth, c and b Coad		0	lbw b Patterson	14
Extras lb 1		1	Extras b 4, lb 9	13
Total		103	Total	266

Bonus points — Yorkshire 3

FoW: 1st 1-13 (Lees), 2-25 (Dickson), 3-34 (Steel), 4-41 (Bedingham), 5-61 (Burnham), 6-68 (Eckersley), 7-77 (Coughlin), 8-86 (Raine), 9-103 (Potts), 10-103 (Rushworth)

FoW: 2nd 1-47 (Dickson), 2-71 (Steel), 3-207 (Bedingham), 4-221 (Lees), 5-225 (Burnham), 6-225 (Eckersley), 7-229 (Coughlin), 8-231 (Raine), 9-239 (Potts), 10-266 (Rushworth)

	O	M	R	W		O	M	R	W
Coad	16.4	6	23	4	Coad	25	12	23	0
Fisher	16	5	43	2	Fisher	26	9	54	4
Patterson	13	3	20	1	Patterson	24.2	5	62	3
Thompson	13	6	16	3	Thompson	19	2	53	2
					Shutt	8	0	41	0
					Brook	6	1	17	0
					Lyth	1	0	3	0

First Innings	YORKSHIRE		Second Innings	
A Lyth, c Dickson b Rushworth		10	lbw b Rushworth	4
T Kohler-Cadmore, b Raine		41	lbw b Rushworth	24
W A R Fraine, lbw b Coughlin		14	lbw b Rushworth	0
D J Malan, c Eckersley b Rushworth		30	c Dickson b Lees	73
* S A Patterson, lbw b Coughlin		0		
H C Brook, c Burnham b Potts		41	(5) not out	66
§ J A Tattersall, b Raine		17	(6) not out	2
J A Thompson, lbw b Raine		1		
M D Fisher, c Lees b Rushworth		1		
B O Coad, c Eckersley b Coughlin		28		
J W Shutt, not out		7		
Extras b 4, lb 5		9	Extras lb 3	3
Total		199	Total (4 wkts)	172

Bonus points — Durham 3

FoW: 1st 1-32 (Lyth), 2-66 (Kohler-Cadmore), 3-68 (Fraine), 4-68 (Patterson), 5-120 (Malan), 6-154 (Brook), 7-157 (Thompson), 8-164 (Tattersall), 9-164 (Fisher), 10-199 (Coad)

FoW: 2nd 1-4 (Lyth), 2-4 (Fraine), 3-56 (Kohler-Cadmore), 4-154 (Malan)

	O	M	R	W		O	M	R	W
Rushworth	17	1	69	3	Rushworth	15	3	52	3
Potts	9	3	19	1	Potts	6	2	25	0
Raine	20	8	53	3	Raine	14	3	32	0
Harte	2	1	3	0	Coughlin	8	2	31	0
Coughlin	14.4	3	46	3	Lees	1	0	12	1
					Harte	0.4	0	17	0

Umpires: G D Lloyd and N J Pratt Scorers: W R Dobson and G Maddison

Durham v. Yorkshire

White Rose off to a flyer

HARRY BROOK
Eye-catching sixes

Yorkshire secured an opening-round victory built upon a memorable bowling performance across both innings from their quartet of seamers and some valuable batting contributions from debutant Dawid Malan and Harry Brook.

The 19-point haul was threatened as Durham fought hard after being bowled out for 103, but in new-ball pair Ben Coad and Matthew Fisher, along with captain Steven Patterson and all-rounder Jordan Thompson, they had four relentless seamers controlling the run-rate and striking when the chance arose.

England's Malan and Brook shared fifth and fourth-wicket stands of 52 and 98, Brook underpinning the pursuit of 171 with an unbeaten 66, including four eye-catching sixes, two in succession.

Conditions favoured bowlers during the first two days before the pitch died and only provided significant threat with the new ball. The toss proved a good one to lose for Patterson as Coad finished with four wickets and Thompson three.

Yorkshire lost a few wickets in avoidable fashion in their 199 reply, but players were finding their way after time away.

Opener Alex Lees, 106, then scored his fourth first-class century since leaving Yorkshire in 2018 from late afternoon on day two to shortly after lunch on day three, sharing a third-wicket stand of 136 with South African David Bedingham, 77.

With Durham at 221-3 and leading by 125 Yorkshire's victory hopes were receding, but having kept the run-rate to under three an over a cluster of wickets would put them back in charge. Fisher swung the new to take four for three in 19 balls, including Jack Burnham bowled with a searing yorker. Durham lost for 18 on the way to 266 all out.

Yorkshire slipped to 4-2 in pursuit, with Chris Rushworth later taking his 500th first-class wicket, but Malan, dropped on 32, expertly steered the ship and expanded his game with the finishing line in sight on the way to 73 — something Brook also did — on a rain-affected fourth day.

Bob Willis Trophy — North Group
Nottinghamshire v. Yorkshire

Played at Trent Bridge, Nottingham, on August 8, 9, 10 and 11, 2020
Yorkshire won by 90 runs

Toss won by Yorkshire Yorkshire 21 points, Nottinghamshire 7 points
Close of play: First Day, Nottinghamshire 13-1 (Hameed 8*, Duckett 0*, Second Day, Nottinghamshire 355 all out; Third Day, Yorkshire 259-7 (Tattersall 41*, Olivier 8*)

YORKSHIRE

	First Innings		Second Innings	
A Lyth, lbw b Ball	4	c Mullaney b Patel	50
T Kohler-Cadmore, c Mullaney b Carter	21	c Carter b Chappell	0
§ J M Bairstow, c Patel b Chappell	5	c Hameed b Carter	75
D J Malan, c Moores b Chappell	4	c Hameed b Carter	1
H C Brook, b Nash	62	c Mullaney b Patel	30
J A Tattersall, lbw b Patel	31	c Mullaney b Carter	53
J A Thompson, c Mullaney b Nash	98	c Carter b Chappell	33
* S A Patterson, c Mullaney b Nash	11	c Moores b Chappell	4
D Olivier, lbw b Patel	5	c Moores b Chappell	8
J W Shutt, lbw b Carter	0	(11) not out	0
D J Leech, not out	0	(10) c Mullaney b Carter	1
Extras b 12, lb 2, nb 4	18	Extras b 13, lb 8, nb 2	23
Total	264	Total	278

Bonus points — Yorkshire 2, Nottinghamshire 3

FoW: 1-6 (Lyth), 2-23 (Bairstow), 3-33 (Malan), 4-44 (Kohler-Cadmore), 5-136 (Tattersall), 1st 6-176 (Brook), 7-218 (Patterson), 8-231 (Olivier), 9-232 (Shutt), 10-264 (Thompson)
FoW: 1-4 (Kohler-Cadmore), 2-135 (Lyth), 3-135 (Bairstow), 4-136 (Malan), 5-186 (Brook), 2nd 6-240 (Thompson), 7-246 (Patterson), 8-262 (Olivier), 9-267 (Leech), 10-278 (Tattersall)

	O	M	R	W		O	M	R	W
Ball	14	5	41	1	Ball	3	1	5	0
Chappell	13	3	64	2	Chappell	17	3	59	4
Mullaney	4	0	9	0	Trego	10	3	26	0
Carter	27	8	44	2	Carter	40.2	14	76	4
Patel	17	3	72	2	Mullaney	7	1	16	0
Nash	6.2	0	20	3	Patel	26	5	57	2
					Nash	5	1	18	0

NOTTINGHAMSHIRE

	First Innings		Second Innings	
C D Nash, b Patterson	8	lbw b Olivier	11
H Hameed, c Lyth b Leech	21	c Bairstow b Leech	1
B M Duckett, c Lyth b Olivier	4	c Malan b Olivier	19
J M Clarke, run out (Thompson)	50	c and b Olivier	18
* S J Mullaney, lbw b Lyth	35	c Bairstow b Patterson	5
P D Trego, c Brook b Olivier	39	lbw b Shutt	7
§ T J Moores, b Patterson	106	b Thompson	8
S R Patel, c Brook b Malan	38	c Malan b Shutt	14
Z J Chappell, c Bairstow b Thompson	1	c Shutt b Thompson	0
J T Ball, c Lyth b Malan	0	lbw b Thompson	7
M Carter, not out	15	not out	0
Extras b 11, lb 9, w 6, nb 12	38	ExtraS lb 1, nb 6	7
Total	355	Total	97

Bonus points — Nottinghamshire 4, Yorkshire 3

FoW: 1-13 (Nash), 2-30 (Duckett), 3-55 (Hameed), 4-115 (Clarke), 5-163 (Mullaney), 1st 6-187 (Trego), 7-286 (Patel), 8-293 (Chappell), 9-294 (Ball), 10-355 (Moores)
FoW: 1-16 (Nash), 2-16 (Hameed), 3-46 (Duckett), 4-61 (Clarke), 5-61 (Mullaney), 2nd 6-74 (Trego), 7-82 (Trego), 8-89 (Chappell), 9-97 (Carter), 10-97 (Patel)

	O	M	R	W		O	M	R	W
Olivier	19	4	88	2	Olivier	10	4	29	3
Patterson	21.1	10	38	2	Leech	4	1	20	1
Leech	10	2	42	1	Patterson	7	1	27	1
Thompson	16	5	37	1	Thompson	5	1	6	3
Brook	2	0	5	0	Shutt	3.2	0	14	2
Shutt	8	0	49	0					
Lyth	13	1	52	1					
Malan	6	1	24	2					

Umpires: J D Middlebrook and R T Robinson Scorers: A Cusworth and I J Smith

Yorkshire pounce on Outlaws

JORDAN THOMPSON
Swashbuckling 98, then
clutch of wickets

The 90-run margin of victory was far greater than anyone could have expected when, at just before 12pm on day four, Yorkshire set a target of 188.

Nottinghamshire were marginal favourites on a used pitch still playing pretty well and against a bowling attack shorn of experience — both Ben Coad and Matthew Fisher had suffered injuries at Durham.

What transpired was a *White Rose* bowling performance which screamed: "The future's bright".

Fiery fast bowler Duanne Olivier ripped out three early wickets to pile the pressure on a Nottinghamshire side without a first-class victory since June 2018, leaving them 61-4. Nineteen-year-old new-ball seamer Dom Leech also removed Haseeb Hameed for the second time in his debut match.

Then it was down to two more youngsters to wrap up a second successive North Group win. Jordan Thompson capped off a memorable personal performance with three cheap wickets, including uprooting the middle and leg stumps of first-innings centurion Tom Moores.

In the first innings Thompson missed out on a swashbuckling century by two runs, Yorkshire conceding a lead of 91 to hosts who had opted to use the same pitch for the second game running and play two spinners. Jonny Bairstow top-scored with a battling 75 in the second innings as Yorkshire gave themselves something to bowl at — it was the England wicketkeeper-batsman's first first-class fifty in a week shy of a year.

Nottinghamshire crumbled in pursuit, off-spinner Jack Shutt claiming his first two wickets in first-class cricket. Shutt, 23, had played in the previous match at Durham and looked nervous when bowling there and in the first innings here. Now he put those nerves behind him to strike twice, including taking the winning wicket of Samit Patel, caught at mid-wicket, as Nottinghamshire were bowled out for 97 inside 30 overs.

Shortly after the win was sealed at 3pm the ECB confirmed that the Bob Willis final would be played at Lord's, with Yorkshire's involvement now a realistic prospect.

Bob Willis Trophy — North Group
Yorkshire v. Derbyshire

Played at Emerald Headingley, Leeds, on August 15, 16, 17 and 18, 2020

Match drawn at 5.18pm on the Fourth Day

Toss won by Derbyshire   Yorkshire 15 points, Derbyshire 13 points

Close of play: First Day, Yorkshire 280-4 (Malan 145*, Tattersall 64*); Second Day, Yorkshire 288-4 (Malan 153*, Tattersall 64*); Third Day, Derbyshire 198-6 (Critchley 31*, Dal 15*)

YORKSHIRE

A Lyth, c Hosein b Cohen		31
T Kohler-Cadmore, c Critchley b Aitchison		0
§ J M Bairstow, c Hosein b Dal		22
D J Malan, c Aitchison b du Plooy		219
H C Brook, c Madsen b Cohen		0
J A Tattersall, c Dal b Critchley		66
J A Thompson, not out		36
G C H Hill, not out		4
* S A Patterson		
D Olivier	Did not bat	
D J Leech		
Extras b 8, lb 7, w 5, nb 2		22
Total (6 wkts dec)		400

FoW: 1-2 (Kohler-Cadmore), 2-40 (Bairstow), 3-126 (Lyth), 4-106 (Brook), 5-306 (Tattersall), 6-395 (Malan).

	O	M	R	W
Cohen	22	4	93	2
Aitchison	17	7	43	1
Melton	19	2	80	0
Dal	15	2	38	1
Hughes	10	1	28	0
Critchley	15.1	1	74	1
du Plooy	2	0	25	1
Madsen	1	0	4	0

DERBYSHIRE

T A Wood, c and b Thompson		26
* B A Godleman, c Bairstow b Patterson		54
W L Madsen, lbw b Patterson		0
J L du Plooy, c Kohler- Cadmore b Patterson		30
M J J Critchley, b Leech		63
A L Hughes, c Olivier b Leech		13
§ H R Hosein, c Bairstow b Olivier		7
A K Dal, not out		78
M A R Cohen, not out		6
B W Aitchison		
D R Melton	Did not bat	
Extras b 4, lb 7, w 6, nb 6		23
Total (7 wkts dec)		300

Bonus points — Derbyshire 3, Yorkshire 2

FoW: 1-58 (Wood), 2-58 (Madsen), 3-126 (du Plooy), 4-127 (Godleman), 5-152 (Hughes), 6-174 (Hosein), 7-278 (Critchley)

	O	M	R	W
Olivier	25	8	83	1
Leech	20	2	72	2
Thompson	18	3	45	1
Patterson	22	9	27	3
Hill	13	4	27	0
Lyth	3	1	8	0
Brook	6.1	0	27	0

Umpires: P J Hartley and J D Middlebrook   Scorers: J T Potter and J R Virr

Yorkshire v. Derbyshire

Sublime double for Malan

Dawid Malan's sublime maiden career double century deserved the adulation of the Emerald Headingley faithful...but it was not to be.

On home debut Malan's dreamy 219 off 244 balls — spread across three days because of rain and bad light — was scored in front of empty seats as the North Group's leading teams met.

There was not the wonderful sound of a partisan home crowd accompanying the England left-hander raising his bat before lunch on day three as he took Yorkshire towards 400-6 declared and the maximum five batting points.

Malan drove particularly handsomely on the way to bettering the 199 he scored against Derby while representing Middlesex in 2019. And he lofted four sixes.

He started his innings at 40-2 after Yorkshire had been inserted, and in challenging conditions navigated them

DAWID MALAN
Dreamy spires of sixes

away from danger at 106-4 with the help of Jonny Tattersall's 66. The pair shared a partnership of 200, with Tattersall only too happy to play second fiddle in a *White Rose* record stand for the fifth wicket in matches against Derbyshire.

One hundred and thirty eight overs were lost in the game — 89 on day two, meaning Yorkshire had to declare immediately upon reaching 400 approximately 40 minutes before lunch on day three.

Miserly Steven Patterson claimed 3-16 from 16 overs as the visitors slipped to 174-6 shortly before the close, still 27 runs from the follow-on target. But Yorkshire met resistance from seventh-wicket pair Matt Critchley and Anuj Dal.

There was a further rain delay until 2.30pm on the final day, only for Critchley and Dal to both post fifties and complete a partnership of 104, preventing Yorkshire from securing a third bowling bonus point (300-7 dec). Derby's lead at the North's summit was cut from four points to two, but a clash which had promised to be pivotal in the pursuit of a Lord's final berth was ruined by weather.

Still, Mr Malan will not forget it.

Bob Willis Trophy — North Group
Yorkshire v. Lancashire

Played at Emerald Headingley, Leeds, on August 22, 23, 24 and 25, 2020
Match drawn at 10.30am on the Fourth Day

Toss won by Yorkshire   Yorkshire 11 points, Lancashire 11 points

Close of play: First Day, Yorkshire 8-0 (Lyth 0*, Kohler-Cadmore 4*); Second Day, Yorkshire 178-6 (Lyth 86*, Hill 9*); Third Day, Lancashire 195-5 (Croft 9*, Balderson 7*)

YORKSHIRE

A Lyth, c Jennings b Bailey	......	103
T Kohler-Cadmore, c Jennings b Bailey	......	18
W A R Fraine, c Davies b Lamb	......	5
T W Loten, lbw b Lamb	......	0
H C Brook, c Bohannon b Burrows	......	6
§ J A Tattersall, c Croft b Jennings	......	25
J A Thompson, b Burrows	......	4
G C H Hill, b Lamb	......	29
* S A Patterson, c Jennings b Lamb	......	8
D Oliver, not out	......	20
J D Warner, lbw b Balderson	......	4
Extras b 5, lb 27, w 2, nb 4	......	38
Total	......	260

Bonus points — Yorkshire 2, Lancashire 3

FoW: 1-53 (Kohler-Cadmore), 2-61 (Fraine), 3-61 (Loten), 4-78 (Brook), 5-139 (Tattersall), 6-164 (Thompson), 7-219 (Lyth), 8-221 (Hill), 9-234 (Patterson), 10-260 (Warner)

	O	M	R	W
Bailey	26	13	40	2
Burrows	21	3	89	2
Balderson	15	7	30	1
Lamb	23	6	55	4
Jennings	8	2	14	1

LANCASHIRE

K K Jennings, lbw b Lyth	......	23
§ A L Davies, lbw b Patterson	......	73
J J Bohannon, c Tattersall b Warner	......	5
R P Jones, c Tattersall b Hill	......	21
* D J Vilas, lbw b Olivier	......	41
S J Croft, not out	......	9
G P Balderson, not out	......	7
D J Lamb		
T W Hartley		
G D Burrows	Did not bat	
T E Bailey		
Extras lb 7, w 1, n 8	......	16
Total (5 wkts)	......	195

Bonus points — Yorkshire 1

FoW: 1-104 (Jennings), 2-112 (Bohannon), 3-112 (Davies), 4-177 (Vilas), 5-177 (Jones)

	O	M	R	W
Patterson	19	9	23	1
Olivier	13	0	65	1
Warner	9	0	23	1
Thompson	10	1	38	0
Hill	12	4	27	1
Lyth	6	1	12	1

Umpires: P J Hartley and J D Middlebrook   Scorers: J T Potter and J R Virr

Adam Lyth the only winner

It was groundhog day for Yorkshire as rain ruined their second successive home fixture, with 212 overs lost across the four days of a *Roses* encounter which promised so much.

Only the third day was uninterrupted, with the last-but-one group fixture abandoned as an 11-point draw at 10.30am on the final day following torrential morning rain.

The fourth day was the anniversary of Ben Stokes's 2019 *Ashes* heroics, but the contrast in scenes could hardly have been starker.

After Yorkshire had elected to bat the 10 *Roses* first-class debutants across both sides were left kicking their heals for large parts, with Lancashire's first innings finishing on 195-5 in reply to 260.

Only 2.1 overs were possible on day one, and with the promise of further inclement weather this became an exercise in accruing bonus points

ADAM LYTH: Ended two-year wait for a century

rather than making a huge stride in the race for a final berth.

Adam Lyth was the big winner. His 103 — he was particularly strong through the leg-side, and advanced from an overnight 86 early on day three to end a near two-year wait for a century in any format, discounting the friendly hundred against the same opponents a month earlier.

He pulled a couple of sixes in a superb 235-ball innings, sharing half-century partnerships with Tom Kohler-Cadmore, Jonny Tattersall and fledgling all-rounder George Hill, who encouraged with bat and ball.

Lancashire's Danny Lamb took a career best 4-55, including bowling Hill during the third morning for a confident 29.

In the *Red Rose* response Hill had Rob Jones caught behind driving for his maiden first-class wicket in only his second game. The pacy Jared Warner also claimed his maiden first-class wicket for the county having spent time on loan at Sussex in 2019. It may not have been the most memorable of *Roses* encounters, but this great rivalry remains as fierce as ever, and Yorkshire remained in the hunt for a Lord's final.

Bob Willis Trophy — North Group
Yorkshire v. Leicestershire

Played at Emerald Headingley, Leeds, on September 6, 7, 8 and 9, 2020
Yorkshire won by 10 wickets at 1.29pm on the Fourth Day

Toss won by Yorkshire

Yorkshire 21 points, Leicestershire 3 points

Close of play: First Day, Yorkshire 36-2 (Fraine 11*, Loten 7*); Second Day, no play; Third Day, Leicestershire 78-5 (Ackermann 23*, Lilley 10*)

First Innings	LEICESTERSHIRE	Second Innings	
M H Azad, lbw b Fisher	0	(2) c Tattersall b Thompson	11
S T Evans, lbw b Coad	7	(1) lbw b Coad	4
H E Dearden, c and b Olivier	20	c Tattersall b Thompson	18
* C N Ackermann, lbw b Fisher	1	b Thompson	47
R K Patel, c Lyth b Coad	19	c Shutt b Thompson	5
§ H J Swindells, c Tattersall b Coad	36	c Tattersall b Fisher	0
A M Lilley, lbw b Coad	5	c Fraine b Coad	13
B W M Mike, c Brook b Fisher	17	lbw b Coad	1
D Klein, c Brook b Olivier	5	c Thompson b Olivier	27
G T Griffiths, not out	4	not out	11
H A Evans, c Lyth b Coad	0	b Thompson	15
Extras b 2, lb 6, nb 2	10	Extras b 1, lb 2, nb 6	9
Total	124	Total	161

Bonus points — Yorkshire 3

FoW: 1-7 (Azad), 2-11 (S T Evans), 3-12 (Ackermann), 4-36 (Dearden), 5-59 (Patel),
1st 6-65 (Lilley), 7-98 (Mike), 8-115 (Klein), 9-124 (Swindells), 10-124 (H A Evans)
FoW: 1-4 (S T Evans), 2-34 (Azad), 3-35 (Dearden), 4-47 (Patel), 5-53 (Swindells),
2nd 6-84 (Lilley), 7-92 (Mike), 8-135 (Klein), 9-139 (Ackermann), 10-161 (H A Evans)

	O	M	R	W		O	M	R	W
Coad	13.2	6	18	5	Coad	14	4	23	3
Fisher	12	4	29	3	Fisher	13	4	54	1
Thompson	12	5	20	0	Thompson	11	2	31	5
Olivier	11	0	49	2	Olivier	13	2	50	1

First Innings	YORKSHIRE	Second Innings	
* A Lyth, c Swindells b Klein	4	not out	14
T Kohler-Cadmore, c S T Evans b H A Evans	0	not out	23
W A R Fraine, c Mike b Klein	13		
T W Loten, c Swindells b Klein	11		
H C Brook, c Ackermann b H A Evans	53		
§ J A Tattersall, b Mike	71		
J A Thompson, lbw b Lilley	62		
M D Fisher, c and b Lilley	1		
B O Coad, c S T Evans b Mike	4		
D Olivier, c Ackermann b Lilley	0		
J W Shutt, not out	0		
Extras b 2, lb 18, w 9, nb 4	33	Extras	0
Total	252	Total (0 wkts)	37

Bonus points — Yorkshire 3, Leicestershire 3

FoW: 1-4 (Kohler-Cadmore), 2-4 (Lyth), 3-38 (Fraine), 4-46 (Loten), 5-121 (Brook).
1st 6-237 (Tattersall), 7-239 (Fisher), 8-250 (Thompson), 9-250 (Olivier), 10-252 (Coad)

	O	M	R	W		O	M	R	W
Klein	15	3	44	3	Klein	3	1	17	0
H A Evans	18	5	59	2	Griffiths	3	0	12	0
Griffiths	15	3	53	0	H A Evans	0.2	0	8	0
Mike	15	2	55	2					
Lilley	6	1	21	3					

Umpires: P J Hartley and J D Middlebrook

Scorers: J T Potter and J R Virr

Seamers snare the *Foxes*

Ben Coad shone in an outstanding bowling display from Yorkshire's seamers, helping to cushion the disappointment of missing out on a Lord's final to Somerset and Essex despite topping the North Group.

Coad claimed match figures of 8-41, expertly supported by Matthew Fisher, Duanne Olivier and Jordan Thompson — who bagged his maiden five-wicket haul in the second innings.

Leicestershire were alarmingly below par, but the quality of Yorkshire's first-innings bowling would have ensured they ran through significantly stronger teams for not much more than 124.

Coad took 5-18 in extremely helpful conditions on day one, with his first wicket — Sam Evans lbw — his 150th first-class victim in his 38th appearance. His performance and new-ball partner Fisher's four wickets

BEN COAD: Shone in outstanding bowling display

in their first game since Durham away due to injury led to coaches Rich Pyrah and Andrew Gale eulogising over their quality.

Pyrah tipped them to be county cricket's best new-ball pair, while Gale admitted his surprise that Coad's name is not talked about more for England Test honours, saying he has a bit of "genius".

Yorkshire's final hopes ended during the third day — day two was washed out. With games progressing elsewhere it became evident that Yorkshire needed to win with the maximum 24 points to be one of the two best group winners. A first-innings reply of 400 was imperative.

Two collapses proved costly — 46-4 and losing the last five wickets for 15 runs to slip from 237-5 after half-centuries from Harry Brook, who was particularly fluent, Jonny Tattersall and Thompson.

Leicester, 78-5 at the close on day three and 161 all out, narrowly avoided an innings defeat, but Thompson capped an excellent personal campaign with 5-31 to help to set a 34-target, achieved just after lunch on day four as the *White Rose* pipped Derbyshire to seal top place in the North Group despite losing 476 overs to weather in three home games.

165

BOB WILLIS TROPHY 2020

FINAL

Somerset (301 and 272-7 dec) drew with Essex (337-8 innings closed and 179-6)
Essex took the Trophy on first-innings score

NORTH GROUP

	P	W	L	D	Tied	Abdn	Bonus Points BAT	Bonus Points BOWL	Pen	Points
1 Yorkshire	5	3	0	2	0	0	11	12	0	87
2 Derbyshire	5	2	1	2	0	0	13	13	0	74
3 Lancashire	5	2	1	2	0	0	7	11	0	66
4 Nottinghamshire	5	0	2	3	0	0	20	15	0	59
5 Leicestershire	5	1	2	2	0	0	4	13	0	49
6 Durham	5	0	2	3	0	0	7	10	0	41

CENTRAL GROUP

	P	W	L	D	Tied	Abdn	Bonus Points BAT	Bonus Points BOWL	Pen	Points
1 Somerset	5	4	0	1	0	0	10	15	0	97
2 Worcestershire	5	2	1	2	0	0	14	12	0	74
3 Warwickshire	5	0	1	4	0	0	7	14	0	53
4 Northamptonshire	5	1	2	2	0	0	4	13	0	49
5 Gloucestershire	5	1	2	2	0	0	3	10	0	45
6 Glamorgan	5	0	2	3	0	0	6	13	0	43

SOUTH GROUP

	P	W	L	D	Tied	Abdn	Bonus Points BAT	Bonus Points BOWL	Pen	Points
1 Essex	5	4	0	1	0	0	6	12	0	90
2 Kent	5	3	1	1	0	0	12	15	1	82
3 Middlesex	5	2	2	1	0	0	8	14	0	62
4 Hampshire	5	2	2	1	0	0	4	13	0	57
5 Surrey	5	1	4	0	0	0	8	12	0	36
6 Sussex	5	1	4	0	0	0	9	11	24	12

Kent deducted 1 point for slow over rate
Sussex deducted 24 points for disciplinary reasons in match v. Middlesex on August 20

YORKSHIRE AVERAGES 2020

BOB WILLIS TROPHY

| Played 5 | Won 3 | Lost 0 | Drawn 2 |

BATTING AND FIELDING

Player	M.	I.	N.O.	Runs	H.S.	100s	50s	Avge	ct/st
D J Malan	3	5	0	332	219	1	1	66.40	2
J A Thompson	5	6	1	234	98	0	2	46.80	2
J A Tattersall	5	7	1	265	71	0	3	44.16	9/0
H C Brook	5	7	1	258	66*	0	3	43.00	4
J M Bairstow	2	3	0	102	75	0	1	34.00	5/0
G C H Hill	2	2	1	33	29	0	0	33.00	0
A Lyth	5	8	1	220	103	1	1	31.42	5
T Kohler-Cadmore	5	8	1	127	41	0	0	18.14	1
B O Coad	2	2	0	32	28	0	0	16.00	1
D Olivier	4	4	1	33	20*	0	0	11.00	3
W A R Fraine	3	4	0	32	14	0	0	8.00	1
J W Shutt	3	4	3	7	7*	0	0	7.00	2
S A Patterson	4	4	0	23	11	0	0	5.75	0
T W Loten	2	2	0	11	11	0	0	5.50	0
J D Warner	1	1	0	4	4	0	0	4.00	0
M D Fisher	2	2	0	2	1	0	0	1.00	2
D J Leech	2	2	1	1	1	0	0	1.00	0

BOWLING

Player	Overs	Mdns	Runs	Wkts	Avge	Best	5wI	10wM
B O Coad	69	28	87	12	7.25	5 -18	1	0
D J Malan	6	1	24	2	12.00	2 -14	0	0
J A Thompson	104	25	246	15	16.40	5 -31	1	0
S A Patterson	106.3	37	197	11	17.90	3 -27	0	0
M D Fisher	67	22	180	10	18.00	4 -54	0	0
J D Warner	9	0	23	1	23.00	1 -23	0	0
D J Leech	34	5	134	4	33.50	2 -72	0	0
D Olivier	91	18	364	10	36.40	3 -29	0	0
A Lyth	23	3	75	2	37.50	1 -12	0	0
J W Shutt	19.2	0	104	2	52.00	2 -14	0	0
G C H Hill	25	8	54	1	54.00	1 -27	0	0
H C Brook	14.1	1	49	0	—	—	0	0

THE LONG VIEW: Yorkshire members will emerge from the Coronavirus restrictions to enter a refurbished East Stand Long Room, with work completed midway through last year. The renovation boasts contemporary decor, a modern bar, a comfortable lounging area and historical cricket memorabilia. There is also a gallery of *Yorkshire Firsts*, celebrating achievements at Headingley such as the county's first one-one-day Trophy success in 1965 and Sachin Tendulkar becoming Yorkshire's first overseas player in 1992.

VITALITY BLAST HIGHLIGHTS OF 2020

VITALITY BLAST WINNERS

Nottinghamshire Outlaws, who beat Surrey by 6 wickets

Totals of 150 and over (6)

220-5	v. Derbyshire at Leeds (won)
198-3	v. Durham at Chester-le-Street (won)
190	v. Nottinghamshire at Nottingham (lost)
188-6	v. Leicestershire at Leicester (lost)
171-4	v. Derbyshire at Leeds (won)
160-6	v. Lancashire at Manchester (lost)

Match aggregates of 350 and over (3)

384	Yorkshire (190) lost to Nottinghamshire (194-4) by 6 wickets at Nottingham
380	Yorkshire (188-6) lost to Leicestershire (192-7) by 3 wickets at Leicester
367	Yorkshire (198-3) defeated Durham (169) by 29 runs at Chester-le Street

Century Partnerships (None)

4 wickets in an innings (None)

3 catches in an innings (1)

H C Brook (1)

3	v. Durham at Leeds

3 dismissals in an innings (None)

Debuts (6)

T20 (5): G C H Hill, J H Wharton, M L Revis, S A Wisniewski and B D Birkhead
For Yorkshire (1): D J Malan

VITALITY BLAST in 2020

NORTH GROUP

		P	W	L	T	NR/A	PTS	NRR
1	Nottinghamshire Outlaws (N 2) *	10	7	1	0	2	16	1.315
2	Lancashire Lightning (N 1) *	10	5	3	0	2	12	-0.250
3	Leicestershire Foxes (N 9) *	10	4	3	0	3	11	-0.180
4	Durham (N 6)	10	4	5	0	1	9	0.421
5	**Yorkshire Vikings (N 5)**	**10**	**3**	**5**	**0**	**2**	**8**	**0.297**
6	Derbyshire Falcons (N 6)	10	1	7	0	2	4	-1.583

CENTRAL GROUP

		P	W	L	T	NR/A	PTS	NRR
1	Gloucestershire (S 2) *	10	7	2	0	1	15	1.017
2	Northamptonshire Steelbacks (N 7) *	10	5	4	0	1	11	0.053
3	Birmingham Bears (N 8)	10	5	4	0	1	11	-0.634
4	Somerset (S 6)	10	4	5	0	1	9	0.653
5	Glamorgan (S 9)	10	4	5	0	1	9	-0.304
6	Worcestershire Rapids (N 4)	10	2	7	0	1	5	-0.789

SOUTH GROUP

		P	W	L	T	NR/A	PTS	NRR
1	Surrey (S 8) *	10	7	1	1	1	16	0.651
2	Sussex Sharks (S 1) *	10	6	3	0	1	13	0.377
3	Kent Spitfires (S 5) *	10	5	3	1	1	12	0.108
4	Middlesex (S 3)	10	3	5	1	1	8	-0.296
5	Essex Eagles (S 4)	10	2	6	1	1	6	-0.003
6	Hampshire (S 7)	10	2	7	0	1	5	-0.803

* Qualified for the Quarter-Finals

(2019 group positions in brackets)

Yorkshire v. Nottinghamshire

At Emerald Headingley, Leeds, on August 27, 2020
Match abandoned without a ball bowled

Toss: None   Yorkshire 1 point, Nottinghamshire 1 point

Umpires: P J Hartley and N A Mallender   Scorers: J T Potter and J R Virr

Yorkshire v. Derbyshire

Played at Emerald Headingley, Leeds, on August 30, 2020
Yorkshire won by 99 runs

Toss won by Yorkshire   Yorkshire 2 points, Derbyshire 0 points

YORKSHIRE

* T Kohler-Cadmore, c McKiernan b Hudson-Prentice ..	16
A Lyth, c du Plooy b McKiernan	61
J E Root, c Hudson-Prentice b McKiernan	64
H C Brook, c Godleman b Reece	23
W A R Fraine, not out	44
M D Fisher, c Godleman b Reece	0
J A Thompson, not out	5
§ J A Tattersall	
G C H Hill Did not bat	
M W Pillans	
J E Poysden	
Extras lb 5, w 2	7
Total (5 wkts, 20 overs)	220

FoW: 1-32 (Kohler-Cadmore), 2-116 (Lyth), 3-160 (Root), 4-197 (Brook), 5-198 (Fisher)

	O	M	R	W
McKiernan	3	0	22	2
Cohen	2	0	24	0
Hudson- Prentice	4	0	52	1
Conners	2	0	19	0
Critchley	4	0	42	0
Hughes	2	0	25	0
Reece	3	0	31	2

DERBYSHIRE

L M Reece, b Fisher	2
* B A Godleman, lbw b Root	4
W L Madsen, c Thompson b Fisher	11
J L du Plooy, c Hill b Root	0
M J J Critchley, c Fisher b Brook	26
A L Hughes, c Fraine b Poysden	12
F J Hudson- Prentice, c Kohler-Cadmore b Poysden	16
M H McKiernan, c Lyth b Fisher	16
§ B D Guest, not out	14
M A R Cohen, c Tattersall b Hill	7
S Conners, not out	2
Extras lb 1, w 8, nb 2	11
Total (9 wkts, 20 overs)	121

FoW: 1-4 (Reece), 2-19 (Madsen), 3-19 (Godleman), 4-20 (du Plooy), 5-38 (Hughes), 6-70 (Hudson-Prentice), 7-76 (Critchley), 8-101 (McKiernan), 9-119 (Cohen)

	O	M	R	W
Lyth	3	0	11	0
Fisher	4	0	21	3
Root	2	0	7	2
Poysden	4	0	30	2
Thompson	2	0	11	0
Pillans	2	0	18	0
Hill	2	0	9	1
Brook	1	0	13	1

Man of the Match: A Lyth

Umpires: N A Mallender and J D Middlebrook   Scorers: J T Potter and J R Virr

Vitality Blast — North Group
Nottinghamshire v. Yorkshire

Played at Trent Bridge, Nottingham, on August 31, 2020

Nottinghamshire won by 6 wickets

Toss won by Yorkshire   Nottinghamshire 2 points, Yorkshire 0 points

YORKSHIRE

* T Kohler-Cadmore, st Moores b Carter	6
A Lyth, c Christian b Mullaney	53
J E Root, c Hales b Fletcher	65
H C Brook, c Duckett b Ball	39
W A R Fraine, c Hales b Fletcher	16
M D Fisher, b Fletcher	0
J A Thompson, c Hales b Ball	1
§ J A Tattersall, b Ball	0
G C H Hill, b Fletcher	1
M W Pillans, c Hales b Fletcher	5
J E Poysden, not out	0
Extras lb 2, nb 2	4
Total (20 overs)	190

FoW: 1-29 (Kohler-Cadmore), 2-83 (Lyth), 3-147 (Brook), 4-168 (Fraine), 5-168 (Fisher), 6-173 (Thompson), 7-184 (Tattersall), 8-194 (Root), 9-190 (Pillans), 10-190 (Hill).

	O	M	R	W
Carter	4	0	32	1
Ball	4	0	36	3
Fletcher	4	0	43	5
Christian	3	0	25	0
Patel	2	0	26	0
Mullaney	3	0	26	1

NOTTINGHAMSHIRE

C D Nash, lbw b Thompson		51
A D Hales, c Kohler-Cadmore b Lyth		4
J M Clarke, c Lyth b Fisher		6
B M Duckett, not out		86
* D T Christian, c Brook b Thompson		21
§ T J Moores, not out		21
S J Mullaney		
S R Patel		
L J Fletcher	Did not bat	
J T Ball		
M Carter		
Extras lb 2, w 3		5
Total (4 wkts, 19.2 overs)		194

FoW: 1-5 (Hales), 2-16 (Clarke), 3-101 (Nash), 4-143 (Christian).

	O	M	R	W
Lyth	3	0	14	1
Fisher	4	0	40	1
Root	3	0	23	0
Thompson	3	0	25	2
Pillans	3.2	0	45	0
Poysden	2	0	32	0
Hill	1	0	13	0

Man of the Match: B M Duckett

Umpires: N G B Cook and I N Ramage   Scorers: A Cusworth and I J Smith

Vitality Blast — North Group
Yorkshire v. Leicestershire

At Emerald Headingley, Leeds, on September 2, 2020
Match abandoned without a ball bowled

Toss: None
Yorkshire 1 point, Leicestershire 1 point
Umpires: R J Bailey and I N Ramage
Scorers: J T Potter and J R Virr

Durham v. Yorkshire

Played at Emerates Riverside, Chester-le-Street, on September 4, 2020
Yorkshire won by 29 runs

Toss won by Durham
Yorshire 2 points, Durham 0 points

YORKSHIRE

A Lyth, c Trevaskis b Potts		20
T Kohler-Cadmore, not out		85
J E Root, c Carse b Coughlin		25
H C Brook, c Potts b Coughlin		23
W A R Fraine, not out		36
§ J A Tattersall		
* D J Willey		
J A Thompson	Did not bat	
M D Fisher		
M W Pillans		
J E Poysden		
Extras lb 7, w 2		9
Total (3 wkts, 20 overs)		198

FoW: 1-29 (Lyth), 2-91 (Root), 3-133 (Brook)

	O	M	R	W
Potts	4	1	23	1
Steel	3	0	24	0
Carse	3	0	33	0
Rimmington	3	0	39	0
Trevaskis	3	0	35	0
Coughlin	4	0	37	2

DURHAM

G Clark, st Tattersall b Root		68
A Z Lees, c Fraine b Root		24
B A Raine, c Fraine b Poysden		4
§ D G Bedingham, c Fisher b Pillans		18
F Behardien, c Willey b Poysden		11
B A Carse, c Root b Poysden		16
P Coughlin, b Fisher		10
S Steel, lbw b Willey		1
L Trevaskis, lbw b Willey		0
M J Potts, not out		2
* N J Rimmington, c Poysden b Willey		2
Extras lb 6, w 7		13
Total (19.1 overs)		169

FoW: 1-77 (Lees), 2-85 (Raine), 3-102 (Clark), 4-125 (Bedingham), 5-133 (Behardien), 6-152 (Carse), 7-162 (Steel), 8-162 (Trevaskis), 9-166 (Coughlin), 10-169 (Rimmington)

	O	M	R	W
Willey	3.1	0	26	3
Fisher	3	0	26	1
Lyth	2	0	14	0
Root	4	0	29	2
Thompson	1	0	14	0
Poysden	4	0	32	3
Pillans	2	0	22	1

Man of the Match: T Kohler-Cadmore

Umpires: N A Mallender and N Pratt
Scorers: W R Dobson and G Maddison

Leicestershire v. Yorkshire

Played at Fischer County Ground, Grace Road, Leicester, on September 11, 2020
Leicestershire won by 3 wickets

Toss won by Leicestershire   Leicestershire 2 points, Yorkshire 0 points

YORKSHIRE

A Lyth, c Mike b Delany		71
T Kohler-Cadmore, c Mike b Davis		3
* D J Willey, b Davis		27
H C Brook, c Taylor b Delany		15
W A R Fraine, run out (Ackermann)		0
§ J A Tattersall, not out		22
J A Thompson, c Hill b Taylor		44
M D Fisher		
B O Coad	Did not bat	
J E Poysden		
J W Shutt		
Extras lb 4, w 2		6
Total (6 wkts, 20 overs)		188

FoW: 1-28 (Kohler-Cadmore), 2-98 (Willey), 3-110 (Lyth), 4-114 (Fraine), 5-124 (Brook), 6-188 (Thompson).

	O	M	R	W
Parkinson	4	0	34	0
Ackermann	3	0	20	0
Taylor	3	0	35	1
Davis	3	0	32	2
Griffiths	2	0	27	0
Delany	3	0	26	2
Lilley	2	0	10	0

LEICESTERSHIRE

H E Dearden, c Willey b Fisher		7
G J Delany, c Tattersall b Willey		64
A M Lilley, c Brook b Shutt		30
* C N Ackermann, lbw b Willey		58
T A I Taylor, lbw b Coad		0
§ L J Hill, c Kohler-Cadmore b Fisher		2
H J Swindells, c Coad b Fisher		0
B W M Mike, not out		22
C F Parkinson, not out		3
G T Griffiths		
W S Davis	Did not bat	
Extras lb 2, w 2, nb 2		6
Total (7 wkts, 20 overs)		192

FoW: 1-19 (Dearden), 2-61 (Lilley), 3-149 (Delany), 4-158 (Taylor), 5-163 (Hill), 6-164 (Swindells), 7-178 (Ackermann).

	O	M	R	W
Willey	4	0	23	2
Coad	4	0	38	1
Fisher	4	0	35	3
Poysden	3	0	20	0
Shutt	2	0	25	1
Thompson	2	0	38	0
Lyth	1	0	11	0

Man of the Match: G J Delany

Umpires: P R Pollard and I N Ramage   Scorers: P J Rogers and P N Johnson

Vitality Blast — North Group
Yorkshire v. Lancashire

Played at Emerald Headingley, Leeds, on September 14, 2020

Lancashire won by 6 wickets

Toss won by Yorkshire

Lancashire 2 points, Yorkshire 0 points

YORKSHIRE

H C Brook, c Hartley b Wood	17
* A Lyth, st Davies b Hartley	36
D J Malan, c Bohannon b Parkinson	27
G C H Hill, c Vilas b Parkinson	6
W A R Fraine, c Davies b Wood	24
J H Wharton, c Vilas b Parkinson	4
M W Pillans, st Davies b Livingstone	5
J A Thompson, lbw b Wood	1
§ J A Tattersall, not out	15
B O Coad, c Livingstone b Lamb	7
J W Shutt, not out	0
Extras lb 1, w 2	3
Total (9 wkts, 20 overs)	145

FoW: 1-30 (Brook), 2-78 (Lyth), 3-87 (Malan), 4-87 (Hill), 5-104 (Wharton), 6-121 (Pillans), 7-123 (Thompson), 8-124 (Fraine), 9-139 (Coad)

	O	M	R	W
Croft	1	0	15	0
Bailey	1	0	15	0
Wood	4	0	21	3
Lamb	3	0	28	1
Hartley	4	0	17	1
Livingstone	4	0	23	1
Parkinson	3	0	25	3

LANCASHIRE

§ A L Davies, c Pillans b Thompson	5
L S Livingstone, c Tattersall b Pillans	17
S J Croft, run out (Shutt/Tattersall)	27
* D J Vilas, not out	44
J J Bohannon, b Coad	0
R P Jones, not out	38
D J Lamb	
T E Bailey	
T W Hartley Did not bat	
M W Parkinson	
L Wood	
Extras b 1, lb 3, w 9, nb 4	17
Total (4 wkts, 17.5 overs)	148

FoW: 1-24 (Livingstone), 2-35 (Davies), 3-76 (Croft), 4-77 (Bohannon)

	O	M	R	W
Coad	4	0	27	1
Pillans	3.5	0	43	1
Thompson	4	0	28	1
Hill	2	0	14	0
Shutt	4	0	32	0

Man of the Match: M W Parkinson

Umpires: N A Mallender and J D Middlebrook   Scorers: J T Potter and J R Virr

Third Umpire: P K Baldwin

Vitality Blast — North Group
Yorkshire v. Durham

Played at Emerald Headingley, Leeds, on September 16, 2020
Durham won by 43 runs

Toss won by Yorkshire   Durham 2 points, Yorkshire 0 points

DURHAM

G Clark, c Brook b Lyth		28
A Z Lees, c and b Lyth		14
B A Raine, c Tattersall b Shutt		23
§ D G Bedingham, c Hill b Thompson		7
F Behardien, c Brook b Olivier		1
B A Carse, c Tattersall b Thompson		22
P Coughlin, c Thompson b Olivier		16
S Steel, run out (Olivier)		19
L Trevaskis, run out (Tattersall>Coad)		0
M J Potts, c Brook b Coad		0
* N J Rimmington, not out		1
Extras b 1, lb 10, w 3, nb 2		16
Total (19.3 overs)		147

FoW: 1-46 (Lees), 2-57 (Clark), 3-78 (Raine), 4-81 (Behardien), 5-94 (Bedingham), 6-110 (Carse), 7-132 (Coughlin), 8-133 (Trevaskis), 9-135 (Potts), 10-147 (Steel)

	O	M	R	W
Coad	3	0	24	1
Lyth	3	0	28	2
Olivier	4	0	16	2
Thompson	4	0	30	2
Hill	1.3	0	14	0
Shutt	4	0	24	1

YORKSHIRE

* A Lyth, c Lees b Potts		11
H C Brook, c Rimmington b Potts		7
D J Malan, b Potts		0
§ J A Tattersall, lbw b Rimmington		10
W A R Fraine, c Bedingham b Carse		28
G C H Hill, b Coughlin		14
J A Thompson, c Trevaskis b Coughlin		11
J H Wharton, c Clark b Coughlin		8
B O Coad, st Bedingham b Trevaskis		4
D Olivier, b Trevaskis		8
J W Shutt, not out		0
Extras lb 1, w 2		3
Total (16.4 overs)		104

FoW: 1-15 (Lyth), 2-15 (Malan), 3-22 (Brook), 4-48 (Tattersall), 5-73 (Hill), 6-73 (Fraine), 7-85 (Wharton), 8-95 (Coad), 9-97 (Thompson), 10-104 (Olivier)

	O	M	R	W
Trevaskis	2.4	0	22	2
Potts	3	0	14	3
Carse	4	0	28	1
Rimmington	2	0	13	1
Coughlin	4	0	22	3
Steel	1	0	4	0

Man of the Match: M J Potts

Umpires: P J Hartley and N A Mallender   Scorers: J T Potter and J R Virr

Vitality Blast — North Group
Lancashire v. Yorkshire

Played at Emirates Old Trafford, Manchester, on September 18, 2020
Lancashire won by 7 runs

Toss won by Lancashire   Lancashire 2 points, Yorkshire 0 points

LANCASHIRE

A L Davies, c Tattersall b Olivier		2
L S Livingstone, c Brook b Thompson		69
S J Croft, c Shutt b Root		58
* D J Vilas, c and b Thompson		0
R P Jones, st Tattersall b Root		8
§ G I D Lavelle, c Brook b Olivier		6
D J Lamb, not out		16
L Wood, not out		2
M W Parkinson		
S Mahmood	Did not bat	
T W Hartley		
Extras lb 2, w 4		6
Total (6 wkts, 20 overs)		167

FoW: 1-2 (Davies), 2-132 (Livingstone), 3-133 (Vilas), 4-135 (Croft), 5-148 (Jones), 6-148 (Lavelle).

	O	M	R	W
Olivier	4	0	33	2
Lyth	3	0	18	0
Thompson	3	0	32	2
Malan	2	0	16	0
Wisniewski	2	0	15	0
Shutt	2	0	26	0
Root	4	0	25	2

YORKSHIRE

* A Lyth, run out (Davies/Lavelle)		45
D J Malan, c Vilas b Lamb		8
J E Root, run out (Croft)		64
H C Brook, lbw b Livingstone		15
W A R Fraine, run out (Davies)		4
§ J A Tattersall, not out		16
J A Thompson, c Jones b Parkinson		1
M L Revis, not out		0
D Olivier		
J W Shutt	Did not bat	
S A Wisniewski		
Extras lb 2, w 5		7
Total (6 wkts, 20 overs)		160

FoW: 1-24 (Malan), 2-115 (Lyth), 3-132 (Root), 4-140 (Brooks), 5-148 (Fraine), 6-156 (Thompson).

	O	M	R	W
Croft	1	0	7	0
Mahmood	3	0	20	0
Wood	2	0	29	0
Lamb	2	0	15	1
Hartley	4	0	24	0
Livingstone	4	0	36	1
Parkinson	4	0	27	1

Man of the Match: L S Livingstone

Umpires: P J Hartley and S J O'Shaughnessy   Scorers: C Rimmer and G L Morgan
Third Umpire: P R Pollard

Vitality Blast — North Group
Derbyshire v. Yorkshire

Played at Emerald Headingley, Leeds, on September 20, 2020
Yorkshire won by 6 wickets

Toss won by Derbyshire   Yorkshire 2 points, Derbyshire 0 points

DERBYSHIRE

T A Wood, c Thompson b Coad	....	67
* B A Godleman, c Olivier b Root	....	49
W L Madsen, c Lyth b Coad	....	23
J L du Plooy, c Birkhead b Thompson	....	9
L M Reece, not out	....	15
M J J Critchley, c Root b Coad	....	0
A L Hughes, c Fraine b Olivier	....	1
A K Dal, not out	....	0
§ B D Guest		
S Conners	Did not bat	
D R Melton		
Extras lb 3	....	3
Total (6 wkts, 20 overs)	....	167

FoW: 1-109 (Godleman), 2-135 (Wood), 3-150 (du Plooy), 4-152 (Madsen), 5-153 (Critchley), 6-159 (Hughes).

	O	M	R	W
Coad	4	0	40	3
Lyth	4	0	29	0
Root	4	0	28	1
Olivier	3	0	24	1
Wisniewski	2	0	17	0
Thompson	3	0	26	1

YORKSHIRE

* A Lyth, c Guest b Conners	....	11
D J Malan, c Guest b Conners	....	1
J E Root, not out	....	60
W A R Fraine, c Wood b Melton	....	11
J A Thompson, c Melton b Hughes	....	26
H C Brook, not out	....	50
M L Revis		
§ B D Birkhead		
D Olivier	Did not bat	
B O Coad		
S Wisniewski		
Extras lb 2, w 4, nb 6	....	12
Total (4 wkts, 20 overs)	....	171

FoW: 1-12 (Lyth), 2-12 (Malan), 3-41 (Fraine), 4-80 (Thompson).

	O	M	R	W
Madsen	2	0	17	0
Melton	4	0	38	1
Conners	4	0	38	2
Critchley	4	0	28	0
Hughes	4	0	24	1
Reece	2	0	24	0

Man of the Match: J E Root

Umpires: P J Hartley and N A Mallender   Scorers: J R Virr and J T Potter

YORKSHIRE AVERAGES 2020

VITALITY BLAST

Played 8   Won 3   Lost 5   Abandoned 2

BATTING AND FIELDING
(Qualification 4 completed innings)

Player	M.	I.	N.O.	Runs	H.S.	100s	50s	Avge	ct/st
J E Root	5	5	1	278	65	0	4	69.50	2
A Lyth	8	8	0	308	71	0	3	38.50	4
W A R Fraine	8	8	2	163	44*	0	0	27.16	4
H C Brook	8	8	1	189	50*	0	1	27.00	7
J A Thompson	8	7	1	89	44	0	0	14.83	4
D J Malan	4	4	0	36	27	0	0	9.00	0
Also played									
T Kohler-Cadmore	4	4	1	110	85*	0	1	36.66	3
J A Tattersall	7	5	3	63	22*	0	0	31.50	6/2
D J Willey	2	1	0	27	27	0	0	27.00	2
D Olivier	3	1	0	8	8	0	0	8.00	1
G C H Hill	4	3	0	21	14	0	0	7.00	2
J H Wharton	2	2	0	12	8	0	0	6.00	0
B O Coad	4	2	0	11	7	0	0	5.50	1
M W Pillans	4	2	0	10	5	0	0	5.00	1
M D Fisher	4	2	0	0	0	0	0	0.00	1
J E Poysden	4	1	1	0	0*	0	0	—	1
M L Revis	2	1	1	0	0*	0	0	—	0
J W Shutt	4	2	2	0	0*	0	0	—	0
B D Birkhead	1	0	0	0	—	0	0	—	1
S A Wisniewski	2	0	0	0	—	0	0	—	0

BOWLING
(Qualification 4 wickets)

Player	Overs	Mdns	Runs	Wkts	Avge	Best	4wI	RPO
D J Willey	7.1	0	49	5	9.80	3-26	0	6.83
D Olivier	11	0	73	5	14.60	2-16	0	6.63
M D Fisher	15	0	122	8	15.25	3-21	0	8.13
J E Root	17	0	112	7	16.00	2- 7	0	6.58
B O Coad	15	0	129	6	21.50	3-40	0	8.60
J E Poysden	13	0	114	5	22.80	3-32	0	8.76
J A Thompson	22	0	204	8	25.50	2-25	0	9.27
Also bowled								
H C Brook	1	0	13	1	13.00	1-13	0	13.00
A Lyth	19	0	125	3	41.66	2-28	0	6.57
G C H Hill	6.3	0	50	1	50.00	1- 9	0	7.69
J W Shutt	12	0	107	2	53.50	1-24	0	8.91
M W Pillans	11.1	0	128	2	64.00	1-22	0	11.46
S A Wisniewski	4	0	32	0	—	0-15	0	8.00
D J Malan	2	0	16	0	—	0-16	0	8.00

Other Matches played At Emerald Headingley
Vitality Blast — North Group
Leicestershire v. Durham

Played at Emerald Headingley, Leeds, on August 31, 2020
Leicestershire won by 30 runs

Toss won by Leicestershire　　　　　　　　　Leicestershire 2 points, Durham 0 points

LEICESTERSHIRE

H E Dearden, c Bedingham b Coughlin	....	9
G J Delany, c Steel b Trevaskis	....	68
A M Lilley, c Lees b Rimmington	....	69
* C N Ackermann, c Bedingham b Trevaskis	....	0
§ L J Hill, c Lees b Rimmington	....	9
T A I Taylor, c Dickson b Potts	....	12
B W M Mike, not out	....	6
G H Rhodes, not out	....	0
C F Parkinson		
G T Griffiths	Did not bat	
W S Davis		
Extras lb 1, w 3	....	4
Total (6 wkts)	....	177

FoW: 1-18 (Dearden), 2-106 (Delany), 3-113 (Ackermann), 4-139 (Hill), 5-163 (Taylor), 6-172 (Lilley)

	O	M	R	W
Potts	4	0	26	1
Carse	3	0	31	0
Coughlin	3	0	29	1
Rimmington	4	0	42	2
Trevaskis	4	1	30	2
Steel	2	0	18	0

DURHAM

A Z Lees, c Rhodes b Davis	....	36
S Steel, c Davis b Ackermann	....	12
G Clark, b Griffiths	....	7
D G Bedingham, c Mike b Parkinson	....	27
S R Dickson, c Davis b Parkinson	....	5
§ S W Poynter, c Ackerman b Davis	....	23
B A Carse, c and b Parkinson	....	1
P Coughlin, c Taylor b Delany	....	15
L Trevaskis, not out	....	7
M J Potts, not out	....	6
* N J Rimmington	Did not bat	
Extras b 2, lb 3, w 3	....	8
Total (8 wkts)	....	147

FoW: 1-17 (Steel), 2-47 (Clark), 3-61 (Lees), 4-80 (Dickson), 5-100 (Bedingham), 6-102 (Carse), 7-125 (Coughlin), 8-140 (Poynter)

	O	M	R	W
Parkinson	4	0	21	3
Taylor	4	0	23	0
Ackermann	1	0	16	1
Griffiths	4	0	27	1
Davis	4	0	32	2
Delany	3	0	23	1

Man of the Match: A M Lilley

Umpires: J D Middlebrook and R T Robinson　　　Scorers: J T Potter and J R Virr
Third Umpire: P J Hartley

Other Matches played At Emerald Headingley
Vitality Blast — North Group
Derbyshire v. Lancashire

Played at Emerald Headingley, Leeds, on August 31, 2020
Lancashire won by 4 runs

Toss won by Lancashire   Lancashire 2 points, Derbyshire 0 points

LANCASHIRE

K K Jennings, c Dal b Critchley	....	29
§ A L Davies, c du Plooy b Conners	....	82
S J Croft, run out (Critchley/Godleman)	....	38
* D J Vilas, c Reece b Barnes	....	8
J J Bohannon, b Barnes		4
R P Jones, not out	....	8
D J Lamb, not out	....	1
T E Bailey		
T W Hartley	Did not bat	
L J Hurt		
M W Parkinson		
Extras lb 2, w 4, nb 2	....	8
Total (5 wkts)	....	178

FoW: 1-63 (Jennings), 2-137 (Croft), 3-153 (Vilas), 4-167 (Davies), 5-174 (Bohannon)

	O	M	R	W
McKiernan	3	0	28	0
Conners	3	0	33	1
Madsen	1	0	5	0
Barnes	3	0	27	2
Critchley	4	0	30	1
Hughes	3	0	31	0
Reece	3	0	22	0

DERBYSHIRE

M H McKiernan, c Vilas b Croft	....	4
* B A Godleman, b Croft	....	7
L M Reece, c Davies b Lamb	....	39
W L Madsen, c Jones b Hartley	....	44
J L du Plooy, c Jones b Parkinson	....	29
M J J Critchley, run out (Davies)	....	32
A L Hughes, c Hurt b Bailey	....	10
A K Dal, not out	....	3
§ H R Hosein, not out	....	1
E Barnes		
S Conners	Did not bat	
Extras lb 2, w 3	....	5
Total (7 wkts)	....	174

FoW: 1-4 (McKiernan), 2-21 (Godleman), 3-60 (Reece), 4-121 (du Plooy), 5-128 (Madsen), 6-152 (Hughes), 7-173 (Critchley)

	O	M	R	W
Croft	4	0	29	2
Bailey	4	0	31	1
Hurt	2	0	27	0
Lamb	4	0	31	1
Hartley	2	0	13	1
Parkinson	4	0	41	1

Man of the Match: A L Davies

Umpires: P J Hartley and J D Middlebrook   Scorers: J T Potter and J R Virr
Third Umpire: R T Robinson

Other Matches played At Emerald Headingley
Rachael Heyhoe Flint Trophy — North Group
Northern Diamonds v. Central Sparks

Played at Emerald Headingley, Leeds, on September 13, 2020
Central Sparks won by 6 wickets

Toss won by Northern Diamonds   Central Sparks 4 points, Northern Diamonds 0 points

NORTHERN DIAMONDS

* H J Armitage, b Russell	18
R H M Hopkins, st G M Davies b Baker	35
S L Kalis, c Arlott b Russell	87
A Campbell, c Arlott b Baker	4
A L MacDonald, lbw b Baker	0
J L Gunn, b Patel	15
§ B A M Heath, lbw b Patel	0
B A Langston, b Arlott	26
P Graham, lbw b Russell	0
H L Fenby, c Jones b Russell	11
K A Levick, not out	1
Extras b 1, lb 6, w 13	20
Total (50 overs)	217

FoW: 1-28 (Armitage), 2-113 (Hopkins), 3-119 (Campbell), 4-120 (MacDonald), 5-157 (Gunn), 6-157 (Heath), 7-185 (Kalis), 8-185 (Graham), 9-212 (Fenby), 10-217 (Langston)

	O	M	R	W
Russell	9	0	28	4
Arlott	10	0	47	1
Patel	10	0	49	2
Butler	9	0	38	0
Baker	10	0	26	3
Jones	2	0	22	0

CENTRAL SPARKS

* E Jones, c and b Levick		77
§ G M Davies, lbw b Langston		0
M Kelly, lbw b MacDonald		49
P L Davies, not out		31
M Home, lbw b Langston		0
C A E Hill, not out		23
E L Arlott		
H L Baker		
S Butler	Did not bat	
A A Patel		
E A Russell		
Extras b 2, lb 10, w 25, nb 1		38
Total (4 wkts, 46.4 overs)		218

FoW: 1-2 (G M Davies), 2-125 (Kelly), 3-171 (Jones), 4-172 (Home)

	O	M	R	W
Langston	8	0	27	2
Graham	7	0	25	0
Levick	10	0	33	1
Gunn	2	0	14	0
Armitage	6	0	41	0
MacDonald	7.4	0	36	1
Fenby	6	0	30	0

Umpires: P J Hatley and L Nenova   Scorers: J T Potter and J R Virr

Other Matches played At Emerald Headingley
Rachael Heyhoe Flint Trophy — North Group
Northern Diamonds v. Thunder

Played at Emerald Headingley, Leeds, on September 19, 2020
Northern Diamonds won by 6 wickets

Toss won by Thunder
Northern Diamonds 5 points, Thunder 0 points

THUNDER

L Marshall, b Langston		0
G E B Boyce, c Heath b Gunn		29
A Clarke, lbw b Graham		1
§ E Threlkeld, b Graham		13
N Brown, b Smith		32
D L Collins, lbw b Gunn		2
R Duckworth, b Langston		19
A E Dyson, b Levick		2
* A Hartley, lbw b Levick		0
L Heap, b Langston		12
H L Jones, not out		2
Extras b 4, lb 1, w 25, nb 1		31
Total (42.5 overs)		143

FoW: 1-6 (Marshall), 2-8 (Clarke), 3-31 (Threlkeld), 4-91 (Brown), 5-91 (Boyce), 6-100 (Collins), 7-109 (Dyson), 8-109 (Hartley), 9-138 (Heap), 10-143 (Duckworth)

	O	M	R	W
Langston	8.5	1	18	3
Graham	9	0	29	2
Levick	8	2	39	2
Smith	9	3	26	1
Gunn	6	1	18	2
Armitage	2	0	8	0

NORTHERN DIAMONDS

* H J Armitage, c and b Hartley		36
R H M Hopkins, b Jones		2
S L Kalis, not out		55
A Campbell, st Threlkeld b Heap		8
A L MacDonald, run out (Collins/Threlkeld)		1
J L Gunn, not out		26
§ B A M Heath		
L C N Smith		
B A Langston	Did not bat	
P Graham		
K A Levick		
Extras b 1, w 15		16
Total (4 wkts, 29.4 overs)		144

FoW: 1-25 (Hopkins), 2-62 (Armitage), 3-88 (Campbell), 4-90 (MacDonald)

	O	M	R	W
Jones	8	2	28	1
Brown	6.4	0	35	0
Dyson	3	0	18	0
Hartley	8	1	35	1
Heap	4	0	27	1

Umpires: J Ibbotson and I N Ramage   Scorers: J T Potter and J R Virr

RECORDS SECTION

All records in this section relate to First-Class Yorkshire matches except where stated

HONOURS

County Champions (34)
1867, 1870, 1893, 1896, 1898, 1900, 1901, 1902, 1905, 1908, 1912, 1919,
1922, 1923, 1924, 1925, 1931, 1932, 1933, 1935, 1937, 1938, 1939,
1946, 1959, 1960, 1962, 1963, 1966, 1967, 1968, 2001, 2014, 2015

Joint Champions (2)
1869, 1949

Promoted to Division 1
2005, 2012

Gillette Cup Winners (2)
1965, 1969

Cheltenham & Gloucester Trophy (1)
2002

Benson & Hedges Cup Winners (1)
1987

John Player Special League Winners (1)
1983

Fenner Trophy Winners (3)
1972, 1974, 1981

Asda Challenge Winners (1)
1987

Ward Knockout Cup (1)
1989

Joshua Tetley Festival Trophy (7)
1991, 1992 (Joint), 1993, 1994, 1996, 1997 and 1998

Tilcon Trophy Winners (2)
1978 and 1988

Pro-Arch Trophy (1)
2007-08

Emirates Airlines T20 (2)
2015 and 2016

Second Eleven Champions (4)
1977, 1984, 1991, 2003

Joint Champions (1)
1987

Minor Counties Champions (5)
1947, 1957, 1958, 1968, 1971

Under-25 Competition Winners (3)
1976, 1978, 1987

Bain Clarkson Trophy Winners (2)
1988 and 1994

Second Eleven Trophy (1)
2009

YORKSHIRE'S CHAMPIONSHIP CAPTAINS

1867 to 2019

* R Iddison (2)	1867, 1870
Lord Hawke (8)	1893, 1896, 1898, 1900, 1901, 1902, 1905, 1908
Sir Archibald White (1)	1912
D C F Burton (1)	1919
G Wilson (3)	1922, 1923, 1924
A W Lupton (1)	1925
F E Greenwood (2)	1931, 1932
A B Sellers (6)	1933, 1935, 1937, 1938, 1939, 1946
J R Burnet (1)	1959
J V Wilson (2)	1960, 1962
D B Close (4)	1963, 1966, 1967, 1968
D Byas (1)	2001
A W Gale (2)	2014, 2015

Joint Champions

* R Iddison (1)	1869
N W D Yardley (1)	1949

* R Iddison was captain when Yorkshire were Champion county, the County Championship starting in 1890.

RECORDS SECTION INDEX

CHAMPION COUNTIES SINCE 1873

The County Championship

The County Championship was officially constituted in 1890, and before that Yorkshire were generally considered Champions by the Press in 1867 and 1870, and equal top in 1869. From 1873 the list was generally accepted in the form as it is today.

		Yorkshire's Position
1873	{ Gloucestershire / Nottinghamshire	7th
1874	Gloucestershire	4th
1875	Nottinghamshire	4th
1876	Gloucestershire	3rd
1877	Gloucestershire	7th
1878	Middlesex	6th
1879	Nottinghamshire/Lancashire	6th
1880	Nottinghamshire	5th
1881	Lancashire	3rd
1882	Nottinghamshire/Lancashire	3rd
1883	Nottinghamshire	2nd
1884	Nottinghamshire	3rd
1885	Nottinghamshire	2nd
1886	Nottinghamshire	4th
1887	Surrey	3rd
1888	Surrey	2nd
1889	{ Surrey/Lancashire / Nottinghamshire	7th
1890	Surrey	3rd
1891	Surrey	8th
1892	Surrey	6th
1893	**Yorkshire**	**1st**
1894	Surrey	2nd
1895	Surrey	3rd
1896	**Yorkshire**	**1st**
1897	Lancashire	4th
1898	**Yorkshire**	**1st**
1899	Surrey	3rd
1900	**Yorkshire**	**1st**
1901	**Yorkshire**	**1st**
1902	**Yorkshire**	**1st**
1903	Middlesex	3rd
1904	Lancashire	2nd
1905	**Yorkshire**	**1st**
1906	Kent	2nd
1907	Nottinghamshire	2nd
1908	**Yorkshire**	**1st**

		Yorkshire's Position
1909	Kent	3rd
1910	Kent	8th
1911	Warwickshire	7th
1912	**Yorkshire**	**1st**
1913	Kent	2nd
1914	Surrey	4th
1919	**Yorkshire**	**1st**
1920	Middlesex	4th
1921	Middlesex	3rd
1922	**Yorkshire**	**1st**
1923	**Yorkshire**	**1st**
1924	**Yorkshire**	**1st**
1925	**Yorkshire**	**1st**
1926	Lancashire	2nd
1927	Lancashire	3rd
1928	Lancashire	4th
1929	Nottinghamshire	2nd
1930	Lancashire	3rd
1931	**Yorkshire**	**1st**
1932	**Yorkshire**	**1st**
1933	**Yorkshire**	**1st**
1934	Lancashire	5th
1935	**Yorkshire**	**1st**
1936	Derbyshire	3rd
1937	**Yorkshire**	**1st**
1938	**Yorkshire**	**1st**
1939	**Yorkshire**	**1st**
1946	**Yorkshire**	**1st**
1947	Middlesex	7th
1948	Glamorgan	4th
1949	**Yorkshire**/Middlesex	**1st**
1950	Lancashire/Surrey	3rd
1951	Warwickshire	2nd
1952	Surrey	2nd
1953	Surrey	12th
1954	Surrey	2nd
1955	Surrey	2nd
1956	Surrey	7th
1957	Surrey	3rd

	Yorkshire's Position		*Yorkshire's Position*
1958	Surrey 11th	1990	Middlesex 10th
1959	**Yorkshire 1st**	1991	Essex 14th
1960	**Yorkshire 1st**	1992	Essex 16th
1961	Hampshire 2nd	1993	Middlesex 12th
1962	**Yorkshire 1st**	1994	Warwickshire 13th
1963	**Yorkshire 1st**	1995	Warwickshire 8th
1964	Worcestershire 5th	1996	Leicestershire 6th
1965	Worcestershire 4th	1997	Glamorgan 6th
1966	**Yorkshire 1st**	1998	Leicestershire 3rd
1967	**Yorkshire 1st**	1999	Surrey 6th
1968	**Yorkshire 1st**	2000	Surrey 3rd
1969	Glamorgan 13th	**2001**	**Yorkshire 1st**
1970	Kent 4th	2002	Surrey 9th
1971	Surrey 13th	2003	Sussex ....Div 2, 4th
1972	Warwickshire 10th	2004	Warwickshire ....Div 2, 7th
1973	Hampshire 14th	2005	Nottinghamshire .....Div 2, 3rd
1974	Worcestershire 11th	2006	Sussex ....Div 1, 6th
1975	Leicestershire 2nd	2007	Sussex ....Div 1, 6th
1976	Middlesex 8th	2008	Durham ....Div 1, 7th
1977	Kent/Middlesex 12th	2009	Durham ....Div 1, 7th
1978	Kent 4th	2010	Nottinghamshire .....Div 1, 3rd
1979	Essex 7th	2011	Lancashire ....Div 1, 8th
1980	Middlesex 6th	2012	Warwickshire ......Div 2, 2nd
1981	Nottinghamshire 10th	2013	Durham ....Div 1, 2nd
1982	Middlesex 10th	**2014**	**Yorkshire ....Div 1, 1st**
1983	Essex 17th	**2015**	**Yorkshire ....Div 1, 1st**
1984	Essex 14th	2016	Middlesex ....Div 1, 3rd
1985	Middlesex 11th	2017	Essex ....Div 1, 4th
1986	Essex 10th	2018	Surrey ....Div 1, 4th
1987	Nottinghamshire 8th	2019	Essex ....Div 1, 5th
1988	Worcestershire 13th	*2020*	*No matches played due to Covid-19*
1989	Worcestershire 16th		

SEASON-BY-SEASON RECORD OF ALL FIRST-CLASS MATCHES PLAYED BY YORKSHIRE 1863-2020

Season	Played	Won	Lost	Drawn	Abd§	Season	Played	Won	Lost	Drawn	Abd§
1863	4	2	1	1	0	1921	30	17	5	8	0
1864	7	2	4	1	0	1922	33	20	2	11	0
1865	9	0	7	2	0	1923	35	26	1	8	0
1866	3	0	2	1	0	1924	35	18	4	13	0
1867	7	7	0	0	0	1925	36	22	0	14	0
1868	7	4	3	0	0	1926	35	14	0	21	1
1869	5	4	1	0	0	1927	34	11	3	20	1
1870	7	6	0	1	0	1928	32	9	0	23	0
1871	7	3	3	1	0	1929	35	11	2	22	0
1872	10	2	7	1	0	1930	34	13	3	18	2
1873	13	7	5	1	0	1931	33	17	1	15	1
1874	14	10	3	1	0	1932	32	21	2	9	2
1875	12	6	4	2	0	1933	36	21	5	10	0
1876	12	5	3	4	0	1934	35	14	7	14	0
1877	14	2	7	5	0	1935	36	24	2	10	0
1878	20	10	7	3	0	1935-6	3	1	0	2	0
1879	17	7	5	5	0	1936	35	14	2	19	0
1880	20	6	8	6	0	1937	34	22	3	9	1
1881	20	11	6	3	0	1938	36	22	2	12	0
1882	24	11	9	4	0	1939	34	23	4	7	1
1883	19	10	2	7	0	1945	2	0	0	2	0
1884	20	10	6	4	0	1946	31	20	1	10	0
1885	21	8	3	10	0	1947	32	10	9	13	0
1886	21	5	8	8	0	1948	31	11	6	14	0
1887	20	6	5	9	0	1949	33	16	3	14	0
1888	20	7	7	6	0	1950	34	16	6	12	1
1889	16	3	11	2	1	1951	35	14	3	18	0
1890	20	10	4	6	0	1952	34	17	3	14	0
1891	17	5	11	1	2	1953	35	7	7	21	0
1892	19	6	6	7	0	1954	35	16	3	16*	0
1893	23	15	5	3	0	1955	33	23	6	4	0
1894	28	18	6	4	1	1956	35	11	7	17	0
1895	31	15	10	6	0	1957	34	16	5	13	1
1896	32	17	6	9	0	1958	33	10	8	15	2
1897	30	14	7	9	0	1959	35	18	8	9	0
1898	30	18	3	9	0	1960	38	19	7	12	0
1899	34	17	4	13	0	1961	39	19	5	15	0
1900	32	19	1	12	0	1962	37	16	5	16	0
1901	35	23	2	10	1	1963	33	14	4	15	0
1902	31	15	3	13	1	1964	33	12	4	17	0
1903	31	16	5	10	0	1965	33	12	4	17	0
1904	32	10	2	20	1	1966	32	16	6	10	1
1905	33	21	4	8	0	1967	31	16	5	10	2
1906	33	19	6	8	0	1968	32	13	4	15	0
1907	31	14	5	12	2	1969	29	4	7	18	0
1908	33	19	0	14	0	1970	26	10	5	11	0
1909	30	12	5	13	0	1971	27	5	8	14	0
1910	31	11	8	12	0	1972	21	4	5	12	1
1911	32	16	9	7	0	1973	22	3	5	14*	1
1912	35	14	3	18	1	1974	22	6	7	9	1
1913	32	16	5	11	0	1975	21	11	1	9	0
1914	31	16	4	11	2	1976	22	7	7	8	0
1919	31	12	5	14	0	1977	23	7	5	11	1
1920	30	17	6	7	0	1978	24	10	3	11	1

SEASON-BY-SEASON RECORD OF ALL FIRST-CLASS MATCHES PLAYED BY YORKSHIRE 1863-2020 *(Contd.)*

Season	Played	Won	Lost	Drawn	Abd§	Season	Played	Won	Lost	Drawn	Abd§
1979	22	6	3	13	1	1999	17	8	6	3	0
1980	24	5	4	15	0	2000	18	7	4	7	0
1981	24	5	9	10	0	2001	16	9	3	4	0
1982	22	5	1	16	1	2002	16	2	8	6	0
1983	23	1	5	17	1	2003	17	4	5	8	0
1984	24	5	4	15	0	2004	16	3	4	9	0
1985	25	3	4	18	1	2005	17	6	1	10	0
1986	25	4	6	15	0	2006	16	3	6	7	0
1986-7	1	0	0	1	0	2007	17	5	4	8	0
1987	24	7	4	13	1	2008	16	2	5	9	0
1988	24	5	6	13	0	2009	17	2	2	13	0
1989	22	3	9	10	0	2010	18	6	2	10	0
1990	24	5	9	10	0	2011	17	4	6	7	0
1991	24	4	6	14	0	2012	17	5	0	12	0
1991-2	1	0	1	0	0	2013	17	8	2	7	0
1992	22	4	6	12	1	2014	17	8	1	8	0
1992-3	1	0	0	1	0	2015	18	12	1	5	0
1993	19	6	4	9	0	2016	18	5	4	9	0
1994	20	7	6	7	0	2017	15	5	5	5	0
1995	20	8	8	4	0	2018	13	5	5	3	2
1995-6	2	2	0	0	0	2019	15	6	4	5	0
1996	19	8	5	6	0	2020	5	3	0	2	0
1997	20	7	4	9	0						
1998	19	9	3	7	0		3650	1535	667	1448	40

* Includes one tie each season

§ All these matches were abandoned without a ball being bowled, except Yorkshire v Kent at Harrogate, 1904, which was abandoned under Law 9. The two in 1914 and the one in 1939 were abandoned because of war. The four-day match, Yorkshire v. Essex at Leeds in 2018, was abandoned without a ball bowled, but each side received 5 points. All these matches are excluded from the total played.

Of the 1,535 matches won 524 have been by an innings margin, 88 by 200 runs or more, and 135 by 10 wickets. Of the 667 lost 113 have been by an innings margin, 17 by 200 runs or more and 35 by 10 wickets.

ANALYSIS OF RESULTS VERSUS ALL FIRST-CLASS TEAMS 1863-2020

COUNTY CHAMPIONSHIP

Opponents	Played	Won	Lost	Drawn	Tied
Derbyshire	205	103	19	83	0
Durham	36	16	8	12	0
Essex	165	85	28	52	0
Glamorgan	111	53	13	45	0
Gloucestershire	200	102	43	55	0
Hampshire	175	75	20	80	0
Kent	202	85	40	77	0
Lancashire	261	79	52	130	0
Leicestershire	166	84	15	66	1
Middlesex	235	82	59	93	1
Northamptonshire	142	67	26	49	0
Nottinghamshire	258	93	47	118	0
Somerset	179	92	27	60	0
Surrey	248	87	69	92	0
Sussex	199	85	33	81	0
Warwickshire	194	87	32	75	0
Worcestershire	142	71	22	49	0
Cambridgeshire	8	3	4	1	0
Total	3126	1349	557	1218	2

OTHER FIRST-CLASS MATCHES

Opponents	Played	Won	Lost	Drawn	Tied
Derbyshire	3	1	1	1	0
Durham	1	1	0	0	0
Essex	2	2	0	0	0
Hampshire	1	0	0	1	0
Lancashire	13	5	3	5	0
Leicestershire	3	2	1	0	0
Middlesex	1	1	0	0	0
Nottinghamshire	3	2	1	0	0
Surrey	1	0	0	1	0
Sussex	2	0	0	2	0
Warwickshire	2	0	0	2	0
Totals	32	14	6	12	0
Australians	55	6	19	30	0
Indians	14	5	1	8	0
New Zealanders	10	2	0	8	0
Pakistanis	4	1	0	3	0
South Africans	17	1	3	13	0
Sri Lankans	3	0	0	3	0
West Indians	17	3	7	7	0
Zimbabweans	2	0	1	1	0
Bangladesh A	1	1	0	0	0
India A	2	0	0	2	0
Pakistan A	2	1	0	1	0
South Africa A	1	0	0	1	0
Totals	128	20	31	77	0

Opponents	Played	Won	Lost	Drawn	Tied
Cambridge University/U C C E	88	42	17	29	0
Canadians	1	1	0	0	0
Combined Services	1	0	0	1	0
Durham MCCU	1	1	0	0	0
England XI's	6	1	2	3	0
Hon. M.B. Hawke's XI	1	0	1	0	0
International XI	1	1	0	0	0
Ireland	3	3	0	0	0
Jamaica	3	1	0	2	0
Leeds/Bradford MCCU	6	3	0	3	0
Liverpool and District*	3	2	1	0	0
Loughborough UCCE	2	1	0	1	0
MCC	155	55	40	60	0
Mashonaland	1	1	0	0	0
Matabeleland	1	1	0	0	0
Minor Counties	1	1	0	0	0
Oxford University	44	21	3	20	0
Philadelphians	1	0	0	1	0
Rest of England	16	4	5	7	0
Royal Air Force	1	0	0	1	0
Scotland**	11	7	0	4	0
South of England	2	1	0	1	0
C. I. Thornton's XI	5	2	0	3	0
United South of England	1	1	0	0	0
Western Province	2	0	1	1	0
Windward Islands	1	0	0	1	0
I Zingari	6	2	3	1	0
Totals	**364**	**152**	**73**	**139**	**0**
Grand Totals	**3650**	**1535**	**667**	**1446**	**2**

*Matches played in 1889, 1891, 1892 and 1893 are excluded. **Match played in 1878 is included

ABANDONED MATCHES (40)

1889	v. MCC at Lord's		1939	v. MCC at Scarborough (due to war)
1891 (2)	v. MCC at Lord's		1950	v. Cambridge University
	v. MCC at Scarborough			at Cambridge
1894	v. Kent at Bradford		1957	v. West Indians at Bradford
1901	v. Surrey at The Oval		1958 (2)	v. Nottinghamshire at Hull
1902	v. Leicestershire at Leicester (AR)			v. Worcestershire at Bradford
1904	v. Kent at Harrogate (Law 9		1966	v. Oxford University at Oxford
	— now Law 10)		1967 (2)	v. Leicestershire at Leeds
1907 (2)	v. Derbyshire at Sheffield			v. Lancashire at Manchester
	v. Nottinghamshire at Huddersfield		1972	v. Australians at Bradford
1912	v. Surrey at Sheffield		1974	v. Hampshire at Bournemouth
1914 (2)	v. England at Harrogate (due to war)		1977	v. Gloucestershire at Bristol
	v. MCC at Scarborough (due to war)		1978	v. Pakistan at Bradford
1926	v. Nottinghamshire at Leeds		1979	v. Nottinghamshire at Sheffield (AP)
1927	v. Kent at Bradford		1982	v. Nottinghamshire at Harrogate
1930 (2)	v. Derbyshire at Chesterfield*		1983	v. Middlesex at Lord's
	v. Northamptonshire at Harrogate*		1985	v. Essex at Sheffield (AP)
1931	v. Sussex at Hull		1987	v. Sussex at Hastings
1932 (2)	v. Derbyshire at Chesterfield		1992	v. Oxford University at Oxford
	v. Kent at Sheffield		2018	v. Leeds/Bradford MCCU at Leeds*
1937	v. Cambridge University at Bradford		2018	v. Essex at Leeds*

* Consecutive matches

ANALYSIS OF RESULTS ON GROUNDS IN YORKSHIRE USED IN 2019 AND 2020

FIRST-CLASS MATCHES

Ground	Played	Won	Lost	Drawn	Tied
Leeds Headingley 1891-2020	469	178 (37.95%)	82 (17.48%)	209 (44.56%)	0 (0.00%)
Scarborough North Marine Road 1874-2019	259	105 (40.54%)	40 (15.44%)	114 (44.02%)	0 (0.00%)
York Clifton Park 2019	1	0 (0.00%)	1 (100.00%)	0 (0.00%)	0 (0.00%)

HIGHEST MATCH AGGREGATES – OVER 1350 RUNS

Runs	Wkts	
1665	33	Yorkshire (351 and 481) lost to Warwickshire (601:9 dec and 232:4) by 6 wkts at Birmingham, 2002
1606	31	Yorkshire (438 and 363:5 dec) lost to Somerset (326 and 479:6) by 4 wkts at Taunton, 2009
1479	28	Yorkshire (405 and 333:4 dec) lost to Somerset (377 and 364:4) by 6 wkts at Taunton , 2010
1473	17	Yorkshire (600:4 dec. and 231:3 dec.) drew with Worcestershire (453:5 dec. and 189:5) at Scarborough, 1995.
1442	29	Yorkshire (501:6 dec. and 244:6 dec.) beat Lancashire (403:7 dec. and 294) by 48 runs at Scarborough, 1991.
1439	32	Yorkshire (536:8 dec. and 205:7 dec.) beat Glamorgan (482: 7 dec. and 216) by 43 runs at Cardiff, 1996.
1431	32	Yorkshire (388 and 312:6) drew with Sussex (398 and 333:6 dec) at Scarborough, 2011
1417	33	Yorkshire (422 and 193:7) drew with Glamorgan (466 and 336:6 dec) at Colwyn Bay, 2003
1406	37	Yorkshire (354 and 341:8) drew with Derbyshire (406 and 305:9 dec) at Derby, 2004
1400	32	Yorkshire (299 and 439: 4 dec.) drew with Hampshire (296 and 366:8) at Southampton, 2007
1393	35	Yorkshire (331 and 278) lost to Kent (377 and 407:5 dec) by 175 runs at Maidstone, 1994.
1390	34	Yorkshire (431:8 dec and 265:7) beat Hampshire (429 and 265) by 3 wkts at Southampton, 1995.
1390	33	Durham (573 and 124:3) beat Yorkahire (274 and 419) by 7 wkts at Scarborough, 2013.
1376	33	Yorkshire (531 and 158:3) beat Lancashire (373 and 314) by 7 wkts at Leeds, 2001
1376	20	Yorkshire (677: 7 dec.) drew with Durham (518 and 181:3 dec.) at Leeds, 2006
1374	36	Yorkshire (594: 9 dec. and 266:7 dec.) beat Surrey (344 and 170) by 346 runs at The Oval, 2007
1373	36	Yorkshire (520 and 114:6) drew with Derbyshire (216 and 523) at Derby, 2005
1364	35	Yorkshire (216 and 433) lost to Warwickshire (316 and 399:5 dec.) by 66 runs at Birmingham, 2006
1359	25	Yorkshire (561 and 138:3 dec.) drew with Derbyshire (412:4 dec. and 248:8) at Sheffield, 1996.
1359	30	Yorkshire (358 and 321) lost to Somerset (452 and 228:0) by 10 wkts at Taunton, 2011
1353	18	Yorkshire (377:2 dec. and 300:6) beat Derbyshire (475:7 dec. and 201:3 dec.) by 4 wkts at Scarborough, 1990.

LOWEST MATCH AGGREGATES – UNDER 225 RUNS
IN A COMPLETED MATCH

Runs	Wkts	
165	30	Yorkshire (46 and 37:0) beat Nottinghamshire (24 and 58 by 10 wkts at Sheffield, 1888.
175	29	Yorkshire (104) beat Essex (30 and 41) by an innings and 33 runs at Leyton, 1901.
182	15	Yorkshire (4:0 dec. and 88.5) beat Northamptonshire (4:0 dec. and 86) by 5 wkts at Bradford, 1931.
193	29	Yorkshire (99) beat Worcestershire (43 and 51) by an innings and 5 runs at Bradford, 1900.
219	30	Yorkshire (113) beat Nottinghamshire (71 and 35) by an innings and 7 runs at Nottingham, 1881.
222	32	Yorkshire (98 and 14:2) beat Gloucestershire (68 and 42) by 8 wkts at Gloucester, 1924.
223	40	Yorkshire (58 and 51) lost to Lancashire (64 and 50)

LOWEST MATCH AGGREGATES – UNDER 325 RUNS
IN A MATCH IN WHICH ALL 40 WICKETS FELL

Runs	Wkts	
223	40	Yorkshire (58 and 51) lost to Lancashire (64 and 50) by 5 runs at Manchester, 1893.
288	40	Yorkshire (55 and 68) lost to Lancashire (89 and 76) by 42 runs at Sheffield, 1872.
295	40	Yorkshire (71 and 63) lost to Surrey (56 and 105) by 27 runs at The Oval, 1886.
303	40	Yorkshire (109 and 77) beat Middlesex (63 and 54) by 69 runs at Lord's, 1891.
318	40	Yorkshire (96 and 96) beat Lancashire (39 and 87) by 66 runs at Manchester, 1874.
318	40	Yorkshire (94 and 104) beat Northamptonshire (61 and 59) by 78 runs at Bradford, 1955.
319	40	Yorkshire (84 and 72) lost to Derbyshire (106 and 57) by 7 runs at Derby, 1878.
320	40	Yorkshire (98 and 91) beat Surrey (72 and 59) by 58 runs at Sheffield, 1893.
321	40	Yorkshire (88 and 37) lost to I Zingari (103 and 93) by 71 runs at Scarborough, 1877.
321	40	Yorkshire (80 and 67) lost to Derbyshire (129 and 45) by 27 runs at Sheffield, 1879.

LARGE MARGINS OF VICTORY – BY AN INNINGS
AND OVER 250 RUNS

Inns and 397 runs	Yorkshire (548:4 dec.) beat Northamptonshire (58 and 93) at Harrogate, 1921
Inns and 387 runs	Yorkshire (662) beat Derbyshire (118 and 157) at Chesterfield, 1898.
Inns and 343 runs	Yorkshire (673:8 dec) beat Northamptonshire (184 and 146) at Leeds, 2003
Inns and 321 runs	Yorkshire (437) beat Leicestershire (58 and 58) at Leicester, 1908.
Inns and 314 runs	Yorkshire (356:8 dec.) beat Northamptonshire (27 and 15) at Northampton, 1908. (Yorkshire's first match v. Northamptonshire).
Inns and 313 runs	Yorkshire (555:1 dec) beat Essex (78 and 164) at Leyton, 1932.
Inns and 307 runs	Yorkshire (681:5 dec.) beat Sussex (164 and 210) at Sheffield, 1897.
Inns and 302 runs	Yorkshire (660) beat Leicestershire (165 and 193) at Leicester, 1896.
Inns and 301 runs	Yorkshire (499) beat Somerset (125 and 73) at Bath, 1899.
Inns and 294 runs	Yorkshire (425:7 dec.) beat Gloucestershire (47 and 84) at Bristol, 1964.
Inns and 284 runs	Yorkshire (467:7 dec) beat Leicestershire (111 and 72) at Bradford, 1932.
Inns and 282 runs	Yorkshire (481:8 dec) beat Derbyshire (106 and 93) at Huddersfield, 1901.
Inns and 280 runs	Yorkshire (562) beat Leicestershire (164 and 118) at Dewsbury, 1903.
Inns and 271 runs	Yorkshire (460) beat Hampshire (128 and 61) at Hull, 1900.
Inns and 271 runs	Yorkshire (495:5 dec) beat Warwickshire (99 and 125) at Huddersfield, 1922.
Inns and 266 runs	Yorkshire (352) beat Cambridgeshire (40 and 46) at Hunslet, 1869.
Inns and 260 runs	Yorkshire (521: 7dec.) beat Worcestershire (129 and 132) at Leeds, 2007.
Inns and 258 runs	Yorkshire (404:2 dec) beat Glamorgan (78 and 68) at Cardiff, 1922. (Yorkshire's first match v. Glamorgan).
Inns and 256 runs	Yorkshire (486) beat Leicestershire (137 and 93) at Sheffield, 1895.
Inns and 251 runs	Yorkshire (550) beat Leicestershire (154 and 145) at Leicester, 1933.

LARGE MARGINS OF VICTORY – BY OVER 300 RUNS

389 runs	Yorkshire (368 and 280:1 dec) beat Somerset (125 and 134) at Bath, 1906.
370 runs	Yorkshire (194 and 274) beat Hampshire (62 and 36) at Leeds, 1904.
351 runs	Yorkshire (280 and 331) beat Northamptonshire (146 and 114) at Northampton, 1947.
346 runs	Yorkshire (594: 9 dec. and 266: 7 dec.) beat Surrey (344 and 179) at The Oval, 2007.
328 runs	Yorkshire (186 and 318:1 dec) beat Somerset (43 and 133) at Bradford, 1930.
328 runs	Yorkshire (280 and 277:7 dec) beat Glamorgan (104 and 105) at Swansea, 2001
320 runs	Yorkshire (331 and 353:9 dec) beat Durham (150 and 214) at Chester-le-Street, 2004
308 runs	Yorkshire (89 and 420) beat Warwickshire (72 and 129) at Birmingham, 1921.
308 runs	Yorkshire (89 and 420) beat Warwickshire (72 and 129)
305 runs	Yorkshire (370 and 305:4 dec) beat Hampshire (227 and 143) at Leeds, 2015
305 runs	Yorkshire (282 and 263:4 dec) beat Nottinghamshire (94 and 146) at Scarborough 2016

LARGE MARGINS OF VICTORY – BY 10 WICKETS
(WITH OVER 100 RUNS SCORED IN THE 4th INNINGS)

4th Innings

167:0 wkt	Yorkshire (247 and 167:0) beat Northamptonshire 233 and 180) at Huddersfield, 1948.
147:0 wkt	Yorkshire (381 and 147:0) beat Middlesex (384 and 142) at Lord's, 1896.
142:0 wkt	Yorkshire (304 and 142:0) beat Sussex (254 and 188) at Bradford, 1887.
139:0 wkt	Yorkshire (163:9 dec and 139:0) beat Nottinghamshire (234 and 67) at Leeds, 1932.
138:0 wkt	Yorkshire (293 and 138:0) beat Hampshire (251 and 179) at Southampton, 1897.
132:0 wkt	Yorkshire (328 and 132:0) beat Northamptonshire (281 and 175) at Leeds, 2005
129:0 wkt	Yorkshire (355 and 129:0) beat Durham MCCU (196 and 287) at Durham, 2011
127:0 wkt	Yorkshire (258 and 127:0) beat Cambridge University (127 and 257) at Cambridge, 1930.
119:0 wkt	Yorkshire (109 and 119:0) beat Essex (108 and 119) at Leeds, 1931.
118:0 wkt	Yorkshire (121 and 118:0) beat MCC (125 and 113) at Lord's, 1883.
116:0 wkt	Yorkshire (147 and 116:0) beat Hampshire (141 and 120) at Bournemouth, 1930.
114:0 wkt	Yorkshire (135 and 114:0) beat Hampshire (71 and 176) at Bournemouth, 1948.
114:0 wkt	Yorkshire (135 and 114:0) beat Hampshire (71 and 176)
105:0 wkt	Yorkshire (307 and 105:0) beat Worcestershire (311 and 100) at Worcester, 2015

HEAVY DEFEATS – BY AN INNINGS
AND OVER 250 RUNS

Inns and 272 runs	Yorkshire (78 and 186) lost to Surrey (536) at The Oval, 1898.
Inns and 261 runs	Yorkshire (247 and 89) lost to Sussex (597: 8 dec.) at Hove, 2007.
Inns and 255 runs	Yorkshire (125 and 144) lost to All England XI (524) at Sheffield, 1865.

HEAVY DEFEATS – BY OVER 300 RUNS

433 runs	Kent (482-8 dec and 337-7 dec) defeated Yorkshire (269 and 117) at Leeds, 2019
376 runs	Essex (227 and 334-7 dec) defeated Yorkshire (111 and 74) at Chelmsford, 2017
324 runs	Yorkshire (247 and 204) lost to Gloucestershire (291 and 484) at Cheltenham, 1994.
305 runs	Yorkshire (119 and 51) lost to Cambridge University (312 and 163) at Cambridge, 1906.

HEAVY DEFEATS – BY 10 WICKETS
(WITH OVER 100 RUNS SCORED IN THE 4th INNINGS)

4th Innings

228:0 wkt	Yorkshire (358 and 321) lost to Somerset (452 and 228:0) at Taunton, 2011
148:0 wkt	Yorkshire (83 and 216) lost to Lancashire (154 and 148:0) at Manchester, 1875.
119:0 wkt	Yorkshire (92 and 109) lost to Nottinghamshire (86 and 119:0 wkt) at Leeds, 1989.
108:0 wkt	Yorkshire (236 and 107) lost to Hampshire (236 and 108:0 wkt) at Southampton, 2008
100:0 wkt	Yorkshire (95 and 91) lost to Gloucestershire (88 and 100:0) at Bristol, 1956.

NARROW VICTORIES – BY 1 WICKET

Yorkshire (70 and 91:9) beat Cambridgeshire (86 and 74) at Wisbech, 1867.
Yorkshire (91 and 145:9) beat MCC (73 and 161) at Lord's, 1870.
Yorkshire (265 and 154:9) beat Derbyshire (234 and 184) at Derby, 1897.
Yorkshire (177 and 197:9) beat MCC (188 and 185) at Lord's, 1899.
Yorkshire (391 and 241:9) beat Somerset (349 and 281) at Taunton, 1901.
Yorkshire (239 and 168:9) beat MCC (179 and 226) at Scarborough, 1935.
Yorkshire (152 and 90:9) beat Worcestershire (119 and 121) at Leeds, 1946.
Yorkshire (229 and 175:9) beat Glamorgan (194 and 207) at Bradford, 1960.
Yorkshire (265.9 dec and 191:9) beat Worcestershire (227 and 227) at Worcester, 1961.
Yorkshire (329:6 dec and 167:9) beat Essex (339.9 dec and 154) at Scarborough, 1979.
Yorkshire (Innings forfeited and 251:9 beat Sussex (195 and 55.1 dec) at Leeds, 1986.
Yorkshire (314 and 150:9) beat Essex (200 and 261) at Scarborough, 1998.

NARROW VICTORIES – BY 5 RUNS OR LESS

By 1 run	Yorkshire (228 and 214) beat Middlesex (206 and 235) at Bradford, 1976.
By 1 run	Yorkshire (383 and inns forfeited) beat Loughborough UCCE (93: 3 dec. and 289) at Leeds, 2007.
By 2 runs	Yorkshire (108 and 122) beat Nottinghamshire (56 and 172) at Nottingham, 1870.
By 2 runs	Yorkshire (304:9 dec and 135) beat Middlesex (225:2 dec and 212) at Leeds, 1985.
By 3 runs	Yorkshire (446:9 dec and 172:4 dec) beat Essex (300:3 dec and 315) at Colchester, 1991.
By 3 runs	Yorkshire (202 and 283) beat Somerset (224 and 258) at Taunton, 2017
By 5 runs	Yorkshire (271 and 147:6 dec) beat Surrey (198 and 215) at Sheffield, 1950.
By 5 runs	Yorkshire (151 and 176) beat Hampshire (165 and 157) at Bradford, 1962.
By 5 runs	Yorkshire (376:4 and 106) beat Middlesex (325:8 and 152) at Lord's, 1975
By 5 runs	Yorkshire (323:5 dec and inns forfeited) beat Somerset (inns forfeited and 318) at Taunton, 1986.

NARROW DEFEATS – BY 1 WICKET

Yorkshire (224 and 210) lost to Australian Imperial Forces XI (265 and 170:9) at Sheffield, 1919

Yorkshire (101 and 159) lost to Warwickshire (45 and 216:9) at Scarborough, 1934.

Yorkshire (239 and 184:9 dec.) lost to Warwickshire (125 and 302:9) at Birmingham, 1983.

Yorkshire (289 and 153) lost to Surrey (250:2 dec and 193:9) at Guildford, 1991.

Yorkshire (341 and Inns forfeited) lost to Surrey (39:1 dec and 306:9) at Bradford, 1992.

NARROW DEFEATS – BY 5 RUNS OR LESS

By 1 run	Yorkshire (135 and 297) lost to Essex (139 and 294) at Huddersfield, 1897.
By 1 run	Yorkshire (159 and 232) lost to Gloucestershire (164 and 228) at Bristol, 1906.
By 1 run	Yorkshire (126 and 137) lost to Worcestershire (101 and 163) at Worcester, 1968.
By 1 run	Yorkshire (366 and 217) lost to Surrey (409 and 175) at The Oval, 1995.
By 2 runs	Yorkshire (172 and 107) lost to Gloucestershire (157 and 124) at Sheffield, 1913.
By 2 runs	Yorkshire (179:9 dec and 144) lost to MCC (109 and 216) at Lord's, 1957.
By 3 runs	Yorkshire (126 and 181) lost to Sussex (182 and 128) at Sheffield, 1883.
By 3 runs	Yorkshire (160 and 71) lost to Lancashire (81 and 153) at Huddersfield, 1889.
By 3 runs	Yorkshire (134 and 158) lost to Nottinghamshire (200 and 95) at Leeds, 1923.
By 4 runs	Yorkshire (169 and 193) lost to Middlesex (105 and 261) at Bradford, 1920.
By 5 runs	Yorkshire (58 and 51) lost to Lancashire (64 and 50) at Manchester, 1893.
By 5 runs	Yorkshire (119 and 115) lost to Warwickshire (167 and 72) at Bradford, 1969.

HIGH FOURTH INNINGS SCORES – 300 AND OVER

By Yorkshire

To Win:	406:4	beat Leicestershire by 6 wkts at Leicester, 2005
	402:6	beat Gloucestershire by 4 wkts at Bristol, 2012
	400:4	beat Leicestershire by 6 wkts at Scarborough, 2005
	339:6	beat Durham by 4 wkts at Chester-le-Street, 2013
	331:8	beat Middlesex by 2 wkts at Lord's, 1910.
	327:6	beat Nottinghamshire by 4 wkts at Nottingham, 1990.*
	323:5	beat Nottinghamshire by 5 wkts at Nottingham, 1977.
	318:3	beat Glamorgan by 7 wkts at Middlesbrough, 1976.
	316:8	beat Gloucestershire by 2 wkts at Scarborough, 2012
	309:7	beat Somerset by 3 wkts at Taunton, 1984.
	305:8	beat Nottinghamshire by 2 wkts at Worksop, 1982.
	305:5	beat Hampshire by 5 wkts at West End, Southampton, 2015
	305:3	beat Lancashire by 7 wkts at Manchester, 1994.
	304:4	beat Derbyshire by 6 wkts at Chesterfield, 1959.
	300:4	beat Derbyshire by 6 wkts at Chesterfield, 1981.
	300:6	beat Derbyshire by 4 wkts at Scarborough, 1990.*
To Draw:	341:8	(set 358) drew with Derbyshire at Derby, 2004.
	333:7	(set 369) drew with Essex at Chelmsford, 2010
	316:6	(set 326) drew with Oxford University at Oxford, 1948.
	312:6	(set 344) drew with Sussex at Scarborough 2011
	316:7	(set 320) drew with Somerset at Scarborough, 1990.
	300:5	(set 392) drew with Kent at Canterbury, 2010
To Lose:	433	(set 500) lost to Warwickshire by 66 runs at Birmingham, 2006
	380	(set 406) lost to MCC. by 25 runs at Lord's, 1937.
	343	(set 490) lost to Durham by 146 runs at Leeds 2011
	324	(set 485) lost to Northamptonshire by 160 runs at Luton, 1994.
	322	(set 344) lost to Middlesex by 21 runs at Lord's, 1996.
	309	(set 400) lost to Middlesex by 90 runs at Lord's 1878.

*Consecutive matches

By Opponents:

To Win:	479:6	Somerset won by 4 wkts at Taunton, 2009
	472:3	Middlesex won by 7 wkts at Lord's, 2014
	404:5	Hampshire won by 5 wkts at Leeds, 2006
	392:4	Gloucestershire won by 6 wkts at Bristol, 1948
	364:4	Somerset won by 6 wkts at Taunton, 2010
	354:5	Nottinghamshire won by 5 wkts at Scarborough, 1990
	337:4	Worcestershire won by 6 wkts at Kidderminster, 2007
	334:6	Glamorgan won by 4 wkts at Harrogate, 1955
	329:5	Worcestershire won by 5 wkts at Worcester, 1979
	321:6	Hampshire won by 4 wickets at Leeds, 2017
	306:9	Surrey won by 1 wkt at Bradford, 1992
	305:7	Lancashire won by 3 wkts at Manchester, 1980
	302:9	Warwickshire won by 1 wkt at Birmingham, 1983

By Opponents:

To Draw:
366:8	(set 443) Hampshire drew at Southampton, 2007.
334:7	(set 339) MCC. drew at Scarborough, 1911.
322:9	(set 334) Middlesex drew at Leeds, 1988.
317:6	(set 355) Nottinghamshire drew at Nottingham, 1910.
300:9	(set 314) Northamptonshire drew at Northampton, 1990.

To Lose:
370	(set 539) Leicestershire lost by 168 runs at Leicester, 2001
319	(set 364) Gloucestershire lost by 44 runs at Leeds, 1987.
318	(set 324) Somerset lost by 5 runs at Taunton, 1986.
315	(set 319) Essex lost by 3 runs at Colchester, 1991.
314	(set 334) Lancashire lost by 19 runs at Manchester, 1993.
310	(set 417) Warwickshire lost by 106 runs at Scarborough, 1939.
306	(set 413) Kent lost by 106 runs at Leeds, 1952.
300	(set 330) Middlesex lost by 29 runs at Sheffield, 1930.

TIE MATCHES

Yorkshire (351:4 dec and 113) tied with Leicestershire (328 and 136) at Huddersfield, 1954.
Yorkshire (106:9 dec and 207) tied with Middlesex (102 and 211) at Bradford, 1973.

HIGHEST SCORES BY AND AGAINST YORKSHIRE

Yorkshire versus: —

Derbyshire: | **By Yorkshire:** | **Against Yorkshire:**
In Yorkshire:	677:7 dec at Leeds 2013	491 at Bradford, 1949
Away	662 at Chesterfield, 1898	523 at Derby, 2005

Durham:
In Yorkshire:	677:7 dec. at Leeds, 2006	573 at Scarborough, 2013
Away	589-8 dec at Chester-le-Street, 2014	507:8 dec at Chester-le-Street, 2016

Essex:
In Yorkshire:	516 at Scarborough, 2010	622:8 dec. at Leeds, 2005
Away:	555:1 dec. at Leyton, 1932	521 at Leyton, 1905

Glamorgan:
In Yorkshire:	580:9 dec at Scarborough, 2001	498 at Leeds, 1999
Away:	536:8 dec. at Cardiff, 1996	482:7 dec. at Cardiff, 1996

Gloucestershire:
In Yorkshire:	504:7 dec. at Bradford, 1905	411 at Leeds, 1992
Away:	494 at Bristol, 1897	574 at Cheltenham, 1990

Hampshire:
In Yorkshire:	593:9 dec. at Leeds 2016	498:6 dec at Scarborough, 2010
Away	585:3 dec at Portsmouth 1920	599:3 at Southampton, 2011

Kent:
In Yorkshire:	550:9 at Scarborough, 1995	537:9 dec at Leeds, 2012
Away:	559 at Canterbury, 1887	580: 9 dec. at Maidstone, 1998

Lancashire:
In Yorkshire:	590 at Bradford, 1887	517 at Leeds, 2007.
Away	616:6 dec at Manchester, 2014	537 at Manchester, 2005

Leicestershire:
In Yorkshire	562 { at Scarborough, 1901 { at Dewsbury, 1903	681:7 dec. at Bradford, 1996
Away:	660 at Leicester, 1896	425 at Leicester, 1906

HIGHEST SCORES BY AND AGAINST YORKSHIRE *(Continued)*

Yorkshire versus: —

	By Yorkshire:	**Against Yorkshire:**
Middlesex:		
In Yorkshire:	575:7 dec. at Bradford, 1899	527 at Huddersfield, 1887
Away	538:6 dec at Lord's, 1925	573:8 dec at Lord's, 2015
Northamptonshire:		
In Yorkshire:	673:8 dec. at Leeds, 2003	517:7 dec. at Scarborough, 1999
Away	546:3 dec at Northampton, 2014	531:4 dec at Northampton, 1996
Nottinghamshire:		
In Yorkshire:	572:8 dec at Scarborough, 2013	545:7 dec at Leeds, 2010
Away	534:9 dec at Nottingham, 2011	490 at Nottingham, 1897
Somerset:		
In Yorkshire:	525:4 dec. at Leeds, 1953	630 at Leeds, 1901
Away:	589:5 dec at Bath, 2001	592 at Taunton, 1892
Surrey:		
In Yorkshire:	582:7 dec. at Sheffield, 1935	516-7 dec at Leeds, 2017
Away:	704 at The Oval, 1899	634:5 dec at The Oval, 2013
Sussex:		
In Yorkshire:	681:5 dec. at Sheffield, 1897	566 at Sheffield, 1937
Away:	522:7 dec. at Hastings, 1911	597:8 dec. at Hove, 2007
Warwickshire:		
In Yorkshire	561:7 dec at Scarborough 2007	482 at Leeds, 2011
Away:	887 at Birmingham, 1896	601:9 dec. at Birmingham, 2002
	(Highest score by a First-Class county)	
Worcestershire:		
In Yorkshire:	600: 4 dec. at Scarborough, 1995	572:7 dec. at Scarborough 2018
Away:	560:6 dec. at Worcester, 1928	456:8 at Worcester, 1904
Australians:		
In Yorkshire:	377 at Sheffield, 1953	470 at Bradford, 1893
Indians:		
In Yorkshire:	385 at Hull, 1911	490:5 dec. at Sheffield, 1946
New Zealanders:		
In Yorkshire:	419 at Bradford, 1965	370:7 dec. at Bradford, 1949
Pakistanis:		
In Yorkshire:	433:9 dec. at Sheffield, 1954	356 at Sheffield, 1954
South Africans:		
In Yorkshire:	579 at Sheffield, 1951	454:8 dec at Sheffield, 1951
Sri Lankans:		
In Yorkshire:	314:8 dec. at Leeds, 1991	422:8 dec. at Leeds, 1991
West Indians:		
In Yorkshire:	312:5 dec. at Scarborough, 1973	426 at Scarborough, 1995
Zimbabweans:		
In Yorkshire:	298:9 dec at Leeds, 1990	235 at Leeds, 2000
Cambridge University:		
In Yorkshire:	359 at Scarborough, 1967	366 at Leeds, 1998
Away:	540 at Cambridge, 1938	425:7 at Cambridge, 1929
Durham MCCU:		
Away:	355 at Durham, 2011	287 at Durham, 2011
Leeds/Bradford MCCU:		
In Yorkshire	543-5 dec at Leeds, 2017	211 at Leeds, 2012
Away	489-8 dec at Weetwood, Leeds, 2019	219 at Weetwood, Leeds, 2019
Loughborough MCCU:		
In Yorkshire:	383:6 dec at Leeds, 2007	289 at Leeds, 2007

Yorkshire versus: —

MCC: **By Yorkshire:**   **Against Yorkshire:**
In Yorkshire: 557:8 dec. at Scarborough, 1933   478:8 at Scarborough, 1904
Away: 528:8 dec. at Lord's, 1919   488 at Lord's, 1919

Oxford University:
In Yorkshire: 173 at Harrogate, 1972   190:6 dec at Harrogate, 1972
Away: 468:6 dec. at Oxford, 1978   422:9 dec. at Oxford, 1953

LOWEST SCORES BY AND AGAINST YORKSHIRE

Yorkshire versus:

Derbyshire: **By Yorkshire:**   **Against Yorkshire:**
In Yorkshire: 50 at Sheffield, 1894   20 at Sheffield, 1939
Away: 44 at Chesterfield, 1948   26 at Derby, 1880

Durham:
In Yorkshire: 93 at Leeds, 2003   125 at Harrogate, 1995
Away: 108 at Durham, 1992   74 at Chester-le-Street, 1998

Essex:
In Yorkshire: 31 at Huddersfield, 1935   52 at Harrogate, 1900
Away: 50 at Chelmsford, 2018   30 at Leyton, 1901

Glamorgan:
In Yorkshire: 83 at Sheffield, 1946   52 at Hull, 1926
Away: 92 at Swansea, 1956   48 at Cardiff, 1924

Gloucestershire:
In Yorkshire: 61 at Leeds, 1894   36 at Sheffield, 1903
Away: 35 at Bristol, 1959   42 at Gloucester, 1924

Hampshire:
In Yorkshire: 23 at Middlesbrough, 1965   36 at Leeds, 1904
Away: 96 at Bournemouth, 1971   36 at Southampton, 1898

Kent:
In Yorkshire: 30 at Sheffield, 1865   39 { at Sheffield, 1882 / at Sheffield, 1936

Away: 62 at Maidstone, 1889   63 at Canterbury, 1901

Lancashire:
In Yorkshire: 33 at Leeds, 1924   30 at Holbeck, 1868
Away: 51 { at Manchester, 1888 / at Manchester, 1893   39 at Manchester, 1874

Leicestershire: **By Yorkshire:**   **Against Yorkshire:**
In Yorkshire: 93 at Leeds, 1935   34 at Leeds, 1906
Away: 47 at Leicester, 1911   57 at Leicester, 1898

Middlesex:
In Yorkshire: 45 at Leeds, 1898   45 at Huddersfield, 1879
Away: 43 at Lord's, 1888   49 at Lord's in 1890

Northamptonshire:
In Yorkshire: 85 at Sheffield, 1919   51 at Bradford, 1920
Away   64 at Northampton, 1959   15 at Northampton, 1908
   (and 27 in first innings)

Nottinghamshire:
In Yorkshire: 32 at Sheffield, 1876   24 at Sheffield, 1888
Away: 43 at Nottingham, 1869   13 at Nottingham, 1901
   (second smallest total
   by a First-Class county)

LOWEST SCORES BY AND AGAINST YORKSHIRE *(continued)*

Yorkshire versus:

	By Yorkshire:	**Against Yorkshire:**
Somerset:		
In Yorkshire:	73 at Leeds, 1895	43 at Bradford, 1930
Away:	83 at Wells, 1949	35 at Bath, 1898
Surrey:		
In Yorkshire:	54 at Sheffield, 1873	31 at Holbeck, 1883
Away:	26 at The Oval, 1909	44 at The Oval, 1935
Sussex:		
In Yorkshire:	61 at Dewsbury, 1891	20 at Hull, 1922
Away:	42 at Hove, 1922	24 at Hove, 1878
Warwickshire:		
In Yorkshire:	49 at Huddersfield, 1951	35 at Sheffield, 1979
Away:	54 at Birmingham, 1964	35 at Birmingham, 1963
Worcestershire:		
In Yorkshire:	62 at Bradford, 1907	24 at Huddersfield, 1903
Away:	72 at Worcester, 1977	65 at Worcester, 1925
Australians:		
In Yorkshire:	48 at Leeds, 1893	23 at Leeds, 1902
Indians:		
In Yorkshire:	146 at Bradford, 1959	66 at Harrogate, 1932
New Zealanders:		
In Yorkshire:	189 at Harrogate, 1931	134 at Bradford, 1965
Pakistanis:		
In Yorkshire:	137 at Bradford, 1962	150 at Leeds, 1967
South Africans:		
In Yorkshire:	113 at Bradford, 1907	76 at Bradford, 1951
Sri Lankans:		
In Yorkshire:	Have not been dismissed. Lowest is 184:1 dec at Leeds, 1991	287:5 dec at Leeds, 1988
West Indians:		
In Yorkshire:	50 at Harrogate, 1906	58 at Leeds, 1928
Zimbabweans:		
In Yorkshire:	124 at Leeds, 2000	68 at Leeds, 2000
Cambridge University:		
In Yorkshire:	110 at Sheffield, 1903	39 at Sheffield, 1903
Away:	51 at Cambridge, 1906	30 at Cambridge, 1928
Durham MCCU:		
Away	355 at Durham, 2011	196 at Durham, 2011
Leeds/Bradford MCCU:		
In Yorkshire	135 at Leeds, 2012	118 at Leeds, 2013
Away		118 at Weetwood, Leeds, 2019
Loughborough MCCU:		
In Yorkshire	348:5 dec at Leeds, 2010	289 at Leeds, 2007
MCC:		
In Yorkshire:	46 { at Scarborough, 1876 / at Scarborough, 1877	31 at Scarborough, 1877
Away:	44 at Lord's, 1880	27 at Lord's, 1902
Oxford University:		
In Yorkshire:	Have not been dismissed. Lowest is 115:8 at Harrogate, 1972	133 at Harrogate, 1972
Away:	141 at Oxford, 1949	46 at Oxford, 1956

CENTURIES BY ALL PLAYERS 1863-2020

C W J ATHEY (10)

131 *	v. Sussex	1976	123 *	v. Northamptonshire	1981
131	v. Somerset	1978	100	v. Glamorgan	1982
114	v. Northamptonshire	1978	134	v. Derbyshire	1982
125 *	v. Gloucestershire	1980	100	v. Kent	1982
114	v. Warwickshire	1980	114 *	v. Surrey	1982

AZEEM RAFIQ

100	v. Worcestershire	2009

D L BAIRSTOW (9)

106	v. Glamorgan	1976	122 *	v. Derbyshire	1985
145	v. Middlesex	1980	104	v. Derbyshire	1987
100 *	v. Middlesex	1983	128	v. Leicestershire	1987
100 *	v. Leicestershire	1985	101 *	v. Surrey	1989
113 *	v. Derbyshire	1985			

J M BAIRSTOW (15))

205	v. Nottinghamshire	2011	123	v. Leeds/Bradford	2014
136	v. Somerset	2011	161 *	v. Sussex	2014
182	v. Leicestershire	2012	102	v. Hampshire	2015
118	v. Leicestershire	2012	125 *	v. Middlesex	2015
107	v. Kent	2012	219 *	v. Durham **	2015
186	v. Derbyshire	2013	108	v. Warwickshire **	2015

(** Consecutive innings)

139	v. Worcestershire	2015	198	v. Surrey	2016
246	v. Hampshire	2016			

G S BALLANCE (26)

111	v. Warwickshire	2011	112	v. Warwickshire	2013
121 *	v. Gloucestershire	2012	148	v. Surrey 1st inns **	2013
112	v. Leeds/Bradford MCCU	2013	108 *	v. Surrey 2nd inns **	2013
107	v. Somerset	2013	101	v. Leeds/Bradford MCCU **	2014
141	v. Nottinghamshire	2013	174	v. Northamptonshire	2014

(** Consecutive innings)

130	v. Middlesex	2014	109	v. Hampshire	2018
165	v. Sussex	2015	104	v. Nottinghamshire	2018
105	v. MCC	2016	194	v. Worcestershire	2018
132	v. Middlesex	2016	101 *	v. Nottinghamshire	2019
101 *	v. Nottinghamshire	2016	148 *	v. Hampshire	2019
120	v. Hampshire	2017	159	v. Kent	2019
108	v. Hampshire 1st innings	2017	100	v. Hampshire	2019
203 *	v. Hampshire 2nd innings	2017	111	v. Somerset	2019

A T BARBER (1)

100	v. An England XI	1929

W BARBER (27)

108	v. South Africans	1929	103	v. Cambridge University	1934
114	v. Glamorgan	1929	168	v. M C C	1934
102	v. Middlesex	1932	248	v. Kent	1934
162	v. Middlesex	1932	191	v. Sussex	1935
110	v. Leicestershire	1932	107	v. Middlesex	1935
120 *	v. Glamorgan	1933	120	v. Glamorgan	1935
124	v. Warwickshire	1933	255	v. Surrey	1935
109 *	v. Nottinghamshire	1933	158	v. Kent	1936
101	v. Essex	1933	104	v. Sussex	1937

W BARBER *(Continued)*

115	v. Nottinghamshire	1937	100	v. Derbyshire	1939
107 *	v. Gloucestershire	1937	128 *	v. Northamptonshire	1939
157	v. Surrey	1938	141	v. Surrey	1939
111	v. Hampshire	1938	113	v. Somerset	1946
130	v. Leicestershire	1938			

W BATES (8)

102	v. Nottinghamshire	1878	116	v. Nottinghamshire	1884
118	v. Lancashire	1879	106	v. Derbyshire	1886
108	v. Kent	1881	136	v. Sussex	1886
133	v. Cambridge University	1884	103	v. Derbyshire	1887

M G BEVAN (9)

113 *	v. Cambridge University	1995	105	v. West Indies	1995
108	v. Lancashire	1995	136	v. Derbyshire	1996
102	v. Gloucestershire	1995	107	v. Middlesex	1996
107	v. Hampshire	1995	160 *	v. Surrey	1996
153 *	v. Surrey	1995			

H D BIRD (1)

181*	v. Glamorgan	1959

T J D BIRTLES (1)

104	v. Lancashire	1914

R J BLAKEY (12)

101 *	v. Glamorgan	1987	125 *	v. Glamorgan	1992
118	v. Lancashire	1987	112 *	v. Nottinghamshire	1992
108	v. Northamptonshire	1987	109 *	v. Lancashire	1996
204 *	v. Gloucestershire	1987	123	v. Glamorgan	1999
111	v. Somerset	1990	103	v. Warwickshire	2002
196	v. Oxford University	1991	223 *	v. Northamptonshire	2003

G S BLEWETT (1)

190	v. Northamptonshire	1999

J B BOLUS (7)

146 *	v. Hampshire	1960	102 *	v. Nottinghamshire	1961
103 *	v. Rest of England	1960	100	v. Hampshire	1961
133	v. Surrey	1961	108	v. Cambridge University	1962
117	v. Sussex	1961			

M W BOOTH (2)

210	v. Worcestershire	1911	107 *	v. Middlesex	1913

G BOYCOTT (103)

145	v. Lancashire	1963	139	v. Nottinghamshire	1975
113	v. Lancashire	1963	201 *	v. Middlesex	1975
165 *	v. Leicestershire	1963	105 *	v. Lancashire	1975
151	v. Middlesex	1964	161 *	v. Gloucestershire	1976
131	v. Lancashire	1964	207 *	v. Cambridge University	1976
151 *	v. Leicestershire	1964	141	v. Nottinghamshire	1976
122	v. Australians	1964	156 *	v. Glamorgan	1976
177	v. Gloucestershire	1964	103 *	v. Lancashire	1976
123	v. MCC	1966	139 *	v. Somerset	1977
136 *	v. Warwickshire	1966	103	v. Australians	1977
103	v. Nottinghamshire	1966	117	v. Middlesex	1977
105	v. Nottinghamshire	1966	154	v. Nottinghamshire	1977
164	v. Sussex	1966	104	v. Warwickshire	1977
102	v. Glamorgan	1967	115	v. Warwickshire	1978
220 *	v. Northamptonshire	1967	113	v. Northamptonshire	1978
128	v. Pakistanis	1967	103 *	v. New Zealanders	1978
114 *	v. Leicestershire	1968	118	v. Glamorgan	1978
125	v. Gloucestershire	1968	129	v. Nottinghamshire	1978
180 *	v. Warwickshire	1968	151 *	v. Derbyshire	1979
132	v. Leicestershire	1968	130 *	v. Somerset	1979
100	v. Sussex	1968	167	v. Derbyshire	1979
102 *	v. MCC	1968	175 *	v. Nottinghamshire	1979
105 *	v. Somerset	1969	135	v. Lancashire	1980
148	v. Kent	1970	154 *	v. Derbyshire	1980
260 *	v. Essex	1970	124	v. Nottinghamshire	1981
110	v. Warwickshire	1971	122 *	v. Derbyshire	1981
112 *	v. Middlesex	1971	138	v. Northamptonshire	1982
169	v. Nottinghamshire	1971	134	v. Glamorgan	1982
233	v. Essex	1971	159	v. Worcestershire	1982
182 *	v. Middlesex	1971	152 *	v. Warwickshire	1982
133	v. Derbyshire	1971	122 *	v. Sussex	1982
169	v. Lancashire	1971	129	v. Somerset	1982
151	v. Leicestershire	1971	112 *	v. Derbyshire	1983
111	v. Hampshire	1971	101	v. Kent	1983
138 *	v. Warwickshire	1971	214 *	v. Nottinghamshire	1983
124 *	v. Northamptonshire	1971	140	v. Gloucestershire	1983
122 *	v. Somerset	1972	163	v. Nottinghamshire	1983
100	v. Northamptonshire	1972	141 *	v. Nottinghamshire	1983
121	v. Essex	1972	169 *	v. Derbyshire	1983
105	v. Lancashire	1972	104 *	v. Kent	1984
204 *	v. Leicestershire	1972	153 *	v. Derbyshire	1984
105	v. Hampshire	1972	126 *	v. Gloucestershire	1984
141 *	v. Cambridge University	1973	101 *	v. Glamorgan	1984
101	v. Lancashire	1973	114 *	v. Somerset	1985
129	v. Nottinghamshire	1973	115	v. Hampshire	1985
140	v. Cambridge University	1974	105 *	v. Worcestershire	1985
149 *	v. Derbyshire	1974	184	v. Worcestershire	1985
117	v. Sussex	1974	103 *	v. Warwickshire	1985
142 *	v. Surrey	1974	125 *	v. Nottinghamshire	1985
152 *	v. Worcestershire	1975	127	v. Leicestershire	1986
141	v. Gloucestershire	1975	135	v. Surrey	1986
175 *	v. Middlesex	1975			

T T BRESNAN (5)

116	v. Surrey	2007	169 *	v. Durham	2015
101 *	v. Warwickshire	2007	142 *	v. Middlesex	2016
100 *	v. Somerset	2015			

H C BROOK (2)

124	v. Essex	2018	101	v. Somerset	2019

J A BROOKS (1)

109 *	v. Lancashire	2017

G L BROPHY (3)

100 *	v. Hampshire	2007	177 *	v. Worcestershire	2011
103	Warwickshire	2010			

J T BROWN (23)

141	v. Liverpool & Districts	1894	150	v. Sussex	1898
100	v. Gloucestershire	1894	100	v. M C C	1898
168 *	v. Sussex	1895	168	v. Cambridge University	1899
203	v. Middlesex	1896	192	v. Derbyshire	1899
107	v. Nottinghamshire	1896	167	v. Australians	1899
131	v. Leicestershire	1896	129	v. Cambridge University	1900
120	v. Hampshire	1896	128	v. Leicestershire	1900
119	v. Nottinghamshire	1897	121	v. Warwickshire	1901
311	v. Sussex	1897	134 *	v. Warwickshire	1901
107	v. Somerset	1897	110	v. Hampshire	1901
144	v. Lancashire	1898	125	v. Gloucestershire	1903
300	v. Derbyshire	1898			

D C F BURTON (2)

142 *	v. Hampshire	1919	110	v. Leicestershire	1921

D BYAS (28)

112	v. Gloucestershire	1988	213	v. Worcestershire	1995
117	v. Kent	1989	143 *	v. Mashonaland	1996
101	v. Oxford University	1991	138	v. Hampshire	1996
135	v. Derbyshire	1991	126 *	v. Oxford University	1997
153	v. Nottinghamshire	1991	103 *	v. Somerset	1997
122 *	v. Leicestershire	1991	128	v. Nottinghamshire	1997
120	v. Lancashire	1991	101	v. Somerset	1998
100	v. Northamptonshire	1992	103	v. Derbyshire	1998
156	v. Essex	1993	116	v. Leicestershire	1998
102	v. Somerset	1994	101	v. Lancashire	1998
104	v. Lancashire	1994	105 *	v. Glamorgan	2001
181	v. Cambridge University	1995	110 *	v. Northamptonshire	2001
193	v. Lancashire	1995	100	v. Leicestershire	2001
108	v. Gloucestershire	1995	104	v. Glamorgan	2001

P CARRICK (3)

105	v. Lancashire	1978	131 *	v. Northamptonshire	1980
128 *	v. Gloucestershire	1979			

D B CLOSE (33)

123 *	v. Pakistanis	1954	103	v. Sussex	1957
164	v. Combined Services	1954	120	v. Glamorgan	1958
114	v. Cambridge University	1955	144	v. Oxford University	1959
143	v. Somerset	1955	154	v. Nottinghamshire	1959
108	v. Derbyshire	1957	128	v. Lancashire	1959
120	v. Derbyshire	1957	128	v. Somerset	1959

CENTURIES BY ALL PLAYERS 1863-2020 *(Continued)*

D B CLOSE *(Continued)*

102	v. Hampshire	1960	198	v. Surrey	1960
184	v. Nottinghamshire	1960	132	v. Surrey	1961
111	v. Lancashire	1961	103	v. Glamorgan	1961
103	v. Somerset	1961	100	v. Cambridge University	1961
121 *	v. Somerset	1962	140 *	v. Warwickshire	1962
142 *	v. Essex	1962	161	v. Northamptonshire	1963
100 *	v. Surrey	1964	115	v. New Zealanders	1965
117 *	v. South Africans	1965	101 *	v. Surrey	1965
103	v. Cambridge University	1966	105	v. Gloucestershire	1966
115 *	v. Nottinghamshire	1966	146	v. New Zealanders	1969
128	v. Northamptonshire	1969			

A J DALTON (3)

111	v. Oxford University	1971	128	v. Middlesex	1972
119 *	v. Worcestershire	1971			

K R DAVIDSON (2)

101 *	v. MCC	1934	128	v. Kent	1934

D DENTON (61)

113	v. Derbyshire	1896	121	v. MCC	1908
112	v. Somerset	1897	140	v. Warwickshire	1909
141 *	v. Warwickshire	1897	129	v. Leicestershire	1909
110	v. Leicestershire	1899	106	v. Australians	1909
113	v. Middlesex	1899	184	v. Nottinghamshire	1909
101 *	v. Lancashire	1899	130	v. Derbyshire	1909
132	v. C J Thornton's XI	1901	182	v. Derbyshire	1910
127	v. Essex	1902	113	v. Derbyshire	1911
108 *	v. Lancashire	1902	120	v. Somerset	1911
101	v. Cambridge University	1903	137 *	v. Leicestershire	1911
133	v. Leicestershire	1903	118	v. All Indians	1911
104	v. Surrey	1903	101 *	v. Nottinghamshire	1911
105	v. Surrey	1904	101 *	v. Lancashire	1911
111	v. Somerset	1904	107	v. Hampshire	1912
119	v. South Africans	1904	200 *	v. Warwickshire	1912
165	v. Hampshire	1905	182	v. Gloucestershire	1912
172	v. Gloucestershire	1905	221	v. Kent	1912
133 *	v. Hampshire	1905	111	v. Northamptonshire	1912
134	v. Essex	1905	191	v. Hampshire	1912
107	v. Somerset	1905	148	v. Nottinghamshire	1913
132	v. Warwickshire	1905	114	v. An England XI	1913
102	v. Middlesex	1905	168 *	v. Hampshire	1914
153 *	v. Australians	1905	129	v. Middlesex	1914
108	v. Leicestershire	1906	124	v. Sussex	1914
127	v. Middlesex	1906	110	v. Leicestershire	1919
107	v. Nottinghamshire	1906	122	v. Gloucestershire	1919
109 *	v. Nottinghamshire	1906	120	v. Middlesex	1919
112 *	v. West Indians	1906	114	v. Kent	1919
149	v. Gents of Ireland	1907	209 *	v. Worcestershire	1920
110 .	v. Northamptonshire	1908	145	v. Kent	1920
133	v. MCC	1908			

A DRAKE (3)

147 *	v. Derbyshire	1911	108	v. Cambridge University	1913
115	v. Sussex	1911			

M T G ELLIOTT (1)

127	v. Warwickshire	2002			

T EMMETT (1)

104	v. Gloucestershire	1873

G M FELLOWS (1)

108	v. Lancashire	2002

A J FINCH (1)

110	v. Warwickshire	2014

W A R FRAINE (1)

106	v. Surrey	2019

A W GALE (19)

149	v. Warwickshire	2006	101 *	v. Durham	2011
138	v. Hampshire	2008	272	v. Nottinghamshire	2013
150	v. Surrey	2008	103	v. Middlesex	2013
136	v. Lancashire	2008	148	v. Surrey	2013
101	v. Worcestershire	2009	124	v. Durham	2014
121	v. Lancashire	2009	126 *	v. Middlesex	2014
101	v. Somerset	2010	148	v. Nottinghamshire	2015
135	v. Essex	2010	164	v. Worcestershire	2015
151 *	v. Nottinghamshire	2010	125	v. Hampshire	2015
145 *	v. Nottinghamshire	2011			

P A GIBB (2)

157 *	v. Nottinghamshire	1935	104	v. Warwickshire	1946

J N GILLESPIE (1)

123 *	v. Surrey	2007

D GOUGH (1)

121	v. Warwickshire	1996

A K D GRAY (1)

104	v. Somerset	2003

A P GRAYSON (1)

100	v. Worcestershire	1994

F E GREENWOOD (1)

104 *	v. Glamorgan	1929

I GRIMSHAW (4)

115	v. Cambridge University	1884	114	v. Nottinghamshire	1885
129 *	v. Cambridge University	1885	122	v. Derbyshire	1886

S HAIGH (4)

159	v. Nottinghamshire	1901	104	v. Derbyshire	1904
129 *	v. Warwickshire	1904	111	v. All Indians	1911

L HALL (9)

124 *	v. Sussex	1883	160	v. Lancashire	1887
116	v. Cambridge University	1884	110	v. Kent	1887
100	v. Kent	1884	119 *	v. Gloucestershire	1887
128 *	v. Sussex	1884	129 *	v. Gloucestershire	1888
135	v. Middlesex	1884			

H HALLIDAY (12))

130	v. Gloucestershire	1948	120	v. Somerset	1951
105 *	v. Surrey	1948	126 *	v. Oxford University	1952
116	v. Northamptonshire	1948	118	v. Gloucestershire	1952
102	v. Worcestershire	1948	105	v. Gloucestershire	1953
113	v. Cambridge University	1949	108	v. Nottinghamshire	1953
144	v. Derbyshire	1950	100	v. Kent	1953

G M HAMILTON (1)

125	v. Hampshire	2000

J H HAMPSHIRE (34)

120 *	v. Surrey	1963	158	v. Gloucestershire	1974
150	v. Leicestershire	1964	106 *	v. Gloucestershire	1975
110	v. Hampshire	1964	115	v. Somerset	1975
105 *	v. Surrey	1965	127	v. Surrey	1975
110 *	v. Lancashire	1965	155 *	v. Gloucestershire	1976
149 *	v. MCC	1965	133	v. Surrey	1976
107	v. MCC	1967	113	v. Sussex	1976
102	v. Warwickshire	1967	100 *	v. Derbyshire	1977
100	v. Derbyshire	1968	124	v. Nottinghamshire	1978
107	v. Leicestershire	1970	109	v. Northamptonshire	1978
120 *	v. Derbyshire	1970	132	v. Warwickshire	1978
116 *	v. Oxford University	1971	124	v. Somerset	1980
183 *	v. Sussex	1971	101 *	v. Warwickshire	1980
105 *	v. Gloucestershire	1971	112	v. Leicestershire	1981
111	v. Glamorgan	1972	127	v. Surrey	1981
103	v. Middlesex	1972	118 *	v. Hampshire	1981
157 *	v. Nottinghamshire	1974	120	v. Northamptonshire	1981

P S P HANDSCOMB (1))

101 *	v. Lancashire	2017

W E HARBORD (1)

109	v. Oxford University	1930

P J HARTLEY (2)

127 *	v. Lancashire	1988	102	v. Gloucestershire	1993

S N HARTLEY (4)

106	v. Nottinghamshire	1981	104 *	v. Gloucestershire	1984
114	v. Gloucestershire	1982	108 *	v. Oxford University	1985

I J HARVEY (2)

209 *	v. Somerset	2005	103	v. Derbyshire	2005

LORD HAWKE (10)

144	v. Sussex	1886	107 *	v. Kent	1898
125	v. Lancashire	1887	134	v. Warwickshire	1898
126	v. Somerset	1891	127	v. Hampshire	1899
166	v. Warwickshire	1896	126	v. Surrey	1902
110 *	v. Kent	1896	100 *	v. Leicestershire	1904

G H HIRST (56)

115 *	v. Gloucestershire	1894	138	v. Nottinghamshire	1899
107	v. Leicestershire	1896	106	v. Somerset	1900
134	v. Gloucestershire	1897	155	v. Nottinghamshire	1900
130 *	v. Surrey	1898	111	v. Gloucestershire	1900
186	v. Surrey	1899	108	v. Gloucestershire	1900
131	v. Hampshire	1899	214	v. Worcestershire	1901

G H HIRST *(Continued)*

125	v. Nottinghamshire	1901	169	v. Oxford University	1906
134	v. Essex	1902	122	v. Sussex	1906
112 *	v. Lancashire	1902	111	v. Somerset	1906
123	v. Worcestershire	1903	117 *	v. Somerset	1906
120	v. Kent	1903	128 *	v. Derbyshire	1908
142	v. Somerset	1903	140	v. Northamptonshire	1909
153	v. Leicestershire	1903	158	v. Cambridge University	1910
102	v. Cambridge University	1904	137	v. Middlesex	1910
153	v. Oxford University	1904	103	v. Warwickshire	1910
152	v. Hampshire	1904	100	v. Worcestershire	1911
157	v. Kent	1904	156	v. Lancashire	1911
108	v. Surrey	1904	218	v. Sussex	1911
103	v. Middlesex	1904	109	v. Worcestershire	1912
140	v. Essex	1904	102 *	v. Kent	1913
121	v. Sussex	1904	112 *	v. Surrey	1913
108 *	v. Somerset	1905	166 *	v. Sussex	1913
341	v. Leicestershire	1905	146	v. Hampshire	1914
113 *	v. Cambridge University	1905	105 *	v. Northamptonshire	1914
103 *	v. Sussex	1905	107	v. Somerset	1914
232 *	v. Surrey	1905	180 *	v. MCC	1919
101	v. Kent	1906	120	v. Essex	1919
104	v. Warwickshire	1906	120	v. Warwickshire	1919

P HOLMES (60)

100	v. Nottinghamshire	1919	194	v. Leicestershire	1925
133	v. Northamptonshire	1919	159	v. Hampshire	1925
123	v. Lancashire	1919	134	v. MCC	1925
140	v. Leicestershire	1919	128	v. Middlesex	1926
133	v. Middlesex	1919	108	v. Hampshire	1926
149	v. Middlesex	1920	143	v. Lancashire	1926
141	v. Essex	1920	127 *	v. Surrey	1926
104	v. Derbyshire	1920	180	v. Gloucestershire	1927
145 *	v. Northamptonshire	1920	107	v. Glamorgan	1927
126	v. Lancashire	1920	126	v. Somerset	1927
111 *	v. Lancashire	1920	175 *	v. New Zealanders	1927
302 *	v. Hampshire	1920	275	v. Warwickshire	1928
150	v. Derbyshire	1921	179 *	v. Middlesex	1928
277 *	v. Northamptonshire	1921	136	v. Essex	1928
132	v. Lancashire	1921	110	v. Leicestershire	1928
138	v. Glamorgan	1922	105	v. Middlesex	1928
209	v. Warwickshire	1922	101 *	v. Nottinghamshire	1928
129	v. Middlesex	1922	110 *	v. Northamptonshire	1929
107	v. Kent	1922	285	v. Nottinghamshire	1929
220 *	v. Warwickshire	1922	100	v. Derbyshire	1929
126 *	v. Cambridge University	1923	142	v. Surrey	1929
199	v. Somerset	1923	107 *	v. Oxford University	1930
122 *	v. Gloucestershire	1923	102	v. Somerset	1930
118 *	v. Glamorgan	1924	132 *	v. Gloucestershire	1930
112	v. Northamptonshire	1924	130	v. Glamorgan	1930
107	v. Derbyshire	1924	250	v. Warwickshire	1931
105 *	v. Kent	1924	133	v. Nottinghamshire	1931
124	v. Derbyshire	1925	125	v. Leicestershire	1931
315 *	v. Middlesex	1925	110	v. Oxford University	1932
130	v. Glamorgan	1925	224 *	v. Essex	1932

CENTURIES BY ALL PLAYERS 1863-2020 *(Continued)*

L HUTTON (85)

196	v. Worcestershire	1934	103	v. Essex	1948
131	v. Warwickshire	1935	104	v. Lancashire	1948
163	v. Surrey	1936	144 *	v. Essex	1948
101	v. Worcestershire	1937	155	v. Essex	1948
136	v. Kent	1937	107 *	v. MCC	1948
271 *	v. Derbyshire	1937	167	v. New Zealanders	1949
153	v. Leicestershire	1937	104	v. Northamptonshire	1949
124	v. Essex	1937	201	v. Lancashire	1949
161	v. MCC	1937	113	v. Middlesex	1949
135	v. New Zealanders	1937	165	v. Sussex	1949
121	v. Middlesex	1937	100	v. Sussex	1949
107	v. Sussex	1938	146 *	v. Scotland	1949
180	v. Cambridge University	1938	269 *	v. Northamptonshire	1949
141	v. Oxford University	1938	147	v. MCC	1949
106 *	v. MCC	1938	141	v. Somerset	1950
102	v. Cambridge University	1939	107	v. Derbyshire	1950
158	v. Warwickshire	1939	156	v. Essex	1950
280 *	v. Hampshire	1939	153	v. Nottinghamshire	1950
144	v. Glamorgan	1939	104	v. West Indians	1950
151	v. Surrey	1939	141	v. Essex	1951
177	v. Sussex	1939	117	v. Middlesex	1951
105 *	v. Lancashire	1939	151	v. Surrey +	1951
109	v. Worcestershire	1939	194 *	v. Nottinghamshire	1951
100	v. Kent	1939	110 *	v. Gloucestershire	1951
103	v. Sussex	1939	156	v. South Africans	1951
111	v. Leicestershire	1946	119	v. Somerset	1952
101	v. Surrey	1946	152	v. Lancashire	1952
171 *	v. Northamptonshire	1946	108	v. Gloucestershire	1952
183 *	v. Indians	1946	132	v. Middlesex	1952
197	v. Glamorgan	1947	189	v. Kent	1952
106	v. Sussex	1947	104	v. Surrey	1952
137	v. Leicestershire	1947	120	v. Kent	1952
197	v. Essex	1947	103	v. MCC	1952
104	v. Essex	1947	137	v. MCC	1952
270 *	v. Hampshire	1947	178	v. Somerset	1953
103	v. Oxford University	1947	100	v. Worcestershire	1953
120 *	v. Cambridge University	1947	100 *	v. Kent	1953
137	v. South Africans	1947	125	v. Warwickshire	1953
107	v. MCC	1947	103 *	v. MCC	1953
100 *	v. Northamptonshire	1948	163	v. Combined Services	1953
100	v. Lancashire	1948	149 *	v. Nottinghamshire	1954
176 *	v. Sussex	1948	194	v. Nottinghamshire	1954
133	v. Middlesex	1948			

+ 100th century in First Class cricket

R A HUTTON (4)

104	v. Derbyshire	1970	189	v. Pakistanis	1971
101	v. Oxford University	1971	102 *	v. Somerset	1974

R IDDISON (1)

112	v. Cambridge University	1869

CENTURIES BY ALL PLAYERS 1863-2020 *(Continued)*

R ILLINGWORTH (14)

146 *	v. Essex	1953	107	v. Warwickshire	1962
116	v. Essex	1955	127	v. Surrey	1962
138	v. MCC	1955	115	v. Hampshire	1962
150	v. Essex	1959	107 *	v. Warwickshire	1963
162	v. Indians	1959	135	v. Kent	1964
122	v. Sussex	1959	103	v. MCC	1964
105 *	v. MCC	1959	100 *	v. Leicestershire	1968

Hon F S JACKSON (21)

111 *	v. MCC	1893	139	v. Somerset	1898
145	v. Nottinghamshire	1894	160	v. Gloucestershire	1898
131	v. Sussex	1894	133	v. Cambridge University	1899
117	v. Warwickshire	1896	155	v. Middlesex	1899
115	v. Middlesex	1896	114	v. Nottinghamshire	1899
102	v. Sussex	1896	101	v. C J Thornton's XI	1899
124	v. Somerset	1897	101 *	v. Essex	1902
101	v. Middlesex	1898	158	v. Surrey	1904
133	v. Middlesex	1898	110 *	v. Sussex	1904
147	v. Leicestershire	1898	111	v. Derbyshire	1905
134 *	v. Lancashire	1898			

P A JAQUES (7)

115	v. Essex	2004	219	v. Derbyshire	2005
243	v. Hampshire	2004	106	v. Somerset	2005
173	v. Glamorgan	2004	172	v. Durham	2005
176	v. Northamptonshire	2005			

C JOHNSON (2)

107	v. Somerset	1973	102	v. Gloucestershire	1976

W G KEIGHLEY (1)

110	v. Surrey	1951

S A KELLETT (2)

109 *	v. Sri Lankans	1991	125 *	v. Derbyshire	1991

R A KETTLEBOROUGH (1)

108	v. Essex	1996

N KILNER (2)

112	v. Lancashire	1921	102 *	v. Gloucestershire	1923

R KILNER (15)

104	v. Leicestershire	1913	166	v. Northamptonshire	1921
169	v. Gloucestershire	1914	150	v. Northamptonshire	1921
112	v. Gloucestershire	1919	117	v. Worcestershire	1922
120	v. MCC	1919	124	v. Northamptonshire	1922
115 *	v. Gloucestershire	1919	124	v. Warwickshire	1925
206 *	v. Derbyshire	1920	100 *	v. MCC	1925
121	v. Warwickshire	1920	150	v. Middlesex	1926
137	Nottinghamshire	1920			

T KOHLER-CADMORE (5)

106	v. Nottinghamshire	2018	102	v. Somerset	2019
105 *	v. Lancashire	2018	165 *	v. Warwickshire	2019
176	v. Leeds/Bradford MCCU	2019			

B LEADBEATER (1)

140 *	v. Hampshire	1976

CENTURIES BY ALL PLAYERS 1863-2020 *(Continued*

J A LEANING (4)

116	v. Nottinghamshire	2015	110	v. Nottinghamshire	2015
123	v. Somerset	2015	118	v. Lancashire	2017

F LEE (3)

101	v.Nottinghamshire	1885	119	v. Kent	1887
165	v. Lancashire	1887			

A Z LEES (11)

121	v. Leeds/Bradford MCCU	2013	107	v. Nottinghamshire	2016
100	v. Middlesex	2013	114 *	v. Lancashire	2016
275 *	v. Derbyshire	2013	132	v. Durham	2016
108	v. Northamptonshire	2014	100	v. Leeds/Bradford MCCU	2017
108	v. Durham	2014	102	v. Surrey	2017
100	v. Nottinghamshire	2015			

D S LEHMANN (26)

177	v. Somerset	1997	252	v. Lancashire	2001
100	v. Surrey	1997	106 *	v. Surrey	2001
163 *	v. Leicestershire	1997	193	v. Leicestershire	2001
182	v. Hampshire	1997	119 *	v. Leicestershire	2002
136	v. Kent	1998	216	v. Sussex	2002
131	v. Nottinghamshire	1998	187	v. Lancashire	2002
200	v. Worcestershire	1998	120	v. Durham	2004
133	v. Derbyshire	2000	150	v. Warwickshire	2006
136	v. Durham	2000	193	v. Kent	2006
115	v. Leicestershire	2000	130 *	v. Sussex	2006
116	v. Kent	2000	130	v. Lancashire	2006
187 *	v. Somerset	2001	172	v. Kent	2006
104	v. Leicestershire	2001	339	v. Durham	2006

J S LEHMANN (1)

116	v. Somerset	2016	

E I LESTER (24)

127	v. Derbyshire	1947	130 *	v. Leicestershire	1952
142	v. Northamptonshire	1947	101 *	v. Nottinghamshire	1952
126	v. Nottinghamshire	1947	178	v. Nottinghamshire	1952
149	v. Oxford University	1948	110 *	v. Indians	1952
110	v. Gloucestershire	1948	109	v. Hampshire	1952
125 *	v. Lancashire	1948	130 *	v. Surrey	1952
132	v. Lancashire	1948	157	v. Cambridge University	1953
112	v. Sussex	1949	103 *	v. Surrey	1953
102	v. Essex	1949	150	v. Oxford University	1954
140 *	v. Derbyshire	1949	121 *	v. Derbyshire	1954
186	v. Warwickshire	1949	163	v. Essex	1954
118	v. Nottinghamshire	1951	142	v. Surrey	1954

M LEYLAND (62)

133 *	v. Lancashire	1924	118	v. New Zealanders	1927
199 *	v. Hampshire	1924	204 *	v. Middlesex	1927
138	v. Worcestershire	1925	127	v. Essex	1927
110	v. Middlesex	1925	247	v. Worcestershire	1928
131 *	v. Glamorgan	1925	89 *	v. Glamorgan	1928
133	v. Surrey	1926	149	v. Derbyshire	1928
118	v. Hampshire	1926	139	v. Surrey	1928
116	v. Leicestershire	1926	133 *	v. Essex	1928
109	v. Warwickshire	1926	134	v. Essex	1929
191	v. Glamorgan	1926	104	v. Hampshire	1929

CENTURIES BY ALL PLAYERS 1863-2020 *(Continued)*

M LEYLAND *(Continued)*

105	v. Kent	1930	126	v. Glamorgan	1934
211 *	v. Lancashire	1930	125	v. Oxford University	1935
172	v. Middlesex	1930	133 *	v. Rest of England	1935
186	v. Derbyshire	1930	115	v. Jamaica	1936
112	v. Kent	1930	263	v. Essex	1936
124	v. Surrey	1931	163 *	v. Surrey	1936
189	v. Middlesex	1932	107	v. Middlesex	1936
153	v. Leicestershire	1932	113	v. Worcestershire	1936
113	v. Derbyshire	1932	107	v. Surrey	1936
166	v. Leicestershire	1932	141	v. Oxford University	1936
153 *	v. Hampshire	1932	100 *	v. Cambridge University	1936
105	v. Rest of England	1932	167	v. Worcestershire	1937
133	v. Worcestershire	1933	118 *	v. Leicestershire	1937
119	v. Northamptonshire	1933	101	v. Sussex	1937
133	v. Hampshire	1933	100	v. Oxford University	1938
134	v. Nottinghamshire	1933	114	v. Essex	1938
210 *	v. Kent	1933	127	v. Glamorgan	1938
117 *	v. Worcestershire	1933	135	v. Lancashire	1938
133	v. MCC	1933	112	v. Gloucestershire	1939
104 *	v. MCC	1934	180 *	v. Middlesex	1939
100	v. Oxford University	1934	114	v. Surrey	1939

E LOCKWOOD *(6)*

103	v. Surrey	1869	109	v. Surrey	1881
121	v. Surrey	1872	104 *	v. I Zingari	1882
107	v. Gloucestershire	1878	208	v. Kent	1883

J D LOVE *(13)*

163	v. Nottinghamshire	1976	154	v. Lancashire	1981
129	v. Warwickshire	1977	110	v. Derbyshire	1982
107	v. Oxford University	1978	123	v. Surrey	1982
170 *	v. Worcestershire	1979	112	v. Somerset	1984
104	v. Warwickshire	1980	106	v. Oxford University	1985
105 *	v. Lancashire	1980	109	v. Northamptonshire	1986
161	v. Warwickshire	1981			

F A LOWSON *(30)*

104	v. Middlesex	1949	101	v. MCC	1953
112	v. Northamptonshire	1950	115	v. Somerset	1954
112	v. Essex	1950	107	v. Cambridge University	1954
104	v. Hampshire	1950	107	v. Middlesex	1954
103	v. Hampshire	1950	165	v. Sussex	1954
141 *	v. Northamptonshire	1950	164	v. Essex	1954
113	v. Middlesex	1951	150 *	v. Kent	1954
155	v. Kent	1951	116	v. Middlesex	1955
104	v. Oxford University	1951	183 *	v. Oxford University	1956
115	v. South Africans	1951	115	v. Scotland	1956
155	v. Worcestershire	1952	154	v. Somerset	1956
120	v. Lancashire	1952	103 *	v. Nottinghamshire	1956
166	v. Scotland	1953	154	v. Cambridge University	1957
103	v. Surrey	1953	100	v. Glamorgan	1957
259 *	v. Worcestershire	1953	116	v. Middlesex	1957

M J LUMB *(8)*

122	v. Leicestershire	2001	103 *	v. Bangladesh 'A'	2005
124	v. Surrey	2002	130	v. Somerset	2005
115 *	v. Hampshire	2003	144	v. Middlesex	2006
105	v. Durham	2003	105	v. Hampshire	2006

CENTURIES BY ALL PLAYERS 1863-2020 *(Continued)*

R G LUMB (22)

114	v. Lancashire	1973	113	v. Northamptonshire	1979
103	v. Sussex	1973	129 *	v. Northamptonshire	1979
103	v. West Indians	1973	118	v. Warwickshire	1979
123 *	v. Northamptonshire	1974	159	v. Somerset	1979
100	v. Derbyshire	1974	110	v. Essex	1979
101	v. Gloucestershire	1975	118	v. Worcestershire	1980
118	v. Surrey	1975	129	v. Glamorgan	1980
132	v. Gloucestershire	1976	101	v. Gloucestershire	1980
118	v. Essex	1976	145	v. Derbyshire	1981
107	v. Oxford University	1978	165 *	v. Gloucestershire	1984
103	v. Leicestershire	1978	144	v. Glamorgan	1984

A LYTH (23)

132	v. Nottinghamshire	2008	251	v. Lancashire	2014
142	v. Somerset	2010	122	v. Nottinghamshire	2014
133	v. Hampshire	2010	113	v. MCC	2015
100	v. Lancashire	2010	111	v. Hampshire	2016
248 *	v. Leicestershire	2012	106	v. Somerset	2016
111	v. Leeds/Bradford MCCU	2013	202	v. Surrey	2016
105	v. Somerset	2013	114 *	v. Durham	2016
130	v. Leeds/Bradford MCCU	2014	194	v. Leeds/Bradford MCCU	2017
104	v. Durham	2014	100	v. Lancashire	2017
230	v. Northamptonshire	2014	134 *	v. Hampshire	2018
143	v. Durham	2014	103	v. Lancashire	2020
117	v. Middlesex	2014			

G G MACAULAY (3)

125 *	v. Nottinghamshire	1921	108	v. Somerset	1926
101 *	v. Essex	1922			

D J MALAN (1)

219	v. Derbyshire	2020

S E MARSH (1)

125 *	v. Surrey	2017

D R MARTYN (1)

238	v. Gloucestershire	2003

G J MAXWELL (1)

140	v. Durham	2015

A McGRATH (34)

101	v. Kent	1996	173 *	v. Worcestershire	2005
137	v. Hampshire	1996	158	v. Derbyshire	2005
105 *	v. Oxford University	1997	123 *	v. Kent	2006
141	v. Worcestershire	1997	127	v. Hampshire	2006
142 *	v. Middlesex	1999	140 *	v. Durham	2006
133	v. Kent	2000	102	v. Lancashire	2006
116	v. Surrey	2001	100	v. Kent	2007
165	v. Lancashire	2002	188 *	v. Warwickshire	2007
127 *	v. Glamorgan	2003	120	v. Kent	2007
126	v. Durham	2004	144	v. Kent	2008
174	v. Derbyshire	2004	128	v. Somerset	2008
109	v. Derbyshire	2004	120	v. Worcestershire	2009
165 *	v. Leicestershire	2005	211	v. Warwickshire	2009
133 *	v. Durham	2005	105	v. Durham	2010
134	v. Derbyshire	2005	112	v. Essex	2010

CENTURIES BY ALL PLAYERS 1863-2020 *(Continued)*

A McGRATH (Continued)

124 *	v. Durham	2010	115	v. Hampshire	2011
106 *	v. Hampshire	2012	104	v. Derbyshire	2012

A A METCALFE (25)

122	v. Nottinghamshire +	1983	113	v. Glamorgan	1989
109	v. Oxford University	1985	112	v. Warwickshire	1989
108	v. Worcestershire	1986	138	v. Warwickshire	1989
151	v. Northamptonshire	1986	162	v. Gloucestershire	1990
123	v. Kent	1986	102	v. Somerset	1990
108	v. Nottinghamshire	1986	146	v. Lancashire	1990
151	v. Lancashire	1986	150 *	v. Derbyshire	1990
149	v. Glamorgan	1986	194 *	v. Nottinghamshire	1990
113	v. Sussex	1987	107	v. Nottinghamshire	1990
152	v. MCC	1987	113 *	v. Lancashire	1991
115	v. Derbyshire	1988	123	v. Glamorgan	1991
216 *	v. Middlesex	1988	133 *	v. Cambridge University	1993
			100	v. West Indians	1995

+ His first First Class innings

A MITCHELL (39)

189	v. Northamptonshire	1926	150 *	v. Worcestershire	1933
105	v. Leicestershire	1927	158	v. MCC	1933
113	v. Kent	1928	104	v. Glamorgan	1934
105	v. Middlesex	1928	121	v. Lancashire	1934
126	v. South Africans	1929	152	v. Hampshire	1934
122 *	v. Worcestershire	1929	102 *	v. Middlesex	1934
136 *	v. Leicestershire	1930	181	v. Surrey	1934
130 *	v. Somerset	1930	111	v. Northamptonshire	1934
105 *	v. Middlesex	1930	101 *	v. Jamaica	1936
176	v. Nottinghamshire	1930	103	v. Derbyshire	1936
101 *	v. Kent	1930	127	v. MCC	1936
119 *	v. Hampshire	1931	100	v. Leicestershire	1937
134	v. Somerset	1931	105	v. Glamorgan	1937
140	v. Gloucestershire	1932	100	v. Cambridge University	1938
177 *	v. Gloucestershire	1932	133	v. Northamptonshire	1938
102	v. MCC	1932	124	v. Warwickshire	1938
108 *	v. Glamorgan	1933	100	v. Sussex	1938
123	v. Lancashire	1933	136	v. Lancashire	1939
142	v. Worcestershire	1933	102 *	v. Northamptonshire	1939
138	v. Nottinghamshire	1933			

F MITCHELL (10)

100	v. Gloucestershire	1899	106 *	v. Surrey	1901
194	v. Leicestershire	1899	162	v. Warwickshire	1901
121	v. Middlesex	1899	122	v. Leicestershire	1901
100	v. Hampshire	1901	116 *	v. Warwickshire	1901
100	v. Middlesex	1901	106	v. Lancashire	1901

R MOORHOUSE (3)

105	v. MCC	1890	113	v. Somerset	1896
102 *	v. Warwickshire	1895			

M D MOXON (41)

116	v. Essex	1981	108	v. Northamptonshire	1991
111	v. Derbyshire	1981	200	v. Essex	1991
153	v. Lancashire	1983	115	v. Lancashire	1991
110	v. Kent	1984	141	v. Surrey	1992
126 *	v. Worcestershire	1984	112	v. Somerset	1992
153	v. Somerset	1985	183	v. Gloucestershire	1992
168	v. Worcestershire	1985	103	v. Glamorgan	1992
127	v. Lancashire	1985	101 *	v. Northamptonshire	1992
123	v. Indians	1986	171 *	v. Kent	1993
112 *	v. Indians	1986	161 *	v. Lancashire	1994
147	v. Lancashire	1986	122	v. Kent	1994
105	v. Windward Islands	1987	116	v. Warwickshire	1994
130	v. Derbyshire	1987	274 *	v. Worcestershire	1994
104	v. Essex	1987	130	v. Cambridge University	1995
106	v. Worcestershire	1988	203 *	v. Kent	1995
132	v. Sri Lankans	1988	104	v. Middlesex	1995
191	v. Northamptonshire	1988	134	v. Matabeleland	1996
162 *	v. Surrey	1989	213	v. Glamorgan	1996
130	v. Zimbabweans	1990	131	v. Warwickshire	1996
123	v. Nottinghamshire	1990	155	v. Pakistan 'A'	1996
218 *	v. Sussex	1990			

J T NEWSTEAD (1)

100 *	v. Nottinghamshire	1908

C M OLD (5)

116	v. Indians	1974	107	v. Warwickshire $	1977
115 *	v. Leicestershire	1975	100 *	v. Lancashire	1978
112	v. Northamptonshire	1976			

$ Third fastest century in First Class cricket — made in 37 minutes

E OLDROYD (37)

125	v. Warwickshire	1921	110	v. Northamptonshire	1927
103	v. Hampshire	1921	111	v. Somerset	1927
127 *	v. Gloucestershire	1921	162 *	v. Glamorgan	1928
144	v. Surrey	1921	124	v. Surrey	1928
151 *	v. Glamorgan	1922	119	v. Nottinghamshire	1928
121	v. Worcestershire	1922	119	v. Worcestershire	1928
138 *	v. Warwickshire	1922	112	v. Essex	1928
143	v. Glamorgan	1922	108	v. Middlesex	1928
128	v. Leicestershire	1922	101	v. Leicestershire	1928
194	v. Worcestershire	1923	111	v. Cambridge University	1929
138	v. Sussex	1924	147	v. MCC	1929
122 *	v. Hampshire	1924	168	v. Glamorgan	1929
103	v. Surrey	1924	143	v. An England XI	1929
109 *	v. Northamptonshire	1925	100 *	v. Hampshire	1929
104	v. Warwickshire	1926	140	v. Surrey	1929
135	v. Sussex	1926	143 *	v. Essex	1930
109	v. Hampshire	1926	164	v. Somerset	1930
114	v. Cambridge University	1927	127	v. Gloucestershire	1930
110	v. Gloucestershire	1927			

CENTURIES BY ALL PLAYERS 1863-2020 *(Continued)*

D E V PADGETT (29)

115	v. Warwickshire	1955	107 *	v. Oxford University	1962
107	v. Scotland	1956	115 *	v. Gloucestershire	1962
161 *	v. Oxford University	1959	125 *	v. Surrey	1962
100	v. Lancashire	1959	101	v. Kent	1963
122	v. Somerset	1959	142	v. Derbyshire	1963
139 *	v. Nottinghamshire	1959	112	v. Derbyshire	1964
130	v. Somerset	1960	110	v. Nottinghamshire	1964
146	v. Sussex	1960	111	v. Middlesex	1967
117	v. Surrey	1960	139	v. Nottinghamshire	1967
120	v. Northamptonshire	1960	136 *	v. Middlesex	1968
113	v. Warwickshire	1960	105	v. Lancashire	1968
114	v. Nottinghamshire	1961	106	v. Hampshire	1970
112 *	v. Northamptonshire	1961	108	v. Nottinghamshire	1970
106	v. Nottinghamshire	1961	133	v. Glamorgan	1971
101	v. Somerset	1961			

B PARKER (2)

127	v. Surrey	1994	138 *	v. Oxford University	1997

R PEEL (6)

158	v. Middlesex	1889	111	v. Sussex	1896
128	v. Sussex	1891	106	v. Sussex	1896
210 *	v. Warwickshire	1896	115	v. Leicestershire	1897

L E PLUNKETT (1)

126	v. Hampshire	2016

C A PUJARA ((1)

133 *	v. Hampshire	2015

R M PYRAH (3)

106	v. Loughborough UCCE	2007	117	v. Lancashire	2011
134 *	v. Loughborough UCCE	2007			

A U RASHID (10)

108	v. Worcestershire	2007	180	v. Somerset	2013
111	v. Sussex	2008	110 *	v. Warwickshire	2013
117 *	v. Hampshire	2009	103	v. Somerset	2013
157 *	v. Lancashire	2009		*(2013 consecutive innings)*	
108	v. Somerset	2014	127	v. Durham	2015
159 *	v. Lancashire	2014			

W RHODES (46)

105	v. MCC	1901	199	v. Sussex	1909
107	v. Surrey	1904	101	v. MCC	1909
196	v. Worcestershire	1904	111	v. Sussex	1910
201	v. Somerset	1905	100	v. Derbyshire	1911
108	v. Somerset	1905	125	v. Sussex	1911
119	v. Leicestershire	1906	128	v. MCC	1911
115 *	v. Somerset	1906	115	v. MCC	1911
109	v. MCC	1906	107	v. Lancashire	1912
112	v. Leicestershire	1907	176	v. Nottinghamshire	1912
140	v. Northamptonshire	1908	110	v. Gloucestershire	1913
122	v. Leicestershire	1908	102	v. Cambridge University	1913
146	v. Worcestershire	1908	110	v. Northamptonshire	1913
114	v. Essex	1909	152	v. Leicestershire	1913
101	v. Kent	1909	105 *	v. Lancashire	1914
108	v. Australians	1909	113	v. Sussex	1914

W RHODES *(Continued)*

135	v. Hampshire	1919	106	v. Hampshire	1922
167 *	v. Nottinghamshire	1920	126	v. Middlesex	1923
267 *	v. Leicestershire	1921	102	v. Essex	1923
104 *	v. Northamptonshire	1921	100	v. Somerset	1924
102 *	v. Essex	1921	157	v. Derbyshire	1925
110	v. Glamorgan	1922	114 *	v. Somerset	1925
108 *	v. Essex	1922	132	v. Essex	1926
105	v. Middlesex	1922	100 *	v. Worcestershire	1928

R B RICHARDSON (1)

112	v. Warwickshire	1993

E ROBINSON (7)

100	v. Derbyshire	1921	108 *	v. Glamorgan	1925
115	v. Sussex	1921	124 *	v. Glamorgan	1926
135 *	v. Leicestershire	1921	108	v. Hampshire	1930
112 *	v. Northamptonshire	1925			

P E ROBINSON (7)

104 *	v. Kent	1986	150 *	v. Derbyshire	1990
129 *	v. Nottinghamshire	1988	100	v. Sri Lankans	1991
147	v. Kent	1989	189	v. Lancashire	1991
117	v. Lancashire	1989			

J E ROOT (7)

160	v. Sussex	2011	236	v. Derbyshire	2013
222 *	v. Hampshire	2012	213	v. Surrey	2016
125	v. Northamptonshire	2012	130 *	v. Nottinghamshire	2019
182	v. Durham	2013			

J W ROTHERY (3)

118	v. Hampshire	1905	134	v. Derbyshire	1910
161	v. Kent	1908			

J ROWBOTTOM (3)

101	v. Surrey	1869	113	v. Surrey	1873
100	v. Nottinghamshire	1869			

J A RUDOLPH (18)

122	v. Surrey	2007	198	v. Worcestershire	2009
129 *	v. Worcestershire	2007	191	v. Somerset	2009
111	v. Durham	2007	127	v. Lancashire	2009
220	v. Warwickshire	2007	149	v. Nottinghamshire	2009
104 *	v. Nottinghamshire	2008	228 *	v. Durham	2010
121	v. Surrey	2008	106	v. Essex	2010
155	v. Somerset	2008	141	v. Nottinghamshire	2010
129	v. Kent	2008	100	v. Durham	2010
146	v. Kent	2008	120	v. Sussex	2011

H RUDSTON (1)

164	v. Leicestershire	1904

J J SAYERS (9)

104	v. Leicestershire	2005	187	v. Kent	2007
115	v. Bangladesh 'A'	2005	173	v. Warwickshire	2009
122 *	v. Middlesex	2006	152	v. Somerset	2009
149 *	v. Durham	2007	139	v. Durham MCCU	2011
123	v. Worcestershire	2007			

A SELLERS (2)

105	v. Middlesex	1893	103	v. Somerset 1893

A B SELLERS (4)

104	v. Australians	1934	109	v. Kent 1937
204	v. Cambridge University	1936	103 *	v. Nottinghamshire 1937

K SHARP (11)

100 *	v. Middlesex	1980	132	v. Glamorgan 1984
116	v. Sri Lankans	1981	173	v. Derbyshire 1984
115	v. Indians	1982	181	v. Gloucestershire 1986
121	v. Gloucestershire	1983	114 *	v. Warwickshire 1986
139	v. Surrey	1983	128	v. Sri Lankans 1988
104	v. Derbyshire	1984		

P J SHARPE (23)

141	v. Somerset	1958	100	v. Warwickshire 1965
203 *	v. Cambridge University	1960	197	v. Pakistanis 1967
152	v. Kent	1960	143 *	v. Nottinghamshire 1968
108 *	v. Lancashire	1962	125	v. Surrey 1968
104	v. Nottinghamshire	1962	114	v. Glamorgan 1968
138	v. Somerset	1962	101	v. MCC 1969
132	v. Surrey	1962	108	v. Kent 1970
110	v. Northamptonshire	1962	120	v. Middlesex 1970
112	v. Lancashire	1962	172 *	v. Glamorgan 1971
136 *	v. Pakistanis	1962	133	v. Somerset 1973
138 *	v. Derbyshire	1963	110	v. Derbyshire 1973
106	v. Lancashire	1963		

A SIDEBOTTOM (1)

124	v. Glamorgan	1977

T F SMAILES (3)

109	v. Warwickshire	1937	116	v. Surrey 1938
117	v. Glamorgan	1938		

E SMITH Morley (2)

129	v. Hampshire	1899	116 *	v. Sussex 1900

G A SMITHSON (2)

107 *	v. Surrey	1947	169	v. Leicestershire 1947

G B STEVENSON (2)

111	v. Derbyshire	1980	115 *	v. Warwickshire 1982

W B STOTT (17)

181	v. Essex	1957	116	v. Kent 1960
139	v. Leicestershire	1957	124	v. Hampshire 1960
114	v. Nottinghamshire	1957	186	v. Warwickshire 1960
126	v. Middlesex	1958	116	v. Hampshire 1961
141	v. Sussex	1958	114 *	v. Derbyshire 1961
110	v. Lancashire	1959	100	v. Nottinghamshire 1961
130 *	v. Hampshire	1959	145	v. Derbyshire 1962
144 *	v. Worcestershire	1959	143	v. Lancashire 1963
138 *	v. Sussex	1960		

H SUTCLIFFE (112)

145	v. Northamptonshire	1919	173 *	v. Cambridge University	1931
118	v. Gloucestershire	1919	129	v. Warwickshire	1931
132	v. Lancashire	1919	120 *	v. Middlesex	1931
103	v. Middlesex	1919	107	v. Hampshire	1931
174	v. Kent	1919	230	v. Kent	1931
112	v. Worcestershire	1920	183	v. Somerset	1931
107	v. Nottinghamshire	1920	195	v. Lancashire	1931
125 *	v. Essex	1920	187	v. Leicestershire	1931
131	v. Hampshire	1920	101 *	v. Surrey	1931
114	v. Surrey	1922	109	v. Warwickshire	1932
232	v. Surrey	1922	104 *	v. Hampshire	1932
101 *	v. MCC	1922	153 *	v. Warwickshire	1932
105 *	v. Cambridge University	1923	313	v. Essex	1932
139	v. Somerset	1923	270	v. Sussex	1932
108 *	v. Cambridge University	1924	132	v. Gloucestershire $	1932
255 *	v. Essex	1924	135	v. Lancashire	1932
213	v. Somerset	1924	182	v. Derbyshire	1932
160	v. Sussex	1924	194	v. Essex	1932
108	v. MCC	1924	136	v. Somerset	1932
235	v. Middlesex	1925	112	v. Hampshire	1932
130	v. Warwickshire	1925	122 *	v. Sussex	1932
121	v. Glamorgan	1925	205	v. Warwickshire	1933
206	v. Warwickshire	1925	113	v. Northamptonshire	1933
129	v. Leicestershire	1925	177	v. Middlesex	1933
171	v. MCC	1925	174	v. Leicestershire	1933
124	v. Rest of England	1925	107	v. MCC	1933
102	v. Warwickshire	1926	114 *	v. Rest of England	1933
200	v. Leicestershire	1926	152	v. Cambridge University	1934
131 *	v. Surrey	1926	166	v. Essex	1934
107	v. MCC	1926	203	v. Surrey	1934
109 *	v. MCC	1926	187 *	v. Warwickshire	1934
134	v. Gloucestershire	1927	135	v. Glamorgan	1935
176	v. Surrey	1927	200 *	v. Worcestershire	1935
169	v. Nottinghamshire	1927	110	v. Kent	1935
135	v. Lancashire	1927	100	v. Hampshire	1935
129	v. Essex	1928	121	v. Glamorgan	1935
140	v. Lancashire	1928	135	v. Nottinghamshire	1935
147 *	v. Glamorgan	1928	212	v. Leicestershire	1935
111	v. Derbyshire	1928	138	v. Worcestershire	1935
111	v. Nottinghamshire	1928	129	v. Surrey	1936
100 *	v. Nottinghamshire	1928	202	v. Middlesex	1936
104	v. Middlesex	1928	189	v. Leicestershire	1937
126	v. Lancashire	1928	138	v. Surrey	1937
119	v. Leicestershire	1928	122	v. Lancashire $$	1937
138	v. Derbyshire	1928	109	v. Leicestershire	1937
228	v. Sussex	1928	110	v. Gloucestershire	1938
113	v. South Africans	1929	142	v. Warwickshire	1938
150	v. Northamptonshire	1929	104	v. Northamptonshire	1938
133 *	v. Essex	1929	105	v. Leicestershire	1938
106	v. Lancashire	1929	100	v. Nottinghamshire	1938
123 *	v. Surrey	1929	125 *	v. Oxford University	1939
108	v. Essex	1929	165	v. Lancashire	1939
150 *	v. Essex	1929	116	v. Hampshire	1939
132 *	v. Glamorgan	1930	234 *	v. Leicestershire	1939
173	v. Sussex	1930	175	v. Middlesex	1939
102 *	v. MCC	1930	107 *	v. Northamptonshire	1939

$ 100th First Class century. $$ 100th First Class century for Yorkshire

W H H SUTCLIFFE (6)

171 *	v. Worcestershire	1952	107	v. Kent	1955
181	v. Kent	1952	161 *	v. Glamorgan	1955
105	v. Northamptonshire	1954	133	v. Derbyshire	1955

I G SWALLOW (1)

114	v. MCC	1987

J A TATTERSALL (1)

135 *	v. Leeds/Bradford MCCU	2019

K TAYLOR (16)

168 *	v. Nottinghamshire	1956	141	v. Worcestershire	1961
140 *	v. Nottinghamshire	1957	115	v. Sussex	1961
104	v. Surrey	1958	163	v. Nottinghamshire	1962
103	v. Nottinghamshire	1959	178 *	v. Oxford University	1962
144	v. Derbyshire	1959	153	v. Lancashire	1964
130 *	v. Sussex	1960	160	v. Australians	1964
203 *	v. Warwickshire	1961	106	v. MCC	1966
159	v. Leicestershire	1961	162	v. Worcestershire	1967

T L TAYLOR (8)

147	v. Surrey	1900	106	v. Derbyshire	1902
113	v. Leicestershire	1901	142 *	v. Derbyshire	1902
156	v. Hampshire	1901	114	v. Leicestershire	1902
135 *	v. England X I	1901	120	v. Nottinghamshire	1902

S R TENDULKAR (1)

100	v. Durham	1992

J THEWLIS (1)

108	v. Surrey	1868

F S TRUEMAN (2)

104	v. Northamptonshire	1963	101	v. Middlesex	1965

J TUNNICLIFFE (22)

104	v. Nottinghamshire	1895	145	v. Derbyshire	1901
101	v. Middlesex	1895	127	v. Kent	1902
147	v. Sussex	1897	105	v. Nottinghamshire	1902
107 *	v. Gloucestershire	1898	104	v. Nottinghamshire	1902
108 *	v. Kent	1898	119	v. Nottinghamshire	1904
102	v. Lancashire	1898	128	v. Hampshire	1904
243	v. Derbyshire	1898	135	v. Kent	1904
101	v. Surrey	1900	139 *	v. Surrey	1904
138	v. Hampshire	1900	102	v. Warwickshire	1905
158	v. Worcestershire	1900	141	v. Warwickshire	1907
100 *	v. Nottinghamshire	1900	103 *	v. Surrey	1907

C TURNER (2)

130	v. Somerset	1936	115 *	v. Hampshire	1936

C T TYSON (1)

100 *	v. Hampshire $	1921

$ *His first First Class innings*

CENTURIES BY ALL PLAYERS 1863-2020 *(Continued)*

G ULYETT (15)

107	v. Scotland	1878	199 *	v. Derbyshire	1887
109	v. Gloucestershire	1878	124	v. Kent	1887
141	v. Surrey	1880	104	v. Gloucestershire	1887
112	v. Surrey	1881	107	v. Gloucestershire	1890
120	v. Surrey	1882	118	v. Somerset	1891
146 *	v. MCC	1884	109	v. Sussex	1891
107	v. Middlesex	1884	111	v. Middlesex	1892
111 *	v. Sussex	1887			

M P VAUGHAN (20)

106 *	v. Oxford University	1994	177	v. Durham	1998
105	v. Somerset	1994	107	v. Middlesex	1998
117	v. Northamptonshire	1994	100	v. Essex	1999
106	v. Matabeleland	1996	151	v. Essex	1999
183	v. Glamorgan	1996	153	v. Kent	1999
135	v. Surrey	1996	155 *	v. Derbyshire	2000
183	v. Northamptonshire	1996	118	v. Durham	2000
109	v. Oxford University	1997	133	v. Northamptonshire	2001
161	v. Essex	1997	113	v. Essex	2001
105	v. Lancashire	1997	103	v. Northamptonshire	2003

H VERITY (1)

101	v. Jamaica	1936

A WADDINGTON (1)

114	v. Worcestershire	1927

D J WAINWRIGHT (2)

104 *	v. Sussex	2008	102 *	v. Warwickshire	2009

E WAINWRIGHT (18)

105	v. Australians	1888	103	v. Nottinghamshire	1897
104	v. Sussex	1892	153	v. Leicestershire	1899
107	v.Warwickshire	1894	228	v. Surrey	1899
126	v. Warwickshire	1896	100	v. Kent	1899
145	v. Sussex	1896	116	v. Kent	1900
100	v. Gloucestershire	1897	109	v. Somerset	1900
171	v. Middlesex	1897	117	v. C I Thornton's XI	1900
118 *	v. Hampshire	1897	108 *	v. Derbyshire	1901
104 *	v. Sussex	1897	116	v. South Africans	1901

T A WARDALL (2)

105	v. Gloucestershire	1892	106	v. Gloucestershire	1893

W A I WASHINGTON (1)

100 *	v. Surrey	1902

W WATSON (26)

153 *	v. Surrey	1947	147	v. Worcestershire	1947
108	v. Northamptonshire	1948	172	v. Derbyshire	1948
119	v. Leicestershire	1949	115	v. Warwickshire	1949
122	v. Somerset	1950	132	v. Northamptonshire	1950
114	v. Kent	1950	108	v. Derbyshire	1951
103 *	v. Nottinghamshire	1952	114	v. Gloucestershire	1952
107 *	v. Essex	1952	162 *	v. Somerset	1953
163	v. Sussex	1955	105	v. Essex	1955
174	v. Lancashire	1955	214 *	v. Worcestershire	1955
117	v. MCC	1956	149	v. Middlesex	1956

CENTURIES BY ALL PLAYERS 1863-2020 *(Continued)*

W WATSON (Continued)

139 *	v. Somerset	1956	103 *	v. Warwickshire	1956
134	v. Scotland	1957	162	v. Northamptonshire	1957
102	v. Worcestershire	1957	116	v. Warwickshire	1957

C WHITE (19)

146	v. Durham	1993	104	v. Kent	2002
108 *	v. Essex	1994	161	v. Leicestershire	2002
107	v. Leicestershire	1995	173 *	v. Derbyshire	2003
110	v. Northamptonshire	1995	135 *	v. Durham	2003
107 *	v. Worcestershire	1995	110	v. Lancashire	2005
181	v. Lancashire	1996	104	v. Sussex	2006
172 *	v. Worcestershire	1997	116	v. Lancashire	2006
104 *	v. Surrey	1998	147	v. Nottinghamshire	2006
186	v. Lancashire	2001	117	v. Surrey	2007
183	v. Glamorgan	2001			

H WILKINSON (1)

113	v. MCC	1904

W H WILKINSON (1)

103	v. Sussex	1909

K S WILLIAMSON (1)

189	v. Sussex	2014

B B WILSON (15)

109	v. Derbyshire	1908	150	v. Warwickshire	1912
102	v. Warwickshire	1909	104	v. Gloucestershire	1913
116	v. Sussex	1909	108	v. Sussex	1913
109	v. Leicestershire	1909	106	v. Essex	1914
108	v. Nottinghamshire	1910	101	v. Derbyshire	1914
115	v. Worcestershire	1910	102	v. Gloucestershire	1914
109	v. Sussex	1910	208	v. Sussex	1914
125	v. Middlesex	1911			

E R WILSON (1)

104 *	v. Essex	1913

J V WILSON (29)

111	v. Surrey	1948	121	v. Surrey	1952
140	v. Derbyshire	1948	113	v. Hampshire	1953
157 *	v. Sussex	1949	138	v. Leicestershire	1954
110 *	v. Scotland	1949	111	v. Middlesex	1954
139	v. Gloucestershire	1950	130 *	v. Lancashire	1954
157	v. Essex	1950	110	v. Cambridge University	1955
142	v. Nottinghamshire	1950	109 *	v. Somerset	1955
139	v. Hampshire	1951	132 *	v. Warwickshire	1955
166 *	v. Sussex	1951	132	v. Essex	1955
114 *	v. Surrey	1951	165	v. Oxford University	1956
120	v. Derbyshire	1951	132	v. Oxford University	1957
107	v. Leicestershire	1951	105	v. Rest of England	1959
223 *	v. Scotland	1951	134	v. Warwickshire	1962
154	v. Oxford University	1952	134	v. Nottinghamshire	1962
230	v. Derbyshire	1952			

A WOOD (1)

123 *	v. Worcestershire	1935

CENTURIES BY ALL PLAYERS 1863-2020 *(Continued)*

M J WOOD (16)

103	v. Derbyshire	1998	124	v. Glamorgan	2001
108	v. Hampshire	1998	157	v. Northamptonshire	2003
200 *	v. Warwickshire	1998	207	v. Somerset	2003
118 *	v. Sussex	1998	155	v. Hampshire	2003
100 *	v. Derbyshire	2000	126	v. Glamorgan	2003
124	v. Somerset	2001	116	v. Gloucestershire	2003
102	v. Leicestershire	2001	123	v. Derbyshire	2004
115	v. Lancashire	2001	202 *	v. Bangladesh 'A'	2005

J D WOODFORD (1)

101	v. Warwickshire	1971

N W D YARDLEY (17)

101	v. Surrey	1937	114	v. Surrey	1948
140 *	v. Cambridge University	1939	134 *	v. New Zealanders	1949
108	v. Warwickshire	1939	104	v. Surrey	1950
108	v. Sussex	1939	120 *	v. Somerset	1950
137	v. Nottinghamshire	1946	119	v. Lancashire	1950
137	v. Glamorgan	1947	101	v. Scotland	1950
100	v. Leicestershire	1947	183 *	v. Hampshire	1951
177	v. Derbyshire	1947	100 *	v. Gloucestershire	1955
136	v. Hampshire	1947			

YOUNUS KHAN (3)

106	v. Hampshire	2007	213 *	v. Kent	2007
202 *	v. Hampshire	2007			

SUMMARY OF CENTURIES
FOR AND AGAINST YORKSHIRE 1863-2020

FOR YORKSHIRE				AGAINST YORKSHIRE		
Total	In Yorkshire	Away		Total	In Yorkshire	Away
111	66	45	Derbyshire	57	27	30
32	16	16	Durham	25	13	12
76	34	42	Essex	46	21	25
68	38	30	Glamorgan	23	13	10
87	41	46	Gloucestershire	53	27	26
101	44	57	Hampshire	61	27	34
82	37	45	Kent	64	32	32
118	59	59	Lancashire	116	58	58
97	52	45	Leicestershire	46	23	23
97	49	48	Middlesex	92	38	54
81	35	46	Northamptonshire	53	25	28
131	60	71	Nottinghamshire	87	33	54
105	53	52	Somerset	62	23	39
120	51	69	Surrey	114	41	73
90	42	48	Sussex	77	33	44
106	36	70	Warwickshire	75	29	46
75	32	43	Worcestershire	45	17	28
1	1	0	Cambridgeshire	0	0	0
1578	**746**	**832**	**Totals**	**1096**	**480**	**616**
9	9	0	Australians	16	16	0
9	9	0	Indians	7	7	0
8	8	0	New Zealanders	3	3	0
5	5	0	Pakistanis	1	1	0
9	9	0	South Africans	7	7	0
5	5	0	Sri Lankans	1	1	0
5	5	0	West Indians	6	6	0
1	1	0	Zimbabweans	0	0	0
3	3	0	Bangladesh 'A'	1	1	0
0	0	0	India 'A'	3	3	0
1	1	0	Pakistan 'A'	1	1	0
45	1	44	Cambridge University	20	2	18
2	2	0	Combined Services	0	0	0
1	0	1	Durham MCCU	1	0	1
4	3	1	England XIs	3	2	1
0	0	0	International XI	1	1	0
1	0	1	Ireland	0	0	0
3	0	3	Jamaica	3	0	3
10	8	2	Leeds/Bradford MCCU	0	0	0
1	0	1	Liverpool and District	0	0	0
2	2	0	Loughborough MCCU	1	1	0
1	0	1	Mashonaland	0	0	0
2	0	2	Matabeleland	1	0	1
54	38	16	MCC	52	34	18
39	0	39	Oxford University	11	0	11
6	0	6	Rest of England	15	0	15
9	5	4	Scotland	1	0	1
3	3	0	C L Thornton's XI	4	4	0
0	0	0	Western Province	1	0	1
1	1	0	I Zingari	1	1	0
239	**118**	**121**	**Totals**	**161**	**91**	**70**
1817	**864**	**953**	**Grand Totals**	**1257**	**571**	**686**

FOUR CENTURIES IN ONE INNINGS

		F S Jackson 117
		E Wainwright 126
1896	v. Warwickshire	Lord Hawke 166
	at Birmingham	R Peel *210

(First instance in First-Class cricket)

THREE CENTURIES IN ONE INNINGS

1884	v. Cambridge University	L Hall 116
	at Cambridge	W Bates 133
		I Grimshaw 115
1887	v. Kent	G Ulyett 124
	at Canterbury	L Hall 110
		F Lee 119
1897	v. Sussex	J T Brown 311
	at Sheffield	J Tunnicliffe 147
		E Wainwright *104
1899	v. Middlesex	F S Jackson 155
	at Bradford	D Denton 113
		F Mitchell 121
1904	v. Surrey	D Denton 105
	at The Oval	G H Hirst 104
		J Tunnicliffe *139
1919	v. Gloucestershire	H Sutcliffe 118
	at Leeds	D Denton 122
		R Kilner *115
1925	v. Glamorgan	P Holmes 130
	at Huddersfield	H Sutcliffe 121
		E Robinson *108
1928	v. Middlesex	P Holmes 105
	at Lord's	E Oldroyd 108
		A Mitchell 105
1928	v. Essex	H Sutcliffe 129
	at Leyton	P Holmes 136
		M Leyland *133
1929	v. Glamorgan	E Oldroyd 168
	at Hull	W Barber 114
		F E Greenwood *104
1933	v. MCC	H Sutcliffe 107
	at Scarborough	A Mitchell 158
		M Leyland 133
1936	v. Surrey	H Sutcliffe 129
	at Leeds	L Hutton 163
		M Leyland *163
1937	v. Leicestershire	H Sutcliffe 189
	at Hull	L Hutton 153
		M Leyland *118
1947	v. Leicestershire	L Hutton 137
	at Leicester	N W D Yardley 100
		G.A Smithson 169

228

THREE CENTURIES IN ONE INNINGS *(Continued)*

1971	v.	Oxford University	J H Hampshire	*116
		at Oxford	R A Hutton	101
			A J Dalton	111
1975	v.	Gloucestershire	G Boycott	141
		at Bristol	R G Lumb	101
			J H Hampshire	*106
1995	v.	Cambridge University	M D Moxon	130
		at Cambridge	D Byas	181
			M G Bevan	*113
2001	v.	Leicestershire	M J Wood	102
		at Leeds	M J Lumb	122
			D S Lehmann	104
2001	v.	Glamorgan	C White	183
		at Scarborough	M J Wood	124
			D Byas	104
2007	v.	Surrey	J A Rudolph	122
		at The Oval	T T Bresnan	116
			J N Gillespie	*123
2014	v.	Leeds/Bradford MCCU	A Lyth	130
		at Leeds	G S Ballance	101
			J M Bairstow	123
2016	v.	Hampshire	A Lyth	111
		at Leeds	J M Bairstow	246
			L E Plunkett	126
2019	v.	Somerset	G S Ballance	111
		at Leeds	T Kohler-Cadmore	102
			H C Brook	101

CENTURY IN EACH INNINGS

D Denton	107 and 109*	v. Nottinghamshire at Nottingham, 1906
G H Hirst	111 and 117*	v. Somerset at Bath, 1906
D Denton	133 and 121	v. MCC at Scarborough, 1908
W Rhodes	128 and 115	v. MCC at Scarborough, 1911
P Holmes	126 and 111*	v. Lancashire at Manchester, 1920
H Sutcliffe	107 and 109*	v. MCC at Scarborough, 1926
H Sutcliffe	111 and 100*	v. Nottinghamshire at Nottingham, 1928
E I Lester	126 and 142	v. Northamptonshire at Northampton, 1947
L Hutton	197 and 104	v. Essex at Southend, 1947
E I Lester	125* and 132	v. Lancashire at Manchester, 1948
L Hutton	165 and 100	v. Sussex at Hove, 1949
L Hutton	103 and 137	v. MCC at Scarborough, 1952
G Boycott	103 and 105	v. Nottinghamshire at Sheffield, 1966
G Boycott	163 and 141*	v. Nottinghamshire at Bradford, 1983
M D Moxon	123 and 112*	v. Indians at Scarborough, 1986
A A Metcalfe	194* and 107	v. Nottinghamshire at Nottingham, 1990
M P Vaughan	100 and 151	v. Essex at Chelmsford, 1999
Younus Khan	106 and 202*	v. Hampshire at Southampton, 2007
G S Ballance	148 and 108*	v. Surrey at The Oval, 2013
G S Ballance	108 and 203*	v. Hampshire at West End, 2017

HIGHEST INDIVIDUAL SCORES
FOR AND AGAINST YORKSHIRE

Highest For Yorkshire:
341 G H Hirst v. Leicestershire at Leicester, 1905
Highest Against Yorkshire:
318* W G Grace for Gloucestershire at Cheltenham, 1876

Yorkshire versus:

Derbyshire	*For Yorkshire:*	300 — J T Brown at Chesterfield, 1898
	Against:	270* — C F Hughes at Leeds, 2013
Most Centuries	*For Yorkshire:*	G Boycott 9
	Against:	K J Barnett and W Storer 4 each
Durham	*For Yorkshire:*	339 — D S Lehmann at Leeds, 2006
	Against:	221* — K K Jennings at Chester-le-Street, 2016
Essex	*For Yorkshire:*	313 — H Sutcliffe at Leyton, 1932
	Against:	219* — D J Insole at Colchester, 1949
Most Centuries	*For Yorkshire:*	H Sutcliffe 9
	Against:	F L Fane, K W R Fletcher, G A Gooch and D J Insole 3 each
Glamorgan	*For Yorkshire:*	213 — M D Moxon at Cardiff, 1996
	Against:	202* — H Morris at Cardiff, 1996
Most Centuries	*For Yorkshire:*	G Boycott, P Holmes and H Sutcliffe 5 each
	Against:	H Morris 5
Gloucestershire	*For Yorkshire:*	238 — D R Martyn at Leeds, 2003
	Against:	318*— W G Grace at Cheltenham, 1876
Most Centuries	*For Yorkshire:*	G Boycott 6
	Against:	W G Grace 9
Hampshire	*For Yorkshire:*	302* — P Holmes at Portsmouth, 1920
	Against:	300* — M A Carberry at Southampton, 2011
Most Centuries	*For Yorkshire:*	H Sutcliffe and G S Ballance 6 each
	Against:	C P Mead 10
Kent	*For Yorkshire:*	248 — W Barber at Leeds, 1934.
	Against:	237 — D I Stevens at Leeds, 2019
Most Centuries	*For Yorkshire:*	A McGrath 6
	Against:	F E Woolley 5
Lancashire	*For Yorkshire:*	252 — D S Lehmann at Leeds, 2001
	Against:	225 — G D Lloyd at Leeds, 1997 (Non-Championship)
		206 — S G Law at Leeds, 2007
Most Centuries	*For Yorkshire:*	G Boycott and H Sutcliffe 9 each
	Against:	M A Atherton and C H Lloyd 6 each.
Leicestershire	*For Yorkshire:*	341— G H Hirst at Leicester, 1905
	Against:	218— J J Whitaker at Bradford, 1996
Most Centuries	*For Yorkshire:*	H Sutcliffe 10
	Against:	J J Whitaker and C J B Wood 5 each
Middlesex	*For Yorkshire:*	315*— P Holmes at Lord's, 1925
	Against:	243*— A J Webbe at Huddersfield, 1887
Most Centuries	*For Yorkshire:*	P Holmes and H Sutcliffe 7 each
	Against:	M W Gatting 8

HIGHEST INDIVIDUAL SCORES FOR AND AGAINST
YORKSHIRE *(continued)*

Yorkshire versus

Northamptonshire	*For Yorkshire:*	277* — P Holmes at Harrogate, 1921
	Against:	235 — A J Lamb at Leeds, 1990
Most Centuries	*For Yorkshire:*	H Sutcliffe 5
	Against:	W Larkins 5
Nottinghamshire	*For Yorkshire:*	285 — P Holmes at Nottingham, 1929
	Against:	251* — D J Hussey at Leeds, 2010
Most Centuries	*For Yorkshire:*	G Boycott 15
	Against:	R T Robinson 6
Somerset	*For Yorkshire:*	213 — H Sutcliffe at Dewsbury, 1924
	Against:	297 — M J Wood at Taunton, 2005
Most Centuries	*For Yorkshire:*	G Boycott 6
	Against:	L C H Palairet, IVA. Richards, M E Trescothick 5 each
Surrey	*For Yorkshire:*	255 — W Barber at Sheffield, 1935
	Against:	273 — T W Hayward at The Oval, 1899
Most Centuries	*For Yorkshire:*	H Sutcliffe 9
	Against:	J B Hobbs 8
Sussex	*For Yorkshire:*	311 — J T Brown at Sheffield, 1897
	Against:	274* — M W Goodwin at Hove, 2011
Most Centuries	*For Yorkshire:*	L Hutton 8
	Against:	C B Fry 7
Warwickshire	*For Yorkshire:*	275 — P Holmes at Bradford, 1928
	Against:	225 — D P Ostler at Birmingham, 2002
Most Centuries	*For Yorkshire:*	G Boycott and H Sutcliffe 8 each
	Against:	D L Amiss, H E Dollery, R B Khanhai and W G Quaife 4 each.
Worcestershire	*For Yorkshire:*	274* — M D Moxon at Worcester, 1994
	Against:	259 — D Kenyon at Kidderminster, 1956
Most Centuries	*For Yorkshire:*	M Leyland 6
	Against:	D Kenyon and G M Turner 5 each
Australians	*For Yorkshire:*	167 — J T Brown at Bradford, 1899
	Against:	193* — B C Booth at Bradford, 1964
Most Centuries	*For Yorkshire:*	G Boycott and D Denton 2 each
	Against:	N C O'Neill 2
Indians	*For Yorkshire:*	183* — L Hutton at Bradford, 1946
	Against:	244* — V S Hazare at Sheffield, 1946
Most Centuries	*For Yorkshire:*	M D Moxon 2
	Against:	V S Hazare, VMankad, PR Umrigar D K Gaekwad, G A Parkar and R Lamba 1 each
New Zealanders	*For Yorkshire:*	175 — P Holmes at Bradford, 1927
	Against:	126 — W M Wallace at Bradford, 1949
Most Centuries	*For Yorkshire:*	L Hutton and DB Close 2 each
	Against:	H G Vivian, WM Wallace and J G Wright 1 each
Pakistanis	*For Yorkshire:*	197 — P J Sharpe at Leeds, 1967
	Against:	139 — A H Kardar at Sheffield, 1954
Most Centuries	*For Yorkshire:*	P J Sharpe 2
	Against:	A H Kardar 1

Yorkshire versus

South Africans	For Yorkshire:	156 — L Hutton at Sheffield, 1951
	Against:	168 — I J Seidle at Sheffield, 1929
Most Centuries	For Yorkshire:	L Hutton 2
	Against:	H B Cameron, J D Lindsay, B Mitchell, D P B Morkel, I J Seidle, L J Tancred, C B van Ryneveld 1 each
Sri Lankans	For Yorkshire:	132 — M D Moxon at Leeds, 1988
	Against:	112 — S A R Silva at Leeds, 1988
Most Centuries	For Yorkshire:	K Sharp 2
	Against:	S A R Silva 1
West Indians	For Yorkshire:	112* — D Denton at Harrogate, 1906
	Against:	164 — S F A Bacchus at Leeds, 1980
Most Centuries	For Yorkshire:	M G Bevan, D Denton, L Hutton, R G Lumb and A A Metcalfe 1 each
	Against:	S F A Bacchus, C O Browne, S Chanderpaul P A Goodman, C L Hooper and G St A Sobers 1 each
Zimbabweans	For Yorkshire:	113 — M D Moxon at Leeds, 1990
	Against:	89 — G J Whittall at Leeds, 2000
Most Centuries	For Yorkshire:	M D Moxon 1
	Against:	None
Cambridge University	For Yorkshire:	207* — G Boycott at Cambridge, 1976
	Against:	171* — G L Jessop at Cambridge, 1899
		171 — P B H May at Cambridge, 1952
Most Centuries	For Yorkshire:	H Sutcliffe 4
	Against:	G M Kemp 2
Durham MCCU	For Yorkshire:	139 — J J Sayers at Durham, 2011
	Against:	127 — T Westley at Durham, 2011
Most Centuries	For Yorkshire:	J J Sayers 1
	Against:	T Westley 1
Leeds Bradford MCCU	For Yorkshire:	194 — A Lyth at Leeds, 2017
	Against:	69 — A MacQueen at Leeds, 2012
Most Centuries	For Yorkshire:	A Lyth, 3
Loughborough MCCU	For Yorkshire:	134* — R M Pyrah at Leeds, 2010
	Against:	107 — C P Murtagh at Leeds, 2007
Most Centuries	For Yorkshire:	R M Pyrah 2
	Against:	C P Murtagh 1
MCC	For Yorkshire:	180* — G H Hirst at Lord's, 1919
	Against:	214 — E H Hendren at Lord's, 1919
Most Centuries	For Yorkshire:	L Hutton 8
	Against:	R E S Wyatt 5
Oxford University	For Yorkshire:	196 — R J Blakey at Oxford, 1991
	Against:	201 — J E Raphael at Oxford, 1904
Most Centuries	For Yorkshire:	M Leyland 4
	Against:	A A Baig and Nawab of Pataudi (Jun.) 2 each

J B Hobbs scored 11 centuries against Yorkshire – the highest by any individual (8 for Surrey and 3 for the Rest of England).

Three players have scored 10 centuries against Yorkshire – W G Grace (9 for Gloucestershire and 1 for MCC). E H Hendren (6 for Middlesex, 3 for MCC and 1 for the Rest of England) and C P Mead (all 10 for Hampshire).

CARRYING BAT THROUGH A COMPLETED INNINGS

Batsman	Score	Total	Against	Season
G R Atkinson	30*	73	Nottinghamshire at Bradford	1865
L Hall	31*	94	Sussex at Hove	1878
L Hall	124*	331	Sussex at Hove	1883
L Hall	128*	285	Sussex at Huddersfield	1884
L Hall	32*	81	Kent at Sheffield	1885
L Hall	79*	285	Surrey at Sheffield	1885
L Hall	37*	96	Derbyshire at Derby	1885
L Hall	50*	173	Sussex at Huddersfield	1886
L Hall	74*	172	Kent at Canterbury	1886
G Ulyett	199*	399	Derbyshire at Sheffield	1887
L Hall	119*	334	Gloucestershire at Dewsbury	1887
L Hall	82*	218	Sussex at Hove	1887
L Hall	34*	104	Surrey at The Oval	1888
L Hall	129*	461	Gloucestershire at Clifton	1888
L Hall	85*	259	Middlesex at Lord's	1889
L Hall	41*	106	Nottinghamshire at Sheffield	1891
W Rhodes	98*	184	MCC at Lord's	1903
W Rhodes	85*	152	Essex at Leyton	1910
P Holmes	145*	270	Northamptonshire at Northampton	1920
H Sutcliffe	125*	307	Essex at Southend	1920
P Holmes	175*	377	New Zealanders at Bradford	1927
P Holmes	110*	219	Northamptonshire at Bradford	1929
H Sutcliffe	104*	170	Hampshire at Leeds	1932
H Sutcliffe	114*	202	Rest of England at The Oval	1933
H Sutcliffe	187*	401	Worcestershire at Bradford	1934
H Sutcliffe	135*	262	Glamorgan at Neath	1935
H Sutcliffe	125*	322	Oxford University at Oxford	1939
L Hutton	99*	200	Leicestershire at Sheffield	1948
L Hutton	78*	153	Worcestershire at Sheffield	1949
F A Lowson	76*	218	MCC at Lord's	1951
W B Stott	144*	262	Worcestershire at Worcester	1959
D E V Padgett	115*	230	Gloucestershire at Bristol	1962
G Boycott	114*	297	Leicestershire at Bradford	1968
G Boycott	53*	119	Warwickshire at Bradford	1969
G Boycott	182*	320	Middlesex at Lord's	1971
G Boycott	138*	232	Warwickshire at Birmingham	1971
G Boycott	175*	360	Nottinghamshire at Worksop	1979
G Boycott	112*	233	Derbyshire at Sheffield	1983
G Boycott	55*	183	Warwickshire at Leeds	1984
G Boycott	55*	131	Surrey at Sheffield	1985
M J Wood	60*	160	Somerset at Scarborough	2004
J J Sayers	122*	326	Middlesex at Scarborough	2006
J J Sayers	149*	414	Durham at Leeds	2007
A Lyth	248*	486	Leicestershire at Leicester	2012

44 instances, of which L Hall (14 times), G Boycott (8) and H Sutcliffe (6) account for 28 between them.

The highest percentage of an innings total is 61.17 by H. Sutcliffe (104* v. Hampshire at Leeds in 1932) but P Holmes was absent ill, so only nine wickets fell.

Other contributions exceeding 55% are:

59.48%	G Boycott	(138*	v. Warwickshire at Birmingham, 1971)
56.87%	G Boycott	(182*	v. Middlesex at Lord's, 1971)
56.43%	H Sutcliffe	(114*	v. Rest of England at The Oval, 1933)
55.92%	W Rhodes	(85*	v. Essex at Leyton, 1910)

2,000 RUNS IN A SEASON

Batsman	Season	M	I	NO	Runs	HS	Avge	100s
G H Hirst	1904	32	44	3	2257	157	55.04	8
D Denton	1905	33	52	2	2258	172	45.16	8
G H Hirst	1906	32	53	6	2164	169	46.04	6
D Denton	1911	32	55	4	2161	137*	42.37	6
D Denton	1912	36	51	4	2088	221	44.23	6
P Holmes	1920	30	45	6	2144	302*	54.97	7
P Holmes	1925	35	49	9	2351	315*	58.77	6
H Sutcliffe	1925	34	48	8	2236	235	55.90	7
H Sutcliffe	1928	27	35	5	2418	228	80.60	11
P Holmes	1928	31	40	4	2093	275	58.13	6
H Sutcliffe	1931	28	33	8	2351	230	94.04	9
H Sutcliffe	1932	29	41	5	2883	313	80.08	12
M Leyland	1933	31	44	4	2196	210*	54.90	7
A Mitchell	1933	34	49	10	2100	158	53.84	6
H Sutcliffe	1935	32	47	3	2183	212	49.61	8
L Hutton	1937	28	45	6	2448	271*	62.76	8
H Sutcliffe	1937	32	52	5	2054	189	43.70	4
L Hutton	1939	29	44	5	2316	280*	59.38	10
L Hutton	1947	19	31	2	2068	270*	71.31	10
L Hutton	1949	26	44	6	2640	269*	69.47	9
F A Lowson	1950	31	54	5	2067	141*	42.18	5
D E V Padgett	1959	35	60	8	2158	161*	41.50	4
W B Stott	1959	32	56	2	2034	144*	37.66	3
P J Sharpe	1962	36	62	8	2201	138	40.75	7
G Boycott	1971	18	25	4	2221	233	105.76	11
A A Metcalfe	1990	23	44	4	2047	194*	51.17	6

1,000 RUNS IN A SEASON

Batsman		Runs scored	Runs scored	Runs scored
C W J Athey	(2)	1113 in 1980	1339 in 1982	—
D L Bairstow	(3)	1083 in 1981	1102 in 1983	1163 in 1985
J M Bairstow	(2)	1015 in 2011	1108 in 2015	—
G S Ballance	(3)	1363 in 2013	1023 in 2017	1014 in 2019
W Barber	(8)	1000 in 1932	1595 in 1933	1930 in 1934
		1958 in 1935	1466 in 1937	1455 in 1938
		1501 in 1939	1170 in 1946	—
M G Bevan	(2)	1598 in 1995	1225 in 1996	—
R J Blakey	(5)	1361 in 1987	1159 in 1989	1065 in 1992
		1236 in 1994	1041 in 2002	—
J B Bolus	(2)	1245 in 1960	1970 in 1961	—
M W Booth	(2)	1189 in 1911	1076 in 1913	—
G Boycott	(19)	1628 in 1963	1639 in 1964	1215 in 1965
		1388 in 1966	1530 in 1967	1004 in 1968
		1558 in 1970	2221 in 1971	1156 in 1972
		1478 in 1974	1915 in 1975	1288 in 1976
		1259 in 1977	1074 in 1978	1160 in 1979
		1913 in 1982	1941 in 1983	1567 in 1984
		1657 in 1985	—	—
J T Brown	(9)	1196 in 1894	1260 in 1895	1755 in 1896
		1634 in 1897	1641 in 1898	1375 in 1899
		1181 in 1900	1627 in 1901	1291 in 1903
D Byas	(5)	1557 in 1991	1073 in 1993	1297 in 1994
		1913 in 1995	1319 in 1997	

1,000 RUNS IN A SEASON *(Continued)*

Batsman	Runs scored	Runs scored	Runs scored
D B Close .... (13)	1192 in 1952	1287 in 1954	1131 in 1955
	1315 in 1957	1335 in 1958	1740 in 1959
	1699 in 1960	1821 in 1961	1438 in 1962
	1145 in 1963	1281 in 1964	1127 in 1965
	1259 in 1966	—	—
K R Davidson .... (1)	1241 in 1934	—	—
D Denton .... (20)	1028 in 1896	1357 in 1897	1595 in 1899
	1378 in 1900	1400 in 1901	1191 in 1902
	1562 in 1903	1919 in 1904	2258 in 1905
	1905 in 1906	1128 in 1907	1852 in 1908
	1765 in 1909	1106 in 1910	2161 in 1911
	2088 in 1912	1364 in 1913	1799 in 1914
	1213 in 1919	1324 in 1920	—
A Drake .... (2)	1487 in 1911	1029 in 1913	—
A W Gale .... (2)	1076 in 2013	1045 in 2015	—
A P Grayson .... (1)	1046 in 1994	—	—
S Haigh .... (1)	1031 in 1904	—	—
L Hall .... (1)	1120 in 1887	—	—
H Halliday .... (4)	1357 in 1948	1484 in 1950	1351 in 1952
	1461 in 1953	—	—
J H Hampshire .... (12)	1236 in 1963	1280 in 1964	1424 in 1965
	1105 in 1966	1244 in 1967	1133 in 1968
	1079 in 1970	1259 in 1971	1124 in 1975
	1303 in 1976	1596 in 1978	1425 in 1981
Lord Hawke .... (1)	1005 in 1895	—	—
G H Hirst .... (19)	1110 in 1896	1248 in 1897	1546 in 1899
	1752 in 1900	1669 in 1901	1113 in 1902
	1535 in 1903	2257 in 1904	1972 in 1905
	2164 in 1906	1167 in 1907	1513 in 1908
	1151 in 1909	1679 in 1910	1639 in 1911
	1119 in 1912	1431 in 1913	1655 in 1914
	1312 in 1919	—	—
P Holmes .... (14)	1876 in 1919	2144 in 1920	1458 in 1921
	1614 in 1922	1884 in 1923	1610 in 1924
	2351 in 1925	1792 in 1926	1774 in 1927
	2093 in 1928	1724 in 1929	1957 in 1930
	1431 in 1931	1191 in 1932	—
L Hutton .... (12)	1282 in 1936	2448 in 1937	1171 in 1938
	2316 in 1939	1322 in 1946	2068 in 1947
	1792 in 1948	2640 in 1949	1581 in 1950
	1554 in 1951	1956 in 1952	1532 in 1953
R Illingworth .... (5)	1193 in 1957	1490 in 1959	1029 in 1961
	1610 in 1962	1301 in 1964	—
F S Jackson .... (4)	1211 in 1896	1300 in 1897	1442 in 1898
	1468 in 1899	—	—
P A Jaques .... (2)	1118 in 2004	1359 in 2005	—
S A Kellett .... (2)	1266 in 1991	1326 in 1992	—
R Kilner .... (10)	1586 in 1913	1329 in 1914	1135 in 1919
	1240 in 1920	1137 in 1921	1132 in 1922
	1265 in 1923	1002 in 1925	1021 in 1926
	1004 in 1927	—	—
T Kohler-Cadmore .... (1)	1004 in 2019	—	—

1,000 RUNS IN A SEASON *(Continued)*

Batsman	Runs scored	Runs scored	Runs scored
A Z Lees	(2) 1018 in 2014	1285 in 2016	—
D S Lehmann	(5) 1575 in 1997	1477 in 2000	1416 in 2001
	1136 in 2002	1706 in 2006	
E I Lester	(6) 1256 in 1948	1774 in 1949	1015 in 1950
	1786 in 1952	1380 in 1953	1330 in 1954
M Leyland	(17) 1088 in 1923	1203 in 1924	1560 in 1925
	1561 in 1926	1478 in 1927	1554 in 1928
	1407 in 1929	1814 in 1930	1127 in 1931
	1821 in 1932	2196 in 1933	1228 in 1934
	1366 in 1935	1621 in 1936	1120 in 1937
	1640 in 1938	1238 in 1939	—
J D Love	(2) 1161 in 1981	1020 in 1983	
F A Lowson	(8) 1678 in 1949	2067 in 1950	1607 in 1951
	1562 in 1952	1586 in 1953	1719 in 1954
	1082 in 1955	1428 in 1956	—
M J Lumb	(1) 1038 in 2003	—	—
R G Lumb	(5) 1002 in 1973	1437 in 1975	1070 in 1978
	1465 in 1979	1223 in 1980	
A Lyth	(3) 1509 in 2010	1619 in 2014	1153 in 2016
A McGrath	(3) 1425 in 2005	1293 in 2006	1219 in 2010
A A Metcalfe	(6) 1674 in 1986	1162 in 1987	1320 in 1988
	1230 in 1989	2047 in 1990	1210 in 1991
A Mitchell	(10) 1320 in 1928	1633 in 1930	1351 in 1932
	2100 in 1933	1854 in 1934	1530 in 1935
	1095 in 1936	1602 in 1937	1305 in 1938
	1219 in 1939	—	—
F Mitchell	(2) 1678 in 1899	1801 in 1901	—
R Moorhouse	(1) 1096 in 1895	—	—
M D Moxon	(11) 1016 in 1984	1256 in 1985	1298 in 1987
	1430 in 1988	1156 in 1989	1621 in 1990
	1669 in 1991	1314 in 1992	1251 in 1993
	1458 in 1994	1145 in 1995	—
E Oldroyd	(10) 1473 in 1921	1690 in 1922	1349 in 1923
	1607 in 1924	1262 in 1925	1197 in 1926
	1390 in 1927	1304 in 1928	1474 in 1929
	1285 in 1930	—	—
D E V Padgett	(12) 1046 in 1956	2158 in 1959	1574 in 1960
	1856 in 1961	1750 in 1962	1380 in 1964
	1220 in 1965	1194 in 1966	1284 in 1967
	1163 in 1968	1078 in 1969	1042 in 1970
R Peel	(1) 1193 in 1896	—	—
W Rhodes	(17) 1251 in 1904	1353 in 1905	1618 in 1906
	1574 in 1908	1663 in 1909	1355 in 1910
	1961 in 1911	1030 in 1912	1805 in 1913
	1325 in 1914	1138 in 1919	1329 in 1921
	1368 in 1922	1168 in 1923	1030 in 1924
	1256 in 1925	1071 in 1926	—
E Robinson	(2) 1104 in 1921	1097 in 1929	—
P E Robinson	(3) 1173 in 1988	1402 in 1990	1293 in 1991
J A Rudolph	(4) 1078 in 2007	1292 in 2008	1366 in 2009
	1375 in 2010	—	—

1,000 RUNS IN A SEASON *(Continued)*

Batsman		Runs scored	Runs scored	Runs scored
J J Sayers	(1)	1150 in 2009	—	—
A B Sellers	(1)	1109 in 1938	—	—
K Sharp	(1)	1445 in 1984	—	—
P J Sharpe	(10)	1039 in 1960	1240 in 1961	2201 in 1962
		1273 in 1964	1091 in 1965	1352 in 1967
		1256 in 1968	1012 in 1969	1149 in 1970
		1320 in 1973		
W B Stott	(5)	1362 in 1957	1036 in 1958	2034 in 1959
		1790 in 1960	1409 in 1961	
H Sutcliffe	(21)	†1839 in 1919	1393 in 1920	1235 in 1921
		1909 in 1922	1773 in 1923	1720 in 1924
		2236 in 1925	1672 in 1926	1814 in 1927
		2418 in 1928	1485 in 1929	1636 in 1930
		2351 in 1931	2883 in 1932	1986 in 1933
		1511 in 1934	2183 in 1935	1295 in 1936
		2054 in 1937	1660 in 1938	1416 in 1939

† First season in First-Class cricket – The record for a debut season.

Batsman		Runs scored	Runs scored	Runs scored
W H H Sutcliffe	(1)	1193 in 1955	—	—
K Taylor	(6)	1306 in 1959	1107 in 1960	1494 in 1961
		1372 in 1962	1149 in 1964	1044 in 1966
T L Taylor	(2)	1236 in 1901	1373 in 1902	
S R Tendulkar	(1)	1070 in 1992	—	—
J Tunnicliffe	(12)	1333 in 1895	1368 in 1896	1208 in 1897
		1713 in 1898	1434 in 1899	1496 in 1900
		1295 in 1901	1274 in 1902	1650 in 1904
		1096 in 1905	1232 in 1906	1195 in 1907
C Turner	(1)	1153 in 1934	—	—
G Ulyett	(4)	1083 in 1878	1158 in 1882	1024 in 1885
		1285 in 1887		
M P Vaughan	(4)	1066 in 1994	1235 in 1995	1161 in 1996
		1161 in 1998		
E Wainwright	(3)	1492 in 1897	1479 in 1899	1044 in 1901
W A I Washington	(1)	1022 in 1902		
W Watson	(8)	1331 in 1947	1352 in 1948	1586 in 1952
		1350 in 1953	1347 in 1954	1564 in 1955
		1378 in 1956	1455 in 1957	
W H Wilkinson	(1)	1282 in 1908	—	—
B B Wilson	(5)	1054 in 1909	1455 in 1911	1453 in 1912
		1533 in 1913	1632 in 1914	
J V Wilson	(12)	1460 in 1949	1548 in 1950	1985 in 1951
		1349 in 1952	1531 in 1953	1713 in 1954
		1799 in 1955	1602 in 1956	1287 in 1957
		1064 in 1960	1018 in 1961	1226 in 1962
A Wood	(1)	1237 in 1935	—	—
M J Wood	(4)	1080 in 1998	1060 in 2001	1432 in 2003
		1005 in 2005		
N W D Yardley	(4)	1028 in 1939	1299 in 1947	1413 in 1949
		1031 in 1950	—	—

BATSMEN WHO HAVE SCORED OVER 10,000 RUNS

Player	M	I	NO	Runs	HS	Av'ge	100s
H Sutcliffe	602	864	96	38558	313	50.20	112
D Denton	676	1058	61	33282	221	33.38	61
G Boycott	414	674	111	32570	260*	57.85	103
G H Hirst	717	1050	128	32024	341	34.73	56
W Rhodes	883	1195	162	31075	267*	30.08	46
P Holmes	485	699	74	26220	315*	41.95	60
M Leyland	548	720	82	26180	263	41.03	62
L Hutton	341	527	62	24807	280*	53.34	85
D B Close	536	811	102	22650	198	31.94	33
J H Hampshire	456	724	89	21979	183*	34.61	34
J V Wilson	477	724	75	20548	230	31.66	29
D E V Padgett	487	774	63	20306	161*	28.55	29
J Tunnicliffe	472	768	57	19435	243	27.33	22
M D Moxon	277	476	42	18973	274*	43.71	41
A Mitchell	401	550	69	18189	189	37.81	39
P J Sharpe	411	666	71	17685	203*	29.72	23
E Oldroyd	383	509	58	15891	194	35.23	37
J T Brown	345	567	41	15694	311	29.83	23
W Barber	354	495	48	15315	255	34.26	27
R Illingworth	496	668	131	14986	162	27.90	14
D Byas	268	449	42	14398	213	35.37	28
G Ulyett	355	618	31	14157	199*	24.11	15
R J Blakey	339	541	84	14150	223*	30.96	12
A McGrath	242	405	29	14091	211	37.47	34
W Watson	283	430	65	13953	214*	38.22	26
F A Lowson	252	404	31	13897	259*	37.25	30
Lord Hawke	510	739	91	13133	166	20.26	10
R Kilner	365	478	46	13018	206*	30.13	15
D L Bairstow	429	601	113	12985	145	26.60	9
K Taylor	303	505	35	12864	203*	27.37	16
N W D Yardley	302	420	56	11632	183*	31.95	17
R G Lumb	239	395	30	11525	165*	31.57	22
E Wainwright	352	545	30	11092	228	21.53	18
S Haigh	513	687	110	10993	159	19.05	4
E I Lester	228	339	27	10616	186	34.02	24
A A Metcalfe	184	317	19	10465	216*	35.11	25
C White	221	350	45	10376	186	34.01	19
Hon F S Jackson	207	328	22	10371	160	33.89	21
J D Love	247	388	58	10263	170*	31.10	13
A Lyth	161	271	14	10046	251	39.08	22

PLAYERS WHO HAVE SCORED CENTURIES
FOR AND AGAINST YORKSHIRE

Player		For	Venue	Season
C W J Athey (5)	114*	Gloucestershire	Bradford	1984
(10 for Yorkshire)	101	Gloucestershire	Gloucester	1985
	101*	Gloucestershire	Leeds	1987
	112	Sussex	Scarborough	1993
	100	Sussex	Eastbourne	1996
M G Bevan (1)	142	Leicestershire	Leicester	2002
(9 for Yorkshire)				
J B Bolus (2)	114	Nottinghamshire	Bradford	1963
(7 for Yorkshire)	138	Derbyshire	Sheffield	1973
D B Close (1)	102	Somerset	Taunton	1971
(33 for Yorkshire)				
M T G Elliott (1)	125	Glamorgan	Leeds	2004
(1 for Yorkshire)				
P A Gibb (1)	107	Essex	Brentwood	1951
(2 for Yorkshire)				
P A Jaques (1)	222	Northamptonshire	Northampton	2003
(7 for Yorkshire)				
N Kilner (2)	119	Warwickshire	Hull	1932
(2 for Yorkshire)	197	Warwickshire	Birmingham	1933
A Z Lees (1)	106	Durham	Chester-le-Street	2020
(11 for Yorkshire)				
M J Lumb (1)	135	Nottinghamshire	Scarborough	2013
(8 for Yorkshire)				
P J Sharpe (1)	126	Derbyshire	Chesterfield	1976
(23 for Yorkshire)				

RECORD PARTNERSHIPS FOR YORKSHIRE

1st wkt	555	P Holmes (224*)	and H Sutcliffe (313)	v. Essex at Leyton	1932
2nd wkt	346	W Barber (162)	and M Leyland (189)	v. Middlesex at Sheffield	1932
3rd wkt	346	J J Sayers (173)	and A McGrath (211)	v. Warwickshire at Birmingham	2009
4th wkt	372	J E Root (213)	and J M Bairstow (198)	v. Surrey at Leeds	2016
5th wkt	340	E Wainwright (228)	and G H Hirst (186)	v. Surrey at The Oval	1899
6th wkt	296	A Lyth (251)	and A U Rashid (159*)	v. Lancashire at Manchester,	2014
7th wkt	366*	J M Bairstow (219*)	and T T Bresnan (169*)	v, Durham at Chester-le-Street	2015
8th wkt	292	R Peel (210*)	and Lord Hawke (166)	v. Warwickshire at Birmingham	1896
9th wkt	246	T T Bresnan (116)	and J N Gillespie (123*)	v. Surrey at The Oval	2007
10th wkt	149	G Boycott (79)	and G B Stevenson (115*)	v. Warwickshire at Birmingham	1982

RECORD PARTNERSHIPS AGAINST YORKSHIRE

1st wkt	372	R R Montgomerie (127)	and M B Loye (205)	for Northamptonshire at Northampton	1996
2nd wkt	417	K J Barnett (210*)	and TA Tweats (189)	for Derbyshire at Derby	1997
3rd wkt	523	M A Carberry (300*)	and N D McKenzie (237)	for Hampshire at Southampton	2011
4th wkt	447	R Abel (193)	and T Hayward (273)	for Surrey at The Oval	1899
5th wkt	261	W G Grace (318*)	and W O Moberley (103)	for Gloucestershire at Cheltenham	1876
6th wkt	346	S W Billings (138)	and D I Stevens (237)	for Kent at Leeds	2019
7th wkt	315	D M Benkenstein (151)	and O D Gibson (155)	for Durham at Leeds	2006
8th wkt	178	A P Wells (253*)	and B T P Donelan (59)	for Sussex at Middlesbrough	1991
9th wkt	233	I J L Trott (161*)	and J S Patel (120)	for Warwickshire at Birmingham	2009
10th wkt	132	A Hill (172*)	and M Jean-Jacques (73)	for Derbyshire at Sheffield	1986

CENTURY PARTNERSHIPS FOR THE FIRST WICKET
IN BOTH INNINGS

128	108	G Ulyett (82 and 91)	and L Hall (87 and 37)	v. Sussex at Hove	1885
		(First instance in First-Class cricket)			
138	147*	J T Brown (203 and 81*)	and J Tunnicliffe (62 and 63*)	v. Middlesex at Lord's	1896
		(Second instance in First-Class cricket)			
105	265*	P Holmes (51 and 127*)	and H Sutcliffe (71 and 131*)	v. Surrey at The Oval	1926
184	210*	P Holmes (83 and 101*)	and H Sutcliffe (111 and 100*)	v. Nottinghamshire at Nottingham	1928
110	117	L Hutton (95 and 86)	and W Watson (34 and 57)	v. Lancashire at Manchester	1947
122	230	W B Stott (50 and 114)	and K Taylor (79 and 140)	v. Nottinghamshire at Nottingham	1957
136	138	J B Bolus (108 and 71)	and K Taylor (89 and 75)	v. Cambridge University at Cambridge	1962
105	105	G Boycott (38 and 64)	and K Taylor (85 and 49)	v. Leicestershire at Leicester	1963
116	112*	K Taylor (45 and 68)	and J H Hampshire (68 and 67*)	v. Oxford University at Oxford	1964
104	104	G Boycott (117 and 49*)	and R G Lumb (47 and 57)	v. Sussex at Leeds	1974
134	185*	M D Moxon (57 and 89*)	and A A Metcalfe (216* and 78*)	v. Middlesex at Leeds	1988
118	129*	G S Ballance (72 and 73*)	and J J Sayers (139 and 53*)	v. Durham MCCU at Durham	2011

CENTURY PARTNERSHIPS FOR THE FIRST WICKET
IN BOTH INNINGS BUT WITH CHANGE OF PARTNER

109		W H H Sutcliffe (82) and F A Lowson (46)
	143	W H H Sutcliffe (88) and W Watson (52) v. Canadians at Scarborough, 1954
109		G Boycott (70) and R G Lumb (44)
	135	G Boycott (74) and J H Hampshire (58) v. Northamptonshire at Bradford, 1977

CENTURY PARTNERSHIPS

FIRST WICKET (Qualification 200 runs)

555	P Holmes (224*) and H Sutcliffe (313)	v. Essex at Leyton, 1932
554	J T Brown (300) and J Tunnicliffe (243)	v. Derbyshire at Chesterfield, 1898
378	J T Brown (311) and J Tunnicliffe (147)	v. Sussex at Sheffield, 1897
375	A Lyth (230) and A Z Lees (138)	v. Northamptonshire at Northampton, 2014
362	M D Moxon (213) and M P Vaughan (183)	v. Glamorgan at Cardiff, 1996
351	G Boycott (184) and M D Moxon (168)	v. Worcestershire at Worcester, 1985
347	P Holmes (302*) and H Sutcliffe (131)	v. Hampshire at Portsmouth, 1920
323	P Holmes (125) and H Sutcliffe (195)	v. Lancashire at Sheffield, 1931
315	H Sutcliffe (189) and L Hutton (153)	v. Leicestershire at Hull, 1937
315	H Sutcliffe (116) and L Hutton (280*)	v. Hampshire at Sheffield, 1939
309	P Holmes (250) and H Sutcliffe (129)	v. Warwickshire at Birmingham, 1931
309	C White (186) and M J Wood (115)	v. Lancashire at Manchester, 2001
290	P Holmes (179*) and H Sutcliffe (104)	v. Middlesex at Leeds, 1928
288	G Boycott (130*) and R G Lumb (159)	v. Somerset at Harrogate, 1979
286	L Hutton (156) and F A Lowson (115)	v. South Africans at Sheffield, 1951
282	M D Moxon (147) and A A Metcalfe (151)	v. Lancashire at Manchester, 1986
281*	W B Stott (138*) and K Taylor (130*)	v. Sussex at Hove, 1960
279	P Holmes (133) and H Sutcliffe (145)	v. Northamptonshire at Northampton, 1919
274	P.Holmes (199) and H Sutcliffe (139)	v. Somerset at Hull, 1923
274	P Holmes (180) and H Sutcliffe (134)	v. Gloucestershire at Gloucester, 1927
272	P Holmes (194) and H Sutcliffe (129)	v. Leicestershire at Hull, 1925
272	M J Wood (202*) and J J Sayers (115)	v. Bangladesh 'A' at Leeds, 2005
270	A Lyth (143) and A Z Lees (108)	v. Durham at Leeds, 2014
268	P Holmes (136) and H Sutcliffe (129)	v. Essex at Leyton, 1928
267	W Barber (248) and L Hutton (70)	v. Kent at Leeds, 1934
265*	P Holmes (127*) and H Sutcliffe (131*)	v. Surrey at The Oval, 1926
264	G Boycott (161*) and R G Lumb (132)	v. Gloucestershire at Leeds, 1976
253	P Holmes (123) and H Sutcliffe (132)	v. Lancashire at Sheffield, 1919
248	G Boycott (163) and A A Metcalfe (122)	v. Nottinghamshire at Bradford, 1983
245	L Hutton (152) and F A Lowson (120)	v. Lancashire at Leeds, 1952
244	J A Rudolph (149) and J J Sayers (86)	v Nottinghamshire at Nottingham, 2009
241	P Holmes (142) and H Sutcliffe (123*)	v. Surrey at The Oval, 1929
240	G Boycott (233) and P J Sharpe (92)	v. Essex at Colchester, 1971
238*	P Holmes (126*) and H Sutcliffe (105*)	v. Cambridge University at Cambridge, 1923
236	G Boycott (131) and K Taylor (153)	v. Lancashire at Manchester, 1964
235	P Holmes (130) and H Sutcliffe (132*)	v. Glamorgan at Sheffield, 1930
233	G Boycott (141*) and R G Lumb (90)	v. Cambridge University at Cambridge, 1973
233	H Halliday (116) and W Watson (108)	v. Northamptonshire at Northampton, 1948
231	M P Vaughan (151) and D Byas (90)	v. Essex at Chelmsford, 1999
230	H Sutcliffe (129) and L Hutton (163)	v. Surrey at Leeds, 1936
230	W B Stott (114) and K Taylor (140*)	v. Nottinghamshire at Nottingham, 1957
228	H Halliday (90) and J V Wilson (223*)	v. Scotland at Scarborough, 1951
228	G Boycott (141) and R G Lumb (101)	v. Gloucestershire at Bristol, 1975
227	P Holmes (110) and H Sutcliffe (119)	v. Leicestershire at Leicester, 1928
225	R G Lumb (101) and C W J Athey (125*)	v. Gloucestershire at Sheffield, 1980
224	C W J Athey (114) and J D Love (104)	v. Warwickshire at Birmingham, 1980
222	W B Stott (141) and K Taylor (90)	v. Sussex at Bradford, 1958
221	P Holmes (130) and H Sutcliffe (121)	v. Glamorgan at Huddersfield, 1925
221	M D Moxon (141) and A A Metcalfe (73)	v. Surrey at The Oval, 1992
221	A Lyth (111) and A Z Lees (121)	v. Leeds/Bradford MCCU at Leeds, 2013
219	P Holmes (102) and A Mitchell (130*)	v. Somerset at Bradford, 1930
218	M Leyland (110) and H Sutcliffe (235)	v. Middlesex at Leeds, 1925
218	R G Lumb (145) and M D Moxon (111)	v. Derbyshire at Sheffield, 1981
210*	P Holmes (101*) and H Sutcliffe (100*)	v. Nottinghamshire at Nottingham, 1928
210	G Boycott (128) and P J Sharpe (197)	v. Pakistanis at Leeds, 1967
209	F A Lowson (115) and D E V Padgett (107)	v. Scotland at Hull, 1956

208	A Mitchell (85) and E Oldroyd (111) v. Cambridge University at Cambridge, 1929
207	A Mitchell (90) and W Barber (107) v. Middlesex at Lord's, 1935
206	G Boycott (118) and R G Lumb (87) v. Glamorgan at Sheffield, 1978
204	M D Moxon (66) and A A Metcalfe (162) v. Gloucestershire at Cheltenham, 1990
203	L Hutton (119) and F A Lowson (83) v. Somerset at Huddersfield, 1952
203	M D Moxon (117) and S A Kellett (87) v. Somerset at Middlesbrough, 1992
203	M D Moxon (134) and M P Vaughan (106) v. Matebeleland at Bulawayo, 1996
200*	P Holmes (107*) and H Sutcliffe (80*) v. Oxford University at Oxford, 1930

Note: P Holmes and H Sutcliffe shared 69 century opening partnerships for Yorkshire;
G Boycott and R G Lumb 29; L Hutton and F A Lowson 22; M D Moxon and A A Metcalfe 21;
J T Brown and J Tunnicliffe 19; H Sutcliffe and L Hutton 15; G Boycott and P J Sharpe 13, and
L Hall and G Ulyett 12.

SECOND WICKET (Qualification 200 runs)

346	W Barber (162) and M Leyland (189) v. Middlesex at Sheffield, 1932
343	F A Lowson (183*) and J V Wilson (165) v. Oxford University at Oxford, 1956
333	P Holmes (209) and E Oldroyd (138*) v. Warwickshire at Birmingham, 1922
314	H Sutcliffe (255*) and E Oldroyd (138) v. Essex at Southend-on-Sea, 1924
311	A Z Lees (275*) and P A Jaques (139) v. Derbyshire at Chesterfield, 2013
305	J W.Rothery (134) and D Denton (182) v. Derbyshire at Chesterfield, 1910
302	W Watson (172) and J V Wilson (140) v. Derbyshire at Scarborough, 1948
301	P J Sharpe (172*) and D E V Padgett (133) v. Glamorgan at Swansea, 1971
288	H Sutcliffe (165) and A Mitchell (136) v. Lancashire at Manchester, 1939
280	L Hall (160) and F Lee (165) v. Lancashire at Bradford, 1887
266*	K Taylor (178*) and D E V Padgett (107*) v. Oxford University at Oxford, 1962
264	P A Jaques (152) and K S Williamson (97) v. Durham at Scarborough, 2013
261*	L Hutton (146*) and J V Wilson (110*) v. Scotland at Hull, 1949
260	R G Lumb (144) and K Sharp (132) v. Glamorgan at Cardiff, 1984
258	H Sutcliffe (230) and E Oldroyd (93) v. Kent at Folkestone, 1931
253	B B Wilson (150) and D Denton (200*) v. Warwickshire at Birmingham, 1912
248	H Sutcliffe (200) and M. Leyland (116) v. Leicestershire at Leicester, 1926
244	P. Holmes (138) and E Oldroyd (151*) v. Glamorgan at Cardiff, 1922
243	G Boycott (141) and J D Love (163) v. Nottinghamshire at Bradford, 1976
243	C White (183) and M J Wood (124) v. Glamorgan at Scarborough, 2001
237	H Sutcliffe (118) and D Denton (122) v. Gloucestershire at Leeds, 1919
237	M D Moxon (132) and K Sharp (128) v. Sri Lankans at Leeds, 1988
236	F A Lowson (112) and J V Wilson (157) v. Essex at Leeds, 1950
235	M D Moxon (130) and D Byas (181) v. Cambridge University at Cambridge, 1995
230	L Hutton (180) and A Mitchell (100) v. Cambridge University at Cambridge, 1938
230	M P Vaughan (109) and B Parker (138*) v. Oxford University at Oxford, 1997.
227	M J Wood (102) and M J Lumb (122) v. Leicestershire at Leeds, 2001
225	H Sutcliffe (138) and E Oldroyd (97) v. Derbyshire at Dewsbury, 1928
223	M D Moxon (153) and R J Blakey (90) v. Somerset at Leeds, 1985
222	H Sutcliffe (174) and D Denton (114) v. Kent at Dover, 1919
219	F S Jackson (155) and D Denton (113) v. Middlesex at Bradford, 1899
217	R G Lumb (107) and J D Love (107) v. Oxford University at Oxford, 1978
216	M P Vaughan (105) and D Byas (102) v. Somerset at Bradford, 1994
215	A W Gale (136) and A McGrath (99) v. Lancashire at Manchester, 2008
215	S E Marsh (125*) and A Z Lees (102) v. Surrey at The Oval, 2017
211	J A Rudolph (141) and A McGrath (80) v. Nottinghamshire at Leeds, 2010
207	P A Jaques (115) and A McGrath (93) v. Essex at Chelmsford, 2004
206	J Tunnicliffe (102) and F S Jackson (134*) v. Lancashire at Sheffield, 1898
206	H Sutcliffe (187) and M Leyland (90) v. Leicestershire at Leicester, 1931
205	H Sutcliffe (174) and A Mitchell (95) v. Leicestershire at Leicester, 1933
205	G Boycott (148) and P J Sharpe (108) v. Kent at Sheffield, 1970
203	A T Barber (100) and E Oldroyd (143) v. An England XI at Sheffield, 1929
203	J J Sayers (187) and A McGrath (100) v. Kent at Tunbridge Wells, 2007
202*	W Rhodes (115*) and G H Hirst (117*) v. Somerset at Bath, 1906
202	G Boycott (113) and C W J Athey (114) v. Northamptonshire at Northampton, 1978

THIRD WICKET (Qualification 200 runs)

346	J J Sayers (173) and A McGrath (211) v. Warwickshire at Birmingham, 2009
323*	H Sutcliffe (147*) and M Leyland (189*) v. Glamorgan at Huddersfield, 1928
317	A McGrath (165) and D S Lehmann (187) v. Lancashire at Leeds, 2002
310	A McGrath (134) and P A Jaques (219) v. Derbyshire at Leeds, 2005
301	H Sutcliffe (175) and M Leyland (180*) v. Middlesex at Lord's, 1939
293*	A A Metcalfe (150*) and P E Robinson (150*) v. Derbyshire at Scarborough, 1990
269	D Byas (101) and R J Blakey (196) v. Oxford University at Oxford, 1991
258*	J T Brown (134*) and F Mitchell (116*) v. Warwickshire at Bradford, 1901
253*	G S Ballance (101*) and J E Root (130*) v. Nottinghamshire at Nottingham, 2019
252	D E V Padgett (139*) and D B Close (154) v. Nottinghamshire at Nottingham, 1959
249	D E V Padgett (95) and D B Close (184) v. Nottinghamshire at Scarborough, 1960
248	C Johnson (102) and J H Hampshire (155*) v. Gloucestershire at Leeds, 1976
247	P Holmes (175*) and M Leyland (118) v. New Zealanders at Bradford, 1927
244	D E V Padgett (161*) and D B Close (144) v. Oxford University at Oxford, 1959
240	L Hutton (151) and M Leyland (95) v. Surrey at Leeds, 1939
237	J A Rudolph (198) and A McGrath (120) v. Worcestershire at Leeds, 2009
236	H Sutcliffe (107) and R Kilner (137) v. Nottinghamshire at Nottingham, 1920
236	M J Wood (94) and D S Lehmann (200) v. Worcestershire at Worcester, 1998
234*	D Byas (126*) and A McGrath (105*) v. Oxford University at Oxford, 1997.
233	L Hutton (101) and M Leyland (167) v. Worcestershire at Stourbridge, 1937
230	D Byas (103) and M J Wood (103) v. Derbyshire at Leeds, 1998
229	L Hall (86) and R Peel (158) v. Middlesex at Lord's, 1889
228	A Mitchell (142) and M Leyland (133) v. Worcestershire at Sheffield, 1933
228	W Barber (141) and M Leyland (114) v. Surrey at The Oval, 1939
228	J V Wilson (132*) and D E V Padgett (115) v. Warwickshire at Birmingham, 1955
226	D E V Padgett (117) and D B Close (198) v. Surrey at The Oval, 1960
224	J V Wilson (110) and D B Close (114) v. Cambridge University at Cambridge, 1955
224	G Boycott (140*) and K Sharp (121) v. Gloucestershire at Cheltenham, 1983
221	A Mitchell (138) and M Leyland (134) v. Nottinghamshire at Bradford, 1933
219	L Hall (116) and W Bates (133) v. Cambridge University at Cambridge, 1884
218	J A Rudolph (127) and A W Gale (121) v. Lancashire at Manchester, 2009
217	A McGrath (144) and J A Rudolph (129) v. Kent at Canterbury, 2008
216	R G Lumb (118) and J H Hampshire (127) v. Surrey at The Oval, 1975
215	A Mitchell (73) and M Leyland (139) v. Surrey at Bradford, 1928
213	E Oldroyd (168) and W Barber (114) v. Glamorgan at Hull, 1929
208	J V Wilson (157*) and E I Lester (112) v. Sussex at Leeds, 1949
206	A McGrath (105) and J A Rudolph (228*) v Durham at Leeds, 2010
205*	E Oldroyd (122*) and M Leyland (100*) v. Hampshire at Harrogate, 1924
205	F S Jackson (124) and D Denton (112) v. Somerset at Taunton, 1897
205	D E V Padgett (83) and D B Close (128) v. Somerset at Bath, 1959
204	M P Vaughan (113) and A McGrath (70) v. Essex at Scarborough, 2001
203	D Denton (132) and J Tunnicliffe (102) v. Warwickshire at Birmingham, 1905
203	A A Metcalfe (216*) and P E Robinson (88) v. Middlesex at Leeds, 1988
201	J Tunnicliffe (101) and T L Taylor (147) v. Surrey at The Oval, 1900
201	H Sutcliffe (87) and W Barber (130) v. Leicestershire at Leicester, 1938
200	M D Moxon (274*) and A P Grayson (100) v. Worcestershire at Worcester, 1994

FOURTH WICKET (Qualification 175 runs)

372	J E Root (213) and J M Bairstow (198) v. Surrey at Leeds, 2016
358	D S Lehmann (339) and M J Lumb (98) v. Durham at Leeds, 2006
330	M J Wood (116) and D R Martyn (238) v. Gloucestershire at Leeds, 2003
312	D Denton (168*) and G H Hirst (146) v. Hampshire at Southampton, 1914
299	P Holmes (277*) and R Kilner (150) v. Northamptonshire at Harrogate, 1921
272	D Byas (138) and A McGrath (137) v. Hampshire at Harrogate, 1996
271	B B Wilson (208) and W Rhodes (113) v. Sussex at Bradford, 1914
259	A Drake (115) and G H Hirst (218) v. Sussex at Hastings, 1911
258	J Tunnicliffe (128) and G H Hirst (152) v. Hampshire at Portsmouth, 1904

258 P E Robinson (147) and D Byas (117) v. Kent at Scarborough, 1989
255 A W Gale (148) and J A Leaning (110) v. Nottinghamshire at Leeds, 2015
254 A W Gale (164) and J M Bairstow (139) v. Worcestershire at Scarborough, 2015
249 W B Stott (143) and G Boycott (145) v. Lancashire at Sheffield, 1963
247* R G Lumb (165*) and S N Hartley (104*) v. Gloucestershire at Bradford, 1984
247 M Leyland (263) and L Hutton (83) v. Essex at Hull, 1936
238 D S Lehmann (216) and M J Lumb (92) v. Sussex at Arundel, 2002
233 D Byas (120) and P E Robinson (189) v. Essex at Scarborough, 1991
231 J E Root (236) and J M Bairstow (186) v. Derbyshire at Leeds, 2013
226 W H Wilkinson (89) and G H Hirst (160) v. Northamptonshire at Hull, 1909
225 C H Grimshaw (85) and G H Hirst (169) v. Oxford University at Oxford, 1906
212 B B Wilson (108) and G H Hirst (166*) v. Sussex at Hastings, 1913
212 G Boycott (260*) and J H Hampshire (80) v. Essex at Colchester, 1970
211 J V Wilson (120) and W Watson (108) v. Derbyshire at Harrogate, 1951
210* A Mitchell (150*) and M Leyland (117*) v. Worcestershire at Worcester, 1933
210 E I. Lester (178) and W Watson (97) v. Nottinghamshire at Nottingham, 1952
207 D Byas (213) and C White (107*) v. Worcestershire at Scarborough, 1995
206 J A Rudolph (121) and A W Gale (150) v. Surrey at The Oval, 2008
205* G Boycott (151*) and P J Sharpe (79*) v. Leicestershire at Leicester, 1964
205 E Oldroyd (121) and R Kilner (117) v. Worcestershire at Dudley, 1922
205 W Watson (162*) and E I Lester (98) v. Somerset at Leeds, 1953
205 A Lyth (111) and J M Bairstow (246) v. Hampshire at Leeds, 2016
204 A W Gale (148) and G S Ballance (90) v. Surrey at Leeds, 2013
201* J H Hampshire (105*) and D B Close (101*) v. Surrey at Bradford, 1965
203 P A Jaques (160) and G S Ballance (121*) v. Gloucestershire at Bristol, 2012
201 W H H Sutcliffe (181) and L Hutton (120) v. Kent at Canterbury, 1952
200 J V Wilson (92) and W Watson (122) v. Somerset at Taunton, 1950
198 A A Metcalfe (138) and D Byas (95) v. Warwickshire at Leeds, 1989
198 A W Gale (124) and J M Bairstow (95) v. Durham at Chester-le-Street, 2014
197 N W D Yardley (177) and A Coxon (58) v. Derbyshire at Scarborough, 1947
197 A Lyth (248*) and J M Bairstow (118) v. Leicestershire at Leicester, 2012
196 M D Moxon (130) and D L Bairstow (104) v. Derbyshire at Harrogate, 1987
193 A Drake (85) and G H Hirst (156) v. Lancashire at Manchester, 1911
192 J V Wilson (132) and W Watson (105) v. Essex at Bradford, 1955
191 M Leyland (114) and C Turner (63) v. Essex at Ilford, 1938
190 A W Gale (125) and J A Leaning (76) v. Hampshire at West End, Southampton, 2015
188 H Myers (60) and G H Hirst (158) v. Cambridge University at Cambridge, 1910
188 G S Ballance (159) and J A Leaning (69) v. Kent at Canterbury, 2019
187 E Oldroyd (168) and F E Greenwood (104*) v. Glamorgan at Hull, 1929
187 K Taylor (203*) and W B Stott (57) v. Warwickshire at Birmingham, 1961
186 D S Lehmann (193) and D Byas (100) v. Leicestershire at Leicester, 2001
184 J H Hampshire (96) and R Illingworth (100*) v. Leicestershire at Sheffield, 1968
182* E I Lester (101*) and W Watson (103*) v. Nottinghamshire at Bradford, 1952
180* G Boycott (207*) and B Leadbeater (50*) v. Cambridge University
                                 at Cambridge, 1976
180 J Tunnicliffe (139*) and G H Hirst (108) v. Surrey at The Oval, 1904
179 J H Hampshire (179) and S N Hartley (63) v. Surrey at Harrogate, 1981
179 M D Moxon (171*) and R J Blakey (71) v. Kent at Leeds, 1993
178 E I Lester (186) and J V Wilson (71) v. Warwickshiire at Scarborough, 1949
177 J D Love (105*) and J H Hampshire (89) v. Lancashire at Manchester, 1980
175 L Hutton (177) and W Barber (84) v. Sussex at Scarborough, 1939
175 A McGrath (188*) and J A Rudolph (82) v. Warwickshire at Birmingham, 2007

FIFTH WICKET (Qualification 150 runs)

340 E Wainwright (228) and G H Hirst (186) v. Surrey at The Oval, 1899
329 F Mitchell (194) and E Wainwright (153) v. Leicestershire at Leicester, 1899
297 A W Gale (272) and G S Ballance (141) v. Nottinghamshire at Scarborough, 2013
276 W Rhodes (104*) and R Kilner (166) v. Northamptonshire at Northampton, 1921
273 L Hutton (270*) and N W D Yardley (136) v. Hampshire at Bournemouth, 1947

245*	H Sutcliffe (107*) and W Barber (128*) v. Northamptonshire at Northampton, 1939
229	D S Lehmann (193) and C White (79) v. Kent at Canterbury, 2006
217	D B Close (140*) and R Illingworth (107) v. Warwickshire at Sheffield, 1962
213	T Kohler-Cadmore (176) and J A Tattersall (135*) v. Leeds/Bradford MCCU at Weetwood, Leeds, 2019
207	G S Ballance (107) and A U Rashid (180) v. Somerset at Leeds, 2013
200	D J Malan (219) and J A Tattersall (66) v. Derbyshire at Leeds, 2020
198	E Wainwright (145) and R Peel (111) v. Sussex at Bradford, 1896
198	W Barber (168) and K R Davidson (101*) v. MCC at Lord's, 1934
196*	R Kilner (115*) and G H Hirst (82*) v. Gloucestershire at Leeds, 1919
195	M J Lumb (93) and C White (173*) v. Derbyshire at Derby, 2003
194*	Younus Khan (202*) and G L Brophy (100*) v. Hampshire at Southampton, 2007
193	A Mitchell (189) and W Rhodes (88) v. Northamptonshire at Northampton, 1926
193	J D Love (106) and S N Hartley (108) v. Oxford University at Oxford, 1985
192	C W J Athey (114*) and J D Love (123) v. Surrey at The Oval, 1982
191*	L Hutton (271*) and C Turner (81*) v. Derbyshire at Sheffield, 1937
191	M G Bevan (105) and A A Metcalfe (100) v. West Indians at Scarborough, 1995
190*	R J Blakey (204*) and J D Love (79*) v. Gloucestershire at Leeds, 1987
189	J E Root (160) and G S Ballance (87) v. Sussex at Scarborough 2011
188	D E V Padgett (146) and J V Wilson (72) v. Sussex at Middlesbrough, 1960
187	J V Wilson (230) and H Halliday (74) v. Derbyshire at Sheffield, 1952
185	G Boycott (104*) and K Sharp (99) v. Kent at Tunbridge Wells, 1984
182	E Lockwood (208) and E Lumb (40) v. Kent at Gravesend, 1882
182	B B Wilson (109) and W Rhodes (111) v. Sussex at Hove, 1910
182	D B Close (164) and J V Wilson (55) v. Combined Services at Harrogate, 1954
182	A W Gale (126*) and J A Leaning (76) v. Middlesex at Scarborough, 2014
181	A A Metcalfe (149) and J D Love (88) v. Glamorgan at Leeds, 1986
177	Hon F S Jackson (87) and G H Hirst (232*) v. Surrey at The Oval, 1905
176	L Hutton (176*) and A Coxon (72) v. Sussex at Sheffield, 1948
175	A Drake (108) and R Kilner (71) v. Cambridge University at Cambridge, 1913
173	H Sutcliffe (206) and R Kilner (124) v. Warwickshire at Dewsbury, 1925
170	W Rhodes (157) and R Kilner (87) v. Derbyshire at Leeds, 1925
170	J V Wilson (130*) and N W D Yardley (67) v. Lancashire at Manchester, 1954
169	W Watson (147) and A B Sellers (92) v. Worcestershire at Worcester, 1947
168	A T Barber (63) and A Mitchell (122*) v. Worcestershire at Worcester, 1929
167	J M Bairstow (136) and G S Ballance (61) v. Somerset at Taunton 2011
165	E Oldroyd (143) and W Rhodes (110) v. Glamorgan at Leeds, 1922
165	K Sharp (100*) and P Carrick (73) v. Middlesex at Lord's, 1980
164	A A Metcalfe (151) and D L Bairstow (88) v. Northamptonshire at Luton, 1986
159*	J D Love (170*) and D L Bairstow (52*) v. Worcestershire at Worcester, 1979
159	D B Close (128) and R Illingworth (74) v. Lancashire at Sheffield, 1959
159	J H Hampshire (183*) and C Johnson (53) v. Sussex at Hove, 1971
158*	G Boycott (153*) and P E Robinson (74*) v. Derbyshire at Harrogate, 1984
157	T L Taylor (135*) and G H Hirst (72) v. An England XI at Hastings, 1901
157	G H Hirst (142) and F Smith (51) v. Somerset at Leeds, 1903
157	W Barber (87) and N W D Yardley (101) v. Surrey at The Oval, 1937
156	A McGrath (158) and I J Harvey (103) v. Derbyshire at Derby, 2005
155	J M Bairstow (102) and J A Leaning (82) v. Hampshire at Leeds, 2015
153	S N Hartley (87) and M D Moxon (112*) v. Indians at Scarborough, 1986
152	J H Hampshire (83) and S N Hartley (106) v. Nottinghamshire at Nottingham, 1981
151*	G H Hirst (102*) and R Kilner (50*) v. Kent at Bradford, 1913
151	G H Hirst (120) and F Smith (55) v. Kent at Leeds, 1903
151	W Rhodes (57) and R Kilner (90) v. Nottinghamshire at Nottingham, 1925

SIXTH WICKET (Qualification 150 runs)

296	A Lyth (251) and A U Rashid (159*) v. Lancashire at Manchester, 2014
276	M Leyland (191) and E Robinson (124*) v. Glamorgan at Swansea, 1926
252	C White (181) and R J Blakey (109*) v. Lancashire at Leeds, 1996
248	G J Maxwell (140) and A U Rashid (127) v. Durham at Scarborough, 2015
233	M W Booth (210) and G H Hirst (100) v. Worcestershire at Worcester, 1911

229	W Rhodes (267*) and N Kilner (112) v. Leicestershire at Leeds, 1921
225	E Wainwright (91) and Lord Hawke (127) v. Hampshire at Southampton, 1899
217*	H Sutcliffe (200*) and A Wood (123*) v. Worcestershire at Sheffield, 1935
214	W Watson (214*) and N W D Yardley (76) v. Worcestershire at Worcester, 1955
205	G H Hirst (125) and S Haigh (159) v. Nottinghamshire at Sheffield, 1901
200	D Denton (127) and G H Hirst (134) v. Essex at Bradford, 1902
198	M Leyland (247) and W Rhodes (100*) v. Worcestershire at Worcester, 1928
190	W Rhodes (126) and M Leyland (79) v. Middlesex at Bradford, 1923
190	J A Rudolph (122) and A U Rashid (86) v. Surrey at The Oval, 2007
188	W Watson (174) and R Illingworth (53) v. Lancashire at Sheffield, 1955
188	M P Vaughan (161) and R J Blakey (92) v. Essex at Ilford, 1997.
188	G S Ballance (111) and A U Rashid (82) v. Warwickshire at Birmingham 2011
184	R Kilner (104) and M W Booth (79) v. Leicestershire at Leeds, 1913
183	G H Hirst (131) and E Smith (129) v. Hampshire at Bradford, 1899
183	W Watson (139*) and R Illingworth (78) v. Somerset at Harrogate, 1956
178*	D Denton (108*) and G H Hirst (112*) v. Lancashire at Manchester, 1902
178*	N W D Yardley (100*) and R Illingworth (71*) v. Gloucestershire at Bristol, 1955
178	E Robinson (100) and D C F Burton (83) v. Derbyshire at Hull, 1921
178	H Sutcliffe (135) and P A Gibb (157*) v. Nottinghamshire at Sheffield, 1935
175	G M Fellows (88) and R J Blakey (103) v. Warwickshire at Birmingham, 2002
174	D S Lehmann (136) and G M Hamilton (73) v. Kent at Maidstone, 1998
173	T Kohler-Cadmore (81) and A J Hodd (85) v. Somerset at Leeds, 2018
172	A J Dalton (119*) and D L Bairstow (62) v. Worcestershire at Dudley, 1971
170*	A U Rashid 103*) and A J Hodd (68*) v. Somerset at Taunton, 2013
170	A W Gale (101) and T T Bresnan (97) v. Worcestershire at Worcester, 2009
169	W Barber (124) and H Verity (78*) v. Warwickshire at Birmingham, 1933
169	R Illingworth (162) and J Birkenshaw (37) v. Indians at Sheffield, 1959
166	E Wainwright (116) and E Smith (61) v. Kent at Catford, 1900
166	D B Close (161) and F S Trueman (104) v. Northamptonshire at Northampton, 1963
162*	G Boycott (220*) and J G Binks (70*) v. Northamptonshire at Sheffield, 1967
161*	D L Bairstow (100*) and P Carrick (59*) v. Middlesex at Leeds, 1983
159*	D S Lehmann (187*) and R J Blakey (78*) v. Somerset at Bath, 2001
159	J M Bairstow (182) and A McGrath (90) v. Leicestershire at Scarborough, 2012
156	W Rhodes (82*) and E Robinson (94) v. Derbyshire at Chesterfield, 1919
154	C Turner (84) and A Wood (79) v. Glamorgan at Swansea, 1936
153*	J A Rudolph (92*) and A U Rashid (73*) v. Worcestershire at Kidderminster, 2007
153	J A Rudolph (69*) and J M Bairstow (81) v. Warwickshire at Birmingham, 2010
151	D Denton (91) and W Rhodes (76) v. Middlesex at Sheffield, 1904
151	G Boycott (152*) and P Carrick (75) v. Warwickshire at Leeds, 1982
150	G Ulyett (199*) and J M Preston (93) v. Derbyshire at Sheffield, 1887

SEVENTH WICKET (Qualification 125 runs)

366*	J M Bairstow (219*) and T T Bresnan (169*) v. Durham at Chester-le-Street, 2015
254	W Rhodes (135) and D C F Burton (142*) v. Hampshire at Dewsbury, 1919
247	P Holmes (285) and W Rhodes (79) v. Nottinghamshire at Nottingham, 1929
227	J M Bairstow (246) and L E Plunkett (126) v. Hampshire at Leeds, 2016
215	E Robinson (135*) and D C F Burton (110) v. Leicestershire at Leicester, 1921
197	G S Ballance (165*) and T T Bresnan (78) v. Sussex at Hove, 2015
185	E Wainwright (100) and G H Hirst (134) v. Gloucestershire at Bristol, 1897
183	G H Hirst (341) and H Myers (57) v. Leicestershire at Leicester, 1905
183	J A Rudolph (220) and T T Bresnan (101*) v. Warwickshire at Scarborough, 2007
180	C Turner (130) and A Wood (97) v. Somerset at Sheffield, 1936
170	G S Blewett (190) and G M Hamilton (84*) v. Northamptonshire at Scarborough, 1999
168	G L Brophy (99) and A Rashid (157*) v. Lancashire at Leeds, 2009
166	R Peel (55) and I Grimshaw (122*) v. Derbyshire at Holbeck, 1886
162	E Wainwright (109) and S Haigh (73) v. Somerset at Taunton, 1900
162	R J Blakey (90) and R K J Dawson (87) v. Kent at Canterbury, 2002
162	A W Gale (149) and G L Brophy (97) v. Warwickshire at Scarborough, 2006

CENTURY PARTNERSHIPS *(Continued)*

161	R G Lumb (118) and C M Old (89) v. Worcestershire at Bradford, 1980
160	J Tunnicliffe (158) and D Hunter (58*) v. Worcestershire at Worcester, 1900
157*	F A Lowson (259*) and R Booth (53*) v. Worcestershire at Bramall Lane, 1953
157	K S Williamson (189) and T T Bresnan (61) v. Sussex at Scarborough, 2014
155	D Byas (122*) and P Carrick (61) v. Leicestershire at Leicester.1991.
154*	G H Hirst (76*) and J T Newstead (100*) v. Nottinghamshire at Nottingham, 1908
148	J Rowbotham (113) and J Thewlis (50) v. Surrey at The Oval, 1873
147	E Wainwright (78) and G Ulyett (73) v. Somerset at Taunton, 1893
147	M P Vaughan (153) and R J Harden (64) v. Kent at Scarborough, 1999
143	C White (135*) and A K D Gray (60) v. Durham at Chester-le-Street, 2003
141	G H Hirst (108*) and S Haigh (48) v. Worcestershire at Worcester, 1905
141	J H Hampshire (149*) and J G Binks (72) v. MCC at Scarborough, 1965
140	E Wainwright (117) and S Haigh (54) v. CI Thornton's XI at Scarborough, 1900
140	D Byas (67) and P J Hartley (75) v. Derbyshire at Chesterfield, 1990
138	D Denton (78) and G H Hirst (103*) v. Sussex at Leeds, 1905
136	GH Hirst (93) and S Haigh (138) v. Warwickshire at Birmingham, 1904
136	E Robinson (77*) and A Wood (65) v. Glamorgan at Scarborough, 1931
133*	W Rhodes (267*) and M Leyland (52*) v. Leicestershire at Leeds, 1921
133*	E I Lester (86*) and A B Sellers (73*) v. Northamptonshire at Northampton, 1948
133	D Byas (100) and P W Jarvis (63) v. Northamptonshire at Scarborough, 1992
132	W Rhodes (196) and S Haigh (59*) v. Worcestershire at Worcester, 1904
132	A J Hodd (96*) and Azeem Rafiq (74) v. Nottinghamshire at Scarborough, 2016
131*	D L Bairstow (79*) and A Sidebottom (52*) v. Oxford University at Oxford, 1981
130	P J Sharpe (64) and J V Wilson (134) v. Warwickshire at Birmingham, 1962
128	W Barber (66) and T F Smailes (86) v. Cambridge University at Cambridge, 1938
128	D B Close (88*) and A Coxon (59) v. Essex at Leeds, 1949
126	E Wainwright (171) and R Peel (46) v. Middlesex at Lord's, 1897
126	W Rhodes (91) and G G Macaulay (63) v. Hampshire at Hull, 1925
126	J C Balderstone (58) and J G Binks (95) v. Middlesex at Lord's, 1964
126	J M Bairstow (70) and A U Rashid (59) v. Kent at Canterbury, 2010
125	A B Sellers (109) and T F Smailes (65) v. Kent at Bradford, 1937

EIGHTH WICKET (Qualification 125 runs)

292	R Peel (210*) and Lord Hawke (166) v. Warwickshire at Birmingham, 1896
238	I J Harvey (209*) and T T Bresnan (74) v. Somerset at Leeds, 2005
192*	W Rhodes (108*) and G G Macaulay (101*) v. Essex at Harrogate, 1922
192	A U Rashid (117*) and A Shahzad (78) v. Hampshire at Basingstoke, 2009
180	W Barber (191) and T F Smailes (89) v. Sussex at Leeds, 1935
167	J A Leaning (118) and J A Brooks (109*) v. Lancashire at Manchester, 2017
165	S Haigh (62) and Lord Hawke (126) v. Surrey at The Oval, 1902
163	G G Macaulay (67) and A Waddington (114) v. Worcestershire at Leeds, 1927
159	E Smith (95) and W Rhodes (105) v. MCC at Scarborough, 1901
157	A Shahzad (88) and D J Wainwright (85*) v. Sussex at Hove, 2009
156	G S Ballance (112) and R J Sidebottom (40) v. Leeds/Bradford MCCU at Leeds, 2013
152	W Rhodes (98) and J W Rothery (70) v. Hampshire at Portsmouth, 1904
151	W Rhodes (201) and Lord Hawke (51) v. Somerset at Taunton, 1905
151	R J Blakey (80*) and P J Hartley (89) v. Sussex at Eastbourne, 1996
149	G L Brophy (177*) and R J Sidebottom (61) v. Worcestershire at Worcester 2011
147	J P G Chadwick (59) and F S Trueman (101) v. Middlesex at Scarborough, 1965
146	S Haigh (59) and Lord Hawke (89) v. Nottinghamshire at Sheffield, 1901
144	G L Brophy (85) and D J Wainwright (102*) v. Warwickshire at Scarborough, 2009
138	E Wainwright (100) and Lord Hawke (81) v. Kent at Tonbridge, 1899
137	E Wainwright (171) and Lord Hawke (75) v. Middlesex at Lord's, 1897
135	P W Jarvis (55) and P J Hartley (91) v. Nottinghamshire at Scarborough, 1992
133	R Illingworth (61) and F S Trueman (74) v. Leicestershire at Leicester, 1955
132	G H Hirst (103) and E Smith (59) v. Middlesex at Sheffield, 1904
132	W Watson (119) and J H Wardle (65) v. Leicestershire at Leicester, 1949
131	P E Robinson (85) and P Carrick (64) v. Surrey at Harrogate, 1990
130	E Smith (98) and Lord Hawke (54) v. Lancashire at Leeds, 1904

CENTURY PARTNERSHIPS *(Continued)*

128	H Verity (96*) and T F Smailes (77) v. Indians at Bradford, 1936
128	D L Bairstow (145) and G B Stevenson (11) v. Middlesex at Scarborough, 1980
127	E Robinson (70*) and A Wood (62) v. Middlesex at Leeds, 1928
126	R Peel (74) and E Peate (61) v. Gloucestershire at Bradford, 1883
126	M W Booth (56) and E R Wilson (104*) v. Essex at Bradford, 1913
126	J D Middlebrook (84) and C E W Silverwood (70) v. Essex at Chelmsford, 2001
126	M J Lumb (115*) and D Gough (72) v. Hampshire at Southampton, 2003

NINTH WICKET (Qualification 100 runs)

246	T T Bresnan (116) and J N Gillespie (123*) v. Surrey at The Oval, 2007
192	G H Hirst (130*) and S Haigh (85) v. Surrey at Bradford, 1898
179	R A Hutton (189) and G A Cope (30*) v. Pakistanis at Bradford, 1971
176*	R Moorhouse (59*) and G H Hirst (115*) v. Gloucestershire at Bristol, 1894
173	S Haigh (85) and W Rhodes (92*) v. Sussex at Hove, 1902
171	G S Ballance (194) and A Brooks (82) v. Worcestershire at Worcester, 2018
167	H Verity (89) and T F Smailes (80) v. Somerset at Bath, 1936
162	W Rhodes (94*) and S Haigh (68) v. Lancashire at Manchester, 1904
161	E Smith (116*) and W Rhodes (79) v. Sussex at Sheffield, 1900
154	R M Pyrah (117) and R J Sidebottom (52) v. Lancashire at Leeds 2011
151	J M Bairstow (205) and R J Sidebottom (45*) v. Nottinghamshire at Nottingham 2011
150	Azeem Rafiq (100) and M J Hoggard (56*) v. Worcestershire at Worcester, 2009
149*	R J Blakey (63*) and A K D Gray (74*) v. Leicestershire at Scarborough, 2002
149	G H Hirst (232*) and D Hunter (40) v. Surrey at The Oval, 1905
146	G H Hirst (214) and W Rhodes (53) v. Worcestershire at Worcester, 1901
144	T T Bresnan (91) and J N Gillespie (44) v. Hampshire at Leeds, 2006
140	A U Rashid (111) and D J Wainwright (104) v. Sussex at Hove, 2008
136	R Peel (210*) and G H Hirst (85) v. Warwickshire at Birmingham, 1896
125*	L Hutton (269*) and A Coxon (65*) v. Northamptonshire at Wellingborough, 1949
124	P J Hartley (87*) and P W Jarvis (47) v. Essex at Chelmsford, 1986
120	G H Hirst (138) and W Rhodes (38) v. Nottinghamshire at Nottingham, 1899
119	A B Sellers (80*) and E P Robinson (66) v. Warwickshire at Birmingham, 1938
118	S Haigh (96) and W Rhodes (44) v. Somerset at Leeds, 1901
114	E Oldroyd (194) and A Dolphin (47) v. Worcestershire at Worcester, 1923
114	N Kilner (102*) and G G Macaulay (60) v. Gloucestershire at Bristol, 1923
113	G G Macaulay (125*) and A Waddington (44) v. Nottinghamshire at Nottingham, 1921
113	A Wood (69) and H.Verity (45*) v. MCC at Lord's, 1938
112	G H Hirst (78) and Lord Hawke (61*) v. Essex at Leyton, 1907
109	Lees Whitehead (60) and W Rhodes (81*) v. Sussex at Harrogate, 1899
108	A McGrath (133*) and C E W Silverwood (80) v. Durham at Chester-le-Street, 2005
106	L E Plunkett (86) and S A Patterson (43) v. Warwickshire at Leeds, 2014
105	J V Wilson (134) and A G Nicholson (20*) v. Nottinghamshire at Leeds, 1962
105	C M Old (100*) and H P Cooper (30) v. Lancashire at Manchester, 1978
105	C White (74*) and J D Batty (50) v. Gloucestershire at Sheffield, 1993
104	L Hall (129*) and R Moorhouse (86) v. Gloucestershire at Clifton, 1888
100	G Pollitt (51) and Lees Whitehead (79) v. Hampshire at Bradford, 1899

TENTH WICKET (Qualification 100 runs)

149	G Boycott (79) and G B Stevenson (115*) v. Warwickshire at Birmingham, 1982
148	Lord Hawke (107*) and D Hunter (47) v. Kent at Sheffield, 1898
144	A Sidebottom (124) and A L Robinson (30*) v. Glamorgan at Cardiff, 1977
121	J T Brown (141) and D Hunter (25*) v. Liverpool & District at Liverpool, 1894
118	Lord Hawke (110*) and D Hunter (41) v. Kent at Leeds, 1896
113	P J Hartley (88*) and R D Stemp (22) v. Middlesex at Lord's, 1996
110	C E W. Silverwood (45*) and R D Stemp (65) v. Durham at Chester-le-Street, 1996
109	A Shahzad (70) and R J Sidebottom (28*) v. Worcestershire at Scarborough, 2011
108	Lord Hawke (79) and Lees Whitehead (45*) v. Lancashire at Manchester, 1903
108	G Boycott (129) and M K Bore (37*) v. Nottinghamshire at Bradford, 1973
106	A B Sellers (79) and D V Brennan (30) v. Worcestershire at Worcester, 1948
106	A Dolphin (62*) and E Smith (49) v. Essex at Leyton, 1919
102	D Denton (77*) and D Hunter (45) v. Cambridge University at Cambridge, 1895

FIFTEEN WICKETS OR MORE IN A MATCH

**A complete list of 12, 13 and 14 wickets in a match up to and including 2007
is to be found in the 2008 edition**

W E BOWES (1)

16 for 35 (8 for 18 and 8 for 17) v. Northamptonshire at Kettering, 1935

A DRAKE (1)

15 for 51 (5 for 16 and 10 for 35) v. Somerset at Weston-super-Mare, 1914

T EMMETT (1)

16 for 38 (7 for 15 and 9 for 23) v. Cambridgeshire at Hunslet, 1869

G H HIRST (1)

15 for 63 (8 for 25 and 7 for 38) v. Leicestershire at Hull, 1907

R ILLINGWORTH (1)

15 for 123 (8 for 70 and 7 for 53) v. Glamorgan at Swansea, 1960

R PEEL (1)

15 for 50 (9 for 22 and 6 for 28) v. Somerset at Leeds, 1895

W RHODES (1)

15 for 56 (9 for 28 and 6 for 28) v. Essex at Leyton, 1899

H VERITY (4)

17 for 91 (8 for 47 and 9 for 44) v. Essex at Leyton, 1933
15 for 129 (8 for 56 and 7 for 73) v. Oxford University at Oxford, 1936
15 for 38 (6 for 26 and 9 for 12) v. Kent at Sheffield, 1936
15 for 100 (6 for 52 and 9 for 48) v. Essex at Westcliffe-on-Sea, 1936

J H WARDLE (1)

16 for 112 (9 for 48 and 7 for 64) v. Sussex at Hull, 1954

TEN WICKETS IN A MATCH
(including best analysis)

61	W Rhodes	15 for	56	v Essex	at Leyton	1899
48	H Verity	17 for	91	v Essex	at Leyton	1933
40	G H Hirst	15 for	63	v Leicestershire	at Hull	1907
31	G G Macaulay	14 for	92	v Gloucestershire	at Bristol	1926
28	S Haigh	14 for	43	v Hampshire	at Southampton	1898
27	R Peel	14 for	33	v Nottinghamshire	at Sheffield	1888
25	W E Bowes	16 for	35	v Northamptonshire	at Kettering	1935
25	J H Wardle	16 for	112	v Sussex	at Hull	1954
22	E Peate	14 for	77	v Surrey	at Huddersfield	1881
20	F S Trueman	14 for	123	v Surrey	at The Oval	1960
19	T Emmett	16 for	38	v Cambridgeshire	at Hunslet	1869
17	R Appleyard	12 for	43	v Essex	at Bradford	1951
15	E Wainwright	14 for	77	v Essex	at Bradford	1896
11	R Illingworth	15 for	123	v Glamorgan	at Swansea	1960
10	A Waddington	13 for	48	v Northamptonshire	at Northampton	1920
9	M W Booth	14 for	160	v Essex	at Leyton	1914
9	R Kilner	12 for	55	v Sussex	at Hove	1924
8	W Bates	11 for	47	v Nottinghamshire	at Nottingham	1881
8	G Freeman	13 for	60	v Surrey	at Sheffield	1869
7	E P Robinson	13 for	115	v Lancashire	at Leeds	1939
7	D Wilson	13 for	52	v Warwickshire	at Middlesbrough	1967
6	G A Cope	12 for	116	v Glamorgan	at Cardiff (Sophia Gardens)	1968
6	A Hill	12 for	59	v Surrey	at The Oval	1871

6 T F Smailes	14 for 58	v Derbyshire	at Sheffield	1939
5 P Carrick	12 for 89	v Derbyshire	at Sheffield (Abbeydale Pk)	1983
5 J M Preston	13 for 63	v MCC	at Scarborough	1888
5 E Robinson	12 for 95	v Northamptonshire	at Huddersfield	1927
4 J T Newstead	11 for 72	v Worcestershire	at Bradford	1907
3 T W Foster	11 for 93	v Liverpool & District	at Liverpool	1894
3 G P Harrison	11 for 76	v Kent	at Dewsbury	1883
3 F S Jackson	12 for 80	v Hampshire	at Southampton	1897
3 P W Jarvis	11 for 92	v Middlesex	at Lord's	1986
3 S P Kirby	13 for 154	v Somerset	at Taunton	2003
3 A G Nicholson	12 for 73	v Glamorgan	at Leeds	1964
3 R K Platt	10 for 87	v Surrey	at The Oval	1959
3 A Sidebottom	11 for 64	v Kent	at Sheffield (Abbeydale Pk)	1980
3 R J Sidebottom	11 for 43	v Kent	at Leeds	2000
3 G Ulyett	12 for 102	v Lancashire	at Huddersfield	1889
2 T Armitage	13 for 46	v Surrey	at Sheffield	1876
2 R Aspinall	14 for 65	v Northamptonshire	at Northampton	1947
2 J T Brown (Darfield)	12 for 109	v Gloucestershire	at Huddersfield	1899
2 R O Clayton	12 for 104	v Lancashire	at Manchester	1877
2 D B Close	11 for 116	v Kent	at Gillingham	1965
2 B O Coad	10 for 102	v. Warwickshire	at Birmingham	2017
2 M J Cowan	12 for 87	v Warwickshire	at Birmingham	1960
2 A Coxon	10 for 57	v Derbyshire	at Chesterfield	1949
2 D Gough	10 for 80	v Lancashire	at Leeds	1995
2 G M Hamilton	11 for 72	v Surrey	at Leeds	1998
2 P J Hartley	11 for 68	v Derbyshire	at Chesterfield	1995
2 R A Hutton	11 for 62	v Lancashire	at Manchester	1971
2 E Leadbeater	11 for 162	v Nottinghamshire	at Nottingham	1950
2 K A Maharaj	10 for 127	v. Somerset	at Leeds	2019
2 M A Robinson	12 for 124	v Northamptonshire	at Harrogate	1993
2 M Ryan	10 for 77	v Leicestershire	at Bradford	1962
2 E Smith (Morley)	10 for 97	v MCC	at Scarborough	1893
2 G B Stevenson	11 for 74	v Nottinghamshire	at Nottingham	1980
2 S Wade	11 for 56	v Gloucestershire	at Cheltenham	1886
2 E R Wilson	11 for 109	v Sussex	at Hove	1921
1 A B Bainbridge	12 for 111	v Essex	at Harrogate	1961
1 J Birkenshaw	11 for 134	v Middlesex	at Leeds	1960
1 A Booth	10 for 91	v Indians	at Bradford	1946
1 H P Cooper	11 for 96	v Northamptonshire	at Northampton	1976
1 A Drake	15 for 51	v Somerset	at Weston-Super-Mare	1914
1 L Greenwood	11 for 71	v Surrey	at The Oval	1867
1 P M Hutchison	11 for 102	v Pakistan 'A'	at Leeds	1997
1 L Hutton	10 for 101	v Leicestershire	at Leicester (Aylestone Rd)	1937
1 R Iddison	10 for 68	v Surrey	at Sheffield	1864
1 M Leyland	10 for 94	v Leicestershire	at Leicester (Aylestone Rd)	1933
1 J D Middlebrook	10 for 170	v Hampshire	at Southampton	2000
1 F W Milligan	12 for 110	v Sussex	at Sheffield	1897
1 H Myers	12 for 192	v Gloucestershire	at Dewsbury	1904
1 C M Old	11 for 46	v Gloucestershire	at Middlesbrough	1969
1 D Pickles	12 for 133	v Somerset	at Taunton	1957
1 A U Rashid	11 for 114	v Worcestershire	at Worcester	2011
1 W Ringrose	11 for 135	v Australians	at Bradford	1905
1 C E W Silverwood	12 for 148	v Kent	at Leeds	1997
1 W Slinn	12 for 53	v Nottinghamshire	at Nottingham	1864
1 J Waring	10 for 63	v Lancashire	at Leeds	1966
1 F Wilkinson	10 for 129	v Hampshire	at Bournemouth	1938
1 A C Williams	10 for 66	v Hampshire	at Dewsbury	1919

TEN WICKETS IN AN INNINGS

Bowler				*Year*
A Drake	10 for 35	v.	Somerset at Weston-super-Mare	1914
H Verity	10 for 36	v.	Warwickshire at Leeds	1931
*H Verity	10 for 10	v.	Nottinghamshire at Leeds	1932
T F Smailes	10 for 47	v.	Derbyshire at Sheffield	1939

*Includes the hat trick.

EIGHT WICKETS OR MORE IN AN INNINGS

(Ten wickets in an innings also listed above)

A complete list of seven wickets in an innings up to and including 2007 is to be found in the 2008 edition

R APPLEYARD (1)

8 for 76 v. MCC at Scarborough, 1951

R ASPINALL (1)

8 for 42 v. Northamptonshire at Northampton, 1947

W BATES (2)

8 for 45 v. Lancashire at Huddersfield, 1878
8 for 21 v. Surrey at The Oval, 1879

M W BOOTH (4)

8 for 52 v. Leicestershire at Sheffield, 1912
8 for 47 v. Middlesex at Leeds, 1912
8 for 86 v. Middlesex at Sheffield, 1913
8 for 64 v. Essex at Leyton, 1914

W E BOWES (9)

8 for 77 v. Leicestershire at Dewsbury, 1929
8 for 69 v. Middlesex at Bradford, 1930
9 for 121 v. Essex at Scarborough, 1932
8 for 62 v. Sussex at Hove, 1932
8 for 69 v. Gloucestershire at Gloucester, 1933
8 for 40 v.Worcestershire at Sheffield, 1935
8 for 18 v. Northamptonshire at Kettering, 1935
8 for 17 v. Northamptonshire at Kettering, 1935
8 for 56 v. Leicestershire at Scarborough, 1936

J T BROWN (Darfield) (1)

8 for 40 v. Gloucestershire at Huddersfield, 1899

P CARRICK (2)

8 for 33 v. Cambridge University at Cambridge, 1973
8 for 72 v. Derbyshire at Scarborough, 1975

R O CLAYTON (1)

8 for 66 v. Lancashire at Manchester, 1877

D B CLOSE (2)

8 for 41 v. Kent at Leeds, 1959
8 for 43 v. Essex at Leeds, 1960

H P COOPER (1)

8 for 62 v. Glamorgan at Cardiff, 1975

EIGHT WICKETS OR MORE IN AN INNINGS *(Continued)*

G A COPE (1)

8 for 73 v. Gloucestershire at Bristol, 1975

M J COWAN (1)

9 for 43 v. Warwickshire at Birmingham, 1960

A COXON (1)

8 for 31 v. Worcestershire at Leeds, 1946

A DRAKE (2)

8 for 59 v. Gloucestershire at Sheffield, 1913
10 for 35 v. Somerset at Weston-super-Mare, 1914

T EMMETT (8)

9 for 34 v. Nottinghamshire at Dewsbury, 1868
9 for 23 v. Cambridgeshire at Hunslet, 1869
8 for 31 v. Nottinghamshire at Sheffield, 1871
8 for 46 v. Gloucestershire at Clifton, 1877
8 for 16 v. MCC at Scarborough, 1877
8 for 22 v. Surrey at The Oval, 1881
8 for 52 v. MCC at Scarborough, 1882
8 for 32 v. Sussex at Huddersfield, 1884

S D FLETCHER (1)

8 for 58 v. Essex at Sheffield, 1988

T W FOSTER (1)

9 for 59 v. MCC at Lord's, 1894

G FREEMAN (2)

8 for 11 v. Lancashire at Holbeck, 1868
8 for 29 v. Surrey at Sheffield, 1869

L GREENWOOD (1)

8 for 35 v. Cambridgeshire at Dewsbury, 1867

S HAIGH (5)

8 for 78 v. Australians at Bradford, 1896
8 for 35 v. Hampshire at Harrogate, 1896
8 for 21 v. Hampshire at Southampton, 1898
8 for 33 v. Warwickshire at Scarborough, 1899
9 for 25 v. Gloucestershire at Leeds, 1912

P J HARTLEY (2)

8 for 111 v. Sussex at Hove, 1992
9 for 41 v. Derbyshire at Chesterfield, 1995

G H HIRST (8)

8 for 59 v. Warwickshire at Birmingham, 1896
8 for 48 v. Australians at Bradford, 1899
8 for 25 v. Leicestershire at Hull, 1907
9 for 45 v. Middlesex at Sheffield, 1907
9 for 23 v. Lancashire at Leeds, 1910
8 for 80 v. Somerset at Sheffield, 1910
9 for 41 v. Worcestershire at Worcester, 1911
9 for 69 v. MCC at Lord's, 1912

EIGHT WICKETS OR MORE IN AN INNINGS *(Continued)*

R ILLINGWORTH (5)

8 for 69 v. Surrey at The Oval, 1954
9 for 42 v. Worcestershire at Worcester, 1957
8 for 70 v. Glamorgan at Swansea, 1960
8 for 50 v. Lancashire at Manchester, 1961
8 for 20 v. Worcestershire at Leeds, 1965

R KILNER (2)

8 for 26 v. Glamorgan at Cardiff, 1923
8 for 40 v. Middlesex at Bradford, 1926

S P KIRBY (1)

8 for 80 v. Somerset at Taunton, 2003

E LEADBEATER (1)

8 for 83 v. Worcestershire at Worcester, 1950

M LEYLAND (1)

8 for 63 v. Hampshire at Huddersfield, 1938

G G MACAULAY (3)

8 for 43 v. Gloucestershire at Bristol, 1926
8 for 37 v. Derbyshire at Hull, 1927
8 for 21 v. Indians at Harrogate, 1932

H MYERS (1)

8 for 81 v. Gloucestershire at Dewsbury, 1904

A G NICHOLSON (2)

9 for 62 v. Sussex at Eastbourne, 1967
8 for 22 v. Kent at Canterbury, 1968

E PEATE (6)

8 for 24 v. Lancashire at Manchester, 1880
8 for 30 v. Surrey at Huddersfield, 1881
8 for 69 v. Sussex at Hove, 1881
8 for 32 v. Middlesex at Sheffield, 1882
8 for 5 v. Surrey at Holbeck, 1883
8 for 63 v. Kent at Gravesend, 1884

R PEEL (6)

8 for 12 v. Nottinghamshire at Sheffield, 1888
8 for 60 v. Surrey at Sheffield, 1890
8 for 54 v. Cambridge University at Cambridge, 1893
9 for 22 v. Somerset at Leeds, 1895
8 for 27 v. South of England XI at Scarborough, 1896
8 for 53 v. Kent at Halifax, 1897

J M PRESTON (2)

8 for 27 v. Sussex at Hove, 1888
9 for 28 v. MCC at Scarborough, 1888

W RHODES (18)

9 for 28 v. Essex at Leyton, 1899
8 for 38 v. Nottinghamshire at Nottingham, 1899
8 for 68 v. Cambridge University at Cambridge, 1900
8 for 43 v. Lancashire at Bradford, 1900
8 for 23 v. Hampshire at Hull, 1900
8 for 72 v. Gloucestershire at Bradford, 1900
8 for 28 v. Essex at Harrogate, 1900
8 for 53 v. Middlesex at Lord's, 1901
8 for 55 v. Kent at Canterbury, 1901
8 for 26 v. Kent at Catford, 1902
8 for 87 v. Worcestershire at Worcester, 1903
8 for 61 v. Lancashire at Bradford, 1903
8 for 90 v. Warwickshire at Birmingham, 1905
8 for 92 v. Northamptonshire at Northampton, 1911
8 for 44 v. Warwickshire at Bradford, 1919
8 for 39 v. Sussex at Leeds, 1920
8 for 48 v. Somerset at Huddersfield, 1926
9 for 39 v. Essex at Leyton, 1929

W RINGROSE (1)

9 for 76 v. Australians at Bradford, 1905

E ROBINSON (3)

9 for 36 v. Lancashire at Bradford, 1920
8 for 32 v. Northamptonshire at Huddersfield, 1927
8 for 13 v. Cambridge University at Cambridge, 1928

E P ROBINSON (2)

8 for 35 v. Lancashire at Leeds, 1939
8 for 76 v. Surrey at The Oval, 1946

M A ROBINSON (1)

9 for 37 v. Northamptonshire at Harrogate, 1993

A SIDEBOTTOM (1)

8 for 72 v. Leicestershire at Middlesbrough, 1986

T F SMAILES (2)

8 for 68 v. Glamorgan at Hull, 1938
10 for 47 v. Derbyshire at Sheffield, 1939

G B STEVENSON (2)

8 for 65 v. Lancashire at Leeds, 1978
8 for 57 v. Northamptonshire at Leeds, 1980

F S TRUEMAN (8)

8 for 70 v. Minor Counties at Lord's, 1949
8 for 68 v. Nottinghamshire at Sheffield, 1951
8 for 53 v. Nottinghamshire at Nottingham, 1951
8 for 28 v. Kent at Dover, 1954
8 for 84 v. Nottinghamshire at Worksop, 1962
8 for 45 v. Gloucestershire at Bradford, 1963
8 for 36 v. Sussex at Hove, 1965
8 for 37 v. Essex at Bradford, 1966

EIGHT WICKETS OR MORE IN AN INNINGS *(Continued)*

H VERITY (20)

9 for 60 v. Glamorgan at Swansea, 1930
10 for 36 v. Warwickshire at Leeds, 1931
8 for 33 v. Glamorgan at Swansea, 1931
8 for 107 v. Lancashire at Bradford, 1932
8 for 39 v. Northamptonshire at Northampton, 1932
10 for 10 v. Nottinghamshire at Leeds, 1932
8 for 47 v. Essex at Leyton, 1933
9 for 44 v. Essex at Leyton, 1933
9 for 59 v. Kent at Dover, 1933
8 for 28 v. Leicestershire at Leeds, 1935
8 for 56 v. Oxford University at Oxford, 1936
8 for 40 v. Worcestershire at Stourbridge, 1936
9 for 12 v. Kent at Sheffield, 1936
9 for 48 v. Essex at Westcliff-on-Sea, 1936
8 for 42 v. Nottinghamshire at Bradford, 1936
9 for 43 v. Warwickshire at Leeds, 1937
8 for 80 v. Sussex at Eastbourne, 1937
8 for 43 v. Middlesex at The Oval, 1937
9 for 62 v. MCC at Lord's, 1939
8 for 38 v. Leicestershire at Hull, 1939

A WADDINGTON (3)

8 for 34 v. Northamptonshire at Leeds, 1922
8 for 39 v. Kent at Leeds, 1922
8 for 35 v. Hampshire at Bradford, 1922

E WAINWRIGHT (3)

8 for 49 v. Middlesex at Sheffield, 1891
9 for 66 v. Middlesex at Sheffield, 1894
8 for 34 v. Essex at Bradford, 1896

J H WARDLE (4)

8 for 87 v. Derbyshire at Chesterfield, 1948
8 for 26 v. Middlesex at Lord's, 1950
9 for 48 v. Sussex at Hull, 1954
9 for 25 v. Lancashire at Manchester, 1954

C WHITE (1)

8 for 55 v. Gloucestershire at Gloucester, 1998

A C WILLIAMS (1)

9 for 29 v. Hampshire at Dewsbury, 1919

R WOOD (1)

8 for 45 v. Scotland at Glasgow, 1952

SIX WICKETS IN AN INNINGS AT LESS THAN FOUR RUNS EACH

A complete list of 5 wickets at less than 4 runs each up to and including 2007 is to be found in the 2008 edition

R APPLEYARD (2)

6 for 17 v. Essex at Bradford, 1951
6 for 12 v. Hampshire at Bournemouth, 1954

T ARMITAGE (1)

6 for 20 v. Surrey at Sheffield, 1876

R ASPINALL (1)

6 for 23 v. Northamptonshire at Northampton, 1947

W BATES (5)

6 for 11 v. Middlesex at Huddersfield, 1879
6 for 22 v. Kent at Bradford, 1881
6 for 17 v. Nottinghamshire at Nottingham, 1881
6 for 12 v. Kent at Sheffield, 1882
6 for 19 v. Lancashire at Dewsbury, 1886

A BOOTH (1)

6 for 21 v. Warwickshire at Birmingham, 1946

W E BOWES (4)

6 for 17 v. Middlesex at Lord's, 1934
6 for 16 v. Lancashire at Bradford, 1935
6 for 20 v. Gloucestershire at Sheffield, 1936
6 for 23 v. Warwickshire at Birmingham, 1947

J T BROWN (Darfield) (1)

6 for 19 v. Worcestershire at Worcester, 1899

R.O CLAYTON (1)

6 for 20 v. Nottinghamshire at Sheffield, 1876

A COXON (1)

6 for 17 v. Surrey at Sheffield, 1948

T EMMETT (6)

6 for 7 v. Surrey at Sheffield, 1867
6 for 13 v. Lancashire at Holbeck, 1868
6 for 21 v. Middlesex at Scarborough, 1874
6 for 12 v. Derbyshire at Sheffield, 1878
6 for 19 v. Derbyshire at Bradford, 1881
6 for 22 v. Australians at Bradford, 1882

H FISHER (1)

6 for 11 v. Leicestershire at Bradford, 1932

SPARKLING GEMS: Jenny Gunn on the sweep during her match-clinching unbeaten 50 for Northern Diamonds against Loughborough Lightning at Grace Road. Below left: fast bowler Phoebe Graham in action at the Rachael Heyhoe Flint Trophy Final and, right, Alex MacDonald during her brilliant 92 against North West Thunder at Liverpool. *(Photos: JOHN HEALD)*

YORKSHIRE'S NEW FACES

Introducing seven young men who made their first-team or competition debuts for the White Rose in 2020.

***

JAMES WHARTON

Joe Root is this top-order batsman's hero, and you can see why when watching him at the crease.

At a glance it is not easy to tell the pair apart. Now 19, the Huddersfield-born right-hander played two *T20* Blast games in late 2020.

DOM LEECH

Turned 20 in January, a few months after removing former England batsman Haseeb Hameed twice on debut in the Bob Willis Trophy win over Nottinghamshire at Trent Bridge in August.

The tall seamer from Middlesbrough claimed four wickets in two four-day appearances. They were his only senior outings in 2020.

***

GEORGE HILL
A highly-rated all-rounder from Keighley, who has developed his game at Sedbergh School.

After representing the England Under-19s Hill's first-team Yorkshire bow came in the home Bob Willis Trophy draw with Derbyshire.

He made six four-day and Blast appearances in all in 2020.

***

JACK SHUTT
The most experienced of the debutants. The Barnsley off-spinner built on impressive Blast form in 2019 with his first taste of first-class cricket in 2020 in the form of three Bob Willis Trophy games, taking two wickets.

YORKSHIRE'S NEW FACES

***

SAM WISNIEWSKI
A net bowler for England in the 2018 summer when they were trying to master playing against Pakistan leg-spinner Yasir Shah.

A left-arm wrist spinner from Huddersfield, he played two season-ending Blast games last year, and also won a contract to play *T10* cricket in Abu Dhabi in January.

***

MATTHEW REVIS
Opened the batting in the 2019 Championship defeat against Kent at Headingley when 43-year-old Darren Stevens starred with runs and wickets.

Revis, then aged 17 and from Steeton, also played two Blast games late last year.

YORKSHIRE'S NEW FACES

***

BEN BIRKHEAD
The Halifax-born wicketkeeper had made his first-team debut in the rain-affected one-day Cup clash with Durham in 2019 and got his second bite of the cherry in the season-ending Blast win over Derbyshire at Emerald Headingley in September.

...AND A GRAND OLD FAITHFUL

TIM BRESNAN: Yorkshire and England all-rounder who has ended a 19-year career with the *White Rose* and departed for Warwickshire.

FIRST MATCH AFTER LOCKDOWN: Lewis Gomersall, wearing a headband, and Jonathan Wiggan touch elbows instead of hands to celebrate a wicket taken by Gomersall at the Leeds Modernians' ground in their First XI home match against Skipton in the Airedale and Wharfedale Senior Cricket League on Saturday, July 18, 2020. League cricket was back after three months of the season had been lost to the Coronavirus pandemic restrictions, but the players were still expected to observe social-distancing guidelines.

(Photo: JOHN HEALD)

GUESS WHO: Ex-Leeds United and England goalkeeper Nigel Martyn indulges his love for cricket by turning out for the Yorkshire and North East branch of the Forty Club XI.

Martyn donned the wicketkeeping gloves, above, and pulled powerfully, right, in a six-wicket defeat against the Yorkshire Gentleman at St Margaret's School, Escrick.

The Forty Club is reputed to be the largest wandering cricket club in the world. It can only play away. Founded in 1936, it recently moved away from fielding players aged 40 or above.

In 2020 it played against teams such as Lancashire Over-50s, Yorkshire Cricket Board and Sheffield Collegiate CC.

ARISE, SIR GEOFFREY: Yorkshire legend Geoffrey Boycott with his wife, Rachael, and daughter, Emma, after receiving the accolade of knighthood. Sir Geoffrey was nominated in outgoing Prime Minister Theresa May's Resignation Honours List.

FIRST LADY: Janet Bairstow became the first Yorkshire female vice-president at last year's AGM.

A long-serving and integral member of the cricket-operations staff, Janet said: "I feel very privileged and honoured that the club has given me this accolade."

Right: Janet with son Jonny when he received the Man of the Match Award after the Second Test against Sri Lanka at Headingley in 2016.

SIX WICKETS IN AN INNINGS AT LESS THAN FOUR RUNS EACH *(Continued)*

S HAIGH (10)

6 for 18 v. Derbyshire at Bradford, 1897
6 for 22 v. Hampshire at Southampton, 1898
6 for 21 v. Surrey at The Oval, 1900
6 for 23 v. Cambridge University at Cambridge, 1902
6 for 19 v. Somerset at Sheffield, 1902
6 for 22 v. Cambridge University at Sheffield, 1903
6 for 21 v. Hampshire at Leeds, 1904
6 for 21 v. Nottinghamshire at Sheffield, 1905
6 for 13 v. Surrey at Leeds, 1908
6 for 14 v. Australians at Bradford, 1912

A HILL (2)

6 for 9 v. United South of England XI at Bradford, 1874
6 for 18 v. MCC at Lord's, 1881

G H HIRST (7)

6 for 23 v. MCC at Lord's, 1893
6 for 20 v. Lancashire at Bradford, 1906
6 for 12 v. Northamptonshire at Northampton, 1908
6 for 7 v. Northamptonshire at Northampton, 1908
6 for 23 v. Surrey at Leeds, 1908
6 for 23 v. Lancashire at Manchester, 1909
6 for 20 v. Surrey at Sheffield, 1909

R ILLINGWORTH (2)

6 for 15 v. Scotland at Hull, 1956
6 for 13 v. Leicestershire at Leicester, 1963

F S JACKSON (1)

6 for 19 v. Hampshire at Southampton, 1897

R KILNER (5)

6 for 22 v. Essex at Harrogate, 1922
6 for 13 v. Hampshire at Bournemouth, 1922
6 for 14 v. Middlesex at Bradford, 1923
6 for 22 v. Surrey at Sheffield, 1923
6 for 15 v. Hampshire at Portsmouth, 1924

G G MACAULAY (10)

6 for 10 v. Warwickshire at Birmingham, 1921
6 for 3 v. Derbyshire at Hull, 1921
6 for 8 v. Northamptonshire at Northampton, 1922
6 for 12 v. Glamorgan at Cardiff, 1922
6 for 18 v. Northamptonshire at Bradford, 1923
6 for 19 v. Northamptonshire at Northampton, 1925
6 for 22 v. Leicestershire at Leeds, 1926
6 for 11 v. Leicestershire at Hull, 1930
6 for 22 v. Leicestershire at Bradford, 1933
6 for 22 v. Middlesex at Leeds, 1934

SIX WICKETS IN AN INNINGS AT LESS THAN FOUR
RUNS EACH *(Continued)*

E PEATE (5)

6 for 14 v. Middlesex at Huddersfield, 1879
6 for 12 v. Derbyshire at Derby, 1882
6 for 13 v. Gloucestershire at Moreton-in-Marsh, 1884
6 for 16 v. Sussex at Huddersfield, 1886
6 for 16 v. Cambridge University at Sheffield, 1886

R PEEL (4)

6 for 21 v. Nottinghamshire at Sheffield, 1888
6 for 19 v. Australians at Huddersfield, 1888
6 for 22 v. Gloucestershire at Bristol, 1891
6 for 19 v. Leicestershire at Scarborough, 1896

A C RHODES (1)

6 for 19 v. Cambridge University at Cambridge, 1932

W RHODES (12)

6 for 21 v. Somerset at Bath, 1898
6 for 16 v. Gloucestershire at Bristol, 1899
6 for 4 v. Nottinghamshire at Nottingham, 1901
6 for 15 v. MCC at Lord's, 1902
6 for 16 v. Cambridge University at Cambridge, 1905
6 for 9 v. Essex at Huddersfield, 1905
6 for 22 v. Derbyshire at Glossop, 1907
6 for 17 v. Leicestershire at Leicester, 1908
6 for 13 v. Sussex at Hove, 1922
6 for 23 v. Nottinghamshire at Leeds, 1923
6 for 22 v. Cambridge University at Cambridge, 1924
6 for 20 v. Gloucestershire at Dewsbury, 1927

W RINGROSE (1)

6 for 20 v. Leicestershire at Dewsbury, 1903

R J SIDEBOTTOM (1)

6 for 16 v. Kent at Leeds, 2000

W SLINN (1)

6 for 19 v. Nottinghamshire at Nottingham, 1864

G B STEVENSON(1)

6 for 14 v. Warwickshire at Sheffield, 1979

F S TRUEMAN (4)

6 for 23 v. Oxford University at Oxford, 1955
6 for 23 v. Oxford University at Oxford, 1958
6 for 18 v. Warwickshire at Birmingham, 1963
6 for 20 v. Leicestershire at Sheffield, 1968

H VERITY (5)

6 for 11 v. Surrey at Bradford, 1931
6 for 21 v. Glamorgan at Swansea, 1931
6 for 12 v. Derbyshire at Hull, 1933
6 for 10 v. Essex at Ilford, 1937
6 for 22 v. Hampshire at Bournemouth, 1939

SIX WICKETS IN AN INNINGS AT LESS THAN FOUR RUNS EACH *(Continued)*

A WADDINGTON (2)

6 for 21 v. Northamptonshire at Harrogate, 1921
6 for 21 v. Northamptonshire at Northampton, 1923

S WADE (1)

6 for 18 v. Gloucestershire at Dewsbury, 1887

E WAINWRIGHT (4)

6 for 16 v. Sussex at Leeds, 1893
6 for 23 v. Sussex at Hove, 1893
6 for 18 v. Sussex at Dewsbury, 1894
6 for 22 v. MCC at Scarborough, 1894

J H WARDLE (8)

6 for 17 v. Sussex at Sheffield, 1948
6 for 10 v. Scotland at Edinburgh, 1950
6 for 12 v. Gloucestershire at Hull, 1950
6 for 20 v. Kent at Scarborough, 1950
6 for 23 v. Somerset at Sheffield, 1951
6 for 21 v. Glamorgan at Leeds, 1951
6 for 18 v. Gloucestershire at Bristol, 1951
6 for 6 v. Gloucestershire at Bristol, 1955

D WILSON (3)

6 for 22 v. Sussex at Bradford, 1963
6 for 15 v. Gloucestershire at Middlesbrough, 1966
6 for 22 v. Middlesex at Sheffield, 1966

FOUR WICKETS IN FOUR BALLS

A Drake v. Derbyshire at Chesterfield, 1914

FOUR WICKETS IN FIVE BALLS

F S Jackson v. Australians at Leeds, 1902
A Waddington v. Northamptonshire at Northampton, 1920
G G Macaulay v. Lancashire at Manchester, 1933
P J Hartley v. Derbyshire at Chesterfield, 1995
D Gough v. Kent at Leeds, 1995
J D Middlebrook v. Hampshire at Southampton, 2000

BEST BOWLING ANALYSES IN A MATCH
FOR AND AGAINST YORKSHIRE

Best For Yorkshire:
17 for 91 (8 for 47 and 9 for 44) H Verity v Essex at Leyton, 1933

Against Yorkshire:
17 for 91 (9 for 62 and 8 for 29) H Dean for Lancashire at Liverpool, 1913
(non-championship)

County Championship
16 for 114 (8 for 48 and 8 for 66) G Burton for Middlesex at Sheffield, 1888

Yorkshire versus:

Derbyshire	*For Yorkshire:*	14 for 58 (4 for 11 and 10 for 47)
		T F Smailes at Sheffield, 1939
	Against:	13 for 65 (7 for 33 and 6 for 32)
		W Mycroft at Sheffield, 1879
Most 10 wickets	*For Yorkshire:*	P Carrick and E Peate 4 each
in a match	*Against:*	W Mycroft 3
Durham	*For Yorkshire:*	10 for 101 (6 for 57 and 4 for 44)
		M A Robinson at Durham, 1992
	Against:	10 for 144 (7 for 81 and 3 for 63)
		O D Gibson at Chester-le-Street, 2007
Most 10 wickets	*For Yorkshire:*	M A Robinson 1
in a match	*Against:*	G R Breese and O D Gibson 1 each
Essex	*For Yorkshire:*	17 for 91 (8 for 47 and 9 for 44)
		H Verity at Leyton, 1933
	Against:	14 for 127 (7 for 37 and 7 for 90)
		W Mead at Leyton, 1899
Most 10 wickets	*For Yorkshire:*	W Rhodes 7
in a match	*Against:*	J K Lever, W Mead 2 each
Glamorgan	*For Yorkshire:*	15 for 123 (8 for 70 and 7 for 53)
		R Illingworth at Swansea, 1960
	Against:	12 for 76 (7 for 30 and 5 for 46)
		D J Shepherd at Cardiff, 1957
Most 10 wickets	*For Yorkshire:*	H Verity 5
in a match	*Against:*	D J Shepherd, J S Pressdee 1 each
Gloucestershire	*For Yorkshire:*	14 for 64 (7 for 58 and 7 for 6)
		R Illingworth at Harrogate, 1967
	Against:	15 for 79 (8 for 33 and 7 for 46)
		W G Grace at Sheffield, 1872
Most 10 wickets	*For Yorkshire:*	W Rhodes 8
in a match	*Against:*	E G Dennett 5
Hampshire	*For Yorkshire:*	14 for 43 (8 for 21 and 6 for 22)
		S Haigh at Southampton, 1898
	Against:	12 for 145 (7 for 78 and 5 for 67)
		D Shackleton at Bradford, 1962
Most 10 wickets	*For Yorkshire:*	W Rhodes, E Robinson, H Verity 3 each
in a match	*Against:*	A S Kennedy 3

Yorkshire versus

Kent	*For Yorkshire:*	15 for 38 (6 for 26 and 9 for 12)
		H Verity at Sheffield, 1936
	Against:	13 for 48 (5 for 13 and 8 for 35)
		A Hearne at Sheffield, 1885
Most 10 wickets	*For Yorkshire:*	E Peate and J H Wardle 4 each
in a match	*Against:*	C Blythe 6
Lancashire	*For Yorkshire:*	14 for 80 (6 for 56 and 8 for 24)
		E Peate at Manchester, 1880
	Against:	17 for 91 (9 for 62 and 8 for 29)
		H Dean at Liverpool, 1913 (non-championship)
		14 for 90 (6 for 47 and 8 for 43)
		R Tattersall at Leeds, 1956 (championship)
Most 10 wickets	*For Yorkshire:*	T Emmett 5
in a match	*Against:*	J Briggs 8
Leicestershire	*For Yorkshire:*	15 for 63 (8 for 25 and 7 for 38)
		G H Hirst at Hull, 1907
	Against:	12 for 139 (8 for 85 and 4 for 54)
		A D Pougher at Leicester, 1895
Most 10 wickets	*For Yorkshire:*	G H Hirst 5
in a match	*Against:*	A D Pougher 2
Middlesex	*For Yorkshire:*	13 for 94 (6 for 61 and 7 for 33)
		S Haigh at Leeds, 1900
	Against:	16 for 114 (8 for 48 and 8 for 66)
		G Burton at Sheffield, 1888
Most 10 wickets	*For Yorkshire:*	W Rhodes 5
in a match	*Against:*	J T Hearne 7
Northamptonshire	*For Yorkshire:*	16 for 35 (8 for 18 and 8 for 17)
		W E Bowes at Kettering, 1935
	Against:	15 for 31 (7 for 22 and 8 for 9)
		G E Tribe at Northampton, 1958
Most 10 wickets	*For Yorkshire:*	W E Bowes, G G Macaulay, H Verity,
in a match		A Waddington 3 each
	Against:	G E Tribe 3
Nottinghamshire	*For Yorkshire:*	14 for 33 (8 for 12 and 6 for 21)
		R Peel at Sheffield, 1888
	Against:	14 for 94 (8 for 38 and 6 for 56)
		F Morley at Nottingham, 1878
Most 10 wickets	*For Yorkshire:*	G H Hirst 5
in a match	*Against:*	F Morley, J C Shaw 4 each
Somerset	*For Yorkshire:*	15 for 50 (9 for 22 and 6 for 28)
		R Peel at Leeds, 1895
	Against:	15 for 71 (6 for 30 and 9 for 41)
		L C Braund at Sheffield, 1902
Most 10 wickets	*For Yorkshire:*	G H Hirst 7
in a match	*Against:*	L C Braund 3

Yorkshire versus

Surrey	*For Yorkshire:*	14 for 77 (6 for 47 and 8 for 30) E Peate at Huddersfield, 1881
	Against:	15 for 154 (7 for 55 and 8 for 99) T Richardson at Leeds, 1897
Most 10 wickets *in a match*	*For Yorkshire:*	W Rhodes 7
	Against:	G A Lohmann, T Richardson 6 each
Sussex	*For Yorkshire:*	16 for 112 (9 for 48 and 7 for 64) J H Wardle at Hull, 1954
	Against:	12 for 110 (6 for 71 and 6 for 39) G R Cox at Sheffield, 1907
Most 10 wickets *in a match*	*For Yorkshire:*	R Peel, E Wainwright 3 each
	Against:	Twelve players 1 each
Warwickshire	*For Yorkshire:*	14 for 92 (9 for 43 and 5 for 49) H Verity at Leeds, 1937
	Against:	12 for 55 (5 for 21 and 7 for 34) T W Cartwright at Bradford, 1969
Most 10 wickets *in a match*	*For Yorkshire:*	S Haigh 4
	Against:	E F Field 4
Worcestershire	*For Yorkshire:*	14 for 211 (8 for 87 and 6 for 124) W Rhodes at Worcester, 1903
	Against:	13 for 76 (4 for 38 and 9 for 38) J A Cuffe at Bradford, 1907
Most 10 wickets *in a match*	*For Yorkshire:*	S Haigh, G G Macaulay 4 each
	Against:	N Gifford 2
Australians	*For Yorkshire:*	13 for 149 (8 for 48 and 5 for 101) G H Hirst at Bradford, 1899
	Against:	13 for 170 (6 for 91 and 7 for 79) J M Gregory at Sheffield, 1919
Most 10 wickets *in a match*	*For Yorkshire:*	S Haigh 2
	Against:	C V Grimmett, F R Spofforth, C T B Turner, H Trumble 2 each

BEST BOWLING ANALYSES IN AN INNINGS
FOR AND AGAINST YORKSHIRE

Best For Yorkshire:
10 for 10 H Verity v Nottinghamshire at Leeds, 1932

Against Yorkshire:
10 for 37 C V Grimmett for Australians at Sheffield, 1930
(non-championship)

County Championship
10 for 51 H Howell for Warwickshire at Birmingham, 1923

Yorkshire versus:

Derbyshire	*For Yorkshire:*	10 for 47	T F Smailes at Sheffield, 1939
	Against:	9 for 27	J J Hulme at Sheffield, 1894
Most 5 wickets *in an innings*	*For Yorkshire:*	S Haigh, E Peat, W Rhodes 11 each	
	Against:	W Mycroft 10	

BEST BOWLING ANALYSES IN AN INNINGS
FOR AND AGAINST YORKSHIRE *(continued)*

Yorkshire versus

Durham   *For Yorkshire:* 6 for 37   R D Stemp at Durham, 1994
                                      6 for 37   J N Gillespie at Chester-le-Street, 2006
                   Against: 7 for 58   J Wood at Leeds, 1999
Most 5 wickets   *For Yorkshire:*   D Gough and M J Hoggard 2 each
in an innings   *Against:*   G R Breese, S J E Brown, S J Harmison
                                      and G Onions 2 each

Essex   *For Yorkshire:* 9 for 28   W Rhodes at Leyton, 1899
                   Against: 8 for 44   F G Bull at Bradford, 1896
Most 5 wickets   *For Yorkshire:*   W Rhodes 18
in an innings   *Against:*   W Mead 14

Glamorgan   *For Yorkshire:* 9 for 60   H Verity at Swansea, 1930
                   Against: 9 for 43   J S Pressdee at Swansea, 1965
Most 5 wickets   *For Yorkshire:*   H Verity 12
in an innings   *Against:*   D J Shepherd 6

Gloucestershire *For Yorkshire:* 9 for 25   S Haigh at Leeds, 1912
                    Against: 9 for 36   C W L Parker at Bristol, 1922
Most 5 wickets   *For Yorkshire:* W Rhodes 22
in an innings   *Against:*   T W J Goddard 17

Hampshire   *For Yorkshire:* 9 for 29   A C Williams at Dewsbury, 1919
                   Against: 8 for 49   O W Herman at Bournemouth, 1930
Most 5 wickets   *For Yorkshire:*   G H Hirst 10
in an innings   *Against:*   A S Kennedy 10

Kent   *For Yorkshire:* 9 for 12   H Verity at Sheffield, 1936
                   Against: 8 for 35   A Hearne at Sheffield, 1885
Most 5 wickets   *For Yorkshire:*   W Rhodes 12
in an innings   *Against:*   A P Freeman 14

Lancashire   *For Yorkshire:* 9 for 23   G H Hirst at Leeds, 1910
                   Against: 9 for 41   A Mold at Huddersfield, 1890
Most 5 wickets   *For Yorkshire:*   T Emmett 16
in an innings   *Against:*   J Briggs 19

Leicestershire *For Yorkshire:* 8 for 25   G H Hirst at Hull, 1907
                   Against: 9 for 63   C T Spencer at Huddersfield, 1954
Most 5 wickets   *For Yorkshire:*   G H Hirst 15
in an innings   *Against:*   H A Smith 7

Middlesex   *For Yorkshire:* 9 for 45   G H Hirst at Sheffield 1907
                   Against: 9 for 57   F A Tarrant at Leeds, 1906
Most 5 wickets   *For Yorkshire:*   W Rhodes 18
in an innings   *Against:*   J T Hearne 21

Northamptonshire *For Yorkshire:* 9 for 37 M A Robinson at Harrogate, 1993
                     Against: 9 for 30 A E Thomas at Bradford, 1920
Most 5 wickets   *For Yorkshire:* G G Macaulay 14
in an innings   *Against:*   G E Tribe, W Wells 7 each

Nottinghamshire *For Yorkshire:* 10 for 10 H Verity at Leeds, 1932
                    Against: 8 for 32 J C Shaw at Nottingham, 1865
Most 5 wickets   *For Yorkshire:*   W Rhodes 17
in an innings   *Against:*   F Morley 17

BEST BOWLING ANALYSES IN AN INNINGS
FOR AND AGAINST YORKSHIRE *(continued)*

Yorkshire versus

Somerset	*For Yorkshire:*	10 for 35	A Drake at Weston-super-Mare, 1914
	Against:	9 for 41	L C Braund at Sheffield, 1902
Most 5 wickets	*For Yorkshire:*	G H Hirst 16	
in an innings	*Against:*	E J Tyler 8	
Surrey	*For Yorkshire:*	8 for 5	E Peate at Holbeck, 1883
	Against:	9 for 47	T Richardson at Sheffield, 1893
Most 5 wickets	*For Yorkshire:*	W Rhodes 17	
in an innings	*Against:*	W Southerton 19	
Sussex	*For Yorkshire:*	9 for 48	J H Wardle at Hull, 1954
	Against:	9 for 34	James Langridge at Sheffield, 1934
Most 5 wickets	*For Yorkshire:*	W Rhodes 14	
in an innings	*Against:*	G R Cox, J A Snow 6 each	
Warwickshire	*For Yorkshire:*	10 for 36	H Verity at Leeds, 1930
	Against:	10 for 51	H Howell at Birmingham, 1923
Most 5 wickets	*For Yorkshire:*	W Rhodes 18	
in an innings	*Against:*	E F Field, W E Hollies 7 each	
Worcestershire	*For Yorkshire:*	9 for 41	G H Hirst at Worcester, 1911
	Against:	9 for 38	J A Cuffe at Bradford, 1907
Most 5 wickets	*For Yorkshire:*	S Haigh, W Rhodes 11 each	
in an innings	*Against:*	R T D Perks 7	
Australians	*For Yorkshire:*	9 for 76	W Ringrose at Bradford, 1905
	Against:	10 for 37	C V Grimmett at Sheffield, 1930
Most 5 wickets	*For Yorkshire:*	R Peel 7	
in an innings	*Against:*	F R Spofforth 7	

HAT-TRICKS

G Freeman v. Lancashire at Holbeck, 1868
G Freeman v. Middlesex at Sheffield, 1868
A Hill v. United South of England XI at Bradford, 1874
A Hill v. Surrey at The Oval, 1880
E Peate v. Kent at Sheffield, 1882
G Ulyett v. Lancashire at Sheffield, 1883
E Peate v. Gloucestershire at Moreton-in-Marsh, 1884
W Fletcher v. MCC at Lord's, 1892
E Wainwright v. Sussex at Dewsbury, 1894
G H Hirst v. Leicestershire at Leicester, 1895
J T Brown v. Derbyshire at Derby, 1896
R Peel v. Kent at Halifax, 1897
S Haigh v. Derbyshire at Bradford, 1897
W Rhodes v. Kent at Canterbury, 1901
S Haigh v. Somerset at Sheffield, 1902
H A Sedgwick v. Worcestershire at Hull, 1906
G Deyes v. Gentlemen of Ireland at Bray, 1907
G H Hirst v. Leicestershire at Hull, 1907
J T Newstead v. Worcestershire at Bradford, 1907
S Haigh v. Lancashire at Manchester, 1909
M W Booth v. Worcestershire at Bradford, 1911
A Drake v. Essex at Huddersfield, 1912

HAT-TRICKS *(Continued)*

M W Booth v. Essex at Leyton, 1912
A Drake v. Derbyshire at Chesterfield, 1914 (4 in 4)
W Rhodes v. Derbyshire at Derby, 1920
A Waddington v. Northamptonshire at Northampton, 1920 (4 in 5)
G G Macaulay v. Warwickshire at Birmingham, 1923
E Robinson v. Sussex at Hull, 1928
G G Macaulay v. Leicestershire at Hull, 1930
E Robinson v. Kent at Gravesend, 1930
H Verity v. Nottinghamshire at Leeds, 1932
H Fisher v. Somerset at Sheffield, 1932 (all lbw)
G G Macaulay v. Glamorgan at Cardiff, 1933
G G Macaulay v. Lancashire at Manchester, 1933 (4 in 5)
M.Leyland v. Surrey at Sheffield, 1935
E Robinson v. Kent at Leeds, 1939
A Coxon v. Worcestershire at Leeds, 1946
F S Trueman v. Nottinghamshire at Nottingham, 1951
F S Trueman v. Nottinghamshire at Scarborough, 1955
R Appleyard v. Gloucestershire at Sheffield, 1956
F S.Trueman v. MCC at Lord's, 1958
D Wilson v. Nottinghamshire at Middlesbrough, 1959
F S Trueman v. Nottinghamshire at Bradford, 1963
D Wilson v. Nottinghamshire at Worksop, 1966
D Wilson v. Kent at Harrogate, 1966
G A Cope v. Essex at Colchester, 1970
A L Robinson v. Nottinghamshire at Worksop, 1974
P W Jarvis v. Derbyshire at Chesterfield, 1985
P J Hartley v. Derbyshire at Chesterfield, 1995 (4 in 5)
D Gough v. Kent at Leeds, 1995 (4 in 5)
C White v. Gloucestershire at Gloucester, 1998
M J Hoggard v. Sussex at Hove, 2009

52 Hat-Tricks: G G Macaulay and F S Trueman took four each, S Haigh and D Wilson three each. There have been seven hat-tricks versus Kent and Nottinghamshire, and six versus Derbyshire.

200 WICKETS IN A SEASON

Bowler	Season	Overs	Maidens	Runs	Wickets	Average
W Rhodes	1900	1366.4	411	3054	240	12.72
W Rhodes	1901	1455.3	474	3497	233	15.00
G H Hirst	1906	1111.1	262	3089	201	15.36
G G Macaulay	1925	1241.2	291	2986	200	14.93
R Appleyard†	1951	1323.2	394	2829	200	14.14

† First full season in First-Class cricket.

100 WICKETS IN A SEASON

Bowler		Wickets taken	Wickets taken	Wickets taken
R Appleyard	(3)	200 in 1951	141 in 1954	110 in 1956
A Booth	(1)	111 in 1946	—	
M W Booth	(3)	104 in 1912	167 in 1913	155 in 1914
W E Bowes	(8)	117 in 1931	168 in 1932	130 in 1933
		109 in 1934	154 in 1935	113 in 1936
		106 in 1938	107 in 1939	

Bowler		*Wickets taken*	*Wickets taken*	*Wickets taken*
D B Close	(2)	105 in 1949	114 in 1952	—
A Coxon	(2)	101 in 1949	129 in 1950	—
A Drake	(2)	115 in 1913	158 in 1914	—
T Emmett	(1)	112 in 1886	—	—
S Haigh	(10)	100 in 1898	160 in 1900	154 in 1902
		102 in 1903	118 in 1904	118 in 1905
		161 in 1906	120 in 1909	100 in 1911
		125 in 1912		
G H Hirst	(12)	150 in 1895	171 in 1901	121 in 1903
		114 in 1904	100 in 1905	201 in 1906
		169 in 1907	164 in 1908	138 in 1910
		130 in 1911	113 in 1912	100 in 1913
R Illingworth	(5)	103 in 1956	120 in 1961	116 in 1962
		122 in 1964	105 in 1968	—
R Kilner	(4)	107 in 1922	143 in 1923	134 in 1924
		123 in 1925	—	—
G G Macaulay	(10)	101 in 1921	130 in 1922	163 in 1923
		184 in 1924	200 in 1925	133 in 1926
		130 in 1927	117 in 1928	102 in 1929
		141 in 1933	—	—
J T Newstead	(1)	131 in 1908	—	—
A G Nicholson	(2)	113 in 1966	101 in 1967	—
E Peate	(3)	131 in 1880	133 in 1881	165 in 1882
R Peel	(6)	118 in 1888	132 in 1890	106 in 1892
		134 in 1894	155 in 1895	108 in 1896
W Rhodes	(22)	141 in 1898	153 in 1899	240 in 1900
		233 in 1901	174 in 1902	169 in 1903
		118 in 1904	158 in 1905	113 in 1906
		164 in 1907	100 in 1908	115 in 1909
		105 in 1911	117 in 1914	155 in 1919
		156 in 1920	128 in 1921	100 in 1922
		127 in 1923	102 in 1926	111 in 1928
		100 in 1929	—	—
E Robinson	(1)	111 in 1928	—	—
E P Robinson	(4)	104 in 1938	120 in 1939	149 in 1946
		108 in 1947	—	—
T F Smailes	(4)	105 in 1934	125 in 1936	120 in 1937
		104 in 1938	—	—
F S Trueman	(8)	129 in 1954	140 in 1955	104 in 1959
		150 in 1960	124 in 1961	122 in 1962
		121 in 1965	107 in 1966	—
H Verity	(9)	169 in 1931	146 in 1932	168 in 1933
		100 in 1934	199 in 1935	185 in 1936
		185 in 1937	137 in 1938	189 in 1939
A Waddington	(5)	100 in 1919	140 in 1920	105 in 1921
		132 in 1922	105 in 1925	—
E Wainwright	(3)	114 in 1893	157 in 1894	102 in 1896
J H Wardle	(10)	148 in 1948	100 in 1949	172 in 1950
		122 in 1951	169 in 1952	126 in 1953
		122 in 1954	159 in 1955	146 in 1956
		106 in 1957	—	—
D Wilson	(3)	100 in 1966	107 in 1968	101 in 1969

BOWLERS WHO HAVE TAKEN OVER 500 WICKETS

Player	M	Runs	Wkts	Av'ge	Best
W Rhodes	883	57634	3598	16.01	9 for 28
G H Hirst	717	44716	2481	18.02	9 for 23
S Haigh	513	29289	1876	15.61	9 for 25
G G Macaulay	445	30554	1774	17.22	8 for 21
F S Trueman	459	29890	1745	17.12	8 for 28
H Verity	278	21353	1558	13.70	10 for 10
J H Wardle	330	27917	1539	18.13	9 for 25
R Illingworth	496	26806	1431	18.73	9 for 42
W E Bowes	301	21227	1351	15.71	9 for 121
R Peel	318	20638	1311	15.74	9 for 22
T Emmett	299	15465	1216	12.71	9 for 23
D Wilson	392	22626	1104	20.49	7 for 19
P Carrick	425	30530	1018	29.99	8 for 33
E Wainwright	352	17744	998	17.77	9 for 66
D B Close	536	23489	967	24.29	8 for 41
Emmott Robinson	413	19645	893	21.99	9 for 36
A G Nicholson	282	17296	876	19.74	9 for 62
R Kilner	365	14855	857	17.33	8 for 26
A Waddington	255	16203	835	19.40	8 for 34
T F Smailes	262	16593	802	20.68	10 for 47
E Peate	154	9986	794	12.57	8 for 5
Ellis P Robinson	208	15141	735	20.60	8 for 35
C M Old	222	13409	647	20.72	7 for 20
R Appleyard	133	9903	642	15.42	8 for 76
W Bates	202	10692	637	16.78	8 for 21
G A Cope	230	15627	630	24.80	8 for 73
P J Hartley	195	17438	579	30.11	9 for 41
A Sidebottom	216	13852	558	24.82	8 for 72
M W Booth	144	11017	557	19.17	8 for 47
A Hill	140	7002	542	12.91	7 for 14
Hon F S Jackson	207	9690	506	19.15	7 for 42

BOWLERS UNCHANGED IN A MATCH
(IN WHICH THE OPPONENTS WERE DISMISSED TWICE)
There have been 31 instances. The first and most recent are listed below.
A complete list is to be found in the 2008 edition.

First: L Greenwood (11 for 71) and G Freeman (8 for 73) v. Surrey
at The Oval, 1867
Yorkshire won by an innings and 111 runs

Most Recent: E Robinson (8 for 65) and G G Macaulay (12 for 50) v. Worcestershire
at Leeds, 1927
Yorkshire won by an innings and 106 runs

FIELDERS (IN MATCHES FOR YORKSHIRE)

MOST CATCHES IN AN INNINGS

6	E P Robinson	v. Leicestershire	at Bradford, 1938
6	T Kohler- Cadmore		
		v. Kent	at Canterbury, 2019
5	J Tunnicliffe	v. Leicestershire	at Leeds, 1897
5	J Tunnicliffe	v. Leicestershire	at Leicester, 1900
5	J Tunnicliffe	v. Leicestershire	at Scarborough, 1901
5	A B Sellers	v. Essex	at Leyton, 1933
5	D Wilson	v. Surrey	at The Oval, 1969
5	R G Lumb	v. Gloucestershire	at Middlesbrough, 1972

MOST CATCHES IN A MATCH

7	J Tunnicliffe	v. Leicestershire	at Leeds, 1897
7	J Tunnicliffe	v. Leicestershire	at Leicester, 1900
7	A B Sellers	v Essex	at Leyton, 1933
7	E P Robinson	v. Leicestershire	at Bradford, 1938
7	A Lyth	v. Middlesex	at Scarborough, 2014
7	T Kohler-Cadmore		
		v. Hampshire	at West End, Southampton, 2019

MOST CATCHES IN A SEASON

70	J Tunnicliffe	in 1901
70	P J Sharpe	in 1962
61	J Tunnicliffe	in 1895
60	J Tunnicliffe	in 1904
59	J Tunnicliffe	in 1896
57	J V Wilson	in 1955
54	J V Wilson	in 1961
53	J V Wilson	in 1957
51	J V Wilson	in 1951

MOST CATCHES IN A CAREER

665	J Tunnicliffe	(1.40 per match)
586	W Rhodes	(0.66 per match)
564	D B Close	(1.05 per match)
525	P J Sharpe	(1.27 per match)
520	J V Wilson	(1.09 per match)
518	G H Hirst	(0.72 per match)

WICKET-KEEPERS IN MATCHES FOR YORKSHIRE

MOST DISMISSALS IN AN INNINGS

7	(7ct)	D L Bairstow	v. Derbyshire	at Scarborough	1982
6	(6ct)	J Hunter	v. Gloucestershire	at Gloucester	1887
6	(5ct,1st)	D Hunter	v. Surrey	at Sheffield	1891
6	(6ct)	D Hunter	v. Middlesex	at Leeds	1909
6	(2ct,4st)	W R Allen	v. Sussex	at Hove	1921
6	(5ct,1st)	J G Binks	v. Lancashire	at Leeds	1962
6	(6ct)	D L Bairstow	v. Lancashire	at Manchester	1971
6	(6ct)	D L Bairstow	v. Warwickshire	at Bradford	1978
6	(5ct,1st)	D L Bairstow	v. Lancashire	at Leeds	1980
6	(6ct)	D L Bairstow	v. Derbyshire	at Chesterfield	1984
6	(6ct)	R J Blakey	v. Sussex	at Eastbourne	1990
6	(5ct,1st)	R J Blakey	v. Gloucestershire	at Cheltenham	1992
6	(5ct,1st)	R J Blakey	v. Glamorgan	at Cardiff	1994
6	(6ct)	R J Blakey	v. Glamorgan	at Leeds	2003
6	(6ct)	G L Brophy	v. Durham	at Chester-le-Street	2009
6	(6ct)	J M Bairstow	v. Middlesex	at Leeds	2013
6	(6ct)	J M Bairstow	v. Sussex	at Arundel	2014

MOST DISMISSALS IN A MATCH

11	(11ct)	D L Bairstow	v. Derbyshire	at Scarborough	1982
		(Equalled World Record)			
9	(9ct)	J.Hunter	v. Gloucestershire	at Gloucester	1887
9	(8ct,1st)	A Dolphin	v. Derbyshire	at Bradford	1919
9	(9ct)	D L Bairstow	v. Lancashire	at Manchester	1971
9	(9ct)	R J Blakey	v. Sussex	at Eastbourne	1990
8	(2ct,6st)	G Pinder	v. Lancashire	at Sheffield	1872
8	(2ct,6st)	D Hunter	v. Surrey	at Bradford	1898
8	(7ct,1st)	A Bairstow	v. Cambridge University	at Cambridge	1899
8	(8ct)	A Wood	v. Northamptonshire	at Huddersfield	1932
8	(8ct)	D L Bairstow	v. Lancashire	at Leeds	1978
8	(7ct,1st)	D L Bairstow	v. Derbyshire	at Chesterfield	1984
8	(6ct,2st)	D L Bairstow	v. Derbyshire	at Chesterfield	1985
8	(8ct)	R J Blakey	v. Hampshire	at Southampton	1989
8	(8ct)	R J Blakey	v. Northamptonshire	at Harrogate	1993
8	(8ct)	A J Hodd	v. Glamorgan	at Leeds	2012
8	(8ct)	J M Bairstow	v. Middlesex	at Leeds	2013

MOST DISMISSALS IN A SEASON

107	(96ct,11st)	J G Binks, 1960
94	(81ct,13st)	JG Binks, 1961
89	(75ct,14st)	A Wood, 1934
88	(80ct,8st)	J G Binks, 1963
86	(70ct,16st)	J G Binks, 1962
82	(52ct,30st)	A Dolphin, 1919
80	(57ct,23st)	A. Wood, 1935

MOST DISMISSALS IN A CAREER

1186	(863ct,323st)	D Hunter (2.29 per match)
1044	(872ct,172st)	J G Binks (2.12 per match)
1038	(907ct,131st)	D L Bairstow (2.41 per match)
855	(612ct,243st)	A Wood (2.09 per match)
829	(569ct,260st)	A Dolphin (1.94 per match)
824	(768ct, 56st)	R J Blakey (2.43 per match)

YORKSHIRE PLAYERS WHO HAVE
COMPLETED THE "DOUBLE"

(all First-Class matches)

Player	Year	Runs	Average	Wickets	Average
M W Booth (1)	1913	1,228	27.28	181	18.46
D B Close (2)	†1949	1,098	27.45	113	27.87
	1952	1,192	33.11	114	24.08
A Drake (1)	1913	1,056	23.46	116	16.93
S Haigh (1)	1904	1,055	26.37	121	19.85
G H Hirst (14)	1896	1,122	28.20	104	21.64
	1897	1,535	35.69	101	23.22
	1901	1,950	42.39	183	16.38
	1903	1,844	47.28	128	14.94
	1904	2,501	54.36	132	21.09
	1905	2,266	53.95	110	19.94
	††1906	2,385	45.86	208	16.50
	1907	1,344	28.38	188	15.20
	1908	1,598	38.97	114	14.05
	1909	1,256	27.30	115	20.05
	1910	1,840	32.85	164	14.79
	1911	1,789	33.12	137	20.40
	1912	1,133	25.75	118	17.37
	1913	1,540	35.81	101	20.13
R Illingworth (6)	1957	1,213	28.20	106	18.40
	1959	1,726	46.64	110	21.46
	1960	1,006	25.79	109	17.55
	1961	1,153	24.53	128	17.90
	1962	1,612	34.29	117	19.45
	1964	1,301	37.17	122	17.45
F S Jackson (1)	1898	1,566	41.21	104	15.67
R Kilner (4)	1922	1,198	27.22	122	14.73
	1923	1,404	32.24	158	12.91
	1925	1,068	30.51	131	17.92
	1926	1,187	37.09	107	22.52
R Peel (1)	1896	1,206	30.15	128	17.50
W Rhodes (16)	1903	1,137	27.07	193	14.57
	1904	1,537	35.74	131	21.59
	1905	1,581	35.93	182	16.95
	1906	1,721	29.16	128	23.57
	1907	1,055	22.93	177	15.57
	1908	1,673	31.56	115	16.13
	1909	2,094	40.26	141	15.89
	1911	2,261	38.32	117	24.07
	1914	1,377	29.29	118	18.27
	1919	1,237	34.36	164	14.42
	1920	1,123	28.07	161	13.18
	1921	1,474	39.83	141	13.27
	1922	1,511	39.76	119	12.19
	1923	1,321	33.02	134	11.54
	1924	1,126	26.18	109	14.46
	1926	1,132	34.30	115	14.86
T F Smailes (1)	1938	1,002	25.05	113	20.84
E Wainwright (1)	1897	1,612	35.82	101	23.06

† First season in First-Class cricket.
†† The only instance in First-Class cricket of 2,000 runs and 200 wickets in a season.

H Sutcliffe (194) and M Leyland (45) hit 102 off six consecutive overs for Yorkshire v. Essex at Scarborough in 1932.

From 1898 to 1930 inclusive, Wilfred Rhodes took no less than 4,187 wickets, and scored 39,969 runs in First-Class cricket at home and abroad, a remarkable record. He also took 100 wickets and scored 1,000 in a season 16 times, and G H Hirst 14 times.

Of players with a qualification of not less than 50 wickets, Wilfred Rhodes was first in bowling in First-Class cricket in 1900, 1901, 1919, 1920, 1922, 1923 and 1926; Schofield Haigh in 1902, 1905, 1908 and 1909; Mr E R Wilson in 1921; G G Macaulay in 1924; H Verity in 1930, 1933, 1935, 1937 and 1939; W E Bowes in 1938; A Booth in 1946; R Appleyard in 1951 and 1955, and F S Trueman in 1952 and 1963.

The highest aggregate of runs made in one season in First-Class cricket by a Yorkshire player is 3,429 by L Hutton in 1949. This total has been exceeded three times, viz: D C S Compton 3,816 and W J Edrich 3,539 in 1947, and 3,518 by T Hayward in 1906. H Sutcliffe scored 3,336 in 1932.

Three players have taken all 10 Yorkshire wickets in an innings. G Wootton, playing for All England XI at Sheffield in 1865, took all 10 wickets for 54 runs. H Howell performed the feat for Warwickshire at Edgbaston in 1923 at a cost of 51 runs; and C V Grimmett, Australia, took all 10 wickets for 37 runs at Sheffield in 1930.

The match against Sussex at Dewsbury on June 7th and 8th, 1894, was brought to a summary conclusion by a remarkable bowling performance on the part of Edward Wainwright. In the second innings of Sussex, he took the last five wickets in seven balls, including the "hat trick". In the whole match he obtained 13 wickets for only 38 runs.

M D Moxon has the unique distinction of scoring a century in each of his first two First-Class matches in Yorkshire — 116 (2nd inns.) v. Essex at Leeds and 111 (1st inns.) v. Derbyshire at Sheffield, June 1981).

In the Yorkshire v. Norfolk match — played on the Hyde Park Ground, Sheffield, on July 14th to 18th, 1834 — 851 runs were scored in the four innings, of which no fewer than 128 were extras: 75 byes and 53 wides. At that time wides were not run out, so that every wide included in the above total represents a wide actually bowled. This particular achievement has never been surpassed in the annals of county cricket.

L Hutton reached his 1,000 runs in First-Class cricket in 1949 as early as June 9th.

W Barber reached his 1,000 runs in 1934 on June 13th. P Holmes reached his 1,000 in 1925 on June 16th, as also did H Sutcliffe in 1932. J T Brown reached his 1,000 in 1899 on June 22nd. In 1905, D Denton reached his 1,000 runs on June 26th; and in 1906 G H Hirst gained the same total on June 27th.

In 1912, D Denton scored over 1,000 runs during July, while M Leyland and H Sutcliffe both scored over 1,000 runs in August 1932.

L Hutton scored over 1,000 in June and over 1,000 runs in August in 1949.

H Verity took his 100th wicket in First-Class cricket as early as June 19th in 1936 and on June 27th in 1935. In 1900, W Rhodes obtained his 100th wicket on June 21st, and again on the same date in 1901, while G H Hirst obtained his 100th wicket on June 28th, 1906.

In 1930, Yorkshiremen (H Sutcliffe and H Verity) occupied the first places by English players in the batting and the bowling averages of First-Class cricket, which is a record without precedent. H Sutcliffe was also first in the batting averages in 1931 and 1932.

G Boycott was the first player to have achieved an average of over 100 in each of two English seasons. In 1971, he scored 2,503 runs for an average of 100.12, and in 1979 he scored 1,538 runs for an average of 102.53.

FIRST-CLASS MATCHES BEGUN AND FINISHED IN ONE DAY

Yorkshire v. Somerset, at Huddersfield, July 9th, 1894.
Yorkshire v. Hampshire, at Southampton, May 27th, 1898.
Yorkshire v. Worcestershire, at Bradford, May 7th, 1900

For England

YORKSHIRE TEST CRICKETERS 1877-2021 (Correct to to January 26, 2021)

Player	M.	I	NO	Runs	HS.	Av'ge.	100s	50s	Balls	R	W	Av'ge	Best	5wI	10wM	c/st
APPLEYARD, R ...1954-56	9	9	6	51	19*	17.00	—	—	1,596	554	31	17.87	5-51	1	—	4
ARMITAGE, T ...1877	2	3	0	33	21	11.00	—	—	12	15	0	—	—	—	—	0
ATHEY, C W J ...1980-88	23	41	1	919	123	22.97	1	4	—	—	—	—	—	—	—	13
BAIRSTOW, D L ...1979-81	4	7	1	125	59	20.83	—	—	—	—	—	—	—	—	—	12/1
BAIRSTOW, J M ...2012-21	72	127	8	4,169	167*	35.03	6	21	12	5	0	—	—	—	—	186/13
BALLANCE, G S 2013/14-17	23	42	2	1,498	156	37.45	4	7	2	0	1	0.00	1-0	—	—	22
BARBER, W ...1935	2	4	0	83	44	20.75	—	—	—	—	—	—	—	—	—	1
BESS, D M ...2018-21	12	15	5	255	57	25.50	0	1	2196	1026	31	33.09	5-30	2	—	3
BATES, W ...1881-87	15	26	2	656	64	27.33	—	5	2,364	821	50	16.42	7-28	4	1	9
BINKS, J G ...1964	2	4	0	91	55	22.75	—	1	—	—	—	—	—	—	—	8/0
BLAKEY, R J ...1993	2	4	0	7	6	1.75	—	—	—	—	—	—	—	—	—	2/0
BOOTH, M W ...1913-14	2	2	0	46	32	23.00	—	—	312	130	7	18.57	4-49	—	—	0
BOWES, W E ...1932-46	15	11	5	28	10*	4.66	—	—	3,655	1,519	68	22.33	6-33	6	—	2
†BOYCOTT, G ...1964-82	108	193	23	8,114	246*	47.72	22	42	944	382	7	54.57	3-47	—	—	33
BRENNAN, D V ...1951	2	2	0	16	16	8.00	—	—	—	—	—	—	—	—	—	0/1
BRESNAN, T T ...2009-13/14	23	26	4	575	91	26.13	—	3	4,674	2,357	72	32.73	5-48	1	—	8
BROWN, J T ...1894-99	8	16	3	470	140	36.15	1	1	35	22	0	—	—	—	—	7
†CLOSE, D B ...1949-76	22	37	2	887	70	25.34	—	4	1,212	532	18	29.55	4-35	—	—	24
COPE, G A ...1977-78	3	3	0	40	22	13.33	—	—	864	277	8	34.62	3-102	—	—	1
COXON, A ...1948	1	2	0	19	19	9.50	—	—	378	172	3	57.33	2-90	—	—	0
DAWSON, R K J ...2002-03	7	13	3	114	19*	11.40	—	—	1,116	677	11	61.54	4-134	—	—	3
DENTON, D ...1905-10	11	22	1	424	104	20.19	1	1	—	—	—	—	—	—	—	8
DOLPHIN, A ...1921	1	2	0	1	1	0.50	—	—	—	—	—	—	—	—	—	1/0
EMMETT, T ...1877-82	7	13	1	160	48	13.33	—	—	728	284	9	31.55	7-68	1	—	9
GIBB, P A ...1938-46	8	13	0	581	120	44.69	2	3	—	—	—	—	—	—	—	3/1

272

For England

YORKSHIRE TEST CRICKETERS 1877-2021 (Continued)

Player	M.	I	NO	Runs	HS.	Av'ge	100s	50s	Balls	R	W	Av'ge	Best	5wI	10wM	c/st
GOUGH, D 1994-2003	58	86	18	855	65	12.57	—	2	11,821	6,503	229	28.39	6-42	9	—	13
GREENWOOD, A 1877	2	4	0	77	49	19.25	—	—	—	—	—	—	—	—	—	2
HAIGH, S ...1899-1912	11	18	3	113	25	7.53	—	—	1,294	622	24	25.91	6-11	1	—	8
HAMILTON, G.M. ...1999	1	2	0	0	0	0.00	—	—	90	63	0	—	—	—	—	0
HAMPSHIRE, J H ..1969-75	8	16	1	403	107	26.86	1	2	—	—	—	—	—	—	—	9
†HAWKE, LORD ..1896-99	5	8	1	55	30	7.85	—	—	—	—	—	—	—	—	—	3
HILL, A 1877	2	4	2	101	49	50.50	—	—	340	130	7	18.57	4-27	—	—	1
HIRST, G H ...1897-1909	24	38	3	790	85	22.57	—	5	3,967	1,770	59	30.00	5-48	3	—	18
HOGGARD, M J .2000-2008	67	92	27	473	38	7.27	—	—	13,909	7,564	248	30.50	7-61	7	1	24
HOLMES, P 1921-32	7	14	1	357	88	27.46	—	4	—	—	—	—	—	—	—	3
HUNTER, J 1884-85	5	7	2	93	39*	18.60	—	—	—	—	—	—	—	—	—	8/3
†HUTTON, L 1937-55	79	138	15	6,971	364	56.67	19	33	260	232	3	77.33	1-2	—	—	57
HUTTON, R A 1971	5	8	2	219	81	36.50	—	2	738	257	9	28.55	3-72	—	—	9
†ILLINGWORTH, R .1958-73	61	90	11	1,836	113	23.24	2	5	11,934	3,807	122	31.20	6-29	3	—	45
†JACKSON, Hon F S1893-1905	20	33	4	1,415	144*	48.79	5	6	1,587	799	24	33.29	5-52	1	—	10
JARVIS, P W 1988-93	9	15	2	132	29*	10.15	—	—	1,912	965	21	45.95	4-107	—	—	2
KILNER, R 1924-26	9	8	1	233	74	33.28	—	2	2,368	734	24	30.58	4-51	—	—	6
LEADBEATER, E .1951-52	2	2	0	40	38	20.00	—	—	289	218	2	109.00	1-38	—	—	3
LEYLAND, M ...1928-38	41	65	5	2,764	187	46.06	9	10	1,103	585	6	97.50	3-91	—	—	13
LOWSON, F A ...1951-55	7	13	0	245	68	18.84	—	2	—	—	—	—	—	—	—	5
LYTH A 2015	7	13	0	265	107	20.38	1	—	6	0	0	—	—	—	—	8
McGRATH, A 2003	4	5	0	201	81	40.20	—	1	102	56	4	14.00	3-16	—	—	5
MACAULAY, G G .1923-33	8	10	4	112	76	18.66	—	—	1,701	662	24	27.58	5-64	1	—	3
MALAN, D J 2017-18	15	26	0	724	140	27.84	1	6	156	70	0	—	0- 7	—	—	11
MILLIGAN, F W 1899	2	4	0	58	38	14.50	—	—	45	29	0	—	—	—	—	1
MITCHELL, A ...1933-36	6	10	0	298	72	29.80	—	2	6	4	0	—	—	—	—	9

For England

YORKSHIRE TEST CRICKETERS 1877-2021 (Continued)

Player	M.	I	NO	Runs	HS.	Av'ge	100s	50s	Balls	R	W	Av'ge	Best	5wI	10wM	c/st
* MITCHELL, F 1899	2	4	0	88	41	22.00	—	—	48	30	0	—	—	—	—	2
MOXON, M D 1986-89	10	17	1	455	99	28.43	—	3	—	—	—	—	—	—	—	10
OLD, C M 1972-81	46	66	9	845	65	14.82	—	2	8,858	4,020	143	28.11	7-50	4	—	22
PADGETT, D E V 1960	2	4	0	51	31	12.75	—	—	12	8	0	—	—	—	—	2
PEATE, E 1881-86	9	14	8	70	13	11.66	—	—	2,096	682	31	22.00	6-85	2	—	2
PEEL, R 1884-96	20	33	4	427	83	14.72	—	3	5,216	1,715	101	16.98	7-31	5	1	17
PLUNKETT, L E 2005/6-2014	13	20	5	238	55*	15.86	—	1	2,659	1,536	41	37.46	5-64	1	—	3
RASHID, A U 2015/16-19	19	33	5	540	61	19.28	—	2	3,816	2,390	60	39.83	5-49	2	—	4
RHODES, W 1899-1930	58	98	21	2,325	179	30.19	2	11	8,231	3,425	127	26.96	8-68	6	1	60
† ROOT, J E 2012-21	99	181	14	8,249	254	49.39	19	49	2,809	1,463	31	47.19	4-87	—	—	131
SHARPE, P J 1963-69	12	21	4	786	111	46.23	1	4	—	—	—	—	—	—	—	17
SHAHZAD, A 2010	1	1	0	5	5	5.00	—	—	102	63	4	15.75	3-45	—	—	2
SIDEBOTTOM, A 1985	1	1	0	2	2	2.00	—	—	112	65	1	65.00	1-65	—	—	0
SIDEBOTTOM, R J 2001-10	22	31	11	313	31	15.65	—	—	4,812	2,231	79	28.24	7-47	5	—	5
SILVERWOOD, C E W 1997-2003	6	7	3	29	10	7.25	—	—	828	444	11	40.36	5-91	1	—	2
SMAILES, T F 1946	1	1	0	25	25	25.00	—	—	120	62	3	20.66	3-44	—	—	0
SMITHSON, G A 1948	2	3	0	70	35	23.33	—	—	—	—	—	—	—	—	—	—
† STANYFORTH, R T 1927-28	4	6	1	13	6*	2.60	—	—	—	—	—	—	—	—	—	7/2
STEVENSON, G B 1980-81	2	2	1	28	27*	28.00	—	—	312	183	5	36.60	3-111	—	—	0
SUTCLIFFE, H 1924-35	54	84	9	4,555	194	60.73	16	23	—	—	—	—	—	—	—	23
TAYLOR, K 1959-64	3	5	0	57	24	11.40	—	—	12	6	0	—	—	—	—	1
TRUEMAN, F S 1952-65	67	85	14	981	39*	13.81	—	—	15,178	6,625	307	21.57	8-31	17	3	64
ULYETT, G 1877-90	25	39	0	949	149	24.33	1	7	2,627	1,020	50	20.40	7-36	1	—	19
† VAUGHAN M P 1999-2008	82	147	9	5,719	197	41.44	18	18	978	561	6	93.50	2-71	—	—	44
VERITY, H 1931-39	40	44	12	669	66*	20.90	—	3	11,173	3,510	144	24.37	8-43	5	2	30
WADDINGTON, A 1920-21	2	4	0	16	7	4.00	—	—	276	119	1	119.00	1-35	—	—	1

For England

Player	M.	I	NO	Runs	HS	Av'ge	100s	50s	Balls	R	W	Av'ge	Best	5wI	10wM	c/st
WAINWRIGHT, E 1893-98	5	9	0	132	49	14.66	—	—	127	73	0	—	—	—	—	2
WARDLE, J H 1948-57	28	41	8	653	66	19.78	—	2	6,597	2,080	102	20.39	7-36	5	1	12
WATSON, W 1951-59	23	37	3	879	116	25.85	2	3	—	—	—	—	—	—	—	8
WHITE, C 1994-2002	30	50	7	1,052	121	24.46	1	5	3,959	2,220	59	37.62	5-32	3	—	14
WILSON, C E M 1899	2	4	1	42	18	14.00	—	—	—	—	—	—	—	—	—	0
WILSON, D 1964-71	6	7	1	75	42	12.50	—	—	1,472	466	11	42.36	2-17	—	—	1
WILSON, E R 1921	1	2	0	10	5	5.00	—	—	123	36	3	12.00	2-28	—	—	0
WOOD, A 1938-39	4	5	1	80	53	20.00	—	1	—	—	—	—	—	—	—	10/1
†YARDLEY, N W D . .1938-50	20	34	2	812	99	25.37	—	4	1,662	707	21	33.66	3-67	—	—	14

†Captained England
*Also represented and captained South Africa

For South Africa

Player	M.	I	NO	Runs	HS	Av'ge	100s	50s	Balls	R	W	Av'ge	Best	5wI	10wM	c/st
†MITCHELL, F 1912	3	6	0	28	12	4.66	—	—	—	—	—	—	—	—	—	0

†Captained South Africa

Overseas Players

(Qualification: 20 first-class matches for Yorkshire)

For Australia

Player	M.	I	NO	Runs	HS	Av'ge	100s	50s	Balls	R	W	Av'ge	Best	5wI	10wM	c/st
BEVAN, M G 1994-2006	18	30	3	785	91	29.07	—	6	1,285	703	29	24.24	6-82	1	1	8
GILLESPIE, J N . .1996-2006	71	93	28	1,218	201*	18.73	1	2	14,234	6,770	259	26.13	7-37	8	—	27
JAQUES, P A 2005-2008	11	19	0	902	150	47.47	3	6	—	—	—	—	—	—	—	7
LEHMANN, D S . .1999-2004	27	42	2	1,798	177	44.95	5	10	974	412	15	27.46	3-42	—	—	11

For South Africa

Player	M.	I	NO	Runs	HS	Av'ge	100s	50s	Balls	R	W	Av'ge	Best	5wI	10wM	c/st
RUDOLPH, J A 2003-12/13	48	83	9	2,622	222*	35.43	6	11	664	432	4	108.00	1-1	—	—	29

For West Indies

Player	M.	I	NO	Runs	HS	Av'ge	100s	50s	Balls	R	W	Av'ge	Best	5wI	10wM	c/st
RICHARDSON, R B 1983-84/95	86	146	12	5,949	194	44.39	16	27	66	18	0	—	—	—	—	90

CENTURIES FOR ENGLAND

C W J ATHEY (1)

123 v Pakistan at Lord's, 1987

J M BAIRSTOW (6)

150* v. South Africa at Cape Town, 2016
167* v. Sri Lanka at Lord's, 2016
101 v. New Zealand at Christchurch, 2018
140 v. Sri Lanka at Leeds, 2016
119 v. Australia at Perth, 2017
110 v. Sri Lanka at Colombo (SSC), 2018

G S BALLANCE (4)

104* v. Sri Lanka at Lord's, 2014
256 v. India at Southampton, 2014
110 v. India at Lord's, 2014
122 v. West Indies at North Sound, 2015

G BOYCOTT (22)

113 v. Australia at The Oval, 1964
117 v. South Africa at Port Elizabeth, 1965
246* v. India at Leeds, 1967
116 v. West Indies at Georgetown, 1968
128 v. West Indies at Manchester, 1969
106 v. West Indies at Lord's, 1969
142* v. Australia at Sydney, 1971
119* v. Australia at Adelaide, 1971
121* v. Pakistan at Lord's, 1971
112 v. Pakistan at Leeds, 1971
115 v. New Zealand at Leeds, 1973
112 v West Indies at Port-of-Spain, 1974
107 v. Australia at Nottingham, 1977
191 v. Australia at Leeds, 1977
100* v. Pakistan at Hyderabad, 1978
131 v. New Zealand at Nottingham, 1978
155 v. India at Birmingham, 1979
125 v. India at The Oval, 1979
128* v. Australia at Lord's, 1980
104* v. West Indies at St John's, 1981
137 v. Australia at The Oval, 1981
105 v. India at Delhi, 1981

J T BROWN (1)

140 v. Australia at Melbourne, 1895

D DENTON (1)

104 v. South Africa at Old Wanderers, Johannesburg, 1910

P A GIBB (2)

106 v. South Africa at Old Wanderers, Johannesburg, 1938
120 v. South Africa at Kingsmead, Durban, 1939

J H HAMPSHIRE (1)

107 v. West Indies at Lord's, 1969

L HUTTON (19)

100 v. New Zealand at Manchester, 1937
100 v. Australia at Nottingham, 1938
364 v. Australia at The Oval, 1938
196 v. West Indies at Lord's, 1939
165* v. West Indies at The Oval, 1939
122* v. Australia at Sydney, 1947
100 v. South Africa at Leeds, 1947
158 v. South Africa at Ellis Park, J'b'rg, 1948
123 v. South Africa at Ellis Park, J'b'rg, 1949
101 v. New Zealand at Leeds, 1949
206 v. New Zealand at The Oval, 1949
202* v. West Indies at The Oval, 1950
156* v. Australia at Adelaide, 1951
100 v. South Africa at Leeds, 1951
150 v. India at Lord's, 1952
104 v. India at Manchester, 1952
145 v. Australia at Lord's, 1953
169 v. West Indies at Georgetown, 1954
205 v. West Indies at Kingston, 1954

R ILLINGWORTH (2)

113 v. West Indies at Lord's, 1969
107 v. India at Manchester, 1971

Hon. F S JACKSON (5)

103 v. Australia at The Oval, 1893
118 v. Australia at The Oval, 1899
128 v. Australia at Manchester, 1902
144* v. Australia at Leeds, 1905
113 v. Australia at Manchester, 1905

CENTURIES FOR ENGLAND

M LEYLAND (9)

137 v. Australia at Melbourne, 1929
102 v. South Africa at Lord's, 1929
109 v. Australia at Lord's, 1934
153 v. Australia at Manchester, 1934
110 v. Australia at The Oval, 1934

161 v. South Africa at The Oval, 1935
126 v. Australia at Woolloongabba, Brisbane, 1936
111* v. Australia at Melbourne, 1937
187 v. Australia at The Oval, 1938

A LYTH (1)

107 v. New Zealand at Leeds 2015

W RHODES (2)

179 v. Australia at Melbourne, 1912
152 v. South Africa at Old Wanderers, Johannesburg, 1913

J E ROOT (17)

104 v. New Zealand at Leeds, 2013
200* v. Sri Lanka at Lord's, 2014
149* v. India at The Oval, 2014
134 v. Australia at Cardiff 2015
110 v. South Africa at Johannesburg, 2016
124 v. India at Rajkot, 2016
136 v. West Indies at Birmingham, 2017
124 v. Sri Lanka at Pallekele, 2018
226 v, New Zealand at Hamiton, 2019

180 v. Australia at Lord's, 2013
154* v. India at Nottingham, 2014
182* v. West Indies at St George's, 2015
130 v. Australia at Nottingham, 2015
254 v. Pakistan at Manchester, 2016
190 v. South Africa at Lord's, 2017
125 v. India at The Oval, 2018
122 v. West Indies at Gros Islet, 2019

P J SHARPE (1)

111 v. New Zealand at Nottingham, 1969

H SUTCLIFFE (16)

122 v. South Africa at Lord's, 1924
115 v. Australia at Sydney, 1924
176 v. Australia at Melbourne, 1925 (1st Inns)
127 v. Australia at Melbourne, 1925 (2nd Inns)
143 v. Australia at Melbourne, 1925
161 v. Australia at The Oval, 1926
102 v. South Africa at Old Wanderers, Jbg.1927
135 v. Australia at Melbourne, 1929

114 v. South Africa at Birmingham, 1929
100 v. South Africa at Lord's, 1929
104 v. South Africa at The Oval, 1929 (1st inns)
109* v. South Africa at The Oval, 1929 (2nd inns)
161 v. Australia at The Oval, 1930
117 v. New Zealand at The Oval, 1931
109* v. New Zealand at Manchester, 1931
194 v. Australia at Sydney, 1932

G ULYETT (1)

149 v. Australia at Melbourne, 1882

M P VAUGHAN (18)

120 v. Pakistan at Manchester, 2001
115 v. Sri Lanka at Lord's, 2002
100 v. India at Lord's, 2002
197 v. India at Nottingham, 2002
195 v. India at The Oval, 2002
177 v. Australia at Adelaide, 2002
145 v. Australia at Melbourne, 2002
183 v. Australia at Sydney, 2003
156 v. South Africa at Birmingham, 2003

105 v. Sri Lanka at Kandy, 2003
140 v. West Indies at Antigua, 2004
103 v. West Indies at Lord's (1st inns) 2004
101* v. West Indies at Lord's (2nd inns) 2004
120 v. Bangladesh at Lord's, 2005
166 v. Australia at Manchester,2005
103 v. West Indies at Leeds, 2007
124 v. India at Nottingham, 2007
106 v. New Zealand at Lord's, 2008

CENTURIES FOR ENGLAND *(Continued)*

W WATSON (2)

109   v. Australia at Lord's, 1953   116 v. West Indies at Kingston, 1954

C WHITE (1)

121 v. India at Ahmedabad, 2001

Summary of the Centuries

versus	Total	In England	Away
Australia	43	23	20
Bangladesh	1	1	0
India	18	15	3
New Zealand	13	11	2
Pakistan	6	5	1
South Africa	21	11	10
Sri Lanka	8	5	3
West Indies	21	11	10
Totals	131	82	49

For Australia

J N GILLESPIE (1)

201* v. Bangladesh at Chittagong, 2006

P A JAQUES (3)

100   v. Sri Lanka at Brisbane, 2007   108   v. West Indies at Bridgetown, 2008
150   v. Sri Lanka at Hobart, 2007

D S LEHMANN (5)

160   v. West Indies at Port of Spain, 2003   129   v. Sri Lanka at Galle, 2004
110   v. Bangladesh at Darwin, 2003   153   v. Sri Lanka at Columbo, 2004
177   v. Bangladesh at Cairns, 2003

For South Africa

J A RUDOLPH (6)

222* v. Bangladesh at Chittagong, 2003   102   v. Sri Lanka at Galle, 2004
101   v West Indies at Cape Town, 2004   102* v Australia at Perth, 2005
154* v. New Zealand at Auckland, 2004   105* v. New Zealand at Dunedin, 2012

10 WICKETS IN A MATCH FOR ENGLAND

W BATES (1)
14 for 102 (7 for 28 and 7 for 74) v. Australia at Melbourne, 1882

M J HOGGARD (1)
12 for 205 (5 for 144 and 7 for 61) v. South Africa at Johannesburg, 2005

R PEEL (1)
11 for 68 (7 for 31 and 4 for 37) v. Australia at Mancester, 1888

Note: The scorebook for the Australia v. England Test match at Sydney in February 1888
shows that the final wicket to fall was taken by W Attewell, and not by Peel
Peel therefore took 9, and not 10 wickets, in the match
His career totals have been amended to take account of this alteration

W RHODES (1)
15 for 124 (7 for 56 and 8 for 68) v. Australia at Melbourne, 1904

R J SIDEBOTTOM (1)
10 for 139 (4 for 90 and 6 for 49) v. New Zealand at Hamilton, 2008

F S TRUEMAN
11 for 88 (5 for 58 and 6 for 30) v. Australia at Leeds, 1961
11 for 152 (6 for 100 and 5 for 52) v. West Indies at Lord's, 1963*
12 for 119 (5 for 75 and 7 for 44) v. West Indies at Birmingham, 1963*
consecutive Tests

H VERITY (2)
11 for 153 (7 for 49 and 4 for 104) v. India at Chepauk, Madras, 1934
15 for 104 (7 for 61 and 8 for 43) v. Australia at Lord's, 1934

J H WARDLE (1)
12 for 89 (5 for 53 and 7 for 36) v. South Africa at Cape Town, 1957

Summary of Ten Wickets in a Match

versus	Total	In England	Away
Australia	5	3	2
India	1	—	1
New Zealand	1	—	1
Pakistan	—	—	—
South Africa	2	—	2
Sri Lanka	—	—	—
West Indies	2	2	—
Totals	11	5	6

For Australia

M G BEVAN (1)
10 for 113 (4 for 31and 6 for 82) v. West Indies at Adelaide, 1997

5 WICKETS IN AN INNINGS FOR ENGLAND

R APPLEYARD (1)
5 for 51 v. Pakistan at Nottingham, 1954

W BATES (4)
7 for 28 v. Australia at Melbourne, 1882   5 for 31 v. Australia at Adelaide, 1884
7 for 74 v. Australia at Melbourne, 1882   5 for 24 v. Australia at Sydney, 1885

D M BESS (2)
5 for 51 v. South Africa at Port Elizabeth, 2020   5 for 30 v. Sri Lanka at Galle 2021

5 WICKETS IN AN INNINGS FOR ENGLAND *(Continued)*

W E BOWES (6)

6-34	v. New Zealand	at Auckland	1933	5-100	v. South Africa	at Manchester	1935
6-142	v. Australia	at Leeds	1934*	5-49	v. Australia	at The Oval	1938
5-55	v. Australia	at The Oval	1934*	6-33	v. West Indies	at Manchester	1939

consecutive Test matches

T T BRESNAN (1)

5-48 v. India   at Nottingham   2011

T EMMETT (1)

7-68 v. Australia   at Melbourne   1879

D GOUGH (9)

6-49	v. Australia	at Sydney	1995	5-70	v. South Africa	at Johannesburg	1999
5-40	v. New Zealand	at Wellington	1997	5-109	v. West Indies	at Birmingham	2000
5-149	v. Australia	at Leeds	1997	5-61	v. Pakistan	at Lord's	2001
6-42	v. South Africa	at Leeds	1998	5-103	v. Australia	at Leeds	2001
5-96	v. Australia	at Melbourne	1998				

S HAIGH (1)

6-11   v. South Africa   at Cape Town   1909

G H HIRST (3)

5-77	v. Australia	at The Oval	1902	5-58	v. Australia	at Birmingham 1909
5-48	v. Australia	at Melbourne	1904				

M J HOGGARD (7)

7-63	v. New Zealand	at Christchurch	2002	5-73	v. Bangladesh	at Chester-le-Street	
5-92	v. Sri Lanka	at Birmingham	2002				2005
5-144	v. South Africa	at Johannesburg	2005*	6-57	v. India	at Nagpur	2006
7-61	v. South Africa	at Johannesburg	2005*	7-109	v. Australia	at Adelaide	2006

Consecutive Test innings

R ILLINGWORTH (3)

6-29	v. India	at Lord's	1967	5-70	v. India	at The Oval	1971
6-87	v. Australia	at Leeds	1968				

Hon F S JACKSON (1)

5-52 v. Australia   at Nottingham   1905

G G MACAULAY (1)

5-64 v. South Africa   at Cape Town   1923

C M OLD (4)

5-113	v. New Zealand	at Lord's	1973	6-54	v. New Zealand	at Wellington	1978
5-21	v. India	at Lord's	1974	7-50	v. Pakistan	at Birmingham	1978

E PEATE (2)

5-43   v. Australia   at Sydney 1882   6-85   v. Australia   at Lord's   1884

R PEEL (5)

5-51	v. Australia	at Adelaide	1884	6-67	v. Australia	at Sydney	1894
5-18	v. Australia	at Sydney	1888	6-23	v. Australia	at The Oval	1896
7-31	v. Australia	at Manchester	1888				

L E PLUNKETT (1)

5-64 v. Sri Lanka   at Leeds   2014

A U RASHID (2)

5-64 v. Pakistan   at Abu Dhabi   2015   5-49   v. Sri Lanka   at Colombo (SSC)   2018

5 WICKETS IN AN INNINGS FOR ENGLAND *(Continued)*

W RHODES (6)

7-17	v. Australia	at Birmingham	1902		7-56	v. Australia	at Melbourne	1904*
5-63	v. Australia	at Sheffield	1902		8-68	v. Australia	at Melbourne	1904*
5-94	v. Australia	at Sydney	1903*		5-83	v. Australia	at Manchester	1909

consecutive Test innings

C E W SILVERWOOD (1)

5-91   v. South Africa   at Cape Town   2000

R J SIDEBOTTOM (5)

5-88	v. West Indies	at Chester-le-Street			5-105	v. New Zealand	at Wellington	2008
			2007		7-47	v. New Zealand	at Napier	2008
6-49	v. New Zealand	at Hamilton	2008		6-47	v. New Zealand	at Nottingham	2008

F S TRUEMAN (17)

8-31	v. India	at Manchester	1952		6-31	v. Pakistan	at Lord's	1962
5-48	v. India	at The Oval	1952		5-62	v. Australia	at Melbourne	1963
5-90	v. Australia	at Lord's	1956		7-75	v. New Zealand	at Christchurch	1963
5-63	v. West Indies	at Nottingham	1957		6-100	v. West Indies	at Lord's	1963*
5-31	v. New Zealand	at Birmingham	1958		5-52	v. West Indies	at Lord's	1963*
5-35	v. West Indies	at Port-of-Spain	1960		5-75	v. West Indies	at Birmingham	1963*
5-27	v. South Africa	at Nottingham	1960		7-44	v. West Indies	at Birmingham	1963*
5-58	v. Australia	at Leeds	1961*		5-48	v. Australia	at Lord's	1964
6-30	v. Australia	at Leeds	1961*					

G ULYETT (1)

7-36   v. Australia   at Lord's   1884

H VERITY (5)

5-33	v. Australia	at Sydney	1933		8-43	v. Australia	at Lord's	1934*
7-49	v. India	at Chepauk, Madras	1934		5-70	v. South Africa	at Cape Town	1939
7-61	v. Australia	at Lord's	1934*					

J H WARDLE (5)

7-56	v. Pakistan	at The Oval	1954		7-36	v. South Africa	at Cape Town	1957*
5-79	v. Australia	at Sydney	1955		5-61	v. South Africa	at Kingsmead Durban	1957*
5-53	v. South Africa	at Cape Town	1957*					

C WHITE (3)

5-57	v. West Indies	at Leeds	2000		5-32	v. West Indies	at The Oval	2000
	5-127	v. Australia	at Perth	2002				

consecutive Test innings

Summary of Five Wickets in an Innings

versus	Total	In England	Away
Australia	42	22	20
Bangladesh	1	1	0
India	8	6	2
New Zealand	11	3	8
Pakistan	6	5	1
South Africa	14	3	11
Sri Lanka	4	2	2
West Indies	11	10	1
Totals	97	52	45

5 WICKETS IN AN INNINGS

For Australia

M G BEVAN (1)

6-82	v. West Indies	at Adelaide	1997

J N GILLESPIE (8)

5-54	v. South Africa	at Port Elizabeth	1997
7-37	v. England	at Leeds	1997
5-88	v. England	at Perth	1998
5-89	v. West Indies	at Adelaide	2000
6-40	v. West Indies	at Melbourne	2000
5-53	v. England	at Lord's	2001
5-39	v. West Indies	at Georgetown	2003
5-56	v. India	at Nagpur	2004

HAT-TRICKS

W Bates	v. Australia	at Melbourne	1882
D Gough	v. Australia	at Sydney	1998
M J Hoggard	v. West Indies	at Bridgetown	2004
R J Sidebottom	v. New Zealand	at Hamilton	2008

FOUR WICKETS IN FIVE BALLS

C M Old	v. Pakistan	at Birmingham	1978

THREE WICKETS IN FOUR BALLS

R Appleyard	v. New Zealand	at Auckland	1955
D Gough	v. Pakistan	at Lord's	2001

YORKSHIRE PLAYERS WHO PLAYED ALL THEIR TEST CRICKET AFTER LEAVING YORKSHIRE

For England

Player	M.	I	NO	Runs	HS.	Av'ge.	100s	50s	Balls	R	W	Av'ge	Best	5wI	10wM	c/st
BALDERSTONE, J C 1976	2	4	0	39	35	9.75	—	—	96	80	1	80.00	1:80	—	—	1
BATTY G J 2003/4-16/17	9	12	2	149	38	14.90	—	—	1,714	914	15	60.93	3-55	—	—	3
BIRKENSHAW, J 1973-74	5	7	0	148	64	21.14	—	1	1,017	469	13	36.07	5:57	1	—	3
BOLUS, J B 1963-64	7	12	2	496	88	41.33	—	4	18	16	0	—	—	—	—	2
†PARKIN, C H 1920-24	10	16	3	160	36	12.30	—	—	2,095	1,128	32	35.25	5:38	2	—	3
RHODES, S J 1994-95	11	17	5	294	65*	24.50	—	1	—	—	—	—	—	—	—	46/3
†SUGG, F H 1888	2	2	0	55	31	27.50	—	—	—	—	—	—	—	—	—	0
WARD, A 1893-95	7	13	0	487	117	37.46	1	3	—	—	—	—	—	—	—	1
WOOD, B 1972-78	12	21	0	454	90	21.61	—	2	98	50	0	—	—	—	—	6

For South Africa

Player	M.	I	NO	Runs	HS.	Av'ge.	100s	50s	Balls	R	W	Av'ge	Best	5wI	10wM	c/st
THORNTON, P G 1902	1	1	1	1	1*	—	—	—	24	20	1	20.00	1:20	—	—	1

†Born outside Yorkshire

CENTURIES FOR ENGLAND

A WARD (1)
117 v. Australia at Sydney, 1894

5 WICKETS IN AN INNINGS FOR ENGLAND

J BIRKENSHAW (1)
5 : 57 v. Pakistan at Karachi, 1973

C H PARKIN (2)
5 : 60 v. Australia at Adelaide, 1921
5 : 38 v. Australia at Manchester, 1921

283

YORKSHIRE'S TEST CRICKET RECORDS

R APPLEYARD

Auckland 1954-55: took 3 wickets in 4 balls as New Zealand were dismissed for the lowest total in Test history (26).

C W J ATHEY

Perth 1986-87: shared an opening stand of 223 with B C Broad – England's highest for any wicket at the WACA Ground.

J M BAIRSTOW

Cape Town, January 2016: scored his maiden Test Century (150*). His sixth- wicket partnership of 399 with B A Stokes (258) was the highest in Test cricket and the highest First Class partnership for any wicket for England. There was only one higher partnership for England. This was 411 by P B H May and M C Cowdrey for the fourth wicket against the West Indies at Birmingham in 1957.

Chittagong, October 2016: scored 52 in the first innings, which passed his 1,000 Test runs in a calendar year. He became only the third Yorkshire player to do this after M P Vaughan with 1,481 in 2002 and J E Root 1,385 in 2015. He was only the second Test wicket-keeper to pass this mark. His first scoring shot in the second inning broke a 16-year record set by Zimbabwe's A Flower (1,045 in 2000) to give him the highest total of runs scored in a calendar year by a Test wicket-keeper. His final tally for 2016 was 1,470.

Mohali, November 2016: his third catch of India's first innings (U T Yadav) was his 68th dismissal of the year to pass the previous best in a calendar year (67) by I A Healy (Australia) in 1991 and M V Boucher (South Africa) in 1998. Bairstow's final tally for the calendar year was 70 (66 caught and 4 stumped).

W BATES

Melbourne 1882-83 (Second Test): achieved the first hat-trick for England when he dismissed P S McDonnell, G Giffen and G J Bonnor in Australia's first innings. Later in the match, he became the first player to score a fifty (55) and take 10 or more wickets (14 for 102) in the same Test.

W E BOWES

Melbourne 1932-33: enjoyed the unique satisfaction of bowling D G Bradman first ball in a Test match (his first ball to him in Test cricket).

G BOYCOTT

Leeds 1967: scored 246 not out off 555 balls in 573 minutes to establish the record England score against India. His first 100 took 341 minutes (316 balls) and he was excluded from the next Test as a disciplinary measure; shared in hundred partnerships for three successive wickets.

Adelaide 1970-71: with J H Edrich, became the third opening pair to share hundred partnerships in both innings of a Test against Australia.

Port-of-Spain 1973-74: first to score 99 and a hundred in the same Test.

Nottingham 1977: with A P E Knott, equalled England v. Australia sixth-wicket partnership record of 215 – the only England v. Australia stand to be equalled or broken since 1938. Batted on each day of the five-day Test (second after M L Jaisimha to achieve this feat).

Leeds 1977: first to score his 100th First Class hundred in a Test; became the fourth England player to be on the field for an entire Test.

G BOYCOTT *(Continued)*

Perth: 1978-79: eighth to score 2,000 runs for England against Australia.

Birmingham 1979: emulated K F Barrington by scoring hundreds on each of England's six current home grounds.

Perth: 1979-80: fourth to carry his bat through a completed England innings (third v. Australia) and the first to do so without scoring 100; first to score 99 not out in a Test.

Lord's 1981: 100th Test for England – second after M C Cowdrey (1968).

The Oval, 1981: second after Hon F S Jackson to score five hundreds v. Australia in England.

Gained three Test records from M C Cowdrey: exceeded England aggregate of 7,624 runs in 11 fewer Tests (Manchester 1981); 61st fifty – world record (The Oval 1981); 189th innings – world record (Bangalore 1981-82).

Delhi, 4.23p.m. on 23 December 1981: passed G St.A Sobers's world Test record of 8,032 runs, having played 30 more innings and batted over 451 hours (cf. 15 complete five-day Tests); his 22nd hundred equalled the England record.

J T BROWN

Melbourne 1894-95: his 28-minute fifty remains the fastest in Test cricket, and his 95-minute hundred was a record until 1897-98; his third-wicket stand of 210 with A Ward set a Test record for any wicket.

D B CLOSE

Manchester 1949: at 18 years 149 days he became – and remains – the youngest to represent England.

Melbourne 1950-51: became the youngest (19 years 301 days) to represent England against Australia.

T EMMETT

Melbourne 1878-79: first England bowler to take seven wickets in a Test innings.

P A GIBB

Johannesburg 1938-39: enjoyed a record England debut, scoring 93 and 106 as well as sharing second-wicket stands of 184 and 168 with E Paynter.

Durban 1938-39: shared record England v. South Africa second-wicket stand of 280 with W J Edrich, his 120 in 451 minutes including only two boundaries.

D GOUGH

Sydney 1998-99: achieved the 23rd hat-trick in Test cricket (ninth for England and first for England v. Australia since 1899).

Lord's 2001: took 3 wickets in 4 balls v. Pakistan.

S HAIGH

Cape Town 1898-99: bowled unchanged through the second innings with A E Trott, taking 6 for 11 as South Africa were dismissed for 35 in the space of 114 balls.

J H HAMPSHIRE

Lord's 1969: became the first England player to score 100 at Lord's on his debut in Tests.

A HILL

Melbourne 1876-77: took the first wicket to fall in Test cricket when he bowled N Thompson, and held the first catch when he dismissed T P Horan.

YORKSHIRE'S TEST CRICKET RECORDS *(Continued)*

G H HIRST

The Oval: 1902: helped to score the last 15 runs in a match-winning tenth-wicket partnership with W Rhodes.

Birmingham 1909: shared all 20 Australian wickets with fellow left-arm spinner C Blythe (11 for 102).

M J HOGGARD

Bridgetown 2004: became the third Yorkshire player to take a hat-trick in Test cricket (see W Bates and D Gough). It was the 10th hat-trick for England and the third for England versus West Indies.

L HUTTON

Nottingham 1938: scored 100 in his first Test against Australia.

The Oval 1938: his score (364) and batting time (13 hours 17 minutes – the longest innings in English First-Class cricket) remain England records, and were world Test records until 1958. It remains the highest Test score at The Oval. His stand of 382 with M Leyland is the England second-wicket record in all Tests and the highest for any wicket against Australia. He also shared a record England v. Australia sixth-wicket stand of 216 with J Hardstaff Jr. – the first instance of a batsman sharing in two stands of 200 in the same Test innings. 770 runs were scored during his innings (Test record) which was England's 100th century against Australia, and contained 35 fours. England's total of 903 for 7 declared remains the Ashes Test record.

Lord's 1939: added 248 for the fourth wicket with D C S Compton in 140 minutes.

The Oval 1939: shared (then) world-record third-wicket stand of 264 with W R Hammond, which remains the record for England v. West Indies. Hutton's last eight Tests had brought him 1,109 runs.

The Oval 1948: last out in the first innings, he was on the field for all but the final 57 minutes of the match.

Johannesburg 1948-49: shared (then) world-record first-wicket stand of 359 in 310 minutes with C Washbrook on the opening day of Test cricket at Ellis Park; it remains England's highest opening stand in all Tests.

The Oval 1950: scored England's first 200 in a home Test v. West Indies, and remains alone in carrying his bat for England against them; his 202 not out (in 470 minutes) is the highest score by an England batsman achieving this feat.

Adelaide 1950-51: only England batsman to carry his bat throughout a complete Test innings twice, and second after R Abel (1891-92) to do so for any country against Australia.

Manchester 1951: scored 98 not out, just failing to become the first to score his 100th First Class hundred in a Test match.

The Oval 1951: became the only batsman to be out 'obstructing the field' in Test cricket.

1952: first professional to be appointed captain of England in the 20th Century.

The Oval 1953: first captain to win a rubber after losing the toss in all five Tests.

Kingston 1953-54: scored the first 200 by an England captain in a Test overseas.

R ILLINGWORTH

Manchester 1971: shared record England v. India eighth-wicket stand of 168 with P Lever.

YORKSHIRE'S TEST CRICKET RECORDS *(Continued)*

Hon. F S JACKSON

The Oval 1893: his 100 took 135 minutes, and was the first in a Test in England to be completed with a hit over the boundary (then worth only four runs).

The Oval 1899: his stand of 185 with T W Hayward was then England's highest for any wicket in England, and the record opening partnership by either side in England v. Australia Tests.

Nottingham 1905: dismissed M A Noble, C Hill and J Darling in one over (W01W0W).

Leeds 1905: batted 268 minutes for 144 not out – the first hundred in a Headingley Test.

Manchester 1905: first to score five Test hundreds in England.

The Oval 1905: first captain to win every toss in a five-match rubber.

M LEYLAND

Melbourne 1928-29: scored 137 in his first innings against Australia.

1934: first to score three hundreds in a rubber against Australia in England.

Brisbane 1936-37: scored England's only 100 at 'The Gabba' before 1974-75.

The Oval 1938: contributed 187 in 381 minutes to the record Test total of 903 for 7 declared, sharing in England's highest stand against Australia (all wickets) and record second-wicket stand in all Tests: 382 with L Hutton. First to score hundreds in his first and last innings against Australia.

G G MACAULAY

Cape Town 1922-23: fourth bowler (third for England) to take a wicket (G A L Hearne) with his first ball in Test cricket. Made the winning hit in the fourth of only six Tests to be decided by a one-wicket margin.

Leeds 1926: shared a match-saving ninth-wicket stand of 108 with G Geary.

C M OLD

Birmingham 1978: took 4 wickets in 5 balls in his 19th over (0WW no-ball WW1) to emulate the feat of M J C Allom.

R PEEL

Took his 50th wicket in his ninth Test and his 100th in his 20th Test – all against Australia.

W RHODES

Birmingham 1902: his first-innings analysis of 7 for 17 remains the record for all Tests at Edgbaston.

The Oval 1902: helped to score the last 15 runs in a match-winning tenth-wicket partnership with G H Hirst.

Sydney 1903-04: shared record England v. Australia tenth-wicket stand of 130 in 66 minutes with R E Foster.

Melbourne 1903-04: first to take 15 wickets in England v. Australia Tests; his match analysis of 15 for 124 remains the record for all Tests at Melbourne.

Melbourne 1911-12: shared record England v. Australia first-wicket stand of 323 in 268 minutes with J B Hobbs.

Johannesburg 1913-14: took his 100th wicket and completed the first 'double' for England (in 44

Sydney 1920-21: first to score 2,000 runs and take 100 wickets in Test cricket.

Adelaide 1920-21: third bowler to take 100 wickets against Australia.

W RHODES *(Continued)*

The Oval 1926: set (then) record of 109 wickets against Australia.

Kingston 1929-30: ended the world's longest Test career (30 years 315 days) as the oldest Test cricketer (52 years 165 days).

J E ROOT

Chittagong, October 2016: with his score (40) in England's first innings he passed 1,000 runs in a calendar year. He also did this in 2015 (1,385) and became the first Yorkshire player to do this twice. His final tally (1,477) in 2016 left him four short of M P Vaughan's total in 2002

Visakhapatnam, November 2016: Played his 50th Test match, which was also his 100th first-class match

Lord's, July 2017 v. West Indies: His first innings (190) was the highest by an England captain in his first innings in this role.

Galle, January 2021 v. Sri Lanka. In the second Test match Root's first-innings score of 186 took him passed G Boycott's England Test runs total of 8,114, and by the end of that match Root's total runs for England stood at 8,249, leaving him in fourth place behind A N Cook (12,472), G A Gooch (8,900) and A J Stewart (8,463).

Chennai, February 2021 First Test Match v. India. Root with scores of 218 and 40 became the first player to score a double-hundred in their 100th Test Match. Eight others including two England players, M C Cowdrey (1968) and A J Stewart (2000) passed the century mark in their 100th Test Match. Root is now England's third all-time run-scorer.

H SUTCLIFFE

Birmingham 1924: shared the first of 15 three-figure partnerships with J B Hobbs at the first attempt.

Lord's 1924: shared stand of 268 with J B Hobbs, which remains the first-wicket record for all Lord's Tests, and was then the England v. South Africa record.

Sydney 1924-25: his first opening stands against Australia with J B Hobbs realised 157 and 110.

Melbourne 1924-25 (Second Test): with J B Hobbs achieved the first instance of a batting partnership enduring throughout a full day's Test match play; they remain the only England pair to achieve this feat, and their stand of 283 in 289 minutes remains the longest for the first wicket in this series. Became the first to score 100 in each innings of a Test against Australia, and the first Englishman to score three successive hundreds in Test cricket.

Melbourne 1924-25 (Fourth Test): first to score four hundreds in one rubber of Test matches; it was his third 100 in successive Test innings at Melbourne. Completed 1,000 runs in fewest Test innings (12) – since equalled.

Sydney 1924-25: his aggregate of 734 was the record for any rubber until 1928-29.

The Oval 1926: shared first-wicket stand of 172 with J B Hobbs on a rain-affected pitch.

The Oval 1929: first to score hundreds in each innings of a Test twice; only England batsman to score four hundreds in a rubber twice.

Sydney 1932-33: his highest England innings of 194 overtook J B Hobbs's world record of 15 Test hundreds.

YORKSHIRE'S TEST CRICKET RECORDS *(Continued)*

F S TRUEMAN

Leeds 1952: reduced India to 0 for 4 in their second innings by taking 3 wickets in 8 balls on his debut.

Manchester 1952: achieved record England v. India innings analysis of 8 for 31.

The Oval 1952: set England v. India series record with 29 wickets.

Leeds 1961: took 5 for 0 with 24 off-cutters at a reduced pace v. Australia.

Lord's 1962: shared record England v. Pakistan ninth-wicket stand of 76 with T W Graveney.

Christchurch 1962-63: passed J B Statham's world Test record of 242 wickets; his analysis of 7-75 remains the record for Lancaster Park Tests and for England in New Zealand.

Birmingham 1963: returned record match analysis (12-119) against West Indies in England and for any Birmingham Test, ending with a 6-4 spell from 24 balls.

The Oval 1963: set England v. West Indies series record with 34 wickets.

The Oval 1964: first to take 300 wickets in Tests.

G ULYETT

Sydney 1881-82: with R G Barlow shared the first century opening partnership in Test cricket (122).

Melbourne 1881-82: his 149 was the first Test hundred for England in Australia, and the highest score for England on the first day of a Test in Australia until 1965-66.

M P VAUGHAN

Scored 1481 runs in 2002 – more than any other England player in a calendar year, surpassing the 1379 scored by D L Amiss in 1979. It was the fourth highest in a calendar year.

Scored 633 runs in the 2002-3 series versus Australia – surpassed for England in a five Test series versus Australia only by W R Hammond, who scored 905 runs in 1928-29, H Sutcliffe (734 in 1924-25), J B Hobbs (662 in 1911-12) and G Boycott (657 in 1970-71), when he played in five of the six Tests.

Scored six Test Match centuries in 2002 to equal the record set for England by D C S Compton in 1947.

Lord's 2004: scored a century in each innings (103 and 101*) versus West Indies and so became the third player (after G A Headley and G A Gooch) to score a century in each innings of a Test match at Lord's.

Lord's 2005: only the second player (J B Hobbs is the other) to have scored centuries in three consecutive Test match innings at Lord's. Scored the 100th century for England by a Yorkshire player.

H VERITY

Lord's 1934: took 14 for 80 on the third day (six of them in the final hour) to secure England's first win against Australia at Lord's since 1896. It remains the most wickets to fall to one bowler in a day of Test cricket in England. His match analysis of 15 for 104 was then the England v. Australia record, and has been surpassed only by J C Laker.

W WATSON

Lord's 1953: scored 109 in 346 minutes in his first Test against Australia.

N W D YARDLEY

Melbourne 1946-47: dismissed D G Bradman for the third consecutive innings without assistance from the field. Became the first to score a fifty in each innings for England and take five wickets in the same match.

Nottingham 1947: shared record England v. South Africa fifth-wicket stand of 237 with D C S Compton.

* * *

Facts adapted by Bill Frindall from his *England Test Cricketers – The Complete Record from 1877* (Collins Willow, 1989). With later additions.

In his master's footsteps...

When James Wharton strode to the crease for his first-team debut in the Vitality Blast Roses defeat against Lancashire at Emerald Headingley on September 14 one thing was immediately clear. Joe Root is his idol.

Such were his mannerisms at the crease you could have been forgiven for thinking the Vikings had snuck England's Test captain into their side.

The now 20-year-old, a former White Rose Academy captain, scored only four off 10 balls in the first of two Blast appearances — he doubled his score in his other appearance against Durham — but made an impression nonetheless.

"When I first saw Wharts it was a couple of years ago," said coach Andrew Gale. "He came in and did 12th man for us, and Rooty was playing in the game. I made him pad up and bat in the indoor nets with Rooty, who is his idol and just bats exactly the same as him.

"Rooty said, 'This lad just bats like me.' He ended up giving him a bat, I think. He absolutely idolises Joe, and it's not a bad role model to have."

TEST MATCHES AT HEADINGLEY, LEEDS 1899-2019

1899 **Australia 172** (J Worrall 76) and **224** (H Trumble 56, J T Hearne hat-trick). **England 220** (A F A Lilley 55, H Trumble 5 for 60) and **19 for 0 wkt.**
Match drawn
Toss: Australia

1905 **England 301** (Hon F S Jackson 144*) and **295 for 5 wkts dec** (J T Tyldesley 100, T W Hayward 60, W W. Armstrong 5 for 122). **Australia 195** (W W Armstrong 66, A R Warren 5 for 57) and **224 for 7 wkts** (M A Noble 62).
Match drawn
Toss: England

1907 **England 76** (G A Faulkner 6 for 17) and **162** (C B Fry 54). **South Africa 110** (C Blythe 8 for 59) and **75** (C Blythe 7 for 40).
England won by 53 runs
Toss: England

1909 **Australia 188** and **207** (S F Barnes 6 for 63). **England 182** (J Sharp 61, J T Tyldesley 55, C G Macartney 7 for 58) and **87** (A Cotter 5 for 38).
Australia won by 126 runs
Toss: Australia

1912 **England 242** (F E Woolley 57) and **238** (R H Spooner 82, J B Hobbs 55). **South Africa 147** (S F Barnes 6 for 52) and **159**.
England won by 174 runs
Toss: England

1921 **Australia 407** (C G Macartney 115, W W Armstrong 77, C E Pellew 52, J M Taylor 50) and **273 for 7 wkts dec** (T J E Andrew 92). **England 259** (J W H T Douglas 75, Hon L H Tennyson 63, G Brown 57) and **202.**
Australia won by 219 runs
Toss: Australia

1924 **England 396** (E H Hendren 132, H Sutcliffe 83) and **60 for 1 wkt.** **South Africa 132** (H W Taylor 59*, M W Tate 6 for 42) and **323** (H W Taylor 56, R H Catterall 56).
England won by 9 wickets   Toss: England

1926 **Australia 494** (C G Macartney 151, W M Woodfull 141, A J Richardson 100). **England 294** (G G Macaulay 76, C V Grimmett 5 for 88) and **254 for 3 wkts** (H Sutcliffe 94, J B Hobbs 88).
Match drawn
Toss: England

1929 **South Africa 236** (R H Catterall 74, C L Vincent 60, A P Freeman 7 for 115) and **275** (H G Owen-Smith 129). **England 328** (F E Woolley 83, W R Hammond 65, N A Quinn 6 for 92) and **186 for 5 wkts** (F E Woolley 95*).
England won by 5 wickets
Toss: South Africa

1930 **Australia 566** (D G Bradman 334, A F Kippax 77, W M Woodfull 50, M W Tate 5 for 124). **England 391** (W R Hammond 113, C V Grimmett 5 for 135) and **95 for 3 wkts.**
Match drawn
Toss: Australia

1934 **England 200** and **229 for 6 wkts.** **Australia 584** (D G Bradman 304, W H Ponsford 181, W E Bowes 6 for 142).
Match drawn
Toss: England

1935 **England 216** (W R Hammond 63, A Mitchell 58) and **294 for 7 wkts dec** (W R Hammond 87*, A Mitchell 72, D Smith 57). **South Africa 171** (E A B Rowan 62) and **194 for 5 wkts** (B Mitchell 58).
Match drawn
Toss: England

1938 **England 223** (W R Hammond 76, W J O'Reilly 5 for 66) and **123** (W J O'Reilly 5 for 56). **Australia 242** (D G Bradman 103, B A Barnett 57) and **107 for 5 wkts.**
Australia won by 5 wickets
Toss: England

1947 **South Africa 175** (B Mitchell 53, A Nourse 51) and **184** (A D Nourse 57). **England 317 for 7 wkts dec** (L Hutton 100, C Washbrook 75) and **47 for 0 wkt.**
England won by 10 wickets
Toss: South Africa

1948 **England 496** (C Washbrook 143, W .J Edrich 111, L Hutton 81, A V Bedser 79) and **365 for 8 wkts dec** (D C S. Compton 66, C Washbrook 65, L Hutton 57, W J Edrich 54). **Australia 458** (R N Harvey 112, S J E Loxton 93, R R Lindwall 77, K R Miller 58) and **404 for 3 wkts** (A R Morris 182, D G Bradman 173*).
Australia won by 7 wickets
Toss: England

291

1949 **England 372** (D C S Compton 114, L Hutton 101, T B Burtt 5 for 97, J Cowie 5 for 127) and **267 for 4 wkts dec** (C Washbrook 103*, W J Edrich 70). **New Zealand 341** (F B Smith 96, M P Donnelly 64, T E Bailey 6 for 118) and **195 for 2 wkts** (B Sutcliffe 82, F Smith 54*).
Match drawn   Toss: England

1951 **South Africa 538** (E A B Rowan 236, P N F Mansell 90, C B. van Ryneveld 83, R A McLean 67) and **87 for 0 wkt** (E A B Rowan 60*). **England 505** (P B H May 138, L Hutton 100, T E Bailey 95, F A Lowson 58, A M B Rowan 5 for 174).
Match drawn   Toss: South Africa

1952 **India 293** (V L Manjrekar 133, V S Hazare 89) and 165 (D G Phadkar 64, V S Hazare 56). **England 334** (T W Graveney 71, T G Evans 66, Ghulam Ahmed 5 for 100) and **128 for 3 wkts** (R T Simpson 51).
England won by 7 wickets   Toss: India

1953 **England 167** (T W Graveney 55, R R Lindwall 5 for 54) and **275** (W J Edrich 64, D C S Compton 62). **Australia 266** (R N Harvey 71, G B Hole 53, A V Bedser 6 for 95) and **147 for 4 wkts.**
Match drawn   Toss: Australia

1955 **South Africa 171** and **500** (D J McGlew 133, W R Endean 116*, T L Goddard 74, H J Keith 73). **England 191** (D C S Compton 61) and **256** (P B H May 97, T L Goddard 5 for 69, H J Tayfield 5 for 94).
South Africa won by 224 runs   Toss: South Africa

1956 **England 325** (P B H May 101, C Washbrook 98). **Australia 143** (J C Laker 5 for 58) and **140** (R N Harvey 69, J C Laker 6 for 55).
England won by an innings and 42 runs   Toss: England

1957 **West Indies 142** (P J Loader 6 for 36, including hat-trick) and **132**. **England 279** (P B H May 69, M C Cowdrey 68, Rev D S Sheppard 68, F M M Worrell 7 for 70).
England won by an innings and 5 runs   Toss: West Indies

1958 **New Zealand 67** (J C Laker 5 for 17) and **129** (G A R Lock 7 for 51). **England 267 for 2 wkts dec** (P B H May 113*, C A Milton 104*).
England won by an innings and 71 runs   Toss: New Zealand

1959 **India 161** and **149**. **England 483 for 8 wkts dec** (M C Cowdrey 160, K F Barrington 80, W G A Parkhouse 78, G Pullar 75).
England won by an innings and 173 runs   Toss: India

1961 **Australia 237** (R N Harvey 73, C C McDonald 54, F S Trueman 5 for 58) and **120** (R N Harvey 53, F S Trueman 6 for 30); **England 299** (M C Cowdrey 93, G Pullar 53, A K Davidson 5 for 63) and **62 for 2 wkts.**
England won by 8 wickets   Toss: Australia

1962 **England 428** (P H Parfitt 119, M J Stewart 86, D A Allen 62, Munir Malik 5 for 128). **Pakistan 131** (Alimuddin 50) and **180** (Alimuddin 60, Saeed Ahmed 54).
England won by an innings and 117 runs   Toss: Pakistan

1963 **West Indies 397** (G St A Sobers 102, R B Kanhai 92, J S Solomon 62) and **229** (B F Butcher 78, G St.A Sobers 52). **England 174** (G A R Lock 53, C C Griffith 6 for 36) and **231** (J M Parks 57, D B Close 56).
West Indies won by 221 runs   Toss: West Indies

1964 **England 268** (J M Parks 68, E R Dexter 66, N J N Hawke 5 for 75) and 229 (K F Barrington 85). **Australia 389** (P J P Burge 160, W M Lawry 78) and **111 for 3 wkts** (I R Redpath 58*).
Australia won by 7 wickets   Toss: England

1965 **England 546 for 4 wkts dec** (J H Edrich 310*, K F Barrington 163). **New Zealand 193** (J R Reid 54) and **166** (V Pollard 53, F J Titmus 5 for 19).
England won by an innings and 187 runs   Toss: England

1966 **West Indies 500 for 9 wkts dec** (G St A Sobers 174, S M Nurse 137). **England 240** (B L D'Oliveira 88, G St A Sobers 5 for 41) and **205** (R W Barber 55, L R Gibbs 6 for 39).
West Indies won by an innings and 55 runs   Toss: West Indies

1967 **England 550 for 4 wkts dec** (G Boycott 246*, B L D'Oliveira 109, K F Barrington 93, T W Graveney 59) **and 126 for 4 wkts. India 164** (Nawab of Pataudi jnr 64) **and 510** (Nawab of Pataudi jnr 148, A L Wadekar 91, F M Engineer 87, Hanumant Singh 73).
England won by 6 wickets Toss: India

1968 **Australia 315** (I R Redpath 92, I M Chappell 65) **and 312** (I M Chappell 81, K D Walters 56, R Illingworth 6 for 87). **England 302** (R M Prideaux 64, J H Edrich 62, A N Connolly 5 for 72) **and 230 for 4 wkts** (J H Edrich 65).
Match drawn Toss: Australia

1969 **England 223** (J H Edrich 79) **and 240** (G.St A Sobers 5 for 42). **West Indies 161 and 272** (B F Butcher 91, G S Camacho 71).
England won by 30 runs Toss: England

1971 **England 316** (G Boycott 112, B L D'Oliveira 74) **and 264** (B L D'Oliveira 72, D L Amiss 56) **Pakistan 350** (Zaheer Abbas 72, Wasim Bari 63, Mushtaq Mohammad 57) **and 205** (Sadiq Mohammad 91).
England won by 25 runs Toss: England

1972 **Australia 146** (K R Stackpole 52) **and 136** (D L Underwood 6 for 45). **England 263** (R Illingworth 57, A A Mallett 5 for 114) **and 21 for 1 wkt.**
England won by 9 wickets Toss: Australia

1973 **New Zealand 276** (M G Burgess 87, V Pollard 62) **and 142** (G M Turner 81, G G Arnold 5 for 27). **England 419** (G Boycott 115, K W R Fletcher 81, R Illingworth 65, RO Collinge 5 for 74).
England won by an innings and 1 run Toss: New Zealand

1974 **Pakistan 285** (Majid Khan 75, Safraz Nawaz 53) **and 179. England 183 and 238 for 6 wkts** (J H Edrich 70, K W R Fletcher 67*).
Match drawn Toss: Pakistan

1975 **England 288** (D S Steele 73, J H Edrich 62, A W Greig 51, G J Gilmour 6 for 85) **and 291** (D S Steele 92). **Australia 135** (P H Edmonds 5 for 28) **and 220 for 3 wkts** (R B McCosker 95*, I M Chappell 62).
Toss: England

1976 **West Indies 450** (C G Greenidge 115, R C Fredericks 109, I V A Richards 66, L G Rowe 50) **and 196** (C L King 58, R G D Willis 5 for 42). **England 387** (A W Greig 116, A P E Knott 116) **and 204** (A W Greig 76*).
West Indies won by 55 runs Toss: West Indies

1977 **England 436** (G Boycott 191, A P E Knott 57). **Australia 103** (I T Botham 5 for 21) **and 248** (R W Marsh 63).
England won by an innings and 85 runs Toss: England

1978 **Pakistan 201** (Sadiq Mohammad 97). **England 119 for 7 wkts** (Safraz Nawaz 5 for 39).
Match drawn Toss: Pakistan

1979 **England 270** (I T Botham 137). **India 223 for 6 wkts** (S M Gavaskar 78, D B Vengsarkar 65*).
Match drawn Toss: England

1980 **England 143 and 227 for 6 wkts dec** (G A Gooch 55). **West Indies 245.**
Match drawn Toss: West Indies

1981 **Australia 401 for 9 wkts dec** (J Dyson 102, K J Hughes 89, G N Yallop 58, I T Botham 6 for 95) **and 111** (R G D Willis 8 for 43). **England 174** (I T Botham 50) **and 356** (I T Botham 149*, G R Dilley 56, T M Alderman 6 for 135).
England won by 18 runs Toss: Australia

1982 **Pakistan 275** (Imran Khan 67*, Mudassar Nazar 65, Javed Miandad 54) **and 199** (Javed Miandad 52, I T Botham 57). **England 256** (D I Gower 74, I T Botham 57, Imran Khan 5 for 49) **and 219 for 7 wkts** (G Fowler 86).
England won by 3 wickets Toss: Pakistan

1983 **England 225** (C J Tavaré 69, A J Lamb 58, B L Cairns 7 for 74) **and 252** (D I Gower 112*, E J Chatfield 5 for 95). **New Zealand 377** (J G Wright 93, B A Edgar 84, R J Hadlee 75) **and 103 for 5 wkts** (R G D Willis 5 for 35).
New Zealand won by 5 wickets Toss: New Zealand

1984 **England 270** (A J Lamb 100) and **159** (G Fowler 50, M D Marshall 7 for 53). **West Indies 302** (H A Gomes 104*, M A Holding 59, P J W Allott 6 for 61) and **131 for 2 wkts.**
West Indies won by 8 wickets   Toss: England

1985 **Australia 331** (A M J Hilditch 119) and **324** (W B Phillips 91, A M J Hilditch 80, K C Wessels 64, J E Emburey 5 for 82). **England 533** (R T Robinson 175, I T Botham 60, P R Downton 54, M W Gatting 53) and **123 for 5 wkts.**
England won by 5 wickets   Toss: Australia

1986 **India 272** (D B Vengsarkar 61) and **237** (D B Vengsarkar 102*). **England 102** (R M H Binny 5 for 40) and **128.**
India won by 279 runs   Toss: India

1987 **England 136** (D J Capel 53) and **199** (D I Gower 55, Imran Khan 7 for 40). **Pakistan 353** (Salim Malik 99, Ijaz Ahmed 50, N A Foster 8 for 107).
Pakistan won by an innings and 18 runs   Toss: England

1988 **England 201** (A J Lamb 64*) and **138** (G A Gooch 50). **West Indies 275** (R A Harper 56, D L Haynes 54, D R Pringle 5 for 95) and **67 for 0 wkt.**
West Indies won by 10 wickets   Toss: West Indies

1989 **Australia 601 for 7 wkts dec** (S R Waugh 177*, M A Taylor 136, D M Jones 79, M G Hughes 71, A R Border 66) and **230 for 3 wkts dec** (M A Taylor 60, A R Border 60*). **England 430** (A J Lamb 125, K J Barnett 80, R A Smith 66, T M Alderman 5 for 107) and **191.** (G A Gooch 68, T M Alderman 5 for 44).
Australia won by 210 runs   Toss: England

1991 **England 198** (R A Smith 54) and **252** (G A Gooch 154*, C E L Ambrose 6 for 52). **West Indies 173** (I V A Richards 73) and **162** (R B Richardson 68).
England won by 115 runs   Toss: West Indies

1992 **Pakistan 197** (Salim Malik 82*) and **221** (Salim Malik 84*, Ramiz Raja 63, N A Mallinder 5 for 50). **England 320** (G A Gooch 135, M A Atherton 76, Waqar Younis 5 for 117) and **99 for 4 wkts.**
England won by 6 wickets   Toss: Pakistan

1993 **Australia 653 for 4 wkts dec** (A R Border 200*, S R Waugh 157*, D C Boon 107, M J Slater 67, M E Waugh 52). **England 200** (G A Gooch 59, M A Atherton 55, P R Reiffel 5 for 65) and **305** (A J Stewart 78, M A Atherton 63).
Australia won by an innings and 148 runs   Toss: Australia

1994 **England 477 for 9 wkts dec** (M A Atherton 99, A J Stewart 89, G P Thorpe 72, S J Rhodes 65*) and **267 for 5 wkts dec** (G A Hick 110, G P Thorpe 73). **South Africa 447** (P N Kirsten 104, B M McMillan 78, C R Matthews 62*) and **116 for 3 wkts** (G Kirsten 65).
Match drawn   Toss: England

1995 **England 199** (M A Atherton 81, I R Bishop 5 for 32) and **208** (G P Thorpe 61). **West Indies 282** (S L Campbell 69, J C Adams 58, B C Lara 53) and **129 for 1 wkt** (C L Hooper 73*).
West Indies won by 9 wickets   Toss: England

1996 **Pakistan 448** (Ijaz Ahmed 141, Mohin Khan 105, Salim Malik 55, Asif Mujtaba 51, D G Cork 5 for 113) and **242 for 7 wkts dec** (Inzamam-ul-Haq 65, Ijaz Ahmed sen 52) **England 501** (A J Stewart 170, N V Knight 113, J P Crawley 53).
Match drawn   Toss: England

1997 **England 172** (J N. Gillespie 7 for 37) and **268** (N Hussain 105, J P Crawley 72, P R Reiffel 5 for 49). **Australia 501 for 9 wkts dec** (M T G Elliott 199, R T Ponting 127, P R Reiffel 54*, D Gough 5 for 149).
Australia won by an innings and 61 runs   Toss: Australia

1998 **England 230** (M A Butcher 116) and **240** (N Hussain 94, S M Pollock 5 for 53, A A Donald 5 for 71). **South Africa 252** (W J. Cronje 57, A R C Fraser 5 for 42) and **195** (J N Rhodes 85, B M McMillan 54, D Gough 6 for 42).
England won by 23 runs   Toss: England

2000 **West Indies 172** (R R Sarwan 59*, C White 5 for 57) and **61** (A R Caddick 5 for 14). **England 272** (M P Vaughan 76, G A Hick 59).
England won by an innings and 39 runs   Toss: West Indies

2001 **Australia 447** (R T Ponting 144, D R Martyn 118, M E Waugh 72, D Gough 5 for 103) and **176 for 4 wkts dec** (R T Ponting 72). **England 309** (A J Stewart 76*, G D McGrath 7 for 76) and **315 for 4 wkts** (M A Butcher 173*, N Hussain 52).
England won by 6 wickets   Toss: Australia

2002 **India 628 for 8 wkts dec** (S R Tendulkar 193, R S Dravid 148, S C Ganguly 128, S B Bangar 68). **England 273** (A J Stewart 78*, M P Vaughan 61) and **309** (N Hussain 110.)
India won by an innings and 46 runs   Toss: India

2003 **South Africa 342** (G Kirsten 130, M Zondeki 59, J A Rudolph 55) and **365** (A J Hall 99*, G Kirsten 60). **England 307** (M A Butcher 77, M E Trescothick 59, A Flintoff 55) and **209** (M A Butcher 61, A Flintoff 50, J H Kallis 6 for 54.)
South Africa won by 191 runs   Toss: South Africa

2004 **New Zealand 409** (S P Fleming 97, M H W Papps 86, B B McCullum 54) and **161.** **England 526** (M E Trescothick 132, G O Jones 100, A Flintoff 94, A J Strauss 62) and **45 for 1 wkt**
England won by 9 wickets   Toss: England

2006 **England 515** (K P Pietersen 135, I R Bell 119, Umar Gul 5 for 123) and **345** (A J Strauss 116, M E Trescothick 58, C M W Reid 55). **Pakistan 538** (Mohammad Yousuf 192, Younis Khan 173) and **155.**
England won by 167 runs   Toss: England

2007 **England 570 for 7 wkts dec** (K P Pietersen 226, M P Vaughan 103, M J Prior 75). **West Indies 146** and **141** (D J Bravo 52).
England won by an innings and 283 runs   Toss: England

2008 **England 203** and **327** (S C J Broad 67*, A N Cook 60). **South Africa 522** (A B de Villiers 174, A G Prince 149) and **9 for 0 wkt.**
South Africa won by 10 wickets   Toss: South Africa

2009 **England 102** (P M Siddle 5 for 21) and **263** (G P Swann 62, S C J Broad 61, M G Johnson 5 for 69). **Australia 445** (M J North 110, M J Clarke 93, R T Ponting 78, S R Watson 51, S C J Broad 6 for 91).
Australia won by an innings and 80 runs   Toss: England

2010 **Australia 88** and **349** (R T Ponting 66, M J Clarke 77, S P D Smith 77). **Pakistan 258** (S R Watson 6-33) and **180-7** (Imran Farhat 67, Azhar Ali 51).
Pakistan won by 3 wickets   Toss: Australia
(This was a Home Test Match for Pakistan!)

2012 **South Africa 419** (A N Petersen 182, G C Smith 52) and **258-9 dec** (J A Rudolph 69, GC Smith 52, S C J Broad 5-69). **England 425** (K P Pietersen 149, M J Prior 68) and **130-4.**
Match drawn   Toss: England

2013 **England 354** (J E Root 104, J M Bairstow 64, T A Boult 5-57) and **287-5 dec** (A N Cook 130, I J L Trott 76). **New Zealand 174** and **220** (L R P L Taylor 70, G P Swann 6-90)
England won by 247 runs   Toss: England

2014 **Sri Lanka 257** (K C Sangakkara 79, L E Plunkett 5-64) and **457** (K C Sangakkara 55, DPMD Jayawardene 79, A D Mathews 160). **England 365** (S D Robson 127, G S Ballance 74, I R Bell 64) and **249** (M M Ali 108*, K T G D Prasad 5-50)
Sri Lanka won by 100 runs   Toss: England

2015 **New Zealand 350** (T W M Latham 84, L Ronchi 88, S C J Broad 5-109) and **454-8 dec** (M J Guptill 70, B B McCullum 55, B J Watling 120, M D Craig 58*). **England 350** (A Lyth 107, A N Cook 75) and **255** (A N Cook 56, J C Buttler 73)
New Zealand won by 199 runs   Toss: England

2016 **England 298** (A D Hales 86, J M Bairstow 140). **Sri Lanka 91** (J M Anderson 5-16) and **119** (B K G Mendis 53, J N Anderson 5-29)
England won by an innings and 88 runs   Toss: Sri Lanka

2017 **England 258** (J E Root 58, B A Stokes 100) and **490-8 dec** (M D Stoneman 52, J E Root 72, D J Malan 61, B A Stokes 58, M M Ali 84, C R Woakes 61*). **West Indies 427** (K C Brathwaite 134, S D Hope 147, J M Anderson 5-76) and **322-5** (K C Brathwaite 95, S D Hope 118*).
West Indies won by 5 wickets   Toss: England

2018 **Pakistan 174** (Shadab Khan 56) and **134. England 363** (J C Buttler 80*)
England won by an innings and 55 runs   Toss: Pakistan
2019 **Australia 179** (M Labuschagne 74, J C Archer 6-45) and **246** (M Labuschagne 80).
England 67 (J R Hazlewood 5-65) and **362-9** (J E Root 77, J L Denly 50,
B A Stokes 135*)
England won by 1 wicket
                                                                              Toss: England

SUMMARY OF RESULTS

ENGLAND	First played	Last played	Played	Won	Lost	Drawn
v. Australia	1899	2019	25	8	9	8
v. India	1952	2002	6	3	2	1
v. New Zealand	1949	2015	8	5	2	1
v. Pakistan	1962	2018	10	6	1	3
v. South Africa	1907	2012	13	6	3	4
v. Sri Lanka	2014	2016	2	1	1	0
v. West Indies	1957	2017	13	5	7	1
Totals	1899	2019	77	34	25	18

SIX HIGHEST AGGREGATES

Runs	Wkts	
1723	31	in 1948 (England 496 and 365 for 8 wkts dec; Australia 458 and 404 for 3 wkts)
1553	40	in 2006 (England 515 and 345; Pakistan 538 and 155)
1497	33	in 2017 (England 258 and 490-8 dec; West Indies 427 and 322-5)
1452	30	in 1989 (Australia 601 for 7 wkts dec and 230 for 3 wkts dec; England 430 and 191)
1409	40	in 2015 (New Zealand 350 and 454 for 8 wkts dec; England 350 and 255)
1350	28	in 1967 (England 550 for 4 wkts dec and 126 for 4 wkts; India 164 and 510)

Note: The highest aggregate prior to the Second World War

1141	37	in 1921 (Australia 407 and 272 for 7 wkts dec; England 259 and 202)

SIX LOWEST AGGREGATES

Runs	Wkts	
423	40	in 1907 (England 76 and 162; South Africa 110 and 75)
463	22	in 1958 (New Zealand 67 and 129; England 267 for 2 wkts)
505	30	in 2000 (West Indies 172 and 61; England 272)
508	30	in 2016 (England 298 and 454; Sri Lanka 91 and 119)
553	30	in 1957 (West Indies 142 and 132; England 279)
566	31	in 1972 (Australia 146 and 136; England 263 and 21 for 1 wkt)

SIX HIGHEST TOTALS

653 for 4 wkts dec	Australia v. England, 1993
608 for 8 wkts dec	India v. England, 2002
601 for 7 wkts dec	Australia v. England, 1989
584	Australia v. England, 1934
570 for 7 wkts dec	England v. West Indies, 2007
566	Australia v. England, 1930

SIX LOWEST TOTALS

61	West Indies v. England, 2000
67	New Zealand v. England, 1958
67	England v. Australia, 2019
75	South Africa v. England, 1907
76	England v. South Africa, 1907
87	Australia v England, 1909

SIX HIGHEST INDIVIDUAL SCORES

For England

310*	J H Edrich versus New Zealand, 1965
246*	G Boycott versus India, 1967
226	K P Pietersen versus West Indies, 2007
191	G Boycott versus Australia, 1977
175	R T Robinson versus Australia, 1985
173*	M A Butcher versus Australia, 2001

For Australia

334	D G Bradman, 1930
304	D G Bradman, 1934
200*	A R Border, 1993
199	M T G Elliott, 1997
182	A R Morris, 1948
181	W H Ponsford, 1934

For Pakistan

192	Mohammad Yousuf, 2006
173	Younis Khan, 2006
141	Ijaz Ahmed, 1996
105	Moin Khan, 1996
99	Salim Malik, 1987
97	Sadiq Mohammad, 1978

For India

193	S R Tendulkar, 2002
148	Nawab of Pataudi jnr, 1967
148	R S Dravid, 2002
133	V L Manjrekar, 1952
128	S C Ganguly, 2002
102*	D B Vengsarkar, 1986

For South Africa

236	E A B Rowan, 1951
182	A N Petersen, 2012
174	A B de Villiers, 2008
149	A G Prince, 2008
133	D J McGlew, 1955
130	G Kirsten, 2003

For New Zealand

120	B J Watling , 2015
97	S P Fleming, 2004
96	F B Smith, 1949
93	J G Wright, 1983
88	L Ronchi, 2015
87	M G Burgess, 1973

For Sri Lanka

160*	A D Mathews, 2014
79	K C Sangakkara, 2014
55	K C Sangakkara, 2014
53*	B K G Mendis, 2016
48	H M R K B Herath, 2014
45	L D Chandimal, 2014
45	F D M Karunaratne, 2014

For West Indies

174	G St.A Sobers, 1966
147	S D Hope, 2017 (1st innings)
137	S M Nurse, 1966
134	K C Brathwaite, 2017
118*	S D Hope, 2017 (2nd innings)
115	C G Greenidge, 1976

S D Hope was the first player to score centuries in both innings of a First Class match at Headingley

HUNDRED BEFORE LUNCH

First day

112*	C G Macartney for Australia, 1926
105*	D G Bradman for Australia, 1930

Third day

102	(from 27* to 129) H G Owen-Smith for South Africa, 1929

CARRYING BAT THROUGH A COMPLETED INNINGS

154* out of 252 G A Gooch, England v. West Indies, 1991

MOST CENTURIES IN AN INNINGS

3	1926	C G Macartney (151), W M Woodfull (141) and A J Richardson for Australia
3	1993	A R Border (200*), S R Waugh (157*) and D C Boon (107) for Australia
3	2002	S R Tendulkar (193), R S Dravid (148) and S C Ganguly (128) for India

MOST CENTURIES IN A MATCH

5	1948	C Washbrook (143) and W J Edrich (111) for England; R N Harvey (112), A R Morris (182) and D G Bradman (173*) for Australia
5	2006	K P Pietersen (135), I R Bell (119) and A J Strauss (116) for England; Younis Khan (173) and Mohammad Yousuf (192) for Pakistan
4	1976	C G Greenidge (115) and R C Fredericks (109) for West Indies; A W Greig (116) and A P E Knott (116) for England
4	1996	Ijaz Ahmed (141) and Moin Khan (105) for Pakistan; A J Stewart (170) and N V Knight (113) for England
4	2002	S R Tendulkar (193), R S Dravid (148) and S C Ganguly (128) for India; N Hussain (110) for England
4	2017	B A Stokes (100) for England; K C Brathwaite (134), S D Hope (147 and 118*) for West Indies

CENTURY PARTNERSHIPS

For England
(six highest)
For the 1st wicket

177	A Lyth (107) and A N Cook (75) v. New Zealand, 2015
168	L Hutton (81) and C Washbrook (143) v. Australia, 1948 (1st inns)
168	G A Gooch (135) and M A Atherton (76) v. Pakistan, 1992
158	M E Trescothick (58) and A J Strauss (116) v. Pakistan, 2006
156	J B Hobbs (88) and H Sutcliffe (94) v. Australia, 1926
153	M E Trescothick (132) and A J Strauss (62) v. New Zealand, 2004

For all other wickets

369	(2nd wkt) J H Edrich (310*) and K F Barrington (163) v. New Zealand, 1965
252	(4th wkt) G Boycott (246*) and B L D'Oliveira (109) v. India, 1967
194*	(3rd wkt) C A Milton (104*) and P B H May (113*) v. New Zealand, 1958
193	(4th wkt) M C Cowdrey (160) and K F Barrington (80) v. India, 1959
187	(4th wkt) P B H May (101) and C Washbrook (98) v. Australia, 1956
181	(3rd wkt) M A Butcher (173*) and N Hussain (55) v. Australia, 2001

For Australia
(six highest)
For the 1st wkt – none
For all other wickets

388	(4th wkt) W H Ponsford (181) and D G Bradman (304), 1934
332*	(5th wkt) A R Border (200*) and S R Waugh (157*), 1993
301	(2nd wkt) A R Morris (182) and D G Bradman (173*), 1948
268	(5th wkt) M T G Elliott (199) and R T Ponting (127), 1997
235	(2nd wkt) W M Woodfull (141) and C G Macartney (151), 1926
229	(3rd wkt) D G Bradman (334) and A F Kippax (77), 1930

For other countries in total
India

249	(4th wkt) S R Tendulkar (193) and S C Ganguly (128), 2002
222	(4th wkt) V S Hazare (89) and V L Manjrekar (133), 1952
170	(2nd wkt) S B Bangar (68) and R S Dravid (148), 2002
168	(2nd wkt) F M Engineer (87) and A L Wadekar (91), 1967
150	(3rd wkt) R S Dravid (148) and S R Tendulkar (193), 2002
134	(5th wkt) Hanumant Singh (73) and Nawab of Pataudi jnr (148), 1967
105	(6th wkt) V S Hazare (56) and D G Phadkar (64), 1952

CENTURY PARTNERSHIPS *(Continued)*

New Zealand

169	(2nd wkt) M H W Papps (86) and S P Fleming (97), 2004	
121	(5th wkt) B B McCullum (55) and B J Watling (120), 2015	
120	(5th wkt) M P Donnelly (64) and F B Smith (96), 1949	
120	(6th wkt) T W M Latham (84) and L Ronchi (88), 2015	
116	(2nd wkt) J G Wright (93) and M D Crowe (37), 1983	
112	(1st wkt) B Sutcliffe (82) and V J Scott (43), 1949	
106	(5th wkt) M G Burgess (87) and V Pollard (62), 1973	

Pakistan

363	(3rd wkt) Younis Khan (173) and Mohammad Yousuf (192), 2006
130	(4th wkt) Ijaz Ahmed (141) and Salim Malik (55), 1996
129	(3rd wkt) Zaheer Abbas (72) and Mushtaq Mohammed (57), 1971
112	(7th wkt) Asif Mujtaba (51) and Moin Khan (105), 1996
110	(2nd wkt) Imran Farhat (67) and Azhar Ali (51), 2010 v. Australia
100	(3rd wkt) Mudassar Nazar (65) and Javed Miandad (54), 1982
100	(4th wkt) Majid Khan (75) and Zaheer Abbas (48), 1974

South Africa

212	(5th wkt)	A G Prince (149)	and A B de Villiers (174)	2008
198	(2nd wkt)	E A B Rowan (236)	and C B van Ryneveld (83)	1951
176	(1st wkt)	D J McGlew (133)	and T L Goddard (74)	1955
150	(8th wkt)	G Kirsten (130)	and M Zondeki (59)	2003
120	(1st wkt)	A N Petersen (182)	and G C Smith (52)	2012
120	(1st wkt)	J A Rudolph (69)	and G C Smith (52)	2012
117	(6th wkt)	J N Rhodes (85)	and B M McMillan (54)	1998
115	(7th wkt)	P N Kirsten (104)	and B M McMillan (78)	1994
108	(5th wkt)	E A B Rowan (236)	and R A McLean (67)	1951
103	(10th wkt)	H G Owen-Smith (129)	and A J Bell (26*)	1929

Sri Lanka

149	(8th wkt)	A D Mathews (160)	and H M R K B Herath (48)	2014

West Indies

265	(5th wkt)	S M Nurse (137)	and G St A Sobers (174)	1966
246	(4th wkt)	K C Brathwaite (134)	and S D Hope (147)	2017
192	(1st wkt)	R C Fredericks (109)	and C G Greenidge (115)	1976
144	(3rd wkt)	K C Brathwaite (95)	and S D Hope (118*)	2017
143	(4th wkt)	R B Kanhai (92)	and G St A Sobers (102)	1963
118*	(2nd wkt)	C L Hooper (73*)	and B C Lara (48*)	1995
108	(3rd wkt)	G S Camacho (71)	and B F Butcher (91)	1969
106	(1st wkt)	C G Greenidge (49)	and D L Haynes (43)	1984

6 BEST INNINGS ANALYSES

For England

8-43	R G D Willis	v. Australia	1981
8-59	C Blythe	v. South Africa	1907 (1st inns)
8-107	N A Foster	v. Pakistan	1987
7-40	C Blythe	v. South Africa,	1907 (2nd inns)
7-51	G A R Lock	v. New Zealand	1958
7-115	A P Freeman	v. South Africa	1929

For Australia

7-37	J N Gillespie	1997	
7-58	C G Macartney	1909	
7-76	G D McGrath	2001	
6-33	S R Watson	2010	v. Pakistan
6-85	G J Gilmour	1975	
6-135	T M Alderman	1981	

5 WICKETS IN AN INNINGS

For India (2)
5-40   R M H Binny   1986
5-100   Ghulam Ahmed 1952

For New Zealand (6)
7-74   B L Cairns   1983
5-57   T A Boult   2013
5-74   R O Collinge   1973
5-95   E J Chatfield   1983
5-97   T B Burtt   1949
5-127   J Cowie   1949

For Pakistan (6)
7-40   Imran Khan   1987
5-39   Sarfraz Nawaz   1978
5-49   Imran Khan   1982
5-117   Waqar Younis   1992
5-123   Umar Gul   2006
5-128   Munir Malik   1962

For South Africa (8)
6-17   G A Faulkner   1907
6-92   N A Quinn   1929
6-54   J H Kallis   2003
5-53   S M Pollock   1998
5-69   T L Goddard   1955
5-71   A A Donald   1998
5-94   H J Tayfield   1955
5-174   A M B Rowan   1951

For Sri Lanka
5-50   K T G D Prasad 2014

For West Indies (8)
7-53   M D Marshall   1984
7-70   F M Worrell   1957
6-36   C C Griffith   1963
6-39   L R Gibbs   1996
6-52   C E L Ambrose 1991
5-32   I R Bishop   1995
5-41   G.St.A Sobers   1966
5-42   G.St A Sobers   1969

10 WICKETS IN A MATCH

For England (8)

15-99	(8-59 and 7-40)	C Blythe	v. South Africa	1907
11-65	(4-14 and 7-51)	G A R Lock	v. New Zeland	1958
11-88	(5-58 and 6-30)	F S Trueman	v. Australia	1961
11-113	(5-58 and 6-55)	J C Laker	v. Australia	1956
10-45	(5-16 and 5-29)	J M Anderson	v. Sri Lanka	2016
10-82	(4-37 and 6-45)	D L Underwood	v. Australia	1972
10-115	(6-52 and 4-63)	S F Barnes	v. South Africa	1912
10-132	(4-42 and 6-90)	G P Swann	v. New Zealand	2013
10-207	(7-115 and 3-92)	A P Freeman	v. South Africa	1929

For Australia (3)

11-85	(7-58 and 4-27)	C G Macartney	1909
10-122	(5-66 and 5-56)	W J O'Reilly	1938
10-151	(5-107 and 5-44)	T M Alderman	1989

For New Zealand (1)

10-144	(7-74 and 3-70)	B L Cairns	1983

For Pakistan (1)

10-77	(3-37 and 7-40)	Imran Khan	1987

Note: Best bowling in a match for:

India	7-58	(5-40 and 2-18)	R M H Binney	1986
Sri Lanka	6-125	(1-75 and 5-50)	K T G D Prasad	2014
South Africa	9-75	(6-17 and 3-58)	G A Faulkner	1907
West Indies	9-81	(6 -36 and 3-45)	C C Griffith	1963

HAT-TRICKS

J T Hearne   v. Australia   1899
P J Loader   v. West Indies   1957
S C J Broad   v. Sri Lanka   2014

TEST MATCH AT BRAMALL LANE, SHEFFIELD 1902

1902 **Australia 194** (S F Barnes 6 for 49) and **289** (C Hill 119, V T Trumper 62, W Rhodes 5 for 63) **England 145** (J V Saunders 5 for 50, M A Noble 5 for 51) and **195** (A C MacLaren 63, G L Jessop 55, M A Noble 6 for 52).
Australia won by 143 runs

Toss: Australia

LIST OF PLAYERS AND CAREER AVERAGES IN ALL FIRST-CLASS MATCHES FOR YORKSHIRE 1863-2020

Based on research by John T Potter, Paul E Dyson, Mick Pope and the late Roy D Wilkinson and Anthony Woodhouse

Career records date from the foundation of Yorkshire County Cricket Club in 1863. The Club welcome any help in keeping this list up to date. The compilers do not believe that we should alter the status of matches from that determined when they were played. These averages include the matches versus Gentlemen of Scotland in 1878, and exclude those versus Liverpool and District in 1889, 1891, 1892 and 1893 in line with what appear to have been the decisions of the Club.

* Played as an amateur ◎ Awarded County Cap § Born outside Yorkshire

Player	Date of Birth	Date of Death (if known)	First Played	Last Played	M	Inns	NO	Runs	HS	Av'ge	100s	Runs	Wkts	Av'ge	Ct/St
Ackroyd, A *	Aug. 29, 1858	Oct. 3, 1927	1879	1879	1	1	1	2	2*	—	0	7	—	—	0
Allen, S *	Dec 20, 1893	Oct 9, 1978	1924	1924	1	2	0	8	6	4.00	0	116	2	58.00	0
Allen, W R *	Apr14, 1893	Oct 14, 1950	1921	1925	30	32	10	475	95*	21.59	0	—	—	—	45/21
Ambler, J	Feb 12, 1860	Feb 10, 1899	1886	1886	4	7	0	68	25	9.71	0	22	0	—	2
Anderson, G	Jan 20, 1826	Nov 27, 1902	1863	1869	19	31	6	520	99*	20.80	0	—	—	—	19
Anderson, P N	Apr. 28, 1966		1988	1988	1	1	0	0	0	0.00	0	47	1	47.00	1
Anson, C E *	Oct 14, 1889	Mar 26, 1969	1924	1924	1	2	0	27	14	13.50	0	—	—	—	1
Appleton, C *	May15, 1844	Feb 26, 1925	1865	1865	3	6	1	56	18	11.20	0	—	—	—	1
Appleyard, R	◎ June 27, 1924	Mar 17, 2015	1950	1958	133	122	43	679	63	8.59	0	9,903	642	15.42	70
Armitage, C I *	Apr 24, 1917		1873	1878	3	5	0	26	12	5.20	0	29	0	—	0
Armitage, T	Apr 25, 1848	Sept 21, 1922	1872	1878	52	85	8	1,053	95	13.67	0	1,614	107	15.08	20
Ash, D L	Feb 18, 1944		1965	1965	3	3	0	22	12	7.33	0	22	0	—	0
Ashman, J R	May 20, 1926	Mar 4, 2019	1951	1951	21	19	5	56	10	4.00	0	116	4	29.00	0
Ashraf, Moin A	Jan 5, 1992		2010	2013	36	48	8	763	75*	19.07	0	1,268	43	29.48	2
Aspinall, R	◎ Oct 26, 1918	Aug 16, 1999	1946	1950	3	3	0	16	14	5.33	0	2,670	131	20.38	18
Aspinall, W	Mar 24, 1858	Jan 27, 1910	1880	1880	2	3	0	0	0	0.00	0	—	—	—	0
Asquith, F T	Feb 5, 1870	Jan 11, 1916	1903	1903	1	2	0	0	0	0.00	0	—	—	—	2
Athey, C W J	◎ Sept 27, 1957		1976	1983	151	246	21	6,320	134	28.08	10	1,003	21	47.76	144/2
Atkinson, G R	Sept 21, 1830	May 3, 1906	1863	1870	27	38	8	399	44	13.30	0	1,146	54	21.22	14
Atkinson, H T	Feb 1, 1881	Dec 23, 1959	1907	1907	1	2	0	0	0	0.00	0	17	0	—	0
§ Azeem Rafiq	◎ Feb 27, 1991		2009	2017	35	41	4	814	100	22.00	1	2,511	63	39.85	14
Backhouse, E N	May 13, 1901	Nov 1, 1936	1931	1931	1	1	0	2	2	2.00	0	4	0	—	0
Badger, H D *	Mar 7, 1900	Aug 10, 1975	1921	1922	2	4	2	6	6*	3.00	0	145	6	24.16	1
Bainbridge, A B	Oct 15, 1932		1961	1963	5	10	0	93	24	9.30	0	358	20	17.90	3

LIST OF PLAYERS AND CAREER AVERAGES IN ALL FIRST-CLASS MATCHES FOR YORKSHIRE (Continued)

Player	Date of Birth	Date of Death (if known)	First Played	Last Played	M	Inns	NO	Runs	HS	Av'ge	100s	Runs	Wkts	Av'ge	Ct/St
Baines, F E *	June 18, 1864	Nov 17, 1948	1888	1888	1	1	0	0	0	0.00	0	—	—	—	—
Bairstow, A	Aug 14, 1868	Dec 7, 1945	1896	1900	24	24	10	69	12	4.92	0	—	—	—	41/18
Bairstow, D L	Sept 1, 1951	Jan 5, 1998	1970	1990	429	601	113	12,985	145	26.60	0	192	6	32.00	907/131
Bairstow, J M	**Sept 26, 1989**		2009	2020	94	149	22	6,445	246	50.74	15	1	0	—	240/10
Baker, G R	Apr 18, 1862	Feb 6, 1938	1884	1884	7	11	1	42	13	4.20	0	—	—	—	5
Baker, R *	July 3, 1849	June 21, 1896	1875	1875	3	5	1	45	22	11.25	0	43	0	—	3
Balderstone, J C	Nov 16, 1940	Mar 6, 2000	1961	1969	68	81	6	1,332	82	17.76	0	790	37	21.35	24
§ **Ballance, G S**	**Nov 22, 1989**		2008	2019	117	188	20	7,913	203*	47.10	26	143	0	—	67
Barber, A T *	June 17, 1905	Mar 10, 1985	1929	1930	42	54	3	1,050	100	20.58	1	0	0	—	40
Barber, W	Apr 18, 1901	Sept 10, 1968	1926	1947	354	495	48	15,315	255	34.26	27	404	14	28.85	169
Barraclough, E S	Mar 30, 1923	May 21, 1999	1949	1950	2	4	2	43	24*	21.50	0	136	4	34.00	4
Bates, W	Nov 19, 1855	June 8, 1900	1877	1887	202	331	12	6,499	136	20.37	8	10,692	637	16.78	163
Bates, W E	Mar 5, 1884	Jan 17, 1957	1907	1913	113	167	15	2,634	81	17.32	0	57	2	28.50	64
Batty G J	Oct 13, 1977		1997	1997	1	2	0	18	18	9.00	0	70	2	35.00	0
Batty, J D	May 15, 1971		1989	1994	64	67	20	703	51	14.95	0	5,286	140	37.75	25
Bayes, G W	Feb 27, 1884	Dec 6, 1960	1910	1921	18	24	11	165	36	12.69	0	1,534	48	31.95	7
Beaumont, H	Oct 14, 1916	Nov 15, 2003	1946	1947	28	46	6	716	60	17.90	0	236	9	26.22	11
Beaumont, J	Sept 16, 1854	May 1, 1920	1877	1878	5	9	3	60	24	10.00	0	50	2	25.00	2
Bedford, H	July 17, 1907	July 5, 1968	1928	1928	5	9	1	57	24	14.25	0	179	8	22.37	2
Bedford, W	Feb 24, 1879	July, 1939	1903	1903	2	2	1	38	30*	38.00	0	117	2	58.50	1
Bell, J T	June 16, 1895	Aug 8, 1974	1921	1923	7	8	1	125	54	17.85	0	—	—	—	1
Berry, John	Jan 10, 1823	Feb 26, 1895	1864	1867	18	32	2	492	78	16.40	0	149	8	18.62	12
Berry, Joseph	Nov 29, 1829	Apr 20, 1894	1863	1874	3	4	0	68	30	17.00	0	—	—	—	1
Berry, P J	Dec 28, 1966		1986	1990	7	5	1	76	31*	19.00	0	401	7	57.28	6
§ **Bess, D M**	**July 22, 1997**		2019	2019	4	5	1	156	91*	39.00	0	234	7	33.42	1
§ Best T L	Aug 26, 1981		2010	2010	9	9	4	56	44*	9.55	0	793	18	44.05	4
Betts, G	Sept 26, 1841	Sept 26, 1902	1873	1874	2	4	1	56	44*	18.66	0	—	—	—	—
§ Bevan, M G	May 8, 1970		1995	1996	32	56	8	2,823	160*	58.81	9	720	10	72.00	24
Binks, J G	Oct 5, 1935		1955	1969	491	587	128	6,745	95	14.69	0	66	0	—	872/172
Binns, J	Mar 31, 1870	Dec 8, 1934	1898	1898	1	1	0	4	4	4.00	0	—	—	—	0/3

302

LIST OF PLAYERS AND CAREER AVERAGES IN ALL FIRST-CLASS MATCHES FOR YORKSHIRE (Continued)

Player	Date of Birth	Date of Death (if known)	First Played	Last Played	M	Inns	NO	Runs	HS	Av'ge	100s	Runs	Wkts	Av'ge	Ct/St
Bird, H D	Apr 19, 1933		1956	1959	14	25	2	613	181*	26.65	1	—	—	—	3
Birkenshaw, J	Nov 13, 1940		1958	1960	30	42	7	588	42	16.80	0	1,819	69	26.36	21
Birtles, T J D	Oct 26, 1886	Jan 13, 1971	1913	1924	37	57	11	876	104	19.04	1	20	0	—	19
Blackburn, J D H *	Oct 27, 1924	Feb 19, 1987	1956	1956	1	2	1	18	15	9.00	0	—	—	—	—
Blackburn, J S	Sept 24, 1852	July 8, 1922	1876	1877	6	11	1	102	28	10.20	0	—	—	—	4
§ Blackburn, W E *	Nov 24, 1888	June 3, 1941	1919	1920	10	13	6	26	6*	3.71	0	173	7	24.71	2
§ Blain J A R	Jan 4, 1979		2004	2010	15	17	7	137	28*	13.70	0	1,113	45	24.73	4
Blake, W	Nov 29, 1854	Nov 28, 1931	1880	1880	2	3	0	44	21	14.66	0	1,312	38	34.52	4
Blakey, R J	©Jan 15, 1967		1985	2003	339	541	84	14,150	223*	30.96	12	17	1	17.00	768/56
Blamires, E	July 31, 1850	Mar 22, 1886	1877	1877	1	2	0	23	17	11.50	0	68	1	68.00	5
§ Blewett, G S	©Oct 28, 1971		1999	1999	12	23	2	655	190	31.19	1	82	5	16.40	5
Bloom, G R	Sept 13, 1941		1964	1964	1	1	0	2	2	2.00	0	212	5	42.40	2
Bocking, H	Dec 10, 1835	Feb 22, 1907	1865	1865	1	2	0	14	11	7.00	0	—	—	—	1
Boden, J G *	Dec 27, 1848	Jan 3, 1928	1878	1878	1	2	0	6	6	6.00	0	—	—	—	—
Bolus, J B	©Sept 23, 1861	Nov 18, 1910	1890	1891	4	6	0	25	11	4.16	0	—	—	—	1
Bolton, A	Nov 3, 1902	Aug 17, 1974	1931	1947	107	179	18	4,712	146*	29.26	7	252	13	19.38	45
Booth, M W	©Dec 10, 1886	July 1, 1916	1908	1914	144	218	31	4,244	210	22.69	2	11,017	557	19.77	114
Booth, P A	Sept 5, 1965		1982	1989	36	36	16	114	29	5.70	0	1,684	122	13.80	10
Booth, R	Oct 1, 1926	May 2, 2017	1951	1955	23	29	9	193	33*	9.65	0	407	13	31.30	79/29
Bore, M K	June 2, 1947		1969	1977	65	76	28	730	53*	15.20	0	1,517	35	43.34	7
Borrill, P D	July 4, 1951		1971	1971	74	78	21	481	37*	8.43	0	4,866	162	30.03	27
Bosomworth W E	Mar 8, 1847	June 7, 1891	1872	1880	4	7	1	20	7	3.33	—	61	5	12.20	—
Bottomley, I H *	Apr 9, 1855	Apr 23, 1922	1878	1880	9	12	0	166	32	13.83	0	140	9	15.55	2
Bottomley, T	Dec 26, 1910	Feb 19, 1977	1934	1935	6	7	0	142	51	20.28	0	75	1	75.00	—
Bower, W H	Oct 17, 1857	Jan 31, 1943	1883	1883	1	2	0	10	5	5.00	0	188	1	188.00	5
Bowes, W E	©July 25, 1908	Sept 4, 1987	1929	1947	301	257	117	1,251	43*	8.93	0	21,227	1,351	15.71	118
Boycott, G	Oct 21, 1940		1962	1986	414	674	111	32,570	260*	57.85	103	665	28	23.75	200
Brackin, T	Jan 5, 1859	Oct 7, 1924	1882	1882	3	4	0	12	9	2.00	0	—	—	—	—
§ Brathwaite, K C	Dec 1, 1992		2017	2017	2	4	0	40	18	10.00	0	—	—	—	1

LIST OF PLAYERS AND CAREER AVERAGES IN ALL FIRST-CLASS MATCHES FOR YORKSHIRE *(Continued)*

Player	Date of Birth	Date of Death (if known)	First Played	Last Played	M	Inns	NO	Runs	HS	Av'ge	100s	Runs	Wkts	Av'ge	Ct/St
Brayshay, P B *	Oct 14, 1916	July 6, 2004	1952	1952	2	3	0	20	13	6.66	0	104	3	34.66	0
Brearley, H *	June 26, 1913	Aug 14, 2007	1937	1937	1	2	0	17	9	8.50	0	—	—	—	0
Brennan, D V * ..... ©	Feb 10, 1920	Jan 9, 1985	1947	1953	204	221	66	1,653	47	10.66	0	—	—	—	280/100
Bresnan, T T * ...... ©	Feb 28, 1985		2003	2019	163	232	35	5,594	169*	28.39	5	13,663	445	30.70	89
Britton, G	Feb 7, 1843		1867	1867	1	2	0	3	3	1.50	0	—	—	—	0
Broadbent, A	June 7, 1879	Jan 3, 1910	1909	1910	3	5	0	66	29	13.20	0	252	5	50.40	1
Broadhead, W B	May 31, 1903	July 19, 1958	1929	1929	1	3	0	5	3	2.50	0	—	—	—	0
Broadhurst, M	June 20, 1974	Apr 2, 1986	1991	1994	5	3	1	7	6	2.33	0	231	7	33.00	0
Brook, H C	**Feb 22, 1999**		**2016**	**2020**	**33**	**54**	**1**	**1,285**	**124**	**24.24**	**2**	**181**	**1**	**181.00**	**19**
Brooke, J W	Feb 1, 1897		1923	1923	1	1	0	0	0*	0.00	0	—	—	—	0
Brooke, B	Mar 3, 1930	Mar.3 1989	1950	1950	2	4	0	16	14	4.00	0	191	2	95.50	0
§ Brooks, J A ...... ©	June 4, 1984		2013	2018	81	102	34	1,229	109*	18.07	1	8,341	316	26.39	21
§ Brophy, G L ...... ©	Nov 26, 1975		2006	2012	73	112	12	3,012	177*	30.12	3	6	0	—	176/15
Broughton, P N	Oct 22, 1935		1956	1956	2	5	2	19	12	6.33	0	365	16	22.81	1
Brown, A	June 10, 1854	Nov 2, 1900	1872	1872	3	5	0	9	5	3.00	0	47	3	15.66	4
Brown, J T (Driffield) ©	Aug 20, 1869	Nov 4, 1904	1889	1904	345	567	41	15,694	311	29.83	23	5,183	177	29.28	188
Brown, J T (Darfield) ©	Nov 24, 1874	Apr 12, 1950	1897	1903	30	32	3	333	37*	11.48	0	2,071	97	21.35	18
Brown, W	Nov 19, 1876	July 27, 1945	1902	1908	2	2	1	2	2	2.00	0	84	4	21.00	0
Brownhill, T	Oct 10, 1838	Jan 6, 1915	1863	1871	14	20	3	185	25	10.88	0	—	—	—	7
Brumfitt, J *	Feb. 18, 1917	Mar 16, 1987	1938	1938	1	1	0	9	9	9.00	0	—	—	—	0
Buller, J S	Aug 23, 1909	Aug 7, 1970	1930	1930	1	2	0	5	3	2.50	0	—	—	—	0
Bulmer, J R L	Dec 28, 1867	Jan 20, 1917	1891	1891	1	2	0	0	0*	0.00	0	—	—	—	2
Burgess, T	Oct 1, 1859	Feb 15, 1922	1895	1895	1	2	1	0	0*	0.00	0	79	1	79.00	0
Burgin, E	Jan 4, 1924	Nov 16, 2012	1952	1953	12	10	3	92	32	13.14	0	795	31	25.64	2
Burman, J	Oct 5, 1838	May 14, 1900	1867	1867	1	1	0	1	1*	1.00	0	—	—	—	0
Burnet, J R * ...... ©	Oct 11, 1918	Mar 6, 1999	1958	1959	54	75	6	889	54	12.88	0	26	1	26.00	7
§ Burrows, M	Aug 18, 1855	May 29, 1893	1880	1880	6	10	0	82	23	8.20	0	—	—	—	2
Burton, D C F * ...... ©	Sept 13, 1887	Sept 24, 1971	1907	1921	104	130	15	2,273	142*	19.76	2	—	—	—	44
Burton, R C *	Apr 11, 1891	Apr 30, 1971	1914	1914	2	2	0	47	47	23.50	0	73	6	12.16	2
Butterfield, E B *	Oct 22, 1848	May 6, 1899	1870	1870	1	2	0	18	10	9.00	0	—	—	—	0

LIST OF PLAYERS AND CAREER AVERAGES IN ALL FIRST-CLASS MATCHES FOR YORKSHIRE (Continued)

Player	Date of Birth	Date of Death (if known)	First Played	Last Played	M	Inns	NO	Runs	HS	Av'ge	100s	Runs	Wkts	Av'ge	Ct/St
Byas, D	© Aug 26, 1963		1986	2001	268	449	42	14,398	213	35.37	28	727	12	60.58	351
Byrom, J L*	July 20, 1851	Aug 24, 1931	1874	1874	2	4	0	19	11	4.75	0	—	—	—	1
Callis, E	Nov 8, 1994		2016	2017	2	3	1	131	84	65.50	0	—	—	—	1
Cammish, J W	May 21, 1921	July 16, 1974	1954	1954	2	2	1	0	0	0.00	0	155	3	51.66	0
Carrick, P	© July, 16 1952	Jan 11, 2000	1970	1993	425	543	102	9,994	131*	22.66	3	30,530	1,018	29.99	183
Carter, Rev E S*	Feb 3, 1845	May 23, 1923	1876	1881	14	21	2	210	39*	11.05	0	104	8	13.00	4
Cartman, W H	June 20, 1861	Jan 16, 1935	1891	1891	3	6	0	57	49	9.50	0	—	—	—	0
Carver, K	Mar 26, 1996		2014	2018	7	13	6	108	20	15.42	0	543	18	30.16	4
Cawthray, G	Sept 28, 1913	Jan 5, 2001	1939	1952	4	6	0	114	30	19.00	0	304	4	76.00	1
Chadwick, J P G	Nov 8, 1934		1960	1965	14	9	3	106	59	17.66	0	67	2	33.50	7
Champion, A	Dec 27, 1851	June 26, 1909	1876	1879	14	23	4	148	29	7.78	0	17	1	17.00	7
Chapman, C A	June 8, 1971		1990	1998	8	13	2	238	80	21.63	0	—	—	—	13/3
Charlesworth, A P	Feb 19, 1865	May 11, 1926	1894	1895	7	12	1	241	63	21.90	0	—	—	—	2
§ Chichester-Constable, R C J*	Dec 21, 1890	May 26, 1963	1919	1919	1	1	1	6	6	0.00	0	6	—	—	1
Clarkson, A	Sept 5, 1939		1963	1963	6	8	1	80	30	11.42	0	92	5	18.40	5
Claughton, H M	Dec 24, 1891	Oct 17, 1980	1914	1919	4	6	0	39	15	6.50	0	176	3	58.66	1
§ Claydon, M E	Nov 25, 1982		2005	2006	3	2	0	38	38	19.00	0	263	3	87.66	0
§ Clayton, R O	Jan 1, 1844	Nov 26, 1901	1870	1879	70	115	23	992	62	10.78	0	2,478	153	16.19	26
§ Cleary, M F	July 19, 1980		2005	2005	2	2	0	23	12	11.50	0	250	8	31.25	2
Clegg, H	Dec 8, 1850	Dec 30, 1920	1881	1881	6	8	1	63	25*	9.00	0	—	—	—	2
Clifford, C C	July, 5, 1942		1972	1972	11	12	4	39	12*	4.87	0	666	26	25.61	5
Close, D B	© Feb 24, 1931	Sept 14, 2015	1949	1970	536	811	102	22,650	198	31.94	33	23,489	967	24.29	564
Clough, G D	May 23, 1978		1998	1998	3	3	0	34	33	17.00	0	11	0	—	1
Coad, B O	**© Jan 10, 1994**		**2016**	**2020**	**38**	**50**	**16**	**519**	**48**	**15.26**	**0**	**3,130**	**157**	**19.93**	**2**
Collinson, R W*	Nov 6, 1875	Dec 26, 1963	1897	1897	2	3	0	58	34	19.33	0	—	—	—	2
Cooper, H P	Apr 17, 1949		1971	1980	98	107	29	1,159	56	14.85	0	6,327	227	27.87	60
Cooper, P E*	Feb 11, 1885	May 21, 1950	1910	1910	1	2	0	0	0	0.00	0	—	—	—	0
Cope, G A	© Feb 23, 1947		1966	1980	230	249	89	2,241	78	14.00	0	15,627	630	24.80	64
Corbett, A M	Nov 25, 1855	Oct 7, 1934	1881	1881	1	2	0	0	0	0.00	0	—	—	—	1

LIST OF PLAYERS AND CAREER AVERAGES IN ALL FIRST-CLASS MATCHES FOR YORKSHIRE (Continued)

Player	Date of Birth	Date of Death (if known)	First Played	Last Played	M	Inns	NO	Runs	HS	Av'ge	100s	Runs	Wkts	Av'ge	Ct/St
Coverdale, S P	Nov 20, 1954	—	1973	1980	6	4	0	31	18	7.75	0	—	—	—	11/4
Coverdale, W *	July 8, 1862	—	1888	1888	2	2	0	2	1	1.00	0	—	—	—	1
Cowan, M J	© June 10, 1933	—	1953	1962	91	84	48	170	19*	4.72	0	6,389	266	24.01	37
Cownley, J M	Feb 24, 1929	Nov 7, 1998	1952	1952	2	2	1	19	19	19.00	0	119	1	119.00	0
Coxon, A	© Jan 18, 1916	Jan 22, 2006	1945	1950	142	182	33	2,747	83	18.43	0	9,528	464	20.53	124
Craven, V J	July 31, 1980	—	2000	2004	33	55	6	1,206	81*	24.61	0	584	15	38.93	18
Crawford, G H	Dec 15, 1890	June 28, 1975	1914	1926	9	8	0	46	21	5.75	0	541	21	25.76	3
Crawford, M G *	July 30, 1920	Dec 2, 2012	1951	1951	1	2	0	22	13	11.00	0	—	—	—	3
Creighton, E	July 9, 1859	Feb 17, 1931	1888	1888	4	8	2	33	10	5.50	0	181	10	18.10	1
Crick, H	Jan 29, 1910	Feb 10, 1960	1937	1947	8	10	0	88	20	8.80	0	—	—	—	18/4
Crookes, R	Oct 9, 1846	Feb 15, 1897	1879	1879	1	2	1	2	2*	2.00	0	14	0	—	0
Crossland, S M	Aug 16, 1851	April 11, 1906	1883	1886	4	6	0	32	20	8.00	0	—	—	—	3/5
Crowther, A	Aug 1, 1878	Nov 4, 1946	1905	1905	1	2	0	0	0	0.00	0	—	—	—	1
Cuttell, W	Jan 28, 1835	June 10, 1896	1863	1871	15	27	6	271	56	12.90	0	596	36	16.55	4
Dalton, A J	Mar 14, 1947	—	1969	1972	21	31	3	710	128	24.48	3	—	—	—	6
§ Darnton, T	Feb 12, 1836	Oct 18, 1874	1864	1868	13	22	1	314	81*	14.95	0	349	12	29.08	3
Davidson, K R	© Dec 24, 1905	Dec 25, 1954	1933	1935	30	46	5	1,331	128	32.46	2	196	5	39.20	18
Dawes, J	Feb 14, 1836	Not known	1865	1865	5	9	2	93	28*	13.28	0	—	—	—	3
Dawood, I	July 23, 1976	—	2004	2005	20	31	9	636	75	26.50	0	—	—	—	46/3
Dawson, E	May 1, 1835	Dec 1, 1888	1863	1874	16	25	1	224	20	9.33	0	—	—	—	5
Dawson, R K J	© Jan 4, 1980	—	2001	2006	72	106	19	2,179	87	22.46	0	6,444	157	41.04	39
Dawson, W A *	Dec 3, 1850	Mar 6, 1916	1870	1870	1	2	0	0	0	0.00	0	—	—	—	1
Day, A G *	Sept 20, 1865	Oct 16, 1908	1885	1888	6	10	0	78	25	7.80	0	—	—	—	3
Dennis, F	© June 11, 1907	Nov 21, 2000	1928	1933	89	100	28	1,332	67	18.50	0	4,517	156	28.95	58
Dennis, S J	© Oct 18, 1960	—	1980	1988	67	62	24	338	53*	8.89	0	5,548	173	32.06	19
Denton, D	© July 4, 1874	Feb 16, 1950	1894	1920	676	1,058	61	33,282	221	33.38	61	957	34	28.14	360/1
Denton, J	Feb 3, 1865	July 19, 1946	1887	1888	15	24	1	222	59	9.65	0	—	—	—	6
Dewse, H	Feb 23, 1836	July 8, 1910	1873	1873	1	1	0	14	12	7.00	0	15	0	—	1
Deyes, G	Feb 11, 1878	Jan 11, 1963	1905	1907	17	24	4	44	12	2.20	0	944	41	23.02	6
Dick, R D *	Apr 16, 1889	Dec 14, 1983	1911	1911	1	1	0	2	2	2.00	0	37	2	18.50	1

LIST OF PLAYERS AND CAREER AVERAGES IN ALL FIRST-CLASS MATCHES FOR YORKSHIRE (Continued)

Player	Date of Birth	Date of Death (if known)	First Played	Last Played	M	Inns	NO	Runs	HS	Av'ge	100s	Runs	Wkts	Av'ge	Ct/St
Dobson, A	Feb 22, 1854	Sept 17, 1932	1879	1879	2	3	0	1	1	0.33	0	—	—	—	1
Doidge, M J	July 2, 1970		1990	1990								106	0	—	0
Dolphin, A	Dec 24, 1885	Oct 23, 1942	1905	1927	427	446	157	3,325	66	11.50	0	28	0	—	569/260
Douglas, J S ◎	Apr 4, 1903	Dec 27, 1971	1925	1934	23	26	8	125	19	6.94	0	1,310	49	26.73	14
Drake, A ◎	Apr 16, 1884	Feb 14, 1919	1909	1914	156	244	24	4,789	147*	21.76	3	8,623	479	18.00	93
Drake, J	Sept 1, 1893	May 22, 967	1923	1924	2	4	1	21	10	7.00	0	117	1	117.00	1
Driver, J	May 16, 1861	Dec 10, 1946	1889	1889	2	4	1	24	8	8.00	0	—	—	—	2
Dury, T S *	June 12, 1854	Mar 20, 1932	1878	1881	13	24	1	329	46	14.30	0	21	0	—	2
Dyson, W L *	Dec 11, 1857	May 1, 1936	1887	1887	2	4	0	8	6	2.00	0	—	—	—	3
Earnshaw, W	Sept 20, 1867	Nov 24, 1941	1893	1896	6	7	3	44	23	11.00	0	349	11	31.72	6/2
Eastwood, D	Mar 30, 1848	May 17, 1903	1870	1877	29	51	2	591	68	12.06	0	—	—	—	16
Eckersley, R	Sept 4, 1925	May 30, 2009	1945	1945	1	1	0	9	9*	9.00	0	62	0	—	0
Elam, F W *	Sept 13, 1871	Mar 19, 1943	1900	1902	2	3	1	48	28	24.00	0	—	—	—	0
§ Elliot, M T G	Sept 28, 1971		2002	2002	5	10	1	487	127	54.11	1	77	1	77.00	7
Ellis, J E	Nov 10, 1864	Dec 1, 1927	1888	1892	11	15	6	14	4*	1.55	0	—	—	—	11/10
Ellis, S *	Nov 23, 1851	Oct 28, 1930	1880	1880	2	3	0	12	9	4.00	0	—	—	—	2
Elms, J E	Dec 24, 1874	Nov 1, 1951	1905	1905	1	2	0	20	10	10.00	0	28	1	28.00	0
Elstub, C J	Feb 3, 1981		2000	2002	6	7	4	28	18*	28.00	0	356	9	39.55	2
Emmett, T ◎	Sept 3, 1841	June 29, 1904	1866	1888	299	484	65	6,315	104	15.07	1	15,465	1,216	12.71	179
Farrar, A	Apr 29, 1883	Dec 25, 1954	1906	1906	1	1	0	2	2	2.00	0	—	—	—	1
Fearnley, M C	Aug 21, 1936	July 7, 1979	1962	1964	3	4	2	19	11*	9.50	0	133	6	22.16	1
Featherby, W D	Aug 18, 1888	Nov 20, 1958	1920	1920	1	2	0				0	12	0	—	0
Fellows, G M	July 30, 1975		1998	2003	46	71	6	1,526	109	23.47	1	1,202	32	37.56	23
Fiddling, K	Oct 13, 1917	June 19, 1992	1938	1946	18	24	6	182	25	10.11	0	—	—	—	24/13
§ Finch, A J ◎	Nov 17, 1986		2014	2015	8	10	1	415	110	46.11	1	40	1	40.00	11
Firth, A *	Sept 3, 1847	Jan 16, 1927	1869	1869	1	1	0	4	4	4.00	0	—	—	—	1
Firth, Rev E B *	Apr 11, 1863	July 25, 1905	1894	1894	1	1	0	1	1	1.00	0	—	—	—	0
§ Firth, E L *	Mar 7, 1886	Jan 8, 1949	1912	1912	2	4	0	43	37	10.75	0	—	—	—	1
Firth, J	June 26, 1917	Sept 6, 1981	1949	1950	8	8	5	134	67*	44.66	0	—	—	—	14/2

LIST OF PLAYERS AND CAREER AVERAGES IN ALL FIRST-CLASS MATCHES FOR YORKSHIRE (Continued)

Player	Date of Birth	Date of Death (if known)	First Played	Last Played	M	Inns	NO	Runs	HS	Av'ge	100s	Runs	Wkts	Av'ge	Ct/St
Fisher, H	© Aug 3, 1903	Apr 16, 1974	1928	1936	52	58	14	681	76*	15.47	0	2,621	93	28.18	22
Fisher, I D	Mar 31, 1976		1996	2001	24	32	9	545	68*	23.69	0	1,382	43	32.13	1
Fisher, M D	**Nov 9, 1997**		**2015**	**2020**	**13**	**17**	**3**	**242**	**47***	**17.28**	**0**	**1,257**	**41**	**30.65**	**5**
Flaxington, S	Oct 14, 1860	Mar 10, 1895	1882	1882	4	8	0	121	57	15.12	0	—	—	—	—
§ Fleming, S P	Apr 1, 1973		2003	2003	7	14	2	469	98	39.08	0	—	—	—	13
Fletcher, S D	© June 8, 1964		1983	1991	107	91	31	414	28*	6.90	0	7,966	234	34.04	25
Fletcher, W	Feb 16, 1866	June 1, 1935	1892	1892	5	8	1	80	31*	11.42	0	157	7	22.42	4
Foord, C W	June 11, 1924	July 8, 2015	1947	1953	51	34	16	114	35	6.33	0	3,412	126	27.07	19
Foster, E	Nov 23, 1873	April 16, 1956	1901	1901	1	1	0	2	2	2.00	0	27	—	—	—
Foster, M J	Sept 17, 1972		1993	1994	5	7	1	165	63*	27.50	0	150	6	25.00	6
§ Foster, T W *	Nov 12, 1871	Jan 31, 1947	1894	1895	14	20	5	138	25*	9.20	0	952	58	16.41	6
Fraine, W A R	**June 13, 1996**		**2019**	**2020**	**11**	**19**	**1**	**425**	**106**	**23.61**	**1**	**—**	**—**	**—**	**9**
Frank, J *	Dec 7, 1857	Oct 22, 1940	1881	1881	1	2	0	10	7	5.00	0	17	1	17.00	3
Frank, R W *	May 29, 1864	Sept 9, 1950	1889	1903	18	28	4	298	58	12.41	0	9	—	—	8
Freeman, G	July 27, 1843	Nov 18, 1895	1865	1880	32	54	2	752	53	14.46	0	2,079	209	9.94	16
Gale, A W	© Nov 28, 1983		2004	2016	149	235	17	7,726	272	35.44	19	238	1	238.00	46
Geldart, C J	Dec 17, 1991		2010	2011	2	2	0	51	34	25.50	0	—	—	—	1
Gibb, P A *	© July 11, 1913	Dec 7, 1977	1935	1946	36	54	0	1,545	157*	32.87	2	82	3	27.33	25/8
Gibson, B P **	Mar 31, 1996		2011	2011	1	1	0	0	1*	—	0	—	—	—	6/0
Gibson, R	Jan 22, 1996		2016	2016	1	1	0	0	0	0.00	0	42	1	42.00	0
§ Gifkins, C J *	Feb 19, 1856	Jan 31, 1897	1880	1880	2	3	0	30	23	10.00	0	—	—	—	1
Gilbert, C R	Apr 16, 1984		2007	2007	2	3	0	64	64	64.00	0	11	0	—	1
Gill, F	Sept 3, 1883		1906	1906	2	4	0	18	11	4.50	0	—	—	—	1
§ Gillespie, J N	©April 19, 1975		2006	2007	26	34	11	640	123*	27.82	1	2,013	59	34.11	4
Gillhouley, K N	Aug 8, 1934		1961	1961	24	31	7	323	56*	13.45	0	1,702	77	22.10	16
Gough, D	Sept 18, 1970		1989	2008	146	188	29	2,922	121	18.37	0	12,487	453	27.56	30
Goulder, A	Aug 16, 1907	June 11, 1986	1929	1929	2	1	0	3	3	3.00	0	90	3	30.00	—
§ Gray, A K D	May 19, 1974		2001	2004	18	26	3	649	104	28.21	0	1,357	30	45.23	16

308

** At 15 years and 27 days on April 27, 2011, First Day of Yorkshire's match v. Durham MCCU, he became the youngest ever English First Class cricketer.

Player	Date of Birth	Date of Death (if known)	First Played	Last Played	M	Inns	NO	Runs	HS	Av'ge	100s	Runs	Wkts	Av'ge	Ct/St
Grayson, A P	Mar 31, 1971	—	1990	1995	52	80	10	1,958	100	27.97	1	846	13	65.07	36
Greenwood, A	Aug 20, 1847	Feb 12, 1889	1869	1880	95	166	12	2,762	91	17.93	0	—	—	—	33
Greenwood, F E *	Sept 28, 1905	July 30, 1963	1929	1932	57	66	8	1,558	104*	26.86	1	36	2	18.00	37
Greenwood, L	July 13, 1834	Nov 1, 1909	1864	1874	50	84	8	885	83	12.29	0	1,615	85	19.00	24
Grimshaw, C H	May 12, 1880	Sept 25, 1947	1904	1908	54	75	7	1,219	85	17.92	0	221	7	31.57	42
Grimshaw, I	May 4, 1857	Jan 18, 1911	1880	1887	125	194	14	3,354	129*	18.63	4	—	—	—	76/3
Guy S M	Nov 17, 1978	—	2000	2011	37	52	6	742	52*	16.13	0	8	0	—	98/12
Haggas, S	Apr 18, 1856	Mar 14, 1926	1878	1882	31	47	3	478	43	10.86	0	—	—	—	10
Haigh, S	© Mar 19, 1871	Feb 27, 1921	1895	1913	513	687	110	10,993	159	19.05	4	29,289	1,876	15.61	276
Hall, B	Sept 16, 1929	Feb 27, 1989	1952	1952	1	2	0	14	10	7.00	0	55	1	55.00	1
Hall, C H	Apr 5, 1906	Dec 11, 1976	1928	1934	23	22	9	69	15*	5.15	0	1,226	45	27.24	11
§ Hall, J	Nov 11, 1815	Apr 17, 1888	1863	1863	1	2	0	4	3	2.00	0	—	—	—	1
Hall. L	© Nov 1, 1852	Nov 19, 1915	1873	1894	275	477	58	9,757	160	23.28	12	781	15	52.06	173
Halliday, H	Feb 9, 1920	Aug 27, 1967	1938	1953	182	279	18	8,361	144	32.03	12	3,119	101	30.88	140
Halliley, C	Dec 5, 1852	Mar 23, 1929	1872	1872	3	5	0	27	17	5.40	0	—	—	—	1
Hamer, A	Dec 8, 1916	Nov 3, 1993	1938	1938	2	2	0	3	3	1.50	0	64	1	64.00	2
§ Hamilton, G M	© Sept 16, 1974	—	1994	2003	73	108	18	2,228	125	24.75	1	5,479	222	24.68	25
Hampshire, A W	Oct 18, 1950	—	1975	1975	1	2	0	18	17	9.00	0	—	—	—	1
Hampshire, J	Oct 5, 1913	May 23, 1997	1937	1937	3	2	0	5	5	2.50	0	109	5	21.80	1
§ Hampshire, J H	© Feb 10, 1941	March 1, 2017	1961	1981	456	724	89	21,979	183*	34.61	34	1,108	24	46.16	367
§ Handscomb, P S P	Apr 26, 1991	—	2017	2017	9	14	1	441	101*	33.92	1	—	—	—	7
Hannon-Dalby, O J	Jun 20, 1989	—	2008	2012	24	25	10	45	11*	3.00	0	1,938	43	45.06	7
§ Harbord, W E *	Dec 15, 1908	July 28, 1992	1929	1935	16	21	1	411	109	20.55	1	—	—	—	7
§ Harden, R J	Aug 16, 1965	—	1999	2000	12	22	3	439	69	23.10	0	—	—	—	2
Hardisty, C H	Dec 10, 1885	Mar 2, 1968	1906	1909	38	55	5	991	84	19.82	0	—	—	—	18
§ Hargreaves, H S	Mar 22, 1912	Sept 29, 1990	1934	1938	18	20	6	51	9	3.64	0	1,145	55	20.81	3
§ Harrison, S J	Oct 23, 1978	—	2012	2012	3	3	0	25	23	8.33	0	195	8	24.37	1
Harris, W	Nov 21, 1861	May 23, 1923	1884	1887	3	4	2	45	25	7.50	0	18	0	—	1
Harrison, G P	© Feb 11, 1862	Sept 14, 1940	1883	1892	59	87	26	407	28	6.67	0	3,276	226	14.49	36
Harrison, H	Jan 26, 1885	Feb 11, 1962	1907	1907	2	1	1	4	4*	—	0	39	2	19.50	1

LIST OF PLAYERS AND CAREER AVERAGES IN ALL FIRST-CLASS MATCHES FOR YORKSHIRE (Continued)

Player	Date of Birth	Date of Death (if known)	First Played	Last Played	M	Inns	NO	Runs	HS	Av'ge	100s	Runs	Wkts	Av'ge	Ct/St
Harrison, W H	May 27, 1863	July 15, 1939	1888	1888	3	6	1	12	7	2.40	0	—	—	—	0
Hart, H W *	Sept 21, 1859	Nov 2, 1895	1888	1888	2	5	0	6	6	3.00	0	32	2	16.00	0
Hart, P R	Jan 12, 1947		1981	1981	3	5	0	23	11	4.60	0	140	2	70.00	1
Hartington, H E	Sept 18, 1881	Feb 16, 1950	1910	1911	10	10	4	51	16	8.50	0	764	23	33.21	2
Hartley, P J	©Apr 18, 1960		1985	1997	195	237	51	3,844	127*	20.66	2	17,438	579	30.11	60
Hartley, S N	©Mar 18, 1956		1978	1988	133	199	27	4,193	114	24.37	4	2,052	42	48.85	47
§ Harvey, I J	Apr 10, 1972		2004	2005	20	31	1	1,045	209*	36.03	2	1,218	37	32.91	12
Hatton, A G	Mar 25, 1937		1960	1961	3	1	0	4	4*	—	0	202	6	33.66	2
§ Hawke, Lord *	Aug 16, 1860	Oct 10, 1938	1881	1911	510	739	91	13,133	166	20.26	10	16	0	—	159
Hayley, H	Feb 22, 1860	June 3, 1922	1884	1898	7	12	1	122	24	11.09	0	48	0	—	3
Haywood, W J	Feb 25, 1841	Jan 7, 1912	1878	1878	1	2	0	7	7	3.50	0	14	1	14.00	0
§ Head, T M	Dec 29, 1993		2016	2016	1	2	0	56	54	28.00	0	16	0	—	0
Hicks, J	Dec 10, 1850	June 10, 1912	1872	1876	15	25	3	313	66	14.22	0	17	0	—	12
Higgins, J	Mar 13, 1877	July 19, 1954	1901	1905	9	14	5	93	28*	10.33	0	—	—	—	10/3
Hill, J	Nov 15, 1843	Aug 28, 1910	1871	1882	140	223	25	1,705	49	8.61	0	7,002	542	12.91	91
Hill, G G H	**Jan 24, 2001**		**2020**	**2020**	**2**	**2**	**1**	**33**	**33**	**33.00**	**0**	**54**	**1**	**54.00**	**0**
Hill, H *	Nov 29, 1858	Aug 14, 1935	1888	1891	14	27	2	337	34	13.48	0	—	—	—	10
Hill, L G *	Nov 2, 1860	Aug 27, 1940	1882	1882	1	2	0	13	8	6.50	0	—	—	—	1
Hirst, E T *	May 6, 1857	Oct 26, 1914	1877	1888	21	33	2	328	87*	10.58	0	—	—	—	7
Hirst, E W *	Feb 27, 1855	Oct 24, 1933	1881	1881	2	3	0	33	28	11.00	0	3	0	—	0
Hirst, G H	©Sept 7, 1871	May 10, 1954	1891	1921*	717	1,050	128	32,024	341	34.73	56	44,716	2,481	18.02	518
Hirst, T H	May 21, 1865	Apr 3, 1927	1899	1899	1	1	0	5	5*	—	0	27	0	—	0
§ Hodd, A J	©Jan 12, 1984		2012	2018	57	79	10	1,803	96*	26.13	0	14	0	—	165/11
Hodgson, D M	Feb 26, 1990		2014	2015	2	3	0	72	35	24.00	0	—	—	—	2
Hodgson, G	July 24, 1828	Nov 24, 1867	1864	1866	1	1	0	4	4	4.00	0	—	—	—	0/2
Hodgson, L	Nov 15, 1828		1863	1866	21	35	14	164	21*	7.80	0	1,537	88	17.46	11
Hodgson, L J	Jun 29, 1986		2009	2010	13	6	3	99	34	33.00	0	158	2	79.00	1
Hodgson, P	Sept 21, 1935	Mar 30, 2015	1954	1956	6	6	2	33	8*	8.25	0	648	22	29.45	6
Hoggard, M J	©Dec 31, 1976		1996	2009	102	120	34	956	89*	11.11	0	8,956	331	27.05	23
Holdsworth, W E N	Sept 17, 1928	July 31, 2016	1952	1953	27	26	12	111	22*	7.92	0	1,598	53	30.15	7

Player	Date of Birth	Date of Death (if known)	First Played	Last Played	M	Inns	NO	Runs	HS	Av'ge	100s	Runs	Wkts	Av'ge	Ct/St
Holgate, G	June 23, 1839	July 11, 1895	1865	1867	12	19	0	174	38	9.15	0	124	1	124.00	17/1
Holmes, P	© Nov 25, 1886	Sept 3, 1971	1913	1933	485	699	74	26,220	315*	41.95	60	—	—	—	319
Horner, N F	© May 10, 1926	Dec 24, 2003	1950	1950	2	4	1	114	43	28.50	0	—	—	—	2
Houseman I J	Oct 12, 1969	—	1989	1991	5	2	1	18	18	18.00	0	311	3	103.66	2
Hoyle, T H	Mar 19, 1884	June 2, 1953	1919	1919	1	1	0	7	7	3.50	0	—	—	—	0/1
Hudson, R	June 29, 1851	Nov 11, 1901	1880	1880	1	2	0	13	5	3.25	0	—	—	—	2
Hunter, D	Feb 23, 1860	Jan 11, 1927	1888	1909	517	681	323	4,177	58*	11.66	0	43	0	—	863/323
Hunter, J	Aug 3, 1855	Jan 4, 1891	1878	1888	143	213	61	1,183	60*	7.78	0	—	—	—	207/102
Hutchison, P M	© June 9, 1977	—	1996	2001	39	39	23	187	30	11.68	0	—	—	—	8
Hutton, L	© June 23, 1916	Sept 6, 1990	1934	1955	341	527	62	24,807	280*	53.34	85	3,244	143	22.68	278
Hutton, R A	© June 23, 1942	—	1962	1974	208	292	45	4,986	189	20.18	0	4,221	154	27.40	160
Iddison, R	Sept 15, 1834	Mar 19, 1890	1863	1876	72	108	15	1,916	112	20.60	1	1,540	102	15.09	70
Illingworth, R	June 8, 1932	—	1951	1983	496	668	131	14,986	162	27.90	14	26,806	1,431	18.73	286
§ Imran Tahir	Mar 27, 1979	—	2007	2007	1	2	0	5	5	2.50	0	141	0	—	0
Ingham, P G	Sept 28, 1956	—	1979	1981	8	14	0	290	64	20.71	0	—	—	—	0
Inglis, J W	Oct 19, 1979	—	2000	2000	1	2	0	4	2	2.00	0	—	—	—	0
§ Inzamam-ul-Haq	Mar 3, 1970	—	2007	2007	3	4	0	89	51	22.25	0	—	—	—	5
Jackson, Hon F S *	© Nov 21, 1870	Mar 9, 1947	1890	1907	207	328	22	10,371	160	33.89	21	9,690	506	19.15	129
Jackson, S R *	July 15, 1859	July 19, 1941	1891	1891	1	2	0	9	9	4.50	0	—	—	—	0
Jacques, T A *	Feb 19, 1905	Feb 23, 1986	1927	1936	28	20	7	162	35*	12.46	0	1,786	57	31.33	12
Jakeman, F	Jan 10, 1921	May 17, 1986	1946	1947	10	16	2	262	51	18.71	0	—	—	—	3
James, B	Apr 23, 1934	May 26, 1999	1954	1954	4	5	3	22	11*	11.00	0	228	8	28.50	3
§ Jaques, P A	© May 3, 1979	—	2004	2013	53	82	3	4,039	243	51.12	11	112	1	112.00	46
Jarvis, P W	© June 29, 1965	—	1981	1993	138	160	46	1,898	80	16.64	0	11,990	449	26.70	36
Johnson, C	© Sept 5, 1947	—	1969	1979	100	152	14	2,960	107	21.44	2	265	4	66.25	50
Johnson, J	May 16, 1916	Jan 16, 2011	1936	1939	3	4	2	5	4*	5.00	0	27	5	5.40	1
Johnson, M	Apr 23, 1958	—	1981	1981	4	4	2	2	2	1.00	0	301	7	43.00	3
Joy, J	Dec 29, 1825	Sept 27, 1889	1863	1867	4	5	0	107	74	21.40	0	5	0	—	0
Judson, A	July 10, 1885	Apr 8, 1975	1920	1920	1	—	—	—	—	—	—	5	0	—	0

LIST OF PLAYERS AND CAREER AVERAGES IN ALL FIRST-CLASS MATCHES FOR YORKSHIRE (Continued)

Player	Date of Birth	Date of Death (if known)	First Played	Last Played	M	Inns	NO	Runs	HS	Av'ge	100s	Runs	Wkts	Av'ge	Ct/St
§ Katich, S M	Aug 21, 1975		2002	2002	2	2	0	37	21	18.50	0	25	0	—	1
Kaye, Harold S *	May 9, 1882	Nov 6, 1953	1907	1908	18	25	1	243	37	10.12	0				9
Kaye, Haven	June 11, 1846	Jan 24, 1892	1872	1873	8	14	0	117	33	8.35	0				3
Keedy, G	Nov 27, 1974		1994	1994	1	1	0	1	1	1.00	0				0
§ Keighley, W G * ... ©	Jan 10, 1925	June 14, 2005	1947	1951	35	51	5	1,227	110	26.67	1	18	0	—	12
Kellett, S A	Oct 16, 1967		1989	1995	86	147	10	4,204	125*	30.68	2	7	0	—	74
Kennie, G	May 17, 1904	Apr 11, 1994	1927	1927	1	2	0	6	6	3.00	0				1
Kettleborough, R A	Mar 15, 1973		1994	1997	13	19	2	446	108	26.23	1				9
Kilburn, N	Oct 16, 1868	Sept 25, 1940	1896	1896	1	1	0	8	8	8.00	0	153	3	51.00	
Kilner, N	July 21, 1895	Apr 28, 1979	1919	1923	69	73	7	1,253	112	18.98	0				34
© Kilner, R	Oct 17, 1890	Apr 5, 1928	1911	1927	365	478	46	13,018	206*	30.13	15	14,855	857	17.33	231
King, A M	Oct 8, 1932		1955	1955	4	1	0	12	12	12.00	0	279	8	34.87	
Kippax, P J	Oct 15, 1940		1961	1962	4	7	2	37	12	7.40	0				11
Kirby, S P	Oct 4, 1977		2001	2004	47	61	14	342	57	7.27	0	5,143	182	28.25	11
§ Kohler-Cadmore, T ©	**Apr 19, 1994**		**2017**	**2020**	**29**	**48**	**4**	**1,696**	**176**	**38.54**	**5**				**40**
© Kruis, G J	May 9, 1974		2005	2009	54	64	31	617	50*	18.69	0	5,431	154	35.26	11
Lambert, G A	Jan 4, 1980		2000	2000	2	3	2	6	3*	6.00	0	133	4	33.25	1
Lancaster, W W	Feb 4, 1873	Dec 30, 1938	1895	1895	3	10	0	163	51	16.30	0	29	0	—	1
§ Landon, C W *	May 30, 1850	Mar 5, 1903	1878	1882	9	13	0	51	18	3.92	0	74	0	—	7
Law, W *	Apr 9, 1851	Dec 20, 1892	1871	1873	4	7	0	51	22	7.28	0				3
Lawson, M A K	Oct 24, 1985		2004	2007	15	21	5	197	44	12.31	0	1,699	42	40.45	7
Leadbeater, B ... ©	Aug 14, 1943		1966	1979	144	236	27	5,247	140*	25.10	1	5	1	5.00	80
Leadbeater, E	Aug 15, 1927	Apr 17, 2011	1949	1956	81	94	29	898	91	13.81	0	5,657	201	28.14	49
Leadbeater, F *	Dec 31, 1863	Oct 9, 1928	1884	1890	6	10	2	141	65	17.62	0				4
§ Leaning, J A	Oct 18, 1993		2013	2019	68	108	11	2,955	123	30.46	4	455	8	56.87	52
Leatham, G A B *	Apr 30, 1851	June 19, 1932	1874	1886	12	18	5	61	14	4.69	0				21/7
Leatham, R S *	Aug 17, 1880	Jan 3, 1913	1906	1906	1	2	0	19	14	9.50	0				0
Lee, C	Mar 17, 1924	Sept 4, 1999	1952	1952	2	4	0	98	74	24.50	0				
© Lee, F	Nov 18, 1856	Sept 13, 1896	1882	1890	105	182	10	3,622	165	21.05	3				53/1

312

LIST OF PLAYERS AND CAREER AVERAGES IN ALL FIRST-CLASS MATCHES FOR YORKSHIRE (Continued)

Player	Date of Birth	Date of Death (if known)	First Played	Last Played	M	Inns	NO	Runs	HS	Av'ge	100s	Runs	Wkts	Av'ge	Ct/St
Lee, G H	Aug 24, 1854	Oct 4, 1919	1879	1879	1	2	0	13	9	6.50	0	—	—	—	0
Lee, Herbert	July 2, 1856	Feb 4, 1908	1885	1885	5	6	0	20	12	3.33	0	—	—	—	2
Lee, J E *	Mar 23, 1838	Apr 2, 1880	1867	1867	2	3	0	9	6	3.00	0	—	—	—	2
Lee, J E	Dec 23, 1988		2006	2009	2	3	1	24	21*	12.00	0	—	—	—	1
Leech, D J	**Jan 10, 2001**		**2020**	**2020**	**2**	**2**	**1**	**1**	**1***	**1.00**	**0**	**134**	**4**	**33.50**	**0**
Lees, A Z	Apr 14, 1993		2010	2018	82	140	11	4,528	275*	35.10	11	149	2	74.50	56
Legard, A D *	June 19, 1878	Aug 15, 1939	1910	1910	4	5	0	50	15	10.00	0	—	—	—	1
© § Lehmann, D S	Feb 5, 1970		1997	2006	88	137	8	8,871	339	68.76	26	26	0	—	35
§ Lehmann, J S	Jul 8, 1992		2016	2016	4	8	1	384	116	54.85	1	—	—	—	2
© Lester, E I	Feb 18, 1923	Mar 23, 2015	1945	1956	228	339	27	10,616	186	34.02	24	160	3	53.33	106
Leyland, M	July 20, 1900	Jan 1, 1967	1920	1946	548	720	82	26,180	263	41.03	62	11,079	409	27.08	204
Lilley, A E	Apr 17, 1992		2011	2011	1	1	0	0	0	0.00	0	—	—	—	0
Linaker, L	Apr 8, 1885	Nov 17, 1961	1909	1909	1	2	0	0	0	0.00	0	28	1	28.00	2
Lister, B	Dec 9, 1850	Dec 3, 1919	1874	1878	7	11	1	36	10	3.60	0	34	0	—	2
Lister, J *	May 14, 1930	Jan 28, 1991	1954	1954	2	4	0	35	13	8.75	0	—	—	—	2
© § Lister-Kaye, K A *	Mar 27, 1892	Feb 28, 1955	1928	1928	2	2	1	13	7*	13.00	0	64	1	64.00	2
Lockwood, E	Apr 4, 1845	Dec 19, 1921	1868	1884	214	364	29	7,789	208	23.25	6	2,265	141	16.06	164/2
Lockwood, H	Oct 20, 1855	Feb 18, 1930	1877	1882	16	27	2	408	90	16.32	0	37	0	—	8
Lodge, J T	Apr 16, 1921	July 9, 2002	1948	1948	2	3	0	48	30	16.00	0	17	0	—	0
Logan, J E G	**Oct 12, 1997**		**2018**	**2020**	**3**	**3**	**1**	**33**	**20***	**16.50**	**0**	**85**	**4**	**21.25**	**0**
Loten, T W	**Jan 8, 1999**		**2019**	**2020**	**3**	**3**	**0**	**69**	**58**	**23.00**	**0**	**—**	**—**	**—**	**1**
Love, J D	Apr 22, 1955		1975	1989	247	388	58	10,263	170*	31.10	13	835	12	69.58	123
Love, G E	Jan 12, 1877	Aug 15, 1932	1902	1902	1	1	1	5	5*	—	0	—	—	—	0
Lowe, J R	Oct 19, 1991		2010	2010	1	1	0	5	5	5.00	0	15	0	—	0
Lowson, F A	July 1, 1925	Sept 8, 1984	1949	1958	252	404	31	13,897	259*	37.25	30	—	—	—	180
§ Lucas, D S	Aug 19, 1978		2005	2005	1	1	0	5	5	5.00	0	—	—	—	0
© Lumb, E *	Sept 12, 1852	Apr 5, 1891	1872	1886	14	23	4	311	70*	16.36	0	84	8	10.50	5
© § Lumb, M J	Feb 12, 1980		2000	2006	78	135	12	4,194	144	34.09	8	199	5	39.80	43
© Lumb, R G	Feb 27, 1950		1970	1984	239	395	30	11,525	165*	31.57	22	5	0	—	129
© Lupton, A W *	Feb 23, 1879	Apr 14, 1944	1908	1927	104	79	15	668	43*	10.43	0	88	0	—	25

LIST OF PLAYERS AND CAREER AVERAGES IN ALL FIRST-CLASS MATCHES FOR YORKSHIRE (Continued)

Player	Date of Birth	Date of Death (if known)	First Played	Last Played	M	Inns	NO	Runs	HS	Av'ge	100s	Runs	Wkts	Av'ge	Ct/St
Lynas, G G	Sept 7, 1832	Dec 8, 1896	1867	1867	2	3	1	4	4*	2.00	0				2
§Lyth, A	Sept 25, 1987		2007	2020	166	279	15	10,266	251	38.88	23	1,699	36	47.19	224
Macaulay, G G	Dec 7, 1897	Dec 13, 1940	1920	1935	445	430	112	5,717	125*	17.97	3	30,554	1,774	17.22	361
McGrath, A	Oct 6, 1975		1995	2012	242	405	29	14,091	211	37.47	34	4,652	128	36.34	168
McHugh, F P	Nov 15, 1925		1949	1949	3							147	4	36.75	1
§Maharaj, K A	Feb 7, 1990		2019	2020	5	9	0	239	85	26.55	0				2
§Malan, D J	Sept 3, 1987		2020	2020	3	5	0	332	219	66.40	1	24	2	12.00	2
§Marsh, S E	Jul 9, 1983		2017	2017	3	3	1	225	125*	112.50	1				2
Marshall, A	July 10, 1849	Aug 3, 1891	1874	1874	1	2	0	2	2	1.00	0	11	0		
§Martyn, D R	Oct 21, 1971		2003	2003	1	2	0	342	238	171.00	1				3
Mason, A	May 2, 1921	Mar 22, 2006	1947	1950	18	19	3	105	16	6.56	0	1,473	51	28.88	6
Maude, E *	Dec 31, 1839	July 2, 1876	1866	1866	4	2	0	17		8.50	0				
Maxwell, G J	Oct 14, 1988		2015	2015	4	7	1	244	140	40.66	1	144	4	36.00	
Metcalfe, A A	Dec 25, 1963		1983	1995	184	317	19	10,465	216*	35.11	25	344	3	114.66	72
Micklethwait, W H *	Dec 13, 1885	Oct 7, 1947	1911	1911	1	1	0	44	44	44.00	0				1
Middlebrook, J D	May 13, 1977		1998	2015	29	38	3	534	84	15.25	0	1,899	66	28.77	17
Middlebrook, W	May 23, 1858	Apr 26, 1919	1888	1889	17	27	7	88	19*	4.40	0	895	50	17.90	3
Midgley, C A *	Nov 13, 1877	June 24, 1942	1906	1906	4	6	2	115	59*	28.75	0	149	8	18.62	0
Milburn, S M	Sept 29, 1972		1992	1995	6	8	2	22	22	3.66	0	431	14	30.78	
§Milligan, F W *	Mar 19, 1870	Mar 31, 1900	1894	1898	81	113	10	1,879	189	18.24	1	2,736	112	24.42	40
Mitchell, A	Sept 13, 1902	Dec 25, 1976	1922	1945	401	550	69	18,189	179	37.81	39	291	5	58.20	406
Mitchell, F *	Aug 13, 1872	Oct 11, 1935	1894	1904	83	125	5	4,104	194	34.20	10	16	1	16.00	52
Monks, G D	Sept 3, 1929	Jan 3, 2011	1952	1952	1	1	0			3.00					0
Moorhouse, R	Sept 7, 1866	Jan 7, 1921	1888	1899	206	315	45	5,217	113	19.32	3	1,232	43	28.65	92
§Morkel, M	Oct 6, 1984		2008	2008	1	2	0	8	8	4.00	0	33	1	33.00	0
Morris, A C	Oct 4, 1976		1995	1997	16	23	2	362	60	17.23	0	508	9	56.44	12
Mosley, H	Mar 8, 1850	Nov 29, 1933	1881	1881	2	4	0	1	1	0.25	0	34	3	11.33	1
Motley, A *	Feb 5, 1858	Sept 28, 1897	1879	1879	2	2	1	10	8*	10.00	0	135	7	19.28	1
Mounsey, J T	Aug 30, 1871	Apr 6, 1949	1891	1897	92	145	21	1,939	64	15.63	0	444	10	44.40	45

LIST OF PLAYERS AND CAREER AVERAGES IN ALL FIRST-CLASS MATCHES FOR YORKSHIRE (Continued)

Player	Date of Birth	Date of Death (if known)	First Played	Last Played	M	Inns	NO	Runs	HS	Av'ge	100s	Runs	Wkts	Av'ge	Ct/St
Moxon, M D	May 4, 1960		1981	1997	277	476	42	18,973	274*	43.71	41	1,213	22	55.13	190
Myers, H	Jan 2, 1875	June 12, 1944	1901	1910	201	289	46	4,450	91	18.31	0	7,095	282	25.15	106
Myers, M	Apr 12, 1847	Dec 8, 1919	1876	1878	22	40	4	537	49	14.91	0	20			11
§ Naved-ul-Hasan, Rana	Feb 28, 1978		2008	2009	11	16	3	207	32	15.92	0	1,018	26	39.15	3
Naylor, J E	Dec 11, 1930	June 27, 1996	1953	1953	1	1						88	0		1
Newstead, J T	Sept 8, 1877	Mar 25, 1952	1903	1913	96	128	17	1,791	100*	16.13	1	5,555	297	18.70	75
Nicholson, A G	June 25, 1938	Nov 3, 1985	1962	1975	282	267	125	1,667	50	11.73	0	17,296	876	19.74	85
Nicholson, N G	Oct 17, 1963		1988	1989	5	8	3	134	56*	26.80	0	25	0		5
Oates, William	Jan 1, 1852	Dec 9, 1940	1874	1875	7	13	7	34	14*	5.66	0				5/1
Oates, W F	June 11, 1929	May 15, 2001	1956	1956	3	3	0	20	9	6.66	0				0
Old, C M	Dec 22, 1948		1966	1982	222	262	56	4,785	116	23.22	0	13,409	647	20.72	131
Oldham, S	July 26, 1948		1974	1985	59	39	18	212	50	10.09	0	3,849	130	29.60	18
Oldroyd, E	Oct 1, 1888	Dec 27, 1964	1910	1931	383	509	58	15,891	194	35.23	37	1,658	42	39.47	203
§ Olivier, D	May 9, 1992		2019	2020	18	21	12	163	24	18.11	0	1,822	57	31.96	6
Oyston, C	May 12, 1869	July 15, 1942	1900	1909	15	21	8	96	22	7.38	0	872	31	28.12	3
Padgett, D E V	July 20, 1934		1951	1971	487	774	63	20,306	161*	28.55	29	208	6	34.66	250
Padgett, G H	Oct 9, 1931		1952	1952	6	7	4	56	32*	18.66	0	336	4	84.00	5
Padgett, J	Nov 21, 1860	Aug 2, 1943	1882	1889	6	9	0	92	22	10.22	0				2
Parker, B	June 23, 1970		1992	1998	44	71	10	1,839	138*	30.14	2	3	0		19
§ Parkin, C H	Feb 18, 1886	June 15, 1943	1906	1906	1	1	0	1	1	0.00	0	25	0		0
§ Parratt, J	Mar 24, 1859	May 6, 1905	1888	1890	2	2	0	11	11	5.50	0	75	1	75.00	4
§ Parton, J W	Jan 31, 1863	Jan. 30, 1906	1889	1889	2	2	0	16	14	8.00	0	4	1	4.00	0
§ Patel, A Y	Oct 21, 1988		2019	2019	2	2	1	20	20	20.00	0	231	2	115.50	0
Patterson, S A	Oct 3, 1983		2005	2020	159	190	43	2,377	63*	16.17	0	11,651	420	27.74	34
Pearson, H E	Aug 7, 1851	July 8, 1903	1878	1880	4	7	5	31	10*	15.50	0	90	5	18.00	1
Pearson, J H	May 14, 1915	May 13, 2007	1934	1936	3	3	0	54	44	18.00	0				0
Peate, E	Mar 2, 1855	Mar 11, 1900	1879	1887	154	226	61	1,793	95	10.86	0	9,986	794	12.57	97
Peel, R	Feb 12, 1857	Aug 12, 1941	1882	1897	318	510	42	9,322	210*	19.91	6	20,638	1,311	15.74	141
Penny, J H	Sept 29, 1856	July 29, 1902	1891	1891	1	1	0	8	8*		0	31	2	15.50	1

LIST OF PLAYERS AND CAREER AVERAGES IN ALL FIRST-CLASS MATCHES FOR YORKSHIRE (Continued)

Player	Date of Birth	Date of Death (if known)	First Played	Last Played	M	Inns	NO	Runs	HS	Av'ge	100s	Runs	Wkts	Av'ge	Ct/St
Pickles, C S	Jan 30, 1966		1985	1992	58	76	21	1,336	66	24.29	0	3,638	83	43.83	24
Pickles D	Nov 16, 1935	June 22, 2020	1957	1960	41	40	20	74	12	3.70	0	2,062	96	21.47	10
§ Pillans, M W	Jul 4, 1991		2018	2019	2	2	0	11	8	5.50	0	189	2	94.50	0
Pinder, G	July 15, 1841	Jan 15, 1903	1867	1880	125	199	44	1,639	57	10.57	0	325	19	17.10	145/102
Platt, R K	© Dec 26, 1932		1955	1963	96	103	47	405	57*	7.23	0	6,389	282	22.65	35
Plunkett, L E	Apr 6, 1985		2013	2017	36	51	7	1,241	126	28.20	1	2,925	98	29.84	20
Pollard, D	Aug 7, 1835	Mar 26, 1909	1865	1865	1	2	1	3	3	1.50	0	19	0	—	0
Pollitt, G	June 3, 1874	May 19, 1942	1899	1899	1	2	0	51	51	51.00	0	—	—	—	0
§ Poysden, J E	Aug 8, 1991		2018	2018	3	5	2	25	20*	8.33	0	259	7	37.00	0
Prest, C H *	Dec 9, 1841	Mar 4, 1875	1864	1864	2	4	0	57	31	14.25	0	—	—	—	3
Preston, J M	Aug 23, 1864	Nov 26, 1890	1885	1889	79	134	11	1,935	93	15.73	0	3,232	178	18.15	36
Pride, T	July 23, 1864	Feb 16, 1919	1887	1887	1	1	0	1	1	1.00	0	—	—	—	4/3
Priestley, I M	Sept 25, 1967		1989	1989	2	4	2	25	23	12.50	0	119	4	29.75	1
Pullan, P	Mar 29, 1857	Mar 3, 1901	1884	1884	1	1	0	14	14	14.00	0	5	0	—	1
Pujara, C A	© Jan 25, 1988		2015	2018	10	18	1	436	133*	25.64	1	5	0	—	6
Pyrah, R M	© Nov 1, 1982		2004	2015	51	61	8	1,621	134*	30.58	3	2527	55	45.94	22
§ Radcliffe, E J R H *	Jan 27, 1884	Nov 23, 1969	1909	1911	64	89	13	826	54	10.86	0	134	2	67.00	21
Ramage, A	Nov 29, 1957		1979	1983	23	22	9	219	52	16.84	0	1,649	44	37.47	4
Ramsden, G	Mar 2, 1983		2000	2000	1	1	1	0	0*	—	0	68	1	68.00	0
Randhawa, G S	Jan 25, 1992		2011	2011	2	1	0	5	5	5.00	0	62	2	31.00	0
Raper, J R S *	Aug 9, 1909	Mar 9, 1997	1936	1947	3	4	0	24	15	6.00	0	—	—	—	2
Rashid, A U *	© **Feb 17, 1988**		**2006**	**2017**	**140**	**196**	**33**	**5,620**	**180**	**34.47**	**10**	**14,136**	**420**	**33.65**	**70**
§ Raval, J A	© May 22, 1988		2018	2018	4	7	0	84	20	12.00	0	498	21	23.71	3
Rawlin, E R	Oct 14, 1897	Jan 11, 1943	1927	1936	8	10	1	72	35	8.00	0	258	11	23.45	2
Rawlin, J T	Nov 10, 1856	Jan 19, 1924	1880	1885	27	36	2	274	31	8.05	0	62	5	12.40	13
Rawlinson, E B	Apr 10, 1867	Feb 17, 1892	1867	1875	37	68	5	991	55	15.73	0	—	—	—	16
Read, J	Feb 2, 1998		2016	2016	1	1	0	14	14	14.00	0	—	—	—	4
Redfearn, J	May 13, 1862	Jan 14, 1931	1890	1890	1	1	0	5	5	5.00	0	—	—	—	0
Render, G W A	Jan 5, 1887	Sept 17, 1922	1919	1919	1	1	0	5	5	5.00	0	—	—	—	0
Revis, M L *	© **Nov 15, 2001**		**2019**	**2019**	**1**	**2**	**0**	**9**	**8**	**4.50**	**0**	—	—	—	**1**

LIST OF PLAYERS AND CAREER AVERAGES IN ALL FIRST-CLASS MATCHES FOR YORKSHIRE (Continued)

Player	Date of Birth	Date of Death (if known)	First Played	Last Played	M	Inns	NO	Runs	HS	Av'ge	100s	Runs	Wkts	Av'ge	Ct/St
Rhodes, A C ©	Oct 14, 1906	May 21, 1957	1932	1934	61	70	19	917	64*	17.98	0	3,026	107	28.28	45
§ Rhodes, H E *	Jan 11, 1852	Sept 10, 1889	1878	1883	10	16	1	269	64	17.93	0	—	—	—	1
Rhodes, S J	June 19, 1964		1981	1984	3	3	2	41	35	41.00	0	—	—	—	3
Rhodes, Wilfred ©	Oct 29, 1877	July 8, 1973	1898	1930	883	1,195	162	31,075	267*	30.08	46	57,634	3,598	16.01	586
Rhodes, W M H	Mar 4, 1883	Aug 5, 1941	1911	1911	1	1		40	1*	—	0	—	—	—	0
§ Rhodes, W M H	Mar 2, 1995		2015	2016	15	25	2	689	95	29.95	0	551	16	34.43	8
Richardson, J A *	Aug 4, 1908	Apr 2, 1985	1936	1947	7	12	2	308	61	30.80	0	90	2	45.00	3
§ Richardson, R B ©	Jan 12, 1962		1993	1994	23	39	1	1,310	112	34.47	1	23	1	23.00	18
§ Richardson, S A	Sept 5, 1977		2000	2003	13	23	2	377	69	17.95	0	—	—	—	11
Riley, H	Aug 17, 1875	Nov 6, 1922	1895	1900	4	5	1	36	25*	9.00	0	54	1	54.00	1
Riley, W *	Apr 5, 1851	June 1, 1899	1878	1882	17	28	1	361	92	13.37	0	10	0	—	3
Ringrose, W ©	Sept 2, 1871	Sept 14, 1943	1901	1906	57	66	9	353	23	6.19	0	3,224	155	20.80	25
Robinson, A L	Aug 17, 1946		1971	1977	84	69	31	365	30*	9.60	0	4,927	196	25.13	48
Robinson, B L H	May 12, 1858	Dec 14, 1909	1879	1879	1	2		5	4	2.50	0	—	—	—	0
Robinson, Edward *	Dec 27, 1862	Sept 3, 1942	1887	1887	1	2	1	23	23*	23.00	0	20	1	20.00	0
© Robinson, Emmott	Nov 16, 1883	Nov 17, 1969	1919	1931	413	455	77	9,651	135*	25.53	7	19,645	893	21.99	318
Robinson, E P ©	Aug 10, 1911	Nov 10, 1998	1934	1949	208	253	46	2,596	75*	12.54	0	15,141	735	20.60	189
Robinson, M A ©	Nov 23, 1966		1991	1995	90	93	36	240	23	4.21	0	6,866	218	31.49	17
Robinson, P E ©	Aug 3, 1963		1984	1991	132	217	31	6,668	189	35.84	7	238	1	238.00	96
Robinson, W	Nov 29, 1851	Aug 14, 1919	1876	1877	7	14	1	151	68	11.61	0	—	—	—	3
Roebuck C G ©	Aug 14, 1991		2010	2010	1	1	0	23	23	23.00	0	—	—	—	0
Root, J E ©	**Dec 30, 1990**		**2010**	**2019**	**47**	**78**	**9**	**3,119**	**236**	**45.20**	**7**	**827**	**17**	**48.64**	**28**
Roper, E *	Apr 8, 1851	Apr 27, 1921	1878	1880	5	7	1	85	68	14.16	0	—	—	—	2
Rothery, J W ©	Sept 5, 1876	June 2, 1919	1903	1910	150	236	8	4,614	161	21.16	3	44	2	22.00	45
Rowbotham, J	July 8, 1831	Dec 22, 1899	1863	1876	94	162	9	2,624	113	17.15	0	37	3	12.33	52
§ Rudolph J A ©	May 4, 1981		2007	2011	68	112	8	5,429	228*	52.20	18	311	1	311.00	79
Rudston, H	Nov 22, 1878	Apr 14, 1962	1902	1907	21	30	0	609	164	20.30	1	—	—	—	3
Ryan, M ©	June 23, 1933	Nov 16, 2015	1954	1965	150	149	58	682	26*	7.49	0	9,466	413	22.92	59
Ryder, L	Aug 28, 1900	Jan 24, 1955	1924	1924	2	2	1	1	1	1.00	0	151	4	37.75	2

Player	Date of Birth	Date of Death (if known)	First Played	Last Played	M	Inns	NO	Runs	HS	Av'ge	100s	Runs	Wkts	Av'ge	Ct/St
Sanderson B W	Jan 3, 1989		2008	2010	3	2	1	6	6	6.00	0	190	6	31.66	2
Savile, G *	Apr 26, 1847	Sept 4, 1904	1867	1874	5	7	2	140	65	20.00	0				2
Sayers, J J	Nov 5, 1983		2004	2013	97	161	13	4,855	187	32.80	9	166	6	27.66	60
Schofield, C J	Mar 21, 1976		1996	1996	1	1	0	25	25	25.00	0				0
Schofield, D	Oct 9, 1947		1970	1974	3	4	4	13	6*		0	112	5	22.40	1
Scott, E	July 6, 1834	Dec 3, 1898	1864	1864	1	1	0	8	8	8.00	0	27	2	13.50	1
Sedgwick, H A	Apr 8, 1883	Dec 28, 1957	1906	1906	3	5	2	53	34	17.66	0	327	16	20.43	2
Sellers, Arthur *	May 31, 1870	Sept 25, 1941	1890	1899	49	88	1	1,643	105	18.88	2	84	2	42.00	40
Sellers, A B *	Mar 5, 1907	Feb 20, 1981	1932	1948	334	437	51	8,949	204	23.18	4	653	8	81.62	264
Shackleton, W A	Mar 9, 1908	Nov 16, 1971	1928	1934	5	6	0	49	25	8.16	0	130	6	21.66	3
Shahzad, Ajmal	July 27, 1985		2006	2012	45	58	14	1,145	88	26.02	0	4,196	125	33.56	5
Sharp, K	Apr. 6, 1959		1976	1990	195	320	35	8,426	181	29.56	11	836	12	69.66	95
§ Sharpe, C M *	Sept 6, 1851	June 25, 1935	1875	1875	1	1	0	15	15	15.00	0	17	0	—	0
Sharpe, P J	Dec 27, 1936	May 19, 2014	1958	1974	411	666	71	17,685	203*	29.72	23	140	2	70.00	526
Shaw C	Feb 17, 1964		1984	1988	61	58	27	340	31	10.96	0	4,101	123	33.34	9
Shaw, James	Mar 12, 1865	Jan 22, 1921	1896	1897	3	3	0	8	7	2.66	0	181	7	25.85	2
Shaw, Joshua	Jan 3, 1996		2016	2019	8	11	2	144	42	16.00	0	617	12	51.41	1
Sheepshanks, E R *	Mar 22, 1910	Dec 31, 1937	1929	1929	1	1	0	26	26	26.00	0				0
Shepherd, D A *	Mar 10, 1916	May 29, 1998	1938	1938	1	1	1	0	0	0.00	0				0
Shotton, W	Dec 1, 1840	May 26, 1909	1865	1874	2	4	0	13	7	3.25	0				0
Shutt, J W	**June 24, 1997**		**2020**	**2020**	**3**	**4**	**3**	**7**	**7***	**7.00**	**0**	**104**	**2**	**52.00**	**2**
Sidebottom, A	Apr 1, 1954		1973	1991	216	249	50	4,243	124	22.33	1	13,852	558	24.82	60
Sidebottom, R J	Jan 15, 1978		1997	2017	137	172	55	1,674	61	14.30	0	10,128	450	22.50	37
Sidgwick, R *	Aug 7, 1851	Oct 23, 1933	1882	1882	9	13	0	64	17	4.92	0				7
Silverwood, C E W *	Mar 5, 1975		1993	2005	131	179	33	2,369	80	16.22	0	11,413	427	27.62	30
Silvester, S	Mar 12, 1951		1976	1977	6	7	4	30	14	10.00	0	313	12	26.08	2
Simpson, E T B *	Mar 20, 1867	Mar 20, 1944	1889	1889	1	2	0	1	1	0.50	0				0
§ Sims, Rev H M *	Mar 15, 1853	Oct 5, 1885	1875	1877	5	10	1	109	35*	12.11	0				2
Slinn, W	Dec 13, 1826	June 17, 1888	1863	1864	9	14	3	22	11	2.00	0	742	48	15.45	5

318

LIST OF PLAYERS AND CAREER AVERAGES IN ALL FIRST-CLASS MATCHES FOR YORKSHIRE (Continued)

Player	Date of Birth	Date of Death (if known)	First Played	Last Played	M	Inns	NO	Runs	HS	Av'ge	100s	Runs	Wkts	Av'ge	Ct/St
Smales, T F ©	Mar 27, 1910	Dec 1, 1970	1932	1948	262	339	42	5,686	117	19.14	3	16,593	802	20.68	153
Smales, K	Sept 15, 1927	Mar 10, 2015	1948	1950	13	19	3	165	45	10.31	0	766	22	34.81	4
Smith, A F	Mar 7, 1847	Jan 6, 1915	1868	1874	28	49	4	692	89	15.37	0	—	—	—	11
Smith, E (Morley) * ©	Oct 19, 1869	April 9, 1945	1888	1907	154	234	18	4,453	129	20.61	2	6,278	248	25.31	112
Smith, E (Barnsley)	July 11, 1888	Jan 2, 1972	1914	1926	16	21	5	169	49	10.56	0	1,090	46	23.69	5
Smith, Fred (Yeadon)	Dec 18, 1879	Oct 20, 1905	1903	1903	13	19	1	292	55	16.22	0	—	—	—	3
Smith, Fred (Idle)	Dec 26, 1885	Not known	1911	1911	1	1	0	11	11	11.00	0	45	2	22.50	0
Smith, G	Jan 19, 1875	Jan 16, 1929	1901	1906	2	1	0	7	7	7.00	0	62	—	—	3
Smith, J	Mar 23, 1833	Feb 12, 1909	1865	1865	2	3	0	28	16	9.33	0	72	6	12.00	3
Smith, N	Apr 1, 1949		1970	1971	8	11	5	82	20	13.66	0	—	—	—	14/3
Smith, R	Apr 6, 1944	Mar 4, 2003	1969	1970	5	8	3	99	37*	19.80	0	—	—	—	0
Smith, Walter	Aug 19, 1845	June 2, 1926	1874	1874	5	9	0	152	59	16.88	0	—	—	—	3
§ Smith, William	Nov 1, 1839	Apr 19, 1897	1865	1874	11	19	3	260	90	16.25	0	—	—	—	8
Smithson, G A ©	Nov 1, 1926	Sept 6, 1970	1946	1950	39	60	5	1,449	169	26.34	2	84	1	84.00	21
Smurthwaite, J	Oct 17, 1916	Oct 20, 1989	1938	1939	7	9	5	29	20*	7.25	0	237	12	19.75	4
Sowden, A	Dec 1, 1853	July 5, 1921	1878	1887	8	11	0	137	37	12.45	0	22	0	—	4
Squire, D	Dec 31, 1864	Apr 28, 1922	1893	1893	1	2	0	0	0	0.00	0	25	0	—	0
Squires, P J	Aug 4, 1951		1972	1976	49	84	8	1,271	70	16.72	0	32	0	—	14
Stanley, H C *	Feb 16, 1888	May 18, 1934	1911	1913	8	13	0	155	42	11.92	0	—	—	—	6
§ Stanyforth, R T *	May 30, 1892	Feb 20, 1964	1928	1928	3	3	0	26	10	8.66	0	—	—	—	2
§ Starc, M A	Jan 30, 1990		2012	2012	2	1	1	28	28*	—	0	—	—	—	2
Stead, B	June 21, 1939	Apr 15, 1980	1959	1959	2	3	0	8	8	2.66	0	153	7	21.85	0
§ Stemp, R D ©	Dec 11, 1967		1993	1998	104	135	36	1,267	65	12.79	0	115	7	16.42	49
Stephenson, J	June 5, 1832	July 5, 1898	1863	1873	36	61	2	803	67	14.33	0	8,557	241	35.50	30/27
Stephenson, J S *	Nov 10, 1903	Oct 7, 1975	1923	1926	16	19	2	182	60	10.70	0	65	0	—	6
Stevenson, G B ©	Dec 16, 1955		1973	1986	177	217	32	3,856	115*	20.84	2	13,254	464	28.56	73
Stott, W B	July 18, 1934		1952	1963	187	309	19	9,168	186	31.61	17	112	7	16.00	91
Stringer, P M	Feb 23, 1943		1967	1969	19	17	8	101	15*	11.22	0	696	32	21.75	7
Stuchbury, S	June 22, 1954		1978	1981	3	3	2	7	4*	7.00	0	236	8	29.50	0

Player	Date of Birth	Date of Death (if known)	First Played	Last Played	M	Inns	NO	Runs	HS	Av'ge	100s	Runs	Wkts	Av'ge	Ct/St
§ Sugg, F H	Jan 11, 1862	May 29, 1933	1883	1883	8	12	4	80	13*	10.00	0	—	—	—	4/1
§ Sugg, W	May 21, 1860	May 21, 1933	1881	1881	1	1	0	9	9	9.00	0	—	—	—	—
Sullivan, J H B *	Sept 21, 1890	Feb 8, 1932	1912	1912	1	2	0	41	26	20.50	0	43	—	—	—
Sutcliffe, H ©	Nov 24, 1894	Jan 22, 1978	1919	1945	602	864	96	38,558	313	50.20	112	381	8	47.62	402
Sutcliffe, W H H *	Oct 10, 1926	Sept 16, 1998	1948	1957	177	273	34	6,247	181	26.13	6	152	6	25.33	80
Swallow, I G	Dec 18, 1962		1983	1989	61	82	18	1,296	114	20.25	0	3,270	64	51.09	28
§ Swanepoel, P J	Mar 30, 1977		2003	2003	2	3	0	20	17	6.66	0	129	3	43.00	1
§ Tait, T	Jan 7, 1872	Sept 6, 1954	1898	1899	2	3	1	7	3	3.50	0	—	—	—	—
Tasker, J *	Feb 4, 1887	Aug 24, 1975	1912	1913	31	43	4	586	67	15.02	0	—	—	—	14
Tattersall, G * ©	Apr 21, 1882	June 29, 1972	1905	1905	1	2	0	26	26	13.00	0	—	—	—	—
Tattersall, J A	**Dec 15, 1994**		**2018**	**2020**	**27**	**41**	**4**	**1,273**	**135***	**34.40**	**1**	—	—	—	**64/4**
Taylor, C R	Feb 21, 1981		2001	2008	16	27	0	416	52*	17.33	0	—	—	—	8
Taylor, H	Dec 18, 1900	Oct 28, 1988	1924	1925	13	13	0	153	36	11.76	0	—	—	—	1
Taylor, H S	Dec 11, 1856	Nov 16, 1896	1879	1879	3	5	0	36	22	7.20	0	—	—	—	0
Taylor, J	Apr 2, 1850	May 27, 1924	1880	1881	9	13	1	107	44	8.91	0	—	—	—	4
Taylor, K	Aug 21, 1935		1953	1968	303	505	35	12,864	203*	27.37	16	3,680	129	28.52	146
Taylor, N S	June 2, 1963		1982	1983	8	6	4	4	2*	2.00	0	720	22	32.72	2
Taylor, T L * ©	May 25, 1878	Mar. 16, 1960	1899	1906	82	122	10	3,933	156	35.11	8	—	—	—	47/2
§ Tendulkar, S R ©	Apr 24, 1973		1992	1992	16	25	2	1,070	100	46.52	1	195	4	48.75	10
Thewlis, H	Aug 31, 1865	Nov 30, 1920	1888	1888	2	4	0	4	2*	1.33	0	—	—	—	2
Thewlis, John Sen.	Mar 11, 1828	Dec 29, 1899	1863	1875	44	80	3	1,280	108	16.62	0	—	—	—	21/1
Thewlis, John Jun.	Sept 21, 1850	Aug 9, 1901	1879	1879	3	4	0	21	10	5.25	0	—	—	—	—
Thompson, J A	**Oct 9, 1996**		**2019**	**2020**	**7**	**9**	**1**	**270**	**98**	**33.75**	**0**	**351**	**20**	**17.55**	**2**
Thormcroft, N D	Jan 23, 1985		2002	2007	7	10	4	50	30	8.33	0	545	16	34.06	2
Thornton, A	July 20, 1854	Apr 18, 1915	1881	1881	3	4	0	21	7	5.25	0	—	—	—	2
Thornton, G *	Dec 24, 1867	Jan 31, 1939	1891	1891	3	4	0	21	16	5.25	0	74	2	37.00	2
Thorpe, G	Feb 20, 1834	Mar 2, 1899	1864	1864	1	2	1	14	9*	14.00	0	—	—	—	0
Threapleton, J W	July 30, 1857	July 10, 1918	1881	1881	1	1	0	8	8*		0	—	—	—	2/1
Tinsley, H J	Feb 20, 1865	Dec 10, 1938	1890	1891	9	13	0	56	15	4.30	0	57	4	14.25	1

LIST OF PLAYERS AND CAREER AVERAGES IN ALL FIRST-CLASS MATCHES FOR YORKSHIRE (Continued)

Player	Date of Birth	Date of Death (if known)	First Played	Last Played	M	Inns	NO	Runs	HS	Av'ge	100s	Runs	Wkts	Av'ge	Ct/St
Townsley, R A J	June 24, 1952		1974	1975	2	4	0	22	12	5.50	0	0	—	—	1
Towse, A D	Apr 22, 1968		1988	1988	1	1	0	1	1	1.00	0	50	3	16.66	1
Trueman, F S	Feb 6, 1931	© July 1, 2006	1949	1968	459	533	81	6,852	104	15.15	2	29,890	1,745	17.12	325
Tunnicliffe, J	Aug 26, 1866	© July 11, 1948	1891	1907	472	768	57	19,435	243	27.33	22	388	7	55.42	665
Turner, A	Sept 2, 1885		1910	1911	9	16	1	163	37	10.86	0	—	—	—	7
Turner, B	July 25, 1938	Dec 27, 2015	1960	1961	2	4	2	7	3*	3.50	0	47	4	11.75	2
Turner, C	Jan 11, 1902	Nov 19, 1968	1925	1946	200	266	32	6,132	130	26.20	2	5,320	173	30.75	181
Turner, F I	Sept 3, 1894	Oct 18, 1954	1924	1924	5	7	0	33	12	4.71	0	—	—	—	2
Tyson, C T	Jan 24, 1889	Apr 3, 1940	1921	1921	5	5	2	232	100*	77.33	1	—	—	—	1
Ullathorne, C E	Apr 11, 1845	May 2, 1904	1868	1875	27	46	8	283	28	7.44	0	—	—	—	19
Ulyett, G	Oct 21, 1851	June 18, 1898	1873	1893	355	618	31	14,157	199*	24.11	15	8,181	457	17.90	235
§ Usher, J	Feb 26, 1859	Aug 9, 1905	1888	1888	1	2	0		5	3.50	—	31	2	15.50	1
van Geloven, J	Jan 4, 1934	© Aug 21, 2003	1955	1955	3	2	1	17	16	17.00	0	224	6	37.33	2
§ Vaughan, M P	© Oct 29, 1974		1993	2009	151	267	14	9,160	183	36.20	20	4,268	92	46.39	55
§ Verelst, H W *	July 2, 1846	Apr 5, 1918	1868	1869	3	4	1	66	33*	22.00	0	—	—	—	1
Verity, H	May 18, 1905	July 31, 1943	1930	1939	278	294	77	3,898	101	17.96	1	21,353	1,558	13.70	191
Waddington, A	Feb 4, 1893	© Oct 28, 1959	1919	1927	255	250	65	2,396	114	12.95	1	16,203	835	19.40	222
Wade, S	Feb 8, 1858	© Nov 5, 1931	1886	1890	65	111	20	1,438	74*	15.80	0	2,498	133	18.78	31
Wainwright, D J	Mar 21, 1985		2004	2011	29	36	11	914	104*	36.56	2	2,480	69	35.94	6
Wainwright, E	Apr 8, 1865	© Oct 28, 1919	1888	1902	352	545	36	11,092	228	21.53	18	17,744	998	17.77	327
Wainwright, W	Jan 21, 1882	Dec 31, 1961	1903	1905	24	36	3	648	62	19.63	0	582	19	30.63	21
Waite, M J	**Dec 24, 1995**		**2017**	**2019**	**8**	**11**	**1**	**160**	**42**	**16.00**	**0**	**583**	**23**	**25.34**	**1**
Wake, W R *	May 21, 1852	Mar 14, 1896	1881	1881	3	3	0	13	11	4.33	0	—	—	—	2
Walker, A *	June 22, 1844	May 26, 1927	1863	1870	9	16	1	138	26	9.20	0	74	1	74.00	3
Walker, C	June 27, 1919	Dec 3, 1992	1947	1948	5	9	2	268	91	38.28	0	71	2	35.50	3
Walker, T	Apr 3, 1854	Aug 28, 1925	1879	1880	14	22	2	179	30	8.95	0	7	0	—	1
Waller, G	Dec 3, 1864	Dec 11, 1937	1893	1894	3	4	0	17	13	4.25	0	70	4	17.50	1

LIST OF PLAYERS AND CAREER AVERAGES IN ALL FIRST-CLASS MATCHES FOR YORKSHIRE (Continued)

Player	Date of Birth	Date of Death (if known)	First Played	Last Played	M	Inns	NO	Runs	HS	Av'ge	100s	Runs	Wkts	Av'ge	Ct/St
Wallgate, L *	Nov 12, 1849	May 9, 1887	1875	1878	3	3	0	9	6	3.00	0	17	1	17.00	3
Ward, A	Nov 21, 1865	Jan 6, 1939	1886	1886	4	7	1	41	22	6.83	0	—	0	—	1
Ward, F	Aug 31, 1881	Feb 28, 1948	1903	1903	1	1	0	0	0	0.00	0	16	0	—	1
Ward, H P *	Jan 20, 1899	Dec 16, 1946	1920	1920	1	1	1	10	10*	—	0	—	—	—	1
Wardall, T A ...©	Apr 19, 1862	Dec 20, 1932	1884	1894	43	73	2	1,003	106	14.12	2	489	23	21.26	25
Wardlaw, I	Jun 29, 1985		2011	2012	4	3	2	31	17*	31.00	0	368	4	92.00	2
Wardle, J H ...©	Jan 8, 1923	July 23, 1985	1946	1958	330	418	57	5,765	79	15.96	0	27,917	1,539	18.13	210
Waring, J S	Oct 1, 1942		1963	1966	28	27	15	137	26	11.41	0	1,122	53	21.16	17
Waring, S ...*	Nov 4, 1838	Apr 17, 1919	1870	1870	1	1	0	9	4	9.00	0	—	—	—	0
Warner, J D ...©	Nov 14, 1996		2020	2020	1	1	0	4	4	4.00	0	23	1	23.00	0
Washington, W A 1 ...©	Dec 11, 1879	Oct 20, 1927	1900	1902	44	62	6	1,290	100*	23.03	1	—	—	—	18
Watson, H	Sept 26, 1880	Nov 24, 1951	1908	1914	29	35	11	141	41	5.87	0	—	—	—	46/10
Watson, W ...©	Mar 7, 1920	Apr 24, 2004	1939	1957	283	430	65	13,953	214*	38.22	26	75	0	—	170
Waud, B W *	June 4, 1837	May 31, 1889	1863	1864	6	10	1	165	42	18.33	0	—	—	—	2
Webster, C	June 9, 1838	Jan 6, 1881	1868	1868	3	5	1	30	10	7.50	0	—	—	—	1
Webster, H H	May 8, 1844	Mar 5, 1915	1868	1868	2	3	0	10	10	3.33	0	—	—	—	0
§ Weekes, L C	July 19, 1971		1994	2000	2	2	0	20	10	10.00	0	191	10	19.10	0
West, J	Oct 16, 1844	Jan 27, 1890	1868	1876	38	64	13	461	41	9.03	0	853	53	16.09	14
Wharf, A G	June 4, 1975		1994	1997	7	9	1	186	62	23.25	0	454	11	41.27	2
Whatmough, F J	Dec 4, 1856	June 3, 1904	1878	1882	7	11	1	51	20	5.10	0	111	5	22.20	4
Wheater, C H *	Mar 4, 1860	May 11, 1885	1880	1880	2	4	1	45	27	15.00	0	—	—	—	3
White, Sir A W * ...©	Oct 14, 1877	Dec 16, 1945	1908	1920	97	128	28	1,457	55	14.57	0	7	0	—	50
White, C	Dec 16, 1969		1990	2007	221	350	45	10,376	186	34.01	19	7,649	276	27.71	140
Whitehead, J P	Sept 3, 1925	Aug 15, 2000	1946	1951	37	38	17	387	58*	18.42	0	2,610	96	27.47	11
Whitehead, Lees ...©	Mar 14, 1864	Nov 22, 1913	1889	1904	119	172	38	2,073	67*	15.47	0	2,408	99	24.32	68
Whiteley, Luther	June 25, 1869	Jan 17, 1931	1893	1893	2	4	0	21	13	5.25	0	—	—	—	0
Whiteley, J P	Feb 28, 1955		1978	1982	45	38	17	231	20	11.00	0	2,410	70	34.42	21
Whiting, C P	Apr 18, 1888	Jan 14, 1959	1914	1920	6	10	2	92	26	11.50	0	416	15	27.73	2

LIST OF PLAYERS AND CAREER AVERAGES IN ALL FIRST-CLASS MATCHES FOR YORKSHIRE (*Continued*)

Player	Date of Birth	Date of Death (if known)	First Played	Last Played	M	Inns	NO	Runs	HS	Av'ge	100s	Runs	Wkts	Av'ge	Ct/St
Whitwell, J F *	Feb 22, 1869	Nov 6, 1932	1890	1890	1	2	0	8	4	4.00	0	11	1	11.00	0
§ Whitwell, W F *	Dec 12, 1867	Apr 12, 1942	1890	1890	10	14	2	67	26	5.58	0	518	25	20.72	2
Widdup, S	Nov 10, 1977		2000	2001	11	18	1	245	44	14.41	0	22	1	22.00	5
Wigley, D H	Oct 26, 1981		2002	2002	5	2	1	19	15	19.00	0	116	1	116.00	0
§ Wilkinson, A J A *	May 28, 1835	Dec 11, 1905	1865	1868	5	6	0	129	53	21.50	0	57	0	—	1
Wilkinson, F	Mar 23, 1914	Mar 26, 1984	1937	1939	14	14	1	73	18*	5.61	0	590	26	22.69	12
Wilkinson, H *	Dec 11, 1877	Apr 15, 1967	1903	1905	48	75	3	1,382	113	19.19	1	121	3	40.33	19
Wilkinson, R	Nov 11, 1977		1998	1998	1	1	0	9	9	9.00	0	35	1	35.00	0
© Wilkinson, W H	Mar 12, 1881	June 4, 1961	1903	1910	126	192	14	3,812	103	21.41	1	971	31	31.32	93
§ **Willey, D J**	**Feb 28, 1990**		**2016**	**2019**	**13**	**18**	**2**	**298**	**46**	**18.62**	**0**	**1015**	**30**	**33.83**	**3**
Williams, A C	Mar 1, 1887	June 1, 1966	1911	1919	12	14	10	95	48*	23.75	0	678	30	22.60	6
§ Williamson, K S	Aug 8, 1990		2013	2018	19	32	3	1,292	189	44.55	1	475	11	43.18	20
© Wilson, B B	Dec 11, 1879	Sept 14, 1957	1906	1914	185	308	12	8,053	208	27.50	15	278	2	139.00	53
§ Wilson, C E M *	May 15, 1875	Feb 8, 1944	1896	1899	9	13	3	256	91*	25.60	0	257	12	21.41	3
© Wilson, D	Aug 7, 1937	July 21, 2012	1957	1974	392	502	85	5,788	83	13.88	0	22,626	1,104	20.49	235
Wilson, E R *	Mar 25, 1879	July 21, 1957	1899	1923	66	72	18	902	104*	16.70	0	3,106	197	15.76	30
Wilson, Geoffrey *	Aug 21, 1895	Nov 29, 1960	1919	1924	92	94	5	983	70	12.28	0	11	0	—	33
Wilson, G A *	Feb 2, 1916	Sept 24, 2002	1936	1939	15	25	5	352	55*	17.60	0	138	1	138.00	7
Wilson, John *	June 30, 1857	Nov 11, 1931	1887	1888	4	5	1	17	13*	4.25	0	165	12	13.75	3
© Wilson, J P *	Apr 3, 1889	Oct 3, 1959	1911	1912	9	14	1	81	36	6.23	0	24	1	24.00	2
© Wilson, J V	Jan 17, 1921	June 5, 2008	1946	1962	477	724	75	20,548	230	31.66	29	313	3	104.33	520
Wood, A	Aug 25, 1898	Apr 1, 1973	1927	1946	408	481	80	8,579	123*	21.39	1	33	1	33.00	612/243
Wood, B	Dec 26, 1942		1964	1964	5	7	2	63	35	12.60	0	—	—	—	4
Wood, C W	July 23, 1934	June 28, 2006	1959	1959	4	4	1	22	10	7.33	0	319	11	29.00	1
Wood, G W	Nov 18, 1862	Dec 4, 1948	1895	1895	2	2	0	2	1	1.00	0	—	—	—	0/1
Wood, H *	Mar 22, 1855	July 31, 1941	1879	1881	10	16	1	156	36	10.40	0	212	10	21.20	8
Wood, J H *			1881	1881	2	1	0	14	14	14.00	0	—	—	—	0
© Wood, M J	Apr 6, 1977		1997	2007	128	222	20	6,742	207	33.37	16	27	2	13.50	113

LIST OF PLAYERS AND CAREER AVERAGES IN ALL FIRST-CLASS MATCHES FOR YORKSHIRE (Continued)

Player	Date of Birth	Date of Death (if known)	First Played	Last Played	M	Inns	NO	Runs	HS	Av'ge	100s	Runs	Wkts	Av'ge	Ct/St
Wood, R	June 3, 1929	May 22, 1990	1952	1956	22	18	4	60	17	4.28	0	1,346	51	26.39	5
Woodford, J D	Sept 9, 1943		1968	1972	38	61	2	1,204	101	20.40	1	185	4	46.25	12
Woodhead, F E *	May 29, 1868	Aug 25, 1943	1893	1894	4	8	0	57	18	7.12	0	—	—	—	3
Woodhouse, W H *	Apr 16, 1856	Mar 4, 1938	1884	1885	9	13	0	218	63	16.76	0	—	—	—	6
Wormald, A	May 10, 1855	Feb 6, 1940	1885	1891	7	11	3	161	80	20.12	0	—	—	—	10/2
Worsley, W A * ©	Apr 5, 1890	Dec 4, 1973	1928	1929	60	50	4	722	60	15.69	0	—	—	—	32
Wrathmell, L F	Jan 22, 1855	Sept 16, 1928	1886	1886	1	2	0	18	17	9.00	0	—	—	—	0
Wright, R	July 19, 1852	Jan 2, 1891	1877	1877	2	4	1	28	22	9.33	0	—	—	—	0
Wright, T J *	Mar 5, 1900	Nov 7, 1962	1919	1919	1	1	0	12	12	12.00	0	—	—	—	0
Yardley, N W D * ©	Mar 19, 1915	Oct 3, 1989	1936	1955	302	420	56	11,632	183*	31.95	17	5,818	195	29.83	220
Yeadon, J	Dec 10, 1861	May 30, 1914	1888	1888	3	6	2	41	22	10.25	0	—	—	—	5/3
§ Younus Khan *	Nov 29, 1977		2007	2007	13	19	2	824	217*	48.47	3	342	8	42.75	11
§ Yuvraj Singh	Dec 12, 1981		2003	2003	7	12	2	145	56	14.50	0	130	3	43.33	12

In the career averages it should be noted that the bowling analysis for the second Cambridgeshire innings at Ashton-under-Lyne in 1865 has not been found. G R Atkinson took 3 wickets, W Cuttell 2, G Freeman 4 and R Iddison 1. The respective bowling averages have been calculated excluding these wickets.

MOST FIRST-CLASS APPEARANCES FOR YORKSHIRE

Matches	Player	Matches	Player
883	W Rhodes (1898-1930)	477	J V Wilson (1946-1962)
717	G H Hirst (1891-1929)	472	J Tunnicliffe (1891-1907)
676	D Denton (1894-1920)	459	F S Trueman (1949-1968)
602	H Sutcliffe (1919-1945)	456	J H Hampshire (1961-1981)
548	M Leyland (1920-1947)	445	G G Macaulay (1920-1935)
536	D B Close (1949-1970)	429	D L Bairstow (1970-1990)
517	D Hunter (1888-1909)	427	A Dolphin (1905-1927)
513	S Haigh (1895-1913)	425	P Carrick (1970-1993)
510	Lord Hawke (1881-1911)	414	G Boycott (1962-1986)
496	R Illingworth (1951-1983)	413	E. Robinson (1919-1931)
491	† J G Binks (1955-1969)	411	P J Sharpe (1958-1974)
487	D E V Padgett (1951-1971)	408	A Wood (1927-1946)
485	P Holmes (1913-1933)	401	A Mitchell (1922-1945)

† Kept wicket in 412 consecutive Championship matches 1955-1969

MOST TOTAL APPEARANCES FOR YORKSHIRE
(First-Class, Domestic List A and t20)

Matches	Player	Matches	Player
883	W Rhodes (1898-1930)	513	S Haigh (1895-1913)
832	D L Bairstow (1970-1990)	510	Lord Hawke (1881-1911)
729	P Carrick (1970-1993)	502	P J Sharpe (1958-1974)
719	R J Blakey (1985-2004)	485	P Holmes (1913-1933)
717	G H Hirst (1891-1929)	477	J V Wilson (1946-1962)
690	J H Hampshire (1961-1981)	472	J Tunnicliffe (1891-1907)
678	G Boycott (1962-1986)	470	F S Trueman (1949-1968)
676	D Denton (1894-1920)	467	J D Love (1975-1989)
602	H Sutcliffe (1919-1945)	453	D Wilson (1957-1974)
583	A McGrath (1995-2012)	452	A Sidebottom (1973-1991)
581	D Byas (1986-2001)	445	G G Macaulay(1920-1935)
568	D B Close (1949-1970)	443	C M Old (1966-1982)
548	M Leyland (1920-1947)	427	A Dolphin (1905-1927)
546	C White (1990-2007)	414	P J Hartley (1985-1997)
544	D E V Padgett (1951-1971)	413	E Robinson (1919-1931)
537	R Illingworth (1951-1983)	408	A Wood (1927-1946)
521	J G Binks (1955-1969)	402	A G Nicholson (1962-1975)
517	D Hunter (1888-1909)	401	A Mitchell (1922-1945)
514	M D Moxon (1980-1997)		

ONE DAY RECORDS SECTION

Yorkshire County Cricket Club thanks Statistician JOHN T. POTTER, who in 2014 revamped and streamlined Yorkshire's One-Day Records Section. John's symbols in the pages that follow are:

$ = Sunday and National Leagues, Pro 40, Clydesdale Bank 40 and Yorkshire Bank 40

\# = Benson & Hedges Cup

+ = Gillette Cup, NatWest Trophy, Cheltenham & Gloucester Trophy, Friends Provident Trophy and Royal London Cup

Yorkshire played no List A matches in 2020 because of the Covid-19 pandemic

WINNERS OF THE GILLETTE CUP, NATWEST TROPHY, CHELTENHAM & GLOUCESTER TROPHY FRIENDS PROVIDENT TROPHY AND ROYAL LONDON ONE-DAY CUP

Yorkshire's Position

GILLETTE CUP

1963	Sussex	Quarter-Final
1964	Sussex	Round 2
1965	**Yorkshire**	**Winner**
1966	Warwickshire	Round 2
1967	Kent	Quarter-Final
1968	Warwickshire	Round 2
1969	**Yorkshire**	**Winner**
1970	Lancashire	Round 1
1971	Lancashire	Round 2
1972	Lancashire	Round 1
1973	Gloucestershire	Round 1
1974	Kent	Quarter-Final
1975	Lancashire	Round 2
1976	Northamptonshire	Round 1
1977	Middlesex	Round 2
1978	Sussex	Quarter-Final
1979	Somerset	Quarter-Final
1980	Middlesex	Semi-Final

NATWEST TROPHY

1981	Derbyshire	Round 1
1982	Surrey	Semi-Final
1983	Somerset	Round 2
1984	Middlesex	Round 1
1985	Essex	Round 2
1986	Sussex	Quarter-Final
1987	Nottinghamshire	Quarter-Final
1988	Middlesex	Round 2
1989	Warwickshire	Round 2
1990	Lancashire	Quarter-Final
1991	Hampshire	Round 1

Yorkshire's Position

1992	Northamptonshire	Round 2
1993	Warwickshire	Quarter-Final
1994	Worcestershire	Round 2
1995	Warwickshire	Semi-Final
1996	Lancashire	Semi-Final
1997	Essex	Quarter-Final
1998	Lancashire	Round 2
1999	Gloucestershire	Semi-Final
2000	Gloucestershire	Round 4

CHELTENHAM & GLOUCESTER TROPHY

2001	Somerset	Quarter-Final
2002	**Yorkshire**	**Winner**
2003	Gloucestershire	Round 4
2004	Gloucestershire	Semi-Final
2005	Hampshire	Semi-Final
2006	Sussex	North 7 (10)

FRIENDS PROVIDENT TROPHY

2007	Durham	North 5 (10)
2008	Essex	Semi-Final
2009	Hampshire	Group C 3 (5)

ROYAL LONDON ONE-DAY CUP

2014	Durham	Quarter-Final
2015	Gloucestershire	Semi-Final
2016	Warwickshire	Semi-Final
2017	Nottinghamshire	Quarter-Final
2018	Hampshire	Semi-Final
2019	Somerset	North 6 (9)
2020	*Not played: COVID-19 restrictions*	

WINNERS OF THE NATIONAL AND SUNDAY LEAGUES, PRO 40, CLYDESDALE BANK 40 AND YORKSHIRE BANK 40 1969-2014

SUNDAY LEAGUE

		Yorkshire's Position
1969	Lancashire	8th
1970	Lancashire	14th
1971	Worcestershire	15th
1972	Kent	4th
1973	Kent	2nd
1974	Leicestershire	=6th
1975	Hampshire	=5th
1976	Kent	15th
1977	Leicestershire	=13th
1978	Hampshire	7th
1979	Somerset	=4th
1980	Warwickshire	=14th
1981	Essex	=7th
1982	Sussex	16th
1983	**Yorkshire**	**1st**
1984	Essex	=14th
1985	Essex	6th
1986	Hampshire	8th
1987	Worcestershire	=13th
1988	Worcestershire	8th
1989	Lancashire	11th
1990	Derbyshire	6th
1991	Nottinghamshire	7th
1992	Middlesex	15th
1993	Glamorgan	9th
1994	Warwickshire	5th
1995	Kent	12th
1996	Surrey	3rd
1997	Warwickshire	10th
1998	Lancashire	9th

NATIONAL LEAGUE

		Yorkshire's Position
1999	Lancashire	5th Div 1
2000	Gloucestershire	2nd Div 1
2001	Kent	6th Div 1
2002	Glamorgan	4th Div 1
2003	Surrey	8th Div 1
2004	Glamorgan	4th Div 2
2005	Essex	8th Div 2
2006	Essex	9th Div 2
2007	Worcestershire	6th Div 2
2008	Sussex	2nd Div 2
2009	Sussex	7th Div 1

CLYDESDALE BANK 40

		Yorkshire's Position
2010	Warwickshire	Group B 1 (7) (Semi-Final)
2011	Surrey	Group A 6 (7)
2012	Hampshire	Group C 5 (7)
2013	Nottinghamshire	Group C 6 (7)

BENSON & HEDGES WINNERS 1972-2002

		Yorkshire's Position
1972	Leicestershire	Final
1973	Kent	Group N 3 (5)
1974	Surrey	Quarter-Final
1975	Leicestershire	Quarter-Final
1976	Kent	Group D 3 (5)
1977	Gloucestershire	Group D 3 (5)
1978	Kent	Group D 4 (5)
1979	Essex	Semi-Final
1980	Northamptonshire	Group B 4 (5)
1981	Somerset	Quarter-Final
1982	Somerset	Group A 5 (5)
1983	Middlesex	Group B 5 (5)
1984	Lancashire	Semi-Final
1985	Leicestershire	Group B 3 (5)
1986	Middlesex	Group B 3 (5)
1987	**Yorkshire**	**Winner**
1988	Hampshire	Group B 4 (5)
1989	Nottinghamshire	Group C 3 (5)
1990	Lancashire	Group C 3 (5)
1991	Worcestershire	Semi-Final
1992	Hampshire	Group C 5 (5)
1993	Derbyshire	Round One
1994	Warwickshire	Round One
1995	Lancashire	Quarter-Final
1996	Lancashire	Semi-Final
1997	Surrey	Quarter-Final
1998	Essex	Semi-Final
1999	Gloucestershire	Final
2000	Gloucestershire	Quarter-Final
2001	Surrey	Semi-Final
2002	Warwickshire	Quarter-Final

Season	Played	Won	Lost	Tie	N R	Abd	Season	Played	Won	Lost	Tie	N R	Abd
1963	2	1	1	0	0	0	1993	21	10	10	0	1	0
1964	1	0	1	0	0	0	1994	19	11	8	0	0	1
1965	4	4	0	0	0	1	1995	27	15	11	0	1	1
1966	1	0	1	0	0	0	1996	27	18	9	0	0	0
1967	2	1	1	0	0	0	1997	25	14	10	1	0	0
1968	1	0	1	0	0	0	1998	25	14	10	0	1	0
1969	19	12	7	0	0	2	1999	23	13	10	0	0	0
1970	17	5	10	0	2	0	2000	24	13	10	0	1	0
1971	15	5	10	0	0	2	2001	26	13	13	0	0	0
1972	25	15	8	0	2	1	2002	27	16	11	0	0	1
1973	21	14	7	0	0	0	2003	18	6	12	0	0	0
1974	22	12	9	0	1	1	2004	23	13	8	0	2	0
1975	22	12	10	0	0	0	2005	22	8	14	0	0	0
1976	22	9	13	0	0	0	2006	15	4	10	0	1	2
1977	19	5	10	0	4	2	2007	17	8	7	0	2	1
1978	22	10	11	0	1	2	2008	18	10	4	1	3	0
1979	21	12	6	0	3	3	2009	16	6	9	0	1	0
1980	23	9	14	0	0	0	2010	13	10	3	0	0	0
1981	19	9	8	0	2	3	2011	12	5	7	0	0	0
1982	23	7	14	1	1	1	2012	11	4	7	0	0	1
1983	19	11	7	0	1	3	2013	13	4	9	0	0	0
1984	23	10	13	0	0	0	2014	10	6	4	0	0	0
1985	19	9	9	0	1	3	2015	10	5	3	0	2	0
1986	22	11	9	1	1	1	2016	10	5	4	0	1	0
1987	24	14	9	0	1	2	2017	10	6	3	0	1	0
1988	21	9	9	0	3	1	2018	9	6	3	0	0	1
1989	23	10	13	0	0	0	2019	8	2	3	2	0	0
1990	22	13	9	0	0	1	2020	No matched played due to Covid-19					
1991	24	13	10	0	1	0							
1992	21	8	13	0	0	2		998	495	455	6	41	40

Abandoned matches are not included in the list of matches played.

ABANDONED LIST A MATCHES (40)

1965 v. South Africa at Bradford	1985 (3) v. Derbyshire at Scarborough $
1969 (2) v. Warwickshire at Harrogate $	v. Warwickshire at Birmingham $
v. Lancashire at Manchester $	v. Lancashire at Leeds $
1971 (2) v. Gloucestershire at Sheffield $	1986 v. Kent at Canterbury $
v. Somerset at Weston-Super-Mare $	1987 (2) v. Sussex at Hull $
1972 v. Sussex at Leeds $	v. Hampshire at Leeds $
1974 v. Warwickshire at Leeds $	1988 v. Northamptonshire
1977 (2) v. Warwickshire at Birmingham $	at Northampton $
v. Surrey at Leeds $	1990 v. Glamorgan at Newport $
1978 (2) v. Essex at Bradford $	1992 (2) v. Sussex at Hove $
v. Gloucestershire at Hull $	v. Durham at Darlington $
1979 (3) v. Leicestershire at Middlesbrough $	1994 v. Essex at Leeds $
v. Kent at Huddersfield $	1995 v. Derbyshire at Chesterfield #
v. Worcestershire at Worcester $	1997 v. Sussex at Scarborough $
1981 (3) v. Warwickshire at Birmingham $	2002 v. Nottinghamshire at Nottingham $
v. Lancashire at Leeds #	2006 (2) v. Nottinghamshire at Leeds +
v. Sussex at Hove $	v. Derbyshire at Derby $
1982 v. Glamorgan at Bradford $	2007 v. Warwickshire at Birmingham +
1983 (3) v. Derbyshire at Chesterfield #	2012 v. Northamptonshire at Leeds $
v. Surrey at Leeds $	2018 v. Nottinghamshire at Leeds +
v. Essex at Chelmsford $	

ANALYSIS OF LIST A RESULTS V. ALL TEAMS 1963-2019
DOMESTIC MATCHES

Opponents	Played	HOME				AWAY				Abd
		Won	Lost	Tied	N. R.	Won	Lost	Tied	N. R.	
Derbyshire	65	20	9	1	1	20	9	1	4	4
Durham	31	10	5	0	1	7	7	0	1	1
Essex	47	12	12	0	0	11	12	0	0	3
Glamorgan	39	9	8	0	0	9	13	0	0	2
Gloucestershire	55	12	12	0	2	8	19	0	0	2
Hampshire	45	11	9	0	1	9	15	0	2	2
Kent	55	13	11	0	1	10	20	0	0	2
Lancashire	64	10	17	0	2	15	18	0	2	3
Leicestershire	68	20	16	0	0	13	16	1	2	1
Middlesex	48	14	4	0	3	9	16	0	2	0
Northamptonshire	60	18	11	0	3	20	7	0	1	2
Nottinghamshire	60	19	8	1	2	10	17	0	3	3
Somerset	54	13	14	0	1	11	15	0	0	1
Surrey	56	12	15	0	0	11	18	0	0	2
Sussex	46	11	11	0	1	11	12	0	0	5
Warwickshire	63	11	18	1	2	13	17	1	0	6
Worcestershire	65	13	20	0	2	17	13	0	0	1
Bedfordshire	1	0	0	0	0	1	0	0	0	0
Berkshire	2	0	0	0	0	2	0	0	0	0
Cambridgeshire	3	2	0	0	0	1	0	0	0	0
Cheshire	1	0	0	0	0	1	0	0	0	0
Combined Universities	3	0	2	0	0	1	0	0	0	0
Devon	4	0	0	0	0	4	0	0	0	0
Dorset	1	0	0	0	0	1	0	0	0	0
Durham (M C)	3	1	1	0	0	1	0	0	0	0
Herefordshire	1	0	0	0	0	1	0	0	0	0
Ireland	4	3	0	0	0	1	0	0	0	0
Minor Counties	11	6	0	0	0	5	0	0	0	0
Netherlands	4	1	1	0	0	1	1	0	0	0
Norfolk	2	1	0	0	0	1	0	0	0	0
Northumberland	1	1	0	0	0	0	0	0	0	0
Scotland	16	8	0	0	0	8	0	0	0	0
Shropshire	2	0	0	0	0	1	1	0	0	0
Unicorns	4	2	0	0	0	2	0	0	0	0
Wiltshire	1	0	0	0	0	1	0	0	0	0
Yorkshire Cricket Board	1	0	0	0	0	1	0	0	0	0
Total	**986**	**253**	**204**	**3**	**22**	**238**	**246**	**3**	**17**	**39**

OTHER MATCHES

	Played	Won	Lost	Tied	N. R.	Won	Lost	Tied	N. R.	Abd
Australia	3	0	1	0	2	0	0	0	0	0
Bangladesh A	1	1	0	0	0	0	0	0	0	0
South Africa	0	0	0	0	0	0	0	0	0	0
South Africa A	1	0	0	0	1	0	0	0	0	1
Sri Lanka A	3	0	3	0	0	0	0	0	0	0
West Indies	1	1	0	0	0	0	0	0	0	0
West Indies A	1	0	1	0	0	0	0	0	0	0
Young Australia	1	1	0	0	0	0	0	0	9	0
Zimbabwe	1	1	0	0	0	0	0	0	0	0
Total	**12**	**4**	**5**	**0**	**3**	**0**	**0**	**0**	**0**	**1**
Grand Total	**998**	**257**	**209**	**3**	**25**	**238**	**246**	**3**	**17**	**40**

Abandoned matches are not included in the list of matches played.

LIST A HIGHEST AND LOWEST SCORES BY AND AGAINST YORKSHIRE
PLUS INDIVIDUAL BEST BATTING AND BOWLING

The lowest score is the lowest all-out total or the lowest score at completion of the allotted overs, 10-over matches not included

Yorkshire versus:

Derbyshire

		By Yorkshire		Against Yorkshire	
Highest Score:	In Yorkshire	349:7	at Leeds 2017 +	334:8	at Leeds 2017 +
	Away	288:6	at Derby 2002 #	268:8	at Chesterfield 2010 $
Lowest Score:	In Yorkshire	117	at Huddersfield 1978 $	87	at Scarborough 1973 $
	Away	132	at Chesterfield 1986 $	127	at Chesterfield 1972 #
Best Batting:	In Yorkshire	140 P S P Handscomb	at Leeds 2017 +	112 W L Madsen	at Leeds 2017 +
	Away	115* M J Wood	at Derby 2002 #	109* C J Adams	at Derby 1997 $
Best Bowling:	In Yorkshire	6-32 S A Patterson	at Leeds 2010 $	4-20 F E Rumsey	at Bradford 1973 #
	Away	5-35 C W J Athey	at Chesterfield 1981 $	5-24 C J Tunnicliffe	at Derby 1981 #

Durham

		By Yorkshire		Against Yorkshire	
Highest Score:	In Yorkshire	339:4	at Leeds 2017 +	335:5	at Leeds 2017 +
	Away	328:4	at Chester-le-Street 2018 +	281:7	at Chester-le-Street 2018 +
Lowest Score:	In Yorkshire	133	at Leeds 1995 $	121	at Leeds 1995 $
	Away	122	at Chester-le-Street 2007 $	136	at Chester-le-Street 1996 $
Best Batting:	In Yorkshire	174 J M Bairstow	at Leeds 2017 +	114 W Larkins	at Leeds 1993 $
	Away	164 T Kohler-Cadmore	at Chester-le-Street 2018 +	124* J P Maher	at Chester-le-Street 2006 +
Best Bowling:	In Yorkshire	4-18 C White	at Scarborough 1997 $	4-20 S J E Brown	at Leeds 1995 $
	Away	4-26 C E W Silverwood	at Chester-le-Street 1996 $	4-31 P D Collingwood	at Chester-le-Street 2000 #

Essex

		By Yorkshire		Against Yorkshire	
Highest Score:	In Yorkshire	290:6	at Scarborough 2014 +	291:5	at Scarborough 2014 +
	Away	307:3	at Chelmsford 1995 +	285:8	at Chelmsford 2008 +
Lowest Score:	In Yorkshire	54	at Leeds 2003 $	108	at Leeds 1996 $
	Away	119:8	at Colchester 1987 $	123	at Colchester 1974 $
Best Batting:	In Yorkshire	111* J A Leaning	at Scarborough 2014 +	119* R N ten Doeschate	at Scarborough 2014 +
	Away	125* A W Gale	at Chelmsford 2010 $	136* N Hussain	at Chelmsford 2002 #
Best Bowling:	In Yorkshire	4-20 G B Stevenson	at Barnsley 1977 #	6-18 R E East	at Hull 1969 $
	Away	4-31 A L Robinson	at Leyton 1976 $	5-20 R E East	at Colchester 1979 $

LIST A HIGHEST AND LOWEST SCORES BY AND AGAINST YORKSHIRE
PLUS INDIVIDUAL BEST BATTING AND BOWLING (Continued)

Yorkshire versus:

Glamorgan

		By Yorkshire		Against Yorkshire	
Highest Score:	In Yorkshire	253:4	at Leeds 1991 $	216:6	at Leeds 2013 $
	Away	257	at Colwyn Bay 2013 $	285:7	at Colwyn Bay 2013 $
Lowest Score:	In Yorkshire	139	at Hull 1981 $	83	at Leeds 1987 +
	Away	93-8	at Swansea 1985 $	90	at Neath 1969 $
Best Batting:	In Yorkshire	96 A A Metcalfe	at Leeds 1991 $	97* G P Ellis	at Leeds 1976 $
	Away	141* M D Moxon	at Cardiff 1991 #	127 A R Butcher	at Cardiff 1991 #
Best Bowling:	In Yorkshire	5-22 P Carrick	at Leeds 1991 $	5-26 D S Harrison	at Leeds 2002 $
	Away	6-40 R J Sidebottom	at Cardiff 1998 $	5-16 G C Holmes	at Swansea 1985 $

Gloucestershire

		By Yorkshire		Against Yorkshire	
Highest Score:	In Yorkshire	263:9	at Leeds 2015 +	269	at Leeds 2009 +
	Away	262:7	at Bristol 1996 $	294:6	at Cheltenham 2010 $
Lowest Score:	In Yorkshire	115	at Leeds 1973 $	91	at Scarborough 2001 $
	Away	133	at Cheltenham 1999 $	90	at Tewkesbury 1972 $
Best Batting:	In Yorkshire	118 J A Rudolph	at Leeds 2009 +	146* S Young	at Leeds 1997 $
	Away	100* J D Love	at Gloucester in 1985 $	143* C M Spearman	at Bristol 2004 $
		100* R J Blakey	at Cheltenham 1990 $		
Best Bowling:	In Yorkshire	5-42 N D Thornicroft	at Leeds 2003 $	5-33 M C J Ball	at Leeds 2003 $
	Away	4-25 R D Stemp	at Bristol 1996 $	5-42 M C J Ball	at Cheltenham 1999 $

Hampshire

		By Yorkshire		Against Yorkshire	
Highest Score:	In Yorkshire	259:4	at Middlesbrough 1985 $	257:6	at Middlesbrough 1985 $
	Away	264:2	at Southampton 1995 $	348:9	at West End, Southampton, 2018 +
Lowest Score:	In Yorkshire	74:9	at Hull 1970 $	50	at Leeds 1991 +
	Away	118	at Southampton 1990 +	133	at Bournemouth 1976 $
Best Batting:	In Yorkshire	104* D Byas	at Leeds 1999 #	155* B A Richards	at Hull 1970 $
	Away	97* M G Bevan	at Southampton 1995 $	171 J M Vince	at West End, Southampton, 2018 +
Best Bowling:	In Yorkshire	5-16 G M Hamilton	at Leeds 1998 $	5-33 A J Murtagh	at Huddersfield 1977 $
	Away	5-33 A U Rashid	at Southampton 2014 +	5-31 D W White	at Southampton 1969 $

LIST A HIGHEST AND LOWEST SCORES BY AND AGAINST YORKSHIRE PLUS INDIVIDUAL BEST BATTING AND BOWLING (*Continued*)

Yorkshire versus:

Kent

		By Yorkshire		Against Yorkshire	
Highest Score:	In Yorkshire	299:3	at Leeds 2002 $	232:8	at Leeds 2011 $
	Away	263:3	at Maidstone 1998 $	266:5	at Maidstone 1998 $
Lowest Score:	In Yorkshire	75	at Leeds 1995 $	133	at Leeds 1974 $
				133	at Leeds 1979 $
				105	at Canterbury 1969 $
Best Batting:	Away	114	at Canterbury 1978 #		
	In Yorkshire	130* R J Blakey	at Scarborough 1991 $	118* M H Denness	at Scarborough 1976 $
	Away	102 A McGrath	at Canterbury 2001 $	118* C J Tavare	at Canterbury 1981 +
Best Bowling:	In Yorkshire	4-15 A G Nicholson	at Leeds 1974 $	6-32 M T Coles	at Leeds 2012 $
	Away	6-18 D Wilson	at Canterbury 1969 $	5-25 B D Julien	at Canterbury 1971 +

Lancashire

		By Yorkshire		Against Yorkshire	
Highest Score:	In Yorkshire	310	at Leeds 2019 +	311:6	at Leeds 2019 +
	Away	379:7	at Manchester 2018 +	363	at Manchester 2018 +
Lowest Score:	In Yorkshire	81	at Leeds 1998 $	68	at Leeds 2000 $
		81	at Leeds 2002 #		
	Away	125	at Manchester 1973 #	84	at Manchester 2016 +
Best Batting:	In Yorkshire	111* D Byas	at Leeds 1996 $	102* N J Speak	at Leeds 1992 $
	Away	144 A Lyth	at Manchester 2018 +	141* B J Hodge	at Manchester 2007 +
Best Bowling:	In Yorkshire	5-25 C White	at Leeds 2000 #	6-25 G Chapple	at Leeds 1998 $
	Away	4-18 G S Blewett	at Manchester 1999 +	5-49 M Watkinson	at Manchester 1991 #

Leicestershire

		By Yorkshire		Against Yorkshire	
Highest Score:	In Yorkshire	379:7	at Leeds 2019 +	302:7	at Leeds 2008 $
	Away	376:3	at Leicester 2016 +	298:9	at Leicester 1997 $
Lowest Score:	In Yorkshire	93	at Leeds 1998 $	141	at Hull 1975 $
	Away	89:9	at Leicester 1989 $	53	at Leicester 2000 $
Best Batting:	In Yorkshire	156 G S Ballance	at Leeds 2019 +	108 N E Briers	at Bradford 1984 $
	Away	176 T M Head	at Leicester 2016 +	108 E J H Eckersley	at Leicester 2013 $
Best Bowling:	In Yorkshire	5-29 M W Pillans	at Leeds 2019 +	5-24 C W Henderson	at Leeds 2004 $
	Away	5-16 S Stuchbury	at Leicester 1982 $	4-25 J Ormond	at Leicester 2001 #

LIST A HIGHEST AND LOWEST SCORES BY AND AGAINST YORKSHIRE PLUS INDIVIDUAL BEST BATTING AND BOWLING (Continued)

Yorkshire versus:

Middlesex

Stat	Location	By Yorkshire			Against Yorkshire		
Highest Score:	In Yorkshire	271:7		at Scarborough 1990 $	245:8		at Scarborough 2010 $
	Away	275:4		at Lord's 2011 $	273:6		at Southgate 2004 $
Lowest Score:	In Yorkshire	148		at Leeds 1974 $	23		at Leeds 1974 $
	Away	90		at Lord's 1964 +	107		at Lord's 1979 #
Best Batting:	In Yorkshire	124*	J A Rudolph	at Scarborough 2010 $	104	P N Weekes	at Leeds 1996 #
	Away	116	A A Metcalfe	at Lord's 1991	125*	O A Shah	at Southgate 2004 $
Best Bowling:	In Yorkshire	4-6	R Illingworth	at Hull 1983 $	4-24	N G Cowans	at Leeds 1986 +
	Away	4-28	H P Cooper	at Lord's 1979 #	5-44	T M Lamb	at Lord's 1975 #

Northamptonshire

Stat	Location	By Yorkshire			Against Yorkshire		
Highest Score:	In Yorkshire	314:8		at Scarborough 2016 +	314:4		at Leeds 2007 +
	Away	341:3		at Northampton 2006 +	351		at Northampton 2019 +
Lowest Score:	In Yorkshire	129		at Leeds 2000 $	127		at Huddersfield 1974 $
	Away	112		at Northampton 1975 $	109		at Northampton 2000 $
Best Batting:	In Yorkshire	125	A Lyth	at Scarborough 2016 +	132	U Afzaal	at Leeds 2007 +
	Away	152*	G S Ballance	at Northampton in 2017 +	161	D J G Sales	at Northampton 2006 +
Best Bowling:	In Yorkshire	5-38	C M Old	at Sheffield 1972 $	5-16	B S Crump	at Bradford 1969 $
	Away	5-29	P W Jarvis	at Northampton 1992 $	5-15	Sarfraz Nawaz	at Northampton 1975 $

Nottinghamshire

Stat	Location	By Yorkshire			Against Yorkshire		
Highest Score:	In Yorkshire	352:6		at Scarborough 2001 $	251:5		at Scarborough 1996 $
	Away	280:4		at Nottingham 2007 +	251:9		at Scarborough 2016 +
					291:6		at Nottingham 2004 $
Lowest Score:	In Yorkshire	120:9		at Scarborough 1998 +	66		at Bradford 1969 $
	Away	147		at Nottingham 1975 $	134:8		at Nottingham 1973 $
Best Batting:	In Yorkshire	191	D S Lehmann	at Scarborough 2001 $	101	M J Harris	at Hull 1973 #
	Away	103	R B Richardson	at Nottingham 1993 $	123	D W Randall	at Nottingham 1987 $
Best Bowling:	In Yorkshire	5-17	A G Nicholson	at Hull 1972 $	5-41	C L Cairns	at Scarborough 1996 $
	Away	4-12	C M Old	at Nottingham 1977 $	5-30	F D Stephenson	at Nottingham 1991 #

LIST A HIGHEST AND LOWEST SCORES BY AND AGAINST YORKSHIRE PLUS INDIVIDUAL BEST BATTING AND BOWLING (Continued)

Yorkshire versus:

Somerset

		By Yorkshire		Against Yorkshire	
Highest Score:	In Yorkshire	283:9	at Scarborough 2002 $	338:5	at Leeds 2013 $
	Away	343:9	at Taunton 2005 $	345:4	at Taunton 2005 $
Lowest Score:	In Yorkshire	110	at Scarborough 1977 $	103	at Sheffield 1972 $
	Away	120	at Taunton 1992 #	63	at Taunton 1965 +
Best Batting:	In Yorkshire	127 J A Rudolph	at Scarborough 2007 $	113 R T Ponting	at Scarborough 2004 $
	Away	148 A McGrath	at Taunton 2006 $	140* P D Trego	at Taunton 2013 $
Best Bowling:	In Yorkshire	6-36 A G Nicholson	at Sheffield 1972 $	4-10 I T Botham	at Scarborough 1979 $
	Away	6-15 F S Trueman	at Taunton 1965 +	5-27 J Garner	at Bath 1985 $

Surrey

		By Yorkshire		Against Yorkshire	
Highest Score:	In Yorkshire	289:9	at Leeds 2017 +	375:4	at Scarborough 1994 $
	Away	334.5	at The Oval 2005 $	329:8	at The Oval 2009 +
Lowest Score:	In Yorkshire	76	at Harrogate 1970 +	90	at Leeds 1996 $
	Away	128.8	at The Oval 1971 $	134	at The Oval 1969 +
Best Batting:	In Yorkshire	118* J D Love	at Leeds 1987 $	136 M A Lynch	at Bradford 1985 $
	Away	146 G Boycott	at Lord's 1965 +	177 S A Newman	at The Oval 2009 +
Best Bowling:	In Yorkshire	5-25 D Gough	at Leeds 1998 $	7-33 R D Jackman	at Harrogate 1970 +
	Away	5-29 R Illingworth	at Lord's 1965 +	5-22 R D Jackman	at The Oval 1978 $

Sussex

		By Yorkshire		Against Yorkshire	
Highest Score:	In Yorkshire	302:4	at Scarborough 2011 $	267	at Scarborough 2011 $
	Away	270	at Hove 1963 +	292	at Hove 1963 +
Lowest Score:	In Yorkshire	89:7	at Huddersfield 1969 $	85	at Bradford 1972 #
	Away	89	at Hove 1998 $	108	at Hove 1971 $
Best Batting:	In Yorkshire	132* J A Rudolph	at Scarborough 2011 $	129 A W Greig	at Scarborough 1976 $
	Away	111* J H Hampshire	at Hastings 1973 $	103 L J Wright	at Hove 2012 $
Best Bowling:	In Yorkshire	5-34 G M Hamilton	at Scarborough 2000 $	4-15 Imran Khan	at Sheffield 1985 $
	Away	5-13 D Gough	at Hove 1994 $	4-10 M H Yardy	at Hove 2011 $

LIST A HIGHEST AND LOWEST SCORES BY AND AGAINST YORKSHIRE PLUS INDIVIDUAL BEST BATTING AND BOWLING (Continued)

Yorkshire versus:

Warwickshire

		By Yorkshire		Against Yorkshire	
Highest Score:	In Yorkshire	274:3	at Leeds 2003 $	283:6	at Leeds 2016 +
	Away	281:8	at Birmingham 2017 +	309-3	at Birmingham 2005 $
Lowest Score:	In Yorkshire	158	at Scarborough 2012 $	59	at Leeds 2001 $
	Away	56	at Birmingham 1995 $	158:9	at Birmingham 2003 $
Best Batting:	In Yorkshire	139* S P Fleming	at Leeds 2003 $	118 I J L Trott	at Leeds 2016 +
	Away	100* J H Hampshire	at Birmingham 1975 $	137 I R Bell	at Birmingham 2005 $
Best Bowling:	In Yorkshire	5-31 M D Moxon	at Leeds 1991 #	4-16 N M Carter	at Scarborough 2012 $
	Away	4-27 H P Cooper	at Birmingham 1973 $	7-32 R G D Willis	at Birmingham 1981 #

Worcestershire

		By Yorkshire		Against Yorkshire	
Highest Score:	In Yorkshire	346:9	at Leeds 2018 +	350:6	at Leeds 2018 +
	Away	346:6	at Worcester 2015 +	342	at Worcester 2017 +
Lowest Score:	In Yorkshire	88	at Leeds 1995 #	86	at Leeds 1969 $
	Away	90	at Worcester 1987 $	122	at Worcester 1975 $
Best Batting:	In Yorkshire	101 M G Bevan	at Scarborough 1995 $	113* G A Hick	at Scarborough 1995 $
		101 C A Pujara	at Leeds 2018 +	115 Younis Ahmed	at Worcester 1980 #
	Away	142 G Boycott	at Worcester 1980 #		
Best Bowling:	In Yorkshire	7-15 R A Hutton	at Leeds 1969 $	5-36 Kabir Ali	at Leeds 2002 $
	Away	6-14 H P Cooper	at Worcester 1976 $	5-25 W D Parnell	at Worcester 2019 +

Bedfordshire +

		By Yorkshire		Against Yorkshire	
Highest Score:	Away	212:6	at Luton 2001	211:9	at Luton 2001
Best Batting:	Away	88 D S Lehmann	at Luton 2001	34 O J Clayton	at Luton 2001
Best Bowling:	Away	4-39 R J Sidebottom	at Luton 2001	4-54 S R Rashid	at Luton 2001

Berkshire +

		By Yorkshire		Against Yorkshire	
Highest Score:	Away	131:3	at Reading 1983	128:9	at Reading 1983
Lowest Score:	Away			105	at Finchampstead 1988
Best Batting:	Away	74* A A Metcalfe	at Finchampstead 1988	29 G R J Roope	at Reading 1983
Best Bowling:	Away	5-27 G B Stevenson	at Reading 1983	1-15 M Lickley	at Reading 1983

LIST A HIGHEST AND LOWEST SCORES BY AND AGAINST YORKSHIRE PLUS INDIVIDUAL BEST BATTING AND BOWLING (Continued)

Yorkshire versus:

Cambridgeshire +

Category	Venue	By Yorkshire	Against Yorkshire
Highest Score:	In Yorkshire	177:1 — at Leeds 1986	176:8 — at Leeds 1986
	Away	299:5 — at March 2003	214:8 — at March 2003
Lowest Score:	In Yorkshire		176:8 — at March 2003
	Away	299:5 M D Moxon — at March 2003	
Best Batting:	In Yorkshire	75 M D Moxon — at Leeds 1986	85 J D R Benson — at Leeds 1986
	Away	118* M J Wood — at March 2003	53 N T Gadsby — at March 2003
Best Bowling:	In Yorkshire	3-11 A G Nicholson — at Castleford 1967	2-8 D H Fairey — at Castleford 1967
	Away	3-37 A K D Gray — at March 2003	3-53 Ajaz Akhtar — at March 2003

Cheshire +

Category	Venue	By Yorkshire	Against Yorkshire
Highest Score:	Away	160:0 — at Oxton 1985	159:7 — at Oxton 1985
Best Batting:	Away	82* M D Moxon — at Oxton 1985	46 K Teasdale — at Oxton 1985
Best Bowling:	Away	2-17 G B Stevenson — at Oxton 1985	

Combined Universities

Category	Venue	By Yorkshire	Against Yorkshire
Highest Score:	In Yorkshire	197:8 — at Leeds 1990	200:8 — at Leeds 1990
	Away	151:1 — at Oxford 1980	150:7 — at Oxford 1980
Lowest Score:	In Yorkshire	197:8 — at Leeds 1990	200:8 — at Leeds 1990
	Away	151:1 — at Oxford 1980	150:7 — at Oxford 1980
Best Batting:	In Yorkshire		63 S P James — at Leeds 1990
	Away	74* C W J Athey — at Oxford 1980	63 J O D Orders — at Oxford 1980
Best Bowling:	In Yorkshire	3-34 P J Hartley — at Leeds 1990	3-44 M E W Brooker — at Barnsley 1976
	Away	2-43 H P Cooper — at Oxford 1980	1-16 C J Ross — at Oxford 1980

Devon +

Category	Venue	By Yorkshire	Against Yorkshire
Highest Score:	Away	411:6 — at Exmouth 2004	279:8 — at Exmouth 2004
Lowest Score:	Away	259:5 — at Exmouth 2002	80 — at Exmouth 1998
Best Batting:	Away	160 M J Wood — at Exmouth 2004	83 P M Roebuck — at Exmouth 1994
Best Bowling:	Away	4-26 D S Lehmann — at Exmouth 2002	2-42 A O F Le Fleming — at Exmouth 1994

LIST A HIGHEST AND LOWEST SCORES BY AND AGAINST YORKSHIRE PLUS INDIVIDUAL BEST BATTING AND BOWLING (Continued)

Yorkshire versus:

		By Yorkshire		Against Yorkshire	
Dorset +					
Highest Score:	Away	101:2	at Bournemouth 2004	97 at Bournemouth 2004	
Best Batting:	Away	71* M J Wood	at Bournemouth 2004	C L Park 23	at Bournemouth 2004
Best Bowling:	Away	4-18 C E W Silverwood	at Bournemouth 2004	D J Worrad 2-31	at Bournemouth 2004
Durham M C +					
Highest Score:	In Yorkshire	249:6	at Middlesbrough 1978	138:5	at Middlesbrough 1978
	Away	214:6	at Chester-le-Street 1979	213:9	at Chester-le-Street 1979
Lowest Score:	In Yorkshire	135	at Harrogate 1973	136:7	at Harrogate 1973
	Away			213:9	at Chester-le-Street 1979
Best Batting:	In Yorkshire	110 J H Hampshire	at Middlesbrough 1978	N A Riddell 52	at Middlesbrough 1978
	Away	92 G Boycott	at Chester-le-Street 1979	Wasim Raja 52	at Chester-le-Street 1979
Best Bowling:	In Yorkshire	4-9 C M Old	at Middlesbrough 1978	B R Lander 5-15	at Middlesbrough 1978
	Away	3-39 H P Cooper	at Chester-le-Street 1979	B L Cairns 2-35	at Chester-le-Street 1979
Herefordshire +					
Highest Score:	Away	275:8	at Kington 1999	124:5	at Kington 1999
Best Batting:	Away	77 G S Blewett	at Kington 1999	R D Hughes 39	at Kington 1999
Best Bowling:	Away	2-22 G M Hamilton	at Kington 1999	C W Boroughs 2-41	at Kington 1999
Ireland +					
Highest Score:	In Yorkshire	299:6	at Leeds 1995	228:7	at Leeds 1995
	Away	202:4	at Belfast 2005	201:7	at Belfast 2005
Lowest Score:	In Yorkshire	249	at Leeds 1997	53	at Leeds 1997
	Away			201:7	at Belfast 2005
Best Batting:	In Yorkshire	113 C White	at Leeds 1995	S J S Warke 82	at Leeds 1995
	Away	58 M P Vaughan	at Belfast 2005	E J G Morgan 59	at Belfast 2005
Best Bowling:	In Yorkshire	7-27 D Gough	at Leeds 1997	P McCrum 3-26	at Leeds 1997
	Away	4-43 C White	at Belfast 2005	W K McCallan 1-29	at Belfast 2005

Yorkshire versus:

		By Yorkshire		Against Yorkshire	
Minor Counties #					
Highest Score:	In Yorkshire	309:5	at Leeds 1997	206:6	at Leeds 1988
	Away	218:3	at Scunthorpe 1975	182	at Scunthorpe 1975
		218:9	at Jesmond 1979		
Lowest Score:	In Yorkshire	309:5	at Leeds 1997	109	at Leeds 1974
	Away	218:3	at Scunthorpe 1975	85	at Jesmond 1979
		218:9	at Jesmond 1979		
Best Batting:	In Yorkshire	109* A McGrath	at Leeds 1997	80* J D Love	at Leeds 1991
	Away	83* G Boycott	at Chester-le-Street 1973	61 N A Folland	at Jesmond 1989
Best Bowling:	In Yorkshire	6-27 A G Nicholson	at Middlesbrough 1972	3-37 S Oakes	at Leeds 1997
	Away	5-32 S Oldham	at Scunthorpe 1975	3-27 I E Conn	at Jesmond 1989
Netherlands $					
Highest Score:	In Yorkshire	204:6	at Leeds 2010	200:8	at Leeds 2010
	Away	158:5	at Rotterdam 2010	154:9	at Rotterdam 2010
Lowest Score:	In Yorkshire	188:9	at Leeds 2011	190:8	at Leeds 2011
	Away	123	at Amsterdam 2011	154:9	at Rotterdam 2010
Best Batting:	In Yorkshire	83* J A Rudolph	at Leeds 2010	62 M G Dighton	at Leeds 2010
	Away	46* J M Bairstow	at Rotterdam 2010	34 P W Borren	at Amsterdam 2011
Best Bowling:	In Yorkshire	3-34 S A Patterson	at Leeds 2010	3-26 Mudassar Bukhari	at Leeds 2011
	Away	4-24 R M Pyrah	at Rotterdam 2010	3-28 Mudassar Bukhari	at Amsterdam 2011
Norfolk +					
Highest Score:	In Yorkshire	106:0	at Leeds 1990	104	at Leeds 1990
	Away	167	at Lakenham 1969	78	at Lakenham 1969
Lowest Score:	In Yorkshire			104	at Leeds 1990
	Away	167	at Lakenham 1969	78	at Lakenham 1969
Best Batting:	In Yorkshire	56* M D Moxon	at Leeds 1990	25 R J Finney	at Leeds 1990
	Away	55 J H Hampshire	at Lakenham 1969	21 G J Donaldson	at Lakenham 1969
Best Bowling:	In Yorkshire	3-8 P Carrick	at Leeds 1990		
	Away	3-14 C M Old	at Lakenham 1969	6-48 T I Moore	at Lakenham 1969

LIST A HIGHEST AND LOWEST SCORES BY AND AGAINST YORKSHIRE PLUS INDIVIDUAL BEST BATTING AND BOWLING (Continued)

Yorkshire versus:

Northumberland +

		By Yorkshire		Against Yorkshire	
Highest Score:	In Yorkshire	138:2	at Leeds 1992	137	at Leeds 1992
Best Batting:	In Yorkshire	38 S A Kellett	at Leeds 1992	47 G R Morris	at Leeds 1992
Best Bowling:	In Yorkshire	3-18 M A Robinson	at Leeds 1992	2-22 S Greensword	at Leeds 1992

Scotland

		By Yorkshire		Against Yorkshire	
Highest Score:	In Yorkshire	317:5	at Leeds 1986 #	244	at Leeds 2008 +
	Away	259:8	at Edinburgh 2007 +	217	at Edinburgh 2007 +
Lowest Score:	In Yorkshire	228:6	at Bradford 1981 +	142	at Leeds 1996 #
	Away	199:8	at Edinburgh 2004 $	129	at Glasgow 1995 $
Best Batting:	In Yorkshire	118* J D Love	at Bradford 1981 #	73 I L Philip	at Leeds 1989 +
	Away	91 A A Metcalfe	at Glasgow 1987 #	78 J A Beukes	at Edinburgh 2005 $
Best Bowling:	In Yorkshire	5-28 C E W Silverwood	at Leeds 1996 #	2-22 P J C Hoffman	at Leeds 2006 $
	Away	4-20 R K J Dawson	at Edinburgh 2004 $	3-42 Asim Butt	at Linlithgow 1998 #

Shropshire +

		By Yorkshire		Against Yorkshire	
Highest Score:	Away	192	at Telford 1984	229:5	at Telford 1984
Lowest Score:	Away	192	at Telford 1984	185	at Wellington 1976
Best Batting:	Away	59 J H Hampshire	at Wellington 1976	80 Mushtaq Mohammad	at Telford 1984
Best Bowling:	Away	3-17 A L Robinson	at Wellington 1976	3-26 Mushtaq Mohammad	at Telford 1984

Unicorns $

		By Yorkshire		Against Yorkshire	
Highest Score:	In Yorkshire	266:6	at Leeds 2013	234	at Leeds 2013
	Away	191:5	at Chesterfield 2013	189:9	at Chesterfield 2013
Lowest Score:	In Yorkshire			150:6	at Leeds 2012
	Away			184	at Scarborough 2012
Best Batting:	In Yorkshire	139 G S Ballance	at Leeds 2013	107 M S Lineker	at Leeds 2013
	Away	103* G S Ballance	at Scarborough 2012	83* T J New	at Scarborough 2012
Best Bowling:	In Yorkshire	5-22 J A Leaning	at Leeds 2013	2-25 R J Woolley	at Leeds 2013
	Away	3-34 R M Pyrah	at Chesterfield 2013	2-31 W W Lee	at Chesterfield 2013

LIST A HIGHEST AND LOWEST SCORES BY AND AGAINST YORKSHIRE PLUS INDIVIDUAL BEST BATTING AND BOWLING (Continued)

Yorkshire versus:

Wiltshire +

	By Yorkshire				Against Yorkshire		
Highest Score:	Away	304:7		at Trowbridge 1987	175		at Trowbridge 1987
Best Batting:	Away	85	A A Metcalfe	at Trowbridge 1987	62	J J Newman	at Trowbridge 1987
Best Bowling:	Away	4-40	K Sharp	at Trowbridge 1987	2-38	R C Cooper	at Trowbridge 1987

Yorkshire Cricket Board +

	By Yorkshire				Against Yorkshire		
Highest Score:	Away	240:5		at Harrogate 2000	110		at Harrogate 2000
Best Batting:	Away	70	M P Vaughan	at Harrogate 2000	31	R A Kettleborough	at Harrogate 2000
Best Bowling:	Away	5-30	D Gough	at Harrogate 2000	1-25	A E McKenna	at Harrogate 2000

Australians

	By Yorkshire				Against Yorkshire		
Highest Score:	In Yorkshire	188		at Leeds 1989	297:3		at Leeds 1989
Lowest Score:	In Yorkshire	140		at Bradford 1972	297:3		at Leeds 1989
Best Batting:	In Yorkshire	105	G Boycott	at Bradford 1972	172	D C Boon	at Leeds 1989
Best Bowling:	In Yorkshire	2-23	D Wilson	at Bradford 1972	3-30	D J Colley	at Bradford 1972

Bangladesh A

	By Yorkshire				Against Yorkshire		
Highest Score:	In Yorkshire	198		at Leeds 2013	191		at Leeds 2013
Best Batting:	In Yorkshire	47*	L E Plunkett	at Leeds 2013	69	Anamul Haque	at Leeds 2013
Best Bowling:	In Yorkshire	5-30	Azeem Rafiq	at Leeds 2013	3-25	Elias Sunny	at Leeds 2013

South Africa A

	By Yorkshire				Against Yorkshire		
Highest Score:	In Yorkshire				129:4		at Leeds 2017
Best Batting:	In Yorkshire				56*	K Zonda	at Leeds 2017
Best Bowling:	In Yorkshire	2-16	S A Patterson	at Leeds 2017			

Sri Lanka A

	By Yorkshire				Against Yorkshire		
Highest Score:	In Yorkshire	249		at Leeds 2014	275:9		at Leeds 2014
Lowest Score:	In Yorkshire	179:7		at Leeds 2004			
Best Batting:	In Yorkshire	81	A W Gale	at Leeds 2007	100	L D Chandimal	at Leeds 2014
Best Bowling:	In Yorkshire	5-51	A Shahzad	at Leeds 2007	4-42	S Prasanna	at Leeds 2014

LIST A HIGHEST AND LOWEST SCORES BY AND AGAINST YORKSHIRE
PLUS INDIVIDUAL BEST BATTING AND BOWLING (Continued)

Yorkshire versus:

		By Yorkshire			Against Yorkshire		
West Indians							
Highest Score:	In Yorkshire	253:4			242		at Scarborough 1995
Best Batting:	In Yorkshire	106	A McGrath		54	R B Richardson	at Scarborough 1995
Best Bowling:	In Yorkshire	3-42	G M Hamilton		3-48	R Dhanraj	at Scarborough 1995
West Indians A							
Highest Score:	In Yorkshire	139			140:2		at Leeds 2002
Best Batting:	In Yorkshire	48	M J Wood		57	D Ganga	at Leeds 2002
Best Bowling:	In Yorkshire	1-31	C J Elstub		4-24	J J C Lawson	at Leeds 2002
Young Australians							
Highest Score:	In Yorkshire	224:6			156		at Leeds 1995
Best Batting:	In Yorkshire	76	M P Vaughan		51	A C Gilchrist	at Leeds 1995
Best Bowling:	In Yorkshire	5-32	A C Morris		2-21	S Young	at Leeds 1995
Zimbabwe							
Highest Score:	In Yorkshire	203:7			202		at Sheffield 1982
Best Batting:	In Yorkshire	98*	G Boycott		53	D A G Fletcher	at Sheffield 1982
Best Bowling:	In Yorkshire	3-47	P W Jarvis		3-30	D A G Fletcher	at Sheffield 1982

341

LIST A HIGHEST TEAM TOTALS

BY YORKSHIRE

411:6	v.	Devon at Exmouth	2004 +
379:7	v.	Lancashire at Manchester	2018 +
379:7	v.	Leicestershire at Leeds	2019 +
376:3	v.	Leicestershire at Leicester	2016 +
352:6	v.	Nottinghamshire at Scarborough	2001 $
349:7	v.	Derbyshire at Leeds	2017 +
346:9	v.	Worcestershire at Leeds	2018 +
345:5	v.	Nottinghamshire at Leeds	1996 +
345:6	v.	Worcestershire at Worcester	2015 +
343:9	v.	Somerset at Taunton	2005 $
341:3	v.	Northamptonshire at Northampton	2006 +
339:4	v.	Durham at Leeds	2017 +
334:5	v.	Surrey at The Oval	2005 $
330:6	v	Surrey at The Oval	2009 +
328:4	v.	Durham at Chester-le-Street	2018 +
325:7	v.	Lancashire at Manchester	2016 +
324:7	v.	Lancashire at Manchester	2014 +
318:7	v.	Leicestershire at Leicester	1993 $
317:4	v.	Surrey at Lord's	1965 +
317:5	v.	Scotland at Leeds	1986 #
314:8	v.	Northamptonshire at Scarboough	2016 +
310:5	v.	Leicestershire at Leicester	1997 +
310	v.	Lancashire at Leeds	2019 +
309:5	v.	Minor Counties at Leeds	1997 #
307:3	v.	Essex at Chelmsford	1995 +
307:4	v.	Somerset at Taunton	2002 $
304:7	v.	Wiltshire at Trowbridge	1986 +

AGAINST YORKSHIRE

375:4	for Surrey at Scarborough	1994 $
363	for Lancashire at Manchester	2018 +
351	for Northamptonshire at Northampton	2019 +
350:6	for Worcestershire at Leeds	2018 +
348:9	for Hampshire at West End	2018 +
345:4	for Somerset at Taunton	2005 $
342	for Worcestershire at Worcester	2017 +
339:7	for Northamptonshire at Northampton	2006 +
338:5	for Somerset at Leeds	2013 $
335:5	for Durham at Leeds	2017 +
334:8	for Derbyshire at Leeds	2017 +
329:8	for Surrey at The Oval	2009 +
325:7	for Northamptonshire at Northampton	1992 $
314:4	for Northamptonshire at Leeds	2007 +
313:7	for Surrey at Leeds	2017 +
311:6	for Lancashire at Leeds	2019 +
310:7	for Northamptonshire at Scarborough	2016 +
309:3	for Warwickshire at Birmingham	2005 $
308:6	for Surrey at The Oval	1995 $
306:8	for Somerset at Taunton	2002 $
302:7	for Leicestershire at Leeds	2008 $
298:9	for Leicestershire at Leicester	1997 $
297:3	for Australians at Leeds	1989
294:6	for Gloucestershire at Cheltenham	2010 $
293:7	for Worcestershire at Worcester	2019 +
293:9	for Lancashire at Manchester	1996 +
293:9	for Leicestershire at Leicester	2018 +
292	for Sussex at Hove	1963 +

LIST A HIGHEST INDIVIDUAL SCORES

BY YORKSHIRE

191	D S Lehmann	v.	Nottinghamshire at Scarborough	2001	$
175	T M Head	v.	Leicestershire at Leicester	2016	+
174	J M Bairstow	v.	Durham at Leeds	2017	+
164	T Kohler-Cadmore	v.	Durham at Chester-le-Street	2018	+
160	M J Wood	v.	Devon at Exmouth	2004	+
156	G S Ballance	v.	Leicestershire at Leeds	2019	+
152 *	G S Ballance	v.	Northamptonshire at Northampton	2017	+
148	C White	v.	Leicestershire at Leicester	1997	$
148	A McGrath	v.	Somerset at Taunton	2006	$
146	G Boycott	v.	Surrey at Lord's	1965	+
144	A Lyth	v.	Lancashire at Manchester	2018	+
142	G Boycott	v.	Worcestershire at Worcester	1980	+
141*	M D Moxon	v	Glamorgan at Cardiff	1991	#
140	P S P Handscomb	v.	Derbyshire at Leeds	2017	+
139*	S P Fleming	v.	Warwickshire at Leeds	2003	$
139	G S Ballance	v.	Unicorns at Leeds	2013	$

AGAINST YORKSHIRE

177	S A Newman	for	Surrey at The Oval	2009	+
172	D C Boon	for	Australia at Leeds	1989	
171	J M Vince	for	Hampshire at West End	2018	+
161	D J G Sales	for	Northamptonshire at Northampton	2006	+
155*	B A Richards	for	Hampshire at Hull	1970	$
146*	S Young	for	Gloucestershire at Leeds	1997	$
143*	C M Spearman	for	Gloucestershire at Bristol	2004	$
141*	B J Hodge	for	Lancashire at Manchester	2007	+
140*	P D Trego	for	Somerset at Taunton	2013	$
137*	M Klinger	for	Gloucestershire at Leeds	2015	+
137	I R Bell	for	Warwickshire at Birmingham	2005	$
136*	N Hussain	for	Essex at Chelmsford	2002	#
136	M A Lynch	for	Surrey at Bradford	1985	$
135*	D J Bicknell	for	Surrey at The Oval	1989	+
133	A D Brown	for	Surrey at Scarborough	1994	$

MOST RUNS IN LIST A MATCHES

742	v.	Lancashire at Manchester	2018 +	Y 379:7	L 363
696	v.	Worcestershire at Leeds	2018 +	W 350:6	Y 346:9
690	v.	Devon at Exmouth	2004 +	Y 411:6	D 279:8
688	v.	Somerset at Taunton	2005 $	S 345:4	Y 343:9
683	v.	Derbyshire at Leeds	2017 +	Y 349:7	D 334:8
680	v.	Northamptonshire at Northampton	2006 +	Y 342:3	N 339:7
674	v.	Durham at Leeds	2017 +	D 335:5	Y: 339-4
659	v.	Surrey at The Oval	2009 +	S 329:8	Y 330:6
633	v.	Worcestershire at Worcester	2017 +	W 342	Y 291
625	v.	Surrey at The Oval	2005 $	S 334:8	S 291
624	v.	Northamptonshire at Scarborough	2016 +	N 310:7	Y 314:8
621	v.	Lancashire at Leeds	2019 +	L 311:6	Y 310
613	v.	Somerset at Taunton	2002 $	Y 307:4	S 306:8
605	v.	Leicestershire at Leeds	2008 $	Y 303:4	L 302:7
604	v.	Surrey at The Oval	1995 $	S 308:6	Y 296:6
602	v.	Surrey at Leeds	2017 +	S 313:7	Y 289:9
601	v.	Lancashire at Manchester	2014 +	Y 324:7	L 277

LIST A BEST BOWLING

BY YORKSHIRE

7-15	R A Hutton	v.	Worcestershire at Leeds	1969 $
7-27	D Gough	v.	Ireland at Leeds	1997 +
6-14	H P Cooper	v.	Worcestershire at Worcester	1975 $
6-15	F S Trueman	v	Somerset at Taunton	1965 +
6-18	D Wilson	v.	Kent at Canterbury	1969 $
6-27	A G Nicholson	v	Minor Counties at Middlesbrough	1972 #
6-27	P W Jarvis	v.	Somerset at Taunton	1989 $
6-32	S A Patterson	v.	Derbyshire at Leeds	2010 $
6-36	A G Nicholson	v	Somerset At Sheffield	1972 $
6-40	R J Sidebottom	v	Glamorgan at Cardiff	1998 $
5-13	D Gough	v.	Sussex at Hove	1994 $
5-16	S Stuchbury	v.	Leicestershire at Leicester	1982 $
5-16	G M Hamilton	v.	Hampshire at Leeds	1998 $
5-17	A G Nicholson	v.	Nottinghamshire at Hull	1972 $
5-18	P W Jarvis	v.	Derbyshire at Leeds	1990 $

AGAINST YORKSHIRE

7-32	R G D Willis	for	Warwickshire at Birmingham	1981 #
7-33	R D Jackman	for	Surrey at Harrogate	1970 +
6-15	A A Donald	for	Warwickshire at Birmingham	1995 $
6-18	R E East '	for	Essex at Hull	1969 $
6-25	G Chapple	for	Lancashire at Leeds	1998 $
6-32	M T Coles	for	Kent at Leeds	2012 $
6-48	T I Moore	for	Norfolk at Lakenham	1969 +
5-15	B R Lander	for	Durham M C at Harrogate	1973 +
5-15	Sarfraz Nawaz	for	Northamptonshire at Northampton	1975 $
5-16	B S Crump	for	Northamptonshire at Bradford	1969 $
5-16	G C Holmes	for	Glamorgan at Swansea	1985 $
5-20	R E East	for	Essex at Colchester	1979 $
5-22	R D Jackman	for	Surrey at The Oval	1978 $
5-24	C J Tunnicliffe	for	Derbyshire at Derby	1981 #
5-24	C W Henderson	for	Leicestershire at Leeds	2004 $

LIST A ECONOMICAL BOWLING

BY YORKSHIRE

11-9-3-1	C M Old	v.	Middlesex at Lord's	1979 #
8-5-3-3	A L Robinson	v.	Derbyshire at Scarborough	1973 $

AGAINST YORKSHIRE

8-4-6-2	P J Sainsbury	for	Hampshire at Hull	1970 $
8-5-6-3	M J Procter	for	Gloucestershire at Cheltenham	1979 $

LIST A MOST EXPENSIVE BOWLING

BY YORKSHIRE

9-0-87-1	T T Bresnan	v.	Somerset at Taunton	2005 $

AGAINST YORKSHIRE

12-1-96-0	M E Waugh	for	Essex at Chelmsford	1995 +

LIST A HAT-TRICKS FOR YORKSHIRE (4)

P W Jarvis	v. Derbyshire at Derby 1982 $	D Gough	v. Ireland at Leeds 1997 +
D Gough	v. Lancashire at Leeds 1998 $	C White	v. Kent at Leeds 2000 $

LIST A MAN-OF-THE-MATCH AWARDS (137)

M D Moxon	12	M P Vaughan	5	M J Wood	3
G Boycott	11	A Sidebottom	4	R J Blakey	2
D L Bairstow	8	C E W Silverwood	4	G L Brophy	2
C White	8	D Byas	3	P Carrick	2
A A Metcalfe	7	D Gough	3	R A Hutton	2
J H Hampshire	6	P J Hartley	3	L E Plunkett	2
D S Lehmann	6	J D Love	3	P J Sharpe	2
C W J Athey	5	A McGrath	3	G B Stevenson	2
M G Bevan	5	C M Old	3		

One each: T T Bresnan, D B Close, M T G Elliott, G M Fellows, S D Fletcher, G M Hamilton, S N Hartley, P M Hutchinson, R Illingworth, C Johnson, S A Kellett, B Leadbeater, M J Lumb, A G Nicholson, S Oldham, S A Patterson, R M Pyrah, P E Robinson, R D Stemp, F S Trueman and D Wilson.

ALL LIST A CENTURIES 1963-2019 (117)

C W J ATHEY (2)

118	v.	Leicestershire	at Leicester	1978 $
115	v.	Kent	at Leeds	1980 +

D L BAIRSTOW (1)

103 *	v.	Derbyshire	at Derby	1981 #

J M BAIRSTOW (2)

114	v.	Middlesex	at Lord's	2011 $
174	v.	Durham	at Leeds	2017 +

G S BALLANCE (4)

139	v.	Unicorns	at Leeds	2013 $
103 *	v.	Unicorns	at Scarborough	2012 $
152 *	v.	Northamptonshire	at Northampton	2017 +
156	v.	Leicestershire	at Leeds	2019 +

M G BEVAN (2)

103 *	v.	Gloucestershire	at Middlesbrough	1995 $
101	v.	Worcestershire	at Scarborough	1995 $

G BOYCOTT (7)

146	v.	Surrey	at Lord's	1965 +
142	v.	Worcestershire	at Worcester	1980 #
108 *	v.	Northamptonshire	at Huddersfield	1974 $
106	v.	Northamptonshire	at Bradford	1984 #
105	v.	Australians	at Bradford	1972
104 *	v.	Glamorgan	at Colwyn Bay	1973 $
102	v.	Northamptonshire	at Middlesbrough	1977 #

R J BLAKEY (3)

130	v.	Kent	at Scarborough	1991 $
105 *	v.	Warwickshire	at Scarborough	1992 $
100 *	v.	Gloucestershire	at Cheltenham	1990 $

ALL LIST A CENTURIES 1963-2019 *(Continued)*

H C BROOK (1)

103	v	Leicestershire	at Leeds	2019 +

D BYAS (5)

116 *	v.	Surrey	at The Oval	1996 #
111 *	v.	Lancashire	at Leeds	1996 $
106 *	v.	Derbyshire	at Chesterfield	1993 $
104 *	v.	Hampshire	at Leeds	1999 #
101 *	v.	Nottinghamshire	at Leeds	1994 $

M T G ELLIOTT (3)

128 *	v.	Somerset	at Lord's	2002 +
115 *	v.	Kent	at Leeds	2002 $
109	v.	Leicestershire	at Leicester	2002 $

S P FLEMING (1)

139 *	v.	Warwickshire	at Leeds	2003 $

M J FOSTER (1)

118	v.	Leicestershire	at Leicester	1993 $

A W GALE (2)

125 *	v.	Essex	at Chelmsford	2010 $
112	v.	Kent	at Canterbury	2011 $

J H HAMPSHIRE (7)

119	v.	Leicestershire	at Hull	1971 $
114 *	v.	Northamptonshire	at Scarborough	1978 $
111 *	v.	Sussex	at Hastings	1973 $
110	v.	Durham M C	at Middlesbrough	1978 +
108	v.	Nottinghamshire	at Sheffield	1970 $
106 *	v.	Lancashire	at Manchester	1972 $
100 *	v.	Warwickshire	at Birmingham	1975 $

P S P HANDSCOMB (1)

140	v. Derbyshire	at Leeds	2017 +

T M HEAD (1))

175	v. Leicestershire	at Leicester	2016 +

P A JAQUES (1)

105	v. Sussex	at Leeds	2004 $

S A KELLETT (2)

118 *	v. Derbyshire	at Leeds	1992 $
107	v. Ireland	at Leeds	1995 +

T KOHLER-CADMORE (1)

164	v. Durham	at Chester-le-Street	2018 +

J A LEANING (2)

131 *	v. Leicestershire	at Leicester	2016 +
111 *	v. Essex	at Scarborough	2014 +

A Z LEES (1)

102	v. Northamptonshire	at Northampton	2014 +

D S LEHMANN (8)

191	v. Nottinghamshire	at Scarborough	2001 $
119	v. Durham	at Leeds	1998 #
118 *	v. Northamptonshire	at Northampton	2006 +
105	v. Glamorgan	at Cardiff	1995 +
104	v. Somerset	at Taunton	2002 $
103	v. Derbyshire	at Leeds	2001 #
103	v. Leicestershire	at Scarborough	2001 $
102 *	v. Derbyshire	ar Derby	1998 #

J D LOVE (4)

118 *	v. Scotland	at Bradford	1981 #
118 *	v. Surrey	at Leeds	1987 $
104 *	v. Nottinghamshire	at Hull	1986 $
100 *	v. Gloucestershire	at Gloucester	1985 $

R G LUMB (1)

101	v. Nottinghamshire	at Scarborough	1976 $

A LYTH (5)

144	v. Lancashire	at Manchester	2018 +
136 §	v. Lancashire	at Manchester	2016 +
132*	v. Leicestershire	at Leicester	2018 +
125 §	v. Northamptonshire	at Scarborough	2016 +
109 *	v. Sussex	at Scarborough	2009 $

(§ consecutive days)

A McGRATH (7)

148	v. Somerset	at Taunton	2006 $
135 *	v. Lancashire	at Leeds	2007 +
109 *	v. Minor Counties	at Leeds	1997 #
106	v. West Indies	at Scarborough	1995
105 *	v. Scotland	at Leeds	2008 +
102	v. Kent	at Canterbury	2001 $
100	v. Durham	at Leeds	2007 +

G J MAXWELL (1)

111	v. Worcestershire	at Worcester	2015 +

A A METCALFE (4)

127 *	v. Warwickshire	at Leeds	1990 +
116	v. Middlesex	at Lord's	1991 $
115 *	v. Gloucestershire	at Scarborough	1984 $
114	v. Lancashire	at Manchester	1991 #

M D MOXON (7)

141 *	v. Glamorgan	at Cardiff	1991 #
137	v. Nottinghamshire	at Leeds	1996+
129 *	v. Surrey	at The Oval	1991 $
112	v. Sussex	at Middlesbrough	1991 $
107 *	v. Warwickshire	at Leeds	1990 +
106 *	v. Lancashire	at Manchester	1986 #
105	v. Somerset	at Scarborough	1990 $

ALL LIST A CENTURIES 1963-2019 *(Continued)*

C A PUJARA (1)

101	v. Worcestershire	at Leeds	2018 +

R B RICHARDSON (1)

103	v. Nottinghamshire	at Nottingham	1993 $

J A RUDOLPH (9)

132 *	v. Sussex	at Scarborough	2011 $
127	v. Somerset	at Scarborough	2007 $
124 *	v. Middlesex	at Scarborough	2010 $
120	v. Leicestershire	at Leeds	2008 $
118	v. Gloucestershire	at Leeds	2009 +
106	v. Warwickshire	at Scarborough	2010 $
105	v. Derbyshire	at Chesterfield	2010 $
101 *	v. Essex	at Chelmsford	2010 $
100	v. Leicestershire	at Leeds	2007 +

K SHARP (3)

114	v. Essex	at Chelmsford	1985 $
112 *	v. Worcestershire	at Worcester	1985 $
105 *	v. Scotland	at Leeds	1984 #

S R TENDULKAR (1)

107	v. Lancashire	at Leeds	1992 $

M P VAUGHAN (3)

125 *	v. Somerset	at Taunton	2001 #
116 *	v. Lancashire	at Manchester	2004 +
116 *	v. Kent	at Leeds	2005 $

C WHITE (5)

148	v. Leicestershire	at Leicester	1997 $
113	v. Ireland	at Leeds	1995 +
112	v. Northamptonshire	at Northampton	2006 +
101 *	v. Durham	at Chester-le-Street	2006 +
100 *	v. Surrey	at Leeds	2002 +

D J WILLEY (1)

131	v. Lancashire	at Manchester	2018 +

M J WOOD (5)

160	v. Devon	at Exmouth	2004 +
118 *	v. Cambridgeshire	at March	2003 +
115 *	v. Derbyshire	at Derby	2002 #
111	v. Surrey	at The Oval	2005 $
105 *	v. Somerset	at Taunton	2002$

YOUNUS KHAN (1)

100	v. Nottinghamshire	at Nottingham	2007 +

274	3rd wkt	T M Head (175)	and J A Leaning (131*)	v. Leicestershire at Leicester
				2016+
242*	1st wkt	M D Moxon (107*)	and A A Metcalfe (127*)	v. Warwickshire at Leeds 1990 +
235	2nd wkt	A Lyth (144)	and D J Willey (131)	v. Lancashire at Manchester
				2018 +
233*	1st wkt	A W Gale (125*)	and J A Rudolph (101*)	v. Essex at Chelmsford 2010 $
213	1st wkt	M D Moxon (141*)	and A A Metcalfe (84)	v. Glamorgan at Cardiff 1991 #
211*	1st wkt	M D Moxon (93*)	and A A Metcalfe (94*)	v. Warwickshire at Birmingham
				1987 #
211	4th wkt	H C Brook (103)	and G S Ballance (156)	v. Leicestershire at Leeds 2019 +
207	4th wkt	S A Kellett (107)	and C White (113)	v. Ireland at Leeds 1995 +
202	2nd wkt	G Boycott (87)	and C W J Athey (115)	v. Kent at Leeds 1980 +
201	1st wkt	J H Hampshire (86)	and C W J Athey (118)	v. Leicestershire at Leicester
				1978 $
198*	4th wkt	M T G Elliott (115*)	and A McGrath (85*)	v. Kent at Leeds 2002 $
195	1st wkt	A Lyth (84)	and A Z Lees (102)	v. Northamptonshire
				at Northampton 2014 +
192	1st wkt	G Boycott (146)	and D B Close (79)	v. Surrey at Lord's 1965 +
190	1st wkt	G Boycott (89*)	and R G Lumb (101)	v. Nottinghamshire
				at Scarborough 1976 $
190	5th wkt	R J Blakey (96)	and M J Foster (118)	v. Leicestershire at Leicester
				1993 $
189	2nd wkt	J M Bairstow (174)	and J E Root (55)	v. Durham at Leeds 2017 +
186	1st wkt	G Boycott (99)	and J H Hampshire (92*)	v. Gloucestershire
				at Scarborough 1975 $
186	1st wkt	G S Blewett (71)	and D Byas (104*)	v. Hampshire at Leeds 1999 #
184	3rd wkt	M P Vaughan (70)	and D S Lehmann (119)	v. Durham at Leeds 1998 #
181	5th wkt	M T G Elliott (109)	and A McGrath (78)	v. Leicestershire at Leicester
				2002 $
176	3rd wkt	R J Blakey (86)	and S R Tendulkar (107)	v. Lancashire at Leeds 1992 $
176	2nd wkt	T Kohler-Cadmore (164)		
			and C A Pujara (82)	v. Durham at Chester-le-Street
				2018 +
172	2nd wkt	D Byas (86)	and D S Lehmann (99)	v. Kent at Maidstone 1998 $
172	3rd wkt	A McGrath (38)	and D S Lehmann (191)	v. Nottinghamshire
				at Scarborough 2001 $
171	1st wkt	M D Moxon (112)	and A A Metcalfe (68)	v. Sussex at Middlesbrough 1991 $
170	4th wkt	M J Wood (105*)	and D S Lehmann (104)	v. Somerset at Taunton 2002 $
170	1st wkt	A W Gale (89)	and J A Rudolph (120)	v. Leicestershire at Leeds 2008 $
167*	6th wkt	M G Bevan (95*)	and R J Blakey ((80*)	v. Lancashire at Manchester
				1996 #
167*	1st wkt	C White (100*)	and M J Wood (57*)	v. Surrey at Leeds 2002 +
167	1st wkt	M D Moxon(64)	and A A Metcalfe (116)	v. Middlesex at Lord's 1991 $
167	1st wkt	M J Wood (65)	and S P Fleming (139*)	v. Warwickshire at Leeds 2003 $
166	1st wkt	M D Moxon (82*)	and A A Metcalfe (70)	v. Northamptonshire at Leeds
				1988 #
165	1st wkt	M D Moxon (80)	and D Byas (106*)	v. Derbyshire at Chesterfield
				1993 $
165	1st wkt	M D Moxon (70)	and D Byas (88*)	v. Northamptonshire at Leeds
				1993 $
164*	2nd wkt	G Boycott (91*)	and C W J Athey (79*)	v. Worcestershire at Worcester
				1981 $

LIST A PARTNERSHIPS OF 150 AND OVER *(Continued)*

164	3rd wkt	A McGrath (105*)	and J A Rudolph (82)	v. Scotland at Leeds	2008 +
164	3rd wkt	J A Rudolph (84)	and A McGrath (73)	v. Glamorgan at Scarborough	2008 $
161	1st wkt	M D Moxon (74)	and A A Metcalfe (85)	v. Wiltshire at Trowbridge	1987 +
160*	1st wkt	G Boycott (70*)	and M D Moxon (82*)	v. Cheshire at Oxton	1985 +
160*	5th wkt	G M Fellows (80*)	and C White (73*)	v. Surrey at Leeds	2001 +
160*	3rd wkt	A Lyth (60*)	and G S Ballance (103*)	v. Unicorns at Scarborough	2012 $
160	1st wkt	G Boycott (67)	and J H Hampshire (84)	v. Warwickshire at Birmingham	1973 $
159	2nd wkt	G Boycott (92)	and D B Close (96)	v. Surrey at The Oval	1969 +
157	2nd wkt	K Sharp (71)	and R J Blakey (79)	v. Worcestershire at Worcester	1990 $
157	1st wkt	T Kohler-Cadmore (79)	and A Lyth (78)	v. Derbyshire at Leeds	2019 +
156	4th wkt	P S P Handscomb (140)	and G S Ballance (63)	v. Derbyshire at Leeds	2017 +
155*	1st wkt	A Lyth (67*)	and A Z Lees (69*)	v. Derbyshire at Scarborough	2014 +
154*	2nd wkt	J H Hampshire (111*)	and B Leadbeater (57*)	v. Sussex at Hove	1973 $
153	4th wkt	Younus Khan (100)	and A W Gale ((69*)	v. Nottinghamshire at Nottingham	2007 +
153	1st wkt	A Lyth (132*)	and T Kohler-Cadmore (74)	v. Leicestershire at Leicester	2018 +
150*	5th wkt	S N Hartley (67*)	and J D Love (82*)	v. Hampshire at Middlesbrough	1983 $

LIST A HIGHEST PARTNERSHIPS FOR EACH WICKET

1st wkt	242*	M D Moxon (107*)	and A A Metcalfe (127*)	v Warwickshire at Leeds	1990 +
2nd wkt	235	A Lyth (144)	and D J Willey (131)	v. Lancashire at Manchester	2018 +
3rd wkt	274	T M Head (175)	and J A Leaning (131*)	v.Leicestershire at Leicester	2016+
4th wkt	211	H C Brook (103)	and G S Ballance (156)	v.Leicestershire at Leeds	2019 +
5th wkt	190	R J Blakey (96)	and M J Foster (118)	v. Leicestershire at Leicester	1993 +
6th wkt	167*	M G Bevan (95*)	and R J Blakey ((80*)	v. Lancashire at Manchester	1996 #
7th wkt	149*	J D Love (118*)	and C M Old (78*)	v. Scotland at Bradford	1981 #
8th wkt	89	R J Blakey (60)	and R K J Dawson (41)	v. Leicestershire at Scarborough	2002 $
9th wkt	88	S N Hartley (67)	and A Ramage (32*)	v. Middlesex at Lord's	1982 #
10th wkt	80*	D L Bairstow (103*)	and M Johnson (4*)	v. Derbyshire at Derby	1981 #

ALL LIST A 5 WICKETS IN AN INNINGS 1963-2019 (57)

C W J ATHEY (1)
5-35	v	Derbyshire	at Chesterfield	1981 $

AZEEM RAFIQ (1)
5-30	v	Bangladesh A	at Leeds	2013

M G BEVAN (1)
5-29	v	Sussex	at Eastbourne	1996 $

P CARRICK (2)
5-22	v	Glamorgan	at Leeds	1991 $
5-40	v	Sussex	at Middlesbrough	1991 $

H P COOPER (2)
6-14	v	Worcestershire	at Worcester	1975 $
5-30	v	Worcestershire	at Middlesbrough	1978 $

D GOUGH (4)
5-13	v	Sussex	at Hove	1994 $
7-27	v	Ireland	at Leeds	1997 +
5-25	v	Surrey	at Leeds	1998 $
5-30	v	Yorkshire C B	at Harrogate	2000 +

G M HAMILTON (2)
5-16	v	Hampshire	at Leeds	1998 $
5-34	v	Sussex	at Scarborough	2000 $

P J HARTLEY (4)
5-36	v	Sussex	at Scarborough	1993 $
5-38	v	Worcestershire	at Worcester	1990 $
5-43	v	Scotland	at Leeds	1986 #
5-46	v	Hampshire	at Southampton	1990 +

M J HOGGARD (3)
5-28	v	Leicestershire	at Leicester	2000 $
5-30	v	Northamptonshire	at Northampton	2000 $
5-65	v	Somerset	at Lord's	2002 +

R A HUTTON (1)
7-15	v	Worcestershire	at Leeds	1969 $

R ILLINGWORTH (1)
5-29	v	Surrey	at Lord's	1965 +

P W JARVIS (3)
6-27	v	Somerset	at Taunton	1989 $
5-18	v	Derbyshire	at Leeds	1990 $
5-29	v	Northamptonshire	at Northampton	1992 $

J A LEANING (1)
5-22	v	Unicorns	at Leeds	2013 $

A C MORRIS (1)
5-32	v	Young Australia	at Leeds	1995

M D MOXON (1)
5-31	v	Warwickshire	at Leeds	1991 #

A G NICHOLSON (4)
6-27	v	Minor Counties	at Middlesbrough	1972 #
6-36	v	Somerset	at Sheffield	1972 $
5-17	v	Nottinghamshire	at Hull	1972 $
5-24	v	Derbyshire	at Bradford	1975 #

C M OLD (2)

5-33	v	Sussex	at Hove	1971 $
5-38	v	Northamptonshire	at Sheffield	1972 $

S OLDHAM (1)

5-32	v	Minor Counties	at Scunthorpe	1975 #

S A PATTERSON (2)

6-32	v	Derbyshire	at Leeds	2010 $
5-24	v	Worcestershire	at Worcester	2015 +

M W PILLANS (1)

5-29	v	Leicestershire	Leeds	2019 +

A U RASHID (1)

5-33	v	Hampshire	at Southampton	2014 +

A SHAHZAD (1)

5-51	v	Sri Lanka A	at Leeds	2007

C SHAW (1)

5-41	v	Hampshire	at Bournemouth	1984 $

A SIDEBOTTOM (2)

5-27	v	Worcestershire	at Bradford	1985 #
5-27	v	Glamorgan	at Leeds	1987 +

R J SIDEBOTTOM (2)

6-40	v	Glamorgan	at Cardiff	2003 $
5-42	v	Leicestershire	at Leicester	2003 $

C E W SILVERWOOD (1)

5-28	v	Scotland	at Leeds	1996 #

G B STEVENSON (4)

5-27	v	Berkshire	at Reading	1983 +
5-28	v	Kent	at Canterbury	1978 #
5-41	v	Leicestershire	at Leicester	1976 $
5-50	v	Worcestershire	at Leeds	1982 #

S STUCHBURY (1)

5-16	v	Leicestershire	at Leicester	1982 $

N D THORNICROFT (1)

5-42	v	Gloucestershire	at Leeds	2003 $

F S TRUEMAN (1)

6-15	v	Somerset	at Taunton	1965 +

C WHITE (2)

5-19	v	Somerset	at Scarborough	2002 $
5-25	v	Lancashire	at Leeds	2000 #

D WILSON (2)

6-18	v	Kent	at Canterbury	1969 $
5-25	v	Lancashire	at Bradford	1972 #

ALL LIST A PLAYERS WHO HAVE TAKEN 4 WICKETS IN AN INNINGS 1963-2019 (167) AND BEST FIGURES

11	C M Old	4-9	v	Durham M C	at Middlesbrough	1978 +
10	C White	4-14	v	Lancashire	at Leeds	2000 $
		4-14	v	Surrey	at The Oval	2005 $
9	A Sidebottom	4-15	v	Worcestershire	at Leeds	1987 #
8	P W Jarvis	4-13	v	Worcestershire	at Leeds	1986 $
8	D Gough	4-17	v	Nottinghamshire	at Nottingham	2000 #
8	G B Stevenson	4-20	v	Essex	at Barnsley	1977 #
7	S D Fletcher	4-11	v	Kent	at Canterbury	1988 $
6	C E W Silverwood	4-11	v	Leicestershire	at Leicester	2000 $
6	H P Cooper	4-18	v	Leicestershire	at Leeds	1975 +
5	S Oldham	4-13	v	Nottinghamshire	at Nottingham	1989 $
5	R M Pyrah	4-24	v	Netherlands	at Rotterdam	2010 $
4	P Carrick	4-13	v	Derbyshire	at Bradford	1983 $
4	R K J Dawson	4-13	v	Derbyshire	at Derby	2002 $
4	T T Bresnan	4-25	v	Somerset	at Leeds	2005 $
4	G M Hamilton	4-27	v	Warwickshire	at Birmingham	1995 $
3	R A Hutton	4-18	v	Surrey	at The Oval	1972 $
3	A G Nicholson	4-15	v	Kent	at Leeds	1974 $
3	P J Hartley	4-21	v	Scotland	at Glasgow	1995 #
3	A L Robinson	4-25	v	Surrey	at The Oval	1974 $
3	R D Stemp	4-25	v	Gloucestershire	at Bristol	1996 $
3	M P Vaughan	4-27	v	Gloucestershire	at Bristol	2000 $
3	S A Patterson	4-28	v	Worcestershire	at Worcester	2011 $
3	A U Rashid	4-38	v	Northamptonshire	at Northampton	2012 $
2	M K Bore	4-21	v	Sussex	at Middlesbrough	1970 $
		4-21	v	Worcestershire	at Worcester	1970 $
2	J D Woodford	4-23	v	Northamptonshire	at Northampton	1970 $
		4-23	v	Warwickshire	at Middlesbrough	1971 $
2	G J Kruis	4-17	v	Derbyshire	at Leeds	2007 $
2	D Wilson	4-22	v	Nottinghamshire	at Bradford	1969 $
2	V J Craven	4-22	v	Kent	at Scarborough	2003 $
2	M A Robinson	4-23	v	Northamptonshire	at Leeds	1993 $
2	S N Hartley	4-32	v	Derbyshire	at Leeds	1989 #
2	A U Rashid	4-38	v	Northamptonshire	at Northampton	2012 $
2	A McGrath	4-41	v	Surrey	at Leeds	2003 $
2	D J Willey	4-47	v	Derbyshire	at Derby	2018 +
1	R Illingworth	4-6	v	Middlesex	at Hull	1983 $
1	M Johnson	4-18	v	Scotland	at Bradford	1981 #
1	G S Blewett	4-18	v	Lancashire	at Manchester	1999 +
1	G M Fellows	4-19	v	Durham	at Leeds	2002 $
1	A P Grayson	4-25	v	Glamorgan	at Cardiff	1994 $
1	C J Elstub	4-25	v	Surrey	at Leeds	2001 $
1	D S Lehmann	4-26	v	Devon	at Exmouth	2002 +
1	C Shaw	4-29	v	Middlesex	at Leeds	1988 +
1	A G Wharf	4-29	v	Nottinghamshire	at Leeds	1996 #
1	F S Trueman	4-30	v	Nottinghamshire	at Middlesbrough	1963 +
1	J D Batty	4-33	v	Kent	at Scarborough	1991 $
1	P M Hutchinson	4-34	v	Gloucestershire	at Gloucester	1998 $
1	A K D Gray	4-34	v	Kent	at Leeds	2002 $

1	A Shahzad	4-34	v	Middlesex	at Lord's	2010 $
1	P M Stringer	4-35	v	Derbyshire	at Sheffield	1969 $
1	C S Pickles	4-36	v	Somerset	at Scarborough	1990 $
1	M J Hoggard	4-39	v	Surrey	at Leeds	2000 #
1	R J Sidebottom	4-39	v	Bedfordshire	at Luton	2001 +
1	K Sharp	4-40	v	Wiltshire	at Trowbridge	1987 +
1	T L Best	4-46	v	Essex	at Chelmsford	2010 $
1	Azeem Rafiq	4-47	v.	Lancashire	at Leeds	2017 +
1	A C Morris	4-49	v	Leicestershire	at Leicester	1997 $
1	L E Plunkett	4-52	v	Kent	Canterbury	2016 +
1	D B Close	4-60	v	Sussex	at Hove	1963 +
1	B O Coad	4-63	v.	Derbyshire	at Leeds	2017 +
1	M J Waite	4-65	v.	Worcestershire	at Worcester	2017 +

CAREER AVERAGES FOR YORKSHIRE
ALL LIST A MATCHES OF 40 TO 65 OVERS 1963-2019

Player	M	Inns	NO	Runs	HS	Av'ge	100s	50s	Runs	Wkts	Av'ge	Ct/St
Ashraf, M A	22	6	4	3	3*	1.50	0	0	895	23	38.91	4
Athey, C W J ...	140	129	14	3,662	118	31.84	2	25	431	19	22.68	46
Azeem Rafiq ...	30	21	8	222	52*	17.07	0	1	1,160	41	28.29	12
Bairstow, D L ..	403	317	71	5,180	103*	21.05	1	19	17	0	—	390/31
Bairstow, J M .	**43**	**39**	**4**	**1,051**	**174**	**30.02**	**2**	**3**	**0**	**0**	**—**	**33/3**
Baker, T M	4	1	0	3	3	3.00	0	0	89	4	22.25	3
Balderstone, J C	13	11	2	173	46	19.22	0	0	38	2	19.00	3
Ballance, G S ..	**67**	**62**	**9**	**2,853**	**156**	**53.83**	**4**	**18**	**0**	**0**	**—**	**23**
Batty, J D	38	16	7	50	13*	5.55	0	0	1,297	42	30.88	18
Berry, P J	1	0	0	0	—	—	0	0	28	0	—	0
Best, T L	5	1	1	8	8*	—	0	0	166	10	16.60	1
Bevan, M G	48	45	12	2,110	103*	63.93	2	19	540	28	19.28	11
Binks, J G	30	21	3	247	34	13.72	0	0	0	0	—	26/8
Birkhead, B D .	**1**	**0**	**0**	**0**	**—**	**—**	**0**	**0**	**0**	**0**	**—**	**1**
Blain, J A R ...	15	8	3	34	11*	6.80	0	0	462	14	33.00	3
Blakey, R J	373	319	84	7,361	130*	31.32	3	35	0	0	—	369/59
Blewett, G S ...	17	17	0	345	77	20.29	0	2	196	11	17.81	7
Booth, P A	5	2	1	7	6*	7.00	0	0	147	3	49.00	1
Bore, M K	55	24	10	90	15	6.42	0	0	1,600	50	32.00	15
Boycott, G	264	255	38	8,699	146	40.08	7	63	1,095	25	43.80	92
Bresnan, T T ..	**181**	**130**	**31**	**2,124**	**95***	**21.45**	**0**	**6**	**6,536**	**196**	**33.34**	**52**
Broadhurst, M ..	1	0	0	0	—	—	0	0	27	0	—	0
Brook, H C ..	**15**	**12**	**1**	**343**	**103**	**31.18**	**1**	**1**	**19**	**0**	**—**	**4**
Brooks, J A	12	4	1	7	6	2.33	0	0	461	15	30.73	3
Brophy, G L ...	68	57	12	1,240	93*	27.55	0	9	0	0	—	67/14
Byas, D	313	301	35	7,782	116*	29.25	5	44	659	25	26.36	128
Callis, E	1	1	0	0	0	0.00	0	0	0	0	—	0
Carrick, P	304	206	53	2,159	54	14.11	0	2	7,408	236	31.38	70
Carver, K	15	4	4	52	35*	—	0	0	440	14	31.42	2
Chapman, C A ..	10	7	4	94	36*	31.33	0	0	0	0	—	7
Claydon, M E ..	7	2	0	15	9	7.50	0	0	293	8	36.62	0
Cleary, M F	4	3	1	50	23*	25.00	0	0	159	2	79.50	0
Close, D B	32	31	2	631	96	21.75	0	3	475	23	20.65	14
Coad, B O	**17**	**6**	**5**	**15**	**9**	**15.00**	**0**	**0**	**748**	**20**	**37.40**	**5**
Cooper, H P ...	142	74	34	483	29*	12.07	0	0	4,184	177	23.63	26
Cope, G A	37	20	13	96	18*	13.71	0	0	1,020	24	42.50	9
Coverdale, S P ..	3	3	2	18	17*	18.00	0	0	0	0	—	4
Craven, V J	42	39	5	580	59	17.05	0	2	353	21	16.80	14
Dalton, A J	17	16	1	280	55	18.66	0	1	0	0	—	7
Dawood, I	25	20	4	260	57	16.25	0	1	0	0	—	18/8
Dawson, R K J .	92	58	12	431	41	9.36	0	0	2,784	91	30.59	31
Dennis, S J	56	24	11	114	16*	8.76	0	0	1,736	42	41.33	7
Elliott, M T G ..	6	6	3	394	128*	131.33	3	0	0	0	—	0
Elstub, C J	10	4	4	6	4*	—	0	0	290	12	24.16	0
Fellows, G M ...	95	79	15	1,342	80*	20.96	0	6	836	22	38.00	27
Fisher, I D	28	12	3	68	20	7.55	0	0	708	29	24.41	6
Fisher, M D ...	**27**	**14**	**9**	**201**	**36***	**40.20**	**0**	**0**	**1,039**	**27**	**38.48**	**5**
Fleming, S P ...	7	7	1	285	139*	47.50	1	1	0	0	—	3
Fletcher, S D ...	129	32	18	109	16*	7.78	0	0	4,686	164	28.57	34
Foster, M J	20	14	1	199	118	15.30	1	0	370	6	61.66	6
Fraine, W A R .	**1**	**0**	**0**	**0**	**—**	**—**	**0**	**0**	**0**	**0**	**—**	**0**
Gale, A W	125	116	11	3,256	125*	31.00	2	17	0	0	—	24

Player	M	Inns	NO	Runs	HS	Av'ge	100s	50s	Runs	Wkts	Av'ge	Ct/St
Gibson, R	6	4	1	19	19	6.33	0	0	158	5	31.60	2
Gilbert, C R	5	4	0	55	37	13.75	0	0	199	8	24.87	2
Gillespie, J N	18	4	1	29	15*	9.66	0	0	601	18	33.38	6
Gough, D	214	120	33	1,280	72*	14.71	0	1	6,798	291	23.36	43
Gray, A K D	31	19	7	130	30*	10.83	0	0	843	25	33.72	8
Grayson, A P	66	49	8	587	55	14.31	0	1	1,441	39	36.94	19
Guy, S M	32	23	4	282	40	14.84	0	0	0	0	—	35/11
Hamilton, G M	101	70	18	1,059	57*	20.36	0	2	2,803	121	23.16	15
Hampshire, A W	4	3	0	3	3	1.00	0	0	0	0	—	1
Hampshire, J H	234	223	24	6,296	119	31.63	7	36	26	1	26.00	69
Hannon-Dalby, O J	5	1	1	21	21*	—	0	0	202	5	40.40	3
Handscomb, P S P	9	9	1	504	140	63.00	1	3	0	0	—	5
Harden, R J	19	16	2	230	42	16.42	0	0	0	0	—	1
Hartley, P J	219	145	49	1,609	83	16.76	0	4	7,476	283	26.41	40
Hartley, S N	171	154	31	2,815	83*	22.88	0	13	2,153	67	32.13	52
Harvey, I J	28	27	2	637	74	25.48	0	3	950	30	31.66	8
Head, T M	4	4	0	277	175	69.25	1	1	0	0	—	1
Hodd, A J	32	23	5	368	69*	20.44	0	1	0	0	—	39/8
Hodgson, D M	12	10	1	272	90	30.22	0	3	0	0	—	10/2
Hodgson, L J	6	2	0	9	9	4.50	0	0	161	4	40.25	1
Hoggard, M J	83	28	19	41	7*	4.55	0	0	2,682	118	22.72	7
Hutchison, P M	32	11	8	18	4*	6.00	0	0	844	43	19.62	3
Hutton, R A	107	80	25	1,075	65	19.54	0	4	3,000	128	23.43	27
Illingworth, R	41	15	11	171	45	42.75	0	0	793	40	19.82	14
Ingham, P G	12	10	4	312	87*	52.00	0	2	0	0	—	2
Inzamam ul Haq	3	3	0	69	53	23.00	0	1	0	0	—	0
Jaques, P A	43	42	2	1,588	105	39.70	1	13	0	0	—	16
Jarvis, P W	144	74	28	529	42	11.50	0	0	4,684	213	21.99	33
Johnson, C	129	102	22	1,615	73*	20.18	0	4	28	2	14.00	33
Johnson, M	14	6	3	34	15*	11.33	0	0	455	12	37.91	2
Katich, S M	3	3	2	79	40*	79.00	0	0	0	0	—	2
Kellett, S A	56	51	3	1,207	118*	25.14	2	4	16	0	—	13
Kettleborough, R A	10	6	3	71	28	23.66	0	0	72	3	24.00	4
Kirby, S P	29	12	3	38	15	4.22	0	0	1,061	24	44.20	6
Kohler-Cadmore, T	**17**	**16**	**0**	**762**	**164**	**47.62**	**1**	**6**	**0**	**0**	**—**	**16**
Kruis, G J	55	22	11	138	31*	12.54	0	0	1,793	62	28.91	9
Lawson, M A K	4	4	0	30	20	7.50	0	0	141	3	47.00	1
Leadbeater, B	105	100	19	2,245	90	27.71	0	11	95	5	19.00	26
Leaning, J A	47	40	7	1,024	131*	31.03	2	5	204	7	29.14	24
Lee, J E	4	0	0	0	—	—	0	0	116	7	16.57	0
Lees, A Z	42	39	2	1,109	102	29.97	1	8	0	0	—	15
Lehmann, D S	130	126	20	5,229	191	49.33	8	38	1,990	79	25.18	41
Lester, E I	1	1	0	0	0	0.00	0	0	0	0	—	0
Loten, T W	**1**	**0**	**0**	**0**	**—**	**—**	**0**	**0**	**0**	**0**	**—**	**0**
Love, J D	220	203	33	4,298	118*	25.28	4	18	129	5	25.80	44
Lucas, D S	5	2	0	40	32	20.00	0	0	187	3	62.33	1
Lumb, M J	104	98	8	2,606	92	28.95	0	18	28	0	—	31
Lumb, R G	137	123	13	2,784	101	25.30	1	16	0	0	—	0
Lyth, A	**121**	**114**	**8**	**3,754**	**144**	**35.41**	**5**	**18**	**373**	**6**	**62.16**	**53**
McGrath, A	275	253	39	7,220	148	33.73	7	44	2,514	79	31.82	91
Maxwell, G J	8	7	1	312	111	52.00	1	2	144	3	48.00	4
Metcalfe, A A	194	189	15	5,584	127*	32.09	4	36	44	2	22.00	44
Middlebrook, J D	18	11	3	61	15*	7.62	0	0	530	13	40.76	5

Player	M	Inns	NO	Runs	HS	Av'ge	100s	50s	Runs	Wkts	Av'ge	Ct/St
Milburn, S M ..	4	2	1	14	13*	14.00	0	0	118	2	59.00	1
Miller, D A	3	3	0	45	44	15.00	0	0	0	0	—	3
Morris, A C	27	17	5	212	48*	17.66	0	0	464	21	22.09	5
Moxon, M D ..	237	229	21	7,380	141*	35.48	7	49	1,202	34	35.35	77
Nicholson, A G .	120	46	22	155	15*	6.45	0	0	2,951	173	17.05	16
Nicholson, N G .	2	2	1	1	1*	1.00	0	0	0	0	—	2
Old, C M	221	169	38	2,572	82*	19.63	0	10	5,841	308	18.96	56
Oldham, S	106	40	21	192	38*	10.10	0	0	3,136	142	22.08	17
Olivier, D ..	**5**	**3**	**3**	**17**	**8***	**—**	**0**	**0**	**262**	**2**	**131.00**	**1**
Padgett, D E V .	57	54	3	1,069	68	20.96	0	2	25	1	25.00	13
Parker, B	73	61	8	965	69	18.20	0	1	18	0	—	12
Patterson, S A .	**94**	**39**	**20**	**248**	**25***	**13.05**	**0**	**0**	**3,436**	**118**	**29.11**	**17**
Pickles, C S ...	71	48	20	375	37*	13.39	0	0	2,403	63	38.14	23
Pillans, M W ..	**7**	**5**	**1**	**54**	**31**	**13.50**	**0**	**0**	**344**	**16**	**21.50**	**2**
Plunkett, L E ...	28	21	10	327	53	29.72	0	1	1,060	33	32.12	17
Poysden, J E ..	**8**	**4**	**1**	**2**	**1**	**0.66**	**0**	**0**	**303**	**6**	**50.50**	**0**
Pyrah, R M	114	75	20	978	69	17.78	0	2	3,572	133	26.85	35
Pujara, C A	8	8	1	370	101	52.85	1	3	0	0	—	4
Ramage, A	34	17	8	134	32*	14.88	0	0	1,178	30	39.26	3
Ramsden, G	1	0	0	0	—	—	0	0	26	2	13.00	0
Rana Naved -ul-Hasan	17	16	1	375	74	25.00	0	3	681	26	26.19	5
Rashid, A U ...	**107**	**75**	**22**	**1,063**	**71**	**20.05**	**0**	**1**	**3,986**	**137**	**29.09**	**34**
Read, J	1	0	0	0	—	—	0	0	0	0	—	1
Rhodes, S J	2	1	0	6	6	6.00	0	0	0	0	—	3
Rhodes, W M H	21	17	2	252	46	16.80	0	0	364	11	33.09	8
Richardson. R B	28	28	6	993	103	45.13	1	8	0	0	—	5
Richardson, S A	1	1	0	7	7	7.00	0	0	0	0	—	0
Robinson, A L ..	92	36	19	127	18*	7.47	0	0	2,588	105	24.64	14
Robinson, M A .	89	30	16	41	7	2.92	0	0	2,795	91	30.71	7
Robinson, O E..	3	2	2	16	12*	—	0	0	66	0	—	4
Robinson, P E ..	135	123	15	2,738	78*	25.35	0	14	0	0	—	47
Root, J E	**23**	**22**	**3**	**747**	**83**	**39.31**	**0**	**5**	**280**	**7**	**40.00**	**10**
Rudolph, J A ...	65	62	10	3,090	132*	59.42	9	19	37	0	—	32
Ryan, M	3	2	1	7	6*	7.00	0	0	149	5	29.80	3
Sadler, J L	1	1	0	19	19	19.00	0	0	0	0	—	0
Sanderson, B W	10	2	1	14	12*	14.00	0	0	247	8	30.87	5
Sayers, J J	31	30	2	594	62	21.21	0	5	79	1	79.00	2
Scofield, D	3	1	0	0	0	0.00	0	0	111	2	55.50	1
Shahzad, A	30	22	7	243	59*	16.20	0	1	1,182	34	34.76	9
Sharp, K	206	191	18	4,776	114	27.60	3	28	48	4	12.00	68
Sharpe, P J	91	86	4	1,515	89*	18.47	0	8	11	0	—	53
Shaw, C	48	20	10	127	26	12.70	0	0	1,396	58	24.06	8
Sidebottom, A ..	236	131	47	1,279	52*	15.22	0	1	6,918	260	26.60	51
Sidebottom, R J .	113	51	22	303	30*	10.44	0	0	3,631	124	29.28	24
Silverwood, C E W	166	94	33	892	61	14.62	0	4	5,212	224	23.26	25
Smith, N	7	2	1	5	5	5.00	0	0	0	0	—	1
Smith, R	3	2	0	17	17	8.50	0	0	0	0	—	1
Squires, P J	56	48	5	708	79*	16.46	0	3	4	0	—	10
Starc, M A	4	2	2	5	4*	—	0	0	181	8	22.62	1
Stemp, R D	88	28	10	118	23*	6.55	0	0	2,996	100	29.96	14
Stevenson, G B .	217	158	23	1,710	81*	12.66	0	2	6,820	290	23.51	38
Stott, W B	2	2	0	30	30	15.00	0	0	0	0	—	0

Player	M	Inns	NO	Runs	HS	Av'ge	100s	50s	Runs	Wkts	Av'ge	Ct/St
Stringer, P M ...	11	8	6	29	13*	14.50	0	0	256	15	17.06	0
Stuchbury, S ...	22	8	4	21	9*	5.25	0	0	677	29	23.34	2
Swallow, I G ...	8	5	3	37	17*	18.50	0	0	198	2	99.00	5
Swanepoel, P J .	3	2	2	9	8*	—	0	0	100	3	33.33	0
Tattersall, J A .	**15**	**11**	**2**	**375**	**89**	**41.66**	**0**	**4**	**0**	**0**	**—**	**16/3**
Taylor, C R	6	5	0	102	28	20.40	0	0	0	0	—	0
Taylor, K	10	10	0	135	30	13.50	0	0	168	11	15.27	3
Taylor, N S ...	1	0	0	0	0	—	0	0	45	1	45.00	1
Tendulkar, S R .	17	17	2	540	107	36.00	1	1	167	6	27.83	3
Thompson, J A	**1**	**0**	**0**	**0**		**—**	**0**	**0**	**43**	**0**	**—**	**0**
Thornicroft, N D	14	7	4	52	20	17.33	0	0	591	17	34.76	3
Townsley, R A J	5	4	1	81	34	27.00	0	0	62	0	—	1
Trueman, F S ..	11	9	1	127	28	15.87	0	0	348	21	16.57	5
Vaughan, M P ..	183	178	13	4,966	125*	30.09	3	29	1,860	60	31.00	56
Wainman, J C ..	4	3	1	51	33	25.50	0	0	201	5	40.20	1
Wainwright, D J	48	21	13	150	26	18.75	0	0	1,427	38	37.55	16
Waite, M E	**13**	**11**	**3**	**278**	**71**	**34.75**	**0**	**1**	**522**	**16**	**32.62**	**0**
Wardlaw, I	17	10	4	56	18	9.33	0	0	686	24	28.58	3
Waring, J	1	1	1	1	1*	—	0	0	11	0	—	0
Warner, J D ...	**1**	**0**	**0**	**0**		**—**	**0**	**0**	**32**	**0**	**—**	**0**
Warren, A C ...	1	1	0	3	3	3.00	0	0	35	1	35.00	0
Wharf, A G	6	1	1	2	2*	—	0	0	176	8	22.00	1
White, C	292	266	39	6,384	148	28.12	5	28	6,120	248	24.67	84
Whiteley, J P ...	6	4	0	19	14	4.75	0	0	195	2	97.50	1
Widdup, S	4	4	0	49	38	12.25	0	0	0	0	—	2
Wigley, D H ...	1	1	0	0	0	0.00	0	0	38	0	—	0
Willey, D J ...	**20**	**16**	**2**	**448**	**131**	**32.00**	**1**	**2**	**808**	**33**	**24.48**	**5**
Williamson, K A	13	11	0	279	70	25.36	0	1	42	1	42.00	6
Wilson, D	61	47	8	430	46	11.02	0	0	1,527	76	20.09	22
Wood, G L	1	1	0	26	26	26.00	0	0	0	0	—	0
Wood, M J	145	134	14	3,270	160	27.25	5	14	76	3	25.33	57
Woodford, J D ..	72	57	14	890	69*	20.69	0	2	1,627	77	21.12	25
Younus Khan ...	11	8	0	248	100	31.00	1	0	144	2	72.00	5
Yuvraj Singh ...	9	9	0	196	50	21.77	0	1	197	3	65.66	1

LIMITED-OVERS INTERNATIONAL MATCHES
AT NORTH MARINE ROAD, SCARBOROUGH 1976-1978

1976 **England 202 for 8 wkts** (55 overs) (G D Barlow 80*, A M E Roberts 4 for 32).
West Indies 207 for 4 wkts (41 overs) (I V A Richards 119*).
West Indies won by 6 wickets   **Award: I V A Richards**

1978 **England 206 for 8 wkts** (55 overs) (G A Gooch 94, B L Cairns 5 for 28).
New Zealand 187 for 8 wkts (55 overs) (B E Congdon 52*).
England won by 19 runs   **Award: G A Gooch**

For England   YORKSHIRE ONE-DAY INTERNATIONAL CRICKETERS 1971-2020 (Correct to December 8, 2020)

Player	M	I	NO	Runs	HS	Av'ge	100s	50s	Balls	Runs	W	Av'ge	Best	4wI	Ct/St
ATHEY, C W J 1980-88	31	30	3	848	142*	31.40	2	4	—	—	—	—	—	0	16
BAIRSTOW, D L ...1979-84	21	20	6	206	23*	14.71	0	0	—	—	—	—	—	0	17/4
BAIRSTOW, J M ...2011-20	83	76	8	3,207	141*	47.16	10	13	—	—	—	—	—	0	39/2
BALLANCE, G S .2013-14/15	16	15	1	297	79	21.21	0	2	—	—	—	—	—	0	8
BLAKEY, R J 1992-93	3	2	0	25	25	12.50	0	0	—	—	—	—	—	0	2/1
BOYCOTT, G 1971-81	36	34	4	1,082	105	36.06	1	9	168	105	5	21.00	2-14	0	5
BRESNAN, T T ...2006-15	85	64	20	871	80	19.79	0	1	4,221	3,813	109	34.98	5-48	4	20
COPE, G A 1977-78	2	1	1	1*	1*	—	0	0	112	35	1	17.50	1-16	0	0
GOUGH, D 1994-2006	158	87	38	609	46*	12.42	0	0	8,422	6,154	234	26.29	5-44	10	24
HAMPSHIRE, J H ...1971-72	3	3	1	48	25*	24.00	0	0	—	—	—	—	—	0	0
HOGGARD, M J ...2001-06	26	6	2	17	7	4.25	0	0	1,306	1,152	32	36.00	5-49	1	5
JARVIS, P W 1988-93	16	8	2	31	16*	5.16	0	0	879	672	24	28.00	5-35	1	1
LOVE, J D 1981	3	3	0	61	43	20.33	0	0	—	—	—	—	—	0	1
MALAN, D J 2019	1	1	0	24	24	24.00	0	0	12	27	1	27.00	1-27	0	0
McGRATH, A 2003-04	14	12	2	166	52	16.60	0	1	228	175	4	43.75	1-13	0	4
MOXON, M D 1985-88	8	8	0	174	70	21.75	0	1	—	—	—	—	—	0	5
OLD, C M 1973-81	32	25	7	338	51*	18.77	0	1	1,755	999	45	22.20	4-8	2	8
PLUNKETT, L E 2005/6-2019	89	50	19	646	56	20.83	0	1	4,137	4,010	135	29.70	5-52	7	24
RASHID, A U ...2009-20	106	48	14	644	69	18.94	0	1	5,255	4,910	155	31.67	5-27	9	31
ROOT, J E 2012/13-20	149	140	21	5,962	133*	50.10	16	33	1,552	1,491	26	57.34	3-52	0	74
SHAHZAD, A 2010-11	11	8	2	39	9	6.50	0	0	588	490	17	28.82	3-41	0	4
SIDEBOTTOM, R J .2001-10	25	18	8	133	24	13.30	0	0	1,277	1,039	29	35.82	3-19	0	6
SILVERWOOD, C E W 1996-2001	7	4	0	17	12	4.25	0	0	306	244	6	40.66	3-43	0	0
STEVENSON, G B ..1980-81	4	4	3	43	28*	43.00	0	0	192	125	7	17.85	4-33	1	2
VAUGHAN, M P ..2001-07	86	83	10	1,982	90*	27.15	0	16	796	649	16	40.56	4-22	0	25
WHITE, C 1994-2003	51	41	5	568	57*	15.77	0	0	2,364	1,726	65	26.55	5-21	2	12
WILLEY, D J ...2015-2020	49	29	13	377	51	23.56	0	2	2,143	2,037	60	33.95	5-30	3	22

For Scotland YORKSHIRE ONE-DAY INTERNATIONAL CRICKETERS 1971-2020 (Correct to December 8, 2020)

Player	M	I	NO	Runs	HS	Av'ge	100s	50s	Balls	Runs	W	Av'ge	Best	4wl	Cl/St
BLAIN, J A R ...1999-2009	33	25	6	284	41	14.94	0	0	1,329	1,173	41	28.60	5-22	4	8
HAMILTON, G M .1999-2010	38	38	3	1,231	119	35.17	2	7	220	160	3	53.33	2-36	0	6/1
WARDLAW, I ...2012/14/15	22	14	8	21	7*	3.50	0	0	1,108	1,036	36	28.77	4-22	2	1

YORKSHIRE PLAYERS WHO PLAYED ALL THEIR ONE-DAY INTERNATIONAL CRICKET AFTER LEAVING YORKSHIRE

For England

Player	M	I	NO	Runs	HS	Av'ge	100s	50s	Balls	Runs	W	Av'ge	Best	4wl	Cl/St
BATTY, G J 2002-09	10	8	2	30	17	5.00	0	0	440	366	5	73.20	2-40	—	4
CLOSE, D B 1972	3	3	0	49	43	16.33	0	0	18	21	0	—	—	—	—
GRAYSON, A P ...2000-01	2	2	0	6	6	3.00	0	0	90	60	3	20.00	3-40	—	1
ILLINGWORTH, R .1971-72	3	2	2	5	4	2.50	0	0	130	84	4	21.00	3-50	—	1
LUMB, M J 2013/14	3	3	0	165	106	55.00	1	0	—	—	—	—	—	—	1
RHODES, S J 1989-95	9	8	2	107	56	17.83	0	1	—	—	—	—	—	—	9/2
WHARF, A G 2004-05	13	5	3	19	9	9.50	0	0	584	428	18	23.77	4-24	1	1
WOOD, B 1972-82	13	12	2	314	78*	31.40	0	2	420	224	9	24.88	2-14	—	6

Overseas Players
(Qualification: 24 List A matches for Yorkshire)

For Australia

Player	M	I	NO	Runs	HS	Av'ge	100s	50s	Balls	Runs	W	Av'ge	Best	4wl	Cl/St
BEVAN, M G ...1994-2004	232	196	67	6,912	108*	53.58	6	46	1,966	1,655	36	45.97	3-36	—	128
HARVEY, I J ..1997/98-2004	73	51	11	715	48*	17.87	0	0	3,279	2,577	85	30.31	4-16	4	17
JAQUES, P A ...2006-2007	6	6	0	125	94	20.83	0	1	—	—	—	—	—	—	3
LEHMANN, D S .1996-2005	117	101	22	3,078	119	38.96	4	17	1,793	1,445	52	27.78	4-7	1	26

For South Africa

Player	M	I	NO	Runs	HS	Av'ge	100s	50s	Balls	Runs	W	Av'ge	Best	4wl	Cl/St
RUDOLPH, J A ...2003-06	43	37	6	1,157	81	37.32	0	7	24	26	0	—	—	—	11

For West Indies

Player	M	I	NO	Runs	HS	Av'ge	100s	50s	Balls	Runs	W	Av'ge	Best	4wl	Cl/St
RICHARDSON, R B .1983-96	224	217	30	6,248	122	33.41	5	44	58	46	1	46.00	1-4	—	75

YORKSHIRE PLAYERS IN WORLD CUPS FOR ENGLAND

BATTING AND FIELDING

Player	Seasons	M	I	NO	Runs	HS	100s	50s	Avge	SR	ct/st
J M Bairstow	2019	11	11	0	532	111	2	2	48.36	92.84	9
G S Ballance	2015	4	4	0	36	10	0	0	9.00	50.70	1
G Boycott	1979	5	5	1	92	57	0	1	23.00	42.90	0
T T Bresnan	2011	7	5	1	41	20*	0	0	10.25	82.00	0
D Gough	1996										
	&1999	11	6	2	95	26*	0	0	23.75	73.07	2
C M Old	1975										
	&1979	9	7	2	91	51*	0	1	18.20	122.97	2
A U Rashid	2019	11	5	1	45	25	0	0	11.25	118.42	3
J E Root *	2015										
	&2019	17	16	2	758	121	3	3	54.14	88.03	20
A Shahzad	2011	2	2	1	7	6*	0	0	7.00	140.00	0
M P Vaughan	2003										
	&2007	14	14	0	348	79	0	3	24.85	71.02	3
C White	1996										
	&2003	7	5	1	92	35	0	0	23.00	98.92	1

* Joe Root's catching tally is an England record. Collingwood has 13, so he is way out in front. Only Ricky Ponting, of Australia, on 28, is ahead.

BOWLING

Player	Overs	Mdns	Runs	Wkts	Avge	BpW	Best	4wi	RPO
G Boycott	27	1	94	5	18.80	32.40	2-14	0	3.48
T T Bresnan	63	5	309	9	34.33	42.00	5-48	1	4.90
D Gough	99.4	8	430	15	28.66	39.86	4-34	1	4.31
C M Old	90.3	18	243	16	15.18	33.93	4- 8	1	2.68
A U Rashid	92	0	526	11	47.81	50.18	3-54	0	5.71
J E Root	19	0	111	3	37.00	38.00	2-27	0	5.84
A Shahzad	18	0	96	3	32.00	36.00	3-43	0	5.33
M P Vaughan	30	0	128	4	32.00	45.00	3-39	0	4.26
C White	51.3	6	202	9	22.44	34.33	3-33	0	3.91

Paul E Dyson

LIMITED-OVERS INTERNATIONAL MATCHES
AT HEADINGLEY, LEEDS 1973-2019

1973 **West Indies 181** (54 overs) (R B Kanhai 55). **England 182 for 9 wkts** (54.3 overs) (M H Denness 66).
England won by 1 wicket   **Award: M H Denness**

1974 **India 265** (53.5 overs) (B P Patel 82, A L Wadekar 67). **England 266 for 6 wkts** (51.1 overs) (J H Edrich 90).
England won by 4 wickets   **Award: J H Edrich**

1975 **Australia 278 for 7 wkts** (60 overs) (R Edwards 80*). **Pakistan 205** (53 overs) (Majid Khan 65, Asif Iqbal 53, D K Lillee 5 for 34).
Australia won by 73 runs   **Award: D K Lillee**

1975 **East Africa 120** (55.3 overs). **India 123 for 0 wkt** (29.5 overs) (S M Gavaskar 65* F M Engineer 54*).
India won by 10 wickets   **Award: F M Engineer**

1975 **England 93** (36.2 overs) (G J Gilmour 6 for 14). **Australia 94 for 6 wkts** (28.4 overs).
Australia won by 4 wickets   **Award: G J Gilmour**

1979 **Canada 139 for 9 wkts** (60 overs). **Pakistan 140 for 2 wkts** (40.1 overs) (Sadiq Mohammed 57*).
Pakistan won by 8 wickets   **Award: Sadiq Mohammed**

1979 **India 182 (55.5 overs)** (S M Gavaskar 55). **New Zealand 183 for 2 wkts** (57 overs) (B A Edgar 84*).
New Zealand won by 8 wickets   **Award: B A Edgar**

1979 **England 165 for 9 wkts** (60 overs). **Pakistan 151** (56 overs) (Asif Iqbal 51, M Hendrick 4 for 15)
England won by 14 runs   **Award: M Hendrick**

1980 **West Indies 198** (55 overs) (C G Greenidge 78). **England 174** (51.2 overs) (C J Tavaré 82*).
West Indies won by 24 runs   **Award: C J Tavaré**

1981 **Australia 236 for 8 wkts** (55 overs) (G M Wood 108). **England 165** (46.5 overs) (R M Hogg 4 for 29).
Australia won by 71 runs   **Award: G M Wood**

1982 **India 193** (55 overs) (Kapil Dev 60, I T Botham 4 for 56). **England 194 for 1 wkt** (50.1 overs) (B Wood 78*, C J Tavaré 66).
England won by 9 wickets   **Award: B Wood**

1983 **West Indies 252 for 9 wkts** (60 overs) (H A Gomes 78). **Australia 151** (30.3 overs) (W W Davis 7 for 51).
West Indies won by 101 runs   **Award: W W Davis**

1983 **Pakistan 235 for 7 wkts** (60 overs) (Imran Khan 102*, Shahid Mahboob 77, A L F de Mel 5 for 39). **Sri Lanka 224** (58.3 overs) (S Wettimuny 50, Abdul Qadir 5 for 44).
Pakistan won by 11 runs   **Award: Abdul Qadir**

1983 **Sri Lanka 136** (50.4 overs). **England 137 for 1 wkt** (24.1 overs) (G Fowler 81*).
England won by 9 wickets   **Award: R G D Willis**

1986 **New Zealand 217 for 8 wkts** (55 overs) (J J Crowe 66). **England 170** (48.2 overs).
New Zealand won by 47 runs   **Award: J J Crowe**

1988 **England 186 for 8 wkts** (55 overs). **West Indies 139** (46.3 overs).
England won by 47 runs   **Award: D R Pringle**

1990 **England 295 for 6 wkts** (55 overs) (R A Smith 128, G A Gooch 55). **New Zealand 298 for 6 wkts** (54.5 overs) (M J Greatbatch 102*, J G Wright 52, A H Jones 51).
New Zealand won by 4 wickets   **Award: M J Greatbatch**

1990 **England 229** (54.3 overs) (A J Lamb 56, D I Gower 50). **India 233 for 4 wkts** (53 overs) (S V Manjrekar 82, M Azharuddin 55*)
India won by 6 wickets   **Award: A Kumble**

1996 **India 158** (40.2 overs). **England 162 for 4 wkts** (39.3 overs) (G P Thorpe 79*).
England won by 6 wickets   **Award: G P Thorpe**

1997 **Australia 170 for 8 wkts** (50 overs).**England 175 for 4 wkts** (40.1 overs) (G P Thorpe 75*, A J Hollioake 66*).
England won by 6 wickets   **Award: G P Thorpe**

1998 **South Africa 205 for 8 wkts** (50 overs) (S M Pollock 56). **England 206 for 3 wkts** (35 overs) (A D Brown 59, N V Knight 51).
England won by 7 wickets   **Award: A D Brown**

1999 **Pakistan 275 for 8 wkts** (50 overs) (Inzamam-ul-Haq 81, Abdur Razzaq 60). **Australia 265** (49.5 overs) (M G Bevan 61, Wasim Akram 4-40).
Pakistan won by 10 runs   **Award: Inzamam-ul-Haq**

1999 **Zimbabwe 175** (49.3 overs) (M A Goodwin 57). **New Zealand 70 for 3 wkts** (15 overs).
No result   **No Award**

1999 **South Africa 271 for 7 wkts** (50 overs) (H H Gibbs 101, D J Cullinan 50). **Australia 275 for 5 wkts** (49.4 overs) (S R. Waugh 120*, R T Ponting 69).
Australia won by 5 wickets   **Award: S R Waugh**

2001 **England 156 (45.2 overs)** (B C Hollioake 53, Waqar Younis 7 for 36). **Pakistan 153 for 4 wkts** (39.5 overs) (Abdur Razzaq 75).
Pakistan won — England conceding the match following a pitch invasion.
Award: Waqar Younis

2002 **Sri Lanka 240 for 7 wkts** (32 overs) (S T Jayasuriya 112). **England 241 for 7 wkts** (31.2 overs) (M E Trescothick 82).
England won by 3 wkts   **Award: S T Jayasuriya**

2003 **England 81 for 4 wkts. Zimbabwe** did not bat.
No result   **No Award**

2004 **West Indies 159** (40.1 overs). **England 160 for 3 wkts** (22 overs) (M E Trescothick 55).
England won by 7 wickets   **Award: S J Harmison**

2005 **Bangladesh 208 for 7 wkts** (50 overs) (Belim 81, A Flintoff 4-29). **England 209 for 5 wkts** (38.5 overs) (A J Strauss 98)
England won by 5 wickets   **Award: A J Strauss**

   Australia 219 for 7 wkts (50 overs) (P D Collingwood 4-34). **England 221 for 1 wkt** (46 overs) (M E Trescothick 104*, M P Vaughan 59*).
England won by 9 wickets   **Award: M E Trescothick**

2006 **England 321 for 7 wkts** (50 overs) (M E Trescothick 121, S L Malinga 4-44). **Sri Lanka 324 for 2 wkts** (37.3 overs) (S T Jayasuriya 152, W U Tharanga 109).
Sri Lanka won by 8 wickets   **Award: S T Jayasuriya**

2007 **India 324 for 6 wkts** (50 overs) (Yuvraj Singh 72, S R Tendulkar 71, S C Ganguly 59, G Gambhir 51). **England 242 for 8 wkts** (39 overs) (P D Collingwood 91*)
India won by 38 runs *(D/L Method)*   **Award: S C Ganguly**

2008 **England 275 for 4 wkts** (50 overs) (K P Pietersen 90*, A Flintoff 78). **South Africa 255** (J H Kallis 52).
England won by 20 runs   **Award: K P Pietersen**

2009 **England v. West Indies**   **Match abandoned without a ball bowled**

2010 **Pakistan 294 for 8 wkts** (50 overs) (Kamran Akmal 74, Asad Shafiq 50, S C J Broad 4-81). **England 295 for 6 wkts** (A J Strauss 126, I J L Trott 53)
England won by 4 wickets   **Award: A J Strauss**

2011 **Sri Lanka 309 for 5 wkts** (50 overs) (D P M D Jayawardene 144, K C Sangakkara 69) **England** 240 all out (E J G Morgan 52)
Sri Lanka won by 69 runs   **Award: D P M D Jayawardene**

2012 **England v. West Indies**   **Match abandoned without a ball bowled**

2013 **England v. Australia**   **Match abandoned without a ball bowled**

2014 **England 294 for 7 wkts** (50 overs) (J E Root 113). **India** 253 all out (48.4 overs)
(R A Jadeja 87)
England won by 41 runs   **Award: J E Root**

2015 **Australia 299 for 6 wkts** (50 overs) (G J Bailey 75, G J Maxwell 85, M S Wade 50*).
England 304 for 7 wkts (48.2 overs) (E J G Morgan 92, P J Cummins 4-49)
England won by 7 wickets   **Award: E J G Morgan**

2016 **Pakistan 247 for 8 wkts** (50 overs) (Azhar Ali 80, Imad Wasim 57*); **England
252 for 6 wkts** (48 overs) (B A Stokes 69, J M Bairstow 61)
England won by 6 wickets   **Award: J M Bairstow**

2017 **England 339 for 7 wkts** (50 overs) (A D Hales 61, E J G Morgan 107, M M Ali 77*)
South Africa 267 (45 overs) (H M Amla 72, F du Plessis 67, C R Woakes 4-38)
England won by 72 runs   **Award M M Ali**

2018 **India 256 for 8 wkts** (50 overs) (V Kohli 71). **England 260 for 2 wkts** (44.3 overs)
(J E Root 100*, E J G Morgan 88*)
England won by 8 wickets   **Award: A U Rashid**

2019 **England 351 for 9 wkts** (50 overs) (J E Root 84, E J G Morgan 76,
Shaheen Afridi 4-82). **Pakistan 297** (46.5 overs) (Babar Azam 80, Sarfaraz Ahmed 97,
C R Woakes 5-54)
England won by 54 runs   **Award: C R Woakes**

2019 **Sri Lanka 232 for 9 wkts** (50 overs) (A D Mathews 85*). **England 212** (47 overs)
(B A Stokes 82*, S L Malinga 4-43)
Sri Lanka won by 20 runs   **Award: S L Malinga**

2019 **Afghanistan 227 for 9 wkts** (50 overs) (Shaheen Afridi 4-47). **Pakistan 230 for 7 wkts**
(49.4 overs)
Pakistan won by 3 wickets   **Award: Imad Wasim**

2019 **West Indies 311 for 6 wkts** (50 overs) (E Lewis 58, S D Hope 77). **Afghanistan 288**
(50 overs) (Rahmat Shah 62, Ikram Ali Khil 86, C R Brathwaite 4-63)
West Indies won by 23 runs   **Award: S D Hope**

2019 **Sri Lanka 264 for 7 wkts** (50 overs) (A D Mathews 113). **India 265 for 3 wkts**
(43.3 overs) (K L Rahul 111, R G Sharma 103)
India won by 7 wickets   **Award: R G Sharma**

SUMMARY OF RESULTS

ENGLAND	Played	Won	Lost
v. Australia	5	3	2
v. Bangladesh	1	1	0
v. India	7	5	2
v. New Zealand	2	0	2
v. Pakistan	5	4	1
v. South Africa	3	3	0
v. Sri Lanka	5	2	3
v. West Indies	4	3	1
v. Zimbabwe	1*	0	0
Totals	33	21	11

*No result. In addition to two matches v. West Indies abandoned
and one match v. Australia abandoned

AFGHANISTAN	Played	Won	Lost
v. Pakistan	1	0	1
v. West Indies	1	0	1
Totals	2	0	2

SUMMARY OF RESULTS *(Continued)*

AUSTRALIA	Played	Won	Lost
v. England	5	2	3
v. Pakistan	2	1	1
v. South Africa	1	1	0
v. West Indies	1	0	1
Totals	9	4	5

In addition to one match abandoned

BANGLADESH	Played	Won	Lost
v. England	1	0	1

INDIA	Played	Won	Lost
v. England	7	2	5
v. East Africa	1	1	0
v. New Zealand	1	0	1
v. Sri Lanka	1	1	0
Totals	10	4	6

NEW ZEALAND	Played	Won	Lost
v. England	2	2	0
v. India	1	1	0
v. Zimbabwe	1*	0	0
Totals	4	3	0

*No result

PAKISTAN	Played	Won	Lost
v. Afghanistan	1	1	0
v. Australia	2	1	1
v. Canada	1	1	0
v. England	5	1	4
v. Sri Lanka	1	1	0
Totals	10	5	5

SOUTH AFRICA	Played	Won	Lost
v. Australia	1	0	1
v. England	2	0	2
Totals	3	0	3

SRI LANKA	Played	Won	Lost
v. England	5	3	2
v. India	1	0	1
v. Pakistan	1	0	1
Totals	7	3	4

WEST INDIES	Played	Won	Lost
v. Afghanistan	1	1	0
v. Australia	1	1	0
v. England	4	1	3
Totals	6	3	3

In addition to two matches abandoned

ZIMBABWE	Played	Won	Lost
v. England	1*	0	0
v. New Zealand	1*	0	0
Totals	2*	0	0

*No result

CANADA	Played	Won	Lost
v. Pakistan	1	0	1

EAST AFRICA	Played	Won	Lost
v. India	1	0	1

CENTURIES

152	S J Jayasuriya	for Sri Lanka	v. England	2006
144	D P M D Jayawardene	for Sri Lanka	v. England	2011
128	R A Smith	for England	v. New Zealand	1990
126	A J Strauss	for England	v. Pakistan	2010
121	M E Trescothick	for England	v. Sri Lanka	2006
120*	S R Waugh	for Australia	v. South Africa	1999
113	J E Root	for England	v. India	2014
113	A M Mathews	for Sri Lanka	v. India	2019
112	S J Jayasuriya	for Sri Lanka	v. England	2002
111	K L Rahul	for India	v. Sri Lanka	2019
109	W U Tharanga	for Sri Lanka	v. England	2006
108	G M Wood	for Australia	v. England	1981
104*	M E Trescothick	for England	v. Australia	2005
103	R G Sharma	for India	v. Sri Lanka	2019
102*	Imran Khan	for Pakistan	v. Sri Lanka	1983
102*	M J Greatbatch	for New Zealand	v. England	1990
101	H H Gibbs	for South Africa	v. Australia	1999
100*	J E Root	for England	v. India	2018

4 WICKETS IN AN INNINGS

7-36	Waqar Younis	for Pakistan	v. England	2001
7-51	W W Davis	for West Indies	v. Australia	1983
6-14	G J Gilmour	for Australia	v. England	1975
5-34	D K Lillee	for Australia	v. Pakistan	1975
5-39	A L F de Mel	for Sri Lanka	v. Pakistan	1983
5-44	Abdul Qadir	for Pakistan	v. Sri Lanka	1983
5-54	C R Woakes	for England	v. Pakistan	2019
4-15	M Hendrick	for England	v. Pakistan	1979
4-29	R M Hogg	for Australia	v England	1981
4-29	A Flintoff	for England	v. Bangladesh	2005
4-34	P D Collingwood	for England	v. Australia	2005
4-38	C R Woakes	for England	v. South Africa	2017
4-40	Wasim Akram	for Pakistan	v. Australia	1999
4-43	S L Malinga	for Sri Lanka	v. England	2019
4-44	S L Malinga	for Sri Lanka	v. England	2006
4-47	Shaheen Afridi	for Pakistan	v. Afghanistan	2019
4-49	P J Cummins	Australia	v. England	2015
4-56	I T Botham	for England	v. India	1982
4-81	S J C Broad	for England	v. Pakistan	2010

YORKSHIRE T20i CRICKETERS 2003-2020 (Correct to December 5, 2020)

For England

Player	M	I	NO	Runs	HS	Av'ge	100s	50s	Balls	Runs	W	Av'ge	Best	4wI	Ct/St
BAIRSTOW, J M ..2011-20	46	40	7	932	86*	28.24	0	6	663	887	24	36.95	3-10	0	33
BRESNAN, T T ..2006-13/14	34	22	9	216	47*	16.61	0	0	12	27	1	27.00	1-27	0	10
MALAN, D J ..2017-2020	19	19	3	855	103*	53.43	1	9	476	627	25	25.08	3-21	0	4
PLUNKETT, L E ..2006-19	22	11	4	42	18	6.00	0	0	1,050	1,316	51	25.80	3-11	0	7
RASHID, A U ..2009-20	52	18	10	56	9*	7.00	0	0	84	139	6	23.16	2- 9	0	12
ROOT, J E ..2012-19	32	30	5	893	90*	35.72	0	5	66	97	3	32.33	2-38	0	18
SHAHZAD, A ..2010-11	3	1	1	0	0*	—	0	0	—	—	—	—	—	—	1
VAUGHAN, M P" ..2005-7	2	2	0	27	27	13.50	0	0	—	—	—	—	—	—	0
WILLEY, D J ..2015-19	28	19	7	166	29*	13.83	0	0	557	761	34	22.38	4- 7	1	12

For Scotland

Player	M	I	NO	Runs	HS	Av'ge	100s	50s	Balls	Runs	W	Av'ge	Best	4wI	Ct/St
BLAIN, J A R ..2007-8	6	3	1	4	3*	2.00	0	0	120	108	6	18.00	2-23	0	1
HAMILTON, G M ..2007-10	12	8	0	90	32	11.25	0	0	—	—	—	—	—	0	3
WARDLAW, I ..2012/13-13/14	4	1	0	1	1	1.00	0	0	96	145	9	16.11	4-40	0	0

YORKSHIRE PLAYERS WHO PLAYED ALL THEIR T20i CRICKET AFTER LEAVING YORKSHIRE

For England

Player	M	I	NO	Runs	HS	Av'ge	100s	50s	Balls	Runs	W	Av'ge	Best	4wI	Ct/St
BATTY, G J ..2009	1	1	0	4	4	4.00	0	0	18	17	0	—	—	0	0
GOUGH, D ..2005-06	2	0	0	0	—	—	0	—	41	49	3	16.33	3-16	0	0
LUMB, M J ..2010-13/14	27	27	1	552	63	21.23	0	3	—	—	—	—	—	—	8
SIDEBOTTOM, R J ..2007-10	18	1	1	5	5*	—	0	0	367	437	23	19.00	3-16	0	5

Overseas Players
(Qualification: 20 t20 matches for Yorkshire)

For South Africa

Player	M	I	NO	Runs	HS	Av'ge	100s	50s	Balls	Runs	W	Av'ge	Best	4wI	Ct/St
RUDOLPH, J A ..2006	1	1	1	6	6*	—	0	0	—	—	—	—	—	0	0

T20 RECORDS SECTION
TROPHY WINNERS 2003-2020

		Yorkshire's Position			*Yorkshire's Position*
2003	Surrey	Group N 2 (6)	2012	Hampshire	Final
2004	Leicestershire	Group N 5 (6)	2013	Northamptonshire	Group N 6 (6)
2005	Somerset	Group N 4 (6)	2014	Warwickshire	Group N 5 (9)
2006	Leicestershire	Quarter-Final	2015	Lancashire	Group N 8 (9)
2007	Kent	Quarter-Final	2016	Northamptonshire	Semi-Final
2008	Middlesex	Group N 3 (6)	2017	Nottinghamshire	Group N 5 (9)
2009	Sussex	Group N 5 (6)	2018	Worcestershire	Group N 5 (9)
2010	Hampshire	Group N 6 (9)	2019	Essex	Group N 5 (9)
2011	Leicestershire	Group N 6 (9)	2020	Nottinghamshire	Group N 5 (6)

SEASON-BY-SEASON RECORD OF ALL T20 MATCHES
PLAYED BY YORKSHIRE 2003-2020

Season	Played	Won	Lost	Tie	N R	Abd	Season	Played	Won	Lost	Tie	N R	Abd
2003	5	3	2	0	0	0	2012/13	6	2	3	0	1	0
2004	5	2	3	0	0	0	2013	10	2	7	1	0	0
2005	8	3	5	0	0	0	2014	11	6	5	0	0	3
2006	9	4	4	0	1	0	2015	14	5	8	1	0	0
2007	8	4	4	0	0	1	2016	15	8	6	0	1	1
2008	9	5	3	1	0	0	2017	12	6	5	1	0	2
2009	10	4	6	0	0	0	2018	16	8	8	0	0	0
2010	16	6	9	1	0	0	2019	10	4	5	1	0	4
2011	15	6	7	0	2	1	2020	8	3	5	0	0	2
2012	12	9	2	0	1	1		199	90	97	6	6	16

ANALYSIS OF T20 RESULTS V. ALL TEAMS 2003-2020
DOMESTIC MATCHES

		HOME				AWAY				
Opponents	*Played*	*Won*	*Lost*	*Tied*	*N. R*	*Won*	*Lost*	*Tied*	*N. R*	*Abd*
Derbyshire	31	9	8	0	0	9	4	0	1	0
Durham	34	10	5	1	0	8	9	0	1	1
Essex	1	0	0	0	0	0	1	0	0	0
Glamorgan	1	0	0	0	0	1	0	0	0	0
Hampshire	1	0	0	0	0	0	1	0	0	0
Lancashire	30	8	6	1	0	4	10	1	0	4
Leicestershire	23	5	5	0	0	4	8	1	0	2
Northamptonshire	13	4	3	0	0	4	1	1	0	3
Nottinghamshire	31	6	7	0	1	4	13	0	0	3
Sussex	2	0	0	0	0	1	1	0	0	0
Warwickshire	14	4	3	1	0	1	3	0	2	2
Worcestershire	10	4	2	0	0	1	3	0	0	1
Total	**191**	**50**	**39**	**3**	**1**	**37**	**54**	**3**	**4**	**16**

Abandoned matches are not included in the list of matches played.

ANALYSIS OF T20 RESULTS V. ALL TEAMS 2003-2020 *(Cont)*
OTHER MATCHES

		HOME				AWAY				
Opponents	Played	Won	Lost	Tied	N. R	Won	Lost	Tied	N. R	Abd
Uva	1	0	0	0	0	1	0	0	0	0
Trinidad and Tobago	1	0	0	0	0	1	0	0	0	0
Sydney Sixers	1	0	0	0	0	0	1	0	0	0
Mumbai	1	0	0	0	0	0	0	0	1	0
Highveld	1	0	0	0	0	0	1	0	0	0
Chennai	1	0	0	0	0	0	1	0	0	0
Lahore Qalandars	1	0	0	0	0	0	1	0	0	0
Hobart Hurricanes	1	0	0	0	1	0	0	0	0	0
Total	**8**	**0**	**0**	**0**	**0**	**3**	**4**	**0**	**1**	**0**
Grand Total	**199**	**50**	**39**	**3**	**1**	**40**	**58**	**3**	**5**	**16**

Abandoned matches are not included in matches played

ABANDONED T20 MATCHES (14)

2007	v. Lancashire at Leeds			Northampton
2008	v. Leicestershire at Leeds		v. Warwickshire at Birmingham	
2011	v. Northamptonshire at Leeds	2019	v. Nottinghamshire at Leeds	
2012	v. Lancashire at Manchester		v. Northamptonshire at	
2014	v. Warwickshire at Birmingham			Northampton
	v. Lancashire at Leeds		v. Lancashire at Manchester	
	v. Worcestershire at Worcester		v. Durham at Leeds	
2016	v. Nottinghamshire at Leeds	2020	v. Nottinghamshire at Leeds	
2017	v. Northamptonshire at		v. Leicestershire at Leeds	

T20 HIGHEST TEAM TOTALS

BY YORKSHIRE

260-4	v.	Northamptonshire at Leeds	2017
255:2	v.	Leicestershire at Leicester	2019
233-6	v.	Worcestershire at Leeds	2017
227-5	v.	Nottinghamshire at Leeds	2017
223-5	v.	Nottinghamshire at Nottingham	2017
226:8	v.	Birmingham Bears at Leeds	2018
223:6	v.	Durham at Leeds	2016
220:5	v.	Derbyshire at Leeds	2020
215:6	v.	Northamptonshire at Leeds	2016
213:7	v.	Worcestershire at Leeds	2010
212:5	v.	Worcestershire at Leeds	2012
211:6	v.	Leicestershire at Leeds	2004
210:3	v.	Derbyshire at Derby	2006
209:4	v.	Nottinghamshire at Leeds	2015
207:7	v.	Nottinghamshire at Nottingham	2004
202:8	v.	Lancashire at Manchester	2015
200:3	v.	Durham at Leeds	2018
200:3	v.	Birmingham Bears at Birmingham	2019
200:5	v.	Nottinghamshire at Leeds	2014

T20 HIGHEST TEAM TOTALS

AGAINST YORKSHIRE

231:6	for Lancashire at Manchester	2015
225:5	for Nottinghamshire at Nottingham	2017
222:6	for Derbyshire at Leeds	2010
221:3	for Leicestershire at Leeds	2004
215:6	for Nottinghamshire at Nottingham	2011
215:6	for Durham at Chester-le-Street	2013
212:5	for Nottinghamshire at Nottingham	2018
210:7	for Nottinghamshire at Nottingham	2004
208:7	for Worcestershire at Worcester	2010
207:5	for Derbyshire at Leeds	2019
207:6	for Lancashire at Manchester	2005
201:4	for Leicestershire at Leicester	2019
201:5	for Nottinghamshire at Leeds	2014
204:7	for Lancashire at Manchester	2016
196:7	for Worcestershire at Leeds	2017
195:8	for Derbyshire at Leeds	2005
195:4	for Nottinghamshire at Nottingham	2006
194:4	for Nottinghamshire at Nottingham	2020
193:5	for Sussex at Hove	2007

T20 HIGHEST INDIVIDUAL SCORES

BY YORKSHIRE

161	A Lyth	v.	Northamptonshire at Leeds	2017
118	D J Willey	v.	Worcestershire at Leeds	2017
109	I J Harvey	v.	Derbyshire at Leeds	2005
108*	I J Harvey	v.	Lancashire at Leeds	2004
102*	J M Bairstow	v	Durham at Chester-le-Street	2014
101*	H H Gibbs	v.	Northamptonshire at Northampton	2010
96*	M J Wood	v.	Nottinghamshire at Nottingham	2004
96*	T Kohler-Cadmore	v.	Leicestershire at Leicester	2019
94*	T Kohler-Cadmore	v.	Birmingham Bears at Birmingham	2019
92*	G J Maxwell	v.	Nottinghamshire at Leeds	2015
92*	J E Root	v.	Lancashire at Manchester	2016
92*	A Lyth	v.	Durham at Leeds	2018
92	P A Jaques	v.	Leicestershire at Leeds	2004
92	J M Bairstow	v.	Durham at Leeds	2015
91	A W Gale	v.	Nottinghamshire at Leeds	2009
89	A J Finch	v.	Nottinghamshire at Leeds	2014
88	A J Finch	v.	Lancashire at Manchester	2014
87	A Lyth	v.	Durham at Leeds	2017

T20 HIGHEST INDIVIDUAL SCORES

AGAINST YORKSHIRE

111	D L Maddy	for	Leicestershire at Leeds	2004
101	S G Law	for	Lancashire at Manchester	2005
101	A D Hales	for	Nottinghamshire at Nottingham	2017
100*	G M Smith	for	Derbyshire at Leeds	2008
100	Sohail Akhtar	for	Lahore Qalandars at Abu Dhabi	2018
97	B J Hodge	for	Leicestershire at Leicester	2003
96*	A B McDonald	for	Leicestershire at Leeds	2011
94	L E Bosman	for	Derbyshire at Leeds	2010
91*	G Clark	for	Durham at Leeds	2015
91*	R A Whiteley	for	Worcestershire at Leeds	2015
91	M A Ealham	for	Nottinghamshire at Nottingham	2004
91	P Mustard	for	Durham at Chester-le-Street	2013
91	M H Wessels	for	Worcestershire at Leeds	2019
90*	S R Patel	for	Nottinghamshire at Leeds	2015
90*	B A Stokes	for	Durham at Leeds	2018
88*	P D Collingwood	for	Durham at Chester-le-Street	2017
85*	B M Duckett	for	Nottinghamshire at Nottingham	2020
85	A Flintoff	for	Lancashire at Leeds	2004

T20 BEST BOWLING

BY YORKSHIRE

6-19	T T Bresnan	v.	Lancashire at Leeds	2017
5-11	J W Shutt	v.	Durham at Chester-le-Street	2019
5-16	R M Pyrah	v.	Durham at Scarborough	2011
5-19	Azeem Rafiq	v.	Northamptonshire at Leeds	2017
5-22	M D Fisher	v.	Derbyshire at Leeds	2015
5-21	J A Brooks	v.	Leicestershire at Leeds	2013
5-31	A Lyth	v.	Nottinghamshire at Nottingham	2019
4-18	M A Ashraf	v.	Derbyshire at Derby	2012
4-18	D J Willey	v.	Northamptonshire at Leeds	2019
4-19	A U Rashid	v.	Durham at Leeds	2017
4-20	R M Pyrah	v.	Durham at Leeds	2008
4-20	A U Rashid	v.	Leicestershire at Leeds	2010
4-21	R M Pyrah	v.	Worcestershire at Leeds	2011
4-21	B W Sanderson	v.	Derbyshire at Derby	2011
4-21	J A Brooks	v.	Derbyshire at Leeds	2013
4-23	Rana Naved	v.	Nottinghamshire at Leeds	2009
4-24	A U Rashid	v.	Nottinghamshire at Nottingham	2008
4-25	R J Sidebottom	v.	Durham at Chester-le-Street	2012

T20 BEST BOWLING

AGAINST YORKSHIRE

5-43	L J Fletcher	for	Nottinghamshire at Nottingham	2020
4- 9	C K Langeveldt	for	Derbyshire at Leeds	2008
4-17	L V van Beek	for	Derbyshire at Leeds	2019
4-19	K H D Barker	for	Warwickshire at Birmingham	2010
4-19	J S Patel	for	Warwickshire at Leeds	2014
4-19	R Rampaul	for	Derbyshire at Chesterfield	2018
4-19	M R J Watt	for	Derbyshire at Chesterfield	2019
4-21	J Needham	for	Derbyshire at Leeds	2009
4-23	A J Hall	for	Northamptonshire at Northampton	2011
4-23	M W Parkinson	for	Lancashire at Leeds	2017
4-25	J A Morkel	for	Derbyshire at Chesterfield	2013
4-25	I G Butler	for	Northamptonshire at Leeds	2014
4-25	M A Wood	for	Durham at Birmingham	2016
4-31	Shakib al Hasan	for	Worcestershire at Worcester	2011
4-32	C A Ingram	for	Glamorgan at Cardiff	2016
4-37	K K Jennings	for	Durham at Chester-le-Street	2015
4-38	S J Harmison	for	Durham at Leeds	2008
3- 3	J K H Naik	for	Leicestershire at Leeds	2011

T20 ECONOMICAL BOWLING

BY YORKSHIRE

4-0-11-5	J W Shutt	v. Durham at Chester-le-Street	2019

AGAINST YORKSHIRE

4-0-9-4	C K Langeveldt for Derbyshire at Leeds		2008

T20 MOST EXPENSIVE BOWLING

BY YORKSHIRE

4-0-65-2	M J Hoggard	v. Lancashire at Leeds	2005

AGAINST YORKSHIRE

4-0-77-0	B W Sanderson for Northamptonshire at Leeds		2017

T20 MAN OF THE MATCH AWARDS (92)

A W Gale	8	Azeem Rafiq	4	A J Finch	2
A Lyth	8	J M Bairstow	3	H H Gibbs	2
A McGrath	6	I J Harvey	3	P A Jaques	2
T Kohler-Cadmore	6	J A Leaning	3	A Z Lees	2
D J Willey	6	D A Miller	3	M J Lumb	2
T T Bresnan	5	A U Rashid	3	J E Root	2
R M Pyrah	5	K S Williamson	3		

One each: G S Ballance, J A Brooks, M E Claydon, M D Fisher, S P Fleming, D S Lehmann, G J Maxwell, J A Rudolph, B W Sanderson, J J Sayers, A Shahzad, J W Shutt, D J Wainwright and C White

T20 HIGHEST AND LOWEST SCORES BY AND AGAINST YORKSHIRE
PLUS INDIVIDUAL BEST BATTING AND BOWLING

The lowest score is the lowest all-out score or the lowest score at completion of the allotted overs, five-over matches not included.

Yorkshire versus:

Derbyshire

Stat		By Yorkshire	Against Yorkshire
Highest Score:	In Yorkshire	220:5 at Leeds 2020	at Leeds 2005 / 222:5 at Leeds 2010
	Away	210:3 at Derby 2006	170:5 at Chesterfield 2018
Lowest Score:	In Yorkshire	102 at Leeds 2018	124 at Chesterfield 2014
	Away	109 at Derby 2012	119:7 at Leeds 2007
Best Batting:	In Yorkshire	109 I J Harvey at Leeds 2005	100* G M Smith at Leeds 2008
	Away	79* A W Gale at Chesterfield 2009	71* B A Godleman at Chesterfield 2018
Best Bowling:	In Yorkshire	5-22 M D Fisher at Leeds 2015	4-9 C K Langeveldt at Leeds 2008
	Away	4-18 M A Ashraf at Derby 2012	4-19 R Rampaul at Chesterfield 2018
			4-19 M R J Watt at Chesterfield 2019

Durham

Stat		By Yorkshire	Against Yorkshire
Highest Score:	In Yorkshire	223:6 at Leeds 2016	191:6 at Leeds 2015
	Away	198:3 at Chester-le-Street 2020	215:6 at Chester-le-Street 2013
Lowest Score:	In Yorkshire	95 at Leeds 2014	116:8 at Leeds 2009
	Away	90:9 at Chester-le-Street 2009	98 at Chester-le-Street 2006
Best Batting:	In Yorkshire	92 J M Bairstow at Leeds 2015	91* G Clark at Leeds 2015
	Away	102* J M Bairstow at Chester-le-Street 2014	91 P Mustard at Chester-le-Street 2013
Best Bowling:	In Yorkshire	5-16 R M Pyrah at Scarborough 2011	4-38 S J Harrison at Leeds 2008
	Away	5-11 J W Shutt at Chester-le-Street 2019	4-25 M A Wood at Birmingham 2016

Essex

Stat		By Yorkshire	Against Yorkshire
Highest Score:	Away	143:7 at Chelmsford 2006	149:5 at Chelmsford 2006
Best Batting:	Away	43 G L Brophy at Chelmsford 2006	48* J S Foster at Chelmsford 2006
Best Bowling:	Away	2-22 A Shahzad at Chelmsford 2006	2-11 T J Phillips at Chelmsford 2006

Glamorgan

Stat		By Yorkshire	Against Yorkshire
Highest Score:	Away	180:8 at Cardiff 2016	90 at Cardiff 2016
Best Batting:	Away	79 D J Willey at Cardiff 2016	26 J A Rudolph at Cardiff 2016
Best Bowling:	Away	4-26 A U Rashid at Cardiff 2016	4-32 C A Ingram at Cardiff 2016

T20 HIGHEST AND LOWEST SCORES BY AND AGAINST YORKSHIRE PLUS INDIVIDUAL BEST BATTING AND BOWLING (Continued)

The lowest score is the lowest all-out score or the lowest score at completion of the allotted overs, five-over matches not included.

Yorkshire versus:

Hampshire

		By Yorkshire		Against Yorkshire	
Highest Score:	Away	140:6	at Cardiff 2012	150:6	at Cardiff 2012
Best Batting:	Away	72* D A Miller	at Cardiff 2012	43 J H K Adams	
Best Bowling:	Away	2-20 R J Sidebottom	at Cardiff 2012	3-26 C P Wood	at Cardiff 2012

Lancashire

		By Yorkshire		Against Yorkshire	
Highest Score:	In Yorkshire	185:8	at Leeds 2015	186:6	at Leeds 2015
	Away	202:8	at Manchester 2015	231:4	at Manchester 2015
Lowest Score:	In Yorkshire	111:8	at Leeds 2009	131:9	at Leeds 2004
	Away	97	at Manchester 2005	104:3	at Manchester 2003
Best Batting:	In Yorkshire	108* I J Harvey	at Leeds 2004	85 A Flintoff	at Leeds 2004
	Away	92* J E Root	at Manchester 2016	101 S G Law	at Manchester 2005
Best Bowling:	In Yorkshire	6-19 T T Bresnan	at Leeds 2017	4-23 M W Parkinson	at Leeds 2017
	Away	3-15 Azeem Rafiq	at Manchester 2011	3-10 D G Cork	at Manchester 2005

Leicestershire

		By Yorkshire		Against Yorkshire	
Highest Score:	In Yorkshire	211:6	at Leeds 2004	221:3	at Leeds 2004
	Away	255:2	at Leicester 2019	201:4	at Leicester 2019
Lowest Score:	In Yorkshire	134	at Leeds 2006	113:9	at Leeds 2013
	Away	105	at Leicester 2013	147:9	at Leicester 2012
Best Batting:	In Yorkshire	92 P A Jaques	at Leeds 2004	111 D L Maddy	at Leeds 2004
	Away	96* T Kohler-Cadmore	at Leicester 2019	97 B J Hodge	at Leicester 2003
Best Bowling:	In Yorkshire	5-21 J A Brooks	at Leeds 2013	3-3 J K H Naik	at Leeds 2011
	Away	3-42 L E Plunkett	at Leicester 2017	3-6 B J Hodge	at Leicester 2003

T20 HIGHEST AND LOWEST SCORES BY AND AGAINST YORKSHIRE PLUS INDIVIDUAL BEST BATTING AND BOWLING (Continued)

The lowest score is the lowest all-out score or the lowest score at completion of the allotted overs, five-over matches not included.

Yorkshire versus:

Northamptonshire

		By Yorkshire		Against Yorkshire	
Highest Score:	In Yorkshire	260:4	at Leeds 2017	165:7	at Leeds 2014
	Away	181:3	at Northampton 2014	180:5	at Northampton 2010
Lowest Score:	In Yorkshire	162:7	at Leeds 2014	107	at Leeds 2019
	Away	144	at Northampton 2011	132:7	at Northampton 2011
Best Batting:	In Yorkshire	161 A Lyth	at Leeds 2017	65 R E Levi	at Leeds 2017
	Away	101* H H Gibbs	at Northampton 2014	76 R E Levi	at Northampton 2014
Best Bowling:	In Yorkshire	5-19 Azeem Rafiq	at Leeds 2017	4-25 I G Butler	at Leeds
	Away	3-15 T T Bresnan	at Northampton 2016	4-23 A J Hall	at Northampton 2011

Nottinghamshire

		By Yorkshire		Against Yorkshire	
Highest Score:	In Yorkshire	227:5	at Leeds 2017	201:4	at Leeds 2014
	Away	223:5	at Nottingham 2017	225:5	at Nottingham 2017
Lowest Score:	In Yorkshire	141:8	at Leeds 2008	155:6	at Leeds 2009
	Away	112:7	at Nottingham 2010	136:6	at Nottingham 2008
Best Batting:	In Yorkshire	92* G J Maxwell	at Leeds 2015	90* S R Patel	at Leeds 2015
	Away	96* M J Wood	at Nottingham 2004	101 A D Hales	at Nottingham 2017
Best Bowling:	In Yorkshire	4-23 Rana Naved-ul-Hasan	at Leeds 2009	3-38 J T Ball	at Leeds 2014
	Away	5-31 A Lyth	at Nottingham 2019	5-43 L J Fletcher	at Nottingham 2020

Sussex

		By Yorkshire		Against Yorkshire	
Highest Score:	Away	172:6	at Cardiff 2012	193:5	at Hove 2007
Lowest Score:	Away	155	at Hove 2007	136:8	at Cardiff 2012
Best Batting:	Away	68* J M Bairstow	at Cardiff 2012	80* C D Nash	at Cardiff 2012
Best Bowling:	Away	2-22 T T Bresnan	at Cardiff 2012	3-22 S B Styris	at Cardiff 2012

T20 HIGHEST AND LOWEST SCORES BY AND AGAINST YORKSHIRE
PLUS INDIVIDUAL BEST BATTING AND BOWLING (Continued)

The lowest score is the lowest all-out score or the lowest score at completion of the allotted overs, five-over matches not included.

Yorkshire versus:

		By Yorkshire		Against Yorkshire	
		Score		Score	
Warwickshire					
Highest Score:	In Yorkshire	226:8	at Leeds 2018	177:4	at Leeds 2019
	Away	200:3	at Birmingham 2019	158:2	at Birmingham 2018
Lowest Score:	In Yorkshire	121:9	at Leeds 2010	145	at Leeds 2015
	Away	131	at Birmingham 2010	181:5	at Birmingham 2019
Best Batting:	In Yorkshire	76* T Kohler-Cadmore		69* L J Evans	at Leeds 2014
	Away	94* T Kohler-Cadmore	at Birmingham 2019	64* S R Hain	at Birmingham 2019
Best Bowling:	In Yorkshire	3-21 T T Bresnan	at Leeds 2017	4-19 J S Patel	at Leeds 2014
	Away	3-25 S A Patterson	at Birmingham 2010	4-19 K H D Barker	at Birmingham 2010
Worcestershire					
Highest Score:	In Yorkshire	233:6	at Leeds 2017	196:7	at Leeds 2017
	Away	187:7	at Worcester 2010	208:7	at Worcester 2010
Lowest Score:	In Yorkshire	117	at Leeds 2015	109	at Leeds 2010
	Away	142	at Worcester 2011	183:7	at Worcester 2011
Best Batting:	In Yorkshire	118 D J Willey	at Leeds 2017	91* R A Whiteley	at Leeds 2015
				91 M H Wessels	at Leeds 2019
	Away	40 G S Ballance	at Worcester 2018	56 A N Kervezee	at Worcester 2011
Best Bowling:	In Yorkshire	4-21 R M Pyrah	at Leeds 2011	3-29 B L d'Oliveira	at Leeds 2015
	Away	3-30 A Shahzad	at Worcester 2011	4-31 Shakib al Hasan	at Worcester 2011
Chennai					
Highest Score:	Away	140:6	at Durban 2012	141:6	at Durban 2012
Best Batting:	Away	58 G S Ballance	at Durban 2012	47 S Badrinath	at Durban 2012
Best Bowling:	Away	3-23 I Wardlaw	at Durban 2012	2-12 J A Morkel	at Durban 2012
Highveld					
Highest Score:	Away	131:7	at Johannesburg 2012	134:5	at Johannesburg 2012
Best Batting:	Away	31 P A Jaques	at Johannesburg 2012	32 Q de Kock	at Johannesburg 2012
Best Bowling:	Away	2-21 S A Patterson	at Johannesburg 2012	2-23 A M Phangiso	at Johannesburg 2012

T20 HIGHEST AND LOWEST SCORES BY AND AGAINST YORKSHIRE PLUS INDIVIDUAL BEST BATTING AND BOWLING (Continued)

The lowest score is the lowest all-out score or the lowest score at completion of the allotted overs, five-over matches not included.

Yorkshire versus:

Hobart Hurricanes

		By Yorkshire	Against Yorkshire
Highest Score:	Away	144:1 at Abu Dhabi 2018	140:7 at Abu Dhabi 2018
Best Batting:	Away	72* T Kohler-Cadmore at Abu Dhabi 2018	38 C P Jewell at Abu Dhabi 2018
Best Bowling:	Away	2-29 K Carver at Abu Dhabi 2018	1-24 J Clark at Abu Dhabi 2018

Lahore Qalandars

		By Yorkshire	Against Yorkshire
Highest Score:	Away	184:5 at Abu Dhabi 2018	189:4 at Abu Dhabi 2018
Best Batting:	Away	37 H C Brook at Abu Dhabi 2018	100 Sohail Akhtar at Abu Dhabi 2018
Best Bowling:	Away	2-26 J E Poysden at Abu Dhabi 2018	2-36 Shaheen Shah Afridi at Abu Dhabi 2018

Mumbai

		By Yorkshire	Against Yorkshire
Highest Score:	Away		156:6 at Cape Town 2012
Best Batting:	Away		37 D R Smith at Cape Town
Best Bowling:	Away	2-36 Azeem Rafiq at Cape Town 2012	

Sydney Sixers

		By Yorkshire	Against Yorkshire
Highest Score:	Away	96:9 at Cape Town 2012	98:2 at Cape Town 2012
Best Batting:	Away	25 J E Root at Cape Town 2012	43* M J Lumb at Cape Town 2012
Best Bowling:	Away	1-21 Azeem Rafiq at Cape Town 2012	3-22 M A Starc at Cape Town 2012

Trinidad and Tobago

		By Yorkshire	Against Yorkshire
Highest Score:	Away	154:4 at Centurion 2012	148:9 at Centurion 2012
Best Batting:	Away	64* G S Ballance at Centurion 2012	59 D Ramdin at Centurion 2012
Best Bowling:	Away	3-13 R J Sidebottom at Centurion 2012	1-16 K Y G Ottley at Centurion 2012

Uva

		By Yorkshire	Against Yorkshire
Highest Score:	Away	151:5 at Johannesburg 2012	150:7 at Johannesburg 2012
Best Batting:	Away	39* D A Miller at Johannesburg 2012	29 S H T Kandamby at Johannesburg 2012
Best Bowling:	Away	2-29 M A Ashraf at Johannesburg 2012	3-32 E M D Y Munaweera at Johannesburg 2012

T20 PARTNERSHIPS OF 100 AND OVER 2003-2020 (25)

150	2nd wkt	A Lyth	(66)	and D J Willey	(79)	v. Northamptonshire at Northampton 2018
137*	2nd wkt	A W Gale	(60*)	and H H Gibbs	(76*)	v. Durham at Leeds 2010
131	1st wkt	A Lyth	(78)	and P A Jaques	(64)	v. Derbyshire at Leeds 2012
129	2nd wkt	A W Gale	(91)	and M P Vaughan	(41*)	v. Nottinghamshire at Leeds 2009
129	2nd wkt	T Kohler-Cadmore	(46)	and D J Willey	(80)	v. Lancashire at Leeds 2018
127	1st wkt	A Lyth	(161)	and T Kohler-Cadmore	(41)	v. Northamptonshire at Leeds 2017
124	2nd wkt	I J Harvey	(109)	and P A Jaques	(37)	v. Derbyshire at Leeds 2005
124	2nd wkt	A Lyth	(161)	and D J Willey	(40)	v. Northamptonshire at Leeds 2017
121	3rd wkt	J A Rudolph	(56)	and A McGrath	(59)	v. Leicestershire at Leicester 2008
121	2nd wkt	T Kohler-Cadmore	(96*)	and N Pooran	(67)	v. Leicestershire at Leicester 2019
116	1st wkt	A W Gale	(70)	and P A Jaques	(48)	v. Leicestershire at Leeds 2012
116	1st wkt	A Lyth	(69)	and T Kohler-Cadmore	(96*)	v. Leicestershire at Leicester 2019
110*	4th wkt	A Lyth	(92*)	and J A Tattersall	(53*)	v. Durham at Leeds 2018
108	1st wkt	I J Harvey	(108*)	and P A Jaques	(39)	v. Lancashire at Leeds 2004
108	2nd wkt	A Lyth	(59)	and H H Gibbs	(40)	v. Worcestershire at Leeds 2010
106	2nd wkt	D J Willey	(74)	and A Z Lees	(35)	v. Northamptonshire at Leeds 2016
104	1st wkt	A W Gale	(43)	and J A Rudolph	(61)	v. Leicestershire at Leicester 2009
104	2nd wkt	A Z Lees	(63)	and J A Leaning	(60*)	v. Warwickshire at Leeds 2015
104	1st wkt	A Lyth	(68)	and T Kohler-Cadmore	(40)	v. Worcestershire at Leeds 2019
103*	5th wkt	G S Ballance	(64*)	and A U Rashid	(33*)	v. Trinidad & Tobago at Centurion 2012/13
103	1st wkt	A W Gale	(65*)	and J A Rudolp	(53)	v. Leicestershire at Leicester 2010
102	1st wkt	T Kohler-Cadmore	(94*)	and A Lyth	(42)	v. Birmingham Bears at Birmingham 2019
101	2nd wkt	M J Wood	(57)	and M J Lumb	(55)	v. Nottinghamshire at Leeds 2003
101	3rd wkt	A J Hodd	(70)	and G J Maxwell	(92*)	v. Nottinghamshire at Leeds 2015
100	4th wkt	A Z Lees	(59)	and J A Leaning	(64)	v. Northamptonshire at Northampton 2016

T20 HIGHEST PARTNERSHIPS FOR EACH WICKET

1st wkt	131	A Lyth	(78)	and P A Jaques	(64)	v. Derbyshire at Leeds 2012
2nd wkt	150	A Lyth	(66)	and D J Willey	(79)	v. Northamptonshire at Northampton 2018
3rd wkt	121	J A Rudolph	(56)	and A McGrath	(59)	v. Leicestershire at Leicester 2008
4th wkt	100	A Z Lees	(59)	and J A Leaning	(64)	v. Northamptonshire at Northampton 2016
5th wkt	103*	G S Ballance	(64*)	and A U Rashid	(33*)	v. Trinidad & Tobago at Centurion 2012/13
6th wkt	76	J E Root	(92*)	and L E Plunkett	(22)	v. Lancashire at Manchester 2016
7th wkt	68*	T T Bresnan	(45*)	and A U Rashid	(29*)	v. Warwickshire at Leeds 2014
8th wkt	54	T T Bresnan	(51)	and J D Middlebrook	(29*)	v. Lancashire at Manchester 2015
9th wkt	33*	A U Rashid	(5*)	and D Gough	(20*)	v. Lancashire at Leeds 2008
10th wkt	28*	A U Rashid	(28*)	and G J Kruis	(12*)	v. Durham at Chester-le-Street 2009

ALL WHO HAVE TAKEN 4 WICKETS IN AN INNINGS (22)

M A ASHRAF (1)
| 4-18 | v. Derbyshire | at Derby | 2012 |

AZEEM RAFIQ (1)
| 5-19 | v. Northamptonshire | at Leeds | 2017 |

T T BRESNAN (1)
| 6-19 | v. Lancashire | at Leeds | 2017 |

J A BROOKS (2)
| 5-21 | v. Leicestershire | at Leeds | 2013 |
| 4-21 | v. Derbyshire | at Leeds | 2013 |

M D FISHER (1)
| 5-22 | v. Derbyshire | at Leeds | 2015 |

A LYTH (1)
| 5-31 | v. Nottinghamshire | at Nottingham | 2019 |

C J MCKAY (1)
| 4-33 | v. Derbyshire | at Leeds | 2010 |

RANA NAVED-UL-HASAN (1)
| 4-23 | v. Nottinghamshire | at Leeds | 2009 |

S A PATTERSON (1)
| 4-30 | v. Lancashire | at Leeds | 2010 |

R M PYRAH (3)
5-16	v. Durham	at Scarborough	2011
4-20	v. Durham	at Leeds	2006
4-21	v. Worcestershire	at Leeds	2011

A U RASHID (5)
4-19	v. Durham	at Leeds	2017
4-20	v. Leicestershire	at Leeds	2011
4-24	v. Nottingham	at Nottingham	2008
4-26	v. Lancashire	at Leeds	2011
4-26	v. Glamorgan	at Cardiff	2016

B W SANDERSON (1)
| 4-21 | v. Derbyshire | at Derby | 2011 |

J W SHUTT (1)
| 5-11 | v. Durham | at Chester-le-Street | 2019 |

R J SIDEBOTTOM (1)
| 4-25 | v. Durham | at Chester-le-Street | 2012 |

D J WILLEY
| 4-18 | v. Northamptonshire | at Leeds | 2019 |

Player	M	Inns	NO	Runs	HS	Av'ge	100s	50s	Runs	Wkts	Av'ge	Ct/St
Ashraf, M A ...	17	1	0	4	4	4.00	0	0	462	17	27.17	1
Azeem Rafiq ...	95	37	24	153	21*	11.76	0	0	2,489	102	24.40	36
Bairstow, J M .	63	58	11	1,231	102*	26.19	1	4	0	0	—	27/8
Ballance, G S ..	79	68	8	1,390	79	23.16	0	4	0	0	—	43
Bess, D M	6	3	1	8	5*	4.00	0	0	174	4	43.50	0
Best, T L	8	3	2	10	10*	10.00	0	0	243	7	34.71	4
Birkhead, B D .	1	0	0	0			0	0	0	0	—	1
Blakey, R J	7	5	1	119	32	29.75	0	0	0	0	—	5/1
Bresnan, T T ..	118	91	35	1,208	51	21.57	0	1	2,918	118	24.72	41
Brook, H C ..	25	25	5	556	50*	27.80	0	1	26	1	26.00	14
Brooks, J A	23	0	0	0		—	0	0	582	22	26.45	11
Brophy, G L ..	54	46	9	717	57*	19.37	0	2	0	0	—	25/7
Carver, K	10	2	1	2	2	2.00	0	0	208	8	26.00	5
Claydon, M E ..	7	2	2	14	12*	—	0	0	188	5	37.60	2
Coad, B O	12	4	1	14	7	4.66	0	0	323	13	24.84	6
Craven, V J	6	6	4	76	44*	38.00	0	0	67	0	—	3
Dawood, I	11	8	3	44	15	8.80	0	0	0	0	—	5/2
Dawson, R K J .	22	8	3	71	22	14.20	0	0	558	24	23.25	7
Finch, A J	16	16	0	332	89	20.75	0	2	24	1	24.00	16
Fisher, M D ..	27	8	4	33	17*	8.25	0	0	781	31	25.19	9
Fleming, S P ...	4	4	0	62	58	15.50	0	1	0	0	—	1
Fraine, W A R .	12	11	3	193	44*	24.12	0	0	0	0	—	10
Gale, A W	104	97	8	2,260	91	25.39	0	16	0	0	—	30
Gibbs, H H	15	15	3	443	101*	36.91	1	2	0	0	—	8
Gibson, R	3	2	0	32	18	16.00	0	0	30	0	—	1
Gilbert, C R	13	9	2	107	38*	15.28	0	0	0	0	—	7
Gillespie, J N ..	17	4	2	14	8*	7.00	0	0	422	17	24.82	5
Gough, D	17	7	3	42	20*	10.50	0	0	416	16	26.00	2
Gray, A K D ...	8	3	0	17	13	5.66	0	0	211	9	23.44	4
Guy, S M	10	6	1	44	13	8.80	0	0	0	0	—	2
Hamilton, G M .	3	3	1	41	41*	20.50	0	0	0	0	—	1
Handscomb, P S P	7	6	0	97	31	16.16	0	0	0	0	—	3/3
Hannon-Dalby, O J	2	0	0	0		—	0	0	58	3	19.33	0
Harvey, I J	10	10	1	438	109	48.66	2	2	258	10	25.80	4
Head, T M	4	4	0	113	40	28.25	0	0	4	0	—	0
Hill, G C H	4	3	0	21	14	7.00	0	0	50	1	50.00	2
Hodd, A J	26	17	4	147	70	11.30	0	1	0	0	—	9/6
Hodgson, D M .	16	14	2	213	52*	17.75	0	1	0	0	—	9/1
Hodgson, L J ...	2	1	1	39	39*		0	0	59	2	29.50	1
Hoggard, M J ..	15	2	1	19	18	19.00	0	0	472	13	36.30	4
Jaques, P A	34	32	3	907	92	31.27	0	6	15	0	—	5
Kirby, S P	3	0	0	0		—	0	0	119	4	29.75	1
Kohler-Cadmore, T	40	40	5	1,226	96*	35.02	0	11	0	0	—	21
Kruis, G J	20	5	3	41	22	20.50	0	0	486	19	25.57	6
Lawson, M A K .	2	1	1	4	4*		0	0	87	3	29.00	1
Leaning, J A ...	52	45	11	952	64	28.00	0	2	45	1	45.00	25
Lees, A Z	37	36	2	857	67*	25.20	0	4	0	0	—	12
Lehmann, D S ..	9	9	3	252	48	42.00	0	0	180	8	22.50	4
Lumb, M J	26	26	3	442	84*	19.21	0	4	65	3	21.66	8

380

CAREER AVERAGES FOR YORKSHIRE

ALL t20 MATCHES 2003-2020 *(Continued)*

Player	M	Inns	NO	Runs	HS	Av'ge	100s	50s	Runs	Wkts	Av'ge	Ct/St
Lyth, A	119	110	3	2,927	161	27.35	1	17	467	21	22.23	57
McGrath, A	66	61	12	1,403	73*	28.63	0	8	698	23	30.34	26
McKay, C J ...	8	6	3	54	21*	18.00	0	0	258	10	25.80	1
Maharaj, K A ..	5	2	2	10	10*	—	0	0	126	2	63.00	2
Malan, D J ...	4	4	0	36	27	9.00	0	0	16	0	—	0
Marsh, S E ...	11	11	4	289	60*	41.28	0	2	0	0	—	1
Maxwell, G J ..	12	12	1	229	92*	20.81	0	1	264	12	22.00	6
Middlebrook, J D	4	2	2	33	29*	—	0	0	101	4	25.25	1
Miller, D A	14	13	4	457	74*	50.77	0	4	0	0	—	7
Olivier, D	8	3	0	10	8	3.33	0	0	264	11	24.00	1
Patterson, S A .	63	9	4	9	3*	1.80	0	0	1,811	61	29.68	10
Pillans, M W ..	9	3	0	18	8	6.00	0	0	246	5	49.20	2
Plunkett, L E ..	42	31	10	353	36	16.80	0	0	1,146	44	26.04	13
Pooran, N	3	3	0	122	67	40.66	0	1	0	0	—	2
Poysden, J E ..	7	1	1	0	0*	—	0	0	187	8	23.37	1
Pyrah, R M .... Rana	105	71	21	593	42	11.86	0	0	2,315	108	21.43	40
Naved-ul-Hasan	8	8	2	63	20*	10.50	0	0	159	11	14.45	2
Rashid, A U ...	103	63	20	577	36*	13.41	0	0	2,668	110	24.25	34
Revis, M L	2	1	1	0	0*	—	0	0	0	0	—	0
Rhodes, W M H	18	16	3	128	45	9.84	0	0	283	13	21.76	2
Robinson, O E . .	7	3	0	5	3	1.66	0	0	162	6	27.00	3
Root, J E	38	34	8	911	92*	35.03	0	8	381	11	34.63	13
Rudolph, J A ...	39	35	5	710	61	23.66	0	3	145	6	24.16	7
Sanderson, B W	4	0	0	0	—	—	0	0	74	6	12.33	0
Sarfraz Ahmed .	5	4	0	53	42	13.25	0	0	0	0	—	3/1
Sayers, J J	17	14	0	253	44	18.07	0	0	0	0	—	5
Shahzad, A ...	22	16	4	129	20	10.75	0	0	576	17	33.88	5
Shaw, J	5	2	1	1	1	1.00	0	0	138	2	69.00	1
Shutt, J W	11	4	3	0	0*	0.00	0	0	271	12	22.58	4
Sidebottom, R J .	40	16	10	87	16*	14.50	0	0	1,069	42	25.45	9
Silverwood, C E W	9	5	2	32	13*	10.66	0	0	264	7	37.71	4
Starc, M A	10	2	1	0	0*	0.00	0	0	218	21	10.38	1
Swanepoel, P J .	2	1	1	2	2*	—	0	0	60	3	20.00	1
Tattersall, J A ..	31	22	8	364	53*	26.00	0-	1	0	0	—	22/6
Taylor, C R ...	2	2	1	10	10*	10.00	0	0	0	0	—	0
Thompson, J A .	26	20	8	202	50	16.83	0	1	640	20	32.00	8
Vaughan, M P ..	16	16	1	292	41*	19.46	0	0	81	1	81.00	3
Wainman, J C ..	2	1	1	12	12*	—	0	0	49	1	49.00	0
Wainwright, D J	26	9	6	23	6*	7.66	0	0	551	21	26.23	9
Waite, M J	6	3	3	34	19*	—	0	0	81	2	40.50	3
Wardlaw, I ...	10	1	1	1	1	—	0	0	179	5	35.80	0
Warren, A C ...	2	0	0	0	—	—	0	0	70	4	17.50	0
Wharton, J H...	2	1	0	12	8	6.00	0	0	0	0	—	0
White, C	33	31	0	570	55	18.38	0	2	132	2	66.00	8
Willey, D J	45	42	1	1,267	118	30.90	1	7	1,181	43	27.46	19
Williamson, K S	12	11	0	302	65	27.45	0	1	37	3	12.33	3
Wisniewski, S A	2	0	0	0	—	—	0	0	32	0	—	0
Wood, M J	15	15	3	328	96*	27.33	0	2	32	2	16.00	11
Younus Khan ...	2	2	0	55	40	27.50	0	0	32	2	16.00	0
Yuvraj Singh ...	5	5	0	154	71	30.80	0	1	51	5	10.20	0

SECOND ELEVEN CHAMPIONS

In the seasons in which Yorkshire have competed. The Championship has been split into two groups since 2009, the group winners playing off for the Championship. These groups were deemed North and South from the 2012 season.

Season	Champions	Yorkshire's Position	Season	Champions	Yorkshire's Position
1959	Gloucestershire	7th	1997	Lancashire	2nd
1960	Northamptonshire	14th	1998	Northamptonshire	9th
1961	Kent	11th	1999	Middlesex	14th
1975	Surrey	4th	2000	Middlesex	5th
1976	Kent	5th	2001	Hampshire	2nd
1977	**Yorkshire**	**1st**	2002	Kent	3rd
1978	Sussex	5th	**2003**	**Yorkshire**	**1st**
1979	Warwickshire	3rd	2004	Somerset	8th
1980	Glamorgan	5th	2005	Kent	10th
1981	Hampshire	11th	2006	Kent	3rd
1982	Worcestershire	14th	2007	Sussex	10th
1983	Leicestershire	2nd	2008	Durham	5th
1984	**Yorkshire**	**1st**	2009	Surrey	A 2nd
1985	Nottinghamshire	12th	2010	Surrey	A 8th
1986	Lancashire	5th	2011	Warwickshire	A 10th
1987	**Yorkshire** and Kent	**1st**	2012	Kent	(North) 9th
1988	Surrey	9th	2013	Lancashire & Middlesex	
1989	Middlesex	9th			(North) 4th
1990	Sussex	17th	2014	Leicestershire	(North) 4th
1991	**Yorkshire**	**1st**	2015	Nottinghamshire	(North) 7th
1992	Surrey	5th	2016	Durham	(North) 5th
1993	Middlesex	3rd	2017	Lancashire	(North) 4th
1994	Somerset	2nd	2018	Durham	(North) 5th
1995	Hampshire	5th	2019	Leicestershire	(North) 2nd
1996	Warwickshire	4th			

SECOND ELEVEN CHAMPIONSHIP 1959-1961 AND 1975-2019

SUMMARY OF RESULTS BY SEASON

Season	Played	Won	Lost	Drawn	Tied	Abandoned	Position in Championship
1959	10	4	1	5	0	0	7
1960	10	1	3	6	0	0	14
1961	9	2	2	5	0	1	11
1975	14	4	0	10	0	0	4
1976	14	5	5	4	0	0	5
1977	**16**	**9**	**0**	**7**	**0**	**1**	**1**
1978	15	5	2	8	0	1	4
1979	16	5	0	11	0	0	3
1980	14	5	2	7	0	1	5
1981	16	2	3	11	0	0	11
1982	16	2	3	11	0	0	14 =
1983	11	5	1	5	0	3	2
1984	**15**	**9**	**3**	**3**	**0**	**0**	**1**
1985	14	3	3	8	0	1	12
1986	16	5	1	10	0	0	5
1987	**15**	**5**	**2**	**8**	**0**	**1**	**1 =**
1988	16	4	1	11	0	0	9
1989	17	2	3	12	0	0	9 =
1990	16	1	6	9	0	0	17
1991	**16**	**8**	**1**	**7**	**0**	**0**	**1**
1992	17	5	2	10	0	0	5
1993	17	6	1	10	0	0	3
1994	17	6	2	9	0	0	2
1995	17	7	1	9	0	0	5
1996	17	6	3	8	0	0	4
1997	16	8	5	3	0	1	2
1998	15	4	2	9	0	0	9
1999	16	3	8	5	0	1	14
2000	14	5	2	7	0	1	5
2001	12	8	2	2	0	1	2
2002	12	5	1	6	0	0	3
2003	**10**	**7**	**1**	**2**	**0**	**0**	**1**
2004	7	2	0	5	0	1	8
2005	12	2	4	6	0	0	10
2006	14	6	4	4	0	0	3
2007	12	4	5	3	0	0	10
2008	12	4	4	4	0	2	5
2009	9	5	0	4	0	0	(Group A) 2
2010	9	2	4	3	0	0	(Group A) 8
2011	9	0	4	4	1	0	(Group A) 10
2012	7	1	2	4	0	2	(North) 9
2013	9	3	4	2	0	0	(North) 4
2014	9	2	1	6	0	0	(North) 4
2015	9	2	4	3	0	0	(North) 7
2016	9	2	3	4	0	0	(North) 5
2017	8	2	0	6	0	1	(North) 4
2018	9	3	1	5	0	0	(North) 5
2019	8	3	1	4	0	0	(North) 2
Totals	618	199	112	305	1	19	

Matches abandoned without a ball bowled are not counted as matches played. The 1976 match between Yorkshire and Northamptonshire at Bradford was cancelled after the fixtures had been published. The Championship was divided into two groups from 2009, each team playng each other once. The two group winners play for the Championship.

ANALYSIS OF RESULTS AGAINST EACH OPPONENT

County	Played	Won	Lost	Drawn	Tied	Abandoned	First Played
Derbyshire	60	14	8	38	0	3	1959
Durham	35	11	6	18	0	2	1992
Essex	13	9	2	2	0	0	1990
Glamorgan	40	11	3	26	0	2	1975
Gloucestershire	10	3	3	4	0	0	1990
Hampshire	12	4	1	7	0	0	1990
Kent	26	5	4	17	0	1	1981
Lancashire	72	14	19	39	0	3	1959
Leicestershire	34	15	8	10	1	1	1975
MCC Young Cricketers	8	4	1	3	0	0	2005
MCC Universities	4	1	1	2	0	0	2011
Middlesex	18	7	2	9	0	0	1977
Northamptonshire	52	16	6	30	0	2	1959
Nottinghamshire	61	17	13	31	0	4	1959
Scotland	2	1	0	1	0	0	2007
Somerset	18	9	3	6	0	0	1988
Surrey	36	9	9	18	0	2	1976
Sussex	16	6	5	5	0	0	1990
Warwickshire	65	24	13	28	0	0	1959
Worcestershire	44	21	6	17	0	0	1961
Totals	626	201	113	311	1	20	

Note: Matches abandoned are not included in the total played.

Largest Victory An innings and 230 runs v. Glamorgan at Headingley, 1986

Largest Defeat An innings and 124 runs v. Gloucestershire at Bradford, 1994

Narrowest Victory By 1 run v. Lancashire at Old Trafford, 2003

Narrowest Defeat By 8 runs v. Derbyshire at Harrogate, 1982

Highest Total

By Yorkshire: 585 for 8 wkts dec v. Lancashire at Scarborough, 2017
Against Yorkshire: 567 for 7 wkts dec by Middlesex at RAF Vine Lane, Uxbridge, 2000

Lowest Total

By Yorkshire 66 v Nottinghamshire at Trent College, 2016
Against Yorkshire: 36 by Lancashire at Elland, 1979

Highest Match Aggregate

1,470 for 39 wkts v. Gloucestershire at Cheltenham, 2001

Highest Individual Score

For Yorkshire: 273* by R J Blakey v. Northamptonshire at Northampton, 1986
Against Yorkshire: 235 by O A Shah for Middlesex at Leeds, 1999

Century in Each Innings

For Yorkshire: C White 209* and 115* v. Worcestershire at Worcester, 1990
(The only instance of two unbeaten centuries in the same match)

K Sharp 150* and 127 v. Essex at Elland, 1991
A A Metcalfe 109 and 136* v. Somerset at North Perrott, 1994
R A Kettleborough 123 and 192* v. Nottinghamshire at Todmorden, 1996
C R Taylor 201* and 129 v. Sussex at Hove, 2005
A W Gale 131 and 123 v. Somerset at Taunton, 2006
J J Sayers 157 and 105 v. Lancashire at Leeds, 2007

Century in Each Innings *(Continued)*

Against Yorkshire: N Nannan   100 and 102* for Nottinghamshire at Harrogate, 1979
                 G D Lloyd   134 and 103   for Lancashire at Scarborough, 1989
                 A J Swann   131 and 100   for Northamptonshire at York, 1998
                 G J Kennis   114 and 114   for Somerset at Taunton, 1999

Most Career Runs

        B Parker   7,450 in 122 matches (average 40.48)

Best Bowling in an Innings

For Yorkshire: 9 for 27 by G A Cope v. Northamptonshire at Northampton, 1979
Against Yorkshire: 8 for 15 by I Folley for Lancashire at Heywood, 1983

Best Bowling in a Match

For Yorkshire: 13 for 92 (6 for 48 and 7 for 44) by M K Bore v. Lancashire
                at Harrogate, 1976
Against Yorkshire: 13 for 100 (7 for 45 and 6 for 55) by N J Perry for Glamorgan
                at Cardiff, 1978

Most Career Wickets

        Paul A Booth   248 in 85 matches, average 29.33

Totals of 450 and over

By Yorkshire (30)

Score	Versus	Ground	Season
585 for 8 wkts dec	Lancashire	Scarborough	2017
538 for 9 wkts dec	Worcestershire	Stamford Bridge	2007
534 for 5 wkts dec	Lancashire	Stamford Bridge	2003
530 for 8 wkts dec	Nottinghamshire	Middlesbrough	2000
526 for 8 wkts dec	MCC Young Cricketers	High Wycombe	2017
514 for 3 wkts dec	Somerset	Taunton	1988
509 for 4 wkts dec	Northamptonshire	Northampton	1986
508	Durham	Riverside	2017
502	Derbyshire	Chesterfield	2003
501 for 5 wkts dec	MCC Young Cricketers	Stamford Bridge	2009
497	Derbyshire	Chesterfield	2005
495 for 5 wkts dec	Somerset	Taunton	2006
488 for 5 wkts dec	Warwickshire	Harrogate	1984
486 for 6 wkts dec	Glamorgan	Leeds	1986
480	Leicestershire	Market Harborough	2013
476 for 3 wkts dec	Glamorgan	Gorseinon	1984
475 for 9 wkts dec	Nottinghamshire	Nottingham	1995
474 for 3 wkts dec	Glamorgan	Todmorden	2003
474	Durham	Stamford Bridge	2003
470	Lancashire	Leeds	2006
469	Warwickshire	Castleford	1999
462	Scotland	Stamford Bridge	2007
461 for 8 wkts dec	Essex	Stamford Bridge	2006
459 for 3 wkts dec	Leicestershire	Oakham	1997
459 for 6 wkts dec	Glamorgan	Bradford	1992
457 for 9 wkts dec	Kent	Canterbury	1983
456 for 5 wkts dec	Gloucestershire	Todmorden	1990
456 for 6 wkts dec	Nottinghamshire	York	1986
454 for 9 wkts dec	Derbyshire	Chesterfield	1959
452 for 9 wkts dec	Glamorgan	Cardiff	2005

Totals of 450 and over

Against Yorkshire (14)

Score	For	Ground	Season
567 for 7 wkts dec	Middlesex	RAF Vine Lane, Uxbridge	2000
555 for 7 wkts dec	Derbyshire	Stamford Bridge	2002
530 for 9 wkts dec	Leicestershire	Hinckley	2015
525 for 7 wkts dec	Sussex	Hove	2005
502 for 4 wkts dec	Warwickshire	Edgbaston Community Foundation Sports Ground	2016
493 for 8 wkts dec	Nottinghamshire	Lady Bay, Nottingham	2002
488 for 8 wkts dec	Warwickshire	Castleford	1999
486	Essex	Chelmsford	2000
485	Gloucestershire	North Park, Cheltenham	2001
477	Lancashire	Headingley	2006
471	Warwickshire	Clifton Park, York	2010
458	Lancashire	Bradford	1997
454 for 7 wkts dec	Lancashire	Todmorden	1993
450 for 7 wkts (inns closed)	Derbyshire	Bradford	1980

Completed Innings under 75

By Yorkshire (6)

Score	Versus	Ground	Season
66	Nottinghamshire	Trent College	2016
67	Worcestershire	Barnt Green (1st inns)	2013
68	Worcestershire	Barnt Green (2nd inns)	2013
69	Lancashire	Heywood	1983
72	Leicestershire	Kibworth	2019
74	Derbyshire	Chesterfield	1960
74	Nottinghamshire	Bradford	1998

Against Yorkshire (10)

Score	By	Ground	Season
36	Lancashire	Elland	1979
49	Leicestershire	Leicester	2008
50	Lancashire	Liverpool	1984
60	Derbyshire	Bradford	1977
60	Surrey	Sunbury-on-Thames	1977
62	MCC YC	High Wycombe	2005
64	Nottinghamshire	Brodsworth	1959
66	Leicestershire	Lutterworth	1977
72	Sussex	Horsham	2003
74	Worcestershire	Barnsley	1978

Individual Scores of 150 and over (68)

Score	Player	Versus	Ground	Season
273*	R J Blakey	Northamptonshire	Northampton	1986
238*	K Sharp	Somerset	Taunton	1988
233	P E Robinson	Kent	Canterbury	1983
230	T Kohler-Cadmore	Derbyshire	York	2017
221*	K Sharp	Gloucestershire	Todmorden	1990
219	G M Hamilton	Derbyshire	Chesterfield	2003
218*	A McGrath	Surrey	Elland	1994
212	G S Ballance	MCC Young Cricketers	Stamford Bridge	2009
209*	C White	Worcestershire	Worcester	1990
205	C R Taylor	Glamorgan	Todmorden	2003
204	B Parker	Gloucestershire	Bristol	1993
203	A McGrath	Durham	Headingley	2005
202*	J M Bairstow	Leicestershire	Oakham	2009
202	A Z Lees	Durham	Riverside	2017
202	M J Wood	Essex	Stamford Bridge	2006
201*	C R Taylor	Sussex	Hove	2005
200*	D Byas	Worcestershire	Worcester	1992
200*	A McGrath	Northamptonshire	Northampton	2012
192*	R A Kettleborough	Nottinghamshire	Todmorden	1996
191	P E Robinson	Warwickshire	Harrogate	1984
191	M J Wood	Derbyshire	Rotherham	2000
191	M J Lumb	Nottinghamshire	Middlesbrough	2000
189*	C S Pickles	Gloucestershire	Bristol	1991
186	A McGrath	MCC Universities	York	2011
184	J D Love	Worcestershire	Headingley	1976
183	A W Gale	Durham	Stamford Bridge	2006
174	G L Brophy	Worcestershire	Stamford Bridge	2007
173	S N Hartley	Warwickshire	Edgbaston	1980
173	A A Metcalfe	Glamorgan	Gorseinon	1984
173	B Parker	Sussex	Hove	1996
173	R A Kettleborough	Leicestershire	Oakham School	1997
173	T Kohler-Cadmore	Northamptonshire	Desborough	2018
172	A C Morris	Lancashire	York	1995
170*	R A J Townsley	Glamorgan	Harrogate	1975
169	J E Root	Warwickshire	York	2010
168	M J Wood	Leicestershire	Oakham School	1997
166	A A Metcalfe	Lancashire	York	1984
166	C A Chapman	Northamptonshire	York	1998
165*	A Lyth	Durham	Stamford Bridge	2006
165	J J Sayers	Sussex	Hove	2006
164*	A W Gale	Leicestershire	Harrogate	2002
164	J C Balderstone	Nottinghamshire	Harrogate	1960
163*	J E Root	Leicestershire	Oakham	2009
163	A A Metcalfe	Derbyshire	Chesterfield	1992
162*	D Byas	Surrey	Scarborough	1987
162*	R Gibson	Leicestershire	York	2016
161	H C Brook	Lancashire	Scarborough	2017
160	A A Metcalfe	Somerset	Bradford	1993
157*	W A R Fraine	Worcestershire	Kidderminster	2019
157	J J Sayers	Lancashire	Headingley	2007
155	S M Guy	Derbyshire	Chesterfield	2005
154*	C R Taylor	Surrey	Whitgift School	2005
153*	A A Metcalfe	Warwickshire	Bingley	1995

Individual Scores of 150 and over *(Continued)*

Score	Player	Versus	Ground	Season
153	C White	Worcestershire	Marske-by-the-Sea	1991
153	R A Stead	Surrey	Todmorden	2002
152	A A Metcalfe	Gloucestershire	Bristol	1993
151*	P E Robinson	Nottinghamshire	York	1986
151*	S J Foster	Kent	Elland	1992
151*	J J Sayers	Durham	Stamford Bridge	2004
151	P J Hartley	Somerset	Clevedon	1989
151	A McGrath	Somerset	Elland	1995
151	V J Craven	Glamorgan	Todmorden	2003
150*	K Sharp	Essex	Elland	1991
150*	G M Fellows	Hampshire	Todmorden	1998
150*	S M Guy	Nottinghamshire	Headingley	2005
150*	J A Leaning	Worcestershire	Worcester	2011
150	K Sharp	Glamorgan	Ebbw Vale	1983
150	S N Hartley	Nottinghamshire	Worksop	1988
150	C R Taylor	Derbyshire	Chesterfield	2003

7 Wickets in an Innings (31)

Analysis	Player	Versus	Ground	Season
9 for 27	G A Cope	Northamptonshire	Northampton	1977
9 for 62	M K Bore	Warwicshire	Scarborough	1976
8 for 33	B O Coad	MCC Young Cricketers	York	2018
8 for 53	S J Dennis	Nottinghamshire	Nottingham	1983
8 for 57	M K Bore	Lancashire	Manchester	1977
8 for 79	P J Berry	Derbyshire	Harrogate	1991
7 for 13	P Carrick	Northamptonshire	Marske-by-the-Sea	1977
7 for 21	S Silvester	Surrey	Sunbury-on-Thames	1977
7 for 22	J A R Blain	Surrey	Purley	2004
7 for 32	P W Jarvis	Surrey	The Oval	1984
7 for 34	P Carrick	Glamorgan	Leeds	1986
7 for 37	P M Hutchison	Warwickshire	Coventry	2001
7 for 39	G M Hamilton	Sussex	Leeds	1995
7 for 40	M K Bore	Worcestershire	Old Hill	1976
7 for 44	M K Bore	Lancashire	Harrogate	1976
7 for 44	J P Whiteley	Worcestershire	Leeds	1979
7 for 51	J D Middlebrook	Derbyshire	Rotherham	2000
7 for 53	J P Whiteley	Warwickshire	Birmingham	1980
7 for 55	C White	Leicestershire	Bradford	1990
7 for 58	K Gillhouley	Derbyshire	Chesterfield	1960
7 for 58	P J Hartley	Lancashire	Leeds	1985
7 for 63	M J Hoggard	Worcestershire	Harrogate	1998
7 for 65	M K Bore	Nottinghamshire	Steetley	1976
7 for 70	J D Batty	Leicestershire	Bradford	1992
7 for 71	J D Batty	Hampshire	Harrogate	1994
7 for 81	K Gillhouley	Lancashire	Scarborough	1960
7 for 84	I J Houseman	Kent	Canterbury	1989
7 for 88	I G Swallow	Nottinghamshire	Nottingham	1983
7 for 90	A P Grayson	Kent	Folkestone	1991
7 for 93	D Pickles	Nottinghamshire	Nottingham	1960
7 for 94	K Gillhouley	Northamptonshire	Redcar	1960

12 Wickets in a Match (6)

Analysis		Player	Versus	Ground	Season
13 for 92	(6-48 and 7-44)	M K Bore	Lancashire	Harrogate	1976
13 for 110	(7-70 and 6-40)	J D Batty	Leicestershire	Bradford	1992
13 for 111	(4-49 and 9-62)	M K Bore	Warwickshire	Scarborough	1976
12 for 69	(5-32 and 7-37)	P M Hutchison	Warwickshire	Coventry	2001
12 for 120	(5-39 and 7-81)	K Gillhouley	Lancashire	Scarborough	1960
12 for 162	(5-78 and 7-84)	I J Houseman	Kent	Canterbury	1989

Hat-tricks (4)

Player	Versus	Ground	Season
I G Swallow	Warwickshire	Harrogate	1984
S D Fletcher	Nottinghamshire	Marske-by-the-Sea	1987
I G Swallow	Derbyshire	Chesterfield	1988
M Broadhurst	Essex	Southend-on-Sea	1992

Second Eleven Performance Of The Year Award

The Trophy was instituted in 2013 to reward a Second Eleven performance with either bat or ball that stood out from the ordinary and turned the course of the game.

2013	M D Fisher	6-25	v. Leicestershire (One-Day Trophy)	
				Grace Road, Leicester
2014	J A Leaning	102	v. Nottinghamshire (T20)	Trent College, Nottingham
2015	M J Waite	143	v. Lancashire (Friendly)	Scarborough
2016	W M H Rhodes	137		
		and 114*	v Lancashire (Friendly)	Liverpool
2017	J W Jack Shutt	4-19	v. Middlesex in the Trophy Final	Headingley
		and 4-12	v. Derbyshire in the T20	Alvaston and Boulton
		to secure two victories.		
2018	J H Wharton	162	v. Leiestershire (Friendly)	Kibworth CC
		in only his second Second Eleven match.		
2019	M L Revis	177	v Sussex (Friendly)	Hove

SECOND ELEVEN TROPHY

WINNERS 1986-2019

1986	**Northamptonshire**, who beat Essex by 14 runs
1987	**Derbyshire**, who beat Hampshire by 7 wickets
1988	**Yorkshire**, who beat Kent by 7 wickets
1989	**Middlesex**, who beat Kent by 6 wickets
1990	**Lancashire**, who beat Somerset by 8 wickets
1991	**Nottinghamshire**, who beat Surrey by 8 wickets
1992	**Surrey**, who beat Northamptonshire by 8 wickets
1993	**Leicestershire**, who beat Sussex by 142 runs
1994	**Yorkshire**, who beat Leicestershire by 6 wickets
1995	**Leicestershire**, who beat Gloucestershire by 3 runs
1996	**Leicestershire**, who beat Durham by 46 runs
1997	**Surrey**, who beat Gloucestershire by 3 wickets
1998	**Northamptonshire**, who beat Derbyshire by 5 wickets
1999	**Kent**, who beat Hampshire by 106 runs.
2000	**Leicestershire**, who beat Hampshire by 25 runs.
2001	**Surrey**, who beat Somerset by 6 wickets
2002	**Kent**, who beat Hampshire by 5 wickets
2003	**Hampshire**, who beat Warwickshire by 8 wickets
2004	**Worcestershire**, who beat Essex by 8 wickets
2005	**Sussex**, who beat Nottinghamshire by 6 wickets
2006	**Warwickshire**, who beat Yorkshire by 93 runs
2007	**Middlesex**, who beat Somerset by 1 run
2008	**Hampshire**, who beat Essex by 7 runs
2009	**Yorkshire,** who beat Lancashire by 2 wickets
2010	**Essex**, who beat Lancashire by 14 runs
2011	**Nottinghamshire**, who beat Lancashire by 4 wickets
2012	**Lancashire**, who beat Durham by 76 runs
2013	**Lancashire**, who beat Nottinghamshire by 76 runs
2014	**Leicestershire**, who beat Lancashire by 168 runs
2015	**Derbyshire**, who beat Durham by 10 runs
2016	**Lancashire,** who beat Somerset by 10 wickets *(DLS)*
2017	**Yorkshire,** who beat Middlesex by 99 runs *(DLS)*
2018	**Middlesex,** who beat Somerset by 1 wicket
2019	**Kent**, who beat Durham by 16 runs

SECOND ELEVEN TWENTY20

WINNERS 2011-2019

2011	**Sussex**, who beat Durham by 24 runs
2012	**England Under-19s**, who beat Sussex by eight wickets
2013	**Surrey**, who beat Middlesex by six runs
2014	**Leicesterhire**, who beat Somerset by 11 runs
2015	**Middlesex**, who beat Kent by four wickets
2016	**Middlesex**, who beat Somerset by two wickets
2017	**Sussex**, who beat Hampshire by 24 runs
2018	**Lancashire**, who beat Essex by 25 runs
2019	**Glamorgan**, beat Hampshire by 1 run

ANNUAL REPORT
and
Statement of Account
for the year ended
December 31, 2020

CHAIRMAN'S STATEMENT

ROGER HUTTON

I was honoured to be appointed the Chair of Yorkshire County Cricket Club almost a year ago. It would be fair to say it has not been the year that I or indeed any of us could have anticipated. The pandemic has brought each and every one of us new and unexpected challenges.

I think we all, from time to time, have felt a little like Brian Close at Old Trafford as Michael Holding whistled down bouncer after bouncer from the far end. I am extremely proud of the courage and resilience with which the Club has faced these challenges, and I truly believe we have emerged stronger and with renewed vigour from the experience.

2020 will not be a year remembered primarily for its cricket, but there have been some moments of light on which to look back. I was very pleased to play my part, alongside others, to persuade the ECB to prioritise red-ball cricket and set up the inaugural Bob Willis Trophy. I was incredibly impressed with our performances in the competition, and we were unlucky to narrowly miss out playing in the first Bob Willis Trophy Final. Great credit must go to the players and skipper, as in my view we were only deprived of success by the number of non-playing days we encountered.

Our white-ball performance has been less successful, and the Club must look at how to make improvements in this arena and deliver better results in the T20 in 2021.

The Northern Diamonds also did their best to brighten up our summer. Following the appointment of James Carr as the Regional Director of Women's Cricket a strengthened and talented team played some great cricket to only narrowly be denied the Rachael Heyhoe Flint Trophy. I am confident the ladies will be shining brightly again in 2021.

However, the real achievements of Yorkshire County Cricket Club in 2020 should not be measured in games won, but games played. The players, coaching staff and the operational team must be applauded for their commitment and hard work in preparing for and competing in fixtures in the face of a global pandemic.

2020 may not be remembered for its cricket, but it will be remembered for the dedication and loyalty of those who had the Club's best interests at heart. I cannot praise the employees of Yorkshire County Cricket Club highly enough, nor sufficiently thank the Membership who showed such tremendous loyalty in helping the Club to survive unprecedented financial times.

Following support from our Membership, loyal sponsors and the ECB I'm pleased to be able to report that the Club's finances held together as Paul Hudson details in his report. This was pivotal for the Club's future, particularly in the face of continued uncertainty for the coming summer.

Through the hard work and endeavour of the YCCC team we have enjoyed record sales for the international matches during the course of next year, with outstanding pre-sales of the Test Match against India and the International T20 against Pakistan. This goes a long way to strengthening the Club's financial position in what still looks to be an uncertain landscape for 2021. Let us hope we can look forward to some great matches and that as many as possible are able to come and enjoy first-class cricket at our wonderful stadium.

I would also like to take the opportunity of thanking the Board for all their hard work in what has been such a challenging and complex year. I have been nothing less than impressed with the tenacity, resilience and resourcefulness of the Executive Committee. I would also like to give special thanks to Katherine Mathew, who has four years of service as a Non Executive Director at the Club. Katherine is to resign from the Board at the AGM, and is leaving a strong and important legacy.

2020 was the year in which societies across the world were challenged to confront racism, improve inclusion and challenge the status quo. This summer the Club faced some serious allegations from a former player as to how it has operated historically. We are clear that there is no room for racism in our society, our sport or our Club, and as a consequence we set up an independent investigation to examine the specific allegations made and also consider if the Club's policies and processes are sufficiently robust.

I will not pretend that this has been an easy or smooth process, but I am confident it has been the right course of action. Very few organisations have held themselves to account in this way, and it has been a difficult and distressing time for all involved with the investigation, but it is hugely important for the future of the Club and for the communities we strive to engage with.

Yorkshire County Cricket Club has a long and proud history in this wonderful game of cricket, and it is determined to be at the vanguard of meaningful change and inclusion. The Club had already established a diversity committee headed by Hanif Malik OBE 18 months before I was involved, and has done some fantastic work with diverse communities across the county, but there is always more we can and must do.

It is critical for the Club to ensure we appeal to all ages, genders and ethnic minorities. Yorkshire is an incredible county crammed with talent and passion, and the more of it that YCCC can attract and harness the better. So, while it was a year full of difficult decisions and conversations I hope 2020 will be remembered for the brilliance, hard work and loyalty of not just our players, but all the employees who worked so hard to deal with the effects of COVID-19.

It is a year that should be remembered for the outstanding loyalty and support of the best Members of any cricket club in the world. It is a year we will look back on and be grateful for the incredible support from all our financial stakeholders and sponsors. It is in my view a year in which we have learned more about ourselves than we could have ever anticipated and found the strength and resilience to move forward with a platform for success and change in 2021.

We are yet to be clear on the challenges to come in this coming season, but I believe we are in the best possible shape to meet them, and I for one am optimistic about YCCC's summer ahead.

ROGER HUTTON
Chairman
The Yorkshire
County Cricket Club

CHIEF EXECUTIVE'S REPORT

At the beginning of 2020 I was really looking forward to the season ahead. I believed, after a few years of transition, that we genuinely had a squad that could compete in all three formats.

We had just experienced an outstanding year in 2019, hosting four ICC World Cup matches and the remarkable Ben Stokes *Ashes* match where England trounced Australia by one wicket.

And I was even looking forward to the AGM, as the Club had produced an outstanding set of figures for the year, resulting in a further reduction of our debt. Although we were not scheduled to host a Test match in 2020 we could look for-

MARK ARTHUR

ward to hosting our first ever T20 Internationals against Australia and Pakistan. So, what could possibly go wrong?

Well, we all know the answer to that. But no one could predict the impact it would have on us as a cricket club or as a business. When the Coronavirus struck we were quick to close down Emerald Headingley to reduce costs and protect our staff and players. The players had just arrived in India for their preseason preparation, but we acted quickly to bring the squad and coaching staff home to their families. We furloughed all but 14 members of staff, who dealt with a new way of running the business from their homes for many months.

Then came the green light to commence the process of returning to the field of play. With new protocols in place and the prospect of behind-closed-doors cricket this was no easy task. And, of course, we were not only dealing with men's cricket. The Northern Diamonds had become part of YCCC.

The Northern Diamonds, with Dani Hazell returning from maternity leave just a few weeks after giving birth to become our Head Coach, performed really well and reached the final of the Rachael Heyhoe Flint Trophy. The Yorkshire first team would have followed suit if we hadn't lost over 450 overs to bad weather, but they produced three wins and two draws as a unit and won our regional league.

It was all rather strange playing cricket without Members and spectators. I do hope we can have crowds at the start of the 2021 Championship. Support makes such a difference to the atmosphere within a cricket ground, and I know our players missed the unrivalled following that Yorkshire Members bring to Emerald Headingley, Scarborough and York. One of the positives to come out of the season was the live streaming of matches, which we will commit to again in 2021.

We have a number of groups to thank for The Yorkshire County Cricket Club coming out of the year 2020 relatively unscathed from a financial perspective. The staff and players stood up magnificently, with each person volunteering to have a pay reduction during the season. We also thank our Members who donated their membership fees in large numbers. We thank our partners and sponsors who stuck with us, particularly The Emerald Group. The ECB made a grant of £500,000 to each of the 18 counties, and we were grateful for the Government's furlough scheme. As you will have gleaned from the accounts, many factors made the financial outcome acceptable.

While on the subject of the ECB, our sincere thanks go to Colin Graves who made a significant difference to the way cricket now operates and is funded during his five-year term as ECB Chair.

Scarborough and York Cricket Clubs missed out on an exciting programme in 2020, and if crowds are permitted in 2021 I hope that as many Members as possible will support the matches at those fabulous grounds.

I hope that you remain healthy in the coming months. When you do come to Emerald Headingley there may well be different protocols in place, and I ask that you to bear with us as we try to adhere to Government and ECB guidelines and keep everyone as safe as possible.

Finally, I would like to thank the non-executive directors who have helped to steer the executive team through these unchartered waters. A tough baptism for our new Chair, Roger Hutton.

I look forward to seeing as many of you as possible during the summer.

MARK ARTHUR
Chief Executive
Yorkshire County Cricket Club

DIRECTOR OF MEN'S CRICKET REPORT

I hope that you are keeping safe and well in these difficult times.

With the incredibly challenging circumstances 2020 presented credit must go to everyone connected with English cricket in enabling the two competitions to take place.

There was an incredible amount of work that went on in preparation. In particular in the drawing up of COVID-19 guidelines and protocols and the setting up of venues to ensure everyone's safety. Our medical staff, ground staff and oper-

MARTYN MOXON

ations team deserve particular praise, but it really was a team effort that everyone bought into.

Like the rest of the country we endured three months of lockdown after returning from Mumbai earlier than planned. However, the players were able to keep a good level of cardiovascular fitness and didn't put on any excess fat. This meant that once we were given the green light to start training again we were able to concentrate on building up their strength and working on their skills. This was done initially on a one-to-one basis, and then gradually moved into small groups.

The biggest challenge was the conditioning of the bowlers, building up their workloads to enable them to manage a challenging schedule. Again, credit should go to both the players and coaching staff for the way they managed this process and the long hours spent in ensuring the players had everything they needed.

Obviously, we only had two competitions to challenge for, namely the Bob Willis Trophy and T20 Blast.

Throughout the Bob Willis Trophy we played some excellent cricket, finishing top of our group with a number of young players coming into the side showing that they have huge potential. It was great to see Dawid Malan settle in well and make two significant contributions in the matches against Durham and Derbyshire. Jordan Thompson capitalised on Matthew Waite's injury, and showed his capabilities with both bat and ball, while it was pleasing to see how well Dominic Leech performed on his debut, and he shows huge potential for the future.

George Hill and Jack Shutt made their first-class debuts during the competition and look promising cricketers. Harry Brook showed more consistency this season, and although he didn't make a big hundred he's certainly showing signs of a growing maturity. It was a shame that our games against Derbyshire and Lancashire were badly affected by the weather. Otherwise we could easily have been competing in the final.

Given last year's performances and the signing of Dominic Bess, I believe we can look forward to the season with confidence and excitement. As has been stated many times we have been through a transitional period, but I feel we now have a squad capable of challenging for the County Championship.

As far as the T20 Blast was concerned it proved to be a very frustrating campaign. We prepared well and in great detail with a new captain in David Willey. The players were given specific roles, and we set out to create an attractive brand of cricket, giving players freedom within their roles while ensuring we were smart and understood what was required to win games.

David Willey missed the early stages of the competition due to his inclusion in the England one-day COVID-19 bubble. However, we did manage to win two out of our first three games. Unfortunately, we lost at Leicester when really we should have won, and after that game, we lost four key players for the remainder of the competition due to COVID-19 protocols. This was a massive blow to lose our captain and three influential players for the run-in. Consequently, we failed to qualify for the knockout stages. It was particularly frustrating, as we got ourselves into a position to win in two of those games, but our inexperience told and we came up short. Having said that we can look on it as good experience for a number who wouldn't normally have played, namely James Wharton, Matthew Revis, Sam Wisniewski, George Hill and Ben Birkhead, who made their T20 debuts.

We also had Joe Root in five games of the competition. As well as his considerable contributions in those games on the field, as ever he was absolutely brilliant with the players off the field. His willingness to support and advise cannot be underestimated, and everyone will have benefited from his presence.

There were no official Second Eleven competitions last season. However, we did have a number of inter-squad games and competitive training days against a couple of other counties. Clearly, it is important that we have a full season of cricket this year to ensure the continuation of our young players' development.

Everyone at the Club is looking forward to this coming season, and we will do everything possible to ensure that we can welcome you back to Emerald Headingley, Scarborough and York safely. We certainly missed you last year, and we hope we can give you some great entertainment over the coming season. In the meantime, take care and stay healthy, and we look forward to seeing you soon.

MARTYN MOXON
Director of Cricket
Yorkshire County Cricket Club

DIRECTOR OF WOMEN'S CRICKET REPORT

JAMES CARR

Year 2020 marked the start of a new strategic cycle for the ECB and one strand of the *Inspiring Generations* strategy is the women and girls action plan, *Transforming Women and Girls' Cricket*. Yorkshire CCC take up the role of regional hosts for the north-east region of England — made up of Northumberland, Durham and Yorkshire.

There are eight regions, made up of clusters of counties, across the country, charged with professionalising the women's game through their elite teams and newly appointed dedicated workforce, which will support our athletes holistically to deliver a year-round training programme — something that has never been done outside of centrally contracted England players.

Having started the role on March 23, 2020, and the country entering a lockdown as a result of the Coronavirus pandemic on March 24, momentum and energy of the women's cricket agenda was somewhat curtailed as the country and cricket reacted to the unprecedented situation, nationally and globally.

By late July it was confirmed a truncated version of the original competition structure would take place in late August and September. All eight regions would play in two geographical groups, culminating with a North versus South final, at Edgbaston. It was at this stage cricket started to mobilise, and the decision was taken for the counties within our region to play one another. The willingness and adaptability of the cricket family confirmed to me what great people we have in our region. The county match-play enabled head coach Dani Hazell to construct a squad for further training camps before competition phase.

Hazell comes with a decade of international playing experience and a year as head coach of the Yorkshire Diamonds from the KIA Super league era. A combination of Dani's style and the girls' hunger for the game and the prestige of entering the professional era provided a chemistry among the squad— the "Northern Way" was born.

Late August bank holiday arrived, and the newly named Rachel Heyhoe-Flint Trophy was upon us with two matches in three days to kick off. Having the England players available for the first weekend yielded 50s and a 100 for Lauren Winfield-Hill, Hollie Armitage and Natalie Sciver respectively. Katherine Brunt made light work of Central Sparks with a five-wicket haul. Being two from two really galvanised the squad, and the hunger to top the group was palpable.

After the opening weekend the England players returned to the bubble for the preparations for their series against the West Indies. Hazell and the squad had to be agile to get through the rigours of the competition with the short lead-in time. The next four matches yielded three wins, securing our place in the final against Southern Vipers, the only loss being the Central Sparks return fixture at Emerald Headingley, where the game was played on an outstanding surface under glorious weather.

What was really encouraging during the group stages was the way the team gelled so easily. At times they well beat teams with clinical performances, but also they won a couple of games from being behind the eight-ball. MacDonald, Kalis, and Gunn all recorded 50s, and that was backed by strong bowling performances led by Langston and Graham.

Sadly, the final was one match too far for the Diamonds. Kalis recorded another 50, this time in vain, as the Vipers won by 38 runs. That the whole team achieved so much in a short space of time and in alien conditions to make a national final live on Sky TV has done wonders to keep the women's game high on the agenda and visible in what has been a turbulent year for the country. I am really proud of the support staff and the players for what they have achieved in a shortened year. They have shown resilience and adaptability to ensure we made it out on the park.

Hopefully, as we enter some normality in 2021 we can really kick on from what is a great start, and it does not stop with the senior team. The whole pathway needs to have depth and be fit for purpose. The addition of a new regional academy this year will go a long way to developing more players and raising the standard of our cricketers.

Exciting times ahead.

JAMES CARR
Director of Cricket
Regional Director of Women's Cricket
Northern Diamonds

FINANCE DIRECTOR'S REPORT

While 2019 was such an exceptionally good year in financial terms, this year has proven a much greater challenge. The Club started the year with a clear financial plan and a good start to ticket sales for the international matches.

However, it very quickly became apparent that we would need to adopt a different approach to remain financially stable and achieve our financial targets. I am very pleased to be able to report that while it was in a manner completely different to envisaged we have managed to maintain financial stability in line with our plans.

PAUL HUDSON

Our conference and banqueting business, together with hospitality for both domestic and international matches, have virtually disappeared during the year, together with a very significant reduction in our commercial income streams and rental incomes from third parties. Domestic ticket sales and memberships were similarly significantly reduced. This was also the first full year of the new Emerald Stand arrangements, which are reflected in the increase in infrastructure and operations overhead costs.

In the backdrop of this bleak picture the Club received support from a large array of sources. This collective group of actions have helped to return the Club's financial outturn in line with our budget. Without any one of these factors the result for this financial year would have been very different. These factors included:

- A significant proportion of members donated their annual membership fees, together with a large proportion of members donating the ticket money from their purchases and notable additional donations from members who wanted to help further. These were all greatly appreciated, and every donation added together to make a real impact;

- Every single member of staff saw a reduction in their pay;

- A thorough review of all suppliers' arrangements during the pandemic and future relationships was conducted achieving strengthened relationships and reduced current-year costs;

- The Club acted at the first opportunity to benefit from the Government's job-furlough scheme, which had a great impact in support for the Club, coupled with a rates holiday for the stadium.

- The ECB also provided significant support through provision of a one-off grant to all counties and a number of cash-flow support initiatives to provide clubs with time to implement their plans;
- Finally, the ECB insurance scheme ensured that the ticket income for international matches was secured for the Club, and there were, of course, no costs incurred in staging the matches.

In addition to the above financial measures, during the summer we were able to complete on our agreement with Leeds Becket University to take over full and unfettered ownership of the pavilion building. This agreement is a positive outturn for both organisations, and gives us total control over the building.

Looking forward into 2021, the Club faces a further year of uncertainty surrounding the pandemic. We have developed a business plan which reflects our current view of cricket and the year ahead. This shows us meeting all our liabilities, including debt-capital repayments to the bank. We have only been able to reach this position through the support of a large number of parties, and I would like to express my own personal thanks to all such people.

This has and continues to be a challenging time for all, and we must continue to pull together.

PAUL HUDSON
Director of Finance
Yorkshire County Cricket Club

RECENT FINANCIAL TRENDS

	2020	2019	2018	2017	2016
	£000	£000	£000	£000	£000
Income:					
International ticket and hospitality revenue	1,485	10,484	2,498	2,686	2,399
Domestic ticket and hospitality revenue	297	1,095	999	932	1,005
Subscriptions	605	812	828	742	740
England and Wales Cricket Board	4,424	2,536	2,119	3,152	2,638
Commercial income	889	3,001	2,353	1,998	1,881
Other	1,086	68	118	150	131
Total Income	**8,786**	**17,996**	**8,915**	**9,660**	**8,794**
Cost of sales	(235)	(4,228)	(2,095)	(2,208)	(2,109)
Cricket expenses	(3,436)	(3,500)	(3,386)	(3,326)	(3,055)
Overheads	(3,837)	(3,817)	(2,920)	(2,982)	(2,554)
EBITDA	**1,278**	**6,451**	**515**	**1,144**	**1,076**
Interest	(800)	(680)	(797)	(805)	(794)
Depreciation and loss on disposal of a fixed asset	(676)	(590)	(556)	(513)	(465)
Capital grants release	213	253	190	188	186
Surplus/(deficit) before exceptional items	**15**	**5,434**	**(648)**	**14**	**3**
Exceptional items	(87)	—	—	(68)	—
(Deficit) / Surplus before taxation	**(72)**	**5,434**	**(648)**	**(54)**	**3**
Loans, borrowing and overdrafts net of cash	**14,789**	**18,340**	**20,636**	**22,942**	**24,636**

CORPORATE GOVERNANCE

The Board is accountable to the Club's members for good corporate governance, and this statement describes how the principles of governance are applied.

THE BOARD

The Board is responsible for approving Club policy and strategy. It meets bi-monthly, or more frequently if business needs require, and has a schedule of matters specifically reserved to it for decision, including all significant commercial issues and all capital expenditure.

The Executive Management Team supply the Board with appropriate and timely information, and Board Members are free to seek any further information they consider necessary. The Board has formed various committees to assist in the governance of the Club's affairs.

NOMINATIONS COMMITTEE

The Nominations Committee is formally constituted with written terms of reference which are defined in the Club Rules and reviewed regularly. It is chaired by the Chair and the other members of the committee are the President, Secretary and one Non-Executive board member, currently Katherine Mathew.

AUDIT, GOVERNANCE AND RISK COMMITTEE

The Audit, Governance and Risk Committee meets to provide oversight of the financial reporting process, the audit process, systems of internal controls and compliance with laws and regulations. It is chaired by Stephen Willis, and meets with the external auditors as part of this process. The other members of the committee are Katherine Mathew and Neil Hartley.

REMUNERATION COMMITTEE

The Remuneration Committee assists the Board in developing and administering a fair remuneration policy for the Club and determining remuneration of senior employees. It is chaired by Stephen Willis, and the other members of the committee are Roger Hutton and Hanif Malik.

MEMBERS' COMMITTEE

The Club encourages effective communication with its members, and the Members' Committee, as defined in the Club Rules, is appointed for that purpose.

EQUALITY AND DIVERSITY WORKING GROUP

The Equality and Diversity Working Group meets four times per year to provide guidance and practical advice to all areas of Yorkshire Cricket, towards improving diversity and inclusion across the organisation. The Group is chaired by Hanif Malik, and the Club is also represented by other Board Members Roger Hutton, Mark Arthur and Martyn Moxon. Liz Neto as HR Manager and PA also represents the Club. The Yorkshire Cricket Board is represented by Andrew Watson and the Yorkshire Cricket Foundation is represented by Will Saville.

INTERNAL CONTROL

The Board acknowledges its responsibility to maintain a sound system of internal control relating to operational, financial and compliance controls and risk management, to safeguard the members' interests and the Club's assets, and will regularly review its effectiveness. Such a system, however, is designed to manage and meet the Club's particular needs and mitigate the risks to which it is exposed, rather than eliminate the risk of failure to achieve business objectives, and can provide only reasonable and not absolute assurance against material mis-statement or loss. The Club considers the key components to provide effective internal control and improve business efficiency are:

- Regular meetings with senior management to review and assess progress made against objectives and deal with any problems which arise from such reviews.

- A financial reporting system of annual budgets, periodic forecasts and detailed monthly reporting which includes cash flow forecasts. Budgets and forecasts are reviewed and approved by the Board.

- A management and organisation structure exists with defined responsibilities and appropriate authorisation limits and short lines of communication to the Non-Executive Chair.

- A Senior Independent Board Member is appointed by the Board, whose role is to serve as a sounding board for the Chair and act as an intermediary for other board members. The position is currently held by Stephen Willis.

BOARD MEMBERS' RESPONSIBILITIES

The Board Members are responsible for preparing the annual report and the financial statements in accordance with applicable law and regulations. Co-operative and Community Benefit Society law requires the Board Members to prepare financial statements for each financial year.

Under that law the Board Members have elected to prepare the financial statements in accordance with United Kingdom Generally Accepted Accounting Practice (United Kingdom Accounting Standards and applicable law). Under Co-operative and Community Benefit Society law the Board Members must not approve the financial statements unless they are satisfied that they give a true and fair view of the state of affairs of the Club and of the income and expenditure of the Club for that period.

In preparing these financial statements the Board Members are required to:

- Select suitable accounting policies and then apply them consistently;
- Make judgements and accounting estimates that are reasonable and prudent;
- Prepare the financial statements on the going-concern basis unless it is inappropriate to presume that the Club will continue in business.

The Board Members are responsible for keeping adequate accounting records that are sufficient to show and explain the Club's transactions and disclose with reasonable accuracy at any time the financial position of the Club and enable them to ensure that the financial statements comply with the Co-operative and Community Benefit Societies Act 2014.

They are also responsible for safeguarding the assets of the Club and hence for taking reasonable steps for the prevention and detection of fraud and other irregularities.

DISCLOSURE OF INFORMATION TO AUDITOR

The members of the Board who held office at the date of approval of the Annual Report and Accounts confirm that, so far as they are aware, there is no relevant information of which the Club's auditor is unaware; or each member has taken all the steps that they ought to have taken as a member to make themselves aware of any relevant audit information or to establish that the Club's auditor is aware of that information.

INDEPENDENT AUDITORS' REPORT

TO THE MEMBERS OF THE YORKSHIRE COUNTY CRICKET CLUB

Opinion

We have audited the financial statements of Yorkshire County Cricket Club Limited (the 'Club') for the year ended December 31, 2020, which comprise the statement of Income and Expenditure account, the Balance Sheet, Cash Flow Statement, Statement of Changes in Equity and notes to the financial statements, including significant accounting policies. The financial reporting framework that has been applied in their preparation is applicable law and United Kingdom Accounting Standards, including FRS 102 The Financial Reporting Standard applicable in the UK and Republic of Ireland (United Kingdom Generally Accepted Accounting Practice).

In our opinion the financial statements:

- Give a true and fair view of the state of the Club's affairs as at December 31, 2020, and of its income and expenditure for the year then ended;
- Have been properly prepared in accordance with United Kingdom Generally Accepted Accounting Practice; and
- Have been prepared in accordance with the requirements of the Co-operative and Community Benefit Societies Act 2014.

Basis for opinion

We conducted our audit in accordance with International Standards on Auditing (UK) (ISAs (UK)) and applicable law. Our responsibilities under those standards are further described in the Auditor's Responsibilities for the Audit of the Financial Statements section of our report. We are independent of the Club in accordance with the ethical requirements that are relevant to our audit of the financial statements in the UK, including the FRC's Ethical Standard, and we have fulfilled our other ethical responsibilities in accordance with these requirements. We believe that the audit evidence we have obtained is sufficient and appropriate to provide a basis for our opinion.

Conclusions relating to going concern

In auditing the financial statements we have concluded that the directors' use of the going-concern basis of accounting in the preparation of the financial statements is appropriate.

Based on the work we have performed, we have not identified any material uncertainties relating to events or conditions that, individually or collectively, may cast significant doubt on the Club's ability to continue as a going concern for a period of at least 12 months from when the financial statements are authorised for issue.

Our responsibilities and the responsibilities of the directors with respect to going concern are described in the relevant sections of this report.

Other information

The other information comprises the Chair's Report, Chief Executive's Report, Director of Cricket's Report, Regional Director of Women's Cricket Report, Director of Finance's Report, Corporate Governance Statement, AGM Minutes, Members' Committee Report, Board Attendance & Players Appearances for 2020, Yorkshire Cricket Foundation Manager's Report, President, Board Members, Staff and Players, Yorkshire Cricket Board Executive Director's report and Notice of AGM and Agenda. Our opinion on the financial statements does not cover the other information and, except to the extent otherwise explicitly stated in our report, we do not express any form of assurance conclusion thereon.

In connection with our audit of the financial statements our responsibility is to read the other information and, in doing so, consider whether the other information is materially inconsistent with the financial statements or our knowledge obtained in the audit or otherwise appears to be materially mis-stated. If we identify such material inconsistencies or apparent material mis-statements we are required to determine whether there is a material mis-statement in the financial statements or a material mis-statement of the other information. If, based on the work we have performed, we conclude that there is a material mis-statement of this other information we are required to report that fact.

Matters on which we are required to report by exception

In the light of the knowledge and understanding of the Club and its environment obtained in the course of the audit we have not identified material mis-statements in the other information.

We have nothing to report in respect of the following matters where the Co-operative and Community Benefit Societies Act 2014 requires us to report to you if, in our opinion:

- Adequate accounting records have not been kept, or returns adequate for our audit have not been received from branches not visited by us; or
- The financial statements are not in agreement with the accounting records and returns; or
- We have not received all the information and explanations we require for our audit.

Extent to which the audit was capable of identifying irregularities, including fraud

We identified areas of laws and regulations that could reasonably be expected to have a material effect on the financial statements from our general commercial and sector experience, through discussion with the board members and other management, and from inspection of the Club's regulatory and legal correspondence, and we discussed with the board members and other management the policies and procedures regarding compliance with laws and regulations. We communicated identified laws and regulations throughout our team and remained alert to any indications of non-compliance during the audit.

The Club is subject to laws and regulations that directly affect the financial statements including financial reporting legislation (including related Co-operative and Community Benefit Societies legislation), pensions legislation and taxation legislation and further laws and regulations that could indirectly affect the financial statements, comprising environmental, health-and-safety legislation and, in the current climate, covid regulations.

We assessed the extent of compliance with these laws and regulations as part of our procedures on the related financial statement items. Auditing standards limit the required audit procedures to identify non-compliance with these laws and regulations to enquiry of the board members and other management and inspection of regulatory and legal correspondence, if any. These procedures did not identify any potentially material actual or suspected non-compliance.

To identify risks of material mis-statement due to fraud we considered the opportunities and incentives and pressures that may exist within the Club to commit fraud. Our risk-assessment procedures included: enquiry of board members to understand the high level policies and procedures in place to prevent and detect fraud, reading Board minutes and considering performance targets and incentive schemes in place for management. We communicated identified fraud risks throughout our team and remained alert to any indications of fraud during the audit.

As a result of these procedures we identified the greatest potential for fraud in the following areas: revenue recognition and in particular the risk that revenue is recorded in the wrong period due to complexities surrounding deferred and accrued income. As required by auditing standards we also identified and addressed the risk of management override of controls.

We performed the following procedures to address the risks of fraud identified:

- Identifying and testing high-risk journal entries through vouching the entries to supporting documentation.
- Assessing significant accounting estimates for bias.
- Sampling testing of deferred and accrued revenue.
- Sales cut-off testing.

Owing to the inherent limitations of an audit there is an unavoidable risk that we may not have detected some material mis-statements in the financial statements, even though we have properly planned and performed our audit in accordance with auditing standards. For example, the further removed non-compliance with laws and regulations is from the events and transactions reflected in the financial statements the less likely the inherently limited procedures required by auditing standards would identify it.

In addition, as with any audit, there remained a higher risk of non-detection of fraud, as these may involve collusion, forgery, intentional omissions, misrepresentations, or the override of internal controls. Our audit procedures are designed to detect material mis-statement. We are not responsible for preventing non-compliance or fraud and cannot be expected to detect non-compliance with all laws and regulations.

Responsibilities of the board

As explained more fully in the board members' responsibilities statement, the board members are responsible for the preparation of the financial statements and for being satisfied that they give a true and fair view, and for such internal control as the board members determine is necessary to enable the preparation of financial statements that are free from material mis-statement, whether due to fraud or error.

In preparing the financial statements the board members are responsible for assessing the Club's ability to continue as a going concern, disclosing, as applicable, matters related to going concern and using the going-concern basis of accounting unless the board members either intend to liquidate the Club or to cease operations, or have no realistic alternative but to do so.

Auditors responsibilities for the audit of the financial statements

Our objectives are to obtain reasonable assurance about whether the financial statements as a whole are free from material mis-statement, whether due to fraud or error, and to issue an auditor's report that includes our opinion. Reasonable assurance is a high level of assurance, but is not a guarantee that an audit conducted in accordance with ISAs (UK) will always detect a material mis-statement when it exists.

Mis-statements can arise from fraud or error and are considered material if, individually or in the aggregate, they could reasonably be expected to influence the economic decisions of users taken on the basis of these financial statements.

A further description of our responsibilities for the audit of the financial statements is located on the Financial Reporting Council's website at: *http://www.frc.org.uk/auditorsresponsibilities*. This description forms part of our auditor's report.

Use of our report

This report is made solely to the Club's members, as a body, in accordance with section 87 of the Co-operative and Community Benefit Societies Act 2014. Our audit work has been undertaken so that we might state to the Club's members those matters we are required to state to them in an auditor's report and for no other purpose. To the fullest extent permitted by law we do not accept or assume responsibility to anyone other than the Club and the Club's members, as a body, for our audit work, for this report, or for the opinions we have formed.

CHRIS BUTT (Senior Statutory Auditor) for and on behalf of Garbutt & Elliott Audit Limited

Chartered Accountants
33 Park Place, Leeds LS1 2RY

February 9, 2021

INCOME AND EXPENDITURE ACCOUNT
for the year ended December 31, 2020

	Note	2020 £	2019 £
Income			
International ticket and hospitality revenue		1,485,362	10,483,782
Domestic ticket and hospitality revenue		296,882	1,095,209
Subscriptions		604,827	811,815
England and Wales Cricket Board		4,424,128	2,536,345
Commercial income		888,849	3,001,265
Other income		1,086,334	67,900
		8,786,382	17,996,316
Cost of sales			
International match and hospitality expenditure		(88,505)	3,362,414
Domestic match and hospitality costs (home fixtures)		189,489	561,569
Commercial costs		134,177	304,533
		(235,161)	(4,228,516)
Cricket expenses			
Staff remuneration and employment expenses		2,752,211	2,714,761
Match expenses (away fixtures)		14,884	227,138
Development expenses		483,573	415,522
Other cricket expenses		185,455	142,574
		(3,436,123)	(3,499,995)
Overheads			
Infrastructure and ground operations		1,902,719	1,514,962
Commercial		869,929	1,100,589
Administration		874,154	962,387
Ticket and membership office		190,593	238,949
		(3,837,395)	(3,816,887)
Earnings before interest, tax, depreciation and amortisation		1,277,703	6,450,918
Interest		(799,997)	(680,183)
Depreciation and loss on disposal of a fixed asset	6	(675,537)	(590,049)
Release of capital grants	10	212,709	252,971
		(1,262,825)	(1,017,261)
Surplus Before Exceptional Items and Taxation		14,878	5,433,657
Exceptional Items	5	(86,800)	—
(Deficit)/Surplus After Exceptional Items But Before Taxation		(71,922)	5,433,657
Taxation	4,11	(53,000)	(1,031,832)
(Deficit)/Surplus After Taxation		(124,922)	4,401,825

BALANCE SHEET

as at December 31, 2020

	Note	2020 £	2020 £	2019 £	2019 £
Assets employed:					
Investments	13		50		50
Fixed assets	6		29,096,526		29,687,706
Current assets:					
Stocks		101,272		132,212	
Debtors	7	1,219,933		1,357,568	
Cash at bank and in hand		3,943,863		319,778	
		5,265,068		1,809,558	
Creditors: amounts falling due within one year	8	(11,383,579)		(5,707,027)	
Net current liabilities			(6,118,511)		(3,897,469)
Total assets less current liabilities			22,978,065		25,790,287
Funded by:					
Creditors: amounts falling due after more than one year	9		16,821,831		19,411,006
Provision for liabilities	15		525,000		450,000
Deferred Income — capital grants	10		4,721,509		4,894,634
			22,068,340		24,755,640
Capital and Reserves					
Called up share capital	12		147		214
Capital redemption reserve			743		676
Income and expenditure account			908,835		1,033,757
			909,725		1,034,647
			22,978,065		25,790,287

These accounts were approved by the Board on February 9, 2021.

ROGER HUTTON, Chair
PAUL HUDSON, Club Secretary

CASH FLOW STATEMENT
for the year ended December 31, 2020

	Note	2020 £	2019 £
Cash flows from Operating Activities			
(Deficit)/Surplus for the year		(124,922)	4,401,825
Adjustments for:			
Depreciation of tangible assets		675,537	586,510
Loss on disposal of tangible fixed asset		—	3,539
Loan interest payable		799,997	680,183
Capital grants released		(212,709)	(252,971)
Taxation		53,000	1,031,832
Decrease/(Increase) in trade and other debtors		159,635	570,445
Decrease/(Increase) in stocks		30,940	(28,001)
Increase/(Decrease) in creditors		3,014,153	(2,851,025)
Interest paid		(641,298)	(680,183)
Net cash inflow from operating activities		**3,754,333**	**3,462,154**
Cash flows from investing activities			
Purchase of tangible fixed assets	6	(84,357)	(1,430,774)
Sale of tangible fixed assets		—	5,500
Capital grants received	10	39,584	259,936
Net cash outflow from investing activities		**(44,773)**	**(1,165,338)**
Cash flows from financing activities			
Repayment of borrowings		(47,975)	(3,725,565)
Repayment of finance lease liabilities		(37,500)	(69,374)
Net cash outflow from financing activites		**(85,475)**	**(3,794,939)**
Increase/(Decrease) in cash in the period		**3,624,085**	**(1,498,123)**
Cash and cash equivalents at January 1		319,778	1,817,901
Cash and cash equivalents at December 31		3,943,863	319,778

STATEMENT OF CHANGES IN EQUITY
for the year ended December 31, 2020

	Called Up Share Capital £	Capital Redemption Reserve £	Income and Expenditure Account £	Total £
Balance at January 1, 2019	228	662	(3,368,068)	(3,367,178)
Reduction in share capital for retiring members	(67)	67	—	—
Surplus for the year after taxation	—	—	4,401,825	4,401,825
Balance at December 31, 2019	**214**	**676**	**1,033,757**	**1,034,647**
Balance at January 1, 2020	214	676	1,033,757	1,034,647
Reduction in share capital for retiring members	(67)	67	—	—
Deficit for the year after taxation	—	—	(124,922)	(124,922)
Balance at December 31, 2020	**147**	**743**	**908,835**	**909,725**

NOTES TO THE ACCOUNTS

for the year ended December 31, 2020

1. Accounting policies

These financial statements were prepared in accordance with Financial Reporting Standard 102. The Financial Reporting Standard applicable in the UK and Republic of Ireland ("FRS 102") as issued in August 2014 and the Co-Operative and Community Benefit Societies Act 2014. The amendments to FRS 102 issued in July 2015 have been applied. The presentation currency of these financial statements is sterling.

Under section 100 of the Co-Operative and Community Benefit Societies Act 2014, neither The Yorkshire Cricket Foundation nor Headingley North-South Stand Limited meet the definition of a subsidiary. The Co-Operative and Community Benefit Societies Act 2014 only requires a consolidation to be prepared where investments meet the definition of a subsidiary. In addition, Under section 9.3(g) of FRS 102, an entity is exempt from preparing consolidated financial statements if not required by the applicable statutory framework (in this case Co-Operative and Community Benefit Societies Act 2014). As such, no consolidated accounts have been prepared.

(a) Income

All income is accounted for on an accruals basis except for donations which are accounted for in the year of receipt.

Income represents amounts receivable from the Club's principal activities. Income is analysed between international ticket and hospitality revenue, domestic ticket and hospitality revenue, subscriptions, England and Wales Cricket Board, commercial and other income.

International ticket and hospitality revenue

Relate to amounts received from ticket sales and hospitality directly attributable to staging international cricket matches in Yorkshire.

Domestic ticket and hospitality revenue

Relate to amounts received from ticket sales and hospitality directly attributable to staging domestic cricket matches in Yorkshire.

Subscriptions

Subscription income comprises amounts receivable from members in respect of the current season. Subscriptions received in respect of future seasons are treated as deferred income.

England and Wales Cricket Board (ECB)

ECB income relates to fees receivable, including performance-related elements, in the current season distributed from central funds in accordance with the County Partnership Agreement (CPA). Also included are any one-off receipts from the ECB outside of the CPA. ECB fees received in respect of future seasons are treated as deferred income. ECB distributions receivable to fund capital projects are treated as deferred income and are released to the Income and Expenditure Account by equal instalments over the expected useful lives of the relevant assets in accordance with accounting policy (c) Fixed assets and depreciation.

Commercial Income

Commercial income relates to amounts received from stadium naming rights, ground advertising, retail operations, catering commissions, indoor cricket-centre facility hire, dinners and other events. Advertising income received in respect of future seasons is treated as deferred income.

Other Income

Other income relates to amounts received from sundry items which mainly consist of income from the Government's Furlough Scheme and any other income not falling into the above categories.

(b) Investments in jointly controlled entity

Investments in jointly controlled entities are carried at cost less impairment.

(c) Fixed assets and depreciation

All expenditure in connection with the development of Emerald Headingley Cricket Ground

414

and the related facilities has been capitalised. Finance costs relating to and incurred during the period of construction were also capitalised. Depreciation is only charged once a discrete phase of the development is completed.

Depreciation is calculated to write down the cost of fixed assets by equal annual installments over their expected useful lives.

The periods generally applicable are:

Emerald Headingley Cricket Ground and Cricket Centre

Buildings	Carnegie Pavilion	125 years
	Other buildings	10-50 years
Fixtures		4 years
Plant & Equipment		4-10 years
Office equipment		2-4 years

Freehold land is not depreciated.

All other expenditure on repairs to Emerald Headingley Cricket Ground and other grounds is written off as and when incurred.

(d) Stocks

Stocks represent goods for resale and are stated at the lower of cost and net realisable value.

(e) Grants

Government grants are recognised at the fair value of the asset received or receivable when there is reasonable assurance that the grant conditions will be met and the grant will be received.

A grant that specifies performance conditions is recognised in income when the performance conditions are met. Where a grant does not specify performance conditions it is recognised in income when the proceeds are received or receivable. A grant received before the recognition criteria are satisfied is recognised as a liability.

Capital grants relating to the development of Emerald Headingley Cricket Ground (including the Yorkshire Cricket Museum) and Cricket Centre are included within the Balance Sheet as deferred income, and are released to the Income and Expenditure Account by equal installments over the expected useful lives of the relevant assets in accordance with accounting policy (c) Fixed assets and depreciation.

Grants of a revenue nature are credited to the Income and Expenditure Account in the same period as their related expenditure.

(f) Cash and cash equivalents

Cash is represented by cash in hand and deposits with financial institutions repayable without penalty on notice of not more than 24 hours. Cash equivalents are highly liquid investments that mature in no more than three months from the date of acquisition and that are readily convertible to known amounts of cash with insignificant risk of change in value.

(g) Financial Instruments

The company has elected to apply the provisions of Section 11 'Basic Financial Instruments' and Section 12 'Other Financial Instruments Issues' of FRS 102 to all of its financial instruments. Financial instruments are recognised in the company's balance sheet when the company becomes party to the contractual provisions of the instrument.

Financial assets and liabilities are offset, with the net amounts presented in the financial statements, when there is a legally enforceable right to set off the recognised amounts and there is an intention to settle on a net basis or to realise the asset and settle the liability simultaneously.

Basic financial assets

Basic financial assets, which include debtors and cash and bank balances, are initially measured at transaction price including transaction costs and are subsequently carried at amortised cost using the effective-interest method unless the arrangement constitutes a financing transaction, where the transaction is measured at the present value of the future receipts discounted at a market rate of interest. Financial assets classified as receivable within one year are not amortised.

Derecognition of financial assets

Financial assets are derecognised only when the contractual rights to the cash flows from the asset expire or are settled, or when the company transfers the financial asset and substantially all the risks and rewards of ownership to another entity, or if some significant risks and rewards of ownership are retained but control of the asset has transferred to another party that is able to sell the asset in its entirety to an unrelated third party.

Classification of financial liabilities

Financial liabilities and equity instruments are classified according to the substance of the contractual arrangements entered into. An equity instrument is any contract that evidences a residual interest in the assets of the company after deducting all of its liabilities.

Basic financial liabilities

Basic financial liabilities, including creditors, bank loans, loans from fellow group companies and preference shares that are classified as debt, are initially recognised at transaction price unless the arrangement constitutes a financing transaction, where the debt instrument is measured at the present value of the future payments discounted at a market rate of interest. Financial liabilities classified as payable within one year are not amortised. Debt instruments are subsequently carried at amortised cost, using the effective interest rate method.

Trade creditors are obligations to pay for goods or services that have been acquired in the ordinary course of business from suppliers. Amounts payable are classified as current liabilities if payment is due within one year or less. If not, they are presented as non-current liabilities. Trade creditors are recognised initially at transaction price and subsequently measured at amortised cost using the effective-interest method.

Derecognition of financial liabilities

Financial liabilities are derecognised when the company's contractual obligations expire or are discharged or cancelled.

(h) Finance Costs

Finance costs are charged to the statement of comprehensive income over the term of the debt using the effective-interest method so that the amount charged is at a constant rate on the carrying amount. Issue costs are initially recognised as a reduction in the proceeds of the associated capital instrument.

(i) Taxation

Tax on the surplus or deficit for the year comprises current and deferred tax. Tax is recognised in the income-and-expenditure account except to the extent that it relates to items recognised directly in equity or other income,

Current tax is the expected tax payable or receivable on the taxable income or deficit for the year, using tax rates enacted or substantively enacted at the balance sheet date, and any adjustment to tax payable in respect of previous years.

Deferred tax is provided in full using the balance sheet liability method. A deferred tax asset is recognised where it is probable that future taxable income will be sufficient to utilise the available relief. Tax is charged or credited to the income statement except when it relates to items charged or credited directly to equity, in which case the tax is also dealt with in equity. Deferred tax liabilities and assets are not discounted.

2. Financial Position

Going concern and Covid-19 Pandemic

The financial statements for the year ending December 31, 2020, have been prepared following a heavily disrupted English summer of cricket as a result of the Covid-19 pandemic, which saw Emerald Headingley lose two international T20 fixtures against Australia and Pakistan due to the need to host them in biosecure bubbles as well as a truncated domestic season, which did not begin until August and saw the Club compete in the Bob Willis Trophy and the T20 Vitality Blast.

Operationally, the pandemic and measures to prevent further spread of the virus caused significant disruption to our business as games had to be staged behind closed doors. This had a material impact on ticket and hospitality sales, sponsorship, retail and catering commissions from both match-day and non-match-day events. This loss of income has been partially offset by a reduction in match-day costs as well as operating overheads, which also includes players and staff taking voluntary paycuts and members donating their annual subscription. The Club has also made use of the Government's Furlough scheme to further mitigate the impact of the lost revenue due to the pandemic.

The Club continues to maintain a strong relationship with its lenders, principally the Graves Family Trusts and HSBC Bank. The Club continues to meet its day-to-day working-capital requirements to pay creditors as they fall due and in addition to the loans also have an overdraft facility of £0.35m (2019: £0.35m) which is repayable on demand and it is assumed that this will be renewed upon its annual expiry in May 2021. Details of the loans and the overdraft maturity analysis which impact on the financial position can be found in Notes 8 and 9. The Board has prepared cash-flow forecasts which show the Club will continue to operate within its current facilities and pay creditors as they fall due for at least the next 12 months from the date of approval of the accounts. These forecasts have been prepared on the basis that cricket starts as it traditionally does in April 2021 and that the Club is able to operate with no reduction to capacity for the fixtures it would reasonably expect to sell out, principally the Test Match between England and India, the IT20 between England and Pakistan and the domestic T20 fixture between Yorkshire and Lancashire. In the event that Covid-19 has an impact on crowd capacity at the international fixtures, then the Club has received confirmation from the England and Wales Cricket Board that they will provide support to the value of tickets sold. To date sales have been strong at £2.5m net of VAT, such that a large element of income is essentially guaranteed. In the event that Covid-19 restricts these fixtures, then the associated costs will also be reduced, creating a potential upside.

The Club's cash-flow forecasts are underpinned by international ticket sales, and sales to date have been stronger than expected. Despite this the Board recognises that Covid-19 is still causing significant ongoing forward-looking uncertainty, and so has considered the potential impact it might have on the business in various scenarios and the impact that this would have on cashflow.

These cash-flow forecasts also include £1m of capital repayment to HSBC, payable in installments in 2021, and it has always been the intention in the normal course of business for the final bullet payment of £1.5m due for repayment on December 31, 2021, to be refinanced. As yet discussions with HSBC have not begun, but throughout regular conversations there has been no indication of any issues with refinancing.

Depending on the severity of any impact of Covid-19 on the Club in 2021 and the resultant impact on cashflow, the Board has identified a number of different actions that it can take to mitigate this impact. Based on the initial forecasts the Board has prepared, additional levers have been identified that can be pulled, including but not limited to: continued use of the furlough scheme as required, use of or extension of overdraft facilities, use of budget contingencies, requests of support from the ECB and ultimately long-term debt restructuring. In light of the extensive options above and the experience of support for the game over the past 12 months the Board is confident the Club will have sufficient funds to continue to meet is liabilities as they fall due for at least 12 months from the approval of these accounts and have therefore prepared the accounts on a going-concern basis.

3. Staff Numbers and Costs

The average number of persons employed by the Club (including board members) during the year, analysed by category, was as follows:

	2020 £	2019 £
Players (including Academy and Northern Diamonds)	46	45
Non-playing full time staff	49	50
Seasonal and casual staff	12	18
	107	113

The aggregate payroll costs of these persons were as follows:

Wages and salaries	3,771,936	3,819,423
Social security costs	409,667	402,502
Contribution to pension plans	286,837	260,535
	4,468,440	4,482,460

The total compensation of key management personnel (including Board Members) as defined in the staff list in the year amounted to £869,029.

4. Taxation

(Deficit)/surplus for the year after taxation	(124,922)	4,401,825
Total tax expense	(53,000)	(1,031,832)
(Deficit)/surplus for the year before taxation	(71,922)	5,433,657

	2020 £	2019 £
Tax at 19.00%	(13,665)	(1,032,395)
Expenses not deductible for taxation purposes	(17,701)	(6,983)
(Increase) reduction in tax rate on deferred tax balances	(18,500)	14,234
Fixed asset permanent differences	(3,134)	(8,936)
Non taxable income	—	61,287
Adjustments in respect of prior periods	—	(59,039)
Total tax expense	(53,000)	(1,031,832)

The Club has utilised corporation-tax losses brought forward in the year, and therefore the tax charge represents movements in deferred tax only.

It was announced in the March 2020 Budget that the reduction in UK corporation-tax rate to 17 per cent would not occur and the corporation-tax rate would remain at 19 per cent from April 1, 2020. Accordingly, deferred tax balances have been remeasured at 19 per cent as this is the tax rate that will apply on reversal.

5. Exceptional Item

The Club has been subject to allegations, and as a result has established an independent panel to review the allegations. This has incurred significant legal costs to date, and these are disclosed as an exceptional item in the accounts.

6. Fixed assets (See next page)

7. Debtors

Trade debtors	514,699	731,662
Deferred tax asset (see Note 11)	347,000	325,000
Other debtors	358,234	300,906
	1,219,933	1,357,568

8. Creditors: amounts falling due within one year

Leeds Beckett University Loan (see Note 9)	141,716	—
ECB Scarborough loan	—	40,000
HSBC Bank (see Note 9)	2,569,014	—
Trade creditors	333,786	1,341,578
Finance leases	—	75,000
Social security and other taxes	1,262,188	293,216
Other creditors	1,481,886	134,633
Accruals	669,358	1,495,407
Deferred income	4,925,631	2,327,193
	11,383,579	5,707,027

9. Creditors: amounts falling due after more than one year

HSBC Bank Loan (see below)	—	2,569,014
Leeds Beckett University Loan (see below)	803,056	—
CJ Graves Accumulation and Maintenance Trust Loan (see below)	4,703,500	4,703,500
J Graves Accumulation and Maintenance Trust Loan (see below)	4,703,500	4,703,500
CJ Graves 1999 Settlement Trust Loan (see below)	5,500,000	5,500,000
Debentures	311,775	319,750
Deferred income	800,000	866,669
Finance leases	—	748,573
	16,821,831	19,411,006

	Cricket Centre		Emerald Headingley Cricket Ground				
	Freehold Land and Buildings £	Plant & Equipment £	Freehold Land and Buildings £	Plant and Equipment £	Improvements to Leasehold Property £	Office Equipment £	Total £
Cost							
At January 1, 2020	608,624	798,891	27,586,665	6,744,544	4,453,421	365,376	40,557,521
Additions	—	—	—	79,336	—	5,021	84,357
At December 31, 2020	608,624	798,891	27,586,665	6,823,880	4,453,421	370,397	40,641,878
Depreciation							
At January 1, 2020	227,430	778,301	3,976,753	5,145,353	409,742	332,236	10,869,815
Charged in the year	17,788	3,918	332,187	258,635	42,522	20,487	675,537
At December 31, 2020	245,218	782,219	4,308,940	5,403,988	452,264	352,723	11,545,352
Net book value							
At December 31, 2020	363,406	16,672	23,277,725	1,419,892	4,001,157	17,674	29,096,526
At December 31, 2019	**381,194**	**20,590**	**23,609,912**	**1,599,190**	**4,043,679**	**33,140**	**29,687,706**

During 2020 the Club became legal owner of the Carnegie Pavilion. As this transaction took place without financial consideration to either party the asset of the Carnegie Pavilion is recognised within the fixed asset register at £nil cost.

	2020 £	2019 £
Loan, borrowing and overdraft maturity analysis:		
In one year or less or on demand	**2,710,730**	115,000
In more than one year but not more than two years	**15,001,478**	2,644,014
In more than two years but not more than five years	**595,210**	15,451,750
In more than five years	**425,142**	448,573
	18,732,560	18,659,337

Loan descriptions

The Club is due to make repayments to HSBC in 2021 totalling £1m in installments and the balance is due on December 31, 2021. The loan carries an interest-rate charge of 2% above the Bank of England base rate. The Club has also given a First Legal Charge to HSBC Bank plc over the Cricket Centre known as 41/43 St Michaels Lane, Headingley, Leeds, and a Third Legal Charge over the property known as Emerald Headingley Cricket Ground, St Michaels Lane, Leeds, in respect of the bank loan and overdrafts. HSBC Bank plc also has a fixed and floating charge over all of the assets of the Club, subject to the other Legal Charges. It has always been the intention in the normal course of business for the final repayment due on December 31, 2021, to be refinanced. As yet discussions with HSBC have not begun, but throughout regular conversations there has been no indication of any issues with refinancing.

CJ Graves Accumulation and Maintenance and J Graves Accumulation and Maintenance Trusts' loans are not due any capital repayments in 2021, and currently bare an interest rate of 4.875% plus any rise in Bank of England base rate above 0.75%. Further repayments are now due to be paid in 2022 and 2023, with the outstanding balance repaid by October 31, 2024. The two Trusts have been granted by the Club joint First Legal Charge over the property known as Emerald Headingley Cricket Ground, St Michaels Lane, Leeds, and joint Second Legal Charge over the Cricket Centre known as 41/43 St Michaels Lane, Headingley, Leeds.

A further £5.5m of debt has also been incurred from the CJ Graves 1999 Settlement Trust. This loan now bares an interest rate of 4.875% plus any rise in Bank of England base rate above 0.75% as of September 1, 2020, due to Mr Graves's term as Chair of the ECB coming to an end. Prior to September 1, 2020, the interest rate charged was 0%. Capital repayment of this loan is due to begin in 2022 with further payments in 2023 before the outstanding balance is repaid on October 31, 2024. The Club has granted Second Legal Charge over the property known as Emerald Headingley Cricket Ground, St Michaels Lane, Leeds, and Third Legal Charge over the property known as the Cricket Centre, known as 41/43 St Michaels Lane, Leeds.

During 2020, the Club took full ownership of the Carnegie Pavilion. The outstanding balance in respect of the fit-out costs on construcion, originally £1.5m in 2009, was due to be recovered by Leeds Beckett University over the remaining lease. Upon the leases falling away the remaining balance being modified to a loan, which is repayable in quarterly installments with the final repayment being June 30, 2030. The loan has a rate of interest of the 3 month LIBOR rate plus 1.35% and is unsecured.

10. Deferred income - capital grants

At 1 January 1, 2020	**4,894,634**	4,887,669
Received in year	**39,584**	259,936
Released to Income and Expenditure Account	**(212,709)**	(252,971)
At December 31, 2020	**4,721,509**	4,894,634

	2020 £	2019 £
11. Deferred tax asset		
At January 1, 2020	**(125,000)**	906,832
to Income and Expenditure Account for the year (see Note 4)	**(53,000)**	(1,031,832)
At December 31, 2020	**(178,000)**	(125,000)
Included within debtors (see Note 7)	**347,000**	325,000
Included within provisions for liabilities (see Note 15)	**(525,000)**	(450,000)
	(178,000)	(125,000)
The elements of recognised deferred tax are as follows:		
Difference between accumulated depreciation and capital allowances	**(525,000)**	(450,000)
Tax losses	**347,000**	325,000
	(178,000)	(125,000)

12. Share capital

	2020	2019
Allotted, called up and fully paid Ordinary shares of 5p each	**147**	214

During the year there was a reduction in qualifying members of 1,340. The total number of qualifying members as at December 31, 2020, was 2,946 (2019: 4,286). Each member of the Club owns one Ordinary share, and the rights attached thereto are contained within the Club's rules which can be found on the Club's website, or from the Secretary on request. Only members who donated their 2020 subscription have been recognised as qualifying members and as such the reduction in number of qualifying members is as a result of the Covid-19 pandemic.

13. Investments

	2020	2019
Cost:at January 1 and December 31	**50**	50

The Club holds 50% of the ordinary share capital of Headingley North-South Stand Limited (HNSS), company number 10747361 of Emerald Headingley Stadium St. Michael's Lane, Headingley, Leeds, LS6 3BR. This company was incorporated to facilitate the redevelopment of the North South Stand.

14. Leasing commitments

Non-cancellable operating lease rentals are payable as follows:

Minimum Lease Payment	2020 £	2019 £
In one year or less	**473,996**	456,240
Between two and five years	**243**	1,298
	474,239	457,538

Operating-lease payments amounting to £623,128 (2019: £232,303) were recognised as an expense in the Income and Expenditure account. In August 2019 the Club began to pay a license fee for use of the redeveloped North-South Stand and incurred a cost of £586,155 to December 2020. The license is to be renewed annually at the discretion of the Club.

The Club has no finances leases.

15. Provision for liabilities

	2020	2019
Deferred tax (see Note 11)	**525,000**	450,000

16. Related Party Transactions

By way of the Articles of Association of The Yorkshire Cricket Foundation (YCF), the Club has the power to appoint two trustees to the board of the YCF. During the year at different points Mark Arthur, Robin Smith and Hanif Malik were Board Members and Trustees of the YCF. During 2020, the YCF awarded non-capital grants of £8,721 (2019: £15,962) to the Club. The balance owed to the Club at December 31, 2020, was £nil (2019: £59). The Club made payments to the YCF of £1,323 (2019 £nil) and the balance owed by the Club at December 31, 2020, was £nil (2019: £nil).

Mark Arthur was also Board Member and Director of the Yorkshire Cricket Board (YCB). During 2020 the Club invoiced sales to the YCB of £53,666 (2019: £92,056). All invoices have been either settled in cash or form part of the trade-debtors balance at the year end. The balance owed at December 31, 2020, was £9,500 (2019: £2,720). The Club has also received invoices from the YCB of £6,441 (2019: £32,745) and this invoice was owed to the YCB as at December 31, 2020, and forms part of the trade creditors balance (2019: £9,476).

The Club is a founding member of Park Avenue Bradford Limited (PABL) along with the YCF and YCB, a private company limited by guarantee, with an investment of £nil. Mark Arthur acted as a Board Member and director of both the Club and PABL while Paul Hudson and Andrew Dawson acted as Board Members of PABL and employees of the Club. During 2020 the Club invoiced sales to PABL of £1,093 (2019: £1,016) for goods or services. The balance owed to the Club at December 31, 2020, was £nil (2019: £1,016).

The Club invested £50 by way of paid-up share capital in Headingley North-South Limited (HNSS) (see Note 13). Mark Arthur, Paul Hudson and Andrew Dawson all acted as directors of this company alongside their roles with the Club. Invoices totalling of £4,800 (2019: £1,461,039) were received by the Club from HNSS in 2020 and were all settled in cash during the year, leaving no balance owing at December 31, 2020 (2019: £nil).

Headingley North-South Stand (Cricket) Limited (HNSS Cricket) is a wholly owned subsidiary of HNSS. During the year the Club received invoices totalling costs of £874,642 (2019: £259,395) from HNSS Cricket and all were settled in cash during the year.

Robin Smith was a Non-Executive Director of the Bartlett Group (Holdings) Limited. Prior to stepping down as the Club's Chair at the AGM on March 21, costs of £3,006 (2019: £3,006) were incurred by the Club from one of its subsidiaries on normal commercial terms, and were settled in cash during the year.

Roger Hutton is a Director of Clarion Solicitors Limited, and following his appointment as a Non-Executive Director he was appointed Chair of the Club at the AGM on March 21, 2020. During the course of the year, on normal commercial terms the Club made invoiced sales to Clarion of £28,788 and at December 31, 2020, a balance of £1,559 was owing to the Club and this forms part of the trade-debtors balance. The Club also received invoices from Clarion totalling £31,089 on normal commercial terms, and these were all settled in cash during the year.

17. Pensions

The Club operates defined contribution pension schemes for the benefit of certain employees. The employee and employer contributions during the year were £397,864 (2019: £347,292). The assets of these schemes are administered in funds independent from those of the Club, and of this £3,590 was unpaid at the end of the year (2019: £57,256).

18. Audit fee and other operating income

In the year the Club paid its auditor £19,000 (2019: £17,500) in respect of the audit of these Financial Statements. The Club also received income grants during the year totaling £918,741 (2019: £nil) in respect of the Government's Coronavirus Job Retention Scheme.

MEMBERS' COMMITTEE
CHAIRMAN'S REPORT

The following served on the Members' Committee during the year.

Chairman:	**Graeme Greenfield**
Elected Members:	**Charlotte Evers**
	Pauline Beesley
	Howard Ray
Appointed Members:	**Graeme Greenfield**
	Richard Levin
	Chris Woodthorpe
In Attendance:	**Mark Arthur,** Chief Executive
	Andy Dawson, Commercial Director
	Paul Hudson, Finance Director
	Treve Whitford, Head of Marcomms and Customer Experience

This year started with my attendance at the AGM. I didn't know then that this would be one of just two visits to Headingley in 2020!

The Members' Committee has continued to meet, but on the *Zoom* platform. All meetings have been minuted and minutes submitted to the board. This year has seen Paul Hudson, (Finance Director), and Treve Whitford (Head of Marcomms and Customer Experience) attend the majority of our Members' meetings. This has allowed for greater transparency and communication with board and staff members.

There continues to be a good working relationship between the members and the board. I am

GRAEME GREENFIELD

still invited to attend the board meetings, either in person or via Zoom, to ensure our members' views are represented.

I would like to take this opportunity to thank both the Immediate Past Chair, Robin Smith, and the new Chair, Roger Hutton, for continuing to invite me, as representative of the Members' Committee, to the board meetings. Much of our time at the Members' Committee meetings has focused on the issue of membership/membership refunds and the effect of Covid on the Club finances and playing of cricket.

In the summer of 2020 the Club held a Members' Open Meeting via *Zoom*, taking questions and comments, and I was invited to join the panel to represent the Members. Feedback shows that this event was welcomed.

I hope that the members have valued the streaming of live matches as part of their membership, although we do realise that nothing beats the real thing.

I would like to thank my fellow Committee Members' for their support and the constructive manner in which meetings are held.

As I write this report we anticipate that we will continue to face some challenges in 2021, but hope that we will all be able to attend YCCC games in the not-too-distant future. I look forward to meeting you in the newly refurbished Long Room before too long.

As ever, if you would like to share your comments and views with committee members please send us an email at:

ycccmemberscommitee@gmail.com.

One of us will be in touch.

> GRAEME GREENFIELD
> Chair,
> Members' Committee
> Yorkshire County Cricket Club

YORKSHIRE CRICKET FOUNDATION

After a brilliant 2019 for cricket 2020 couldn't have been more different, and the impact of this was certainly felt by the Yorkshire Cricket Foundation. The challenges of Covid have meant as a charity we have had to adapt everything we do to support our communities.

In addition we faced the challenge of not being able to fundraise in the summer, as we normally would, to support our work.

However, Covid has also highlighted the importance of our work, supporting the communities in Yorkshire, and moving forwards it will be more vital than ever that we reach out and

WILL SAVILLE

work with more people and communities as we return back to normal.

Throughout the year and the pandemic there has still been some fantastic work undertaken. The Yorkshire Cricket College continues to grow and thrive, providing an excellent education for 16-18-year-olds and supporting them to develop their career aspirations.

We are committed to significantly growing the college over the next few years as we strongly believe Yorkshire Cricket has a major role to play in developing young people in Yorkshire.

In addition to the college we were awarded a National Citizen Service contract, which is a programme aimed at bringing young people from all walks of life together and developing their life skills. We were very proud to run our first NCS scheme, which was hugely successful, and look forward to expanding that over the next few years.

Our *Wicketz* programme funded by Lord's Taverners has continued to work closely with young people in Bradford, Leeds and Hull, supporting them all through these tough times.

As well as our work with the younger generations we have engaged with older adults throughout the lockdowns through our online sporting reminiscence sessions, held weekly on *Zoom*. These are becoming increasingly popular, and have provided a fantastic forum for sports fans to get together.

As we move forwards in 2021 we will be launching our new strategy, which will outline our key priorities over the next four years under our four themes of education, health and well-being, participation and heritage. One of the key projects that we are really excited about is the county-wide rollout of our Crick-Eat programme, which helps to tackle holiday hunger with young people.

All of this work would not be possible without the fantastic support we receive from Emerald Foundation, who have been with us on this journey from the beginning and continue to be a fantastic supporter of the Foundation.

Highlights

- Awarded two national awards for Best Volunteer Programme and Best Community Impact.
- Yorkshire Cricket College increased student numbers to 58 studying full time at Emerald Headingley.
- Yorkshire Cricket College maintained 100 per cent pass rate.
- First summer National Citizen Service programme delivered.
- Enjoy Cricket camps welcomed record numbers of young people taking part:
  - * 2,876 young people participated
  - * 33 clubs ran camps
  - * 47 different courses delivered
  - * 120 days of summer camps
  - * 554 hours of coaching provided
- Record numbers of young people attending the Wicketz programme in Hull during the summer.
- Crick-Eat holiday hunger programme delivered cricket activity and meals to young people in Leeds and is now set for a major, county-wide expansion in 2021.
- Our Sporting Reminiscence programme successfully delivered online to engage cricket and sports fans across the county.
- Sporting reminiscence and legacy Key Stage 3 schools resources were created alongside teacher training, to create more engagement with schools.

WILL SAVILLE
Managing Director,
Yorkshire Cricket Foundation

YORKSHIRE CRICKET BOARD

Who would have thought that following Ben Stokes's heroic innings at Emerald Headingley in the late summer of 2019 we would be facing the severest pandemic in a century with over 100,000 people losing their lives?

As the year unfolded it was clearly evident that the 2020 season would be like no other. However, with the significant help and support from ECB the Recreational Game did commence in July, and by closely following the Government guidelines we did have *Adapted Cricket*, and this was a small price to pay for us to play the game.

ANDREW WATSON

We must also bear in mind that we were the only grassroots sport to come back in this period. Thankfully most clubs and leagues did play, and we did not lose any clubs.

During 2020 most of our staff were on furlough leave, but we provided a quality service through our four Heads of Region. They have worked tirelessly throughout the year supporting all our clubs, leagues and communities — 80 leagues and 750 clubs, while also bringing in excess £3,000,000 of funding outside cricket to support them in these most difficult times. Other examples of support are:

- Dealing with Return to Cricket grant applications/offering advice and processing applications with ECB.
- Safe Hands Management System ensuring all clubs are inputting data.
- Core Cities Urban update.
- Street Chance.
- LA liaison regards tier 3/lockdown and the impact, immediate and into 2021 with regards to outdoor pitches.
- Numerous DBS initiations and verifications.
- Various club issues including lease issues/facility development support/All Stars/Dynamos updates.
- Yorkshire Schools Offer updates and dealing with enquiries.
- Coach Education and Officials Education.
- GOV UK Support Scheme — passing key messages to all clubs and support in applications.
- LA playing pitch strategies.

- Women and Girls Support & Guidance — general catchup with a number of clubs who had committed to developing opportunities in 2020.
- Connecting with Clubs and Leagues — emails/virtual meetings regards facility development/lease support/W&G.

We understand that countless hours of work from thousands of volunteers went into getting ready for the 2020 season. We are so thankful for the huge role that volunteers play in local cricket to ensure the game remains at the heart of our communities.

We know that all clubs, leagues and associations will play a very important role in bringing communities together once we get past this difficult period of time.

We shall continue to support all recreational cricket collectively the best way we possibly can, while ultimately supporting and keeping everyone safe.

The County Club has continued to be extremely supportive of YCB as we continue to enhance our very strong collaboration within Yorkshire Cricket. Mark Arthur, YCCC Chief Executive, has continued to significantly support the impetus of collaborative working — the whole of Yorkshire Cricket is so very grateful for his leadership.

Thanks must be made of the voluntary work of all Board officials and subcommittee secretaries who put in so many unpaid hours for the benefit of the YCB together with all the League Council secretaries and chairmen. We are also absolutely indebted to Ray Knowles, our Senior Safeguarding Officer and to his safeguarding team who work tirelessly as volunteers and deal with all safeguarding matters.

Finally, I would like to record my sincere thanks to my fellow Directors, to everyone involved in Yorkshire Cricket and all at ECB for their support during this difficult and unprecedented year.

ANDREW WATSON,
Managing Director,
Yorkshire Cricket Board

SALUTE TO THE MEMBERS

Yorkshire County Cricket Club wishes to place on record its thanks to all members and supporters who contributed significantly to the county's bid to minimise the financial impact of Coronavirus in 2020 by donating their membership and season-ticket fees.

Eighty-five percent of members, plus *Vitality Blast* season-ticket holders and Club Yorkshire members, donated fees ranging between £35 and £245. The club will be forever grateful to all of you, whether listed here or not. Thank you.

The names listed on these pages follow the style set by the members themselves.

A Baxter
A Coates
A D Mason
A G Cowling
A Glennon
A J Birkett
A J Fletcher
A J Rawnsley
A J Swires
A Nelson
A Nettleton
A Stephenson
A W C Fawcus
A Walmsley
A Y Hutchinson
Ackworth Cricket Club
Adam & Archie Tyler
Adam Binks
Adam Harrison
Adam Redhead
Adrian Brooke
Adrian Roberts
Adrian Smith
Al Coates
Alan Barber
Alan Brown CBE

Alan Coe
Alan Deacon
Alan Greenwood
Alan Hicks
Alan Higgs
Alan Hull
Alan Jinkinson
Alan Kay
Alan Robert Laycock
Alan Rogers
Alan Sixsmith
Alan Skinns
Alan Stewart Kaye
Alan Thomas
Alan W Gibbons
Alec Kokinis
Alex Fairhurst
Alice Pemberton
Alice Worsley
Alice Worsley
Alistair Last
Alistair Moore
Allan J Buchan
Amelia Barclay
Amy Clayton
Amy L Gunby

SALUTE TO THE MEMBERS

Andrea Warner
Andrew Bartle
Andrew Baxter
Andrew C Brown
Andrew Cross
Andrew Dunn
Andrew Durkin
Andrew Hartley
Andrew Hewitt
Andrew Hinchliffe
Andrew Hudson
Andrew J Bailey
Andrew Lee Poole
Andrew Mortimer
Andrew Nicholas Wright
Andrew Parker
Andrew S Freeman
Andrew Smith
Andrew Stocks
Andrew Tyler
Andrew Waite
Andrew Warner
Andrew Whiteley
Andy Bird
Andy Collier
Andy Dawson
Andy Glennon
Andy Jones
Andy Theyers
Andy Walker
Andy Williamson OBE
Andy Wright
Angela Thomas
Angela Thomas
Angus McDonald
Ann Cutting
Ann Hewitson
Ann Simpson

Ann Witty
Anna C Varley
Anne Smith
Anne W Gibbons
Anthony Bennett
Anthony Dowson
Anthony Nelson
Anthony Winstanley
Archie F A Robinson
Arlo Robinson
Arthur M Simpson
Arthur Moore
Asgar Sheriff
B Aconley
B Oliver C Eng MIET
Barbara Atkinson
Barbara Boswell
Barbara Matthews
Barbara Potter
Barbara Tatton
Barrie Goodall
Barrie King
Barry Anthony Simpson
Barry Casterton
Barry W Town
Ben Crosland
Ben Harrison
Ben Potter
Ben Senior
Bernard A Wilson
Bernard Thornton
Betty Britton
Betty Wood
Bill Ball
Bill Morgan
Bill Newham
Bill Tunnicliffe
Bob Haywood

430

SALUTE TO THE MEMBERS

Bob Precious
Bob Watson
Bobby Roberts
Brendan Mitchell
Brian Callaghan
Brian Chambers
Brian Clark
Brian Moore
Brian North
Brian Platt
Brian S Ward
Brian Sanderson
Brian Sargeant
Brian W Harrison
Brian Ward
Brian Whitehead
Brian Yeates
Bryan Ellinthorpe
Bryan Elliott
Bryan Leighton
C & N Rennison
C A J Marshall
C A Michelbach
C Boyne-Whitelegg
C D Hinks
C Edwards
C Freeman
C M Sheerien
C P Douglas
C P Farrar
C P Thomas
C Round
C Storer
C V Harrison
Callum L Noble
Callum Thornton
Campbell Mathieson

Carol Blackburn
Carol Stockton
Carole Clegg
Carolyn Barron
Catherine A Bell
Catherine Sheerien
Cecilia Weston
Charles D Menaul
Charles J Fox
Charles J Kennedy
Charles Peter Brown
Charles Sutcliffe
Charlie Smith
Charlotte Adamson
Charlotte Evers
Chris & Tracy Taylor
Chris Addey
Chris Allen
Chris Booth
Chris Brooksbank
Chris Fitzpatrick
Chris Hardy
Chris Hirst
Chris J Rushworth
Chris Leadbetter
Chris Menaul
Chris Prior
Chris Smailes
Chris Smith
Chris Thompson
Chris Timewell
Chris Weaver
Chris Woodthorpe
Christine Hardman
Christine Kemp
Christine Robbins
Christine Shann

SALUTE TO THE MEMBERS

Christopher Aherne
Christopher D Drake
Christopher Holland
Christopher Moss
Christopher T Jackson
Clare Bramhall
Clare Lynas
Clive Caygill
Clive Porter
Colin Hargreaves
Colin Harker
Colin J Hickford
Colin Morris
Colin Shackleton
Colin Thompson
Colin Watson
Colonel & Mrs Victor J Nicholls
Councillor Stephen King
Craig Greensmith
Craig Hewson
Craigogg
D A Agerskow
D A Hart
D A Howe
D Bramhall
D Cooper
D G Taylor
D G Wright
D Graham Mitchell
D H Burnett
D Herring
D J Drake
D J Hickey
D J Stone
D M Pyrah
D Munro
D R Dickson
D Rawnsley

D S Atkinson
D Sowerby
D Twitchen
D Wilson
Damian Guckian
Dan Normandale
Dan Taylor
Daniel J Randerson
Daniel P Collinson
Daniel Parkinson
Daniel Woodthorpe
Darren Taylor
Dave & Chris Robbins
Dave & Sarah Bishop
Dave Atkinson
Dave Ellison
Dave Horner
Dave Morton
David & Hilary Tingle
David & Kay Watt
David A Hopkin
David Barron
David Bell
David Blythe
David Booth
David Brook
David Brooks
David Bulmer
David Butterfield
David Charlesworth
David Chellingsworth
David Cockcroft
David Day
David E Broadbent
David Earnshaw
David Evans
David Fallon
David Farmer

432

SALUTE TO THE MEMBERS

David Firth
David Flintoft
David Goodchild
David Greenwood
David Grinnell
David Hatliff
David Hawksworth
David Hutchinson
David J Lawton
David J Nuttall
David Jessop
David John Kemp
David John Ward
David Keighley
David Kitson
David Lane
David Lord
David Lowe
David M Walker
David M Wood
David McDermott
David Mills
David Mitchell
David Moore
David Nairn Geekie
David O'Kelly
David Peel
David Quilter
David R Baker
David Rhodes
David Robbins
David Robinson
David Shaw
David Shay
David Simon
David Skilbeck
David Smith
David Smith

David Stringer
David Stroughair
David Sydney Cox
David Todd
David Turner
David W Bramley
David W Coupland
David W Hirst
David Westmoreland
David Wheeeler
David Wilcock
David Woods
Dawn Pollard
Dawn Whiteley MBE
Deborah Robinson
Debra Harker
Deirdre K Bailey
Dennis L Barnett
Dennis Morley
Dennis Stabler
Derek Agar
Derek Norfolk
Derek Simpson
Derek Whitworth
Diane E Mellor
District Judge Adrian Lower
Don Widdows
Donald Verity
Donald Weaver
Donald Wood
Dorothy Thompson
Douglas Child
Douglas E Ombler
Dr Alan C Keighley
Dr Andrew Grainger
Dr C John McHenry
Dr David A Harding
Dr David Thompson

SALUTE TO THE MEMBERS

Dr Greg Lodge
Dr J P Adams
Dr James Moxon
Dr John Adams
Dr John Potter
Dr Jonathan Tummons
Dr Kamal Samanta
Dr M G Walker
Dr O Kayes FRCS
Dr P Oxtoby
Dr Peter Brookes
Dr Peter H A Roebuck
Dr Peter W Dettmar
Dr R & Mrs D Lucas
Dr Richard J Holden
Dr Sean Ennis
Drew Lundy
Dudley Eric Graham GSY
Duncan Agerskow
Dunnington John
E Bush
E Julian Holdroyd
E Sheerien
Eamonn Mullins
Ed Anderson
Eddie Hambleton
Edward M Spiers
Edward Sheerien
Eileen Sanderson
Elaine Keighley
Eli S Mallison
Elisabeth Stringer
Elizabeth North
Elizabeth Sixsmith
Elizabeth Thompson
Ellen Spencely
Emma Barclay
Eoin McDonnell

Eric Heaton
Eric Horsfall
Eric Richley
Erin Grange
Ethan Smith
Finn & Eddie Hemsley
Francis Mullen
Frank Lister
Frank Siddle
Frank Willis Womack
G A Johnson
G C Baglow
G Cockerill
G G Fardell
G Goodall
G Gravil
G M Brown
G M France
G M France
G M Webster
G Moss
G S Harridge
G Watkin Jones
Garth Thistlethwaite
Gary Ashton
Gary Holmes & Susan Allick
Gary Howden
Gary Smith
Geoff Binks
Geoff Cooper
Geoff Foster
Geoff Gittus
Geoff Laycock
Geoff Marshall
Geoff Packer
Geoff Pearson
Geoffrey Dodsworth
Geoffrey Edward Heywood

SALUTE TO THE MEMBERS

George Froggatt
George Mallender
George Thomas
George W Thompson
Gerald Gaunt
Geraldine C Tolan
Geraldo
Gerard & Anne McGrath
Gerard Fox
Gerry Hutchinson
Gill Moody
Gordon Lee
Gordon Wigglesworth
Graeme Acton
Graeme P Robinson
Graeme Pike
Graham C Robinson
Graham Colledge
Graham Cook
Graham Douglas Baker
Graham Fieldsend
Graham Fisher
Graham Haley
Graham Harris
Graham Hustwit
Graham Laing
Graham Lloyd Myers
Graham P Cooper
Graham P Gaunt
Graham Robert Cook
Graham Smith
Graham W V Carter
H Martin V Gray
Hanlon Family
Harold & Vanessa Todd
Harris Dobson
Harry Cowgill
Harry George Henson

Harry Staines
Harry Streeting
Harvey E Morrison
Hazel Marshall
Hazel Rawnsley
Hazel Rawnsley
Helen Bellamy
Helen Clarke
Helen J Hoyle
Helen Thompson
Helen Wood
Helen Woodthorpe
Henry & Albert Rigg
Hilary J Wood
Hilary Oliver
Howard Adamson
Howard Bell
Howard Holmes
Howard Petch
Hugh Platt
I & C Normington
I & C Normington
I C McDougall
I Cavanagh
I Flaxman
I Goodings
I Heaton
I L Askey
I Robinson
Iain Farquhar
Iain Ledingham
Ian & Shirley Hunt
Ian Aldred
Ian Askey
Ian Barraclough
Ian C Thompson
Ian Campbell
Ian Clapham

435

SALUTE TO THE MEMBERS

Ian D Smith
Ian E Torr
Ian Fairhurst
Ian G Wilson
Ian Goodings
Ian Greenhalgh
Ian Hodgson
Ian Ireland
Ian Jackson
Ian L Thomas
Ian Lister
Ian N Gunby
Ian Preston
Ian Riley
Ian Ross Atkinson
Ian Smith
Ian Sutcliffe
Ian Walker
Ian Weatherhead
Ian Wilson
In memory of J Brook
Ivan E Harrison
J A Pickford
J B Turner
J Charlesworth
J Coates
J D Clark
J D Graham Crowther
J E Arundel
J Howden
J K M & K Brearley
J K M Simcox
J K Round
J Leigh
J M Bolland
J Margaret Hellowell
J Michael Parkinson
J Michael Rawnsley

J P Jackson
J Pickering
J R Durdy
J Richard Taylor
J T Cowling
J Taplin
J Wilkie
Jack Merrick
Jack Popplestone
Jack Potter
Jacky Hutchinson
Jacky Martin
Jacqueline Ward
James F C Leathley
James F Sutton
James Halloran
James L Hoyle
James Metcalfe
James Richardson
James W D Moxon
James Walker
James Whitworth
James Woodthorpe
Jane M Wiles
Janet Beaumont
Janet Chapman
Janet Leighton
Janet Teasdale
Jayne Woodthorpe
Jean I Reece
Jef Thompson
Jeff Croft
Jennifer Hoare
Jennifer Millard
Jennifer Whitworth
Jenny & Barry Smith
Jenny Graaf
Jeremy Wimbush

Jill Howden
Jill M A Brewer
Jillian Smith
Jim Collinson
Jim Cork
Jim Henderson
Jim Parkinson
Jim Teasdale
Joan Pickering
Joe Agerskow
Joe Durkin
John & Bridget Shackleton
John & Mary Holmes
John A Cooper
John Ainsley
John B W Summerskill
John Barraclough
John Bird
John Bowker
John Briggs
John Brudenell
John C Clapham
John Carlisle
John Carter
John Currie
John D Spencely
John D. Broadley
John David Turner
John Drake
John E Walker
John Eaton
John Edwards
John F Spencely
John Foster
John G Atkinson
John Garratt
John Gatenby
John Gilbert Foster

John Hall
John Harrison
John Hedley Wainwright
John Hullah
John Ibbotson
John Ingram
John J Storey
John K Boddy
John Kerby
John Leveson
John M Haigh
John Mann
John Marshall
John Mason
John Merrifield
John Michael Seed
John Mortoin
John Neil Preston
John Oxley
John Parkinson
John Pick
John Quickfall
John R Bullamore
John R Strickland
John Rawnsley
John Rhodes
John Ridings
John Robinson
John Rowley
John Stockton
John Stuttard
John Sutcliffe
John Tiernan
John Turner
John W A Clayton
John Walker
John Whitley
John Wilkie

SALUTE TO THE MEMBERS

John Wilkinson
John Wilson
John Zimnoch
Jonathan Bell-Syer
Jonathan Brain
Jonathan Glahome
Jonathan Lynas
Jonathan Merrick
Jonathan Shaw
Jonboy Baildon Bantam
Joyce & Barry Canham
Joyce Bean
Joyce Dinsdale
Joyce Myers
Judith Roberts
Julian Graham-Rack
Julian Horberry
Julie Holmes
Julie Holmes
Julie M Smith
Julie Mincher
Julie Peters
June Coates
K & J Blythe
K A Bickerdike
Karen Borowski
Karen Harris
Karen Preston
Karin Lowson
Kath Dawson
Keith & Edwina Stones
Keith A Bickerdike
Keith Bassitt
Keith Herdman
Keith Hopkinson
Keith Morrison
Keith Parsons
Keith Pearson

Keith Potter
Keith Roberts
Keith S Roberts
Keith Soames
Keith Thompson
Keith Thompson
Keith W Ward
Ken & Marlene Magson
Ken Blackburn
Ken Bruce
Ken Marshall
Ken Redshaw
Kenneth Marshall
Kenneth Williamson
Kennett Crosby
Kerry Evans
Kevan Judge
Kevan Judgr
Kevin & Denise Firth
Kevin Andrew
Kevin F Henry
Kevin G Rourke
Kevin Hardisty
Kevin Morgan
Kevin Stones
L Collinson
L Loft
L Morrell
L Morrissey-Edgley
Laura Killeen
Laurence Guy
Lawrence Hodgson
Lawrie Miller
Les Horner
Les Morrell
Les Stones
Leslie Couldwell
Lily Humphries

SALUTE TO THE MEMBERS

Lisbeth Stabler
Liz Davies
Lord Haselhurst
Lorna Laing
Lorna Laing
Luke Langley
Lynda Sutcliffe
Lynn Hanson
Lynne Adamson
Lynne Ward
M A Beresford
M Ann Busfield
M Asling
M C Morpeth
M C R Marsden
M Daniels
M E Brown
M G Brothwell
M Harrison
M J Elsmore
M J Hardcastle
M J Hunt
M L Ellerton
M McMahon
M Newhouse
M Nixon
M P Lewis
M P Threadgold
M Poad
M Reese
M Stones
M Thompson
M Walmsley
M Walmsley
Mal Denison
Mal Meneaud
Malcolm Brown
Malcolm Denison

Malcolm Ellerton
Malcolm Meneaud
Malcolm North
Malcolm Poad
Malcolm Skinner
Malcolm Taylor
Marcus Robinson
Marcus Woodthorpe
Margaret Hemingway
Margaret Kear
Margaret M Hartley
Margaret Ratcliffe
Margaret Smith
Margaret White
Margaret Williams
Margaret Wright
Marie Barker
Mark & Lynda Mason
Mark Breislin
Mark Carter
Mark Graham
Mark Heap
Mark Hewson Overend
Mark Inman
Mark J Roberts
Mark Kenny
Mark Rayner
Mark Ripley
Mark Thornton
Maroof Khan (Roofa)
Martin Armitage
Martin Brannan
Martin Clark
Martin D Dean
Martin Fincham
Martin Gamble
Martin J Brown
Martin J Dodgson MBE

SALUTE TO THE MEMBERS

Martin Overfield
Martin P Walker
Martin Speake
Martin Stead
Martin Winnard
Martyn Stringer
Mary Teresa Palmer
Master Brett Siddle
Master M J F Walker
Matt Price
Matthew Leddy
Matthew Paul Smith
Matthew Smith
Matthew T Cooper
Maureen Thompson
Maurice & Karen Cowen
Max Cooke
Max Theyers
Mel Brown
Mel Neary
Mel Wiles
Melanie King
Michael & Jennifer Harrison
Michael Barden
Michael Brook
Michael C Gibson
Michael C Jackson
Michael Clegg
Michael Davies
Michael Dods
Michael G Brothwell
Michael H Rhodes
Michael Hare
Michael Harrop
Michael Heard
Michael J Tunbridge
Michael J Vickerman
Michael JF Walker

Michael Jones
Michael Last
Michael Luke
Michael Miller
Michael Myers
Michael Pollard
Michael Ralph Lee
Michael Ralph Lee
Michael Rawnsley
Michael Richley
Michael Richley
Michael Robb
Michael S Turner
Michael Sanderson
Michael Stephenson
Michael Swift
Michael Watson
Michael Wilson
Mick Killeen
Mick McVeigh
Mick Newell
Mike Barrett
Mike Brown
Mike Brown (SG)
Mike Carroll
Mike Cornish
Mike Longthorpe
Mike Lowe
Mike Oldham
Mike Scott
Mike Stadler
Milan Atanaskovic
Miles Kamstra
Miss Alison Frank
Moira Herring
Monty Dodsworth
Mr & Mrs D Hudson
Mr & Mrs E Massheder

SALUTE TO THE MEMBERS

Mr & Mrs G Connell
Mr & Mrs Hagger
Mr & Mrs I R Wood
Mr & Mrs J L Benton
Mr & Mrs John Blackburn
Mr & Mrs K Bramley
Mr & Mrs R Pickard
Mr & Mrs Scruton
Mr & Mrs Stephen Batty
Mr & Mrs W & S Lundy
Mr A P Jackson
Mr Alan Frank
Mr Alan S East
Mr Andrew Shackleton
Mr Angelo Palladino
Mr C C Wilkinson
Mr C Rhodes
Mr Callum Walker
Mr Chris Rigby FRCS
Mr Colin Wordsworth
Mr D & Mrs M Kitchman
Mr D G & Mrs W Copperthwaite
Mr D Garforth
Mr D J Wilson
Mr D M Goodhead
Mr D M Pyrah
Mr D W & Mrs C Beasley
Mr David Alexander Robinson
Mr David Brooks
Mr David Coldwell
Mr David Cornish
Mr David Hoyle
Mr David Martin
Mr David Walker
Mr Ethan Thompson
Mr Geoffrey Bateman
Mr George Burton
Mr Graham Clark

Mr Graham E Hoyle
Mr Harold Turkington
Mr Harry Broderick
Mr Howard Bell
Mr I C Skaife
Mr I Cavanagh
Mr Ian Quirie
Mr J E Gregory
Mr J L & Mrs A M Benton
Mr J T H Walker
Mr James Hayhurst
Mr Jeffrey Charnock
Mr John Banks
Mr John Cook
Mr John Gallagher
Mr John Ward
Mr Joshua TH Walker
Mr Keith Johnstone
Mr M Wells
Mr Martin G Grayshon
Mr Michael Brook
Mr Michael G Walker
Mr Michael Jackman
Mr Michael Ralph Lee
Mr Mike Warburton
Mr Nigel Thorpe
Mr P Boocock
Mr P Church
Mr Peter Armitage
Mr Peter W Ruder
Mr Peter Winteringham
Mr Phill Tweddle
Mr R & Mrs L Steward
Mr R Boldry
Mr R P Smith
Mr R W Noble
Mr R W Rix
Mr Ralph Wright

SALUTE TO THE MEMBERS

Mr Richard Whitelegg
Mr Robin Harvey
Mr S J Llewellyn
Mr S J Reardon
Mr S Morris-Armitage
Mr S Northin
Mr S Woodward
Mr Scott McCord
Mr Stephen Holmes
Mr Stephen Simpson
Mr Steve Northin
Mr Stuart Hardy
Mr T G Wright
Mr T R French
Mr Timothy Gladwin
Mr Tom Booth
Mrs Anne Hoyle
Mrs B Smith
Mrs Betty A Mitchell
Mrs Christine Hayhurst
Mrs Elizabeth Carr
Mrs Gwyneth Todd
Mrs J A Howe
Mrs J Heald
Mrs Janet Clinton
Mrs Jennifer Ellison
Mrs Jennifer Harrison
Mrs Jill Coldwell
Mrs Julie E Bragg
Mrs L Darwin
Mrs L Garforth
Mrs L Woodward
Mrs Margaret Banks
Mrs Margaret Frank
Mrs Mary Wood
Mrs Norma Jean Winteringham

Mrs P J Wilkinson
Mrs P Wells
Mrs Pamela Martin
Mrs Patricia Hicks
Mrs Paula Hoyle
Mrs Sarah Rees
Mrs V A Hackney
Murray Roberts
N A Hector
N Houston
N P Upton
N R B West
Neal French
Neal J Hardcastle
Ned Holt
Neil A Whitaker
Neil Asling
Neil Clay
Neil Hall
Neil Hasty
Neil Spedding
Neil Stephenson
Neil Tempest
Neville Smith
Nicholas Eleanor
Nicholas Hall
Nicholas John Rogers
Nick Bolton
Nick David Taffinder
Nick Gale
Nick Mould
Nick Taylor
Nick Upton
Nicola Lamb
Nigel & Susan Crick
Nigel Carrick

SALUTE TO THE MEMBERS

Nigel Hedley Jones
Nigel J Steels
Noah Smith
Oliver, Archie, Jude & Henry Bareham
Os Osborn
P A G Newing
P A Smith
P Agerskow
P Bracewell
P Cain
P Cookman
P D Battley
P D Whitaker
P H Cadman
P Hudson
P Kitson
P M Banks
P M Beeley
P North
P R White
P S N Kendall
P Sheerien
P Winteringham
Pamela Lumb
Pat
Pat Bailes
Pat Hall
Pat Whitehouse
Patricia Currie
Patricia Spencely
Paul & Joanne Clarke
Paul Abrahams
Paul Campbell
Paul Clegg
Paul D S Fisher

Paul David Robinson
Paul Delaney
Paul Driver
Paul E Buckmaster
Paul Edgar
Paul F I Jackson
Paul Fletcher
Paul Gray
Paul Green
Paul H Johnson
Paul Hemingway
Paul Holmes
Paul Humphries
Paul K Green
Paul Kilvington
Paul Leah
Paul Lund
Paul M Kemp
Paul Millen
Paul Morris
Paul Morritt
Paul N Gaywood
Paul R Devey
Paul R Devey
Paul Richards
Paul Rodgers
Paul Searle
Paul Sutcliffe
Paul Tatton
Paul Thompson
Paul White
Paula Agerskow
Paxton Dewar
Paxton Dewar
Penelope Ibbotson
Pervinder Kaur

SALUTE TO THE MEMBERS

Peter Armitage
Peter Atkinson
Peter B Wright
Peter Ball
Peter Britton
Peter Buckley
Peter Cadman
Peter Dawson
Peter Forster
Peter Hardman
Peter Hayton
Peter Henderson
Peter Horne
Peter Hutchinson
Peter J Hoyle
Peter J Newton
Peter J Thomas
Peter Lees
Peter MacGowan
Peter McKenzie
Peter Moran
Peter Nelson
Peter R Fisher
Peter Richard Fisher
Peter Robinson
Peter Skilbeck
Peter Smithson
Peter Stowe
Peter Walker
Peter Wildsmith
Peter Wilson
Peter Wood
Phil Beaver
Phil Brown
Phil Hardaker
Phil Marsland

Phil Rose
Phil Short
Phil Sutcliffe
Phil Wood
Phil Woodthorpe
Philip Alban Jones
Philip Beckwith
Philip Fisher
Philip Gil
Philip J Foster
Philip W O'Mara
Philip White
Philip Woodward
Phillip Skilbeck
Priti Taylor
Prof J B Hall
Prof J F Tunnicliffe
Prof J Tunnicliffe
Prof Mike Morgan
Prof S Gregory
Professor Shaun Gregory
R A Steeles
R A Steeles
R A Webster
R BALME
R Cartwright
R Darwin
R G Porritt
R Hampstead
R Haywood
R J Adams
R J Hodgson
R J Mitchell
R K Lithgow
R Lancaster
R M Hunt

444

SALUTE TO THE MEMBERS

R M Parkinson
R P Leeman
R Sampson
R Sapey
R Scott Elliot
R T Leathley
R Triggs
R W Bower
R Whitelegg
Rachel Rose
Ralph Scott
Ralph W Middlebrook
Ralph Wright
Ray Helme
Raymond Allatt
Raymond Schofield
Raymond Williams
Rev Dr David R Peel
Rev John Simms
Rhys Williams
Richard A Avison
Richard Benson
Richard Chaffer
Richard Copley
Richard Crompton
Richard Cunningham
Richard Dickinson
Richard Fenn
Richard G Fletcher
Richard Geldard
Richard Harker
Richard Hopkin
Richard Hopwood
Richard Hunt
Richard Huntington
Richard Iball

Richard Jeavons
Richard John Hodgson
Richard Larking & Oliver Larking
Richard Milner
Richard MrPinPool
Richard Mumford
Richard Turner
Rick Thompson
Rob Allison
Rob Chambers
Rob Cowling
Rob Edwards
Rob Fairhurst
Rob Firth
Rober E A Spiers
Robert A Davison
Robert Atkinson
Robert Galvin
Robert Gosling
Robert Graham Porritt
Robert Heppell
Robert Hewitt
Robert Isaac
Robert Kettlewell
Robert M Town
Robert Metcalfe
Robert Smith
Robert Thompson
Robert W Metcalfe
Robert W Smith
Robin Aldersley
Robin Beaumont
Robin Thurlow
Robin Wight
Rod Ash
Roderick Wilson

SALUTE TO THE MEMBERS

Rodney Mellor
Roger & Wendy Statham
Roger Bailes
Roger Balme
Roger Bottomley
Roger Brice
Roger Gibbons
Roger Holles
Roger L Scholey
Roger Mather
Roger W Peacock
Roland Todd
Ron Needham
Rory Ibbotson
Roy Johnson
Roy Lockwood
Roy Newbould
Roy-Edward Walker
Rupert D E Brown
Russ Holroyd
Russ Shimmin
Russell Holroyd
Russell W Langton
S Chatterton
S Donaghy
S J Doughty
S J R Edwards
S Murray
S O'Connor
S P Millard
S Phelps
S Pickering
Sally Harrison
Sam Booth
Sam Cameron
Sam Carrick

Sam Froggatt
Samuel A Smith
Sandy Duncan
Sandy Ibbotson
Scarlett Grange
Scott Elliot Hawick
Seth G Mallison
Sharon-Jane Mills
Shaun Fisher
Shaun Raistrick
Shaun Woodall
Sheila Bennett
Si Bourke
Simon C Garton
Simon Carter
Simon Coulthard
Simon Dwyer
Simon Firth
Simon Gibbs
Simon Graham Wetherell
Simon Meritt
Simon Smith
Simon Wraith
Sir Ian Magee
Stan Dawson
Stanley Jackson
Stephen Baines MBE
Stephen Barclay
Stephen Chell
Stephen George Bridge
Stephen Greaves
Stephen Hodgson
Stephen J Geraghty
Stephen L Heald
Stephen Lambert
Stephen Marklew